G000071181

Lucilius And Horace: A Study In The Classical Theory Of Imitation

George Converse Fiske

In the interest of creating a more extensive selection of rare historical book reprints, we have chosen to reproduce this title even though it may possibly have occasional imperfections such as missing and blurred pages, missing text, poor pictures, markings, dark backgrounds and other reproduction issues beyond our control. Because this work is culturally important, we have made it available as a part of our commitment to protecting, preserving and promoting the world's literature. Thank you for your understanding.

UNIVERSITY OF WISCONSIN STUDIES
IN LANGUAGE AND LITERATURE
NUMBER 7

LUCILIUS AND HORACE

A STUDY IN THE CLASSICAL THEORY OF IMITATION

BY

GEORGE CONVERSE FISKE
ASSOCIATE PROFESSOR OF LATIN

MADISON
1920

αἱ μὲν γὰρ πράξεις προγεγενημέναι κοιναὶ πᾶσιν ἡμῖν κατελείφθησαν, τὸ δ' ἐν καιρῷ ταύταις καταχρήσασθαι καὶ τὰ προσήκοντα περὶ ἑκάστης ἐνθυμηθῆναι καὶ τοῖς ὀνόμασι εὖ διαθέσθαι τῶν εὖ φρονούντων ἴδιόν ἐστιν. ἡγοῦμαι δ' οὕτως ἂν μεγίστην ἐπίδοσιν λαμβάνειν καὶ τὰς ἄλλας τέχνας καὶ τὴν περὶ τοὺς λόγους φιλοσοφίαν, εἴ τις θαυμάζοι καὶ τιμώῃ μὴ τοὺς πρώτους τῶν ἔργων ἀρχομένους, ἀλλὰ τοὺς ἄρισθ' ἕκαστον αὐτῶν ἐξεργαζομένους, μηδὲ τοὺς περὶ τούτων ζητοῦντας λέγειν, περὶ ὧν μηδεὶς πρότερον εἴρηκεν, ἀλλὰ τοὺς οὕτως ἐπισταμένους εἰπεῖν ὡς οὐδεὶς ἂν ἄλλος δύναιτο.   (Isocrates *Panegyricus*, 9 and 10.)

Ainsi donc, dans les arts, l'inventeur est celui
Qui peint ce que chacun peut sentir comme lui.
—ANDRÉ CHÉNIER

To
A. E. F.

CONTENTS

PREFACE

The appearance of the two volumes of Marx's *Lucilius* in 1904 and 1905 and of Cichorius' *Untersuchungen zu Lucilius* in 1908 have given us a new Lucilius. To appreciate the truth of this statement it is only necessary to examine the earlier editions of Lucian Mueller, 1872, and of Lachmann, 1876. Not only do we have a text which is the result of long and discriminating study, but we now have fuller information as to the social, political, and aesthetic environment of the Scipionic epoch than we have of any other period of Roman literary history until we reach the Ciceronian and Augustan age.

These facts are of fundamental importance for all students of Horace's satires, for they at once render necessary a complete revision of judgment in regard to such earlier studies of Lucilian and Horatian relationships as those of M. A. Herwig, *Horatius quatenus recte de Lucilio iudicaverit*, Halle, 1873; J. J. Iltgen, *de Horatio, Lucilii aemulo*, Montabauer, 1872; L. Triemel, *Ueber Lucilius und seine Verhältniss zu Horatius*, Kreusn, 1877 (not accessible to me); V. Zawadzski, *quatenus in satiris Horatius videatur imitatus esse Lucilium*, Erlangen, 1881; R. Y. Tyrell, *Horace and Lucilius*, Hermathena 4, 355, and Tyrrel's Johns Hopkins Lecture on *Horace* published as chapter 6 in his *Latin Poetry*, pp. 162-215. The student who peruses these studies to-day will still find much of value. Certain parallels he will reject, others he will accept, and above all he will concern himself not with the question of sporadic instances of verbal imitation arranged in the familiar parallel columns or of the reinterpretation of the thought of individual passages by Horace, but with the much more fundamental question of the relation between the themes of Lucilian satires and those of Horace.

Traces of this point of view are not wanting in these earlier studies. Iltgen, for example, deserves great credit for pointing out the relationship between certain fragments now included in Lucilius, book 6, which appear to constitute an earlier treat-

9

ment of the theme of the encounter with the bore, the subject of Horace's famous satire 1, 9 and of numerous imitations and paraphrases in French, Italian, and English satire since that time. Tyrrel has deserved well of all students of the classics by his discussion of the relationship between Lucilius and Horace, but the unique value of his central thesis has been somewhat obscured by a mistaken emphasis. He has pointed out correctly the important relationship existing between certain Lucilian and Horatian satires but he has misinterpreted this phenomenon by representing it as derogatory to the originality of Horace, and by presenting Horace's satires too exclusively from the point of view of contemporary paraphrases or modernizations of Lucilian satire. Unquestionably there is a measure of truth in this last point of view, but it quite fails to account for the intricate problem of imitation in all its larger relations with the literary ideals of the Augustan age and Horace's own literary theories and practice.

The students of Marx's commentary and of Cichorius' studies have long been aware of the great advance made towards the solution of the problem of Lucilian and Horatian relationships. For example Marx's commentary gives clear indications of his consciousness of important relationships—and differences—between the critical theories of Lucilius, as presented in certain satires in books 6 and 30 and Horace's critical satires 1, 4, and 1, 10, though he does not always pursue these evidences so far as to make concrete formulations of his point of view. So also he has seen the relationship between certain lines in Lucilius, book 30 and Horace's satire 1, 6. Cichorius, building on the foundation of the remarkable work of Marx, has succeeded in a considerable number of instances in formulating argumentative sequences of still other themes, notably that of the relation of the unsavory satire in 29, 3 on the sexual question to Horace's satires 1, 2, and the relation of the εἰσαγωγή to Iunius Congus to certain themes treated in the *Ars Poetica* of Horace.

In the light of these facts, therefore, a new examination of the whole question of Lucilian and Horatian relationships seems desirable, an examination, however, which shall endeavor to interpret the problem not by the mere citation of parallel passages, but in the light of the theories of literary imitation current in the age of Augustus. With this problem I have been busy in the all too scanty intervals afforded for research by the multifarious duties of an American college teacher during the past seven years.

At this point I seem to hear the voices of many American friends and colleagues in the classical field admonishing me that I am on slippery ground in making any efforts at conjectural reconstructions of fragments, and a fortiori at building up any argumentative sequences based on fragments.

That he is on slippery ground no one knows better than one who has worked with fragments. Such a one realizes only too well that some of his reconstructions will fall to the ground and not permanently meet the approval of critical scholarship. Why then should he pursue the quest? The answer is to be found in the history of the net advance in our knowledge made by successive generations of scholars who have had the courage to persevere in the field of interpreting the fragments both of Greek and Roman literature whether those fragments are scattered in the pages of grammarians or unearthed by the excavations of the Fayum.

Even the most conservative scholar who will examine the successive editions of Gerlach, L. Mueller, and Marx, and the study of Cichorius, will, I think, be forced to acknowledge that a notable advance has been made by each successive student in the field, not only in the interpretation of individual fragments but in the relocation of fragments in more probable contexts, and in the establishment of what measured by the ordinary tests of probability we may fairly call a new theory of the content of certain themes in Lucilius and their relations to Horace. It seems likely that, as the result of archaeological excavations, classical scholars will have more and not fewer problems of this nature to solve in the future. With such material no real progress can be made except through the exercise of the scientific imagination constantly censored by a rigidly scientific criticism on the part of the worker himself and of his professional readers. I will venture to add that where problems of imitation are involved as is the case in Horace's relation to Lucilius, it is necessary not merely to scrutinize the individual fragments but also all pertinent evidence which will tend to establish longer or shorter sequences of thought or argument which by the ordinary rules of scientific evidence may be regarded as probable or possible. At any rate the results of the pursuit of this method in the successive editions of Lucilius should convince anyone except the perversely sceptical that thus a marked advance has been made in our knowledge of Lucilius, an advance which would have been quite impossible had all editors confined the attention exclusively to the text and the interpretation of the individual fragments. In any case he who works in fragments has the same right to present all the data and methods involved in his search for the final appraisal of scholars and to expect that his case will not be ruled out of court by any dogmatic verdict as to the alleged uselessness of the reconstruction of fragments, but that his results will be weighed with the same careful scrutiny, the same insistence upon the claims of the scientific imagination and the same rigid regard for the laws of evidence and probability that he has honestly endeavored to employ during his search for a nearer approach to the ultimate truth.

And here one question of detail may be mentioned, which may serve to illustrate how complex is this question of weighing evidence in the case of fragments. For a long time it was my intention to differentiate by the use of separate type those fragments of Lucilius which I regarded as almost certainly or probably related to certain Horatian contexts and those whose relationship was only one of possibility. When, however, I came to consider the whole aspect of my problem, I rejected this idea in favor of the plan of simply stating in each case my reasoned opinion for believing that that particular fragment both by itself and in the light of its context showed relationship with such and such lines of Horace or probably found a place in a Lucilian context which showed relationships with such and such a parallel context in Horace. To me—and I think other workers familiar with the problems of literary relationships will agree with me—this procedure seems preferable and for this reason. When a sequence of thought is established on the basis of obvious or probable relationship between a block of Lucilian fragments, and when in addition this sequence is found to pursue a course in general parallel to a sequence of thought or argument in Horace, the student then turns to a consideration of the other fragments from the same book of Lucilius. Here he may be said, roughly speaking, to encounter two sets of phenomena. First he will find certain fragments which he cannot relate without an illegitimate forcing process to the general outlines of his thematic sequence. These he must reject. But he will also find other fragments which are still susceptible of several explanations, but which now, so to speak, are floated on the surface of the context he has established as probable. In such a case he must, of course, state all the possibilities in the way of interpretation, but among these possibilities he is justified in preferring that one which seems to him most natural in the light of the sequence on context previously established. Such a fragment or group of fragments then draws relatively nearer the class of fragments which are probably to be related to a Horatian context, and relatively farther away from those fragments which can only be explained in isolation. Such a class of fragments are examples of a relatively common phenomenon. To attempt to differentiate them mechanically by typographical distinctions would be to obscure entirely one of the most complex problems in literary relationships.

In the controversy as to the proper sequence of all Lucilian fragments quoted by Nonius, I am inclined to hold rather with Lindsay than with Marx. Cf. his *Nonius Marcellus' Dictionary of Republican Latin*, Oxford, 1901, and reviews of Marx in *Class. Rev.* 19, 271; 20, 63; *Deutsche Litzeit*, 25, 3088 ff. But to reconstruct the text of Lucilius along the lines suggested by Lindsay is, of course, beyond the scope of this work. Until a text following Lindsay's *principle of sequence* is so constituted, all investigations like the present must necessarily follow Marx on present clear reasons for deviation. Indeed the text of Marx, as Lindsay himself acknowledges, is notably sane in the treatment of the individual fragments. In the meantime it is

obvious that the evidence afforded by the apparent parallel-
isms between certain sequences of Lucilian fragments and
certain satires of Horace present a phenomenon which is of the
utmost importance for the determination of the arrangement
of Lucilian sequences by future editors of the earlier satirist.

Hitherto studies of literary relationships in Greek and Latin
have fallen into two classes. On the one hand we have studies
on the general problems of style, rhetoric, and imitation, such
for instance as those of Stemplinger, *Das Plagiat in der griech-
ischen Literatur*. On the other hand we have a huge body of
studies on the sources of classical authors more or less valuable
and more or less detailed in the citation of parallel passages.
So far as I have observed few scholars have attempted to bring
these two types of studies into any intimate and organized
relation. And yet until this is done the larger aspects of the
problem escape us. Such studies as Hirzel, *Der Dialog*, Reich,
Der Mimus, Misch, *Der Autobiographie*, trace with great learn-
ing and acumen the development and literary environment of
. three important genres, but concern themselves only inciden-
tally with the questions of the sources of the great writers
working within these genres. And yet only in the light thrown
by a somewhat detailed knowledge of the general theories of
imitation and originality, widely current from the rise of
sophistic rhetoric in Greece after the middle of the 5th century
B.C. and its spread by the influence of philosophical, aesthetic,
and rhetorical studies of the fourth and succeeding centuries
to all parts of the Hellenistic and Greco-Roman world can we
hope to view a problem of imitation involving the relation
between the founder of a great genre and his still more famous
successor, the relation of a Horace to a Lucilius in its true aesthe-
tic and historical perspective. This book, therefore, starts
with the assumption that there was such a thing as the Classical
Theory of Imitation, and that it is a dangerous anachronism
to attempt to appraise the literary modes and ideals of a great
classical writer like Horace on the basis of our current romantic
theories of composition, with their over-emphasis on originality
and spontaneity, and their tendency to tear loose the individual
genius from his cultural environment, and their relative dis-

regard of the claims of the great tradition of European literary culture.

I use the term "European literary culture" advisedly because I believe that to understand clearly the content, the scope, the strength and the defects of the Classical Theory of Imitation is to gain a point of view of real value not only for the workers in the classical field, but for students of mediaeval and renaissance literature. After all, with important modifications, misinterpretations, degradations, and revivals, this theory of literary composition was the one most widely prevailing in the long period from the 4th century b.c. to the middle of the 18th century. It is my hope then that this book will make an appeal to all who are interested in literary relationships, and to such cultivated readers as believe it is still necessary to keep open that long road which binds our modern civilizations to those of Greece and Rome. Certainly the first three chapters of this book should contain something of interest to those who wish to study at first hand the evolution of the classical theory of imitation. And there are perhaps still some lovers of Horace who will not be repelled by the more technical chapters in which I try to show Horace the satirist in his workshop. For in my belief Horace the poet and Horace the critic are one. At nearly every turn we find concrete illustrations of Horace's literary theories in his non-critical works, while the critic is guarded from any tendencies to dogmatic or pedantic devotion to abstract theory by his experience in the practical problems of literary composition. In this respect the relation between Horace the literary critic and Horace the Augustan poet is strikingly similar to that between Cicero the rhetorical theorist and Cicero the republican orator. That both men were conscious adherents to a long rhetorical tradition dealing with the problems of composition in prose and verse is a point of view which I have constantly presented in this book.

It is to emphasize my belief that such a study rightly interpreted can in no sense be regarded as derogatory to the originality of Horace that I have selected the two epigraphs of this book and have called the book a Study in the Classical Theory of Imitation. To the classicist at any rate originality does not connote originality of theme, but rather the imaginative power of the creative artist to impress his ideals, from whatsoever source derived, upon his own age and all future ages by means of his complete mastery of those ideals and the technique of the form in which they find most appropriate expression. So Isocrates declares in the *Panegyricus* in words not without their value for the present day: Now I think that a very great advance would be made in every pursuit, and especially in the practical study of literary expression if admiration and honor were to be bestowed in practical affairs not so much on those who take the first step in anything as on those who bring it in each case to the most successful conclusion, *not so much on those who seek a subject on which no one has ever spoken before as on* those who know how to treat their subject in a manner which is beyond the power of anyone else. So André Chénier in *L'Invention* (2, 170) admirably voices the same theory:

Ainsi donc, dans les arts, l'inventeur est celui
Qui peint ce que chacun put sentir comme lui.

Judged in the light of the influences which I have just outlined, the six chapters of this book will be found, I hope, to possess a progressive unity. In Chapter I, which I have called The Classical Theory of Imitation, I shall trace the salient elements in the development of the aesthetic and rhetorical theory of imitation. We shall find that the principles underlying this theory are deduced in the first instance from the sympathetic study of the actual works of the greatest Greek writers in the various genres of poetry and prose. The principles thus discovered were formulated by some of the most discriminating Hellenic minds from the days of Gorgias to those of Plato and Aristotle and the later philosophical rhetoricians of the Academy and the Porch. We shall find that the study of rhetoric was placed on a scientific basis in the Hellenistic period and was nationalized in Rome in the age of the Scipios. Here it underwent still further formulations and developments at the hands of Cicero, Brutus, the Roman Atticists, Horace, Dionysius of Halicarnassus, Quintilian, and many others. We shall find that the rhetorical theory of imitation, which from its wide acceptance in the Hellenistic and Greco-Roman period we may fairly call the classical theory of imitation, regarded the subject matter falling within the pale of the genre as the common property of the workers in the genre, and looked askance both at independent invention and slavish plagiarism. Yet originality was assured because the different genres were both developed and gradually transformed by the study of the great masters made by their successors, who work not in the spirit of verbal imitation, but in that of generous rivalry. But since imitation is quite as much a matter of style as of content we shall further discuss the development of the theory of the three styles, the plain, the middle, and the grand, and other more technical aspects of stylistic imitation, and the relation of these theories to the development of such well-known literary genres as epic, tragedy, comedy, and the free satiric forms, and finally we shall find explicit evidence from Horace's critical works of his complete familiarity and sympathy with the essential elements in the classical theory of imitation.

Our next consideration will be the effect of Horace's acceptance of this theory of imitation upon his relations with his predecessor Lucilius, the inventor or εὑρετής of the *sermo* or satiric discourse in the plain style, the genre in which Horace is the greatest representative. But to answer this question rightly it is necessary to consider in detail the relation of Lucilius and the Scipionic circle to the new Greek learning, and especially to the Stoic rhetoric as expounded by Diogenes of Babylon and Panaetius of Rhodes.

In my second chapter, therefore, The Relations of Lucilius and the Scipionic Circle to the New Greek Learning and Literature, I shall first try to trace the development of the theory of the diction and humor appropriate to the *sermo* or conversational discourse in the plain style, the type of oral and written expression favored by the truth-loving Stoics, formulated for the Romans in the systems of Diogenes of Babylon and Panaetius, and employed as the result of their influence in nearly all the literature emanating from the Scipionic circle. In particular I shall consider the probable relation of Lucilius to such rhetorical theories, and the relation of these earlier theories to

the subsequent rhetorical and stylistic theories of Cicero and
the Roman Atticists as set forth in Cicero's rhetorical works,
notably in his *de oratore*, *orator*, and *Brutus*. Cicero indeed
appears as a great mediating agency between Lucilius and
Horace, because on the one hand he is a deep admirer of the
earlier Roman poetry and thus supplements in countless ways
our knowledge of the literary ideals and the literary environ-
ment of the earlier period; and on the other hand because he
restates, enlarges, transforms, and refines the stylistic theories
which first found expression in the theoretical treatises of the
earlier period.   Above all we learn from Cicero's use of Panae-
tius in the *de officiis*, especially from his summary of Panaetius
de sermone in book 1, the Stoic rules for the content, and tone,
and style of the conversational discourse both oral and written.
By comparative analysis of the *sermones* or discourses in the
plain style of Lucilius we find that he is in essential harmony
with the tenets, both grammatical and stylistic, of this Stoic
rhetoric, save in two important respects.   In the first place
Lucilius apparently because of the influence of the impromptu
satiric forms of the Cynics, τὸ σπουδαιογέλοιον is in sympathy
whether consciously or unconsciously with those tendencies,
which were subsequently formulated as a definite nuance under
the concept of the plain style.   He therefore prefers impromptu
composition and a freer and racier diction than is approved by
the more exacting standards of the later Roman Atticists and
Horace.   In the second place by temperamental bias and
probably also under the influence of the popular Cynic-Stoic
satirical forms, Lucilius was shown to use invective more freely
than was permissible to a strict adherent of the theory of the
plain style.   And finally the relation of the Socratic theory of
irony, the type of liberal humor pervading the conversations of
Socrates, the Platonic dialogues, and widely prevalent in the
Scipionic circle will be shown to be according to rhetorical
theory especially appropriate to the *sermo*.   Here also Lucilius
will be found to be entirely familiar with this rhetorical theory
of ironic humor, and yet to have transgressed the limits of that
theory too freely to meet with the approval of the more urbane
standards of the Augustan age.   Yet it will be shown that

even Lucilius employs humor of the ironic type more freely than has ordinarily been supposed, and probably advocates this type of humor, or at least protests in his critical satires against the charge of employing malicious invective.

In Chapter III, Lucilius and the Greek Satirists, I attempt by a preliminary survey of this most difficult field to outline tentatively the general nature of the relationship between the Greek philosophic satirists of the Hellenistic period, whose tone and spirit is best summed up by the term τὸ σπουδαιογέλοιον and Lucilius. Here results are necessarily problematical, as we are dealing exclusively with fragments, but sufficient evidence is disclosed for making at least a plausible case for a fairly wide acquaintance of Lucilius with the somewhat inchoate expressions of the satiric spirit in Greek literature, especially with the διατριβαί of Bion of Borysthenes. In any case the influence of certain widely spread Greek satiric forms, which have not yet crystallized into a satiric genre, upon Lucilius seems probable.

My purpose in the last three chapters of this book is to make a concrete application of the theoretical principles set forth in the first three chapters to the question of the exact nature of Horace's imitation of Lucilius. Chapter IV, The Satires of Horace's First Book, shows that Horace did in practice use the themes of several Lucilian satires, notably satires 1, 2, 4, 5, and 9, as common material to be transformed by the alembic of his genius into the most perfect examples of the satirist's art in the annals of literary history. An examination of the critical satires 1, 4 and 1, 10 shows that Horace was in all probability a convinced adherent of the later and more refined interpretations of the plain style and the ironic type of humor appropriate to that style. Yet his literary criticism, even his strictures upon Lucilius are presented in a form clearly reminiscent in its essential outlines of the critical satires of Lucilius. Finally Horace, like Lucilius, is found, notably in the first and fourth satires, to be strongly influenced by the Greek satirists, the Cynics and Stoics of the Hellenistic period. My whole analysis is an endeavor to define concretely the nature of Horace's imitation of Lucilius, to show that Horace is at once an imitator as defined by the Classical Theory of Imitation and according to his own explicit admission, and yet a profoundly original poet, who gives consummate expression to his own theories of art and life and to the literary, social, and ethical ideals of the Augustan age. An understanding of the delicacy and the intricacy of this imitative relationship between Lucilius and Horace as revealed in the first book of the satires is, I believe, of great value for an intelligent understanding of the Classical Theory of Imitation.

In Chapter V, The Satires of Book II, I continue the comparative analysis of the satires of Lucilius and Horace. In this book we find a consciousness on the part of Horace that his satire of the first book was in some measure open to the criticism of being *nimis acer*. In consequence we shall find a distinct decline in the employment of purely personal satire and in the use of proper names, accompanied by a notable advance in the use of those popular philosophic themes suited for the expression of social satire and social philosophy. The conscious relationship with the more formally articulated popular philosophic discourses of the Cynics and Stoics is increasingly apparent, notably in such satires as 2, 3, and 7. Horace's concern is with the art of life and in this sense most of the satires of this second book may be said to pave the way for the epistles. And yet we still have abundant evidence in all the satires of the book except the sixth of the continued influence of Lucilian themes or of the Lucilian formulation of well-worn Stoic and Cynic commonplaces and stock examples upon the satires of this book. Horace seems, however, to have shifted his interest to those more general satires of Lucilius, which probably stood in closest relation to Lucilius' expression of his underlying philosophy of life as moulded by the influence of Greek philosophy, and by the popular forms of Greek philosophic exposition. I may add that Horace's relation to Lucilius is now freer and more independent. Such apprentice studies in the Lucilian manner as satire 1, 2, and 1, 7, are conspicuously absent from this book.

In Chapter VI, The Epistles and the Ars Poetica, we shall find the mould of satiric tradition partly broken. Horace, never a slavish imitator, seems to feel that having served his exacting and willing apprenticeship to the laws of satiric composition, and having given concrete illustration of his acceptance of the great classical tradition and the law of his genre (the *lex operis*), he has now attained complete mastery of the form best suited to express his critical judgment upon the ideals of the Augustan age. Out of the material of the Lucilian satiric genre he has evolved the new mould of Horatian satire. We still find in the first book of the epistles distinct traces of Lucilian coloring, but a marked diminution in the direct use of extended Lucilian themes. On the other hand in the *Ars Poetica* he may be almost said to warn us that the perfect mastery of the form such as he reveals in his epistles can only be attained by a reasoned and detailed knowledge of the laws of the genre, the selection of a congenial theme, and the imitative and stylistic development of that theme in almost complete accord with the stylistic theories which I have described in my first three chapters. As if to give concrete proof of this belief, Horace appears to have taken as the point of departure for the form and for certain of the topics treated in his *Ars Poetica*, the εἰσαγωγή addressed by Lucilius to the young historian Iunius Congus. In a very real sense the *Ars Poetica* affords a most interesting demonstration of the essential soundness of the thesis set forth in the theoretical chapters of this book, and a concrete illustration of Horace's reasoned adherence to the Classical Theory of Imitation. Taken in connection with chapters 4 and 5, it emphasizes the essential unity in the theory and practise of Horace the critic and Horace the satirist.

My present work would not have been possible without the remarkable edition of *Lucilius* by Marx and the illuminating *Untersuchungen zu Lucilius* of Cichorius. My indebtedness to these two works will appear constantly in the pages of this book. Equally heavy is my obligation to the editors of Horace. First and foremost among them I must express my deep sense of gratitude and high admiration for the great edition of Lejay. In the appreciation of the importance of Greek satiric influences Lejay's general introduction and his introductions to the individual satires have been of constant value. The text of Horace which I follow is that of the Heinze-Kiessling 4th edition. My indebtedness to the incisive commentary of this edition will be apparent to all my professional readers. In the case of the distinguished company of English and American editors whose humane scholarship has done so much to preserve for Horace his traditional place in the affections of our English speaking race, I must content myself with a general acknowledgment of benefits received. The editions of Wickham, Palmer, Greenough, Rolfe, and Morris have long been my familiar friends.

The point of view presented in my first chapter has been greatly influenced by Stemplinger's study, *Das Plagiat in der Griechischen Literatur*. To the long list of my helpers in the second and third chapters due acknowledgment is made by the constant citations of their works in my notes.

This study has developed in the *milieu* and under the direct inspiration of the remarkable series of studies in the field of Roman satire and Greco-Roman rhetoric made by a group of American colleagues and friends. The studies of Wilson, Knapp, Rolfe, Webb, Ogle, Jackson, Ullman, Hendrickson, and others have been a continuous incentive to me to seek to attain the same thoroughness of scrutiny, restraint in statement, and lucidity of form,—in short, to emulate the virtues of the plain style, the tradition of which they so worthily maintain.

I have profited greatly by the advice of my friend Professor A. G. Laird of the Department of Greek of the University of Wisconsin, who has aided me in the reading of the proof of this book. Professor Clifford H. Moore and my classmate, Professor E. K. Rand, of the Classical Department of Harvard University have given me valuable suggestions upon the fourth and fifth chapters and upon the general scope of the work.

Above all my friends and colleagues, it is a pleasure to express my especial gratitude to Professor George L. Hendrickson of Yale University. Professor Hendrickson has read the MS. of this book, and has given me in unstinted measure the benefit of his wide knowledge in the fields of ancient rhetoric and satire. In numerous places he has by his incisive and sympathetic criticism led me to corrections of fact and to revisions of statement and argument which have helped to a clearer understanding and presentation of the truth.

The publication of this study has been rendered possible by the liberality of the University of Wisconsin, which has freely aided this investigation at every stage of its progress, and which through its committee on publications undertook the entire expense for the publication of this book.

It is with real satisfaction after twenty years of service at the University of Wisconsin that I take this occasion to express my gratitude to the administrative officers of the University of Wisconsin, to my colleagues in the Department of Classics, and to my many friends in the faculty for their encouragement and generous help.

The Index is the work of my former student, Dr. Marie McClernan, to whose scholarship and industry I am deeply indebted.

And finally, it would have been quite impossible to have planned or to have brought to conclusion the present work, which has been largely pursued amid the manifold distractions and engrossing duties of an American citizen in war time, without the patience, encouragement, and unfaltering faith of her to whom this book is dedicated.

GEORGE CONVERSE FISKE

Madison, Wis.
  May 14, 1919

CHAPTER I

THE CLASSICAL THEORY OF IMITATION

In the life of Horace prefixed to Porphyrio's commentary we read:

sermonum duos <libros> Lucilium secutus antiquissimum scriptorem.

Here clearly the verb *sequor* implies imitation, but how did the ancient literary critic and the creative artist interpret such imitation? In what sense and under what limitations of personal temperament and contemporary taste did Horace "follow" his great predecessor Lucilius? The philological and aesthetic interpretation of the two words *Lucilium secutus* is the purpose of this book on Lucilius and Horace.

To answer this question it is necessary, (1) to study the rhetorical theory of imitation and of literary composition current in the Scipionic period and the Augustan age, which, as we can see from the critical writings of Horace himself underlay all that he wrote. (2) It is necessary also by a searching examination of the fragments of Lucilius, and a close comparison of their themes, form, and language with the satires and epistles of Horace to determine the precise relation of Horatian to Lucilian satire. The first of these two questions I shall consider in my first three chapters, the second in the three succeeding chapters of this book.

In these latter chapters I shall analyze the form and content of the first and second books of Horace's satires and of the two books of his epistles. Such a division of the subject is justified not only by reason of the separate publication of the first book of the satires in 35 B.C., the second book in 30 B.C., and the epistles from 20 to 14 B.C., but by the fact that these three works represent three distinct stages in the aesthetic and creative development of Horace. In the first book of the satires Horace is trying his prentice hand. Here his dependence on Lucilius is most clearly discernible in theme, thought, tone, and at times even in language. In the second book while relations to Lucilius (sometimes quite as close) can still be clearly traced, there is visible a greater firmness of structure, a marked restraint in the employment of invective, and a growing tendency to the popular treatment of philosophical themes of Cynic and Stoic origin. The second book of the satires thus paves the way for the epistles, in which Horace moves for the most part quite unconsciously in the field which he has won for himself, casting only an occasional glance backward to his former master Lucilius.[1]

In this introductory chapter it will be necessary to examine certain problems of literary imitation among the Greeks and Romans, and in particular to consider the conscious formulation of certain theories of imitation by the Greek and Roman rhetoricians and literary critics.[2] I shall try to show how far such aesthetic and rhetorical theories of imitation influenced literary composition. But since ancient rhetorical theory was firmly rooted in the study of the great masters in every genre, it is needless for my present purpose to give separate treatment to the work of the rhetorician and the literary artist. And in point of fact their functions were not mutually exclusive in antiquity. Both hold a large field in common, and both work with a common end in view, the perfection of the literary masterpiece.

It will be possible to draw many illustrations of the principles underlying rhetorical imitation from the satires of Lucilius and Horace; but such conceptions circulate through and animate all the literary genres of the ancients: epic, tragedy, comedy, elegy, the pastoral, the philosophic dialogue, the scientific treatise. They do not confine the human spirit in a straitjacket, as would at first seem to be the case to us moderns, with our romantic theories of "expression," "originality," "spontaneity." We may rather compare their effect to such physical systems as the circulation of the blood or the nervous system, which condition and animate the most varied types of physical activity. So these aesthetic systems suffuse and animate the human spirit in its task of expressing in enduring forms the ideals of truth and beauty.

Now the aesthetic theories of the Greeks and Romans, as we shall see, never condemned imitation *per se*, provided the result was a work of art. Rather the general trend of ancient literary tradition, reenforced by the teaching of the rhetorical schools, and formulated by the treatises on literary criticism and rhetoric, was to regard the subject matter of an earlier master in any given genre as the common property of posterity. Hence the duty and privilege of the heir to such a noble heritage is, working in the spirit of generous rivalry, to follow in the steps of his master, to preserve unimpaired the essentials of the great tradition, to perpetuate that ordered freedom which conditioned the growth in Greece and the continuation in Rome of all the literary genres.

While artistic imitation was thus recognized and approved by ancient critical opinion plagiarism was condemned. The ancients understood by plagiarism close verbal imitation or even free paraphrase, especially if the imitator made no direct acknowledgment of his sources, or even deliberately concealed them. Thus the classic example of plagiarism is found in Martial 1, 53 and 1, 66. Fidentius gave a reading of certain unpublished poems of Martial as if they were his own compositions, subsequently publishing them in his own name. Hence Martial calls him both thief (*fur*) and *plagiarius* (1,52,9). That is, as poet, he is the *dominus* of his works as a master is of his slaves. He manumits them as it were by publication. He therefore humorously appeals to the *lex de plagiariis* of the consul Q. Fabius Verrucosus 209 B.C. against the *plagiator* who laid claim to them as his own, and calls upon Quintianus, a rich patron, to appear in his behalf as the *assertor libertatis*, thus protecting the poet's right to his property. Similarly in *epistles* 1, 3, 15–20, Horace speaks of frequent warnings given to Celsus against excessive dependence upon the works in the new library of Apollo on the Palatine, advises him to depend on his own resources, and not to strut like the crow in borrowed plumage.[3]

The successor to a great tradition in any genre must clearly avoid plagiarism. Nevertheless, according to the ancient point of view ample scope was provided for his originality by the high privilege of retelling the ancient message with such additions, omissions, and transformations in the subject matter, and above all, with such stylistic perfection as would inevitably result in a work of art. According to this conception, a work of literary art expresses the result of ages of discrimination devoted to the attainment of a free and harmonious union of form and thought. At the same time it satisfies the sensuous, ethical, and aesthetic ideals of contemporary life and is redolent of that life. This conception of the function of the creative artist, which we may call the Classical Tradition, is closely bound up with imitation in the sense in which I have just defined that term. Its eternal antinomy is the Romantic Tradition, according to which, like Minerva the work of art springs fully armed from the head of each creative Jove.[4]

Thus in the body of this study I shall try to show that Horace in keeping with these general aesthetic and critical laws of composition—and he has himself constantly given utterance to them in his critical works—found the themes of many of his satires in Lucilius, just as Lucilius, in his turn, had found certain of his themes in the popular dialogues of the Cynics and Stoics with their frank criticism of contemporary Hellenistic life. Our judgment of Horace as a satirist, therefore, should be based on that of antiquity, or at least should take antiquity's judgment as a point of departure. We should regard Horace as an author, who gathered the themes of many of his satires as Shakespeare did the plots of his plays, who then following the broad outlines of his Lucilian themes, transmitted them and contemporized them with such perfection of literary art as to mirror in his satires and epistles both the everyday life and the higher aesthetic and social ideals of the Augustan age. Like his great successor Juvenal[5] he knew that the true subject of satire is the struggle, ever won—yet ever lost—between the activities of man, the outward expression of his seething emotions, and the ever changing stream of life down which he is swept:

> quidquid agunt homines, votum, timor, ira, voluptas,
> gaudia, discursus nostri farrago libelli est.

Horace, indeed, as we may see from his own words, regarded himself, except in style, as the follower of Lucilius. Thus in *sat.* 1, 10, 46 ff. he tells us that after the unsuccessful experiments of Varro Atacinus he felt that he could attain a

measurable success in the field of Lucilian satire, though inferior
to its *inventor* or *εὑρετής*, Lucilius:

> Hoc erat, experto frustra Varrone Atacino
> atque quibusdam aliis melius quod scribere possem,
> inventore minor; neque ego illi detrahere ausim
> haerentem capiti cum multa laude coronam.

We may contrast the modesty of this passage with the proud
boast with which at the conclusion of the first collection of the
odes 3, 30, 12 ff., Horace lays claim in lyric poetry to the
imperishable fame due the *inventor*, whose badge is the laurel
crown bestowed by Melpomene herself in recognition of the
poet's proud claim:

> princeps Aeolium carmen ad Italos
> deduxisse modos.   Sume superbiam
> quaesitam meritis et mihi Delphica
> lauro cinge volens, Melpomene, comam.

Later in the same satire, line 65, Lucilius is described as pos-
sessed of a greater degree of polish than one would expect
from the inventor of an entirely new kind of poetry, and one
untouched by the Greeks:[5]

> Fuerit Lucilius, inquam
> comis et urbanus, fuerit limatior idem
> quam rudis et Graecis intacti carminis auctor,
> quamque poetarum seniorum turba.

And again in *sat.* 2, 1, 28 ff., Horace with complete generosity
recognizes himself as the imitator:

> me pedibus delectat claudere verba
> Lucili ritu, nostrum melioris utroque.
>
> . . . .
>
> sequor hunc, Lucanus an Appulus anceps.

In *sat.* 2, 1, 62 ff., Horace gives renewed recognition to the
claims of Lucilius as the inventor of satire:

> cum est Lucilius ausus
> primus in hunc operis componere carmina morem.

And finally in line 74, he affects, certainly not with utter insin-
cerity, to regard himself as inferior to Lucilius in native ability,
as he is in financial standing:

> quidquid sum ego, quamvis
> infra Lucili censum ingeniumque.

In the satires then, Horace explicitly rejects for himself the title of εὑρετής or *inventor*, which he so proudly claims in the odes. He denies any intention of tearing the garland, the symbol of primacy, from the head of Lucilius. Such recognition of the claims of the inventor of the genre is, in fact, a commonplace of Augustan literary theory.[7] The testimony of the life in the commentary of Porphyrio, quoted above, is to this extent confirmed by Horace's own words, and by parallel passages in praise of the εὑρεταί in Augustan poetry.

What, then, was the theory of imitation in which Horace and the great continuators of the Augustan age approached their task? Of the relations of Roman literature to the Greek we may fairly say that the Roman man of letters adopted the attitude later assumed by the humanists of the Italian renaissance to the ancient classics. Thus Horace in the *Ars Poetica* 268 ff., exhorts his countrymen to the unremitting study of the Greeks:

> vos exemplaria Graeca
> nocturna versate manu, versate diurna.

So Petrarch *ep. rer. fam.* 6, 2, p. 315:

> Testatus sum me nihil novum, nihil fere meum dicere, immo vero nihil alienum; omnia enim, undecumque didicimus, nostra, nisi forsan abstulerit ea nobis oblivio.

Now of all periods of Roman literature the Augustan age perhaps stood closest to the Italian renaissance in its insistence on the union in the man of letters of critical theory and creative practice, and consequently in the almost excessive regard in which it held perfection of style.

The works which best express the critical theories current in this and the preceding age, the *de oratore* and *orator* of Cicero, the treatises of Dionysius of Halicarnassus, and the *Ars Poetica* of Horace devote much attention to the critical gradation of φύσις (natural talent, spontaneity, originality), ἐπιστήμη, (knowledge of literature, history, philosophy, and rhetoric), and μελέτη (technical exercises designed to mould the faculties of the man of letters, whether orator or poet). The general trend of Ciceronian and Augustan opinion seems to be summarized in the *Ars Poetica* of Horace, 408 ff.:[8]

Natura fieret laudabile carmen, an arte
quaesitum est: ego nec studium sine divite vena,
nec rude quid prosit video ingenium; alterius sic
altera poscit opem'res et coniurat amice.

Thus we see that the sophisticated Augustan age had reacted
in no small measure from the ancient theory of the poet as the
vessel of a Dionysiac enthusiasm, a theory, which at least as old
as Democritus,[9] is eloquently defended by Plato in the Ion and
Phaedrus.[10] This theory is so far acceptable to Cicero[11] that he
denies that any poem of imaginative sweep can be composed
sine aliquo mentis instinctu. And even the cool-minded Horace,
who in the concluding lines of the *Ars Poetica* (453–476) ridicules
the conception of the *demens poeta*, elsewhere (*odes* 2, 19; 3, 1)
submits to the conventional symbolism of inspiration.

In modern times also critics of distinction have not been
lacking, who asserted this predominant influence of inspiration.
So the youthful Goethe,[12] at first attracted by the formlessness
of Shakspeare cries: Natur, Natur! Nichts so Natur als
Shakspeare's Menschen. Yet both in theory and practice the
sober second thought of men, ancient and modern, has always
recognized that the divine *afflatus* is the breath that permeates
our being only when we have attained the hard won summit of
perfection; or to vary the figure, only a spiritual wrestling with
the divine powers assures their gifts. From this point of view
inspiration may be held to be the child of Talent and of patient
Art. So the aged Goethe on December 13, 1826, to Eckemann:[13]
Ein Talent wird nicht geboren, um sich selbst überlassen zu
bleiben, sondern sich zur Kunst und guten Meistern zu wenden,
die dann etwas aus ihm machen. So Longinus on the Sublime
36, 4: προσήκει . . . βοήθημα τῇ φύσει πάντη πορίζεσθαι τὴν τέχνην.
ἡ γὰρ ἀλληλουχία τούτων ἴσως γένοιτ' ἂν τὸ τέλειον.

By the Augustan age, then, the belief was well established
that the poet must first be born, and then be made. The youth
of talent (φύσις) had first to enlarge his sympathies and develop
his intelligence by the unremitting study of the liberal arts
(ἐπιστήμη). But this did not suffice. He must in addition by
practical exercises in poetical and prose composition, by the
study of the rhetorical principles on which the literary art was
supposed to rest, attain the mastery of fitting literary expression

(τέχνη). Only thus could he hope to attain that half-rational, half-emotional elevation of the spirit in whose union the highest work of art is conceived.

The study of rhetoric, then, was a prerequisite for literary composition in every field. But the art of rhetoric was itself the result of the sympathetic and critical study of the great masterpieces of Greek prose and verse, by some of the most discriminating Hellenic minds from Gorgias to Aristotle and the later rhetoricians of the Academy and the Porch. This study was placed on a scientific basis in the great schools of Athens, Pergamum, Alexandria, Rhodes, and carried to Rome in the age of the Gracchi, where it was warmly welcomed by the Scipionic circle. The belief in the great classical tradition lies at the root of these aesthetic and rhetorical studies of the ancient world. But these studies in their turn reenforced, clarified, and systematized the aesthetic conceptions of the best minds among the Greeks and Romans from the middle of the fifth century B.C. until the Augustan age when rhetoric came to be regarded for better and for worse as *par excellence, the discipline* by whose principles the youth must be moulded, and upon whose mastery all literary composition depended. And so in time it came to pass that each poet and writer in turn transmitted the great tradition by transmuting it. Each spoke to his age with a voice in which the human tones of the present were mingled in the higher and ideal harmony of the human spirit in all the ages.

This traditional interpretation of the poet's calling was not unnatural or constraining, for that calling had been traditional in certain guilds and families in the earlier days in Greece,[14] while in Athens from the days of Pisistratus the festival system exercised a similar unifying influence. Even the earlier Roman poets like Livius Andronicus and Accius belonged to the *collegium poetarum*,[15] which still existed in Augustan Rome, and held its meetings at the temple of Minerva on the Aventine. For all these reasons the ancient writer gave his willing allegiance to claims whose coercive force it is difficult for us to realize today. The spirit in which each poet contributed his part to the permanence of the tradition is well expressed by Bacchylides frag. 14, 1.

ἕτερος ἐξ ἑτέρου σοφὸς τότε πάλαι τότε νῦν.

It was in this spirit that Horace looked up to his master Lucilius. It was from the cumulative force of such traditions, whether corporate, educational, domestic, or spiritual that the different types of literature were evolved in Greece and worthily continued in Rome. The literary artist felt that the highest perfection of his powers was conditioned by the free and glad observance of those unchanging principles of art, which assured the development of his powers in that broad, but well defined spiritual country in which he lived, and moved, and had his being.[16] Since the spiritual law of that land was open to him to read in the great critical and creative masterpieces of Greece and Rome, which he could and did regard as the very charter of his freedom, it would perhaps be fitting that our modern romantic critics should show a somewhat greater diffidence in regarding such necessary restrictions of ordered liberty as fetters placed upon the human imagination.

Let us now examine in somewhat greater detail the operation of this tradition, and the function of rhetorical training in the assimilation of the tradition with literary composition. For these were the great influences affecting the poet in dealing with the material so largely traditional in the genre to which he felt himself attracted by intellect, sympathy, and imagination.

In the first place as regards tradition: the μῦθος or *fama*, that is the story or vulgar tradition must be followed in its main outlines. Thus Aristotle in his *poetics* 6, 9, 9 asserts that the myth is the source and soul of tragedy: ἀρχὴ καὶ ψυχὴ ὁ μῦθος τῆς τραγῳδίας. The Stoics held that it was the substratum of primitive history and physical philosophy.[17] Even the poets of the Alexandrian age, a race of ἐπίγονοι, did not venture in the epic or in the tragic forms to invent myths. Rather, priding themselves upon their antiquarian lore, they sought long-forgotten myths, which lay half-concealed to the side of the paths well worn by Homer and the great Attic tragedians. Thus Callimachus says: hymn *in laud. Pall.* 56:

μῦθος δ' οὐκ ἐμός, ἀλλ' ἑτέρων.

and in frag. 442:

ἀμάρτυρον οὐδὲν ἀείδω.

This intense activity of the *docti poetae* of Alexandria and their Roman imitators in the search of antiquarian lore is perhaps the nearest analogue in antiquity to the feverish striving of the modern romanticists for novelty and their appropriation of neglected mediaeval material. This tendency is displayed in various genres. Thus in the epic we find a clear recognition of the orthodox form of the tradition and the variant versions. In the *Aeneid*, for instance, we hear of such phrases as *fama volat, dicuntur, fertur, ut ferunt Grai*.[18] Of the historian's attitude to tradition Livy says, 7, 6, 6: *fama standum est, ubi certam derogat vetustas fidem.*

Too wide a departure from the tradition in the way of independent invention, transformation of the traditional material, or even supplementary invention might be subject to criticism. So Aristophanes in the Knights, 16 ff., criticizes Euripides for his attempts to reinterpret the myths in term of contemporary rationalism. Here Roman aesthetic theories are in complete agreement with those of the Greeks. Thus Servius criticizes Virgil for unprecedented inventions or variations from.the tradition, but once defends him against criticism on the ground that he follows a variant invention from the Alcestis of Euripides.[19] Horace in the *Ars Poetica*, after emphasizing the point that the delineation of the historical or mythical character of the tradition must be observed—as we can see from such examples as the *honoratus Achilles*, the *Medea ferox invictaque*, the *flebilis Io*, the *perfidus Ixion*, the *tristis Orestes*—admirably sums up the accepted law of composition in the words, 119:

> aut famam sequere aut sibi convenientia finge.

At first sight it would seem that such forms as comedy and satire, which by their very nature mirror realistically the .present, stand in inevitable conflict with such principles. This is, indeed, largely true of the Old Comedy and of political satire so closely related to it in spirit, but the striving of the Greek genius towards the ideal and the typical was one of the many influences that led to the growth of the New Comedy from the Old, to the differentiation from such personal invectives as those of Archilochus and Hipponax of the biting social satire of the Cynics and the Stoics, to the composition in close relation of the χαρακτῆρες of Theophrastus and the comedy of manners. So Horace transforms the personal invective of Lucilius to social satire, illustrated to be sure by contemporary types, which are nevertheless not infrequently disguised under traditional Lucilian names.

The high value thus placed upon tradition fostered the study of rhetoric, which took a dominant place among the arts, and in education. The practical, didactic, and somewhat formalistic temper of the Romans induced them in the later republic and early empire to follow and develop as an educational instrument the intensive study of rhetoric, into which they had been inducted by Hellenistic Greece. Of this Greco-Roman rhetorical tradition a long succession of works on poetical and prose composition is known to us from antiquity. Of these the *Poetics* and *Rhetoric* of Aristotle, the *Manuals* of Theophrastus, the *Ars Poetica* of Neoptolemus of Parium, the *Orator, de Oratore*, and *Brutus* of Cicero, the *Ars Poetica* of Horace, the rhetorical treatises of Dionysius of Halicarnassus, and the institutes of Quintilian may serve to indicate the main line of the tradition. Such manuals of rhetoric and poetics were designed to codify for the benefit of the student the practice and theory of good usage as illustrated by the great classical models in the genres of epic, drama, oratory, history, and the other forms of prose and verse.[20]

But ancient rhetoric did not attain its purpose merely by the study of the general principles of composition as codified by philosophic and aesthetic theory. It insisted equally upon the pursuit of two closely related practical disciplines, which gave breadth and fixity of outline to its teachings, and incidentally lent further reenforcement to the classical tradition. These are (1) the reading and interpretation of the great masters; (2) the unremitting practice of the paraphrase and translation of masterpieces.

From the time of Isocrates reading, ἀνάγνωσις, was the principal medium of instruction in the schools, which were designed to fit the youth of Greece and Rome for the practice of sophistic eloquence. The foundation of reading was laid by the study of poetry, for through poetry the youth was introduced into life itself with its activities and reflections, its sufferings and its joys.[21]   Memorizing was employed to an extent which would grieve the soul of the modern pedagogical expert, and even mnemonic systems were taught.   That Livius Andronicus translated Homer's *Odyssey* into Saturnians as a school text shows how early Roman education followed in the steps of the Greek tradition.   So Horace in the famous lines in the *Ars Poetica* 268 insists on the unremitting study of the masterpieces of Greek literature:

vos exemplaria Graeca
nocturna versate manu versate diurna.

Thus an educational canon of school classics, as we should say, was formed, embracing the works of the poets, philosophers, historians.   Such traditional canons have been often traced,[22] extending in an unbroken sequence from the Hellenistic rhetoricians to the lists of school classics employed in the Byzantine empire.

The importance of reading is to be found in the fact that it lays the spiritual foundation for imitation.   Thus Dionysius of Halicarnassus, in his περὶ μιμήσεως,[23] says that the soul of the reader absorbs a stylistic affinity by continual association. In a passage of lofty poetical coloring Longinus, περὶ ὕψους p. 129, 11H, compares the influence of what is read upon the soul of the reader to the exhalations which stir the Pythia upon the tripod.   So Quintilian, 10, 2, 2, following Greek Peripatetic sources, says: omnis vitae ratio sic constat, ut quae probamus in aliis facere ipsi velimus . . . Similem (bonis) raro natura praestat, frequenter imitatio.[24]

Next to reading, the rhetorical schools employed paraphrase as a means of training.   By paraphrase they understood either grammatical paraphrase, the virtual equivalent of close translation, or rhetorical paraphrase, which implies the transformation of an original with deliberate creative purpose by application of the principles of rhetoric.   Thus Isocrates[25] insisted on the repeated and varied reinterpretation of the same material, and urged that the orator's goal should be ἄμεινον εἰπεῖν, the stylistic improvement of the original.   In the Alexandrian period poets vied with one another in their efforts at variety in the phrasing of the same theme.[26] Similarly Quintilian *Inst. Or.* 10, 5, 4, speaks quite in the Alexandrian temper of the *circa eosdem sensus certamen atque aemulatio.* Cicero, himself, though opposed to paraphrase in the vernacular, was a strong advocate of translations from the Greek.[27] Hermogenes, the Stoic rhetorician, indicates two methods of paraphrase, (1) τάξεως μεταβολή, (2) καὶ μῆκη καὶ βραχύτητες, that is either variation of the sequence in story, or argument, or amplification and condensation. There can be no doubt that the youthful dexterity gained by such scholastic exercises was later reflected in imitations of real literary value. All of these three methods of paraphrase find frequent illustration in Persius' relations to the satires of Horace. There is, indeed, aesthetic and psychological justification for such procedure, if we accept the doctrine of La Bruyère in the 17th chapter of the *Ouvrages de l'esprit:* Entre toutes les differentes expressions qui peuvent rendre une seule de nos pensées il n'y en a qu'une qui soit la bonne. To attain this *solum* and *summum bonum* of literary art is the goal of paraphrase.

Thus the art of composition was really taught, a goal which our modern American universities have so far sought vainly to attain by less thorough-going methods. By constant memorizing and reading the student steeped himself in the works of the great masters. By practical paraphrase in prose and verse he set for himself the same task which they had successfully performed. By means of rhetorical manuals, composed by those who usually combined with their professional functions as teachers the art of literary criticism, the student was in the literal sense of the word informed with those general principles of aesthetics which underlie, whether consciously or unconsciously, all literary composition. Both creative art and critical theory combined to regard the μίμησις τῶν ἀρχαίων, the imitation of the great masters, as the final criterion of a work of art. Thus the *auctor ad Herennium* 4, 2: quid? ipsa auctoritas antiquorum non cum res probabiliores tum hominum studia ad imitandum alacriora reddit.

As the practice of imitation thus became established, various aesthetic theories of its functions and limitations were formulated. It will be worth while to cite a few of these, as they afford striking illustrations of the literary ideals prevalent in the late republic and imperial Rome.[28]

Dionysius of Halicarnassus in his treatise περὶ μιμήσεως frag. 3, p. 197, Usener says: μίμησίς ἐστιν ἐνέργεια διὰ τῶν θεωρημάτων ἐκματτομένη τὸ παράδειγμα: and in his τέχνη 10, 19, p. 394.R: μίμησις . . . οὐ χρῆσίς ἐστι τῶν διανοημάτων ἀλλ' ἡ ὁμοία τῶν παλαιῶν ἔντεχνος μεταχείρισις. The *auctor ad Herennium*, apparently following the Stoic rhetoric of Hermagoras, gives this definition, 1, 2, 3: Imitatio est qua impellimur cum diligenti ratione ut aliquorum similes in dicendo velimus esse. Longinus περὶ ὕψους p. 129 Sp. recommends the imitation and rivalry of the great writers and poets as the surest means to the attainment of a lofty style. The rhetorical treatises of Cicero and Quintilian are permeated with similar theories. Thus Quintilian 10, 2, 1, declares: neque enim dubitari potest quin artis pars magna contineatur imitatione.

If then, imitation as the result of the cumulative influence of literary practice and rhetorical and aesthetic theories is the guiding principle of literary art, it is important to consider in a somewhat more systematic fashion its scope, virtues, and defects as a working creed. Above all we may inquire how the ancients succeeded in reconciling the principles of imitation with the desire for self-expression, for "originality" (as we say today), an aspiration inseparable from any great art.

It will be convenient[29] to consider these questions under the two categories of subject matter or content, and style. Under the category of subject matter I shall try to show, (1) that in the various genres the subject matter or theme was regarded as the common property of posterity, and hence that independent invention was shunned. (2) I shall try to show that within the limits of the genre, the perpetuation of which is a high privilege, originality is given ample scope by means of three principles of composition. These are: (a) the principle of the New Way or νέα ὁδός, as it has been called, that is the reinterpretation of the material in a form inspired by the aesthetic and ethical ideals of the present, and so transformed as to give appropriate utterance to those ideals; (b) the differentiation of the various genres by a formulation of their specific laws as deduced by the study and observation of the works of the great masters and their disciples; (c) the principle of improvement, which says that the writer's attitude to his model shall be that of generous rivalry.

Under the second category of stylistic imitation I wish to consider in some detail the influence of the ancient theory of the three styles of discourse, plain, middle, and grand, upon Horace's theory of satire and upon his criticisms of Lucilius. Also certain technical aspects of poetical composition with special reference to satire require brief treatment. These are parody, contamination, modernizations, the use of commonplaces, and self-citation.[30] Such an extended introduction may at first sight seem needless and wearisome, but it is necessary in order that we may approach our central problem, the nature of Horace's imitation of Lucilius, in full realization of the attitude of the ancients towards imitation, and with some knowledge of ancient imitative practice. Such a study will furthermore act as a check upon the "romantic approach" to ancient literature, from whose prepossessions it is especially difficult for modern scholars and critics to free themselves. Let us then push firmly forward with our task.

The Subject Matter is Common Property

The subject matter or theme, whether it be a myth, an historical epoch, a poetic theme, a humorous anecdote, an ethical reflection, was regarded by the ancients as common property, (δημόσιον or *publica materies*). Isocrates formulates this principle in the *Panegyricus* 8, where he says: αἱ πράξεις αἱ προγεγενημέναι κοιναὶ πᾶσιν ἡμῖν κατελείφθησαν. For the Romans, Seneca, speaking of the proper attitude of the poet to such a well worn theme as the Aetna says, *ep.* 79, 5 ff.: nec illis manus inicit tamquam alienis: sunt enim publica—iuris consulti negant quicquam publicum usucapi.[31] By this last phrase, *usucapi*, Seneca jestingly denies that common property can become private property by the exercise of a sort of literary squatter sovereignty. Similarly in the *Saturnalia* of Macrobius 6, 1, 7 Furius Albinus speaks of a: societas et rerum communio poetis scriptoribusque omnibus inter se exercenda concessa.

Hence the question for the author in any given genre was not so much what to write, but how to write it. If form did not dominate content, it at least shared the throne with it. Iso-crates,[32] who codified for future generations, both Greek and Roman, the tenets of the sophistic rhetoric gives full expression to this ideal in the *Panegyricus* 8, where he asserts that variety of expression upon the same theme is of the very essence of rhetoric; consequently that the grand may be simply expressed, the trivial magnified, the archaic modernized, so as to be brought into harmony with the tradition. Traditional material, therefore, need not be avoided. It represents rather the great cultural inheritance, which it is the task of the educated writer to interpret to his contemporaries in content and style. Such a task is manifestly one of utmost difficulty. Thus Pliny the Elder in the preface to his natural histories declares 12: res ardua vetustis novitatem dare, novis auctoritatem.[33]

THE IMPROVEMENT OF THE FORM AND THE νέα ὁδός

One result of the prevalence of such conceptions was, as we have just seen, that ancient literary theory deliberately dis-couraged independent invention of material. So Horace in the *Ars Poetica* 128 ff., advises the appropriation of epic material by the dramatist (the conventional source of Greek tragedy) a difficult, yet possible task:[34]

> difficile est proprie communia dicere; tuque
> rectius Iliacum carmen deducis in actus
> quam si proferres ignota indictaque primus.

In the New Comedy in particular with its fixed types, its intrigues ever recurring, but ever solved by scenes of recogni-tion, we see this principle of ancient literary art worked out with the extreme of logical consistency, and yet with a minute and deft variety in the delineation of the individual characters and incidents. Goethe in the conversation with Eckemann of September 18, 1823, expounds in strict accordance with these aesthetic principles the advantages in vividness of delineation, in what we call truth to life, gained by the poet, who in this sense accepts the raw material of tradition.

If then, the subject matter is common property and too independent invention is even discouraged, it follows as a corol-lary that the perfection of the form of the genre is all important, the development of its laws, a task worthy of the most loving care, and one affording an adequate recompense to the most aspiring genius. Hence Isocrates in the *Panegyricus* 3, quite logically advises the abandonment of any field in which perfection has already been attained, because further improvement is no longer possible. Horace's reason for writing Lucilian satire as given in *sat.* 1, 10, 40-49 is precisely the same. It was possible for him to write Lucilian satire because the unsuccessful attempts of Varro Atacinus and others left that field still open (for stylistic perfection), while Fundanius in comedy, Pollio in tragedy, Varius in epic, and Virgil in bucolic poetry had already won renown by their efforts to continue and improve by their verse, the great traditions of these genres.

By the Alexandrian age it had come to be felt, at least by Callimachus and his school, that in the epic perfection had already been attained, and consequently that this genre was exhausted. As a result we have the rise of the epyllion with its more limited field and its greater insistence on nicely chiselled strokes. Hence the famous line of Callimachus fr. 359:

τὸ γὰρ μέγα βιβλίον ἴσον τῷ μεγάλῳ κακῷ.

The same disinclination to epic composition is exhibited in the Augustan age by Propertius, Horace, and Ovid. Even Virgil essayed the epic only after long years of hesitation and several trial attempts. As is well known, the *Aeneid* is not a purely Homeric epic but fuses into a new form, elements from the Homeric epic, the Alexandrian epyllion, and the Roman national epic.

In the Alexandrian age this yearning for novelty struggled with partial success against the cumulative force of tradition, as we may see from the growth of such poetical and prose forms as the epigram, epyllion, and mime. Even Callimachus *ep.* 28 goes so far as to say that he hates the *publica materies* the tradition of content left by the great masters:

μισέω καὶ περίφοιτον ἐρώμενον οὐδ' ἀπὸ κρήνης
πίνω· σικχαίνω πάντα τὰ δημόσια.

Yet both for the Alexandrian writers and the Romans the principle of the νέα ὁδός was after all a *via media*. Literary tradition was so powerful that even Callimachus never thinks of the independent fabrication of material, but rather of the

rediscovery of such poetic material as has been hitherto but
little or imperfectly worked. Herein lies the special import
of Callimachus's dictum fr. 442:

ἀμάρτυρον οὐδὲν ἀείδω.

The road may be new, but the forest through which it winds is
hoary with antiquity.[35]

THE FORMULATION OF THE LAWS OF THE GENRES

From the efforts to reinterpret the traditional material
according to the principles of the New Way, there gradually
grew up a body of aesthetic law governing content, tone, and
style, which in each genre was deduced from the study of the
works of the great successors, who through discipleship attained
to the goal of creative art. Thus by the Augustan age, as we
have already seen, the works of certain masters had attained a
sort of canonical literary authority. Virgil, for example, is in
his *Eclogues*, a Roman Theocritus, in his *Georgics* a Roman
Hesiod, in his *Aeneid* the continuator in the main of the Homeric
Epic and the Ennean *Annalis*. Propertius regards himself as a
Roman Callimachus. Horace's lyric poetry is modelled on the
Aeolic lyrics of Sappho, Alcaeus, and Anacreon; his epodes
continue the tradition of personal invective first expressed in
the iambics of Archilochus, and in his satires he follows in the
steps of Lucilius.[36]

As a result of such aesthetic conceptions it followed that
the existence of a great masterpiece which might serve as a
model in any given genre, so far from deterring literary
aspirants acted as a direct challenge to their powers. The
stimulus to personal originality was quite as strong in antiquity
as in modern times under the influence of the romantic tradition,
but the questions of originality hardly ever arose in our modern
sense, because the ancient author adopted a different
attitude towards the function of *inventio* or invention. I mean
that the ancient author found (*invenit*), but did not fabricate
(*fingit*) his material. There is, therefore, no exact technical
equivalent in ancient literature for our term fiction. A letter
of Seneca to a friend upon the the writing of a poem upon such

a conventional subject as Mt. Aetna may serve to illustrate this point: Seneca says *ep.* 79, 6:

> non praeripuisse quae dici poterant, sed aperuisse . . . sed multum interest, utrum ad consumptam materiem an ad subactam accedas: crescit in dies et inventuris inventa non obstant, praeterea condicio optima est ultimi: parata verba invenit quae aliter instructa novam faciem habent.

IMPROVEMENT AND RIVALRY

The last clause of Seneca suggests the third principle of imitation, improvement of the model and generous rivalry with the great master. The subject matter, the very words even were at hand, but in an altered environment they could be made, chameleon-like, to assume a different color by an *opportuna derivatio*. In this effort to improve on the masterpiece the nicest sensitiveness to form and content was cultivated. Among the Greeks—and here again the Romans are their disciples—the narrow gap which separates imitation of content from imitation of form was bridged by what Dion of Prusa, 18 p. 476 R, calls the principles of καλλιειπεῖν and τὰ αὐτὰ ἕτερον τρόπον ὑποβάλλειν; that is, the effort was to attain stylistic perfection, and to reshape more perfectly the identical material. Thus Ovid, for example, makes Odysseus retell "the tale of Troy divine" to Calypso in ever changing form.[37]

The principle of generous rivalry ζῆλος or *aemulatio*, that pursuit of pre-eminence which appears in the games, in the Dionysiac festivals of Athens, in music, in court, in market place, and in the halls of the philosophers[38] was predominant also in ancient literature, Greek and Roman. Thus the author of the pseudo-Platonic *Epinomis*, 10, p. 987D, E, declares proudly: ὅτι περ' ἂν Ἕλληνες βαρβάρων παραλάβωσι κάλλιον τοῦτο εἰς τέλος ἀπεργάζονται. So in the *Saturnalia* of Macrobius 6, 1, 2 ff. Furius Albinus defends the practice of Virgil in dealing with tradition as an *opportuna derivatio*, while Pliny the Elder, *N. H. Praef.* 20 ff., assailing the compilers, describes his own writings as an ἀγώνισμα with the ancients. Quintilian, *inst.* 10, 2, 28 regards the effort *priores superasse* as the chief stimulus to literary composition.

Imitation of a model or borrowing from any source whatsoever was, therefore, never the subject of blame in antiquity, provided the imitator showed independence in the treatment of his material, and aimed at improvement in form or content. Thus Quintilian, continuing in complete accord with this conception, describes the perfect orator as one: qui etiam propria adiecerit ut suppleat quae deerunt, circumcidat, si quid redundabit. Of course an unsuccessful effort at improvement was properly subject to critical censure. According to Gellius, 9, 9, Probus censures Virgil in the fourth book of the *Aeneid* for adapting less successfully than Apollonius of Rhodes the comparison of Nausicaa with Artemis. This is the point of Horace's caution in regard to imitation in the *Ars Poetica* 134 ff.:

nec desilies imitator in artum
unde pedem proferre pudor vetet aut operis lex.

That is, the imitator must not set too narrow limits to his task. On the one hand he must have regard for the dignity of his model (*pudor*), on the other for the principles governing his own independent literary creation, subject however to the general laws of the genre (*lex operis*). Both of these principles will unite to discourage too literal a rendering as we see by the preceding line:

nec verbum verbo curabis reddere fidus.

The related processes by which the ancient literary artist first ranges widely to gain imaginative possession of his store, then laboriously reshapes it in accordance with the promptings of his genius, and finally gives it to the world quite transformed, is aptly compared by ancient literary critics to the operations of the bees in gathering honey, building the comb, and producing honey. For superficial appropriation on the other hand, the daw who struts in borrowed plumage is an equally apt symbol. Macrobius, *Saturnalia* I, *praef.* 4 gives the simile of the bee in a highly imaginative form: apes . . . quodammodo debemus imitari, quae vagantur et flores carpunt, deinde quicquid attulere, disponunt ac per favos dividunt et sucum varium in unum saporem mixtura quadam et proprietate spiritus sui mutant. That is, the collection of the essence of the flowers corresponds to *inventio*, its distribution among the combs to *dispositio*, and the transformation into honey to expression or *elocutio*. This simile of the bee is a favorite one for the poet's

activity. When thus used it clearly implies the acceptance of
what we may call the imitative interpretation of poetic inven-
tion. It is used by Lucretius 3, 10 ff.; and by Horace in the
odes 4, 2, 27 ff.:[39]

> ego apis Matinae.
> more modoque,
> grata carpentis thyma per laborem
> plurimum circa nemus uvidique
> Tiburis ripas operosa parvus
> carmina fingo.

Horace ep. 1, 3, 17 ff., employs the simile of the jackdaw in
borrowed plumage,[40] in urging his friend Celsus to make his
borrowed material his own by the independent exercise of his
poetical power, (in the various technical tasks of composition
we have been enumerating):

> ne, si forte suas repetitum venerit olim
> grex avium plumas, moveat cornicula risum
> furtivis nudata coloribus.

Such transforming imitation, therefore, proceeding upon the
principle of generous rivalry, and aiming at the improvement
of the genre, both Greeks and Romans sharply distinguished
from plagiarism. Thus Longinus περὶ ὕψους, 1,129 H: οὐ κλοπὴ
τὸ πρᾶγμα, ἀλλ' ὡς ἀπὸ καλῶν εἰδῶν ἢ πλασμάτων ἢ δημιουργημάτων
ἀποτύπωσις. Afranius also with perfect self-confidence
defends himself in the prologue of the Compitalia, against the
charge of plagiarism from Menander:

> fateor, sumpsi non ab illo modo,
> sed ut quisque habuit, conveniret quod mihi,
> quodque me non posse melius facere credidi
> etiam a Latino.

So Goethe, Gespräch. mit Eckermann 108G, who in Faust 7,96 ff.
had made Mephistopheles employ a song from Hamlet
expresses himself to almost the same effect:

> So singt mein Mephistopheles ein Lied von Shakespeare und warum
> sollte er das nicht? Warum sollte ich mir Mühe geben, ein eigenes zu
> erfinden, wenn das von Shakespeare eben recht war, und eben das sagte
> was er wollte.

Horace himself in the Ars Poetica 131 ff. has given us the
most concise summary of the three guiding principles on which

artistic imitation should rest. Is it unreasonable to assume, therefore, in view of the extent that similar principles have been shown to determine the nature of literary composition in Greece and Rome, that he observed these principles in the composition of his satires, in which he followed Lucilius as his master?

> publica materies privati iuris erit, si
> non circa vilem patulumque moraberis orbem,[41]
> nec verbum verbo curabis reddere fidus
> interpres, nec desilies imitator in artum,
> unde pedem proferre pudor vetet aut operis lex.

That is the successful appropriation of the common traditional material is dependent upon the observance of these three laws:

(1) Do not journey upon well-travelled ways.

(2) Avoid literal translation.

(3) Do not be a slave to the original, but keep your creative freedom.

Imitation thus freely conceived often develops into independent production, subject only to the general aesthetic laws developed by rhetorical study and by the influence of the earlier masters in the genre upon the later continuators of its high traditions. Thus Horace himself begins in the first book of satires with a number of more or less close studies in the Lucilian form. In the second book of the satires he supplements these with satires much more independently composed and more firmly constructed, illustrated too from contemporary life, satires, however, in the Bionean as well as in the Lucilian manner. Besides these we have even such completely independent studies as that on the Sabine farm.[42] Finally, in the epistles, where he has attained complete and independent mastery of the form we find only scattering Lucilian allusions.[43]

STYLISTIC IMITATION

But such conscious imitation of the content of the work of the great master of the genre with nice regard to aesthetic and rhetorical principles and to the promptings of the writer's own genius is only half the story. Imitation is as much a matter of style as of content; in fact the line which separates style from content is a tenuous one. This fact will appear most clearly when we come to consider the ancient theory of the three styles, plain, middle, and grand; for as epic and tragedy in matter and manner belong to the grand style, so comedy and the satiric forms by the same natural evolution fall under the plain style, the natural medium for the expression of our daily thoughts and emotions.

Moreover, style far more than theme is of the very essence of the man. From this point of view we may look upon the stylistic imitation of the ancients, as the free transformation and application of these rhetorical and aesthetic principles by the literary artist. Lack of space compels me to pass over unconscious imitation.[44] Under the category of what we may call applied theory, there are certain topics belonging to the ordinary technique of the ancient stylist which demand our brief attention. I wish to speak, therefore, of (1) the use of parody, (2) of free translation, (3) of contamination, (4) of modernization, (5) of the use of proverbs and literary commonplaces. Examples of these fundamental principles of literary craftsmanship may be cited from many genres. We shall have occasion to illustrate every one of them as we proceed with our more detailed study of the works of Lucilius and of Horace. We must not, however, lose sight of the larger truth in the study of the phenomenal aspects of the ancient literary forms. Ancient literature is true to form and to type, but in a far higher sense there emerges from such adherence and because of such adherence to type, the higher truth which pervades the world of ideas. For to the ancients imitation is after all the gestation by the human spirit of all the living elements streaming into its depths from the life and culture of the past, and from the works of the great masters mimetic of that life. From this slow process there is born a work of art expressing that larger vision of the individual spirit, which pierces through the shifting shadows of the world of contemporary phenomena and beholds in undimmed clarity the ideals of beauty and truth, seen *sub specie aeternitatis*. It is, however, our immediate task to analyze the phenomena that we may better appreciate the ideal.

PARODY

Parody[45] was especially common in ancient literature on account of the absence of contemporary critical reviews of

the type so common in England in the first half of the nine-
teenth century.   In oratory and philosophy parody seems to be
used as an occasional and ancillary weapon of controversy.
So in the Platonic dialogues there certainly existed—though
we cannot always clearly appraise and analyze their exact
nature today—assaults upon the sophistic tendencies of Antis-
thenes, the rhetorical philosophy of the school of Isocrates,
and the hedonistic tendencies of Aristippus.   The part that
parody plays in the assaults of Demosthenes upon Aeschines
is well known.   The later literature of philosophical controversy,
of which we are today only imperfectly informed through
allusions in Latin philosophical writers, made frequent use of
parody, until in the σπουδαιογέλοιον of the later Cynics and
Stoics parody became one of the favorite vehicles for the diffu-
sion of philosophic truth, and the demolition of error by means
of ridicule.

Long before this period it is possible in poetry, especially in
iambic poetry, in the Old Comedy, and in Satire to observe a
much more thorough-going use of parody as a weapon of literary
criticism.   As examples we may cite from the earlier period the
Homeric parodies of Hipponax and the Batrachomyomachia.
The criticisms of Euripides and Aeschylus in the Frogs of
Aristophanes, the parody on the *Cyclopeia* in the Wasps 130,
on the song of Harmodius in the Wasps 750, on the Homeric
Circe in the *Plutus* 302 ff., will serve to recall how commonly
literary criticism was couched in this form in the Old Comedy.
It was, in fact, Aristophanes in the Frogs 389 ff., who announced
his programme as πολλὰ μὲν γέλοιά μ'εἰπεῖν πολλὰ δὲ σπουδαῖα,
thus anticipating the designation of the genre which in the
hands of the Cynics and Stoics played such an important part in
the development of Greek and Roman satire.   The σίλλοι of
Timon, which genetically we must regard as Homeric parodies,
are perhaps the most striking example of the profound influence
of parody upon the literature of this period.[46]   In Roman satire
parodies upon the epic and the tragic style play an important
part in the satires of Lucilius.[47]   In Horace all readers are
familiar with the epic parodies interspersed in the Journey to
Brundisium.   Persius[48] begins his fifth satire with a stylistic
disquisition upon the characteristics of the plain and the grand

style in which parody plays an important part, while Juvenal[49] perhaps more than any other satirist employs parody as an instrument of satiric effect.

FREE TRANSLATION

Among the Romans, whose normal literary development was transformed by contact with the finished masterpieces of the Greeks at a time when their own crude and popular literary forms had not yet been perfected by a slowly developing evolutionary process, free translation from the Greek was held in even higher esteem than original invention. The aesthetic theories governing such translations are set forth by Cicero, one of the most productive of all the Romans in such translations, and the first discriminating literary critic of the Latin race. Thus in his *de optimo genere dicendi* 14 he prefaces his version of Demosthenes on the Crown, and the reply of Aeschines by some remarks on the relation of artistic to literal translations, strongly advocating a free treatment of the original: nec converti, ut interpres sed ut orator; sententiis iisdem et earum formis tamquam figuris, verbis ad nostram consuetudinem aptis; in quibus non verbum pro verbo necesse habui reddere, sed genus omne verborum uimque servavi non enim ea me adnumerare lectori putavi oportere sed tamquam appendere. Mere literal rendering is likewise condemned in the *de finibus* 3, 4, 15: nec tamen exprimi verbum e verbo necesse erit, ut interpretes indiserti solent. This, he declares in the *acad. posterior.* 10 was the principle adopted by Ennius, Pacuvius, and Accius and the other poets of the pre-Ciceronian period in their translations from the Greek: non verba sed uim Graecorum expresserunt poetarum, words which recall the strictures of Horace in the *Ars Poetica*.[50]

Translation according to this conception does in fact approximate to the ancient theory of independent literary creation. Cicero clearly expresses this conception in the *de oratore* 1,155: hoc adsequebar, ut non solum optimis verbis uterer et tamen usitatis, sed etiam exprimerem verba quaedam imitando, quae nova nostris essent. Hence we find the title *poeta* applied at an early period of Latin literature both to poet and to translator. Thus in the prologue of Terence's *Andria, nova fabula* means a play not previously translated from the Greek. The value set on literary translation may be seen from the fact that free translations from the Greek were in all periods made by writers of established reputation. Thus Catullus made translations from Callimachus, Cornelius Gallus from Euphorion; translations from the φαινόμενα of Aratus were made by Varro Atacinus, Cicero, Virgil, Germanicus, Gordianus, Avienus.

CONTAMINATION

Contamination, the fusing of incidents, scenes, or plots from two or more Greek originals is a favorite device of Latin literature from the time of the *palliata*.[51] But contamination, which arises from the natural desire of the imitator or translator to secure variety and rapidity of action or from the general similarity in theme or illustration between the contaminated originals is, of course, not confined to the *palliata*. It occurs in various literary forms and has left distinct traces in satire. In a paper on Lucilius and Persius[52] I have sought to show that the first satire of Persius was contaminated from certain passages in Lucilius, especially a satire in book 26, and Horace *sat.* 2, 1 for general setting, and the *Ars Poetica* of Horace for aesthetic creed. This study will afford several examples of the employment of contamination by Horace. A few examples must suffice. We shall find that the first satire of Horace's first book combines elements found in books 18 and 19 of Lucilius; the second satire on the sexual question draws on Lucilius books 7, 8, and 29. In the first satire of Horace's second book, a defence of satire and a fuller definition of the satiric genre, already presented in 1, 4 and 1, 10, we have a contamination of satires in Lucilius books 26 and 30. In the third satire of the same book, Horace's use of material from books 17 and 30 may possibly justify the conjecture that Lucilius twice wrote on the favorite Stoic paradox ὅτι πᾶς ἄφρων μαίνεται.[53]

MODERNIZATION

Strictly speaking, what we today understand by the term modernization falls under the broader category called by the Greek rhetoricians διασκευή.[54] In this term they included recension either by the author himself or by some later writer. Of recensions made by the author himself—and of such double versions we have many examples in Greek and Latin literature—it is not necessary to speak. On the other hand, posthumous revisions of the works of earlier masters designed to adapt them to contemporary literary taste and understanding play an important part in the literature of both Greeks and Romans. Indeed this element of modernization enters into the relationship which binds the continuator of a great literary tradition in any given genre to the εὑρετής or founder of the genre. Whether we are to regard the continuator as a creative artist or not depends in large measure upon the inspiration and native genius with which he vivifies his material. In either case the material is in no small degree the same whether worked by one who merely paraphrases with an eye to the present or by the consummate literary artist. The name and fame of the mere modernizer is lost, while that of the creative artist becomes immortal.

Recensions of this modernizing type are well-known to ancient literary critics. Quintilian[65] expressly informs us that the plays of Aeschylus underwent modernization to adapt them to the changed conditions of the Athenian stage. Similar recensions in the New Comedy are well attested. Thus the similarity between the Δεισιδαίμων of Menander and the οἰωνιστής of Antiphanes may best be explained on the supposition that the latter was a recension of the piece of Menander. Somewhat similar, though far freer in scope and method is Shakespeare's modernization of older dramas and novels. Closer to the ancient conception of διασκευή is the manner in which Pope retells the tales of Chaucer in a form suited to the more sophisticated age of Queen Anne. Such is in fact essentially Tyrrel's conception of the relation of Horace's satires to those of Lucilius.[66] As stated by Tyrrel, however, the theory is a half truth which fails to account for some of the most important characteristics of Horatian in distinction from Lucilian satire, and properly to recognize and define the real originality of the Augustan poet. For Horace absolutely reshaped the Lucilian ore and stamped upon it the image of his own life and world, social, intellectual, and spiritual.

The Literary Commonplace

In a realistic genre like satire, which combines vivid individual portraiture with popular exposition of the results of reflection upon the workings of those master passions which in every age determine the recurrence of such types as the miser, the spendthrift, the glutton, the adulterer, the *meretrix*, the soldier of fortune, the lover, the slave, the fortune hunter, and many others, there naturally develops a mass of reflective wisdom expressed in a humorous manner. This wisdom, pointedly expressed and realistically illustrated by anecdote, bulks so large in the works of the popular Cynic and Stoic teachers of the Hellenistic period that they may be regarded as the originators of this type of half-philosophical, half-satirical exposition. As these methods of exposition gained wider influence there were gradually formed collections or anthologies of reflections, maxims, proverbs, apothegms, witty anecdotes, which were drawn upon to add savor to the diatribe and satirical writings of the popular Hellenistic philosophers.[57]

Similar manuals appear also among the Romans apparently containing both Greek and Roman material. How far they were drawn upon by the Roman satirists it is difficult to say. Their existence, however, and the constant employment of the anecdotic method of exposition by the Latin satirists, and the approval accorded to the theory of literary commonplaces by the ancient rhetoricians make it extremely probable that these reservoirs of popular wisdom and humorous anecdote were employed by the Latin satirist with the same freedom with which they were employed by their Greek predecessors of the Cynic and Stoic schools. As an illustration of a collection of anecdotic apothegms we may cite the eleventh book of Lucilius which contained a string of epigrammatic invective and anecdote levelled against the satirist's contemporaries.[58] Collections of apothegms were made by Cato the elder, while we hear of collections of the witty sayings of Caesar and of Cicero.

Somewhat similar is the influence upon Latin satire of the literary conditions which determined the rise in the Hellenistic age of the ἀπομνημονεύματα and χρεῖαι. It will be more convenient to discuss the nature of these forms and their later influence

on Latin satire in connection with the general question of the
Greek sources of Lucilius.[59] We may note in passing that
Horace in speaking in *sat.* 2, 1, 30 of the tone of intimate self-
revelation so characteristic of Lucilius uses language which is
reminiscent of the ὑπομνήματα, and in *sat.* 1, 4, 139, he relates
his own literary practice in the writing of satire to similar
Hellenistic and Lucilian antecedents. In the second book of
Horace's satires, *sat.* 2, 3, 4, and 7, the discourses of Ofellus,
Stertinius, Catius, and Davus clearly follow the expository
methods of the Hellenistic ἀπομνημονεύματα in which the disciple
narrates the teachings of his master.[60] Formally, at least,
such satires are reminiscent—as were also possibly their Lucilian
prototypes, where these can be determined—of such works as
Xenophon's *Memorabilia*, and the collections known to have
existed of the teachings and sayings of Aristippus, the Cyreniac;
of Diogenes and Metrocles, the Cynics; of Zeno, Persaeus,
Aristo of Ceos, and Hecaton, the Stoics. From such sources
indeed Horace may have derived such anecdotes as those of
Aristippus, Diogenes, and others.[61] From the Roman period
we find similar collections under the names of Cato, Cicero,
Trebonius, Furius Bibaculus, Caesar, and Melissus.[62] The
work of the latter as a member of the circle of Maecenas must
certainly have been known to Horace.

The χρεῖαι[63] or utilitarian ethical anecdote is related to such
reminiscent literature on the one hand, and even more closely
by reason of its brevity to the literary commonplace on the
other. The structural influence of such χρεῖαι upon Lucilian
and Horatian satire may be illustrated by the anecdote from
the trial of the Hellenomaniac Albucius in Lucilius book 2,
fragment 88 ff., by the anecdote of the conversion of Polemon
Lucilius frag. 755 and Horace *sat.* 2, 3, 25 ff., by the story of
Rupilius Rex in Horace *sat.* 1, 7, virtually a Roman χρεία.
The cumulative influence of such rhetorical and aesthetic
theories of imitation, and the existence and wide popularity of
these literary forms and methods, the ἀπομνημονεύματα, the
ἀποφθέγματα, and the χρεῖαι, and their later Roman analogues
found its fullest development in the rhetorical theory of the
τόποι κοινοί or *loci communes*.[64] As a result we find a great body
of commonplaces, current probably in oral and literary form,

which like an atmosphere surround and permeate nearly all forms of literature in the Hellenistic and Roman period. Both philosophers and rhetoricians developed a theory as to the relations of such commonplaces to creative literature, which profoundly influenced the writers of the Hellenistic period and their Roman successors. The studious elaborations and the variation of the commonplaces traditional in the genre was not regarded as inimical to originality. Just here is to be found one of those subsidiary results of the ancient rhetorical theory of imitation. Modern romantic literature is for the most part distinguished by an aversion to the employment of such traditional wisdom. It insists upon originality in form and content, however limited, partial, or superficial may be the experience and outlook of the writer and of the age. Ancient literary theory held a radically different conception of the desires of the reader. Thus Aristotle in his rhetoric[65] boldly asserts the fondness of the hearer for such traditional generalizations tested by common human experience: χαίρουσι γὰρ ἐάν τις καθόλου λέγων ἐπιτύχῃ τῶν δοξῶν. So Cicero in his *de oratore* 3, 107, of stock controversial themes: ancipites disputationes, in quibus de universo genere in utramque partem disseri copiose licet. Such themes became in fact a specialty of the Academic and Peripatetic schools. How widely these themes gave utterance to the traditional morality in all the literary genres known to the Romans we may infer from Cicero's *orator* 118, in which the need of such a philosophical and rhetorical arsenal is asserted:

Nec vero dialecticis modo sit instructus, sed habeat omnes philosophiae notos et tractatos locos. Nihil enim de religione, nihil de morte, nihil de pietate, nihil de caritate patriae, nihil de bonis rebus aut malis, nihil de virtutibus aut vitiis, nihil de officio, nihil de dolore, nihil de voluptate, nihil de perturbationibus animi et erroribus, quae saepe cadunt in causas et ieiunius aguntur, nihil, inquam, sine ea scientia quam dixi graviter ample copiose dici et explicari potest.

Quintilian also, 10, 5, 12, expresses himself with clearness and good sense upon the real value for the orator of a thorough familiarity with the sound general principles succinctly expressed which are found in such *loci communes*. Stemplinger well says:[66] So finden sich auch in den Reden aller Gattungen stets wiederkehrends Gemeinplätze; ebenso in den Digressionen der Historiker, Geographien, bei den Moralschriften der Stoiker und Kyniker, in Dramen und Satiren, Elegien und Episteln.

In such a genre as satire with its constant preoccupation with the spirit of the individual and of society, with its insistence upon the principles which mould character, with its frank, popular, and humorous expression of these social and moral laws, there was accumulated, so to speak, a vast mass of human and social material. In so far as human and social experience repeats itself in every age, this material had some measure of fixity. We, therefore, find in satire certain conventional themes elaborated with general, but not too rigid adherence to rhetorical schemes of exposition and even to argumentative sequences. Such schematization may even be traditional in several related genres. In the second place we find a large mass of briefly worded gnomic wisdom and of pointed and humorous anecdote, which is freely drawn upon by all the satirists to furnish concrete illustration for their interpretation and commentary on contemporary life. Since the following pages will afford constant examples of the employment both of traditional themes and of illustrative commonplaces it will hardly be necessary to quote specific examples.

As examples of conventional themes of larger outline, which will be treated more fully below, we may cite the themes of φιλοπλουτία and μεμψιμοιρία,[67] the aesthetic and ethical defence of satire, and comparison of the satirist's technique with that of other literary forms, such as comedy, epic, tragedy,[68] and especially Horace 1, 6,[69] which, as Hendrickson has shown, combines a discussion of the nature of the poet's relation to Maecenas with a eulogy of his patron and a vindication of his sincerity. This whole satire is in fact arranged according to a strict rhetorical sequence under the themes of γένος, τροφή, ἀγωγή, φύσις ψυχῆς καὶ σώματος, ἐπιτηδεύματα, πράξεις. Especially frequent are themes relating to the banquet, which, as we shall see below, are connected with the Greek δεῖπνα, and which are represented by satires in Lucilius books, 4, 5, 13, 20, and 21, and Horace's *satire* 2, 8.[70] Similarly, as Süss has shown,[71] a well established topic of invective with a more or less closely defined sequence of argument had been developed by Greek oratory, comedy and scholastic controversy and recurs in the διατριβαί of the Cynics, the prototype of satire in many respects.[72]

While these traditional themes and shorter commonplaces are sometimes found in several different genres—the epigram and satire for example using much common material—on the whole they tended to accumulate within the pale of a single genre as the natural result of the rhetorical theory of imitation which we have described and of the reverence accorded by each man of letters to the theory and practise of his great predecessors in his chosen genre. So true is this of the Greek διατριβαί that Wendland[73] on the basis of the investigations of Weber and Hense does not hesitate to declare: Was wir von stoischen, kynischen, neupythagoreischen Moraltraktaten haben ist in der Wahl der Themata, Tendenze, Haltung gleichartig, nur in Ton und Nuance verschieden. How largely the same conception permeates the works of the Roman satirists from Lucilius to Juvenal has not yet been clearly realized or investigated, but will become clearer in some degree in the following pages.

But Roman satire teems with the briefer commonplaces, as does the Greek διατριβή so closely related to it. Sometimes these commonplaces are philosophical paradoxes, such as the Stoic maxims ὅτι πᾶς ἄφρων μαίνεται and ὅτι μόνος ὁ σοφὸς ἐλεύθερος. The first paradox is the subject of satires in Lucilius books 27 and 30 and in Horace 2, 3. The second is the subject of Horace's satire 2, 7 and of the fifth satire of Persius. Sometimes there are animal similes, a favorite type of illustration for the Cynic because the animal most nearly lives according to nature. The ant is a symbol of industry in Horace sat. 1, 32 and 40, and Lucilius 561; the dog still dragging the broken chain is a symbol of slavery as in Horace 2, 7, 70 f. Or we have miniature scenes drawn with dramatic vividness—and perhaps in some instances influenced by the Mime and New Comedy—such as the miser watching over his hoard in Horace satires 2, 3, 111 and 142, the laughing heir, the sacrifice of the avaricious man, and numerous other examples from the same third satire of Horace's second book, as set forth in Lejay's introduction to the satire. Again we find mythological types, such as Tantalus, a stock example of insatiate greed Horace sat. 1, 1, 68; or Homeric types like Ulysses, the traditional cynic hero;[74] or professional types like the *mercator* Horace *sat.* 1, 1, 17; or the miser with his dreads in Horace *sat.* 1, 1, 75. It is, therefore, apparent that a satirist like Horace took intense pleasure in adorning his satires with the reflections and illustrations traditional to the genre and largely derived from the Greek διατριβή and other related popular forms of philosophic exposition current in the Hellenistic period.

In this first chapter I have been tracing the general laws of imitation current in the Augustan age to their sources in Greek rhetorical theory. I have endeavored to make clear why Horace by reason of the natural trend of his philosophical and rhetorical studies and under the compelling influence exercised by these studies upon literary composition in all the great fields of Latin poetry, was led by training, temperament, and literary convention to give willing adherence to the principles of rhetorical imitation, and to employ with the freedom of a master those tools of a good craftsman in the satiric workshop; parody, free translation, contamination, modernization, the traditional theme, and the illustrative commonplace. Further, I have endeavored to show by quotations from the critical satires and epistles of Horace that he did give just such allegiance to these widely accepted principles of the literary art.

I wish now to consider the effect of Horace's theoretical and practical acceptance of these general principles of imitation upon his relations to Lucilius and to the Cynic and Stoic philosophers, who worked in a genre closely allied to Lucilian satire. To understand the full nature of this relationship—and such an understanding is indispensable for the more detailed comparison of the satires of Lucilius and of Horace—it will be necessary to consider in detail (1) the relation of Lucilius and the Scipionic circle to the new Greek learning and especially to the Stoic rhetoric; (2) the formulation of the theory of the plain style under the influence of the Stoic rhetoricians in the Scipionic circle, the relation of that theory to Lucilian satire and in its later and fuller development in the Ciceronian and Augustan age to Horatian satire; (3) the relations of the satires of Lucilius to the half-satirical, half-serious works of the Greek Cynic and Stoic philosophers with the resultant modifications of the theory of the plain style as applied to satire. To a consideration of these important problems I now turn. The bond of union between them is to be found in the importance of the relationship of the work of the Scipionic circle to the new Greek learning and in the persistence of that influence, greatly enriched and refined, to be sure, by later study in Greek rhetoric and literature in the literary compositions of the Augustan age. In this larger sense, then, I may call my second chapter, The Relation of Lucilius and the Scipionic Circle to the new Greek Learning and Literature.

Notes on Chapter I

[1] The *Ars Poetica* may perhaps be regarded as an exception, if we accept its relationship to an εἰσαγωγή of Lucilius addressed to Iunius Congus. See *infra*, pp. 446-468.

[2] The study by E. Stemplinger, *Das Plagiat in der griechischen Literatur*, Teubner, 1912, is of especial value. I gratefully recognize my indebtedness to Stemplinger for many points of view and for much of the ancient evidence cited in this chapter.

[3] See Stemplinger, *op. cit.*, pp. 167 ff. κλοπή *im eigentlichen Sinne*.

[4] The spirit of the Classical Tradition finds worthy expression in the words of Doudan, prefixed to *The Recollections of Viscount Morley*, vol. I, p. 1. Quoted *infra* p. 207.

[5] *Sat.* 1, 1, 85 f.

[6] In this much-vexed passage I can see no reference to Ennius. Lucilius, the inventor of satire, a genre influenced by various Greek compositions in the satiric spirit, is compared with the hypothetical inventor of any poetic form that is rude and untouched by the Greeks. This is essentially the interpretation of Morris. Both Rolfe and Morris in their editions of the satires appear to be influenced by the article by Hendrickson, *Lucilius and Horace* in the *Studies in Honor of Gildersleeve*, pp. 163-168, *Excursus: Graecis Intacti Carminis Auctor*. Hendrickson differs from Morris in holding that the reference is exclusively to the hexameter satires of Lucilius. For this there is much to be said. Against this view, however, is the fact that the investigations embodied in this book fail to reveal that Horace made any discrimination in favor of the hexameters in his use of Lucilian material. He was certainly familiar with the whole Lucilian collection of thirty books.

[7] For other instances of the praise of the εὑρετής see Horace, *epp.* 1, 19, 22; Virgil, *ec.* 6, 1; *georg.* 2, 174 ff.; Propertius 3, 1, 3; Manilius 1, 4; and on the εὑρεταί of the different genres, Horace, *A. P.* 75 ff. Also Stemplinger, *op. cit.*, p. 11 *s.v.* Εὑρήματα-Literatur. Lucretius, *de rerum natura* 1, 117 and 926 are similar in tone.

[8] Cicero gave the same answer to this traditional debate of the Greek rhetoricians in the *de oratore* published in the year 55 B.C. His perfect orator is the prose counterpart of Horace's perfect poet. He is the product of the union in a man of high natural gifts of the widest possible culture with the most exacting technical training. *Cf.* such passages as the *de oratore* 1, 20; 72; 3, 54 for his attitude. So in the *orator*, composed in the year 46 B.C. and dedicated to Brutus, a thorough-going Atticist, the ideal orator raised far above the ephemeral controversies of the schools is equally master of "all three styles," and employs each in turn in accordance with the dictates of good taste. This work also implies the same

happy union of wide knowledge and good technical training in an orator of original powers.

Of the attitude of Dionysius of Halicarnassus we are not so clearly informed, but he too seems to have held similar doctrine. Thus in the letter to Pompeius 3 he summarizes the general content of his treatise in three books περὶ μιμήσεως. The first book was devoted to an abstract inquiry into the nature of imitation; the second established the canon of the poets, philosophers, orators, and historians who should be imitated. The third discussed the proper manner of imitation. Material of much value upon the Augustan theories of imitation may be gathered from the other works of Dionysius on literary criticism. The general trend of opinion in the Augustan age upon the debate of originality versus craftsmanship and education seems to agree with the dictum of Aristotle, *rhet.* 2, 19, p. 1392 b: καὶ εἰ ἄνευ τέχνης ἢ παρασκευῆς δυνατὸν γίνεσθαί τι μᾶλλον διὰ τέχνης καὶ ἐπιμελείας δύνατον. See Shorey, φύσις, μελέτη, ἐπιστήμη in *Transc. Am. Phil. Assn.*, vol. 40, pp. 185-201.

⁹ *Fr. 18 d:* ποιητὴς ὅσσα μὲν ἂν γράφῃ, μετ᾽ ἐνθουσιασμοῦ καὶ ἱεροῦ πνεύματος μάλα κάρτα ἐστίν.

¹⁰ *Ion* 534 b; *Phaedrus* 244.

¹¹ *De div.* 1, 80; *de oratore* 2, 46.

¹² *Zum Shakespeare's Tag*, 1771, *Schriften zur Literatur*, 1, vol. 36, p. 6, Jubiläums, Ausgabe, Cotta.

¹³ *Eckermanns Gespräche mit Goethe* (ed. Cotta), p. 173.

¹⁴ Sometimes the poet continued the tradition of the family, sometimes of the guild. Thus in Athens we hear of a guild of Εὐνεῖδαι and a γένος ὀρχηστῶν καὶ κιθαριστῶν. *Cf.* Töpfer, *Att. Geneal.*, p. 181 ff.; *CIA* 3, 274. Tragedy became traditional in the families of Aeschylus and Sophocles. Bacchylides was the nephew of Simonides, and Menander of Alexis. See Stemplinger, *op. cit.*, pp. 88-91.

¹⁵ See the article on the *collegium poetarum* by E. G. Sihler in *A. J. P.*, vol. 26, pp. 1-21 and *infra*, pp. 288-289, 346-347.

¹⁶ Hence the Greeks until the fourth century B.C. usually confined themselves to a single γένος or literary form. See Plato, *Ion* 541; *Resp.* 3, 395. Among the Romans from the very first we find a great relaxation of this principle. Ennius and Horace are both examples of marked success in several different genres. Nevertheless, the careful observance of the laws governing successful creation in any given genre continued in Rome with almost unimpaired force, as we can see from such passages as Horace *sat.* 1, 10, 42 ff.

¹⁷ See Strabo I, 2, 19 ff.

¹⁸ *Aeneid* 8, 135; 3, 551, 578; Ovid, *Met.* 13, 732, and Callimachus, *fr.* 252: τὼς ὁ γέγειος ἔχει λόγος.

¹⁹ For criticism see Servius on *Aeneid* 9, 81; 1, 267; for excuse of a variant authority *idem* on *Aeneid* 3, 46: *hoc purgatur Euripidis exemplo qui de Alcesti hoc dixit.*

²⁰ They are not, however, to be confused with our modern rhetorical textbooks, to which the κανόνες τῶν τεχνῶν, τεχνολογίαι, and παραγγέλματα

τεχνικά more closely correspond. The close connection between ancient rhetoric and the philosophy of style is fundamental. The first and most obvious effect of such works was to spread the belief among the cultivated classes of the Hellenistic states and of Rome that through them was to be gained the *carrière ouverte* to success in all the arts. See Seneca, *rhet.* to Mela, *controv.* 2 *praef.* Stemplinger, *op. cit.*, p. 106. Hence the dilettanteism of which Horace complains in *epp.* 2, 1, 114 ff. and *A. P.* 379 ff. *scribimus indocti doctique poemata passim.* Such deleterious effects of rhetoric show some analogies to those traceable to the prevalence of journalistic ideals in modern America and Europe.

[21] Strabo 1, 2, 3: οἱ παλαιοὶ φιλοσοφίαν τινὰ λέγουσι πρώτην τὴν ποιητικήν, εἰσάγουσαν εἰς τὸν βίον ἡμᾶς ἐκ νέων καὶ διδάσκουσαν ἤθη καὶ πάθη καὶ πράξεις μεθ' ἡδονῆς . . . διὰ τοῦτο καὶ τοὺς παῖδας αἱ τῶν Ἑλλήνων πόλεις πρώτιστα διὰ τῆς ποιητικῆς παιδεύουσιν.

[22] See Stemplinger, *op. cit.*, pp. 113-115.

[23] περὶ μιμ; *frag.* 6 Us.: ἡ γὰρ ψυχὴ τοῦ ἀναγιγνώσκοντος ὑπὸ τῆς συνεχοῦς παρατηρήσεως τὴν ὁμοιότητα τοῦ χαρακτῆρος ἐφέλκεται.

[24] See also Macrobius, *Sat.* 6, 1, 7.

[25] 4, 7 and 4, 8.

[26] See Brinkmann, *Rh. Mus.* 63, pp. 618 ff.

[27] Stemplinger, *op. cit.*, p. 119.

[28] In Rome, as in Greece, the tendency to imitation was greatly stimulated by Atticism, a reaction in favor of the earlier, more simple, and more vigorous models of the best period of Greek literature. Thus in the Augustan age, the Alexandrian influence is still felt but with diminished vigor. Virgil's model for the *Aeneid* is Homer rather than the Alexandrian epyllion. The lyrics of Horace hark back to Sappho and Alcaeus rather than to Callimachus.

[29] I follow Stemplinger's general sequence of argument here. See *op. cit.*, pp. 121-167.

[30] For a fuller treatment of these topics and many other related ones, see Stemplinger, *op. cit.*, Dritter Theil, *Literarische Praxis des Alterthums.*

[31] See also Symmachus to Ausonius, *ep.* 1, 31. Stemplinger compares Lessing's *Briefe die neuest. Literatur betr.* (1762) 233 Br. *Cf.* Stemplinger, *op. cit.*, p. 126 f.

[32] ἐπειδὴ δ' οἱ λόγοι τοιαύτην ἔχουσι φύσιν ὥσθ' οἷόν τ' εἶναι περὶ τῶν αὐτῶν πολλαχῶς ἐξηγήσασθαι, καὶ τά τε μεγάλα ταπεινὰ ποιῆσαι καὶ τοῖς μικροῖς μέγεθος περιθεῖναι, καὶ τά τε παλαιὰ καινῶς διελθεῖν καὶ περὶ τῶν νεωστὶ γεγενημένων ἀρχαίως εἰπεῖν, οὐκέτι φευκτέον ταῦτ' ἐστί, περὶ ὧν ἕτεροι πρότερον εἰρήκασιν.

[33] See also Apuleius, *de dogm. Platonis* 3, p. 362 Hild; Longinus περὶ ὑψ. 1,328 Sp; Lucian, *Zeuxes* 25; Quintilian, *Inst.* 1, 8, 18 advises compilation from earlier sources.

[34] See Lessing, *Hamb. Dramat.* St. 19.

[35] Among the Romans an interpretation of the νέα ὁδός was current by which translation ranked with original production. In this sense Plautus and Terence use the term *nova fabula* of a piece not previously translated from the Greek or brought upon the boards, Rohricht Aug., *quaestiones*

scaenicae, Dissert. Argent. 1885. Virgil, who in the *Georgics* 3, 40 declares *saltus sequamur intactos* and who was blamed because Hesiod and Nicander and others had worked in the same genre, is defended in the Berne scholia thus: *intactos ad Romanos rettulit, quia nullus scripsit.* *Cf.* Pliny, *N. H. praef.* 12. So Cicero boasts that he has introduced philosophy to Latium. See further Stemplinger, *op. cit.,* p. 137 f.

³⁶ Thus Virgil, *ecl.* 6, 1 in allusion to the relation of his bucolic poetry to the Sicilian pastorals of Theocritus, says:

> Prima Syracosio dignata est ludere versu
> nostra neque erubuit silvas habitare Thalia.

So in the *Georgics* 2, 176 he boasts that he is the Roman Hesiod:

> Ascraeumque cano Romana per oppida carmen.

Naturally the objective technique of the epic forbids any direct tribute to Homer in the *Aeneid.* Nevertheless, all Virgil's Roman contemporaries recognized him as the continuator of the Homeric tradition and the generous rival of Homer as the words of Propertius 2, 34, 63 prove. Similarly Horace regards Archilochus as his model in the epodes (*cf. epp.* 1, 19, 23); Lucilius in his satires, *cf. supra,* pp. 6 ff. In the odes he is the follower of the Aeolic poetry of Sappho and Alcaeus, see *odes* 3, 30, and for Alcaeus *epp.* 1, 19, 9 ff. This last passage is of vital importance for the understanding of the relation of Horace's poetry to his Greek originals. *Cf.* also Schanz, *Romische Literaturgeschich* 8, 2³, 1, p. 169. So Propertius regards Callimachus and Philetas as his masters. *Cf.* 3, 1, 1; 3, 9, 43; 4, 6, 3. Aemilius Macer seems to have followed Boios in his *Ornithogonia;* (*Cf.* Schanz, *op. cit.,* 8, 2, 13, p. 199), and Nicander in his *Theriaca.* Cornelius Gallus stood in close relation to Euphorion. ˙*Cf.* Schanz, *op. cit.,* p. 209.

³⁷ *Ars Amatoria* 2, 221.

³⁸ See Billeter, *Der Wettkamp als Mittelpunkt des griechischen Lebens,* 212 ff.

³⁹ Horace's simile of the bee was often imitated in renaissance literature. See Stemplinger, *Das Fortleben des Horaz, Lyrik,* p. 383.

⁴⁰ This fable of Aesop was also applied to Rhetoric by Philodemus II P. II, p. 68, 25 S. by way of criticism to rhetorical ornamentation of a meretricious nature.

⁴¹ According to Stemplinger this line harks back to the Alexandrian controversy between Callimachus and Apollonius of Rhodes upon the question of the continued use of the Cyclic epics.

⁴² See *infra* pp. 405, note 130 on Horace's satires of the second book. Compare Lejay's edition of Horace's satires, pp. 512-523 for an excellent discussion on the form of *sat.* 2, 6.

⁴³ For a similar development in the case of Phaedrus' relations to his Greek originals *cf.* J. J. Hartman, *de Phaedri fabulis commentatio,* Leyden, 1889, p. 11. This is, of course, a natural evolution, we may almost say *the* natural evolution for the ancient man of letters.

⁴⁴ *Cf.* Stemplinger, *op. cit.,* pp. 275-280.

⁴⁵ *Cf.* Stemplinger, *op. cit.,* pp. 203-209; Geffcken, *Studien zur griechischen Satire, N. Jahrb. für das Klass. Alt.,* vol. 27, pp. 394-403.

⁴⁶ *Cf.* Wachsmuth, *Sillographorum Graecorum Reliquiae*, pp. 37 ff.

⁴⁷ *E.g.*, 1, 19, 148, 191, 462, 587, 597, 599, 605, 606. These passages listed by Marx, II *Index auctorum* under *Ennius, imitatio aut irrisio* under Homer, and under *Pacuvius* are worthy of examination. For a more detailed discussion of Lucilius' use of Homer *cf. infra*, pp.153-155.

⁴⁸ Persius, *sat.* 5, 1-20. For a detailed discussion on the relations of this passage to Horace's *Ars Poetica* and general literary doctrines see my paper, *Lucilius, the Ars Poetica of Horace and Persius*, in *Harvard Studies in Classical Philology*, vol. 24, pp. 1-36.

⁴⁹ *E.g.*, 5, 139. *Cf.* Wilson's *Juvenal*, Introd. 26.

⁵⁰ *A. P.*, 139 ff.

⁵¹ *Cf.* the defense of Terence in the prologue of the *Andria*, 15-21.

⁵² *Tr. A. P. A.*, vol. 40, pp. 121-151.

⁵³ See *infra*, pp. 387-398.

⁵⁴ *Cf.* Stemplinger, *op. cit.*, p. 215. For the technical definition of διασκευή *cf.* Galenus 17, 1, p. 79, Kühn.

⁵⁵ *Inst.* 10, 1, 66.

⁵⁶ *Latin Poetry. Johns Hopkins Lectures*, 1893, pp. 162-215.

⁵⁷ See Gerhard, *op. cit.*, pp. 228 ff. *Die gnomische Poesie der Hellenistenzeit.*

⁵⁸ See *infra*, p. 161.

⁵⁹ See *infra*, pp. 156-158 on the ἀπομνημόνευμα; pp. 158-162 on the χρεία.

⁶⁰ See *infra*, p. 156.

⁶¹ On Aristippus *cf. sat.* 2, 3, 100; *epp.* 1, 17, 14 and 23; on Diogenes *epp.* 1, 17, 13.

⁶² *Cf.* Stemplinger, *op. cit.*, pp. 222; Gerhard, *op. cit.*, p. 248, note 8.

⁶³ *Cf.* G. von Wartensleben, *Begriff der gr. Chreia und Beitrage zur Geschichte ihrer Form*, Heidelberg, 1901; Gerhard, *op. cit.*, pp. 248 ff.; Stemplinger, *op. cit.*, pp. 222 ff.; Lejay, *op. cit.*, pp. 17-21.

⁶⁴ *Cf.* Stemplinger, *op. cit.*, pp. 228-241.

⁶⁵ 2, 21.

⁶⁶ *Op. cit.*, p. 229.

⁶⁷ See *infra*, pp. 219-248.

⁶⁸ See *infra*, pp. 277-306.

⁶⁹ See *infra*, pp. 316-324.

⁷⁰ See *infra*, pp. 162-166 on the δεῖπνον and συμπόσιον.

⁷¹ W. Süss, *Ethos*, Leipzig, 1910, II *cap.* 25.

⁷² On the relations of the διατριβαί with satire, see *infra*, pp. 178-180.

⁷³ Paul Wendland, *Die Hellenistische-Romische Kultur*, p. 45.

⁷⁴ See *infra*, pp. 154-155.

CHAPTER II

THE RELATION OF LUCILIUS AND THE SCIPIONIC CIRCLE TO THE NEW GREEK LEARNING AND LITERATURE

My task in this chapter is to consider the relation of Lucilius to the Scipionic circle and to the new Greek learning, enthusiasm for which was perhaps the most potent factor in uniting the members of the circle. These influences, generated in this circle, gained cumulative effect, and new and nicer definition in the period separating the Scipionic from the Augustan period. The critical theories of Horace as to satiric composition must, therefore, be studied as affected by this stream of influence. Before entering upon such a study, however, it is well to recall the existence of certain external resemblances and differences between the life and environment of the two men which in themselves would attract Horace to his great predecessor.

Both Lucilius and Horace, like so many Roman writers, were born in the southern provinces; Lucilius at Suessa Aurunca in Campania, and Horace at Venusia in Apulia. These towns were originally Latin military colonies. The former was founded as a fortress on the old Appian road from Rome to Capua, during the years 314-312 B.C.; the latter, a fortress of the first class, designed to aid in the control over the later extension of that road from Samnium to Tarentum, was founded in 244 B.C. Thus the most impressionable years of both satirists were passed in districts populated by vigorous frontier folk, who would cherish with pride the tradition of Rome's hard won struggles over Oscan and Greek neighbors. Horace certainly was deeply impressed with the warlike atmosphere of Venusia for in *sat.* 2, 1, 34 ff. he associates it with his comparison of the polemical element in his own satire and in Lucilius:

> sequor hunc, Lucanus an Appulus anceps:
> nam Venusinus arat finem sub utrumque colonus,
> missus ad hoc, pulsis, uetus est ut fama, Sabellis,
> quo ne per vacuum Romano incurreret hostis

sive quod Appula gens seu quid Lucania bellum
incuteret violenta sed hic stilus haud petet ultro
quemquam animantem et me veluti custodiet ensis
vagina tectus.

Along the great road, also, must have come to the two
colonies the sturdy Oscan peasant proprietors, who were anxious
to sell the products of their farms. Greek traders with the more
luxurious wares of Capua and of Tarentum brought with them
some suggestion of the complex culture of those great centres
of Greek civilization. Lucilius knew Oscan, and in Ofellus
Horace has sketched for all time the hard-handed and clear-
headed Italian peasant proprietor, not unacquainted with the
elaborate dishes of the *triclinium* of the town, but deliberately
preferring the *tenuis victus*, his plain fare and plain art of living.

But in descent and social position a marked difference
appears. Horace was a freedman's son, descended from some
conquered Lucanian or Apulian family, not from some one of
the 20,000 Roman colonists sent to Venusia in 294 B.C. Lucil-
ius, on the other hand, was probably a Roman citizen, and
possibly of local equestrian rank.[1]

It is surely not fanciful to attribute to this contrast in social
standing some of the differences which in a stratified society
like that of Rome differentiate Lucilius' relations with Scipio
from Horace's relations with Maecenas. In spite of his com-
plete independence of action Horace is not entirely unconscious
of those social and economic gradations which tend to erect
reserves even between the most intimate friends. This feeling
appears in satires 1, 6 and 2, 6, in the fable of the frog who
attempts to imitate the ox at the close of the third satire of
book 2, and in such epistles as the 7th and 17th of the first
book.

I hardly believe that the friendship of Horace and Maecenas
ever relaxed its bonds in such unrestrained frolics as the Com-
mentator Cruquianus attributes to Scipio and Lucilius, in his
note on Horace's *sat.* 2, 1, 71 ff. It is impossible to imagine
the fat little Augustan poet, armed with a twisted napkin
chasing the hypochondriac Maecenas about the dining room.[2]

Nor is the greater restraint with which Horace employs
invective entirely due to the greater stringency of legal enact-

ments and the rise of Augustan urbanity.[3] The freedman's
son is forewarned and forearmed, as he himself tells us in his
conversation with Trebatius Testa, *sat.* 2, 1, 39-46. He does
not have that lust of combat, which Juvenal 1, 165-167, appar-
ently in direct allusion to the defensive conception of satire
advocated by Horace in such a passage as *sat.* 2, 1, 39 ff.,
attributes to Lucilius:

> ense uelut stricto quotiens Lucilius ardens
> infremuit, rubet auditor cui frigida mens est.

But intellectual and spiritual sympathy counted far more
than the influence of provincial environment and descent in
attracting Horace to Lucilius. Both men were Greco-Roman
rather than Italic in their outlook on life and literature. Both
sought to combine all that was best in the old Roman concep-
tion of *virtus* with that broader appreciation of learning and
culture, that sympathetic and emotional interest in the common
fate of mankind, which are connoted by the new word *humani-
tas*. The truly Roman spirit which animates the Lucilian
definition of an originally Stoic *virtus* in fragment 1326 ff. is of
the same strain as that which finds such noble utterance in the
Roman odes of Horace. Neither the one nor the other could
have been written except under the compelling force of an
idealistic Stoic conception of the true citizen in a Roman com-
monwealth.

As Greco-Romans, Horace, and probably Lucilius, sup-
plemented their studies in rhetoric and philosophy on Roman
soil by visits to Athens. A critical analysis of the fragments
of Lucilius reveals[4] an intimacy with Athenian institutions and
social usages, with vulgar and dialectical Greek,[5] which can
hardly have been acquired in any other way than by a sojourn
of some length at Athens. Lucilius was, moreover, acquainted
with the Academic philosopher Clitomachus, who dedicated a
book to him, and may even have studied under Carneades at
Athens.[6] It is possible that this intimate acquaintance with
Athenian life, with Athenian men of letters and philosophers
dated from the year 139 B.C., when Scipio visited Athens.
Similarly Horace studied the Academic philosophy at Athens.[7]
From that scholastic centre he was sucked into the rising tide
of civil war.[8]

This military apprenticeship of the two men has left a distinct impress upon the content and spirit of their satires. Horace served under Brutus at Philippi, where he even commanded a legion as military tribune.[9] Lucilius served a much severer apprenticeship as *eques* under Scipio at the siege of Numantia, where he remained for 15 months in the year 134-133, B.C. Of his experiences in these campaigns he has left us some record in satires in books 11, 14, and 15.[10] But we have also in the remains of book 7 and 30, in the *Incertae sedis fragmenta*, and in other allusions from books 11, 14, and 15, a number of fragments which reveal so minute a familiarity with the troubled course of the Spanish wars from 139-134 B.C. (before the arrival of Scipio) that Cichorius[11] is inclined to believe that Lucilius saw some service within that period.

The seventh satire of Horace's first book is a direct reminiscence of this period of his life. Such common military apprenticeship probably had its influence in inspiring that admiration for disciplinary values which appears so clearly in both satirists. Both satirists repeatedly hold up to ridicule the spendthrifts, the gluttons, the fortune hunters, the whole company of egotists, whose theories and practices threatened to transform the traditional Roman concern with public affairs, *negotium* into a selfish *otium* of pleasure and languid dilettanteism. For Lucilius and Horace alike culture is a robust and hard-won discipline designed to enlarge the sympathies and inform the understanding of the leaders of the state.[12]

We find also certain similarities between the attitude of Lucilius and of Horace to contemporary philosophy and even to scholastic controversies. Both men are eclectic.[13] Their eclecticism is based on the practical Roman perception that ethics, the philosophy of right action, is and should be the main concern of all philosophic inquiry and teaching. But something more than a vague eclecticism unites the two men. With increasing age, deeper study, and riper experience with life, this eclecticism shows a growing sympathy with Stoic ideals of life and conduct, but with Stoic ideals so purged of scholastic rigidity as to constitute a more humane reinterpretation of the old Roman *mos maiorum*. The earlier studies of Lucilius had attached him to the Academic school, and had probably won for him the personal intimacy and regard of such philosophers as Carneades and Clitomachus. His early satire shows a lively interest in Academic philosophy.[14] In this period he may even have assailed the Stoics.[15] As a member of the Scipionic circle, however, although he may at first have upheld his Academic principles he gradually came to adopt a much more sympathetic attitude towards the Stoics. This was the inevitable result of the Stoic atmosphere surrounding Scipio. So Horace was at first, a follower not of the Academy but of Epicureanism, and a witty assailant of Stoicism, as we may see from such satires as the first, second, and third of the first book. Yet in spite of this moderate and somewhat super-ficial personal hedonism he gradually came to feel that regenera-tion for the individual, as for the state, can only be attained through the practice of the Stoic virtues and adherence to a liberally interpreted Stoicism. Hence in the second book of satires the second, third and seventh satires are essentially Stoic. In the third and fourth book of the odes and above all in the epistles Horace constantly interprets the problems of life and conduct from the Stoic point of view.

In mature life both Lucilius and Horace became members of the most important literary and political coterie of their period. By virtue of such association both came to understand and to sympathize with the programme of moderate social and political reform as conceived by the most enlightened body of contemporary statesmen. Moreover, both poets influenced by these ideals of their patrons Augustus, Agrippa, and Maecenas in the later period, Scipio and Laelius in the earlier, sought to win by their writings a wider adherence for those principles of progressive amelioration which played so important a part in the plans of Scipio, Maecenas, and Augustus.[16] It therefore seems desirable to touch briefly upon the personality, social, and political ideals of some of the leading members of the Scipionic circle, that we may have a clearer standard of com-parison with which to measure the ideals of the better known circle of Maecenas.

Publius Cornelius Scipio Africanus Aemilianus,[17] the son of Lucius Aemilius Paulus, the conqueror of Pydna, was born about 185 or 184 B.C. From earliest youth he received a liberal training in which Greek studies played a leading part.[18] Paulus, indeed, turned over to the education of his sons the library of King Perseus, a part of the spoils of Pydna.[19] But the three most important influences on the intellectual life of Scipio were his intimacy with the Greek historian Polybius, the Stoic philosopher Panaetius, and the wise Roman Laelius, all worthy representatives of the well balanced Stoic harmony of lofty idealism with practical citizenship.

Polybius[20] was born in Megalopolis about 200 B.C. As the son of Lycortas, the general of the Achaean league, he took an active part in the effort to unite the Greek states of the Peloponnesus against the Macedonian tyranny of Perseus. In the year 167 B.C., however, as the result of the ascendancy of the extreme partisans of Rome in Greece, Polybius was sent to Rome. Here he remained as one of the 1000 hostages exacted from the league as a pledge for the security of Roman rule in Greece. The military efficiency, scholarship, and statesmanship of this remarkable Greek had already attracted the attention of Lucius Aemilius Paulus, the victor of Pydna. Hence we find Polybius at the very beginning of his career at Rome, a member of the family circle of Paulus, and engaged in the interpretation and discussion of a philosophical work with two sons of the house, who were later to become Fabius and Scipio Africanus Minor. In one of the noblest passages in Greek literature Polybius[21] himself has told us how the ingenuous and sensitive Scipio, the younger son, opened his heart to him in the crowded forum, and how, after expressing his lack of confidence in his ability worthily to maintain the high traditions of his house Scipio begged passionately for the friendship and philosophic guidance of the older man. Then Polybius promised to aid the young man in the quest of virtue and of fame. The quest was one for virtue, for Polybius was in essential harmony with the teachings of the Stoa; it was one for fame, for Polybius was a practical statesman, profoundly impressed with the importance of making the new empire of Rome in the east an instrument of moral discipline, enlightenment, and civilization. He was able to inform the mind of his younger friend with the principles of a real political philosophy, to make him feel that to be a Roman in

the true sense was the highest goal. As Leo well says:[22] dass
Scipio zugleich ein grosser und ein guter Römer wurde dankte
er seiner Natur, aber auch dem Griechen.

Polybius was a convinced adherent of the Stoic philosophy
and of the Stoic rhetoric which found its natural expression
in the shining simplicity and informal tone of the plain style.
In contrast to his rhetorical predecessors, he regarded truth as
indispensable for the historian as the eye for the body (1, 14, 6;
12, 7, 3). He therefore assailed the boastfulness and rich orna-
mentation affected by the historical writers who worked under
the influence of a more pretentious rhetorical tradition, and
whose works accordingly approximate to the canons of the
grand style. He even asserts that a single lie (12, 25a–27)
suffices to destroy an author's credibility. His history, therefore,
as befits the Stoic ideal, is written to teach (*ad docendum*),
not to delight (*ad delectandum*). Moreover, like Panaetius he is a
strong believer in the necessity of the critical analysis of tradi-
tion. Although he rigorously sought historical truth his method
was not that of the modern scientific historian, nor was his
goal the same. He seeks truth not for truth's sake, but for the
practical moral effects that history, which he compares to the
healing art (12, 25d), may have in training the future statesman.
Thus a knowledge of origins and contemporary tendencies helps
to mould sound character and to call forth reasoned action in the
statesman.

In all Stoicism there is a conflict between a somewhat asser-
tive individualism and the feeling of duty to humanity at large.[23]
This conflict may be traced in Polybius, who sometimes asserts
his complete right to freedom of speech and his devotion to
truth even in the face of the claims of the fatherland (1, 14. 16,
17, 8). Like Tacitus' famous *sine ira et odio* he writes of the
development of the constitution: χωρὶς ὀργῆς καὶ φθόνου (6, 9,
11). In 16, 14, 6 he says: ἐγὼ δ' οὔτε λοιδορεῖν ψευδῶς φημὶ δεῖν τοὺς
μονάρχους οὔτε ἐγκωμιάζειν. Such assertions of the right of free
speech on the part of the historian are spiritually related to
those expressions of the satirist's right to free criticism and free
speech, a commonplace developed in the apologetic satires of
all the great Roman satirists from Lucilius to Juvenal. They

represent an application of Cynic and Stoic ideals to two different fields of literature.[24]

On the other hand, Polybius was a confirmed believer in the world order, in the ebb and flow of events under the guidance of τύχη, or as we should say today of manifest destiny. He wished to show how she led the most varied events to a common goal. Hence his universal history regards the Roman rule of the Mediterranean world as the consummation of the will of fate. He acted moreover as a great mediator between Hellenism and Rome.

Like Lucilius book 26, fragments 588, 592, 593, 594, 595, Polybius also wished to address a definite element in the reading public. Here both writers in my judgment are giving expression to Stoic rhetorical theories. Both divide their readers into three classes: Lucilius into the *populus*, the men of average culture, and the learned; Polybius first into the φιλήκοοι who seeks pleasure (τέρψις) and inspiration (ψυχαγωγία), and hence favor an historical style approximating to the grand style with its associations with epic and tragedy. So Lucilius line 587, apparently referring to the claims of a class of readers enamored of tragic grandeur, the φιλήκοοι of Polybius says:

> nisi portenta anguisque uolucris ac pinnatos scribitis.

The second class for whom Polybius will not write are the *literati*, the *doctissimi* of Lucilius. These men are the πολυπράγμονες and περιττοί who demand accounts of colonies, legends of the foundations of cities, and genealogies. The historian wishes rather to address a third class of readers, the πολιτικοί or πραγματικοί, the men performing the practical task of ruling the Roman world, who alone could profit by his history. And it was essentially for the same class that Lucilius wrote his satires.[25]

In point of fact the Stoicism of Polybius is in harmony in most respects with the modified Stoicism represented by Panaetius. Like Panaetius he is favorable to many of the ideals of Aristotle and the Academic and Peripatetic schools, but also like Panaetius he deprecates the scholastic tendency to lose oneself in hair-splitting argumentation. Like Panaetius he reinterprets the

imperialistic Stoic conception of the world state and its citizens
in terms of the newly dawning Roman imperialism. The ideal
constitution for Polybius and Scipio alike is that of Rome,
which by its system of checks and balances, incorporated in an
originally monarchical consulate, an oligarchical senate, and
a democratic *comitia*, assured the continuous existence of a
true πολιτεία.

Panaetius, 189–109 B.C.,[26] appeared in Rome shortly after
the fall of Carthage, 146 B.C., probably arriving at the invitation
of Polybius. From that time until the death of Scipio, 129
B.C., he lived on terms of closest intimacy with his patron.

It is difficult to exaggerate the influence of Panaetius, not
merely on Roman Stoicism, of which he is the real founder, but
also on Roman law, social and political theory, and through his
grammatical and rhetorical interests upon the Roman literary
theory and composition. His temper is that of the scholar of
studied moderation and catholic sympathies. This may be
illustrated by his sympathetic studies in the teachings of the
Platonic Academy,[27] by the liberality with which he admits
into his essentially eclectic system the ethical theories of Aris-
totle and the sceptical epistemology of Carneades. His ethics
are in fact, a sort of aristocratic pragmatism which interprets
the old Stoic *virtus* in term of social service, and lays great stress
upon the doctrine of *noblesse oblige* and propriety, (τὸ
πρέπον, *decus*) in speech[28] and action. His principal treatise,
περὶ τοῦ καθήκοντος as we may see from Cicero's free paraphrase
in the *de officiis*,[29] sets forth Stoicism as the school which will
train the scholar, the gentleman, and the statesman, while he
shrinks from those bolder doctrines, borrowed from the Cynic
school, which conflict with that which is conventional or, as
their opponents say, with that which is becoming. The regular
performance of services (τὰ καθήκοντα *officia*) is the true road by
which virtue is attained. These services are the simple duties
which fall in the way of the ordinary citizen. In this connection
it is interesting to note that the famous fragment of Lucilius on
virtue (1326–1338) seems to contain in a condensed form an
exposition of virtue as accepted in the Scipionic circle from the
lips of Panaetius.[30]

It is clear that such a conception of *virtus* is a sort of transfer from the field of aesthetics to the field of ethics of the principle of τὸ πρέπον, appropriateness. So also in the field of aesthetics and literature, we find questions of diction, structure, and the delineation of character interpreted in the light of the same doctrine of propriety.[21] Hence Arnold remarks with some justice[22] that "the success of the new system might not unfairly be described as a victory of literature over logic, of reasonableness over reason, and of compromise over consistency." But this victory of literature over logic was momentous for the whole history of European culture, for under its influence there grew up in the Scipionic circle that conception of *humanitas* which socially and intellectually determined for centuries the activities and ideals of the more enlightened wing of Roman imperialists. The dealings of this school with a conquered world we see illustrated in the administrative efficiency of an Augustus and a Trajan, in the imperialistic humanism of Horace and Virgil, and above all in the development of the principles of human rights and natural law under the influence of a jurisprudence essentially Stoic. Polybius and Panaetius, Laelius and Scipio thus annexed to the Stoic interpretation of the old Roman *virtus* a new conception of *humanitas*, an ideal truly Greco-Roman. In Terence, that is from the very heart of the Scipionic circle, we receive the broadest definition of that term in the famous line: *homo sum humani nil a me alienum puto.* As understood in this circle, then, the modern conflict between humanism and humanitarianism, the unhappy product of a romantic Rousseauism did not yet exist. The definition of *humanitas* originally embraced and fused both ideals.[23] On the ethical side *humanitas* is closely related to such ideas as *benevolentia, mansuetudo, suavitas, clementia.* Opposed to it are *inhumanitas*, associated with *barbaritas, crudelitas, arrogantia, superbia, durities, acerbitas, severitas.* On the intellectual side it is related to *litterae, doctrina, eruditio, artes.* It is in short the art of life calling into play all the highest faculties of man, intellectual as well as moral, united in a true harmony and finding fitting expression in the bearing, speech, and action of the '*vir illa humanitate praeditus.*' This ideal of the '*vir illa humanitate praeditus*' in letters and in life is the gift of the Scipionic circle to Roman and to human civilization.[34]

Moreover, earnest efforts were made to realize this ideal in contemporary life. Thus the Stoic philosopher Blossius was intimately associated with the reform movement of the Gracchi. Scipio's championship of the cause of the Latins and Italians was in large measure the result of this same humane philosophy. But perhaps of all the members of the circle, C. Laelius, who from his devotion to Stoicism was called *Sapiens*, most nearly realized the ideals of this ameliorated Stoicism. As a literary critic and a student of philosophy he probably surpassed the more versatile Scipio.[35] Indeed the gentleness, geniality, and tact of the older man was one of the most important elements in uniting the members of the circle. It is with good reason, therefore, that Cicero selected Laelius as the spokesman of his dialogue on friendship. Of the other members of the circle it is not necessary to speak here since we are concerned with them rather as representatives through their writings of the Stoic doctrine of the plain style.[36]

When we turn, however, to the circle of Maecenas we are at once confronted by way of contrast with the earlier circle with certain differences as well as with certain similarities in the composition and in the ideals of the later coterie. Like the circle of Scipio, the circle of Maecenas aims to associate a policy of social and moral reform with the highest intellectual enlightenment. It also includes the most famous names in contemporary literature, and stands in a middle position between the remnants of the reactionary senatorial nobility and the radical imperialistic democracy.[37] Its policy also is one of reconciliation, of peace as the necessary condition for the pursuit of the arts, for the work of social and political reconstruction, for the Romanization of the world. In this respect it is not unfair to compare the importance assigned to *otium*[38] by Scipio with the insistence on the peaceful mission of Augustus which permeates all Augustan poetry. Moreover, just as the social, political, and moral ideals of the Hellenized nobility afford the central inspiration of all the writings emanating from the Scipionic circle, so also, but with a clearer consciousness and a more deliberate adaptation of methods, the ideals of the new government of Augustus were consciously spread by the poets of the circle of Maecenas. Thus we find Augustus feeling out public opinion through the poets of this circle even before the actual initiation of reform legislation or strokes of foreign policy. To employ the language of contemporary American life, Augustus succeeds in developing an instrument of publicity which no American university has as yet attempted, a poetical press bureau.[39]

But the circle of Maecenas reveals no common philosophy of life welding its members together. Poetry, which constituted the strongest bond of association, though making a brave and sincere attempt, failed even more completely than philosophy as an effective instrument of social regeneration. The contrast between the cultivated hedonism of the court of Augustus and the circle of Maecenas with its disinclination to face boldly the facts of life, and the Scipionic circle with its ideals of *virtus* and *humanitas* is profound. The conception of pleasure for yourself and duty for your neighbor, which is so apparent in the reform movement of the Augustan age, made impossible such vigorous and sustained efforts as arose from the Scipionic circle. The fashion of moral detachment which marks the wide gulf between Horatian and Lucilian satire is not solely the expression of the temperamental divergencies of the two poets. It is also a measuring rod with which we may estimate the gap which separates a throbbing epoch of humanistic renaissance born in the civic throes of a free city state from the later period of self-conscious creation in the arts, literature, and science, fostered in the atmosphere of an enlightened despotism.[40]

One interesting minor result of the membership of Lucilius and Horace in the two literary circles most closely related to the moderately progressive wing of the aristocracy, is to be seen in their attitude of indifference to the guild of professional poets. This guild which was already formed in the days of Lucilius appears to have had Accius as its leading member. In the Augustan age it still survived under the presidency of Tarpa.[41] Both Lucilius and Horace priding themselves upon their associations with their noble patrons looked askance at an organization in which the crude philistinism of the state had but imperfectly differentiated the high calling of the poet from that of the *scriba* or *librarius*.

Such striking similarities (and differences) in the lives and environment of the two poets might well have attracted Horace to his great predecessor.   But spiritual magnetism working through a common adherence to a rhetorical and philosophical theory of imitation and of style was far more potent.   In order to understand the nature of Horace's imitative discipleship to Lucilius it now becomes necessary to examine in some detail the nature of the Stoic rhetoric and the Stoic theory of the plain style upon the stylistic doctrines and actual compositions of Lucilius.   Such an inquiry is indispensable because in the first instance both Lucilius and Horace are convinced Greco-Romans, and because the grammatical and rhetorical ideals in whose dissemination Diogenes of Babylon and Panaetius played so important a part, were subsequently modified and reinterpreted in the intervening period, notably in the rhetorical works of Cicero and the Roman Atticists.   In this later and more sophisticated form these ideals found wide acceptance in Augustan Rome and are in consequence of vital importance in determining the aesthetic creed of Horace, the nature of his criticism upon Lucilius, and in fact the sense in which Porphyrio's statement that Horace followed Lucilius is to be interpreted. Nor must we forget that the study of rhetoric was pursued quite as ardently in the circle of Maecenas as in the circle of Scipio.

C. Domitius Marsus,[41] an epigrammatist of the circle of Maecenas, wrote a treatise *de urbanitate* in which he treated the theory of pregnant, piquant expression and stylistic restraint.   Undoubtedly the theme stands in close relation to his epigrams and *fabellae*.   We know from Quintilian's use of this work in his discussion of the laughable (6, 3) that Domitius Marsus did not limit the definition of the term to witty sayings alone.   Since Horace in his satires (1, 10, 13) also associated the conception of the *urbanitas* with brevity and stylistic restraint rather than with wit he must have accepted the theory of Domitius Marsus in essence.   Apparently we have in Horace's odes (4, 4, 18 ff.) a learned allusion to the *Amasonis* of Domitius, which gives further corroboration of the inference of Horace's intimacy with his works. C. Valgius Rufus[45] also, who is mentioned among the friends of Horace in satire 1, 10, 82, and to whom Horace dedicates *carm.* 2, 9, wrote on grammar and rhetoric. In rhetoric he seems to have published a revision of the τέχνη or *ars* of Apollodorus of Pergamum which advocated the theoretical and cultural study of rhetoric rather than a mere practical acquaintance with its applications. It seems probable moreover that Horace after 30 B.C. was acquainted with Dionysius of Halicarnassus, who came to Rome in that year.

The nature of the Greek influence on Roman literature from the days of Livius Andronicus to the period of the Macedonian wars has been described by Leo[44] in so masterly a manner that it is needless for me to retraverse that great period of imperialistic and cultural expansion.

With the year 168 B.C., the year of the battle of Pydna, there began at Rome a genuine invasion of educated Greeks. Crates of Mallos came to Rome in this year as the head of an embassy from King Eumenes of Pergamum. In 155 B.C., Athens sent the famous embassy of the three philosophers, the Academician Carneades, the Peripatetic Critolaus, and the Stoic Diogenes of Babylon. Even before this the number of philosophers and rhetoricians was so large in Rome that in 161 B.C., the senate instructed the praetor to banish them from the city as a menace to Roman manners and morals. The arrival of the 1000 Achaean hostages after the battle of Pydna was another great Hellenizing influence. It is in the light of such facts that we must measure the works of Polybius and Panaetius. In truth the position and influence of these two gifted writers differs from that of their less gifted countrymen rather in the lasting effect they exercised upon Roman literature, aesthetics, and philosophy than as regards the immediate results of their influence upon their Roman contemporaries. All classes of educated Greeks aided in the transformation of the Roman nobility into a body of patrons of the Greco-Roman literature and learning. From Grecomaniacs like Albinus nothing was to be expected, but the influence of the Scipios, of Fulvius Nobilior, and of the other patrons of the new literature and learning fertilized the soil in which Latin literature was to be nurtured.

In this period between the first and second Punic wars, if we can trust the testimony of Cicero's *Brutus* (77–82) there arose a large number of orators whose style frankly rested upon the new Greek rhetoric. Under the same influence the serious interest in historical composition now developed among certain of the noble senatorial families. But it was in the Scipionic circle that these influences attained their greatest focal intensity, and gained most adequate expression in all the different fields of literature and philosophy which had stirred the imaginations of the Romans of this great epoch.

Since the rhetorical and literary ideals which pervade all the writings emanating from this famous circle of men are profoundly influenced by the teachings of Diogenes of Babylon and Panaetius, a few words may be said of these two Stoic philosophers, the exponents to the Roman world of the theory of the plain style, and of the Socratic or ironical type of humor associated with that style.

The Stoic theory of the plain style, as taught by Diogenes of Babylon,[45] rests ultimately upon the Aristotelian and Theophrastean antithesis between the λόγος πρὸς τὸ πρᾶγμα and the λόγος πρὸς τὸν ἀκροατήν, the discourse addressed to the subject in hand, and the discourse addressed to the hearer. The object of the former is to apply to rhetoric the style of exact pragmatic discussion appropriate to philosophy and dialectic. It is in a word simply a dialectical rhetoric designed exclusively to inform the hearer (*ad docendum*). The object of the latter is to produce an emotional effect on the mind of the hearer by all the devices of rhetoric, linguistic, rhythmical, psychological. Its ultimate goal is to lead captive[46] the soul, for rhetoric is a ψυχαγωγία. Its immediate aim is to move and delight the hearer (*ad delectandum*) because, as Aristotle declares, we give very different judgments under the influence of pain or pleasure, love or hate. Now a style which should aim only at austere justice would be characterized by the traditional Stoic apathy or ἀπάθεια towards such emotional effects. As Aristotle says:[47] τὸ δίκαιον μηδὲν πλεῖω ζητεῖν περὶ τὸν λόγον ἢ ὡς μήτε λυπεῖν μήτ' εὐφραίνειν. And this and nothing more was the goal of the earlier Stoics. They believed that to speak well was to speak the truth:[48] οἱ Στωικοὶ δὲ τὸ εὖ λέγειν ἔλεγον τὸ ἀληθῆ λέγειν. Furthermore, their theory of ἀπάθεια would naturally inhibit any self-conscious straining at emotional effects.

Smiley, in a Wisconsin doctoral thesis on *Latinitas and* Ἑλληνισμός, well describes the philosophical motives which influenced these stylistic theories:[49]

There were perhaps three considerations which had weight with the Stoics in the formulation of their theory of the plain style. (1) Their belief that to speak well was to speak the truth. (2) Their conception that the function of an orator was merely to teach, and not as Cicero asserted, "to teach, to delight, to move . . ." There was the general Stoic principle, that anything to be ideal, whether in speech or conduct, must be in harmony with nature. Given now an orator, whose function is to speak the truth, to teach, and to use language in harmony with nature it is easy to formulate a theory of style, the virtues of which shall be (1) pure and unperverted speech, (2) clearness, (3) precision, (4) conciseness, (5) appropriateness, (6) freedom from artificial ornamentation. And this was the Stoic theory which bore the name Ἑλληνισμός or *Latinitas*. The reason why the first virtue gave its name to the theory is quite evident, for the first virtue in a sense embraces the other five. Speech that is pure and unperverted and in harmony with nature will of necessity be clear, precise, concise, appropriate, and free from all artificiality.

Such a style, as Diogenes says, has five virtues: ἀρεταὶ δὲ λόγου εἰσὶ πέντε. Its first quality is a correct and pure conversational idiom as opposed to the poetical and elaborated style of conventional rhetoric: Ἑλληνισμὸς μὲν οὖν ἐστι φράσις ἀδιάπτωτος ἐν τῇ τεχνικῇ καὶ μὴ εἰκαίᾳ συνηθείᾳ. Its second quality is clearness, aiming at an exact reproduction of the thought: σαφήνεια δέ ἐστι λέξις γνωρίμως παριστῶσα τὸ νοούμενον. Third, brevity limiting utterance to just what was necessary to set forth the matter: συντομία δέ ἐστι λέξις αὐτὰ τὰ ἀναγκαῖα περιέχουσα πρὸς δήλωσιν. Fourth, appropriateness, that is the appropriateness of the word to the object in hand: πρέπον δέ ἐστι λέξις οἰκεία τῷ πράγματι. Fifth, avoidance of the vulgar: κατασκευὴ δέ ἐστι λέξις ἐκπεφευγυῖα τὸν ἰδιωτισμόν.

On the other hand, in Herodian's system, which is closely related to that of Diogenes, we find six faults, which may in essence be reduced to three opposed to these virtues. These faults are σολοικισμός, βαρβαρισμός, ἀκυρολογία. Under σολοικισμός are included faults in syntax; under βαρβαρισμός faults in spelling, pronunciation, and impurity of diction; under ἀκυρολογία is included the failure to give each object or act its own specific name, that is, inaccuracy in the use of words in their literal or metaphorical sense.

This grammatical rhetoric of Diogenes of Babylon forms the foundation for the more highly articulated rhetorical system of Panaetius. But before turning to this system, it will be desirable to show how wide was the influence of the simpler rhetoric of Diogenes—though doubtless here also the teachings of Panaetius were not without influence—upon the writings emanating from the Scipionic circle.

An inventory of these writings enables us to see in true perspective the stylistic relation of Lucilius to his contemporaries. Furthermore, we gain a realization of the part the Stoic rhetoric played in laying the firm foundations on which rested the subsequent structure of Roman rhetoric and critical theory, as developed in the rhetorical works of Cicero, the movement of the Roman Atticists, the critical works of Horace, and the Institutes of Quintilian. By such an analytical summary, we find that the plain style and the restrained "ironic" humor associated with it obtained full expression in many different fields of literary endeavor. Hence it becomes antecedently probable that Lucilius was influenced by these same critical theories summed up in the ideal of *Latinitas*, the goal of the Stoic theory of the plain style.

For my present purpose it is not necessary to make an exhaustive examination. I shall rather attempt to summarize the general tenor of the stylistic criticisms upon the works emanating from the Scipionic circle. This criticism found in the rhetorical works of Cicero and other Latin writers attests the pervasiveness of the Stoic ideal of *Latinitas* and the related virtues of the grammatical rhetoric of Diogenes of Babylon.

The style of Laelius was marked by the pure Latinity so studiously sought by the Stoic grammarians. Thus Atticus in the *Brutus* 258, after speaking of the *locutio emendata et Latina of* Caesar (*cf.* the φράσις ἀδιάπτωτος of Diogenes, and ὀρθογραφία as a technical term of rhetoric) says: Mitto C. Laelium, P. Scipionem; aetatis illius ista fuit laus tamquam innocentiae sic Latine loquendi. Again in 94, as the representative of the plain style, he is contrasted with the impetuous Galba, the representative of the grand style. His speeches read well because they are studiously filed and polished (limatius dicendi consectantur genus). In 89 of the *Brutus*, he appears as a model of the plain style, nicely wrought and designed to instruct, while Galba is the model of the grand style, designed to move the feelings of the jury. *Elegantia*, the virtue of nice discrimination of word and phrase, was the central quality of Laelius, force, of Galba.

The life and writings of P. Rutilius Rufus, a student of Panaetius, a courageous statesman who was the unflinching champion of the oppressed provincials, were animated by the same Stoic principles. Like Diogenes he believed that to speak well was to speak the truth, for Cicero in *de oratore* 1, 229 declares that his defence against the charge of extortion was characterized by a *simplex ratio veritatis*, a tradition which was continued by his nephew Cotta.[60] In general Cicero found his orations "jejune," a favorite epithet of the plain style. Furthermore, his Stoic tendencies found an even more productive outlet in the law, where his *responsa* enjoyed a high reputation.[61] He exhibits also the same interest in biography which is exhibited by Scipio, who was deeply influenced by the writings of Xenophon, one of the greatest Greek models of the simple narrative style affected by the Stoic rhetoricians. Hence we find Rutilius Rufus writing a *de vita sua* in five books. Such a work, which is closely related to the categories of ἀπομνημονεύματα and ὑπομνήματα or memoirs, helps us to understand how naturally the element of personal confession came to play so important a part in the writings of Lucilius.[62]

But the greatest of these Stoic jurists belonged to the family of the Scaevolas, a family famous for its pontiffs, statesmen, and jurisconsults. At this period P. Mucius Scaevola,[63] the consul of 133 B.C. and Q. Mucius Scaevola, the augur, represent the same Stoic tendencies in jurisprudence and oratory. The former was the teacher of P. Rutilius Rufus in law, the latter was more actively associated with the Scipionic circle. In a fragment of Lucilius, 86, this legally-minded Scaevola alludes to the rhetorical powers of his son-in-law Crassus:

'Crassum habeo generum, ne rhetoricoterus tu *seis*'.

Here the use of the Greek comparative is in part a mocking parody of the fondness of Albucius, Scaevola's legal opponent, for Greek terms, but it also suggests the indifference to rhetorical embellishments natural to a convinced adherent of the unadorned grammatical rhetoric of the Stoics.

Quintus Tubero,[54] the nephew of Scipio, was an enthusiastic student of Panaetius, who dedicated a work to the Greek philosopher.   He was a thorough-going Stoic, who as an orator seems to have followed the most severe Stoic standards.

The two native historians of the Scipionic circle, Gaius Fannius and Sempronius Asellio, seem to have written under the influence of Polybius, who is himself strongly imbued with Stoic tendencies.   Fannius,[55] the son-in-law of Laelius, is best known by his *Annales*.   In this work he recognized and defended the Socratic irony of Scipio, a clear proof of his Stoic predilections.   He, too, was a pupil of Panaetius.   His history, which was marked by moderation of tone and high regard for truth, has some claims to *elegantia*, the quality of nice discrimination in the choice of word and phrase, a prerequisite to the attainment of the Stoic virtue of *Latinitas*.   On the other hand, his style was criticized as dry and thin, *exiguus*, a defect inseparable from the virtues of the plain style.   Sempronius Asellio,[56] like Polybius, whom he directly imitates in one passage, wrote a philosophical pragmatic history of decided Stoic tinge.   He shows also the same patriotic and ethical motives which we find in Polybius.   Like Polybius he omitted any detailed annalistic introduction and plunged directly into the account of contemporaneous events.

Marcus Iunius Congus,[57] the author of a legal treatise *de potestatibus*, has been identified by Cichorius with the Iunius Congus of Lucilius 596.   As Lucilius also wrote to him an εἰσαγωγή or introduction on the writing of history, he was probably a younger member of the same Stoic school of historians and jurists.

Less known members of the circle were Furius Phlius, consul of 136 B.C., perhaps an antiquarian; Sextus Pompeius, through intimacy with whom the foundation of the friendship uniting the Lucilian and the Pompeian families may have arisen. Spurius Mummius, the brother of the conqueror of Corinth, was another educated Stoic of this period. The poetical epistles,[58] which he sent from Corinth, are of importance in the genesis of this form, a genre closely allied to the *sermo* or conversation as developed by the rhetoric of Panaetius, which is represented in Lucilian satire, and finds consummate expression in the epistles of Horace.

As the most famous writer of the whole circle something must be said of the style of Terence. As *puri sermonis amator* he is, of course, in thorough sympathy with the Stoic ideal of Latinitas.[59] As Leo well says:[60] Das Latein des Terenz ist eine neue römische Urbanität wie Menander's Griechisch eine neue Atthis war. Er wiess das sehr gut; *est pura lectio* lässt er den Ambivius in Prolog zum Heautontimoroumenos sagen.

This is recognized by Cicero, usually a severe critic of the plain style. Such a *purus* and *lectus sermo* means the best Latinity of the period.[61] Such purity of tasfe and diction, *elegantia*, would seem to imply thorough familiarity with the strict grammatical, lexicographical, and rhetorical studies of Diogenes and Panaetius.[62] Even in his own lifetime Terence was criticized by his rival Luscius for what soon came to constitute the most characteristic virtues of the plain style, *tenuitas* and *levitas*.[63] So in a later age Caesar in his famous epigram mentions the *levia scripta* of Terence after his *purus sermo*, thereby definitely assigning Terence to the γένος ἰσχνόν or *genus tenue*, the technical designations of the plain style.[64]

Finally, a word as to Scipio himself. The youthful Scipio, enthusiastic, ingenuous, and highly sensitive, was profoundly influenced by his studies in Greek literature, philosophy, and rhetoric. He especially admired Xenophon, a master of the plain style, whose *Cyropaedia* and *Memorabilia* he kept constantly with him. Nor was this love of Greek literature in its simpler forms a mere boyish passion; we may rather regard it as a lasting sympathy if we are to attach any weight to the tone of Socratic irony, the peculiar humor of the plain style, which marked Scipio's oratory.[65] In line 964 Lucilius' mockery of Scipio's pronunciation *pertisum* for *pertaesum* shows Scipio's interest in lexicographical details. The three most important influences on his intellectual life were his intimacy with the Greek historian Polybius, the Stoic philosopher Panaetius, and the wise Roman Laelius, all worthy representatives of the well-balanced Stoic harmony which combined high intellectual and ethical idealism and effective service to the state.

This rapid inventory has been sufficient, I trust, to show how important a part the grammatical rhetoric of Diogenes played in laying the foundation for the plain style, the favorite mode of expression for nearly every writing emanating from the Scipionic circle, however the requirements of the individual genre may have introduced stylistic variations in detail. We may now turn to a much more searching analysis of the rhetorical theories of the philosopher Panaetius, who, accepting the grammatical foundation of his teacher Diogenes, evolved a nicely discriminated theory of the *sermo* or *conversation*, and established the restrained type of ironic or Socratic humor as the appropriate tone for such an unpretentious literary genre.

We know that, as the pupil of Crates of Mallos[66] and of Diogenes of Babylon, Panaetius followed more or less closely the Stoic theories of grammar and rhetoric. Thus he discussed the formation of the pluperfect tense among the Attic writers and in Plato. In contrast to the exclusive ethical interests of the earlier Stoics he also assailed the barbarisms, solecisms, and violent neologisms, so common in the technical writings of the Cynics and Stoics, while he preached and sought to attain a pure and unperverted diction. That is, he held fast to the ideal of Ἑλληνισμός or *Latinitas* as defined by his Stoic teacher Diogenes, but intensively developed the teachings of his master on the rhetorical rather than the grammatical side by the exposition of his theory on appropriateness in language and the type of Socratic humor suited to the *sermo* or conversational form most commonly affected by the plain style.

In the first place, Panaetius assails the aesthetic and moral coarseness of Cynic speech which sins equally against linguistic propriety and social decency. Thus in the *de officiis* 1, 128 he attacks that Cynic παρρησία or brutal frankness of speech which calls a spade a spade. He denies that actions involving moral obliquity or social impropriety must be called by their real names. Those who employ such *verba obscaena* sin against modesty. In such matters we must follow the principle of propriety, which is really identical with that inculcated by the

Stoic doctrine of following nature; that is, we must shun that which is offensive to eye or ear: Nos autem naturam sequamur et ab omni quod ab oculorum auriumque approbatione abhorret fugiamus. It is clear that as applied to speech this test of *approbatio aurium* carries with it certain stylistic implications which find final expression in Horace's conception of *urbanitas* as employed as a touchstone of style in the criticisms levelled against the satires of Lucilius in 1,4; 1,10, and 2,1, and the function assigned to appropriateness in the critical theory of the *Ars Poetica*.[67]

Furthermore propriety of speech is a development of the Aristotelian theory of the mean as we see in the *de officiis* 1, 129: Quibus in rebus duo maxime sunt effugienda, ne quid effeminatum aut molle et ne quid durum aut rusticum sit, a doctrine which is declared to be binding on the orator and the actor.

Again in *de officiis* 1, 148, we are told with even greater emphasis that Cynic coarseness of speech is inimical to moral sensibility, and by clear implication to stylistic sensibility as well: Cynicorum vero ratio tota est eicienda; est enim inimica verecundiae, sine qua nihil rectum esse potest, nihil honestum. In fact it is clear from other passages in the *de officiis* that Panaetius applied his shibboleth of τὸ πρέπον to speech as well as to action by developing a set of principles, rhetorical and yet quasi-ethical, which should govern the *sermo* or conversation both oral and written, as well as the more formal speech of the orator. Negatively, then, the passages just cited show that Panaetius eliminates from the oral or written discourse, *sermo*, the obscenity, over-frankness, and harshness, affected by his Cynic and Stoic predecessors.[68]

In the *de officiis* 1, 132 ff.,[69] Cicero following Panaetius discusses the form, content and the tone of the *sermo*, the ideal literary form for the plain style whether written or spoken. In the spoken discourse *claritas* or distinctness of utterance, and *suavitas* or agreeable harmony are essential. These qualities by a slight shift of meaning correspond to perspicacity and easy charm in the written discourse. The Catuli, who are quoted as models of such a style, both spoken and written, clearly adopt the Stoic principle of *Latinitas*, for Cicero tells us: hi autem optime uti lingua Latina putabantur. Again, in the *Brutus* 132, Cicero, speaking of the elder Catulus, refers to his *suavitas*, and his *incorrupta quaedam Latini sermonis integritas*. Such epithets recall the pure and unperverted diction demanded by the grammatical rhetoric of Diogenes, and the theory of appropriateness of Panaetius.

Now the agreeableness (*suavitas*) of the *Brutus* passage, and such purity of diction as was advocated by Panaetius and realized by Catulus, imply by definition avoidance of foreign idiom, especially of the pedantic and objectionable habit of interlarding Latin with Greek. Panaetius seems to have fully realized this, if we may accept the testimony of the *de officiis* 1, 111, for certainly one of the attributes of propriety τὸ πρέπον is to be true to the dictates of our own nature: quam (i.e., τὸ πρέπον) conservare non possis, si aliorum naturam imitans omittas tuam. Ut enim sermone eo debemus uti, qui innatus est nobis, ne, ut quidam Graeca verba inculcantes iure optimo rideamur, sic in actiones omnemque vitam nullam discrepantiam conferre debemus. Doubtless, therefore, Panaetius, like Diogenes, advocated a style free from barbarisms or solecisms. Moreover, as models for his discourse he would avoid such coarse and careless Cynic or Stoic predecessors, as Diogenes the Cynic, Zeno, or Chrysippus.[70] And here he would only be following the teachings of his master Diogenes of Babylon, who in vii, 59 tests what constitutes a barbarism by the usage of οἱ εὐδοκιμοῦντες Ἕλληνες, the Greek writers of good repute. Can we infer who these Greek writers were who set the standard of good usage?

In the first place we know that Cicero, evidently following Panaetius, in the *de officiis* 1, 134 regarded the Socratici as furnishing the model for the sermo: Sit ergo hic sermo, in quo Socratici maxime excellunt, lenis minimeque pertinax, insit in eo lepos.[71] It is indeed natural that the oral discussions of Socrates and the informal dialogues of his pupils Plato, Xenophon, and others, should be regarded as the models for the *sermo* or conversation. In the first place, the actual conversation of Socrates on the streets of Athens was in a general way in conformity with the definition of Ἑλληνισμός as given above,[72] for it was a conversation in pure style in a form based on the rules of a technical grammar and prosecuted with a definite purpose. In the second place, the written dialogues of Plato, Xenophon, and the other writings of the Academy, held fast to the original stylistic simplicity of tone introduced by Socrates, and in some degree to the Socratic system of question and answer. So Cicero in the *de officiis* 1, 134 expressly argues against conversation becoming a monologue, an injunction which seems to be carefully observed in the dialogues of Plato and in the *sermones* of Lucilius and Horace, though only to a limited degree in the satires of Persius and Juvenal, with their increasing tendency to suppress even the shadowy outlines of the *adversarius*. So Cicero says: nec vero, tamquam in possessionem suam venerit, excludat alios, sed cum reliquis in rebus, tum in sermone communi vicissitudinem non iniquam putet. Moreover, since Socrates and Plato affect the attitude of irony, it is indispensable that they should give the interlocutors a free chance to develop their ignorance.

A third injunction of Cicero recalls a well-known characteristic of Horatian satire, the tendency of conversation to reveal some defect in the speaker's (or writer's) own character, especially when he slanders the absent: in primisque provideat, ne sermo vitium aliquod indicet inesse in moribus; quod maxime tum solet evenire, cum studiose de absentibus detrahendi causa aut per ridiculum aut severe maledice contumelioseque dicitur.

Similarly, in Lucilian and Horatian satire the *adversarius* sometimes turns the tables on the satirist, supposedly the author of a *suspectum genus*, as for instance in Lucilius 1014, 1015, 1016, 1021, and in such Horatian passages as 1, 3, 19; 1, 4, 33–35, 81 ff. In the last passage we are told that the man who slanders an absent friend reveals his own blackness of heart, while in 1, 10, 79, the words *vellicet absentem Demetrius* are used in the same spirit.

While the remarks upon the occasions appropriate to conversation have the oral discourse more distinctly in mind, it is worth noticing that the *mise-en-scène* of several satires also fall under the rubric of the *de officiis* 1, 132. To begin with the last, the δεῖπνα or *cenae* form a distinct genre among Latin satires. Such are the satires in Lucilius books 4 and 20, the dinner of Nasidienus, Horace *satire* 2, 8, the *Cena Trimalchionis* in the satire of Petronius, and the satires 5 and 11 of Juvenal. Such satires as the journey to the Sicilian Straits, Lucilius book 3, the corresponding journey to Brundisium, Horace 1, 5, the satire of Horace 1, 6, which describes the introduction of Horace to Maecenas and defends the poet's position within the circle, and the related lines in Lucilius, book 30, 1009, 1010, 1011, 1227, which record the relations of Lucilius with a new patron;[73] Horace 2, 6, an expression of gratitude for the gift of the Sabine farm, and the satire of Lucilius in book 14, fragments 464, 466 on the embassy of Scipio to the east—all these satires breathe the intimacy of the literary coteries (the *circuli* of Cicero), of Scipio, and Maecenas.   On the other hand, the more formal philosophic satires such as that of Horace, 1, 1, on Avarice, directly dedicated to Maecenas, with its probable Lucilian predecessors in Lucilius books 18 and 19, the discussion of the Stoic paradoxes in Horace 2, 3, and 2, 7, and the related Lucilian satire in book 30, suggest the philosophic discussions or *disputationes* of intimates.   Finally, the intimacy binding together the members of the older and younger circle alike is admirably pictured in the famous lines of Horace's *sat.* 2, 1, 71 ff. where the good Scipio and the wise Laelius unbend in preparation for the plain dinner of cabbage,[74] or in the delightful conversation between Maecenas and Horace in *sat.* 2, 6, 41–46.

The further injunction of Cicero (Panaetius): si seriis severitatem adhibeat, si iocosis leporem, marks the mixture in the tone of satire now grave, now gay, which testifies to its classification under the larger literary family of the σπουδαιο-γέλοιον, whose common object is to convey philosophic truth under cover of a jest.   Of this semi-technical literary term Horace's well-known phrase *ridentem dicere verum quid vetat?* appears to be a deliberate paraphrase.[75]

From a different point of view, the subject matter of satire can be largely fitted into the discussion on the subject matter of the *sermo* with which 135 begins: Habentur autem plerumque sermones aut de domesticis negotiis aut de re publica aut de artium studiis atque doctrina.   Satires of anecdote or of personal concern may be illustrated in Horace by satires 2, 6 and 2, 8 of the second book.   In Lucilius by the satire on the Helleno-

maniac Albucius in book 2, the journey to the Sicilian Straits
in book 3, the complaint of illness in book 5, and the encounter
of Scipio with the bore in book 6.[76] Political satire, a field
inevitably closed to Horace under Augustus, was the constant
weapon of Lucilius, as Horace himself attests in the well-known
passage *sat.* 2, 1, 62–70.

Finally, the part that satire played from the days of Lucilius
to those of Juvenal in popularizing the Stoic philosophy is
constantly manifest. Such an interest falls naturally under the
rubric *aut de artium studiis et doctrina*. Here also deserve to
be mentioned the grammatical and rhetorical studies of Lucilius
especially those in books 9 and 10,[77] and such criticisms on the
theory of the satirist's art as we find in Lucilius books 26 and 30,
and Horace's satires, 1,4 and 10, and 2,1, the literary epistles,
and above all the *Ars Poetica* of Horace. The last is an εἰσαγωγή
or informal introduction to an art addressed by a master to his
youthful protégés, with which Cichorius rightly compares the
satire of Lucilius addressed to Iunius Congus, the youthful
historian.[78]

The passage of Cicero also contains certain hints upon the
manner of the conversation, which distinctly suggest the
rambling and somewhat desultory manner of satire. Thus in
135: Danda igitur opera est, ut, etiamsi aberrare ad alia coe-
perit ad haec revocetur oratio, sed utcumque aderunt; neque
enim isdem de rebus nec omni tempore nec similiter delectamur.
It is needless to quote Horatian examples on this point, but it
is worth noticing that certain transitional lines in Lucilius,
such as 558, 1027, 1032, 1227, 1279, seem to employ the same
desultory method of composition.

The abrupt and witty endings of Horace's satires, sometimes
coupled with ironical mockery of the satirist himself, are in
strict keeping with the concluding injunction of Cicero in this
same section: Animadvertendum est etiam, quatenus sermo
delectationem habeat, et, ut incipiendi ratio fuerit, ita sit
desinendi modus. In illustration of this point we may cite
Horace *sat.* 1, 1, 120; 3, 136 ff.; 4, 140 ff.; 9, 78; 10, 92; 2, 1,
83 ff.; 3, 323 ff. Hitherto it has escaped observation that
Lucilius probably affected a similar abruptness at the end of
his satires, as we may infer from fragment 567, parallel to the

close of Horace's first satire: 1038, parallel to the close of the fourth satire of book 1, 231, clearly the original of Horace's 1, 9, 78, and 1095, parallel to 2, 1, 84–85.

More vital than such corroborative evidence as to details is the evidence concerning the wit and humor appropriate to the oral or written discourse. It is, therefore, important to consider what limits were set to their employment, and what type of humor Panaetius regarded as appropriate to the *sermo*.

This question has already been partially answered by the evidence that the *libri Socratici* are the best models for the *sermo*, which should be easy and not too aggressive, and should have the spice of wit.[79] The tone of the conversation also, as we have just seen, should vary with the subject, now grave, now gay. In this fact, indeed, lies the psychological justification for the apparently informal, yet subtly artistic, development of the σπουδαιογέλοιον by the Greek Cynics and Stoics, and·by the Roman satirists, their successors. In such genres, however, a sharp distinction must be made between the province of humor and that of invective. To the latter belong the iambics of Archilochus, the works of Hipponax, certain of the epigrams of Catullus, and the epodes of Horace. The conversation, whether written or spoken, should not reveal the venom or censoriousness of the writer or real defects in his character. Hence, Horace is extremely careful in the third satire of the first book to differentiate mere censoriousness from the light, but reforming humor of the true satirist. In fact the definition of invective in distinction from the approved Socratic type of ironical humor, with which the *de officiis* 1, 134 closes, seems to correspond essentially to that of βωμολοχία or scurrility in the rhetorical works of Aristotle. Since it can be shown that in a satire in book 30, 6 fragments 1022, 971, 1014, 970, 1015, 1016, Lucilius develops a similar discussion as to the type of humor appropriate for the *sermones* and rebuts charges of backbiting or invective, the question arises whether Panaetius was not one of the most important intermediaries, in naturalizing, so to speak, the Aristotelian theory of liberal humor in the critical satires of Lucilius; (2) whether Horace's theory of the type of humor appropriate to satire was not profoundly influenced by similar current theories on the proper function and limits of

humor, theories of ultimate Aristotelian origin, best represented
to us in the rhetorical works of Cicero. The thoughtful reader
will not fail to notice that the theory of satiric humor set forth
in Horace's satires 1,3; 1,4; 1,10, and 2,1, is in essential harmony
with that set forth in the *de officiis* 1, 101–104 by Cicero, the
translator of Panaetius. Let us turn to the analysis of this
theory.

In these sections Cicero begins by asserting the conflict
between ὁρμή appetite and reason; reason should command,
appetite obey. Hence, every action should be based on reason;
the appetites should neither run ahead of reason nor lag behind
it. The control or rather the wise use of the passions is all
important. Such ordered control is the first law of duty.
Nature did not bring us into the world for play and jest: Neque
enim ita generati a natura sumus, ut ad ludum et iocum facti
esse videamur. Nevertheless, play and jest have their place;
like sleep and rest they are used as a means of relaxation from
serious effort, relaxations which rebuild us in the literal sense
of the word. It follows that jesting is subject to the restraints
of reason; it must not be unrestrained and unrefined, but
refined and witty: Ipsumque genus iocandi non profusum ne
immodestum, sed ingenuum et facetum esse debet. The limits
set to play in the case of children afford a good analogy for the
proper limitation of what we in English call the "play of wit,"
and the Latin satirists called *ludus*, a name actually attached to
his satires by Lucilius.[80] In both cases nothing incompatible
with good conduct is permissible; ordered freedom, but not
license, is the rule: Ut enim pueris non omnem ludendi licentiam
damus, sed eam, quae ab honestatis actionibus non sit aliena,
sic in ipso ioco aliquod probi ingenii lumen eluceat. We have
now brought our paraphrase to the end of 103.

In 104, Cicero, following Panaetius, proceeds to make a
practical application of these principles of propriety and modera-
tion to the field of the laughable, the *genus iocandi*. He announ-
ces that there are two types of jests: the one coarse, rude,
vicious, indecent; the other refined, polite, clever, witty:
Duplex omnino est iocandi genus unum illiberale, petulans,
flagitiosum, obscenum, alterum elegans, urbanum, ingeniosum,
facetum. As examples of the latter type Cicero cites Plautus,

the Old Comedy, the works of the Socratic school, and the collections of witty sayings of which the ancients were so fond. The last example of the liberal jest is represented by the collection of Cato Maior, which bore the general title of ἀποφθέγματα. Further, Panaetius' general theory of propriety may be applied as a test to distinguish the liberal from the vulgar jest; thus the former is well-timed, used in the hours of mental relaxation, which even the most austere allow themselves; the other is unworthy of any freeborn man, since the subject is indecent and the words obscene. Finally, returning to the analogy of the playground, on the basis of which the term *ludus* came to be applied to satiric writing, Cicero asserts that the military exercises of the Campus Martius and hunting are examples of true recreations.

Here again, it is clear that Horace in his critical satires, and notably in the fourth satire of the first book, followed a rhetorical theory of humor having many relations to that set forth by Cicero's paraphrase of Panaetius. He, too, differentiates two types of humor; his fourth satire, as Hendrickson has seen,[31] "is a criticism of literary theory put concretely." That is, Horace writes a satire upon the proper limits of the laughable τὸ γέλοιον from the express point of view of aesthetics and ethics. In 1, 4, 34, it is clear that Horace like Cicero protests against the unrestrained type of humor (*profusum genus iocandi*). Such a method of jesting, as Aristotle had declared long before Cicero (and Panaetius), was that of the βωμολόχος or scurrilous jester, the man who is the slave to the ridiculous; that is, one who does not subject humor to the dictates of reason, is not sparing in his attacks on others, has no regard for his own reputation, or even his personal safety. Similarly, Lucilius in fragments 1015, 1016, seems to put into the mouth of an adversarius a charge of βωμολοχία levelled against himself. He, too, is charged with having disseminated scurrilous attacks in many discourses:

> et male dicendo in multis sermonibus differs.

As Horace shows in line 90, there are limits, which distinguish true freedom of speech from unlicensed invective:

> hic tibi comis et urbanus liberque videtur.

Similarly proper freedom is associated with humor in line 103:

> liberius si dixero quid, si forte iocosius.

Indeed, at the very beginning of the satire, in line 5, Horace gives recognition to the *libertas* of Lucilius, which is directly derived from the Old Comedy. Such *libertas* he can even approve of, when applied in the spirit of the Old Comedy to the task of moral reform within the state. So, in fragment 1033 Lucilius seems to assume the rôle of *censor morum*:

> quem scis scire tuas omnes maculasque notasque.

Here *macula* is glossed by Nonius p. 350, 12 by *turpitudines*. In this connection it is worth noticing that the illiberal jest according to Cicero employs obscene words in the assault upon an indecent subject: alterum (*i.e.*, the genus illiberale iocandi) ne libero quidem, si rerum turpitudini adhibeatur verborum obscenitas.

Similarly, in a discussion upon the province of the laughable in the *de oratore* 2, 235-247, Cicero points out (236) that the laughable is said to originate in what is disgraceful pointed out in a manner not disgraceful. This last definition seems to be derived from Aristotle's *poetics* 6: τὸ γὰρ γελοῖόν ἐστι ἁμάρτημά τι καὶ ἀνώδυνον καὶ οὐ φθαρτικόν.

In the *de oratore* 2, 242, in speaking of the type of wit which turns upon the matter expressed rather than the manner of expression, Cicero urges moderation and care; the mimicking manner employed by the actors in farces, *ethologi*, or in the mimes is excessive, and should be avoided by the orator.[22] The orator should rather adumbrate, *surripiat*, his imitation, that the hearer's imagination may be aroused: orator surripiat oportet imitationem, ut is, qui audiet, cogitet plura, quam videat; praestet idem ingenuitatem et ruborem suum verborum turpitudine et rerum obscenitate vitanda.

Now Horace, at the beginning of *sat.* 1, 4, seems to recognize that Lucilius, whose spiritual descent is from the writers of the Old Comedy, is ethically a humorist of the second or reforming type. His assaults, like that of the Old Comedy, aim at social reform; they attack the *turpitudines* of robbery, adultery, murder, with freedom. Lucilius, like those writers, is *facetus*, or as Horace says in 1, 10, 65 *comis et urbanus*. Stylistically, however, he merits severe criticism because, in spite of his theoretical adherence to the spirit of the Old Comedy, he sinks in practice to the level of the mime. Horace 1, 10, 5, cannot give him a blanket approval though he recognizes his comic power:

nec tamen hoc tribuens dederim quoque cetera.

Otherwise, one would have to praise the mimes of Laberius as beautiful poetry. True comic power, in the best sense of the word, implies certain stylistic qualities, notably restraint and the use of the liberal type of humor; it is not by itself enough to extend the jowl of the hearer in a laugh:

ergo non satis est risu diducere rictum
auditoris.

Evidently then, Horace's opinion was in harmony with that of Cicero in the *de oratore* in regarding the humor of the *ethologi* or impersonators of character skits and *mimi* as excessive, and their language as a sort of *obscenitas*. Certainly this type of humor does not conform to the dictates of reason and moderation enjoined in the *de officiis* 1, 104: Ludendi etiam est quidam modus retinendus, ut ne nimis omnia profundamus elatique voluptate in aliquam turpitudinem delabamur. The implication of Horace's remarks follows the doctrine of this passage. Lucilius, swept away by his passions, "lapses" (delabitur) to the genre of humor represented by the mime, which is marked by complete lack of restraint in its determination to raise a laugh. Led astray by his temperament he is thus unconsciously recreant to the higher type of humor derived from the Old Comedy. Horace, like Cicero,[83] asserts that the methods of the actors of the farce and the mime are to be avoided: sed ut in illo superiore genere vel narrationis vel imitationis vitanda est mimorum et ethologorum similitudo.

Similarly, Lydus[84] characterizes the μιμικὴ κωμῳδία as τεχνικὸν μὲν ἔχουσα οὐδὲν ἀλόγῳ μόνον τὸ πλῆθος ἐπαγοῦσα γέλωτι. This is in fact an appropriate designation for the mime of Laberius, whom Macrobius, *sat.* 3, 7, 2, characterizes as an *actor asperae libertatis*.

Such lapses on the part of the temperamental Lucilius were probably purely unconscious. Theoretically he, like Horace, probably disapproved the broader and coarser strokes of the mime, in which *obscenitas verborum* is added to *turpitudo rerum*. The suit which Lucilius brought against an actor of mimes who assailed him by name and the possible allusion to a *mimus* in fragment 1344, afford some ground for the belief that Lucilius, unlike Caelius, the judge of the trial court, was conscious of an inherent ethical and aesthetic gulf separating the type of humor employed in his satires from that bandied on the stage. The basis of such a distinction was probably in part stylistic, but rested principally upon the high purpose of social reform which Lucilius rightly believed animated his poetry and made him akin to the spirit of the Old Comedy rather than that of the mime which, like our farce comedy, exists solely to portray ridiculous types of character, or grotesque incidents, with the broadest and coarsest strokes.[85] The whole incident of the suit of the *mimus* is worth reviewing here. According to the (*auctor ad Herennium* 2, 13, 19), the judge Caelius acquitted an actor against whom Lucilius brought a damage suit for having assailed him by name from the stage, whereas Publius Mucius Scaevola condemned one who had made a similar assault on Accius.

It seems probable that the actors concerned were both *mimi*, for we are expressly told in the same work 1, 14, 24 that the actor whom Accius sued was a *mimus*, and that his defence was that he had the right to mention by name a writer of plays publicly performed.

The passage from Lucilius fragment 1344 is extremely corrupt but if we accept the reading of Marx, it will stand as follows:

> ut me scire volo *dum* mimi conscius sum(*mum*)
> ne damnum faciam, scire hoc se nescit.

This is further interpreted in the note of Marx: non quemvis hominem in re turpi oportet esse loquacem neque meae domus turpia facta si quae sunt foras efferre: sicut me scire volo, si veluti uxor adulterium fecit dum mimi conscius, summum ne dammum faciam scire hoc se nescit, id est tacet.

Furthermore, we have in line 899 of Lucilius a passage which might be interpreted as referring not to a woman[86] on whom one is showering a stream of abuse, but to an appeal by the poet himself that such *verba obscena* should be far removed from his pages.   The Lucilian line reads:

deum *rex auertat* uerba obscena — ⌣ —

Indeed fragments 895 and 900 seem to refer to amatory scenes which might be classed among *turpitudines*.   It thus seems possible to apply to the humor of the mime as conceived by Horace and possibly by Lucilius, the rhetorical formula of Cicero and Panaetius.   The wit of the mime is an *illiberalis iocus* for in it *obscenitas verborum* is added to *turpitudo rerum*.   The sharp humor of the mime may also be said to be an excellent example of the reprobated manner which precedes *severe, maledice, contumeliose*, against which Cicero protests in the *de officiis* 1, 134.

But it might be argued that the humor of the Old Comedy could hardly be regarded as the representative of the *genus liberale iocandi*.   And in point of fact "to Aristotle himself the old comedy afforded the most conspicuous illustration of illiberal jest."   Yet Aristotle's condemnation of Old Comedy did not prevail generally among later theorists and critics, as Hendrickson has shown.[87]   The Old Comedy, then, was for many reasons frequently classed with the *genus liberale iocandi*.   In the first place, Cicero in the *de officiis* 1, 103 shows that this type of humor must have a certain probity of character: sic in ipso ioco aliquod probi ingenii lumen eluceat.   Now the purpose of ethical and social reform sheds such a light upon the Old Comedy.   This we see clearly in the characterization of the Old Comedy in its relation to the spirit of Lucilian satire with which Horace begins satire 1, 4.   Nor is this an isolated point of view, for Pliny *epist.* 6, 21 says in praise of an imitator of the Old Comedy: ornavit virtutes, insectatus est vitia.

From this point of view, moreover, the spirit of the Old Comedy, in distinction from the spirit animating the iambic verses of Archilochus, or the poetry of Hipponax, or the mime, may be fairly classed with the spirit of the σπουδαιογέλοιον of which the later popular Cynic and Stoic philosophers are the best representatives.   In fact these writers constantly traced their descent from the Old Comedy.   The Old Comedy is serious in that it has a distinct ethical purpose, but it clothes that

purpose in the liberal jest. Perhaps it would be more correct
to say that the Old Comedy was the precursor of the Socratic
literature to whose tone Cynicism owed so much.[88]   Indeed,
the Old Comedy is not infrequently described in language that
clearly implies its association with the σπουδαιογέλοιον.   Thus
Cicero, *ad. Q. fr.* 3, 1, 19, interprets the term, *Aristophaneus
modus* by *suavis et gravis*.   In Lucilius, however, owing to the
undue prominence given to invective, as we shall presently see,
the σπουδαῖον far outweighed the γέλοιον.   Lucilius is, then, only
an imperfect interpreter of the spirit of the Old Comedy; the
true adherent of this genre will have a more refined conception
of the lighter elements entering into its composition.   Herein
lies the point of Horace's lines 1, 10, 10 ff.

> et sermone opus est modo tristi, saepe iocoso,
> defendente vicem modo rhetoris atque poetae,
> interdum urbani, parcentis viribus atque,
> extenuantis eas consulto, ridiculum acri
> fortius et melius magnas plerumque secat res.
> illi scripta quibus comoedia prisca viris est
> hoc stabant, hoc sunt imitandi.

That is the Old Comedy has a style now sharp, *tristis*, now sug-
gestive of the rhetorical and poetical, now *acer*—all words
associated with the seriousness of the grand style—but now
iocosus, *urbanus*, and *ridiculus*, that is, smacking of true comic
informality, ease, and charm—qualities associated with the
conception of the εἴρων because Socrates best realized in actual
life this type of humor, a type bound up with the conception of
the plain style from the days of Socrates and Plato on.   Thus
Cicero in the *Orator* 62, distinctly indicates Plato as the master
of this style and its appropriate type of humor: longe omnium
quicumque scripserunt aut locuti sunt exstitit et gravitate et
suavitate princeps.

In accordance, also, with the practice of Latin literary
criticism of seeking a national parallel to the representative
writers of Greek literary forms, Plautus is regarded by Cicero as
the Latin representative of the type of liberal humor affected by
the Old Comedy, while the sayings of Cato the elder, are paral-
lel to the *bons mots* of which the Greeks were so fond.   If this
judgment of Cicero's on Plautus reflects that of Panaetius it is

one in which Lucilius would probably acquiesce. Thus the
Index Auctorum of Marx shows seven passages in which Lucilius
imitates Plautus, 612 (*Stichus* 736), 669 (*Poenulus* 138), 700
(*Trinummus* 994), 736 (*Mercator* 397), 771 (*Poenulus* 351),
957 (*Asinaria* 23), 1094 (*Miles* 4). An examination of these
passages reveals, as we should expect, the sympathetic familiar-
ity of Lucilius with Plautus. In two of these passages we have
imitations of verse movements in language and rhythm. The
ad amores tuos of Lucilius 612 reproduces the *ad amores tuos*
of Plautus' *Stichus* 736. In 700 the introductory movement
and language of Plautus' *Trinummus* 994 is imitated. In
669 Lucilius employs the abusive Plautine intensive *tricorius*
used in the *Poenulus* 138. In 771 the vigorous Plautine idiom
compendi facere is employed, probably from the *Poenulus* 351,
although the phrase is used elsewhere as well. In 736 in de-
scribing the activities of an *ancilla*, Lucilius clearly follows the
description of Plautus in the *Mercator* 397. Finally, we have
two fragments 957 and 1094 involving close verbal imitation,
the former of the phrase *mihi necesse est eloqui* from the Asinaria
23, the latter of the phrase *praestringat oculorum aciem* from the
Miles 4. Unlike Lucilius' treatment of Afranius, we nowhere
find any abusive parody of the verses of Plautus. Horace,
on the other hand, in a well-known passage in the *Ars Poetica*
270, refused to recognize either the comic power or the metrical
versatility of Plautus:

> at vestri proavi Plautinos et numeros et
> laudavere sales, nimium patienter utrumque
> ne dicam stulte, mirati. Si modo ego et vos
> scimus inurbanum lepido seponere dicto
> legitimumque sonum digitis callemus et aure.

Here the contrast between *inurbanus* and *lepidus* clearly shows
that the quality of *urbanitas* by which Horace and the Augustan
age set so much store, is denied to the Plautine type of humor.

The same judgment in somewhat greater detail appears in
epistles 2, 1, 170 ff. There it is stated that comedy, as being so
close to life, demands more, not less labor of composition.
Horace then proceeds to deny that Plautus has the power of
drawing characters harmoniously. This is illustrated by the
types of the *ephebus, pater, leno*, and parasite. Horace's norm

is that of the New Comedy, while he feels that Plautus in his desire for financial success or popular applause sinks to the standard of Dorsennus, the hungry parasite of the Atellana. It will be noticed that here also as in satires 1,4 and 1,10 the style and the humor of the mime and of the popular native farce the *Atellana*, the tone of which was similar, are contrasted with the more exacting standards of legitimate drama.

Such collected witticisms as those of Cato were not without influence upon the humor of Lucilian and Horatian satire. One of these, the well-known apothegm of Cato on seeing a man leaving a brothel, is alluded to by Horace in *sat.* 1, 2, 31. It is certain that such collections received their original impetus from the χρεῖαι of the Cynics and Stoics. Similar χρεῖαι and apothegms of brief compass may be found embedded in many satires of Lucilius and Horace.[89] In fact in book 11 Lucilius seems to have collected a series of pointed anecdotes relating to his famous Roman contemporaries.

It is clear, then, that the type of humor illustrated by the Old Comedy and χρεῖαι in Greece, by the plays of Plautus and the apothegms of Cato in Rome, was in the main regarded by the critical theories of the Romans as appropriate to the spirit of Latin satire, while the unrestrained, coarse, and obscene humor and lack of moral purpose, characteristic of the mime or *Atellana* met with disapproval. This disapproval was mainly based on the fact that these humorous genres indulge in laughter for laughter's sake. They do not subject laughter to the restraints of reason and ethical purpose demanded by the ancient rhetorical theory of the liberal jest.

But far more than the Old Comedy, the moral anecdotes or χρεῖαι of the Greeks and of Cato, the humor represented by the famous Socratic irony, most profoundly influenced the theory of humor current in the satires of Lucilius and of Horace. Who were the writers included under the canon as used by Horace in the *Ars Poetica* 310, by Lucilius in 707, and as proclaimed in the critical theories of Panaetius and Cicero in the *de officiis* to be *par excellence* the models for the appropriate and liberal type of humor? What was the conception of the Socratic εἴρων and in what relation does this conception stand to the theory of the plain style?

Under the *Socratici libri* were included the dialogues of
Plato, Xenophon, Antisthenes, and Aeschines, as Hirzel has
conclusively shown.[90] These were the models of philosophic
exposition followed by Panaetius. This we may infer from the
title of a non-extant work περὶ τῶν Σωκρατικῶν as well as from
the position accorded to the Socratici in the *de officiis* 1, 134,
where they are quoted as the stylistic norm for the *sermo* or
discourse in contrast to the crude and barbarous style of such
writers as Zeno and Chrysippus: Sit ergo hic sermo, in quo
Socratici maxime excellunt, lenis minimeque pertinax, insit in
eo lepos. Moreover since the Socratic dialectic was carried on
by questions and answers, it follows that under the term *dispu-
tationes*, which in the *de officiis* 1, 132 were expressly included
under the conception of *sermo* we are to understand such philo-
sophic arguments as we find in Plato and other writers of the
Socratic school. It is clear that the whole humorous character
of such dialogues was conditioned by the shrewd and kindly
personality of Socrates. Now the kernel of the Socratic humor
lies in the Socratic irony. It is therefore necessary, omitting
the detailed proof for lack of space, to summarize briefly the
ancient conception of the εἴρων, which received its first embodi-
ment in Socrates.[91]

In brief, the strongly marked character of Socrates and of
the Socratic dialectic caused the terms εἴρων and εἰρωνεία to be
applied to Socrates as indicating a simulated self-depreciation
and humility or a simulated ignorance. From the employment
of the term in Plato it passed over into the rhetorical handbooks.
It is essentially for our present purpose to notice that the word
is employed by Aristotle and the New Comedy in a sense closely
related to its earlier popular usage as a foil to the conception of
the ἀλάζων or boastful braggart. In popular usage, therefore,
the term εἴρων was applied to one who uses words without
serious purpose, to betray, dissuade, mock, jest, or excuse himself,
act the swindler. Hence the term stands in close relation to the
conception of the φλύαρος, ὑποκριτής, ἀλάζων, and κόλαξ. So in
the Coislinian treatise on Comedy, *Aristophanes' Prolegomena
Xd*, the three fundamental types of comedy, ἤθη, were called
τά τε βωμολόχα καὶ τὰ εἰρωνικὰ καὶ τὰ τῶν ἀλαζόνων. Again in the
treatment of the laughable in the *Rhetoric* of Aristotle,[92] 3,

1419, b7, two types are differentiated, εἰρωνεία and βωμολοχία: ἔστι δ' ἡ εἰρωνεία τῆς βωμολοχίας ἐλευθερώτερον ὁ μὲν γὰρ αὐτοῦ ἕνεκα ποιεῖ τὸ γέλοιον. ὁ δὲ βωμολόχος ἑτέρου. In the *Ethics* of Aristotle 2, 7, 20, the εἴρων suppresses or understates the truth, the ἀλάζων or boaster exaggerates it.[98] In the *Ethics* 4, 7, 13, Aristotle asserts that both of these extremes are blameworthy, and that both deviate from the truth, but the εἴρωνες are more congenial (χαριέστεροι) for their motive is not self-advantage, but to avoid bombast; that is, while the ἀλάζων lays claim to what he does not have, the εἴρων depreciates or conceals what he has. Aristotle is also the first to designate Socrates as the type of genuine and fine irony, a reputation which the master maintains for all time, and which was accepted by Roman ethical and aesthetic criticism. To this we now turn.

To the Romans, Socrates was clearly the type of the εἴρων as we may see from Cicero *academica priora* 2, 5, 15 where it is said of Socrates: autem de se ipse detrahens in disputatione plus tribuebat iis quos volebat refellere. Ita cum aliud diceret atque sentiret, libenter uti solitus est ea dissimulatione quam εἰρωνείαν vocant; quam sit etiam in Africano fuisse Fannius idque propterea vitiosum in illo non putandum quod idem fuerit in Socrate. So also in the *de officiis* 1, 108, Cicero clearly represents the opinion of Panaetius in saying of Socrates: De Graecis autem dulcem et facetum festivique sermonis atque in omni oratione simulatorem, quem εἴρωνα Graeci nominarunt, Socratem accepimus. Moreover, such dissimulation is not blameworthy as 109 clearly declares.

Among the eclectic Romans, the agnostic attitude represented by the Socratic irony was in greater favor than with the somewhat dogmatic Epicureans.[94] This is clearly apparent in the treatment of wit assigned to Julius Caesar Strabo in the *de oratore* of 2, 264–290 where irony is given a high place in the six types of wit derived from the substance of the thought.[95] Cicero, accordingly, in 269 defines irony as an *urbana dissimulatio*:

Urbana etiam dissimulatio est, cum alia dicuntur ac sentias, non illo genere, de quo ante dixi. . . . In hoc genere Fannius in annalibus suis Africanum hunc Aemilianum dicit fuisse egregium et Graeco cum verbo appellat εἴρωνα; sed, uti ei ferunt, qui melius haec norunt, Socratem opinor in hac ironia dissimulantiaque longe lepore et humanitate omnibus praestitisse, genus est perelegans et cum gravitate salsum cumque oratoriis actionibus tum urbanis sermonibus adcommodatum.

We have similar testimony in the *Brutus* 292, where Atticus on the basis of this quality of irony, assigns Plato, Xenophon, and Aeschines to the *libri Socratici*:

Tum ille, Ego inquit ironian illam quam in Socrate dicunt fuisse, qua ille in Platonis et Xenophontis et Aeschinis libris utitur, facetum et elegantem puto. Est enim et inepti hominis et eiusdem etiam faceti, cum de sapientia disceptetur hanc sibi ipsum detrahere eis tribuere inludentem qui eam sibi adrogant, ut apud Platonem Socrates in caelum affert laudibus Protagoram, Hippiam, Prodicum, Gorgian ceteros, se autem omnium rerum inscium fingit et rudem. Decet hoc nescio quo modo illum: nec Epicuro, qui id reprehendit, adsentior.[96]

It is certain that this conception of ironic humor was domiciled in the Scipionic circle at Rome probably in large measure by the efforts of Panaetius. The humor of Scipio himself appears to be a Roman approximation to the ideal of the Socratic εἴρων. Indeed Cicero in several passages, some of which have already been quoted, expressly attributes to Scipio the Socratic irony. We thus have explicit evidence of the familiarity of the Scipionic circle with this conception.

Scipio was devoted to Xenophon and Lysias, both masters of the plain style. Now Xenophon holds next to Plato the most prominent position in the canon of the *libri Socratici* with the critical and exegetical study of which Panaetius was so much concerned. Such works as the *Memorabilia* and the *Symposium* of Xenophon were of the utmost importance in formulating the traditional character of Socrates, and in helping to establish the general stylistic criteria of the dialogue, a literary form not without influence upon Latin satire. Moreover, we have in the pages of Cicero and in the fragments of Lucilius some examples of the wit and humor of Scipio which afford us an opportunity to estimate the quality of his irony. These occur in the discussion of the nature of the laughable assigned to Julius Caesar Strabo in Cicero's *de oratore* 2, 217-290.

Thus in 253 we have the witticism of Scipio at the expense of Decius which is found in Lucilius 1280. The most plausible interpretation of this corrupt line is given by Cichorius,[97] whose reading I follow:

Quid Decius? Nuculam an confixum vis facere inquit.

The scene may be during the Numantine war. The point of this jest lies in the meaning of *nucula*. We have, as the context in Cicero shows, the type of jest arising from the employment of a word in a double sense. Since the Praenestines according to Festus 172 M were nicknamed *Nuculae* or "nuts" we may guess that Decius had a quarrel with a man of Praeneste. In this case Scipio's remark would mean: Do you wish to bore through a little "nut"; that is, do you wish to bore through a man of Praeneste? Perhaps to the same effeminate Decius is to be assigned the jest at the expense of Quintus Opimius also found in Lucilius 421 and quoted by Cicero in *de oratore* 2, 277.[98]

In Cicero *de oratore* 258, we have a jest of Scipio at the expense of Asellus, the point of which lies in the interpretation of a name or the application of a proverb. It is not the question of a mere verbal pun such as that in Horace *sat.* 1, 7 on Rupilius Rex, but the application of the double meaning of Asellus as a *cognomen* and as meaning donkey to the enemy of Scipio by quoting the well-known proverb *agas asellum*. The special incident in question seems to concern the censorship of Scipio in 142 B.C. Scipio at that time expelled Asellus from the equestrian order, while in revenge Asellus as tribune prosecuted Scipio for having brought a plague upon Rome by changing the customary prayer made at the lustration from *ut populus Romanus re meliores et ampliores faciant* to *ut populus Romanus res perpetuo incolumis servent*. Asellus then complained of his degradation and boasted of having served in every province. Scipio rejoined by quoting the proverb, the application of which to my mind is "however wide his experience is you can't teach an ass anything"; that is, "to think that I should experience such an act from Asellus who has learned nothing from his provincial experience or his degradation in my censorship."[99]

Another allusion to the same controversy is found in 277 which we may fairly conjecture is derived from Lucilius. Although Scipio had sought to degrade Asellus his purpose was thwarted by the veto of his colleague Mummius, which automatically restored Asellus to his equestrian rank. Scipio then says: infelix "noli" inquit mirari; is enim. qui te ex aere iis exemit lustrum condidit et taurum immolavit. That is, Mummius had to offer the purificatory sacrifice to purge the state from the taint his action had brought upon it.

In 267 we hear a further witticism of Africanus at the expense of C. Metellus, the fourth and least distinguished son of Quintus Metellus Macedonicus. In allusion to the progressive intellectual degradation manifested in the four brothers, Scipio said: si quintum pareret mater eius Asinum fuisse parituram.

The fact that Scipio, who in his own circle was called an εἴρων, is thus quoted four times by Cicero shows how high a reputation for restrained humor he enjoyed in the Ciceronian period. Also the fact that two of these jests are from the pages of Lucilius is proof of the satirist's appreciation of this type of humor. If, as I shall seek to show below,[100] we have in the sixth book of Lucilius a satire on Scipio's encounter with a bore, a theme which anticipates the similar adventure of Horace in 1,9 we may regard this Lucilian satire as a refined example of the *urbana dissimulatio* so characteristic of the εἴρων.

I have so far endeavored to show the vital part played by Diogenes, Polybius, and above all by Panaetius, in establishing in the Scipionic circle the Stoic theory of the plain style and the restrained type of ironic or Socratic humor peculiar to that style. I have also shown that the works of the orators, historians, and jurists, emanating from the Scipionic circle reveal a general adherence to the Stoic philosophy, are composed in the plain style, and are from time to time enlivened by the liberal type of humor. This last is notably true of Scipio and of the plays of Terence. I wish now to show by actual examination of the testimony of ancient literary criticism upon Lucilian satire, and by study of the Lucilian fragments themselves that Lucilius was a conscious adherent of the Stoic theory of the plain style, and in at least occasional sympathy with the ironic type of humor associated with that style.

So firmly are the characteristics of Lucilian satire fixed in our consciousness as a *carmen maledicum ad vitia hominum carpendum* that at first sight it seems almost like a paradox to seek to find in his critical theory, not even to speak of his satirical practice, any traces of sympathy for the more restrained type of humor, which we associate with the plain style. Upon closer examination, however, the matter will appear in a somewhat different light.

In the first place, there exists a considerable mass of ancient literary criticism which not only regards Lucilius as an example of the plain style in the narrower sense of vocabulary, grammar, and diction, but which describes his humor in the same technical vocabulary of rhetoric which we have found Cicero and Panaetius applying to the liberal type of humor. To anyone who has studied the stylistic epithets employed with almost meticulous accuracy to indicate the plain style, this evidence carries complete conviction.

Over against such passages, to be sure, we have a strong mass of criticism which differentiates the χαρακτήρ Lucilianus from the χαρακτήρ Horatianus. More important still, we have the evidence of our own critical judgment, which convinces us that here we have a conception of satire, a wit and humor, standing in strong contrast to that of Horace. To the explanation of this apparent enigma, which really involves no contradiction between the canons of ancient and modern taste, I now turn.

It is true that, in indifference to stylistic finish and in the type of humor he often employs, Lucilius shows a marked divergence from the more finished interpretation of the plain style exemplified in the works of Terence—*par excellence, puri sermonis amator*—and in the more serious writings emanating from the Scipionic circle, and in Horace. These divergencies are partly due to the aggressive temperament of the man; yet it can be shown, I think, that they rest in part upon a freer and looser tradition of the nature and limits of the plain style than we find elsewhere in the Scipionic circle. Naturally, the free satiric form of Lucilius demanded a less rigorous interpretation of the plain style than that affected by Terence in so finished a genre as the New Comedy. Still when all has been said, it comes as a distinct surprise to us who are familiar with the stylistic strictures of Horace upon Lucilius to find that ancient literary criticism almost uniformly groups his writings under the category of the plain style. For the most part, the technical terms characterizing the style of Lucilius are found in the vocabulary which ancient literary criticism employs to give objective characterization to the plain style.

Thus, Lucilius is the model of *gracilitas*, a term reserved for the plain style.[101] *Humilitas*, another common attribute of the plain style, which does not soar, but is a *sermo repens per humum*[102] is applied to him by Petronius. Lucilius is *doctus* and *urbanus*.[103] The former designation is appropriate in view of his wide acquaintance with Greek and Latin literature, with Greek philosophy and rhetoric.[104]   Hence we find Cicero[105] quoting Lucilius as advocating a broad culture and training for the orator. Lucilius' wit justifies the application to him of the adjective *urbanus*[106] not perhaps as judged by the strict puristic standards of the later Atticists and of the Augustan age, but certainly as judged by the standards of his own time, and those dominant in the minds of his archaizing admirers in the Augustan age and later empire.   To Lucilius, also, are applied the epithets *politus, eruditus, elegans*,[107] which in the rhetorical works of Cicero are used to designate the calm revision, sound scholarship, and discrimination in word and phrase which play so prominent a part in the ideals of the plain style.

In the judgment of both Cicero and Horace, Lucilius is *facetus*[108] and *emunctae naris*. Cicero connects this quality of *facetiae* with the Stoic conception of the *purus sermo*, the goal of the plain style as cherished by the Atticists:

Accedunt non Attici, sed salsiores quam illi Atticorum Romani veteres atque urbani sales, ego autem—existimare licet quidlibet—mirifice capior facetiis, maxime nostratibus praesertim cum eas videam primum oblitas. Latio tum cum in urbem nostram est infusa peregrinitas, nunc vero etiam bracatis et transalpinis nationibus, ut nullum veteris leporis vestigium appareat. Itaque te cum video omnis mihi Granios omnis Lucilios, vere ut dicam Crassos quoque et Laelios videre videor.

As to *facetiae* we may notice in passing that in line 963 Lucilius humorously applies the epithet *facetior* to Scipio's somewhat pedantic adherence to the Stoic principle of analogy in the use of *pertisum* instead of *pertaesum* contrary to ordinary usage for the Latin form:[109]

> quo facetior uideare et scire plus quam ceteri,
> pertisum hominum, non pertaesum, dicere humanum genus.

This Ciceronian passage also assigns to Lucilius the quality of *sal* or pungent wit, a gift which borders on *acerbitas*. Thus, in Horace, *sat.* 1, 10, 3, Lucilius is said to have rubbed down the city *sale multo*, and in Quintilian 10, 1, 94, we read: nam eruditio in eo mira et libertas atque inde acerbitas et abunde

salis. In a sense, therefore, this quality marks the transition
from the plain style in the narrower sense of the term to the
element of invective, which is associated rather with the grand
style.

The *comitas*, "geniality" of Lucilius is a quality related to
his *urbanitas*. It is recognized by Horace in *sat.* 1, 10, 65 as
a quality commonly attributed to the earlier satirist. Like
urbanitas, it is in rhetorical theory contrasted with *severitas*
which is associated rather with the grand style, or at least with
serious discourse.[110]

Indeed, a comparison of the *de officiis* 2, 48, the *de officiis*
1,132, the *de oratore* 3,177, and the *orator* 64 shows that *comitas*,
adfabilitas sermonis, *mollitudo*, are characteristics of the plain
style, the style suited to conversation, to the serious philosophic
dialogue, to the half-humorous, half-serious dialogues of Cynics
and Stoics, and so progressively to the Latin satirical *sermones*.

This was the frank, informal, conversational idiom, the
unassuming literary form which Lucilius employed. His books,
as even Horace acknowledges, are self-revelations. They,
therefore, like the works of so many writers of the Socratic
school, most notably perhaps Xenophon, belong to the category
of ὑπομνήματα or memoirs:

> ille velut fidis arcana sodalibus olim
> credebat libris neque si male cessarat usquam
> decurrens alio neque si bene: quo fit ut omnis
> votiva pateat, veluti descripta tabella
> vita senis.[111]

But besides these qualities of tone and mood, the plain
style, as we have seen, made exacting claims upon the gram-
matical and rhetorical scholarship of its followers. Let us
briefly summarize the evidence on these points revealed by a
study of the surviving fragments of Lucilius.

We find Lucilius thoroughly conversant with the principles
of the Stoic grammatical rhetoric as taught by Diogenes of
Babylon. The ninth book affords ample evidence of this, but
we may supplement its testimony by other evidence. Thus in
fragment 1100, Lucilius says there are 100 different kinds of
solecisms and apparently listed them as an aid to a standard
of correct usage.[112] Also in this book we have 16 fragments

dealing with barbarisms, mistakes in spelling or pronunciation, with detailed discussions upon the proper spelling of verbal endings or case endings.[112] We have two humorous fragments, 963 and 1130, in which points of pronunciation are discussed; the pronunciation of *pertisum* instead of *pertaesum* in the former case, the rustic pronunciation of *pretor* for *praetor* in the latter case.

In etymology Lucilius shows much interest. This must in large measure be due to the sensitiveness to the accurate use of words resulting from the Stoic interest in etymology. Hence, in 437 we find Lucilius deriving *tragoedia* from *trux*. In 452 the etymology of *iners* from *ars* is explained.

We have three fragments in which Lucilius shows his interest in κυριολογία, the technical Stoic designation for verbal accuracy. In addition, most of the word plays of which Lucilius was fond may be referred to this category.[114] In 1190 Lucilius criticizes the metaphorical use of *horrere* in Ennius. Ennius applied the term, the literal meaning of which is "to have the goose flesh," to a battlefield bristling with arms. Lucilius ridicules this trope by saying why not add *algere* "shivers." In 1215 we find an exposition of the difference between *intro* and *intus*, *apud* and *ad*. In 519, perhaps in jest, he seems to allude to the legal definition of the terms *mundus* and *penus*.

In addition to these three passages, which more strictly belong to the category of ἀκυρολογία, the following word plays deserve to be catalogued as involving a nice discrimination in the use of words. In fragment 33 a play on *nescire*, in 63 a sharp contrast between the meanings of *praecanto* and *excanto* as applied to the witness Aemilius, whom the speaker will induce as by a magic incantation to give answer to his cross-questioning. In 171 we have a play on *edit* and *comedit*; in 204 on *satis* in the sense of enough and in the connection of a feeling of satisfaction; 1128 on *carcer*, concrete vs. abstract, a jailbird hardly worthy of a jail; in 1134 on *ludet* and *eludet*; in 1284 upon *eques* in the sense of *equus*, and *equitare*; in 1344 upon *scio* and *nescio*.

In technical grammar, therefore, it is beyond question that Lucilius was vitally interested in the study of the three faults reprobated by the Stoic grammarians, σολοικισμός, βαρβαρισμός and ἀκυρολογία. Moreover, the discussion upon *pertisum* or *pertaesum* suggests that, like Panaetius, Lucilius gave only limited adherence to the Stoic principle of analogy.

Finally, we have two fragments, 1111 and 1241, which demand more detailed study. The first seems to imply that Lucilius, in spite of his apparent carelessness of finish, was strongly in sympathy with the best classical models, the οἱ εὐδοκιμοῦντες Ἕλληνες of the rhetoric of Diogenes.[115] Who were these models? Marx believes that the passage refers to Homer; and in fact it is true that Homer occupies a central position among the ancient classics. Lucilius also shows traces of his influence in at least twelve passages.[116] To me, however, the similarity of the wording of the fragment with Horace's *sat.* 1, 4, 1-6 makes an allusion to the Old Comedy more probable. The Lucilian line is:

archaeotera * * unde haec sunt omnia nata.

Here *archaeotera* would summarize the writers of the Old Comedy mentioned in detail by Horace, while there seem to be traces of actual verbal resemblance between *unde haec sunt omnia nata* in Lucilius and *hinc omnis pendet* Lucilius in Horace. I shall discuss the passage more fully in connection with Horace's fourth satire.

In the second passage 1241,[117] a quotation from Cicero (*de oratore* 1, 72), we have a dictum of Lucilius demanding a training for the orator in all the arts. The εἰσαγωγή to Iunius Congus, which is related to the *Ars Poetica* of Horace, also contained a discussion upon the choice of words.[118]

Turning now from grammar to the broader aspects of rhetoric, we find Lucilius as a satirist emphasizing the importance of sincerity, frankness, informality, rather than the rhetorical finish of epic poetry, or tragedy or a highly ornate prose style.[119] Thus in fragment 86, where Scaevola bids his opponent not to be too rhetorical, he represents the attitude of indifference to excessive rhetorical elaboration so common in the simple grammatical rhetoric of the Stoics. In fragment 608, Lucilius seems to defend the plain style from the charge of meanness.[120] In book 27,[121] there was perhaps developed in fragment 693 with its contrast between *rem* and *verba*, the favorite Stoic theory of a rhetoric πρὸς τὰ πράγματα, insisting on dialectic and clear thinking.[112] Such a dialectic springs in ultimate analysis from the *Socraticae chartae* whose influence on the teachings of Panaetius we have traced.

Although Lucilius does not follow the teachings of the more ostentatious rhetoricians, he is perfectly familiar with the technical figures of this rhetoric. In fragment 181, he characterizes the Isocratean ὁμοιοτέλευτον as petty and childish. In line 604 from book 26 the rhetorical device of *commiseratio*, so common in ancient oratory, seems to be held up to ridicule. Perhaps we may trace a similar attitude in 388 to a boastful ἐπίδειξις of some Greek orator. Fragment 1117 may imply a controversy with a sophist, though here other interpretations are not excluded.

To the ordinary and less elaborate figures of rhetoric Lucilius is more friendly. Thus in fragment 1133 he is quoted by Servius as considering climax a *bonum schema*, a good figure, and as discussing *epanalepsis* or repetition in connection with it. In fragment 1132, according to Porphyrio on Horace's *epistles* 2, 2, 94 ff., the two parts of a compound verb are split between the end of one line and the beginning of the following line. In fragment 1137 we have a case of *tmesis* in the reading *conque tubernalem*, a practice common in Lucilius according to Ausonius, 16, 35.

Lucilius was also interested, at least theoretically, in the proper disposition of words in a sentence according to rhythm and sense, a process called *iunctura* by the ancients. He seems to have discussed this and other rhetorical problems in book 10. Thus fragment 386 evidently refers to *iunctura*, while fragment 377 refers to the antithetical vice of *cacosyntheton*.[113] He has also a lively interest in questions of metre and rhythm, which are discussed in fragments 1168, 1209, and 1294. Thus in fragment 1168 he advocates the observance of euphonious combinations of words, preferring *aliut lucenarum* to *aliut lychnorum*. In fragment 1209 he would confine the monosyllabic close of the dactylic hexameter to the names of small animals, a rule also observed by Horace in the *Ars Poetica* in the use of the famous verse-tag, *ridiculus mus*. In fragment 1294 Lucilius employs for the first time in Latin literature the term *numerus* as a translation of the Greek μέτρον or metre. In the same passage he uses *modus* as a translation of the Greek 'ρυθμός. Horace employs the same technical vocabulary in his *satires* 1, 4, 7 and in the *epistles* 1, 18, 59.

From what has been said it is clear that, like Horace, Lucilius made a sharp distinction in vocabulary, metre, and tone between the requirements of the simple and unpretentious *sermo* or discourse of Socratic, Cynic, and Stoic origin, and the older epic and tragic forms in the grand style. It seems reasonable to believe that the basis of this distinction is to be found in the general theories of grammar, rhetoric, and style accepted and realized in the writings of the Scipionic circle as the clearest result of the teachings of Diogenes and Panaetius. In particular, in books 26 and 30, Lucilius wrote satires discussing these problems in detail, and making an ethical and aesthetic defence of the satiric form, which in a very real sense[124] anticipate certain of the arguments set forth by Horace in *satires* 1,4, 1,10 and 2,1. If then, Lucilius was well informed as to the fundamental principles of the plain style, it is likely that such violations of that style as we may detect in the surviving fragments of his satires should be attributed to a divergent theory of the relation of the loose satiric form to the plain style, rather than to ignorance of its principles, or careless indifference to its laws.

Even in the question of the use of Greek, a practice reprobated by Panaetius and Horace alike, it can be shown that Lucilius recognized some limits to a hybrid bilingualism, for in 15 he makes fun of those who use *cliopodas* and *lychnos* for *pedes lecti* and *lucernas*, in 88 he ridicules the Hellenomaniac Albucius, and in ʃ915 he apparently translates the Greek verb ὑποσκελίζω by *supplanto*, besides introducing into the Latin language the term *numerus*, as a technical translation for μέτρον and *modus* for ρυθμός in 1295. In short, his style was undoubtedly the informal mixture of Greek and Latin current in the Scipionic circle. It is in degree rather than in kind that it differs from the informal style of Cicero's letters.

Furthermore, there are certain passages in Lucilius which suggest that he had some regard for the claims of a pure Latinity. Fragment 1322, a quotation from Quintilian, may be cited as showing that Lucilius, like Pollio, distinguished pure

Latinity from provincial usage and attacked a certain Vettius
for employing a provincial dialect, probably Sabine, just as
Pollio assailed the *Patavinitas* of Livy. Similarly in fragment
594, Lucilius, by saying that he feared the judgment of Scipio
and Rutilius and wrote for the people of Tarentum, Consentia,
and the Sicilians, seems to take a side shot at the over-pedantic
interpretation of *Latinitas* current among some distinguished
members of his circle. In this connection, it will be remembered
that in fragment 964 Lucilius criticized Scipio for saying
pertisum instead of *pertaesum*.

Now that we have discussed the Stoic theories of grammar
and rhetoric, have seen the influence of Diogenes and Panaetius
in popularizing these theories in the Scipionic circle, and the
intimate acquaintance of Lucilius with the Stoic theories of
grammar, rhetoric, and style, it remains for us to consider the
chartae or Socratic dialogues, which hold a central place in the
aesthetic theories of Panaetius, as the model, *par excellence*, for
the philosophic *sermo* or conversation.

In at least three passages, 738, 742, and 754, we may fairly
assume the direct influence of Panaetius upon Lucilius. In
fragment 738 Lucilius refers to the indispensable duties
demanded by our common humanity, *viz.*, to point out the road
to the traveler, to give free access to running water, to allow
one to get light from the fire:

> certa sunt, sine detrimento quae inter sese commodent.

Now a comparison with Cicero *de officiis* 1, 51 seems to prove
that this was a favorite doctrine of Panaetius who there (as
interpreted by Cicero) says: quiquid sine detrimento commo-
dari possit, id tribuatur vel ignoto. Again in line 742 we read:

> Socraticum quidam tyranno misse Aristippum autumant.

Now a passage in Diogenes Laertius 2, 83 seems to show that
Aristippus of Cyrene sent three books of Libyan history to
Dionysius, the tyrant. Here the resemblance of the Latin
phrase *tyranno misse* to the Greek phrase Διονυσίῳ ἀπεσταλμένα
seems to argue that both authors drew from a common source,
while the statement of Diogenes 2, 85 seems to indicate that this
source was Panaetius. In further support of this inference we
know that Panaetius was, unlike the earlier Stoics, particularly

favorable to Aristippus. This we may infer from the testimony
of Cicero *de officiis* 1, 148 where Aristippus is classed with
Socrates himself in opposition to the crudity of the Cynics,
which is entirely to be rejected. The third fragment is 754, a
reference to the succession of Xenocrates to the headship of
the Academy. Here Lucilius and Diogenes draw from a com-
mon source, presumably Panaetius, in their description of the
severus philosophus.[125] Furthermore, the indirect evidence
for the influence of Panaetius upon Lucilius emerges from the
critical analysis of the doctrines of Panaetius as to the *sermo* and
the ironic humor, and the comparison of this evidence with the
position assigned to Lucilian satire by ancient rhetorical critics
and the actual critical theories of Lucilius himself. As to the
Socraticae chartae, however, we have explicit evidence that
Lucilius also looked upon them as the most important models
for his *sermones* in fragment 710 where Lucilius definitely
mentions these writings:

> nec sic ubi Graeci? ubi nunc Socratici carti? # quiquid quaeritis, etc.

This passage occurs in a satire in book 27, dealing with literary
criticism, and, as I shall show below,[126] treating certain topics
in close relation to those discussed in the *Ars Poetica* of Horace.
Here, especially, we must compare Horace's *Ars Poetica* 310-312:

> rem tibi Socraticae poterunt ostendere chartae
> verbaque provisam rem non invita sequentur.

Horace here shows that the source of moral knowledge is the
philosophy of Socrates and the Academy. The Roman poet
draws his subject matter from this philosophy, and as a natural
consequence his style as well. But with this study must be
associated familiarity with the Greek poets, who combine
inspiration with style. So Lucilius, referring to the Greek poets,
says "nec sic ubi Graeci" implying that they are great classical
models, just as in 1111 he insisted on the study of the earlier
writers of Greece, probably with especial reference to the
writers of the Old Comedy, so intimately related to Greek
satire. Moreover, we know that Horace was perfectly famil-
·iar with Panaetius and the Socratic dialogues from his own
explicit testimony of *odes* 1, 29, 13 where Iccius is satirized for
first buying up all the works of Panaetius and the Socratic
school and then abandoning them for a military career.

The first-hand intimacy of Lucilius with the teachings of Socrates himself, and with the philosophers and philosophy of the Academy, affords strong corroborative evidence for the essential correctness of my interpretation of the passages just discussed.[127]   Moreover, Lucilius had himself studied in the Academic school, possibly in Athens itself, and was apparently an intimate of Clitomachus, the head of the Academy, who dedicated a book to him, as Cicero informs us in the *Academica* 2, 32, 102.[128]

In spite of these many influences to restraint, moderation, and careful finish, emanating from Diogenes, Panaetius, and the other members of the Scipionic circle—and these influences have been overlooked by modern scholars, who have accepted too literally the strictures of Horace—it remains essentially true that the satires of Lucilius are a *carmen maledicum ad vitia hominum carpendum*—because of the place he accorded the disturbing element of invective within the plain style. In the part thus assigned to invective Lucilius often transgresses the limits associated with the liberal jest by Panaetius, and follows the unrestrained type of humor favored by the popular impromptu Cynic discourse. Moreover, invective, so far as stylistic theory is concerned, belongs rather to the grand style than to the plain style by virtue of its lack of restraint, absence of subtle humor, and boldness of diction. In fact, critics, both ancient and modern, from Horace on, have laid such stress on these qualities that, in spite of his scholarship, sanity, and breadth of intellectual sympathies, Lucilius has suffered the fate meted out to the aggressive humorist in every age, that of having his calmer words and more restrained counsels ignored.

Now invective, according to the rhetorical theories of the ancients, was related not to the plain style, but to the grand style. It depends for its effect upon *amplificatio* or fullness of style. The *auctor ad Herennium* 4, 8, 11 speaks of *amplificatio* in connection with the grand style. Here, as Ullman has seen[129] the thought is of the threefold division of *mollitudo vocis* (3, 13, 23), into *sermo, contentio*, and *amplificatio*. *Sermo,* as we know, is associated with the plain style, while *contentio*, which corresponds pretty closely to our controversial discourse, is described as an *oratio acris*. In 3, 13, 24 of the *auctor ad Herennium* one side of *amplificatio* is described as an *oratio acris, quae in iracundiam inducit,* and later in 24, as an *oratio quae aliquid peccatum amplificans auditorem ad iracundiam adducit.* Panaetius shared this view as to angry outbursts, for in the *de officiis* 1, 136 he reprobates all *perturbationes* as contrary to the general principle of appropriateness, urges that anger be avoided, and that courtesy be shown to those with whom we talk. In cases where reproof is needed, Panaetius permits a more emphatic tone of voice, more forcible and severe terms—the words *verborum gravitate acriore* belong rather to the vocabulary of the grand style—and even an assumption of anger. But we must show that this anger is designed to effect a reform in the character of the person thus reproved; real anger must be far from us.[130]

Even this limited concession is withdrawn to some extent by the further injunction that we restrain our anger in disputes even with our bitterest enemies, and that we maintain our dignity, because what is done under emotional stress cannot be done with perfect self-respect or with the approval of the witnesses.

The definitions, *oratio quae in iracundiam inducit* and *oratio quae auditorem ad iracundiam adducit,* fit admirably the element of wrathful invective, which plays so important a part in Lucilian satire, as Juvenal 1, 165 ff. and Horace *sat.* 1, 4, 3 and 2, 1, 68 clearly perceive. When the style of the satirist—whether he be a Lucilius or a Juvenal—is surcharged with invective, we have a boldness of diction, a sweep, *amplificatio,* alien to the reserve of passion advocated by Panaetius, and often a bitter abandon, equally alien to the restrained humor of the εἴρων, the type of humorist held in such esteem by Panaetius and in some of his moods even by Lucilius himself.[131] Hence *audax,* an epithet associated with the grand style, is frequently applied to Lucilius by ancient literary criticism,[132] whether directly as in Horace's *satire* 2, 1, 62 and in Martial's *epigram* 12, 94, 7, or by clear implication, as in Juvenal 1, 165 and Horace's *satires* 1, 4, 1 and 2, 1, 68.

Such an attitude of mind and such a theory of the admissibility of invective into the canon of humor is bound to affect the diction of the satirist. The theoretical adherent of the *purus sermo* of the Stoics cannot breathe freely in so pure an atmosphere. Hence, the *sermo purus* is contaminated by a consider-able infiltration of the *sermo plebeius* and the argot of the camp, as may be perceived by anyone who will compare the diction of Lucilius with that of Horace.[133] Gallic words, Etruscan words, Syrian words, and words from the Italic dialects, Oscan, Pelig-nian, Praenestine, Sardinian, and Umbrian,[134] even bits of Greek dialect slang, are found in the pages of the earlier satir-ist.[135] This gives the "punch" which the ancient *subbasilicani* valued as much as the modern man on Broadway.

Horace is a sound critic as to these facts. Invective and the plain style are incompatible, for, as Cicero in the *orator* 64 declares of the plain style: nihil iratum habet, nihil invidum, nihil atrox. The style of Lucilius, on the other hand, is racy of the camp, the soil of Italy, and the melting pot of the Roman capital. The theory of humor favored by the writer of such a style, friendly to bold invective, and equally sensitive to the diction of the Scipionic circle and that of the forum, breaks through the more limited definitions of *iocosum* and *ridiculum* favored by the Stoic rhetorical theory, and exemplified by the humor of Scipio, Laelius, and Terence. Frequently, therefore, Lucilius found it impossible in practice to accept the more restrained definitions of the laughable current in the Peripatetic school from the days of Aristotle, and promulgated in the Scipionic circle by his friend Panaetius.[136] His inspiration, except in those important satires where he is consciously theorizing and in satires of simple narrative, goes straight back through the Cynic and Stoic popular philosophers to Eupolis, Cratinus, and Aristophanes with their complete freedom of speech (*libertas* or παρρησία).

Moreover, we must remember that all the members of this circle, living in an age of the rapid assimilation of Greek culture, were unfamiliar with the later refinements upon the Stoic theory of the plain style developed by the meticulous studies of such later Roman Atticists, as Calvus, Catullus, Brutus, and Messala. In particular, the members of the Scipionic circle seem to have laid great stress upon the humorous anecdote in a fashion which should appeal to us Americans. It can be shown that book 11 of Lucilius contained a miscellany of such good stories. By the time of Augustus, however, we find a more refined appreciation of the claims of the more subtle humor, which like an atmosphere pervades Horatian satire.[127]

So far as the net impression made by the actual reading of Lucilius is concerned it must be acknowledged that his style generally speaking is more properly characterized by those ancient literary critics who call him *acer* and *tristis* than by the epithets *iocosus* and *ridiculus*. It is just here that he meets with some of the severest criticisms of Horace in *satires* 1,4; 1,10, and 2,1. When in this mood Lucilius, throwing restraint to the winds, launches forth upon a swollen stream of invective completely at variance with his urbanity elsewhere. This is the quality which Quintilian 10, 1, 94, calls *acerbitas*. Horace, by no means a rigorous adherent of the plain style, recognizes in *satire* 1, 10, 13 that there is occasional need of this quality which is derived from the spirit of the Old Comedy, but more often one needs the genial grace and the linguistic and stylistic reserve, so closely associated with the two related concepts of the *urbanus* and the εἴρων. In these respects Lucilius is frequently deficient. The epithet *acer* thus applied to Lucilius is, moreover, more appropriately and commonly applied to the grand style to which invective inevitably tends to rise, as any modern critic may see if he will reflect upon the effects of the stichomithies in Greek tragedy. Thus Horace employs this epithet in *satire* 1, 10, 43, 46 of Varius, the epic poet. So Cicero in the *orator* 99 applies the epithet to the *grandiloqui*. The related epithet of *tristis* (Greek πικρός), which is apparently applied to the satire of Lucilius either by Lucilius himself or the *adversarius* in 1014, seems to mean biting or bitter or savage. As a general rhetorical term it is associated with the grand style, which Cicero in the *orator* 20 characterizes as a *tristis oratio*. So in Quintilian 8, 3, 49 it is contrasted with *hilaris* with which we may compare Horace's epithet *iocosus*. Lucilius, therefore, unlike the majority of writers in the Scipionic circle is not the heir to the doctrines of Diogenes and Panaetius to the exclusion of all other influences.

On the contrary in the three titles which he selects for his work, *sermo*, *ludus*, and *schedium*, Lucilius shows that the influence of the Cynic popular discourse of satirical tone often held the whip hand over Greek rhetorical theories. The term *sermo* is apparently a translation of the Greek διατριβή, the term applied to a half-improvisatory genre in conversational form, best represented to us by the Cynic philosopher, Bion of Borysthenes. It is broad enough, however, to cover the serious but informal dialogues of Plato, Aeschines, Xenophon, and the other Greek writers who continued the Socratic tradition. It occurs in fragments 1016 and 1039. Its use by Lucilius in view of the theoretical discussion developed by Panaetius[138] on the content, sequence, and humor of the *sermo* is highly significant of the interest and enthusiasm of Lucilius for this form.

But Lucilius also employs the word *ludus* of his satires in fragment 1039. This term refers originally to the light, informal play of humor, so characteristic of the plain style, and indeed a fundamental criterion to distinguish it from such productions in the grand style as epic or tragedy. The term is also employed informally by Horace, as in 1, 10, 37 where he says *haec ego ludo;* and by Persius in 5, 5:[139]

> Pallentes radere mores
> doctus et ingenuuo culpam defigere ludo.

In this passage we have clear evidence of Aristotle's distinction between βωμολοχία or scurrility and εὐτραπελία or refined humor. It will be remembered that one of the MS. titles of the Menippean satire of Seneca upon the death of Claudius is *ludus de morte Claudii Caesaris.* Moreover, *ludus* may be justified as a title for Lucilius' and Seneca's satires upon the basis of the limited recreative function assigned to humor in life by ancient rhetorical theory, as set forth in Aristotle's poetics and ethics, and as restated in the Scipionic circle by Panaetius, whose doctrine is preserved to us in the pages of the *de officiis* of Cicero.[140] In fact the Latin term *ludus* may be an actual translation of the Greek term παίγνιον, which is the name given to a loosely constructed Greek satirical form current in the works of the popular philosophers of the Hellenistic period. It will be noticed that the definition of Anacharsis,[141] παίζειν δ' ὅπως σπουδάζῃ, is the warrant for the literary form τὸ σπουδαιογέλοιον and is reechoed in Horace's famous paraphrase of that term: ridentem dicere verum quid vetat?

On the other hand, the term *schedium* from the Greek σχέδιον which means anything hastily knocked together, like a raft for instance,[142] recalls the improvisatory element in Cynic and Lucilian satirical composition. It is therefore an admirable designation to indicate the method of one who, as Horace said, could dictate two hundred verses an hour standing on one foot. It is probably from a wish to avoid such implications of improvisation and careless composition that Horace deliberately refrains from applying the term *satura* to his *sermones* in book 1.

This more Academic conception of the province of humor in the plain style, using the term Academic in the original sense, may be further illustrated by certain passages in the ancient rhetoricians, which will serve to bring into clearer light the importance of the line of cleavage, which, sometimes in theory and even more often in practice, separates the satires of Horace from those of his master Lucilius.

Cicero in the *de oratore* 2, 236, a passage which seems to contain the theoretical justification for Horace's criticism of Lucilius in such passages as *sat.* 1, 10, 14 ff., tells why wit is superior to biting invective. It seems probable that Horace knew this passage in which Cicero gives his decision in favor of wit: quod ipsum oratorem politum esse hominem significat, quod eruditum, quod urbanum, maxime quod tristitiam ac severitatem mitigat et relaxat odiosasque res saepe, quas argumentis dilui non facile est, ioco risuque dissolvit.

Again the *auctor ad Herennium* 3, 13, 23 describes *iocatio* as *oratio quae ex aliqua re risum pudentem et liberalem potest comparare*; a definition which at once recalls the distinctions of Aristotle and Panaetius between the liberal jest or εὐτραπελία and the scurrilous jest or βωμολοχία.

Cicero's discussion in the *orator* (88–89) of the province of the *ridiculum* is similar. It parallels most of the points characterizing the liberal jest I have already enumerated, and affords such an admirable characterization of the Horatian type of humor in distinction from that of Lucilius that it must be analyzed in detail. It traverses in briefer form the ground covered by the *de oratore* (2, 217 ff.).

At the beginning of 87 Cicero differentiates two different types of wit (*sales*) following the same distinction made in the *de oratore* (2, 218) between *cavillatio* and *dicacitas*. This distinction probably goes back to that made by the Peripatetics between γέλως and χάρις. Cicero in the *orator* employs the two terms *facetiae* and *dicacitas*. It will be noticed that Horace also in *sat.* 1, 4, 34 and 81 ff., assails the quality of *dicacitas*; the *dicax* will hunt for his laugh, will not keep a secret, and will bespatter (*adspergere* also used by Cicero) guests and hosts with his wit. Can such a one be called *comis, urbanus,* and *liber?* Cicero then goes on to say that both forms of wit may be employed, the former (*facetiae*) in graceful (*venuste*) narratives which give pervasive humor to the whole theme. This we may illustrate by Horace's encounter with the bore, or the satire on the Sabine farm. The other type of wit hurls shafts of ridicule.

Cicero then proceeds in 88 exactly as in the *de officiis* to limit the use of the ridiculous: Illud admonemus tamen, ridiculo sic usurum oratorem, ut nec nimis frequenter, ne scurrile sit; nec subobsceno, ne mimicum, nec petulanti, ne improbum, nec in calamitatem, ne inhumanum, nec in facinus, ne odii locum risus occupet, neque aut sua persona aut iudicum aut tempore alienum; haec enim ad illud indecorum referuntur.

The ridiculous, therefore, must not be employed too frequently lest it become buffoonery which corresponds to the βωμολοχία of Aristotle. Such a humor does not observe the proper limitations of time or place. It flows on without cessation. Hence Cicero in the *de oratore* (2, 244) tells that the *scurrilis dicacitas* must be avoided by the orator. Again in (2, 247) Cicero declares: temporis ratio et ipsius dicacitatis moderatio et temperantia et raritas dictorum distinguet oratorem a scurra.

Several of these points may be illustrated by Horace's fourth satire of the first book. The *dicax* according to Horace will pick out the banquet as a proper occasion on which to assail guests and host (86–88). On the other hand, Horace himself values the proprieties of time and place so far as they apply to the publication of his satires. Unlike the empty headed people who recite at the bath and have no tact (*inanis hoc iuvat, haud illud quaerentis num sine sensu tempore num faciant alieno* 76 f.), he will only recite to his friends, and then only under compulsion. How different from the procedure of Lucilius in rubbing down the whole city with his wit! Also, Horace, like

Cicero's ideal orator, prides himself upon his *raritas dictorum*.
Thus in *satire* 1, 4, 18 he says:

> di bene fecerunt inopis me quodque pusilli
> finxerunt animi, raro et perpauca loquentis.

How different from the unrestrained abandon of improvisation
which characterizes Lucilius! As for obscenity, although Luci-
lius may have felt that in keeping with the Stoic theories of
diction he refrained from the use of *verba obscena*,[148] nevertheless
the satires on the sexual questions in books 7, 8 and 29, 3 reveal a
frankness of utterance foreign to the taste of the Augustan
age.[144] Horace's *satire* 1, 2 which reflects the influence of these
Lucilian satires met with such strong disapproval by Horace's
contemporaries that he refrained from further experiments in
this brutally frank manner. Moreover, such coarseness savors
of the mime, which, as we have seen,[145] Horace in complete
sympathy with the theories of Cicero, differentiates from the
more liberal and refined humor associated with the plain style.
Also Horace avoids aggressive humor, and true to his theories
of urbane irony assumes the pose of the defensive satirist (*nec
petulanti ne improbum*) in such passages as *sat.* 2, 1, 40-46.
Here he differs from the frequently more aggressive Lucilius.
His similes in this satire of the wolf and the bull are natural
animal similes for the *petulans* who makes unprovoked attacks.
He also protests against humor at the expense of the unfortunate
which may degenerate into lack of human charity (the *nec in
calamitatem ne inhumanum* of Cicero). So (in *sat.* 1, 3, 44 ff.)
Horace argues for the same charitable attitude towards the
faults of our friends which doting fathers employ when speaking
of the physical misfortunes that have overtaken their children.
The next injunction of Cicero (*nec in facinus ne odii locum risus
occupet*) is clearly influential in the mind of Horace in such a
passage as *sat.* 1, 4, 93 ff., where he protests against the hypo-
critical defense made for Petillius Capitolinus accused of
embezzlement. Such a defense is *sucus nigrae lolliginis* and
aerugo mera: hatred has usurped the place of laughter.

The satirist will, however, spare his friends and will maintain
his own dignity; *parcet et amicitiis et dignitatibus, vitabit
insanabilis contumelias*, says Cicero. A similar injunction is

found in the *de oratore* 2, 237. This obligation of friendship is certainly observed by Lucilius, who shows an undeviating loyalty to his friends within the Scipionic circle, and by Horace in his relations to the circle of Maecenas. Lucilius' enemies are in large measure those of his patron Scipio. Horace's devotion to his literary friends may be illustrated by the famous characterization of the members of the circle of Maecenas in *sat.* 1, 10, 43–45 and 81–90. Moreover in *sat.* 1, 4, 35 (non hic cuiquam parcet amico), he assails the lack of regard exhibited for friendship by the βωμολόχος. Again in line 80 of the same satire he emphatically denies that any of his friends can bring such a charge against him:

> est auctor quis denique eorum
> vixi cum quibus?

The injunction to avoid *insanabilis contumlias* is equally appropriate to the refined humor of Horatian satire.

Finally, Cicero declares in 90 that the orator who belongs to the category of the plain style will follow the Attic standard of wit and humor, a standard which even in Attica is rarely attained: quibus exceptis sic utetur sale et facetiis, ut ego ex istis novis Atticis talem cognoverim neminem, cui id certi vel maxime Atticum. Hanc ego iudico formam *summissi* oratoris, sed magni tamen et germani Attici, quoniam quiquid est salsum aut salubre in oratione id proprium Atticum est. The Attici whom Cicero has in mind here are the great masters of the plain style and Demosthenes, as we may see from the list of names he cites at the close of the section. But this Attic type of humor appropriate to the *orator summissi genus*, that is *urbanitas*, is also, after necessary allowances are made for the modifications inevitable in the change to a metrical conversation—peculiarly appropriate to Horatian satire as a *sermo repens per humum*.[144] In further proof of this point of view one need only cite Horace's praise of the *urbanus* in *sat.* 1, 10, 13; for *urbanitas* from some points of view is the Roman equivalent of Ἀττικισμός, from others the equivalent of ἀστειότης in Greek rhetorical theory.

In spite of the evidence of such passages the rift between Horace's theory of the plain style and the humor appropriate to that style is not exclusively the result of the aggressive iconoclasm of Lucilius.

If we would understand the nature of Lucilius' attitude towards the plain style, and the apparent flaw which vitiates so many of his theories, we must clearly understand that we have in the rhetoric of Cicero a recognition of the doctrine of nuances within the plain style. It is precisely because Horace's quarrel with Lucilius and with the contemporary defenders of Lucilian satire rests upon this conception of nuances within the plain style that the conflict is waged with such bitterness. It is in fact a quarrel within the family. Cicero *orator* 20 is especially illuminating in this connection. Of the writers of the plain style in general Cicero says: et contra tenues acuti omnia docentes et dilucidiora non ampliora facientes, subtili quadam et pressa oratione limati. But the adherents of this style like those of the grand style fall into two classes; the first class, and here Lucilius belongs in most respects, is thus described: in eodem genere alii callidi, sed impoliti et consulto rudium similis et imperitorum. The other class, and here clearly Horace belongs, is thus described: alii in eadem ieiunitate concinniores, id est faceti, florentes etiam et leviter ornati. Here *callidi* suggests the shrewdness or adroitness in argument so characteristic of the Socratic method. Similarly, in the *de oratore* 1, 93 Charmadas, in arguing for the dialectical rhetoric of the Stoics, uses the term *callide* in contrast with *copiose* evidently of the shrewd restraint and argumentative adroitness practiced by all true masters of the plain style, who prefer to lure their opponent to his own defeat rather than to overwhelm him by the wealth of their resources.[147]

A closer application to Lucilian satire may be made of the phrase *consulto rudium similis*, for certainly his use of the term σχέδιον as a description of his satires because of their hasty construction is admirably paraphrased by these words. *Impolitus*, connoting a lack of polish, may perhaps be used for the indifference to the labor of the file, so characteristic of Lucilius, who certainly is not *pressa oratione limatus*.

As for the *imperitorum*, we may notice Lucilius' affectation of speaking not as a *doctus* or expert poet, but as a man of general culture who addresses his friends. This point of view appears in such a passage as book 26, 592 in the pretense of Lucilius of dreading the judgment of Scipio and Rutilius, while he writes for the people of Tarentum, Consentia, and Sicily, untutored in Latin.

On the other hand, the second nuance, although somewhat less definitely, may be applied to Horatian satire. The writers who follow this nuance still work in the same dry medium *in eadem ieiunitate,* but they are *concinniores* or as we should say better, craftsmen. By this quality of *concinnitas* is meant a beauty of style produced by the skilful ordering of words and clauses, in short the *curiosa felicitas,* which constituted Horace's undying claim to fame. The noun *concinnitas* is so used by Cicero in the *orator* 149 where he discusses the principles governing the *collocatio verborum,* the σύνθεσις ὀνομάτων of the Greek rhetoricians, by which we are to understand the proper rhythmic, euphonic, metrical, and rational ordering of words and clauses. The term seems indeed to be synonymous with *iunctura,* as we may see by comparing Quintilian 9, 4, 32. The importance of *iunctura* is especially emphasized by Horace himself in the *Ars Poetica* 47, as a nice tool in the hands of the poet:

> Dixeris egregie notum si callida verbum
> reddiderit iunctura novum.

Horace is also *facetus,* a term associated with the permissible *genus liberale iocandi* and as such peculiarly applicable to Horace, but which may be used as in Quintilian 6, 3, 20, simply in the sense of *decus* or appropriateness and a certain cultivated taste (*exculta quadam elegantia*). Finally he permits polish in moderation (*leviter ornati*) an excellent characterization of the quality of *urbanitas,* of which Horace makes so much.

This term *urbanus*[148] probably developed as a technical rhetorical term towards the close of the republic as the result of the discriminating linguistic studies of the Roman Atticists. It connoted not only wit and cleverness, but also to a much greater degree elegance and refinement.

Now this conception of the *urbanus,* and the related, but in some respects different, type of the εἴρων stand in pretty close relation to the theory of the plain style. The term *urbanitas* implies a type of humor worthy of the ἐλεύθερος or should we rather say of the καλὸς κάγαθός, the alert and intelligent citizen of the Greek city state? But refined humor does not exhaust its meanings. We may rather argue that just as *Latinitas* is the equivalent in the technical vocabulary of the Stoic rhetoric for Ἑλληνισμός so *urbanitas* is the equivalent for Ἀττικισμός or ἀστειότης. In fact in the Ciceronian and Augustan ages this term sums up better than any other the ideals which the Roman Atticists associate with the plain style.

Hence, Horace in *sat.* 1, 10, 9 ff., associates the *urbanus* definitely with the plain style because he restrains his strength (*parcentis viribus*). On the other hand, formal rhetoric is almost synonymous with the grand style as perfected in the lofty and sustained flight of epic and the passionate power of tragedy. *Vis* or *vires* thus connotes a quality frequently applied to the grand style of oratory. But the wise husbanding of strength with its suggestion of reserve power is constantly associated with the plain style. The economy of expression is aptly described by the epithet *parcus*.

Closely related to this conception of aesthetic and linguistic *parsimonia*[149] is the ideal of *elegantia*, the watchword of the Atticists, the quality for which Laelius was famous in the Scipionic circle. The *vir elegantia praeditus*, if we may so describe him, makes wise and restrained selection from the linguistic, emotional, and in the case of a genre like satire above all, from the humorous effects at his disposal, employing only such as are in harmony with his aesthetic purpose. Hence Horace in this passage, as elsewhere in his works, employs the phrase *extenuantis*[150] with direct allusion to his essential sympathy with the tenets of the *genus tenue* or plain style.

Even in the linguistic sense, there is an element of *urbana dissimulatio* about this more finished nuance of the plain style, owing to its studied simplicity, a simplicity which looks easy of attainment, but in reality demands the constant use of the file. It is just here that the related conceptions of the *urbanus* and the εἴρων with their narrower relations to wit and humor interpenetrate the theories of technical composition. Horace understands this perfectly.[151] Thus Pedius Poplicola and Messala sweat out their cases in an effort to sustain a standard of pure Latinity *sat.* 1, 10, 27 ff. Even Lucilius would have paid more heed to our present better understanding of the need of restraint in language if he were alive today and would have applied himself to the labor of the file by which alone such restraint is attained. (Horace *sat.* 1, 10, 66-71). But the clearest statement of what we may call the principle of linguistic irony is in the *Ars Poetica* 240 ff.:

> ex noto fictum carmen sequar ut sibi quisque
> speret idem sudet multum frustraque laboret
> ausus idem.

In short, the stylistic method, ideals, and ironic humor of Socrates admirably fit the refined procedure of Horatian in distinction from Lucilian satire. This insinuating advance into his subject and into the hearts of his readers is admirably characterized by the rhetorical application of irony to the plain style of the *sermo* made by Cicero in the *de oratore* 3, 203: tum illa quae maxime quasi inrepit in hominum mentis, alia dicentis ac significantis dissimulatio; quae est periucunda, cum in oratione non contentione, sed sermone tractatur.[152] Persius must clearly have had this ideal of the εἴρων in mind when he gave his immortal characterization of Horace as a satirist:

> omne vafer vitium ridenti Flaccus amico
> tangit et admissus circum praecordia ludit.

Certainly Horatian satire approximates the Ciceronian definition of a *genus perelegans cum gravitate salsum*. At times it is even *accomodatum oratoriis dictionibus*, a phrase which we may compare with the Horatian *defendente vicem modo rhetoris* (*sat.* 1, 10, 12). Thus Horace permits an occasional encroachment upon the domain of the grand style, whether to give adequate expression to human passion (*sat.* 1, 4, 49), or to characterize the grand style in contrast to that of the satire; as in *sat.* 1, 4, 60, a quotation from Ennius, *sat.* 1, 10, 31 ff., the vision of father Quirinus, *sat.* 2, 1, 13 ff., an epic description of battle, *sat.* 2, 6, 65 ff., the praise of philosophy, followed by a parody of the epic style in lines 79 ff., the fable of the city and the country mouse. It would be easy to multiply examples.

Finally it will be instructive in closing this extended survey of the relations of the two satirists to the grammatical and rhetorical theories of Diogenes of Babylon, Panaetius and the later Roman Atticists if we compare point by point Horace's criticisms on Lucilius in *sat.* 1, 4, and 1, 10 with the definitions of the virtues of the plain style enumerated by Diogenes.

It will be remembered that the first virtue of the plain style was Ἑλληνισμός, *Latinitas*,[153] that. is correctness and purity of conversational idiom employed in accordance with the tenets of technical grammatical theory (ἐν τῇ τεχνικῇ) in the language of colloquial art, but not of the streets (μὴ εἰκαίᾳ συνηθείᾳ) as, for instance, in the conversational dialectic of Socrates and his followers and notably in the Platonic dialogues. Now Horace on the whole follows these principles pretty strictly. Thus in 1, 4, 13 he criticizes Lucilius for his indifference to the labor of correct composition (*atque piger scribendi ferre laborem, scribendi recti*). Here *scribendi recte* is obviously an allusion to the Greek virtue of ὀρθογραφία, a synonym for Ἑλληνισμός. Again in *sat.* 1, 10, 27 *pater Latinus*[154] appears as the guardian of *Latinitas* when Horace thinks of a hybrid form of composition containing both Greek and Latin. Furthermore, Horace's lapses into vulgar idiom are deliberately chosen to produce dramatic effect or to give verisimilitude to the conversation of his characters. His diction recalls the purity of the Platonic dialogues and the other serious productions of the Socratic school. The style of Lucilius, on the other hand, in spite of his intimate knowledge of the principles of the Stoic grammar and rhetoric, and of the theory of the type of humor appropriate for the *sermo* or conversation, cannot fairly be described as infallible from the standpoint of Latinity. We have already seen that he gives full recognition to the colloquialisms of every-day speech τὸ εἰκαῖον, at times quite unrefined by the art of cultivated intercourse, by calling his work *schedium* and *ludus*, and perhaps even *libri saturarum*. Moreover, he does not hesitate to do violence in practice to such nicer conceptions of the *purus sermo* as were developed in the period intervening between Lucilius and Horace by the rhetorical studies of Cicero and the tenets of the Roman Atticists.

We have already discussed these borrowings from Greek, the Italic dialects, and the *sermo castrensis*.[155] In these respects Terence rather than Lucilius is the exemplar in the earlier period of the *purus sermo*. Later I shall have occasion to discuss in detail Horace's criticisms in *sat.* 1, 10, 19 ff. of Lucilius' free admission of Greek into his satires.[156] By contrast Horace holds up the necessity of such travail of composition as is illustrated by the methods of Messala Corvinus, *Latini sermonis observator diligentissimus*. The dream of father Quirinus serves as a further warning against the corruption of pure Latinity even by the introduction of the modicum of Greek, long domiciled in the language of the upper classes of Rome, from the days of Lucilius on. Horace, then, is seen to preach sound Atticistic doctrine, and Lucilius is condemned as recreant to the theory apparently known in the Scipionic circle from the teachings of Panaetius and in some of its aspects approved by Lucilius himself.[157] In the *Ars Poetica* 56 Horace extends the principle by limiting the formation of new compounds to those which have some analogy in the Greek since later Latin usage had come to frown on the freedom of the early Latin tragedians in this respect.[158]

The second quality of the plain style is brevity, συντομία. This is secured by the use of the file which is particularly active against prolixity. Thus Horace in *sat.* 1, 4, 13 ff. thanks heaven that he is brief of speech and declines the challenge of Crispinus who improvises without limit. Again in *sat.* 1, 10, 8 he expressly asserts the creed of brevity:

> est brevitate opus ut currat sententia neu se
> inpediat verbis lassas onerantibus auris.

This criticism is repeated in line 60 ff., where Lucilius as a writer who will readily improvise 400 verses a day is compared with the wretched Etruscan poet Cassius whose funeral pyre is said to have been built of his voluminous writings. And later in line 67 we are told that Lucilius would lop off everything in excess of the mean of perfect composition if he were alive today. He is then *limatior* or prone to the use of the file though from a purely relative standpoint (1, 10, 65). He would dictate 200 verses an hour, standing on one foot; he is garrulous and chafes under the labor of sound composition (*sat.* 1, 4, 9 ff.).

But as I have shown,[159] there is a principle underlying the prolixity of Lucilius. His theory of satire in large measure harks back to the vivid and impromptu utterances of the Cynic and Stoic popular preachers. If transplanted to the Ciceronian age he would have defended his satires as *consulto rudium similis*. Again his prolixity is in part the result of his fondness for invective which leads inevitably to such fullness of utterance as is described in ancient literary criticism by the term *amplificatio*, a manner approximating to the grand style.[100]

Such a theory of poetry in the plain style as is advocated by Horace seems to have clear analogies with Cicero's description of the *orator tenuis*, the ideal of the Atticists.[101] (Orator tenuis) summissus est et humilis consuetudinem imitans ab indisertis re plus quam opinione differens. Itaque eum qui audiunt, quamvis ipsi infantes sint tamen illo modo confidunt se posse dicere: nam orationis subtilitas imitabilis illa quidem videtur, sed . nihil est experienti minus. These last words correspond pretty closely to the fate of the man who seeks to emulate the poetry in the familiar vein (the plain style?) described by Horace in the *Ars Poetica* 240 ff.:

> ex noto fictum carmen sequar, ut sibi quivis
> speret idem, sudet multum frustraque laboret
> ausus idem.

And, in fact, it is not true that two hundred verses of the Horatian type can be composed in an hour, for Horace definitely excludes actual improvisation from the *sermo*. Hence Quintilian[102] justly designates Horatian satire as *tersior ac purus magis* (*i.e., quam Lucilius*).

The third quality of the plain style is clearness, σαφήνεια, which aims at the exact representation of the thought, but Lucilius is muddy *sat.* 1, 4, 11, (*cum flueret lutulentus, erat quod tollere velles*) a fault which results inevitably from his prolixity. This criticism is emphatically repeated in *sat.* 1, 10, 50 ff.:

> at dixi fluere hunc lutulentum, saepe ferentem
> plura quidem tollenda relinquendis.

The fourth virtue of the plain style is appropriateness, τὸ πρέπον, a value raised in the stylistic system of Panaetius to an equality with the generic conception of *Latinitas*. This virtue finds only incidental discussion in Horace's satires, so far as Lucilius himself is concerned, but it is of fundamental importance in the critical theory developed by Horace in the *Ars Poetica*.[103] In the simpler grammatical system of Diogenes of Babylon this virtue is represented largely by κυριολογία (*proprietas verborum*). We have comparatively little criticism of Lucilius by Horace which falls under this category. Nevertheless the virtue of appropriateness seems to be involved in the question of mixing Greek with Latin. To be sure this is a barbarism, but from another point of view it is inappropriate for one who was by nature a Latin to indulge in such a hybrid mixture. Such a practice could only be truly appropriate for one who was bilingual, an inhabitant of Apulian Canusium for instance. Quirinus warns Horace against writing Greek verses therefore. Horace's position is certainly in entire accord with the opinion of Panaetius expressed in Cicero's *de officiis* 1, 111 and it may even be, as we shall see below, that Lucilius theoretically shared the same views.[164]

Horace, moreover, seems to have developed from this theory of appropriateness the doctrine of the law of the genre, the *lex operis*. I cannot find a similar development in Lucilius. In *sat.* 2, 1, 2 Horace declares that some of his critics believe that his excessive sharpness forces the satiric genre beyond its proper law:

> sunt quibus in satura videor nimis acer et ultra
> legem tendere opus.

A similar conception seems to lie at the basis of the phrase *operis lex* in the *Ars Poetica* 135. Certainly also Horace's criticism in *sat.* 1, 10, 36 of the epithet *luteus* as applied to the head of the Rhine may be regarded as directed against the inappropriateness of such a word for the epic.

The fifth virtue of Diogenes is κατασκευή, interpreted as embellishment or ornamentation, in the main as the result of the use of metaphorical language. To the Stoics such ornamentation was largely of that negative sort which consists of the avoidance of the vulgar. In this respect, as we have already seen,[165] Lucilius is at times sadly deficient. Horace, however, seems to feel that more is demanded of the real poet, which the satirist is not, than the use of *pura verba*, words employed in the literal or ordinary sense, the κύρια ὀνόματα of Greek rhetorical theory.[166] Thus in *sat.* 1, 4, 53 he says:

> ergo
> non satis est puris versum perscribere verbis.

Again in the *Ars Poetica* 234 the employment of a style no more adorned than that of comedy is declared to be insufficient for the

writer of the satyr play, which is nearer the level of the grand
style than comedy:

> non ego inornata et dominantia nomina solum
> verbaque, Pisones, Satyrorum scriptor amabo.

Above all Horace would lay far greater stress than Lucilius
did upon another aspect of κατασκευή, namely εὐσυνθεσία. In this
respect Horace appears to be in harmony with the tendencies of
contemporary rhetorical criticism which developed the earlier
and simpler conception of the place of εὐσυνθεσία as the means of
attaining embellishment into a highly elaborate system. Cicero
in the *orator* discusses the theory of σύνθεσις ὀνομάτων in great
detail, 149–236, while the *de compositione verborum* of Dionysius'
of Halicarnassus attests the importance of such theories in the
Augustan age. On the other hand Herodian, whose system
corresponds essentially to that taught in the Scipionic circle
by Diogenes of Babylon, substituted for κατασκευή the two
virtues of κυριολογία and εὐσυνθεσία. By κυριολογία he secures
such embellishment or grace of style as is gained by verbal
precision. By εὐσυνθεσία the early Stoic rhetoricians showed
their regard for the sound values as well as the sense values of
words combined in sentences. In particular they accepted the
doctrine that the sound value of a word depends largely upon
the final sound of the preceding word and the initial sound of
the following word.[167]

Lucilius himself was clearly acquainted with this doctrine
and gave it his theoretical adherence. Thus in line 377 he
discusses as a case of *cacosyntheton*, the unpleasant growling
sound of the letter *r*, which he designates by the term *cacosyn-
theton*, as the vice antithetical to εὐσυνθεσία:

> (a)r(e): non multum (ab)est, hoc cacosyntheton atque canina
> si lingua dico: nihil ad me, nomen *enim* illi est.[168]

Lucilius furthermore favored the collocation of words or sounds
which combined euphoniously. So in fragment 1167 quoted by
the 4th century rhetorician C. Chirius Fortunatianus: quid hic
aliud obseruabimus? ut quae uerba magis sonantia sunt, ea
potius conlocemus, quae Lucilius euphona appellat, id est quasi
uocalia. ut pro Caelio 'aliut fori lumen est, aliut lychnorum,'
cum potiusset etiam structius dicere 'aliut lucernarum.' And

yet even here the 4th century rhetorician feels that the combination *aliut lucernarum* would have shown a nicer sense of phonetic adjustment (*structius*).

Again in book 10, fragment 386 Lucilius clearly has *iunctura* in mind, a Latin term closely related to certain aspects of the Greek concept of εὐσυνθεσία:

> *horum est iudicium, crisis ut discribimus ante,*
> *hoc est, quid sumam, quid non, in quoque locemus.*

In spite of this technical knowledge of the requirements of εὐσυνθεσία Lucilius appeared noticeably deficient to the more refined ears of the Augustan age. In practice also he was far from being the careful metrician that Horace was, while the *curiosa felicitas* of the later poet, a virtue which is so largely the result of the delicate application of the principles, summed up under such Latin terms as *compositio, concinnitas, iunctura* was quite outside his purpose.[168]

With good reason, therefore, Horace as the perfect exponent of the stylistic and euphonic principles summed up under these rhetorical terms criticizes the performance of his master, Lucilius, as harsh in composition, the antonym of *mollis* (1, 4, 8 *durus componere versus*). To this criticism he returns in 1, 10, 1,

> Nempe inconposito dixi pede currere versus.

and he repeats the criticism in lines 56 ff.:

> quid vetat et nosmet Lucili scripta legentis
> quaerere num illius, num rerum, dura negarit
> versiculos natura magis factos et euntis
> mollius ac siquis pedibus quid claudere senis.

In this passage the *magis factos* expresses the idea of a style wrought with conscious artistic purpose. So Cicero *de oratore* 3, 48, 184 speaks of an *oratio quae quidem sit polita atque facta quodam modo*, a passage in which the *facta* seems to be a translation for the technical Greek rhetorical term πεποιημένη.

Even more clearly a study of the *Ars Poetica* shows that Horace regarded *iunctura* as one of the most important rhetorical instruments for the attainment of the style appropriate to the *sermo*. Thus in line 47 he declares:

> dixeris egregie notum si callida verbum
> reddiderit iunctura novum.

And again in 242:

> tantum series iuncturaque pollet.

Finally, if we compare such Lucilian fragments as 628, 629, 630, 671, 675, 1022 with Horace's argument in *sat.* 2, 1, 50 we seem to have a half-jocose, half-serious application to the theory of style of the Stoic doctrine of living in accordance with nature. So also in the passage just quoted from the tenth satire Horace raises the philosophic query whether the harshness of Lucilian composition is an expression of the harshness of the man's nature. Such criticisms are quite justified in view of the insistence of Lucilius that his satire was the spontaneous expression of a natural impulse. So Lucilius declares in 590:

> ego ubi quem ex praecordiis
> ecfero versum.

In point of fact Horace in this satire is quite willing to recognize that satire is the artist's natural weapon of defense, which he may use just as the steer uses his hoofs or the wolf his fangs. While Lucilius, however, makes little effort to restrain his strength or to sheath his natural weapons, but rushes into the attack as he himself says, like a dog, fragment 1095:

> inde canino ritu oculisque
> inuolem

i.e., like the Cynic; Horace, on the other hand, with the ironical restraint of the sophisticated man of the city state, the ideal *urbanus*, keeps his weapon sheathed until it is necessary to draw it in self-defense (lines 38 ff.), a criticism on the part that unrestrained invective too frequently played in Lucilian satire.

This long survey of the diction and humor appropriate to the *sermo* or conversation in the plain style, the form selected by both Lucilius and Horace, was necessary to set in clear light the environment in which the two satirists worked, as well as to bring out the similarities and differences existing between them. It has incidentally served to give added corroboration to the general discussion on the rhetorical theory of imitation which was the subject of my first chapter. The similarities in the theoretical attitude of the two men have been sufficiently indicated. The chief differences separating them are in large measure the results of the temperamental differences of their genius, and the genius of the two vivid epochs in which they lived and worked. Yet we have found reason to believe that Lucilius sometimes consciously, sometimes unconsciously, modified the more restrained definition of the content, tone, and humor of the *sermo* presented by Panaetius, by permitting a strong admixture of popular elements, a freer use of invective, and a more informal and impromptu ideal of composition than Horace, a member of the cultivated circle of Augustus and intimately acquainted with the finished theories of the later Roman Atticists, thought permissible. Finally, we have found definite though scattering indications that Lucilius was influenced in these respects by his acquaintance with the theories of composition and the somewhat inchoate productions of the popular Cynic and Stoic philosophers, half-preachers, half-satirists. To establish with greater clearness the nature of this influence upon Lucilian satire it now becomes necessary to gather together and analyze the widely scattered and uncertain information we possess in regard to these Greek satires of the Cynics and Stoics. If it is impossible to attain certainty in view of the fragmentary nature of our material both Greek and Latin, it is nevertheless important to consider the probable direction in which such streams of influence as we can uncover, flowed.

NOTES ON CHAPTER II

[1] Cichorius, *Untersuchungen zu Lucilius*, pp. 14-22, discussing the social position of Lucilius seeks to refute the contention of Marx, *proleg.*, p. 18, that Lucilius was a Latin. This hypothesis seems to rest on the fact that Lucilius was born in a Latin colony. But many Roman citizens had residence in Latin colonies, and many Latin families also in course of time obtained Roman citizenship. Furthermore, there is good external evidence that Lucilius was a Roman citizen, for such passages as Horace, *sat.* 2, 1, 74-75, Cicero, *de oratore* 1, 72 (*cf.* Cichorius, *op. cit.*, p. 15) can hardly be explained on any other assumption. Internal evidence afforded by such fragments as 1228, 1259, 1287 seems to carry the implication of Roman citizenship. In pp. 19-21 Cichorius argues on the basis of the so-called *senatus consultum of Adramyttium Ep. Epigr.* 4, 213, in which the brother of Lucilius is mentioned as Μάνιος Λευκίλιος Μαάρκου Πωμεντείνα, that the absence of the grandfather's name proves that citizenship had only recently been acquired by the father in the generation before the cutting of the inscription. Finally, in a passage in Velleius Paterculus 2, 29, the phrase *Lucilia stirpis senatoriae* at least makes it plausible that the grandfather of Lucilia, the poet's niece, was a senator.

[2] *Cf. schol Cruq ad loc.* Also Cicero, *de oratore* 2, 22.

[3] On legal restrictions see *infra*, pp. 370-373 under *sat.* 2, 1, and pp. 292-293 under *sat.* 1, 4.

[4] Cichorius, *op. cit.*, pp. 45 ff. reconstructs with much plausibility a banquet of philosophers at Athens, at which philosophical problems were debated by Academicians and Epicureans. See *fragments* 751, 755, 754, 753, 762.

[5] See *fragments* 388, 1104, 1251.

[6] *Cf.* Cicero, *Acad. prior.* 2, 102. Cichorius, *op. cit.*, pp. 43 ff. argues that this intimacy between the two men arose during a visit made by Lucilius to Athens, at which time Lucilius came to know and reverence Clitomachus and his teacher Carneades.

[7] *Epp.* 2, 2, 43.

[8] *Epp.* 2, 2, 47.

[9] *Sat.* 1, 6, 48; *Epp.* 2, 2, 47; *carm.* 2, 7, 9 ff.

[10] See *fragment* 397 ff. in book 11; 467 in book 14; and 490 in book 15 . *Cf.* also Marx, *proleg.*, p. XXV; Cichorius, *op. cit.*, pp. 33 ff.

[11] Cichorius, *op. cit.*, pp. 29-40, and especially *fragment* 405.

[12] *E.g., fragments* 1228 and 1326 for Lucilius; *sat.* 2, 2 and *carm.* 3, 2 and 3 for Horace.

[13] Horace, *Epp.* 1, 1, 14; for Lucilius see *infra*, pp. 185 ff.

[14] See the satire on the banquet of the philosophers in book 28, on which *cf.* Cichorius, *op. cit.*, pp. 44-49. Also *infra*, pp. 150 ff.

[15] Cichorius, *op. cit.*, pp. 149-150.

[16] *Cf.* the relations of Horace's Roman odes, book 3, 1-6, to the reforms of Augustus. Also see the article by Norden, *Virgil's Aeneis im Lichte ihrer zeit, Neujahrbücher für das Klass. Alt.*, vol. 7, pp. 251-265.

[17] On the life and character of Scipio Africanus Minor compare in addition to the standard Roman histories of Mommsen, Heitland, and Greenidge, Schanz, *op. cit.* 8, 1, 1, §73b. 2; Leo, *Geschichte der römischen Literatur*, pp. 315 ff.; and on the philosophical and political ideals of the Scipionic circle Buttner, *Porcius Licinus*, pp. 132-143; Schmekel, *Die Philosophie der mittleren Stoa*, chap. 3, pp. 439-446; Reitzenstein, *Werden und Wesen der Humanität in Alterthum.*

[18] Plutarch, *Aemil. Paul.* 6.

[19] Plutarch, *Aemil. Paul.* 28.

[20] Leo, *op. cit.*, pp. 316 ff., 325 ff. H. Peter, *Wahrheit und Kunst*, pp. 243-264; Hirzel, *Untersuchungen zu Ciceros philosophischen Schriften*, 2, pp. 841-907.

[21] 32, 9.

[22] *Op. cit.*, pp. 318 ff.

[23] Peter, *op. cit.*, pp. 246 ff.

[24] See *infra*, pp. 279-281.

[25] I do not wish to be understood as insisting that there is any case of direct imitation involved between Polybius and Lucilius, but rather that the employment of the threefold division of readers in the historian and the satirist is the free application of a rhetorical commonplace to their respective genres, history and satire.

[26] On Panaetius see Schmekel, *op. cit.*, pp. 1-9, and pp. 439 ff.; Arnold, *Roman Stoicism*, pp. 113-116; Reitzenstein, *op. cit.*; Hirzel, *Untersuchungen zu Ciceros philosophischen Schriften*, Theil 3, pp. 566 ff. and index.

[27] Hirzel, *Untersuchungen zu Cicero's philosophischen Schriften*, Theil 1, pp. 242 ff., II, pp. 335 ff. In the *de finibus* 4, 27, 79 Cicero describes the superiority of Panaetius to his predecessors, who are *horridiores, asperiores, duriores et oratione et moribus*; and of his philosophical tendencies he says: *quam illorum tristitiam atque aspiritatem fugiens Panaetius nec acerbitatem sententiarum nec disserendi spinas probavit, fuitque in altero genere mitior, in altero illustrior semperque habuit in ore Platonem Aristotelem, Xenocratem, Theophrastum, Dicaerchum, ut ipsius scripta declarant, quos quidem tibi studiose et diligenter tractandos esse censeo.*

[28] See *infra*, pp. 84-86 and Chapter VI, p. 443.

[29] Cicero, *ad Att.* 16, 11, 4; *de off.* 3, 2, 7: *quem nos correctione quadam adhibita potissimum secuti sumus*; also *ibid.* 1, 2, 6; 2, 17, 60. Cicero's indebtedness to Panaetius is usually held to be especially great in book 1 of the *de officiis.*

[30] So Schmekel, *op. cit.*, p. 445. Not accepted by Buttner, *Porcius Licinus*, pp. 138-139.

[31] He is in fact the first Stoic since Cleanthes with "a sense of form." See Hirzel, *op. cit.*, vol. I, p. 354.

[32] *Op. cit.*, p. 103.

[33] As Reitzenstein, *op. cit.*, *passim* has clearly shown.

[34] For the influence of Panaetius on Rhetoric, *cf. infra*, pp. 85-99.

[35] *Cf.* Cicero, *Brutus*, 84.

[36] See *infra*, pp. 80-84.

[37] See Mommsen, *Roman History* (Eng. Trans.) book 4, chap. 3.

[38] This reference eludes me. Perhaps some reader will supply the ancient source.

[39] The best discussion on the relation of the government to Augustan literature is that of Norden, *Virgil's Aeneis im Lichte ihrer Zeit, N. Jahrb. für d. kl. Alt.*, vol. 7, pp. 248-282 and 313-334.

[40] In the Florence of the Renaissance we have an example of the swift transition from a renaissance of the first type to one of the second. On the relation between social and political conditions at Rome, see Duff, *Literary History of Rome*, pp. 612-618. Schanz, *op. cit.*, 8, 3, 2, 116-7.

[41] See Lucilius, *fragments* 794, 1028, and Horace, *sat.* 1, 10, 37. Also *infra*, pp. 346-347.

[42] See Schanz, *op. cit.*, 84, 2, 1, 3, §276 a.

[43] See Schanz, *op. cit.*, 8, 2, 1, 3, §273 a.

[44] *Op. cit.*, pp. 34 ff. Chapter 3, *Die Anfänge*, pp. 47-55, 139-143, 259-265, 315-325, 351-368.

[45] See Hendrickson, *The Origin and Meaning of the Ancient Characters of Style* in *A. J. P.* 26, pp. 249 ff.; especially pp. 264 ff.; Smiley, *Latinitas and Ἑλληνισμός*, University of Wisconsin thesis, 1906; Striller, *de Stoicorum Studies rhetoricis*, Breslauer, *Phil. Abhandlungen*, 1.

[46] Aristotle, *Rhetoric* I, 1356 a, 15.

[47] Aristotle, *Rhetoric* 2, 1404 a, 4.

[48] *Anon. Proleg. ad Hermog. Rhet. Graec.* 7, 8. W.

[49] See pp. 211 ff.

[50] See *de oratore* 3, 16; on Rutilius see also *Brutus* 48.

[51] Cicero, *Brutus* 113 f.

[52] See *infra*, pp. 156-158.

[53] On Publius Mucius Scaevola, see Leo, *op. cit.*, p. 349; on Quintus Mucius Scaevola, *ibid.*, p. 349, 421.

[54] Leo, *op. cit.*, p. 348 f.

[55] Leo, *op. cit.*, p. 333.

[56] Leo, *op. cit.*, pp. 334 ff.

[57] See Cichorius, *op. cit.*, p. 121 ff. On the relation of this εἰσαγωγή to the *Ars Poetica* of Horace see *infra*, pp. 446-468.

[58] On the relation of the *epistula* to the *sermo* see Hendrickson, *Are the Letters of Horace Satires?* in *A. J. P.* 18, pp. 312-324. Also Cicero, *ad. Att.* 13, 6, 4.

[59] Caesar, who composed this famous epigram on Terence, was himself an adherent of the plain style; of this epigram I quote the first two lines:

Tu quoque tu in summis, o dimidiate Menander,

poneris, et merito, puri sermonis amator.

[60] *Op. cit.*, p. 253.

[61] See *Brutus* 171.

[62] See *infra*, pp. 107-112.

[63] *Cf. Heautontimoroumenos*, 45.

[64] *Cf.* Leo, *op. cit.*, pp. 251-258 for a discriminating critique on the style of Terence.

[65] See Leo, *op. cit.*, p. 320. On the humor of Scipio compare Cicero, *de oratore* 2, 253, 258, 267, 269, 270. In the last passage we are expressly told that *Fannius* called Scipio εἴρων.

[66] Strabo 14, 53.16; p. 676.

[67] See *infra*, pp. 277-306 for *sat.* 1, 4; pp. 336-349 for *sat.* 1, 10; pp. 369-378 for 2, 1; 446-468 for *Ars Poetica.*

[68] Similarly Galen, *de diff. puls.* 3, p. 32 speaks of the neologisms of Zeno and his violations of the ἔθος of the Greeks.

[69] See Hirzel, *op. cit.*, p. 355.

[70] See Hirzel, *op. cit.*, pp. 356-357.

[71] We may notice in passing that the *excellunt* of Cicero, *de oratore* 134 suggests the Greek οἱ εὐδοκιμοῦντες Ἕλληνες.

[72] See *supra*, p. 79.

[73] See *infra*, pp. 306-316; 316-324.

[74] See also Cicero, *de oratore* 2, 6, 22.

[75] See *infra*, p. 229.

[76] With lines 228 and 229, 230, 231, 232, 233, 235, 236, 241 of book 6, we may associate *dubia* 1138 ff. in the reconstruction of a satire parallel to Horace's encounter with the bore.

[77] See *infra*, pp. 107-109 on grammar; pp. 109-112 on rhetoric.

[78] See *infra*, pp. 446-468.

[79] See *supra*, pp. 86 f.

[80] See *infra*, pp. 145-146.

[81] Horace, *Sermo* 1, 4; *A Protest and a Programme* in *A. J. P.*, vol. 21, pp. 121-142. Also *infra*, pp. 277 ff. *passim.*

[82] *De oratore*, 2, 244.

[83] In Persius, *sat.* 1, 127-132 the disapprobation of a jest involving an attack on a personal infirmity, blindness, reveals the continuance of the same rhetorical disapprobation of the vulgar and unkind humor of the mime:

> *non hic qui in crepidas Graiorum ludere gestit.*

Compare also Hendrickson's *Horace, Sermo* 1, 4, in *A. J. P.*, vol. 21, pp. 121 ff. *Excursus on Persius and the Theory of Satire*, pp. 138-142.

[84] *Lydus de magistratibus*, see 40 ed. *Wuensch.*

[85] Perhaps the fact that slaves and freedmen were the regular actors of the mime helped to suggest such an association of the illiberal type of jest with this form of drama which bore a low reputation for decency.

[86] So Marx, comment. *ad loc.*

[87] See Hendrickson, *op. cit.*, in *A. J. P.*, 21, p. 140, and *Horace and Lucilius* in *Studies in Honor of Gildersleeve*, p. 155.

[88] Hirzel, *op. cit.*, pp. 373 ff. seems to prove this.

[89] In the Augustan age the wide influence of the doctrine of *urbanitas* with its fondness for apt and trenchant sayings facilitated the use of such χρεῖαι. See *infra*, pp. 160-162 and p. 343.

[90] *Op. cit.*, pp. 357-364.

[91] The most detailed discussion of the history of the word is by Otto Ribbeck in the *Rheinisches Museum*, 31, 381 ff.

[92] The following passages of Plato are also cited by Ribbeck: *Sophistes*, p. 268; *Laws*, p. 908d; *Apology*, p. 38a; *Republic*, 1, p. 337a; *Symposium*, p. 216d; *Theatetus*, p. 150.

[93] See also *Ethics Eud.* 3, 1234a, 1; *Etym. M.*, p. 1192a, 31.

[94] For the traditional Stoic and Epicurean attitude towards irony, which even Aristotle regards as a purely relative virtue lying in the mean between ἀλαζονεία and the qualities of the βαυκοπανούργος compare Hirzel, *op. cit.*, p. 366, note 3.

[95] *Vis.*, (1) deceiving of expectation, (2) caricature, (3) comparison with the ugly or distorted, (4) irony, (5) assumed simplicity, (6) lashing of folly.

[96] See Cicero, *Tuscl. Disp.* 2, 26; *ad Q. frat.* 2, 26, 32; Reitzenstein: *Scipio Aemilianus und die Stoische Rhetorik, Strassburger Festschrift zu 46 vers. der deutschen Philologer und Schulmänner*, Strassburg, 1901.

[97] *Op. cit.*, pp. 311 ff.

[98] See Cichorius, *op. cit.*, p. 310.

[99] On the charge of Asellus see Lucilius 394.

[100] See *infra*, pp. 330-336.

[101] On the stylistic position of Lucilius in general, see the *testimonia de vita et poesi C. Lucili* in Marx' *Prolegomena*, pp. cxxv-cxxxiv; also the article *Molle atque Facetum* by C. N. Jackson, in the *Harvard Studies in Classical Philology*, vol. 24, pp. 117-137; the article *Horace, Catullus, Tigellius* by B. L. Ullman, in *C. P.* 10, pp. 270-296. For a criticism on Jackson and Ullman, see article by M. B. Ogle, *Horace an Atticist*, in *C. P.* 11, pp. 156-168. While I cannot agree with Ogle's general point of view he is right in denying any relation between Lucilius and Asianism. On *gracilitas* see A. Gellius 6, 14, 6; Marx, *testimonia* no. 73; Fronto, p. 113 N.; Marx, *testimonia*, no. 74.

[102] Petronius 4, Marx, *testimonia*, no. 77. On *schedium* see *infra*, pp. 146 ff.

[103] See Cicero, *de oratore* 1, 72; Quintilian 10, 1, 94; Marx, *testimonia* nos. 58 and 62.

[104] On the *officia oratoris* which may be connected with the adjective *doctus*, see Cicero, *de oratore* 2, 115; Quintilian, 5 *praef.* 1; also Hendrickson on *The Origin and the Meaning of the Ancient Characters of Style*, in *A. J. P.* 26, 260 and especially note 3.

[105] Cicero, *de oratore* 1, 72; Marx 1241. I can see no valid reason why Marx should be averse to regarding this passage as representing the belief of Lucilius.

[106] Lucilius was probably not *urbanus* in the wide sense in which that word had come to be used in the Augustan age. In the main the term was in his period confined to the sense of pregnant wit, and yet such a fragment as 1322 with its differentiation between the style of the city and that of Praeneste shows that the differentiation between the *urbanus* and the *agrestis* as two opposed types was already known. Cicero, *de*

oratore 1, 72. Horace, *sat.* 1, 10, 64 though a mere argumentative concession, implies the prevalence of such a view even in the Augustan age. Porphyrio's phrase (*ad Horat. serm.* 1, 3, 40) *Lucilius urbanitate usus* seems to mean employing a witty Lucilian expression.

[107] Cicero, *Brutus* 133, 285; also Ullman, *op. cit.*, p. 287.

[108] Cicero, *epist. ad fam.* 9, 15, 2; Horace, *sat.* 1, 4, 16.

[109] On the meaning of *facetior* in this passage see Jackson, *loc. cit.*, p. 131, note 3.

[110] Cicero, *orator* 34.

[111] Horace, *sat.* 1, 10, 30 ff.   On the βρομήματα see *infra*, pp. 157-158.

[112] See Marx, comment. *ad loc.*

[113] *Vis.*, on vowels, 351, 356, 357, 358, 362, 364, 367, 369, 371; on prepositions in composition 373, 374, 375; on consonants 377, 379, 381, 382.

[114] *Vis.*, 33, 63, 171, 204, 1128, 1134, 1284, 1334.

[115] See *supra*, p. 86.

[116] See *infra*, pp. 153-155.

[117] See *supra*, p. 106.

[118] See *infra*, pp. 450-456, and also Lucilius, *fragments* 649 and 650.

[119] See *fragments* 587-590, 632, and *infra*, pp. 450-456.

[120] See *infra*, pp. 456 ff.

[121] See *infra*, pp. 460 ff. on the relation of this satire with the *Ars Poetica*.

[122] See *supra*, pp. 78 ff.

[123] On *iunctura* see also *fragments* 378, 387.

[124] See *infra*, pp. 277-306, for *sat.* 1, 4; pp. 336-349; for *sat.* 1, 10; and pp. 369-378 for *sat.* 2, 1.

[125] See Marx, *ad loc.*

[126] See *infra*, pp. 461 f.

[127] In such *fragments* of Lucilius as those on friendship in books 29 *vis.*, 830, 834, 908, 909, 902, 905, 906, on which see Cichorius, *op. cit.*, pp. 177-179; for Lucilius' interest in the history of philosophy, see 755, 754, 753, 757, 762, apparently forming a satire on a banquet of philosophers, as Cichorius has seen *op. cit.*, pp. 44-46.

[128] *Cf.* also Cichorius, *op. cit.*, pp. 11 f., 40 f., 46 f.

[129] *Op. cit.*, pp. 270-296.

[130] Magnam autem partem clementi castigatione licet uti; gravitate tamen adiuncta, ut severitas adhibeatur et contumelia repellatur, atque etiam illud ipsum, quod acerbitatis habet obiurgatio, significandum est ipsius id causa, qui obiuregtur, esse susceptum.

[131] See *supra*, pp. 100-104.

[132] For these passages see Marx, *testimonia* nos. 53, 54, 55, 56.

[133] See Marx, *index grammaticus s.v. castrensis sermo.*

[134] See Marx, index VI, *vocabula peregrina praeter Graeca.*

[135] Cichorius, *op. cit.*, pp. 40-53.

[136] See *de officiis* I, 128 and 148.   Panaetius disapproves of the Cynic flouting of the proprieties of speech and urges the entire rejection of the

Cynic system: Cynieorum vero ratio tota est eicienda; est enim inimica verecundiae sine qua nihil rectum esse potest, nihil honestum.

[137] So Quintilian 6, 3, 104, quotes the definition of Domitius Marsus on *urbanitas* which might well apply to such a book of Lucilian satire as 11; *urbanitas est virtus quaedam in breve dictum coacta et apta ad delectandos movendosque homines in omnem adfectum animi; maxime idonea ad resistendem vel lacessendum, prout quaeque res aut persona desiderat.* After criticizing this definition especially on the score of the demand for brevity, Quintilian gives his own definition in 107 which fits admirably the discriminating care, perfect finish, and pervasive atmospheric humor of Horatian satire: *Nam meo quidem iudicio illa est urbanitas, in qua nihil absonum, nihil agreste, nihil inconditum, nihil peregrinum neque sensu neque verbis neque ore gestuque possit deprehendi, ut non tam sit in singulis dictis quam in toto colore dicendi, qualis apud Graecos* Ἀττισμὸς *ille redolens, Athenarum proprium sermonem.*

[138] See *supra*, pp. 85-92.

[139] On the relation of this passage to the critical theory of Horace in the *Ars Poetica*, see *Lucilius, the Ars Poetica of Horace, and Persius*, in *Harvard Studies in Classical Philology*, vol. 24, pp. 28 ff. I am now inclined to interpret the phrase *tantum de medio* in Horace's *Ars Poetica*, line 243, as a reference to the *sermo* which reproduces the language of ordinary life. My former interpretation in the sense of a middle genre I believe to be erroneous.

[140] See *supra*, pp. 91-92.

[141] Mullach, *Frag. Phil. Gr.* 1, p. 233, no. 22. Compare also Aristotle's discussion on εὐτραπελία and βωμολοχία in the Nichomachean *Ethics* II 7, 1108a, 24, and the relation of βωμολοχία, εὐτραπελία, and ἀγροικία to play or παιδία. Also the discussion on παιδία in Ethics 10, 6.

[142] On *schedium* see the paper by Ingersoll in *C. P.* 7, pp. 59-65. Also see *infra*, pp. 146 ff.

[143] See *supra*, pp. 85, 93, 96.

[144] See *infra*, pp. 248-274.

[145] See *supra*, pp. 92-96.

[146] In fact *summissus, humilis, humilitas* are probably to be regarded as translations of the Greek rhetorical terms ταπεινός and ταπεινότης. See Geigenmuller, *op. cit.* index.

[147] Dionysius of Halicarnassus uses similar language of the plain style, which he declares is precise and while seeming to be unfinished is in reality a dialect logically consistent and formed by an impeccable and simple reasoning art. Lysias 8 and Demosthenes 2, 6, p. 138, 9. Also Smiley, *op. cit.*, pp. 219-231.

[148] Compare Hendrickson in *C. P.*, 12, pp. 88-92.

[149] On the quality of stylistic reserve see Cicero, *orator* 81 and 83. The discussion of *parsimonia* in 81 is especially in point.

[150] Compare the interesting collection of passages made by Jackson in the article, *Molle atque Facetum*, vol. cit., pp. 132 ff. in proof of Horace's use of *tenuis* and related terms as technical designations of plain style.

[151] For further consideration of these points see my discussion of Horace's *sat.* 1, 4, *passim infra*, pp. 277-306; and 1, 10, *infra*, pp. 336-349.

[152] Yet even in Lucilius we apparently have attempts at this more subtle and pervasive irony in the satire upon the interview with the bore in book 6, for example.

[153] See *supra*, pp. 79-80.

[154] See Hendrickson's article, *Horace and Valerius Cato*, in C. P. 12.

[155] See *supra*, p. 116, note 133.

[156] See *infra*, pp. 338-341.

[157] See *supra*, pp. 122-124.

[158] See Heinze-Kiessling, comment *ad loc.*

[159] See *supra*, pp. 117-118 for evidence of the Lucilian titles.

[160] See *supra*, pp. 114-115.

[161] *Orator* 76.

[162] *Inst.* 10, 1, 94.

[163] See R. K. Hack, *The Doctrine of the Literary Forms*, in *Harvard Studies in Classical Philology*, 27, pp. 1-67 *passim*.

[164] See *infra*, pp. 338-341.

[165] See *supra*, pp. 114-116.

[166] See Heinze-Kiessling's note on *sat.* 1, 4, 53 and *A. P.* 234.

[167] See Smiley, *op. cit.*, p. 215.

[168] See Marx, comment. *ad loc.*

[169] See Marx, *index grammaticus metricus rerum memorabilium*, *passim*.

CHAPTER III

LUCILIUS AND THE GREEK SATIRISTS

It is antecedently probable that Lucilius as a member of a circle permeated with the new Greek learning in the fields of grammar, rhetoric, and philosophy should have sought to familiarize himself with the various expressions of the Greek satiric spirit so widely diffused among the popular and scholastic literary forms of the Hellenistic period. Unfortunately, the works of the popular Cynic and Stoic preachers which afford the nearest analogue to the genre of Lucilius are in fragments. For the study of these fragments of the Cynics and Stoics and for Greek satire in general we have as yet no work approximating to the thorough scholarship and imaginative insight so constantly evidenced in the edition of Marx and in the study of Cichorius on Lucilian satire. A detailed examination of the whole question of the relations between Greek satire and Roman satire is a pressing need, but falls outside the immediate scope of this work.[1] Yet it is necessary if we are to gain a real understanding of the nature of Horace's dependence upon Lucilius to form some idea of the broad outlines of the problem of the relationship between the Greek and Latin satiric forms, and to reconstruct the probable paths of these cultural influences so far as the baffling nature of our Greek and Latin material permits. In view of the strong tendency to stress the Italic elements entering into the development of satire as a genre and the relative neglect of the indications of Greek influence, this preliminary study may at least have the justification of indicating the general nature of the problem.

It is my purpose, therefore: (1) to examine the external evidence for the influence of the popular satirical productions of the Cynic and Stoic schools upon the satires of Lucilius, those informal Greek works, which from their common purpose to convey serious moral teaching under the form of a humorous discourse, whether oral or written, are most conveniently designated by the Greek term τὸ σπουδαιογέλοιον. (2) I shall try to estimate the value of the evidence resting on a similarity of title or metrical form between such Greek works and the satire of Lucilius. (3) I shall try to indicate the net impression gained by comparative analysis of the subject matter and tone of these Greek satirical forms and of Lucilius. (4) I shall examine the question of the possible relation between Bion and Lucilius by the aid of the somewhat uncertain light of our knowledge of the relations between the Greek satirist and Horace.

The external evidence may be briefly dismissed. In the first place we seem to have evidence, the persuasive value of which will be variously estimated,[2] that Nysius, a pupil of Panaetius, whose close relationship with Lucilius I have already established, was regarded as the inventor of a genre known as τὸ σπουδαιοχαρίεν. His name appears in column LXXIV in a catalogue of the Stoics made by Philodemus, but as to the restoration of the name of the genre there is some question. The notice is thus restored by Curt Wachsmuth:[3] Μάρκιος καὶ Νύσιος Σαυν[ῖ]ται. Νύσιος δὲ καὶ / τ[ὸ τ]ῶν σπουδαιο [χ]α / ρ[ιέν]των γένος π[ρ]ῶτος ἐ[π]ενόησεν. The form here restored as σπουδαιοχαρίεν was undoubtedly related to popular Cynic and Stoic forms. We know that Zeno and other Stoic philosophers divided men into two classes, the σπουδαῖοι and the φαῦλοι. The former were frequently called ἀστεῖοι with which χαρίεντες is almost a stylistic synonym. Now we find the corresponding qualities indicated in Latin by lepos and urbanitas emphasized by Panaetius in such passages as the de officiis 1, 104 and 134 as important elements in the restrained type of humor suited to the sermo. It seems possible therefore that the later conceptions of urbanitas as developed by Cicero and Horace may be related to the Greek ideal of ἀστειότης, and that this stylistic concept in an embryonic form may have been known as early as the period of the Scipios.

If on the other hand we accept the reading of τὸ τῶν σπου-δαιοπαρῴδων γένος[4] we shall still be inclined to refer the genre to the category of the popular satires of Cynics and Stoics in which, as we shall presently see,[5] parody played a very important part. But parody of Homer played an extremely important part in Lucilian satire, as I shall demonstrate. Here again therefore we have external indications pointing in the direction of Greek influence exercised upon Lucilian satire.

Rather more definite is the commentary of the pseudo-Acro upon the well-known passage in Horace's epistles 2, 2, 60 in which Horace seems to imply the relation of his *sermones* with those of Bion:

> carmine tu gaudes, hic delectatur iambis,
> ille Bioneis sermonibus et sale nigro.

Upon this passage the scholiast says: Sunt autem disputationes Bionis philosophi, quibus stultitiam vulgi arguit, cui paene consentiunt carmina Luciliana. Without denying the possibility that these words might be taken in the more general sense of spiritual kinship between the Cynic philosophers and Lucilius, it seems to me more probable that they refer to more direc' relationship in tone, method, and subject matter. I shall later seek to corroborate this view more fully by a detailed analysis of the evidence upon the nature of Bion's influence upon the works of Lucilius and Horace.[6] The evidence afforded by the titles selected by Lucilius for his satires is most naturally interpreted as a further indication of his conscious relationship with the somewhat inchoate Greek satirical forms. That the term *ludus*, employed by Lucilius as a designation for his satires in fragment 1039, goes back in ultimate analysis to the limited function assigned to recreation and humor in the ethical and stylistic theories of Aristotle and Panaetius has been shown.[7] One is inclined to relate this designation of the genre with the Greek term παίγνιον. Thus we hear that the Cynic Monimus wrote παίγνια σπουδῇ λεληθυίᾳ i.e., masking a serious purpose. In fact the term παίγνιον seems to go back to the age of the sophists. Gorgias used the term in distinction from ἐπιδείξεις to indicate discourses arbitrarily chosen and not in themselves of serious import, but designed to display the speaker's art for the entertainment of the reader, especially in the way of praise or blame.[8] Such a conception of the importance of the function of play and humor is admirably illustrated by the attitude of the Cynic Crates of Thebes, an influential figure in the development of the Cynic τὸ σπουδαιογέλοιον. According to Plutarch[9] he regarded life as a festival in which gayety and serious teaching were mingled, lived a life of play and laughter, and even

died with the same cheerfulness.[10]   In fact the Cynic conception
of the παίγνιον differs from the ἐρωτοπαίγνιον, a related genre,
principally in this sharp antithesis between humor and serious-
ness.[11]   Quite similar is the attitude of Diogenes, the most
striking figure of all the Cynics, the teacher of Crates.   Thus he
is represented as saying:[12] πενίαν . . . καὶ φυγὴν καὶ ἀδοξίαν
καὶ τὰ τοιαῦτα μηδὲν ἡγεῖσθαι δεινὸν αὐτῷ, ἀλλὰ πάνυ κοῦφα, καὶ
πολλάκις παίζειν ἐν αὐτοῖς τὸν ἄνδρα τὸν τέλειον, ὥσπερ οἱ παῖδες.

Lucilius apparently applied the term *schedium* to individual
satires to designate their informality of tone and impromptu
composition.[13]   In such informality and rapidity of composition
Lucilius' satires resemble the methods of the popular Cynic
and Stoic preachers of the Hellenistic period, as is apparent
from a study of their lives and methods in the Lives of the
Philosophers of Diogenes Laertius.   The Cynic and Stoic
street preachers of Rome followed the same tradition as is
evident from the challenge of Crispinus, a contemporary street
preacher, to Horace (*sat.* 1, 4, 13 ff.) to engage in such an impro-
visatory contest.[14]   Marx in his *prolegomena* properly charac-
terizes this feature of Lucilian satire by the term αὐτοκάβδαλος.
This term, which is used both of persons and things, means
"wrought or done in a careless, slovenly, slight, trivial, or
random manner."   It is so used by Aristotle,[15] and is applied to
a class of buffoons or buffoon actors, who speak offhand.

But the more formal title *sermones* or discourses which Luci-
lius selected for his work shows even more clearly the influence
of the Greek philosophical discourse perfected by Bion under
the title of διατριβή.   It will be more convenient to consider the
development and characteristics of this very important instru-
ment of popular philosophic propaganda in connection with the
question of Bion's influence on Lucilius and Horace.[16]   The
influence of Diogenes of Babylon and Panaetius in popularizing
the grammatical and rhetorical theories of the plain style, the
humor and diction appropriate to the *sermo* we have already
considered in detail.[17]

Such a form of popular philosophic exposition attests the
persistence in literature and in oral discourse of the influence of
the actual conversations carried on by Socrates with the respec-
table citizens and craftsmen of Athens in his efforts to arouse

them to self-examination and reflection upon the fundamental questions of human conduct. It was in fact this popular side of the Socratic tradition which was most ardently cultivated in the Hellenistic period by the vigorous propaganda of the Cynics. Diogenes, the Cynic, is the first to formulate the method and to some extent the content of a long tradition of Cynic-Stoic oral and literary discourses. The favorite themes of such preaching are the disregard of material advantage, the recognition of virtue as the highest good, the self-sufficiency of the ideal wise man, and the need of complete indifference to the ordinary objects of human desire and to the ordinary conventions of society. The method of Diogenes and the whole mendicant tribe of Cynic preachers is popular. They preach by homely examples drawn from every day life. They sum up their teaching in pointed apothegms, often couched in popular language. They enliven their discourse by anecdotes and witty sayings.

Then scholarship intervened and arranged these sayings of the master in rubrics: e.g., Diogenes with the robbers, Diogenes at the slave market, Diogenes and Alexander, Diogenes at Olympia. And new cycles of anecdotes gradually clustered around the more famous names in the Cynic and Stoic schools. The philosophers of other schools also gradually busied themselves with literary adaptations of these informal and successful forms. In adopting the title *sermones*, for his satires, therefore, Lucilius was probably in the minds of his contemporaries consciously associating his work with a complex of loosely jointed forms of half-satirical, half-philosophical exposition widely spread over the Hellenistic world, united only in possessing the common tone of the τὸ σπουδαιογέλοιον and in making their nearest approach to the fixity of generic exposition in the Bionean διατριβή. The cumulative evidence of such Greek influence will emerge in clear light as we proceed with the detailed analysis of the satires of Lucilius and Horace in Chapter IV.

It is probable also that Lucilius besides the terms, *schedium*, *ludus*, and *sermones* applied to his works the more general term of *poemata*.[18] The contrast between lines 1012 and 1013 in bóok 30 seems to suggest a literary polemic between a poet whose compositions do not meet with popular favor, and the poems of Lucilius which enjoy a wide circulation. Thus 1012 reads:

> et sua perciperet retro rellicta iacere.

and 1013:

> et sola ex multis nunc nostra poemata ferri.

There is some reason for thinking that the rival poet may be Accius, with whom Lucilius carried on numerous polemics,[19] and whose *didascalica* present certain parallel literary themes to those treated by Lucilius.[20] Thus we know that fragment 15 from book 9 of the *didascalica* introduced a discussion of the different genres of poetry:

> namquae varia sint genera poematarum, Baebi,
> quamque longe distincta alia ab aliis nosce.

Under these various genres[21] Accius was not likely to omit a considerable discussion of that of Lucilius, which by reason of its miscellaneous contents and variety of metrical forms, was probably called *satura*, a feminine collective singular apparently first used by Ennius to designate a literary miscellany in various metres or to quote the definition of Varro-Suetonius preserved in Diomedes 3, p. 485 Keil, a *carmen quod ex variis poematibus constabat.*[22] Such a definition it will be further noticed suits well the distinction made by Lucilius himself between *poema* and *poesis* in the 9th book, lines 338 ff. The definitions found there look like an answer to a definition given by someone else, quite possibly Accius in the 9th book of the *didascalica*. Lucilius, then, asserts that his opponent did not clearly understand the distinction between ποίησις and *poema*. The former term was by Lucilius applied to works of some compass, like the *Iliad* or the *Annales* of Ennius, from which the poet distinguishes the individual episodes or shorter subdivisions by the name of *poemata*. On the other hand, one independent short poem might be called *poema*:

> epistula item quaeuis non magna poema est.
> illa poesis opus totum, (tota[que] Ilias una
> est, una ut θέσις annales Enni) atque opus unum
> est, maius multo est quam quod dixi ante poema.
> qua propter dico: nemo qui culpat Homerum,

perpetuo culpat, neque quod dixi ante poesin:
uersum unum culpat, uerbum, entymema, *locum* (*unum*).

We may at least infer from this passage that Lucilius'
opponent took exception to the title *poemata* as applied by
Lucilius in the earlier book 30 to his satires. To which Lucilius
rejoins by giving the definition I have just quoted, in which he
perhaps asserts the right of his satires to be classified among
varia genera poematorum and defends his use of the term *poema*,
as a designation appropriate—and in fact quite as appropriate
as *ludus, schedium*, or *sermo*—to the individual satire.

We hear moreover in the Herculanean papyrus 1014²² of
Demetrius περὶ ποιημάτων that there was a discussion of ἀνυπό-
τακτα ποιήματα, that is, poems defying exact classification, a
title which suggests a Greek grammatical category related to
the *varia poemata* grouped by the Latin grammarians under the
generic term of *satura*. Such a designation may have stood in
relation to Ennean and Lucilian *satura* in a position somewhat
similar to such Hellenistic titles as Ἄτακτα and Σύμμικτα.²⁴
All in all then, the net impression emerging from a consideration
of this complex of relationships is one pointing to the probability
of the connection of the term ποιήματα as used by Lucilius with
the Latin concept of a literary miscellany in various metres.
This concept probably in the time of Ennius or at the very
latest by the time of Varro gained more piquant expression
under the colloquial term *satura*.

The variety of metrical forms in which Lucilius experi-
mented before settling on the hexameter is a phenomenon
parallel to the variety of metres represented by Greek satirical
writing, the τὸ σπουδαιογέλοιον of the Hellenistic period. It is
not usually possible, however, to prove a close genetic relation-
ship in form or content between such Greek satirical fragments
and fragments of Lucilius in the same metre. I shall hope,
however, to show that a study of the themes represented in
certain Hellenistic metrical fragments throws some light on
the cultural environment in which the satires of Lucilius must
have been written, and probably written with the direct con-
sciousness of Greek satiric literature. It would be rash to
speak of any direct appropriation of Hellenistic material except
in a few cases. The earliest books which Lucilius published,

books 26 and 27, were written in trochaic tetrameters. This
metre, which is associated with the name of Epicharmus by
Plato,[25] was used by the Cynic satirist, Menippus of Gadara.
As a favorite metre of the Old and the New Comedy it is well
adapted to satiric purposes. Iambic verse was, of course,
consecrated to abusive poetry from the days of Archilochus and
Hipponax.[26] In the gnomic poetry of the Stoics and the Cynics
the iambic trimeter is the ordinary metre. Besides certain iambic
fragments from the professional philosophers of these schools,
we find a number of poets at the beginning of the third or the
close of the fourth century B.C. who betray Cynic influence.
Among these the iambic epigrams of Leonidas of Tarentum
deserve especial mention. Timon of Phlius also beside his
better known Σίλλοι wrote iambics. In general the satiric
literature in iambics developed in close relation to the drama,
especially in connection with tragedy. Of the so-called Cynic
tragedies we lack the proper basis for a critical judgment, but
of the iambics of the philosophers we have clearer examples.
Here we find such themes as the complaint of poverty, the
prosperity of the wicked man, parainetic iambics, and at a later
period fables, maxims of the sages, and many other themes.

Now the subjects selected by Lucilius for treatment in this
metre may fairly be said so far as theme is concerned to point
towards the wide acquaintance of Lucilius with the themes of the
Greek philosophic iambi. Thus in book 28 fragments 751, 752,
753, 755, 756, 762 are taken from a banquet of philosophers at
Athens at which Lucilius may even have been present.[27] Frag-
ment 764 employs the favorite Stoic simile of the dropsical man
as an example of avarice. Fragment 765 seems to refer to the
Philistine who scorns to learn philosophy; one might as well
teach dirt as him; a remark which recalls Diogenes' saying:[28]
Διογένει τῷ Κυνικῷ . . . ἰδόντι μειράκιον πλούσιον ἀπαίδευτον ἔδοξεν
εἰπεῖν· οὗτός ἐστι ῥύπος περιηργυρωμένος. Fragment 766 refers
to a drunken hag who cannot be induced to forsake the
wine cask for philosophy. We also have a group of fragments
in this same book, viz., 773, 774, 775, 776, 777, 778, 779, 780,
781, 782, 783, which seem to refer to an attack on the house of a
leno by an angry lover, who seeks to carry off his mistress by
force, an erotic subject from the field of the New Comedy.

In book 29 we have a series of iambic *senarii* dealing with the Socratic theory of love and friendship, *viz.*, fragments 830–33, 834, 908, 909, 902–905, 906.[29] In fragments 839, 840, 841, 843, 845 we have a scene of comic or satiric origin, that of the excluded lover.[30]

In lines 923–942 Marx groups a number of *senarii* which cannot be assigned with certainty either to books 28 or 29. Here fragment 938 seems to refer to the exclusion of an impecunius lover by the *meretrix* just as the *cobius*, a cheap fish, is thrown out of the net when a rich tunny (*i.e.*, a rich lover) is caught, another subject related to the New Comedy.[31] In fragments 940–941 written either in iambic *senarii* or trochaic *septenarii* we have a poem on Hymnis, the mistress of the poet, in which the lady on the basis of the identity of name may have been brought into relation with the Hymnis of comedy, known through the works of Menander and Caecilius.[32] In fragment 923 we apparently have an allusion to the stock Cynic-Stoic example of the glutton, carried off by one fever or one case of indigestion or one draught of wine, a commonplace which was taken over by the writers of Latin satire.[33] In fragment 926 we have an allusion to the tenacity of the good man in love or hate. In 935 we may have the reply of the parasite to the question where he has left his shield, that his nose and his body are his shield, a passage evidently related to a scene from the New Comedy.

From this brief inventory it is abundantly evident that the iambic verses of Lucilius are steeped in the atmosphere of the New Comedy and of the philosophic iambic of the Hellenistic period, and that the appeal which they made to the highly sophisticated Scipionic circle and the nobles of the period was due quite as much to this Hellenistic atmosphere as to the pictures they give of contemporary Roman life. The influence of such Hellenistic iambic poetry upon Horace and at times clearly upon Lucilius also I have discussed below in connection with the sources of Horace's *sat.* 1, 1 where my readers will find a detailed examination of the relationship of the Hellenistic philosophical commonplaces represented in the ἴαμβος Φοίνικος and the other iambic fragments of the Heidelberg papyrus with Horace's satire.[34] Other relationships may clearly be traced between this literature and commonplaces in other Horatian satires. Since, however, the *tertium quid* of a Lucilian parallel fails us, I must content myself with the expression of the belief that several of the iambic satires of Lucilius probably stood in quite as close relations to this popular Hellenistic philosophy expressed in the form of sententious maxims and witty anecdotes as the satires of Horace.[35]

We have from book 22 of Lucilius two pentameters and an elegiac distich. Cichorius is inclined to believe[36] that books 22–25 contained occasional poems, probably epigrams, composed after the fashion which may in general be designated by the term *nugari Graece*.[37] These poems which Lucilius according to this hypothesis did not deem worthy of publication may have been posthumously published as a *libellus*. Book 22 seems to have contained epigrams on the slaves of the poet. Fragment 585 carries with it the implication that slaves were also treated in book 23. So far as form is concerned, therefore, it is fair to see in the activity of Lucilius with such material an evidence for the influence of the Hellenistic fondness for epigram in pentameter.[38]

Finally we come to the hexameters of Lucilius—the form in which he wrote book 30 and books 1–21. Doubtless the final selection of this metre was in large measure influenced by its relatively high development at the hands of Ennius. And in point of fact the Lucilian hexameter is the Ennean hexameter, adapted, however, to the purposes of informal narrative, and marked by considerable improvement in technique.[39] Nevertheless, we must not neglect the possibility that Lucilius was influenced by the popular Greek hexameters of the Hellenistic period and especially by the employment of the hexameter for purposes of Homeric parody in the Σίλλοι of Timon of Phlius. Indeed parody, one of the most elementary forms of satire, plays a considerable rôle in Lucilian satire.[40]

Even before the Hellenistic period the hexameter had been moulded for philosophic expression by the gnomic epics of Hesiod and Phocylides. In the Hellenistic period, however, the metre was principally employed for the purposes of parody. Yet we find the hexameter as the medium of hortatory poetry by Critias, Crates, the Cynic, Crantor, Menippus, Cleanthes.

Generally speaking, however, it seems clear that with the exception of the Σίλλοι the hexameter as a supple weapon of satiric expression attained its full development only with Roman satire.

Of the Σίλλοι, however, something further may be said. The Σίλλοι of Timon were parodies in hexameter, in which Homeric verses were deftly employed to parody the Homeric Νέκυια. The work is largely taken up by a wordy argument between Timon, the analogue of Ulysses, and the other philosophers resident in Hades.

Now Lucilius also employs the verses of Homer for the purposes of quotation and parody. Homer was in fact regarded by the Cynics and Stoics as a general store-house of wisdom. His heroes were types of the virtues, and hence far above the disputes of the schools. The second epistle of Horace's first book affords an excellent illustration of this Cynic-Stoic method of allegorical interpretation of Homer. In the Lucilian passages in which Homer is quoted or parodied it is impossible to detect any direct influence of Timon but it is perfectly clear that Lucilius' method of using Homer is strikingly similar to that in vogue among the Cynics and Stoics. Thus the council of the gods which sits upon the case of Lupus in book 1 is a parody on the councils of the Olympian divinities in Homer. We have similar parodies in the *Apocolocyntosis* of Seneca and in Lucian.

Within this satire are deftly introduced a number of Homeric allusions or parodies of Homeric lines. Thus in fragment 24, Apollo, who has objected to the epithet *pulcher* because of its use in the derived sense of *exoletus*, refers to the amours of Zeus with Leda and Dia, the wife of Ixion. This line is modelled on Ξ 317 οὐδ' ὁπότ' ἠρασάμην 'Ιξιονίης ἀλόχοιο. Again Neptune regrets his absence from the earlier council (fragment 27), presumably because he had been absent among the blameless Ethiopians (fragment 26). In fragment 37 we have an allusion to a storm to be sent by Jupiter to punish the Romans for the unjust decisions of Lupus (M253, 365, 384). Finally, the decision of Jupiter upon the fate of Lupus in 54 seems to be a parody upon Homeric decisions.[41]

Again in Horace's *sat.* 2, 5 we have a Νέκυια in which Ulysses and Tiresias are employed as types of Cynic-Stoic popular exposition, Ulysses standing for the χρηματιστικὸς of Chrysippus. Since there seems to be evidence for the use of Lucilian material in this satire, it is a fair inference that Lucilius had composed a satire having certain affinities with the parodic satire of Horace.[42]

Also in book 30 Ulysses seems to have been employed as a Cynic-Stoic hero.[43] Thus in fragment 1005 the Sirens' song was allegorically interpreted as meaning the allurements of sloth. To the same context we may refer fragments 996, 998 on the lonely voyage of Ulysses; 997, in which a woman, perhaps Penelope protests her loyalty to her husband; 1000 in which Ulysses recognizes his home once more; 1002 in which Telemachus(?) is unwilling to recognize his father; 1003 on the refusal to admit Ulysses to his own home, and possibly 1004 on the affectionate recognition of Ulysses by his old dog.

Beside these longer passages, which seem to point to a use of Homeric material for purpose of parody we have a number of allusions, adaptations, or translations from lines of Homer.[44]

In book 15, fragment 480 we have a Lucilian passage which demands somewhat fuller treatment. The reference here is to the Cyclops Polyphemus, 200 feet tall, with a staff as big as a ship's mast. The argument of this book seems to deal with philosophy, and more particularly with some of the typical vices assailed by Cynics and Stoics. Thus superstition is treated in lines 480–489, avarice in 492–503, anger in 506–514. The description of the Cyclops, which some think a foolish invention of Homer is taken from 190. The whole passage certainly looks like one of those wonderful tales with which an audience is regaled, just as Odysseus regaled Alcinous with the tale of his wanderings among the Laestrygonians and Cyclopes. With it we may compare Juvenal 15, 13–26:

> attonito cum
> tale super cenam facinus narraret Ulixes
> Alcinoe, bilem aut risum fortasse quibusdam
> moverat, ut mendax aretalogus, 'in mare nemo
> hunc abicit saeva dignum veraque Charybdi,
> fingentem inmanes Laestrygonas atque Cyclopas?
> nam citius Scyllam vel concurrentia saxa
> Cyaneis, plenos et tempestatibus utres
> crediderim, aut tenui percussum verbere Circes,

et cum remigibus grunnisse Elpenora porcis.
tam vacui capitis populum Phaeaca putavit?
sic aliquis merito nondum ebrius et minimum qui
de Corcyraea temetum duxerat urna;
solus enim haec Ithacus nullo sub teste canebat.

In this passage Juvenal declares that Homer makes Ulysses play the part of one of those bankrupt and parasitic Cynics, who told wonderful stories for the amusement of the great at their banquets. This class of *aretalogi* are alluded to by Suetonius *Aug.* 74 as hangers-on at banquets along with actors and players from the crossroads. Similarly Lycophron calls Ulysses a μυθοπλάστης. Even more important in showing the probable setting for such a passage is Lucian's *ver. hist.* 1, 3: ἀρχηγὸς δὲ αὑτοῖς καὶ διδάσκαλος τῆς τοιαύτης βωμολοχίας ὁ τοῦ Ὁμήρου Ὀδυσσεύς, τοῖς περὶ τὸν Ἀλκίνουν διηγούμενος ἀνέμων τε δουλείαν καὶ μονοφθάλμους καὶ ὠμοφάγους καὶ ἀγρίους τινὰς ἀνθρώπους, ἔτι δὲ πολυκέφαλα ζῷα καὶ τὰς ὑπὸ φαρμάκων τῶν ἑταίρων μεταβολάς, οἷα πολλὰ ἐκεῖνος ὡς πρὸς ἰδιώτας ἀνθρώπους ἐτερατεύσατο τοὺς Φαίακας. The ἀληθὴς ἱστορία or veracious narrative which the narrator— Juvenal, Lucian, or whoever he may be—then proceeds to tell, is declared to be even more marvelous than the traditional tale of wonders from Homer and in addition true. (nos miranda quidem, sed nuper consule Iunco etc., Juvenal, 15, line 27.)⁴⁵ Moreover, if we assign fragments 1342 and 1343 to this same book, we have a somewhat closer parallel to the passage in Lucian for these lines seem to describe a one-eyed monster like the Cyclops:

uno oculo, pedibusque duobus, dimidiatus ut porcus

Such wide general familiarity with Homer conjoined with the Cynic tendency to parody Ulysses as a sort of anti-hero makes it certain that Lucilius was entirely at home in the Homeric parodies of the Cynics, and justify our raising the question whether the Σίλλοι of Timon may not have had some influence in determining the final decision of Lucilius in favor of the hexameter as the proper measure for satire.

An even more important argument for the relationship of Lucilius to the Greek satirical literature of the Hellenistic period is found in the general similarity of tone and at times in content between the Lucilian satires and certain forms of popular philosophic exposition. The genres which I wish briefly to consider from this point of view are: (1) the ἀπομνημόνευμα and ὑπόμνημα (2) the χρεία; (3) the συμπόσιον, and δεῖπνον; (4) the αἶνος or fable; (5) the μῖμος; (6) the epistula; (7) the epigram. A consideration of the διατριβή, the most important genre of all, I shall take up in close relation to the question of Bion's influence on Lucilius and Horace.

The term ἀπομνημόνευμα[46] is used to designate a report upon the acts, noteworthy incidents, or speeches of a master made by a pupil on the basis of personal recollection or oral tradition. The narrator is the witness, not the subject of the narrative. The term was first used by Xenophon as a title (in the plural) for his recollections of Socrates, his master. The traditon thus started by Xenophon was continued by the earlier *Stoa* which shared with the Cynics this interest in the study of personality. Hence we find Zeno the Stoic writing ἀπομνημονεύματα of Crates the Cynic.[47] Persaeus' Συμποτικοὶ διάλογοι of Zeno and Stilpo were probably similar. This form was parodied in such reports as those of Lynceus and Aristodemus on the *bons mots* of the Athenian *hetaerae* and parasites, which were published in the period of Theophrastus and Menander.

It is clear that the conventional setting of this form, which presupposes a master whose teachings like those of Socrates and Diogenes the Cynic are given orally influenced certain satires in Horace's second book. Thus in 2, 3 Damasippus reports the discourse of Stertinius. Similarly it is possible to regard Horace in 2, 2 as playing the part of reporter of the teachings of Ofellus, an *abnormis sapiens*, and structurally at least to refer this satire to the class of ἀπομνημονεύματα. Again in *satire* 2, 7, Horace's slave Davus reports the words of wisdom emanating from the *ianitor* in the establishment of Crispinus the philosopher (45).

Although we have evidence that Lucilius also treated the themes of these three satires so that Horace may have derived this device of satiric exposition from him, unfortunately our surviving fragments give us no evidence as to whether Lucilius himself or some reporter acting dramatically as his spokesman reported the words and arguments of the master. There is just one fragment which seems slightly to favor the latter conclusion in the case of a Lucilian satire on the Stoic paradox that all are mad except the sage. Here fragment 1007 seems to refer to the beard of the Stoic philosopher, who is addressed in the second person (neque barbam inmiseris istam) and who might in consequence be regarded as the speaker of a Stoic discourse, mocked by the poet Lucilius as Damasippus was by Horace.

The line which separates the ὑπομνήματα from the ἀπομνημονεύματα is a tenuous one. In general the genres are pretty closely related. The former term seems to correspond to the Latin *Commentarii* and to mean essentially what we in English call memoranda, while the latter means what is written down from memory. ὑπομνήματα[48] are thus virtually the notebooks of writers and philosophers, not designed for publication until they have been revised. It is probable that Horace kept such a notebook from *sat.* 1, 4, 36:

> et quodcumque semel chartis inleverit, omnis
> gestiet a furno redeuntis scire lacuque,
> et pueros et anus.

and from 1, 4, 137 taken in connection with the procedure of ethical observation instilled by Horace's father:

> haec ego mecum
> conpressis agito labris; ubi quid datur oti
> inludo chartis.

Similarly in *sat.* 2, 1, 6 Horace declares that he cannot sleep if he does not write.

It is clear that Lucilius often stopped at this crude preliminary stage of composition and entirely disregarded revision, or even substituted dictation to a slave for the writing of first drafts of his satires. Hence the pages of Lucilius are, as Horace declares, a faithful transcript of his life, *sat.* 2, 1, 30 ff.:

> ille velut fidis arcana sodalibus olim
> credebat libris, neque si male cesserat, usquam
> decurrens alio, neque si bene; quo fit ut omnis
> votiva pateat veluti descripta tabella
> vita senis.

In fragment 1138, a passage which probably recounts Scipio's meeting with a bore, Lucilius uses the word *dicto* of his method of literary composition:

> Cornelius Publius noster Scipiadas, dicto.

Certain of the anecdotic satires of Lucilius and Horace, though not ὑπομνήματα in the strict sense of the word, suggest kinship to this form in view of the strong personal flavor which pervades their narrative. In addition they were perhaps not originally intended for general publication. Here we may mention Lucilius' journey to the Sicilian straits, *sat.* 3, and Horace's paraphrase, the better-known journey to Brundisium.[49] Both narratives were told by the poets themselves and suggest the keeping of an itinerary. Of similar biographical interest and likewise told in the first person is the satire of Horace 1, 6, in which he recounts the circumstances of his introduction to Maecenas. In fragments 1009, 1010, 1011 Lucilius recounts his own introduction to a new patron, possibly Sempronius Tudianus, the victor of the Istrian war.[50] It is clear that the note of personal confession which plays such an important rôle in Lucilian and Horatian satire found apt expression in such forms.

Finally it may be noted that in Horace's *satire* 2,4 we have a satire which structurally shows how tenuous is the line which separates the ὑπομνήματα from the ἀπομνημονεύματα. Horace meets Catius on the street who is hurrying home to commit to writing the gastronomic precepts of an anonymous teacher. He then rehearses these precepts at the request of Horace. It follows that this satire is a ὑπόμνημα, based on mnemonic devices, as far as Catius is concerned, but it is also an ἀπομνημόνευμα like 2, 2; 2, 3; 2, 7, in the sense that Catius recounts the teachings of his master.

We may now turn to the χρεία, a form closely related to those we have just mentioned, but far more influential in disseminating the serious and serio-comic teachings of the Greek philosophers and of the Roman satirists.

Our fullest definition of the χρεία is found in Charisius (Keil, *gram. lat.* 6, p. 273, cf. p. 251): Chria est dicti vel facti praecipua memoratio. The grammarian then proceeds to divide the verbal *chria* into four classes, viz., *propositiva*, involving a proposition; *percunctativa*, or interrogative; *refutativa*, in rebuttal ; fourth, *demonstrativa*, or direct. The definition further quotes examples from the Cynic heroes, Diogenes, Antisthenes, and Cato the censor. This definition is in substantial agreement with that of Hermogenes, *Progymnasmata* 3: χρεία ἐστὶν ἀπομνημόνευμα λόγου τινὸς ἢ πράξεως ἢ συναμφοτέρου, σύντομον ἔχον δήλωσιν, ὡς ἐπὶ τὸ πλεῖστον χρησίμου τινὸς ἕνεκα. The χρεία, therefore, to quote Lejay:[51] est donc un fait significatif, un mot piquant ou sentencieux. La chrie diffère de la maxime (γνώμη) en ce qu'elle est particularisée à une circonstance donnée et a un personnage déterminé. Elle est spirituelle ou ingénieuse. Elle s'encadre dans un recit qui l'explique. Elle comporte une mise en oeuvre plus ou moins dévelopée. Hermogène remarque qu'elle diffère du mémorable par sa brièveté. Cependant elle peut être un court narration ordonné en vue du mot ou du geste de la fin. Les satires septième et huitième du premier livre d'Horace peuvent être comparées aux chries de l'école. The definition of Theon is similar, *Prog.* 6: χρεία ἐστὶ σύντομος ἀπόφρασις ἢ πρᾶξις μετ' εὐστοχίας ἀναφερομένη εἴς τι ὡρισμένον πρόσωπον.

The χρεία was so called because of its utilitarian intent. Hence it is especially associated with the more practical sects of Greek philosophy, notably with the Cynics and the Stoics. It exists, however, as early as the age of the sophists, but it obtains its widest popularity in the Hellenistic period and among the Romans. Among the latter people it is first associated with the name of Cato the censor.

In Greece the χρεία was originally oral. It was thought out in advance, a sort of prepared improvisation designed to lead on the hearer adroitly to the focal point of expression, to employ a convenient metaphor. Hence it was especially common in the meetings between the masters of the rival schools. Thus in one example given by Charisius, Antisthenes is opposed to Aristippus; Aristotle is matched against Diogenes the Cynic.[52] As a weapon admirably adapted to the methods of the popular preacher, the χρεία was virtually endemic in the Cynic and Stoic philosophy. Thus collections of χρεῖαι are attributed to Metrocles, a pupil of Crates, to Persaeus, a pupil of Zeno, to Aristo of Chios, to Cleanthes, and to Hecaton.

The χρεία is not, however, the exclusive weapon of the Cynics and Stoics.[53] On the contrary we find philosophers from all the schools represented by such instructive anecdotes. Nor do the so-called parodic χρεῖαι[54] in which courtesans and parasites appear by the side of philosophers really constitute a distinct genre.   Since all χρεῖαι by their mixture of seriousness and humor constitute a species of τὸ σπουδαιογέλοιον this type differs from the more strictly scholastic χρεῖαι in degree rather than in kind.

The χρεία also reached back into the past for its scenes, actions, and *dramatis personae*.   We have χρεῖαι associated with the pre-Socratic philosophers, with the seven wise men, with Anarchasis and with Aesop.   We have also the so-called Laconian χρεῖαι of whose nature we may form some idea from Plutarch's collection of ἀποφθέγματα Λακωνικά and ἀποφθέγματα Λακαινῶν.   The greatest collection of χρεῖαι which has come down to us from antiquity is the *Gnomologium Vaticanum,*[55] a vast treasure house of commonplaces, associated not only with philosophers, but also with poets, orators, statesmen, and kings.

In Rome the χρεῖαι enjoyed great popularity.   Cato the censor both collected and was the author of such anecdotes. We hear of collections of the *facete dicta* of Cicero made by Tiro, Trebonius, and Furius Bibaculus; also of collections made by Cato the younger, Caesar, and Melissus.   The *fabellae* of Domitius· Marsus, a member of the circle of Maecenas, are evidently of similar nature.   The collection of *ineptiae* of Melissus, the freedman of Maecenas, and the librarian of the portico of Octavia, is said to have compromised 150 books.[56] Moreover it is clear from the testimony of Seneca and Quintilian that the χρεία played an important part in the education of the young. Thus Seneca *ep.* 33 says: Nec dubito, quin multum conferant rudibus adhuc et extrinsecus auscultantibus.   Facilius enim singula insidunt circumscripta et carminis modo inclusa. Ideo pueris et sententias ediscendas damus et has quas Graeci chrias vocant, quia complecti illas puerilis animus potest, qui plus adhuc non capit.   Certi profectus viro captare flosculos turpe est; dicat ista, non teneat.   So Quintilian *Inst.* 1, 9, 3 gives the χρεία a high place among the exercises of the *grammaticus.*

From what has been said it is evident that there were at the disposal of the Roman satirists, Lucilius and Horace, collections of Chreia-like anecdotes, both Greek and Roman.   Lucilius can hardly have been unacquainted with the collections of Cato, and Horace must as a member of the circle of Maecenas have had at his disposal such collections as those of Domitius Marsus and Melissus. It is possible that some of the brief anecdotes of the Greek philosophers which these satirists employ for purposes of moral instruction were drawn from such handbooks. It seems certain that the satirists themselves invented others, or transformed past or contemporary incidents into satiric χρεῖαι of their own, designed to give concrete point to their comments on contemporary life. It is, in fact, difficult to exaggerate the influence of this form upon Roman satire. However, it is beyond the scope of this work to give a complete collection of the χρεῖαι, embedded in the works of Lucilius and Horace. It will be sufficient to cite a few of the more striking examples.

In the first place we have certain χρεῖαι clearly of Greek origin. Thus Lucilius in fragment 742 alludes to a χρεία involving Aristippus and Dionysius of Syracuse. Fragments 754 and 755 seem to imply an account of Polemon's conversion by Xenocrates and his succession to the headship of the academy, a χρεία also found in Horace's *sat.* 2, 3, 250–257. In the pages of Horace also several examples of such Hellenistic χρεῖαι may be detected. Thus in the same satire 2, 3, 99–102 we have a χρεία from the life of Aristippus who orders his slaves to leave the gold in the midst of the Libyan desert. In fact this satire, as we shall see later[57] contains no less than eleven passages belonging to the general category of Cynic commonplaces.

On the other hand the Romans were quick to invent and collect χρεῖαι of their own. Both Lucilius and Horace afford illustrations. Thus the Lucilian fragment 1235 is a χρεία applied to a Roman *sapiens*, Laelius *sophos*, who praises the sorrel to the discomfiture of the gluttons. Another χρεία is that in which the same Laelius as a Stoic advocate of plain living and high thinking is confronted with the glutton Gallonius, who has never dined well in his life though he has squandered his whole substance on a tiny shrimp and a huge sturgeon (fragment 1238). So also in fragment 1316 Lucilius refers to *Valeri sententia dia*, possibly an allusion to the *lex Tappula* of *Valerius Valentinus*.[58] If Cichorius is correct[59]—and the nature of the surviving fragments of the book seems to confirm his inference—book 11 of

Lucilius contained a collection of short χρεία-like anecdotes of well-known contemporaries of the Scipionic period. Fragment 411 seems to suggest a clear consciousness in the satirist's mind of a definition of the form corresponding to that quoted above from Charisius:

conicere in versus dictum praeconis volebam Grani.

The confrontation of two speakers in several of these fragments is a feature especially common in the χρεία. Again, as we shall see later,[60] the story of the discomforture of Albucius, the Hellenomaniac by Scaevola is clearly a somewhat longer χρεία or a χρεία embedded in a longer Lucilian satire.

In Horace the anecdote of Rupilius Rex, *sat.* 1, 7 and the story of Canidia and the witches on the Esquiline *sat.* 1, 8 are both χρεῖαι from contemporary life quite analogous to the Lucilian practice.[61]

The success of the χρεία is grounded on the love of men in all countries and all ages for a good story. No wonder, then, that it is one of the strongest weapons in the whole panoply of the Greek philosophers, and the Roman satirists, their successors. As Cicero says in the *de oratore* 2, 328: sed et festivitatem habet narratio distincta personis et interpuncta sermonibus. So also Pliny *epist.* 5, 81: homines . . . qui sermunculis etiam fabellisque ducentur.

Let us turn next to the συμπόσιον and the δεῖπνον[62] and trace in outline the influence of these forms upon Lucilius. Like so many literary forms of the mirth-loving Hellenistic period these forms were originally employed for serious purposes by Xenophon, Plato, and Aristotle. Such forms inevitably occupy a very important place in the *sermo*, a genre modelled on actual oral discourse, for nowhere is true conversation freer and more inspired than at the table. As Cicero says, *ad Fam.* 9, 24, 3: sermone familiari, qui est in conviviis dulcissimus, ut sapientius nostri quam Graeci: illi συμπόσια aut σύνδειπνα, id est, conpotationes aut concenationes; nos convivia, quod tum maxime simul vivitur.

Hence with the Hellenistic period, when the creative impulse in philosophy was spent, and when the dialogue, the form indis-

solubly attached to Greek philosophical teaching from the days
of Socrates, Plato, and Aristotle had yielded to the letter, the
symposium still held its own as an independent genre, because
it had its roots in the daily life of the Greek people, and especial-
ly in the habits of philosophic schools to discuss the problems of
philosophy at the table. The Diadochoi in their desire to honor
philosophy furnished subventions for such gatherings,[63] or
invited the philosophers and men of learning to their tables
where they were expected to show their wit. Hence on the
model of what was originally at Athens the voluntary and
informal meal of the master and his disciples, the literary and
philosophic symposium became an established institution at
Alexandria, Pergamum, and elsewhere. The existence of such
institutions inevitably reacted upon the literature of the period.
Technical discussions, pedantry, and senseless revelry took the
place of the high seriousness and sparkling humor which marked
the earlier symposia in life as well as in letters.

Under these circumstances the rise of the parodic δεῖπνα was
natural. These are lively descriptions of delicious banquets,
often with parodies of Homeric verses. They are a natural
development from the descriptions of banquets common in
comedy from the days of Epicharmus. We can form a good idea
of the nature of this genre from the δειπνοσοφισταί of Athenaeus
who has quoted whole pages of such poems. A poem by Matron
of Petara, a contemporary of Alexander the Great, was called
δεῖπνον 'Αττικόν.[64] This began with a parody on the first line of
the Odyssey: Δεῖπνα μοι ἔννεπε, Μοῦσα, πολύτροφα καὶ μάλα πολλά.

Of more serious nature are the συμπόσια proper.[66] Aristo-
xenus of Tarentum wrote a work called σύμμικτά συμποτικά,
in which he elucidated problems of musical theory.[67] From such
works the συμπόσια are continued in a closely wrought tradition
by the works of the Peripatetics Hieronymus of Rhodes and
Prytanis, the Symposium of Epicurus, the συμποτικοὶ διάλογοι of
the Stoic Persaeus, the banqueting scenes of Menippus of
Gadara, the Cena Trimalchionis of Petronius, the symposium of
Lucian, the banquet of the seven wise men, the συμποσιακὰ
προβλήματα of Plutarch, and the δειπνοσοφισταί of Athenaeus.

The symposium of the Tarentine Heracleides who lived
about 160 B.C.[68] discussed questions of diet from the point of

view of a physician of the empirical school. Thus the effects of onions, shell fish, and eggs on the human body was considered;[69] whether warm or cold water should be taken after eating figs.[70] One was advised against drinking on an empty stomach. It is worth noticing that in a satire of Lucilius, fragment 1076, the endive is spoken of as causing urination; the context appears to refer to a camp carouse.

The symposium of Epicurus[71] is strongly colored by the personality of the master. It has no dramatic *mise-èn-scene*, for the place is assumed to be the famous garden of the school. We plunge at once into the discussion. The questions discussed were such as were traditional in the Epicurean school; on digestion, on apparitions in fever, on the warming strength of wine, on cohabitation, and above all on the doctrine of the atoms. Epicurus is represented as an old man surrounded by youths. It is interesting to notice in this connection that an *ephebus* appears in the philosophers' banquet of Lucilius, and that the atomic doctrine of the Epicureans is assailed in fragment 753.

With the Stoics the symposium was not a favorite form. The institution played only a minor part in the life of the school, and certain principles of Stoicism were opposed to the symposium, as for instance, the tradition to discuss erotic subjects or wine at the symposium.

On Roman soil the symposium and δεῖπνον received a friendly reception. In the age of the Scipios and the Gracchi luxury at the table was one of the most striking features of the change in manners and morals which appeared at Rome as the most immediate result of the Macedonian wars. Under the influence of Greek and oriental standards, gluttony was rapidly becoming a Roman vice. This we can see by the unsuccessful efforts at sumptuary legislation. Lucilius himself, fragment 1172, mentions the *Fanni centussis misellus*. This law of Fannius passed in 161 B.C. provided (according to Gellius 2, 24, 3) that at the *ludi Romani*, *ludi plebeii*, and certain other festivals 100 asses a day might be spent on meals, and on ten other days in each month a total of 300 asses; on all other days only 10 asses a day. This law was apparently strictly observed by the stingy host of the *cena rustica* in Lucilius' fifth book, as we may see from Marx's note on fragment 193, for the limited expenditures on cabbage, spelt, and wine.

In short there was no more worthy object for frank and biting social satire than table luxury, and Lucilius returns to the attack on this vice again and again, sometimes with scenes clearly borrowed from contemporary life, sometimes in words that suggest Greek influences. Let us briefly indicate the general content of these satires on banquets and the related satires of the art of cooking.

In the fourth book Lucilius in assailing the luxury of the rich lays special stress on the luxury of the table, as we may see from fragments 165, 166, 167, 169, 171, 172 (and possibly here belong *dubia* 1315 and 1150). In the fifth book Lucilius assails a rustic dinner, given by a miserly host, and enumerates many of the simple dishes (fragments 192, 193, 194, possibly 137 and 189, 195, 196, 197, 198, 200, 201, 202 ff.).[72] Books 13 and 14 contain many lines that apparently refer to the banquet. In book 13, fragments 438, 440, 442, 443, 1368(?) 445, 446; in book 14 fragments 454, 455, 456 seem to refer to a *cena*. In book 20 we have a satire on a banquet probably given by the *praeco* Granius, which was the original of Horace's *satire* 2, 8, the banquet of Nasidienus.[73] Horace was also probably familiar with the satire in book 13, for he seems to employ certain situations similar to those indicated in 447, 448, 449, 450 and 451.[74] The banquet of the philosophers described by Lucilius in *satire* 28, 2 affords striking proof of the influence of the Greek[75] symposia upon the satires of Lucilius. Here belong the following fragments: 751, 752, 753, 754, 755, 757, 758, 759, 760, 762, 763. Besides these extended sequences we have a number of scattering fragments, which probably used the banquet or incidents in connection with the banquet frequently for illustrations, just as in Horace we find the banquet frequently serving a similar purpose. Here we may include 665, 1156, 1201, 1205, 1212, 1235, 1250, 1370.

The influence of this Hellenistic form upon the satires of Lucilius is therefore strongly marked. This is natural when we consider that in the Scipionic period the simpler features of the

Roman banquet were being transformed under the influence of the Greek δεῖπνον and συμπόσιον.

The fable is one of the most popular means of conveying moral instruction under cover of entertainment.[76] By definition therefore it falls under the broad category of the τὸ σπουδαιογέλοιον. The fable, αἶνος, μῦθος, λόγος, ἀπόλογος, as we may see from the etymology of its earliest name αἶνος, is a story of didactic character. Hesiod (op. 202 ff.) and Archilochus (fr. 86) especially understand by that term a story of the animal world. In point of fact, however, no sharp line can be drawn between the fable and the short crisp jests, tales, anecdotes, folk-lore, riddles and other similar forms used in the Orient and in Ionia for the amusement and instruction of the idle people in the home or in the market place. All such narratives were originally in prose, but comparatively early came their formulation in iambic trimeters or choliambics, the metrical form which we find in the later collections of Phaedrus and Babrius.

Such stories naturally wander from people to people. Greek fables wander to the Romans, Germans and Indians, and on the other hand the Greeks draw widely from the stores of other lands. Thus many Greek fables come from Egypt, India, Phrygia, Caria, spread by slaves or professional story tellers. In time collections are made. The sophists and rhetoricians[77] finally make such tales an instrument of elementary instruction, carefully classifying their species and authors. The earliest collection of such fables and humorous anecdotes is associated with the name of Aesop.[78]

By its nature the fable, as the Cynics were quick to see, was an instrument especially well adapted to the goal of the τὸ σπουδαιογέλοιον. If one would live in accordance with nature the animals are his best guides, and as a corollary will arise the interest of the Cynics in all stories concerning animals. Agathias in the Palatine Anthology, Chapter 16, Appendix Planudea, 332, 3–8 has an interesting characterization of Aesop's pleasant method of instruction in contrast to the disciplinary theory of the seven wise men, a clear recognition of the fable as falling under the category of τὸ σπουδαιογέλοιον:

Κεῖνοι μὲν ἀνάγκην
ἔμβαλον, οὐ πειθώ, φθέγμασι τοῖς σφετέροις,

ὃς δὲ σοφοῖς μύθοις καὶ πλάσμασι καίρια λέξας,
παίζων ἐν σπουδῇ, πείσει· ἔχε φροντίων.
φευκτὸν δ' ἡ τρηχεῖα παραίνεσις· ἡ Σαμίου δὲ
τὸ γλυκὺ τοῦ μύθου καλὸν ἔχει δέλεαρ.

In recognition of this traditional two-fold aspect of the fable
Phaedrus says in the prologue 3 ff.:

> duplex libelli dos est; quod risum movet
> et quod prudenti vitam consilio monet.

The Cynics were inevitably attracted also to the simple figure
of Aesop, a barbarian and a slave, and to that of his Scythian
comrade Anacharsis. Both approximate, or perhaps we should
rather say were made approximate, to the Cynic conception of
the natural man. Socrates, a real Cynic hero had shown much
interest in the μῦθοι Αἰσώπειοι and the Cynics, the *Socratici
par excellence* followed him.[79]

In the Alexandrian era also the fable attained wide popu-
larity. Thus Demetrius of Phalerum made a collection of Aeso-
pia, whose influence upon Callimachus is manifest. In fact the
fable now blended so naturally with the philosophic χρεία that
the line of demarcation between them is a tenuous one. To the
original animal fables were added anecdotes of philosophers,
such for instance as we find in Phaedrus *apl.* 25. Aesop and
Anacharsis are, so to speak, cynicized and classed with the
seven wise men.

The fable, although originally written in prose, employs
various metrical forms. Of these the earliest was the iambic
trimeter. The use of the hexameter is comparatively late; the
use of the pentameter occasional.[80] As the iambic trimeter was
the prevailing metre, it is clear that Phaedrus must have had
Greek metrical predecessors in this metre even though they
have not come down to us.

In Roman times the fable seems to have become one of the
earliest elements in satire. Ennius[81] tells the story of the tufted
lark in the wheat field, and we have other indications of the
presence of fables in his satire.

In Lucilius the signs of the employment of the fable are
both more numerous and more certain. The longest fable is that
of the sick lion and the fox found in a satire of book 30, frag-
ments 980–989. It is possible that fragment 534 in book 16 is

from a fable in which the ram appears. In fragment 954 the simile of the hired mourners, imitated by Horace in the *Ars Poetica* 431 seems to be an allusion to the fable of Aesop 369 ed. Halm. In fragment 561, from book 19, which contained a satire on αἰσχροκέρδεια of which Horace's satire 1, 1 is a counterpiece, we have the fable of the thrifty ant (Aesop 295, Halm). Finally in book 5, fragments 208, 213 it seems natural to compare the fable of the fox and the weasel told in Horace's *epistle* 1, 7, 29. In fragment 669 we may have an allusion to the fable of the ass in the lion's skin, found also in Horace *sat.* 1, 6, 22 and 2, 1, 64.

In Horace we find the fable used even more widely. Besides the passages just mentioned Horace has the fable of the frog and the ox in *satires* 2, 3, 314-end; the fable of the city mouse and the country mouse in 2, 6, 79–117; perhaps *satire* 2, 1, 77 contains an allusion to the viper and the file; while *satire* 2, 3, 186 is the fable of the fox who imitated the lion.[82]

In the production of the fable as an independent genre in Latin we find traces of satiric influence.[83] Here we have narrations of two types. Thus Phaedrus continues the Aesopic tradition of the apologue in the proper sense of the word, giving speech to animals, plants, mountains and inanimate objects. But after the second book he adds to these apologues, moralizing anecdotes in which men, gods, and personified abstractions speak. He has, then as he boasts in prologue 3, 38, extended the domain of the fable. But the extension is drawn principally from the types of anecdotes employed by the satirists to impart moral instruction. His procedure may in fact be illustrated by the discourse of Stertinius in Horace *sat.* 2, 3 which is full of such anecdotes.

The mime, μῖμος,[84] as its name implies is an imitation of life, the actual definition of Theophrastus:[85] μῖμός ἐστιν μίμησις βίου. The mime is in essence a photographically accurate reproduction in character and language of a typical scene (or scenes) of every day life in the form of a short monologue or dialogue. Such scenes were presented as interludes either at banquets or at contests in the orchestra or stadium. They were individually recited by an actor in costume.

It is not possible to trace the historical development of the mime here even in summary. Its beginnings are associated rather with Sicily than with old Greece. Here its earliest representative, if we exclude from consideration Epicharmus (550–460 B.C.), whose comedies of droll situations and character types paved the way for the mime,[86] is Sophron.

Sophron, a younger contemporary of Epicharmus, is the real founder of the mime as a literary genre. His mimes were written in prose and in the Doric dialect. They are said to have been greatly admired by Plato. Like Epicharmus he also wrote parodies of myths. His language was popular. His influence upon later literature was very strong especially upon Theocritus, whose second and fifteenth idylls are imitations of Sophron. Indeed, we may fairly say that in Sophron the form of prose conversation first attained the dignity of an independent literary form. The relation of the mime with the Socratic dialogue is, therefore, obvious, and so indirectly its influence upon the Roman *sermones* or *satura*.

Such a form at once acquired a new importance in the Hellenistic age, so prone to miniature forms, to realism, and as fearful of the high seriousness of the fifth century, as we are today of the earnestness of the Victorian period. Like the fable the mime is from its very nature a form allied to the conception of the τὸ σπουδαιογέλοιον. Hellenistic and subsequent literary criticism was quick to recognize this fact,[87] and to call the writers of mimes by the epithets of τερπνός, φιλητός, and βιωφελής.

In this period, therefore, the mime became the favorite dramatic form. It consisted sometimes of episodic scenes in monologues or dialogues, sometimes of more extended compositions (ὑποθέσεις), such as we find at Rome from the period of Sulla on. Their existence in Greece before 300 B.C. is attested by an inscription on a terra cotta lamp found at the foot of the Athenian Acropolis representing three actors of mimes.[88]

Only the mimes of Theocritus and of Herondas are fully preserved. These are designed, as their verse measures show, for recitation and fall into scenes from city and from country life. The style of the mime, which in Sophron had been a mixture of prose and popular dialect forms, was in general transformed by Theocritus and Herondas.

The *mimiambi* of Herondas are the invention of the Hellenistic period. They employ the iambic and choliambic metres to give a vivid and realistic picture of the life of the Hellenistic city. The discovery of eight mimes of Herondas in 1890 gave us our first detailed acquaintance with this form.[89] Herondas lived about the middle of the third century under king Ptolemy Euergetes. He was of Doric origin. His mimes were written in choliambics, and he frankly asserts his allegiance to Hipponax (8, 78 ff.), from whom he borrows his Ionic dialect. These mimes frequently represent the more sensual aspects of the life of the Hellenistic city states with such types as the procuress, whoremonger, or sensual wife. Herondas was well known to the Romans of the imperial epoch and had already been imitated in the time of Sulla by Gaius Mattius. Besides these Roman imitations of individual scenes or παίγνια, there were more extended dramatic mimes, as we may infer from the literary mimes of Laberius and Publilius Syrus, composed in the period of Sulla and the years following his dictatorship. Having thus briefly outlined the development of the mime up to the time of its arrival on Roman soil we may now consider its subsequent development and its relation to the satires of Lucilius and Horace.[90]

The oldest evidence for the existence of the mime at Rome is found in a notice of Festus, p. 326, ed. Mueller, where we are told that at the first celebration of the *ludi Appollinares* in 212 B.C. an old freedman, probably a Greek, performed a dance in the nature of a mime to the accompaniment of the flute. From 173 B.C. similar dances of women were celebrated at the Floralia.[91] The burial inscription of an agreeable mime, Protogenes, who gave the people much satisfaction by his jests dates from the middle of the second century B.C.[92] So also Cicero in the *de oratore* 2, 250, whose dramatic date is 91 B.C., makes Crassus speak of an old mime of comic nature entitled the guardian, *Tutor*. The libel suits of Accius and Lucilius against an actor of mimes have already been considered.[93] Such incidents show that at this period the mime attempted to revive direct verbal assaults in the spirit of Naevius. In 115 B.C. the censors banished the lower forms of scenic productions, probably including the mime, from Rome. The grounds for this decision were partly perhaps, the libellous attacks employed by the mime, but principally because the tone of the mime was regarded as inimical to public morals.[94]

We have already seen that both Cicero and Horace looked on the unrestrained laughter and the improvisatory style of the mime with disapproval. Horace in particular in *sat.* 1, 10, 3[95] seems to imply that Lucilius, recreant to the higher standards of the Old Comedy, sinks to the level of the mime; his language is a sort of *obscenitas*; his humor lacks the true principle of restraint. These are the later refinements of the more discriminating Ciceronian and Augustan epochs. Nevertheless, it seems probable that Lucilius felt an aesthetic and ethical difference between the type of humor employed in his satires and that bandied about on the stage by the *mimi*. Such a difference would rest mainly upon the stronger consciousness of reforming purpose, which Lucilius associated with his satires. As we have seen,[96] fragments 899 and 1344 afford some slight confirmation for this view.

Nevertheless, there is something to be said for Horace's quasi-assimilation of Lucilian satire with the mime. In fact there seems some ground for believing that certain general characteristics of satire were influenced by the mime. Nor is this an unreasonable supposition in view of the early Academic and Peripatetic leaning of Lucilius and the high esteem in which the mime was held by Aristotle and Theophrastus.

In the first place, as the mime was an imitation of life in the broadest sense of the word, we have an extraordinary number of types of human character and of professional life. Not only is this number of types much larger than that employed in the New Comedy with its plots of intrigue, but also a much lower level of society is drawn upon. This power of minute delineation of character first endeared the mime to Plato, and led to the current association of Plato's dialogues with the mimes of Sophron. We find an echo of such admiration for the power of characterization in Volcatius Sedigitus, who assigns the palm in this respect to Caecilius.[97]

Caecilio palmam Statio do mimico.

The question of how far Lucilius was influenced by such popular methods of character delineation does not admit of a satisfactory answer in view of the paucity of the fragments alike of the satirist and the mime. There are, however, four types of character that may be considered in this connection:[98] the *sannio*, the *stupidus*, the *scurra*, and the *parasite*. Now the first type is one who makes amusement by his grimaces. Servilius Balatro, with his pretended consolations and his pleasantries at the dinner of Nasidienus (Horace *sat.* 2, 8, 64–77, 83) has something of the *sannio* about him. The *stupidus* is often the unhappy lover, beaten and content as in Horace *sat.* 1, 2, 64–67, and 2, 3, 259. But the excluded lover is a type which also occurs in Lucilius,[99] who introduces this type from the Eunuchus of Terence just as Horace does. Moreover in the *sermo plebeius* the *stupidus* is often called *baro*, a word which we find in Lucilius fragment 1121:

> baronum ac rupicum squarrosa, incondita rostra.

evidently a passage satirizing shaggy, bearded, and unkempt rustics, perhaps even in contrast with the urbane appearance of Scipio and his circle, who, as we know, were the first Romans to shave daily. Lucilius, moreover, explicitly mentions a *scurra* Caelius who is a *conlusor* of Gallonius, because he played ball with him, and judging from the word play on *ludet* and *eludet* went through at the same time some trick or other typical of the *scurra*. In the third satire of Lucilius fragments 117–122, as we shall see later,[100] we have evidence of a contest between two *scurrae* at Capua, which we may compare to that between Sarmentus and Cicirrus in Horace *sat.* 1, 5, 51–70. Moreover, if we accept the note of Festus p. 294, 26M found in Marx's commentary on fragment 1138 we may assume that Lucilius recorded an adventure of Scipio with a *scurra*. This adventure is an earlier analogue of Horace's encounter with the bore *sat.* 1, 9.[101]

The parasite, a type from the comedy of Epicharmus, appears as early as Ennius, in Latin literature,[102] and reappears in Lucilius. Thus in fragment 716 from book 27 we have the cook compared to the parasite in a satire upon the Cynic theme of plain living which is parallel to Horace's *sat.* 2, 2. Similarly in fragment 718 from the same satire the humorous formation *cibicida* (food-slayer) on the model of *parricida* seems to refer to the parasite. The word is perhaps influenced also by such comic Greek formations as σιτόκουρος found in Athenaeus 6, 248a and the Greek comic fragments.

Moreover, it is a fair inference that the nice classification of types of character in the *Ethics* of Aristotle owes much to the ethological coloring of the mime. Aristotle's observations are hardly based on first hand acquaintance with whoremongers, procuresses, gamblers, thieves, highwaymen, misers of various types, and cuminsplitters. This sphere is the domain of Sophron Herondas, and the later Greek and Roman writers of the mimic ethology.[103] Nevertheless Aristotle's knowledge of these classes is clear from the popular character of his designations for many of the types of the *comédie humaine*. Thus Aristotle[104] cites soothsayers and physicians as types of boasters, ἀλάζονες. Now the physician appears as a type in the Laconian mime.[105] So also later in Pomponius we have a *medicus*, while Novius has a mime entitled *medica*. Laberius writes an *augur* while an Atellana of Pomponius is called *haruspex*. It seems clear, therefore, that Aristotle had studied the mimic ethology and that this ethology was not without influence on the Roman comic genres.

Upon the mind of Theophrastus, Aristotle's successor, the methods of character delineation employed in the mime left an even greater impress, as is proved by the publication of his χαρακτῆρες, types of character. This work was published either in 319 B.C. or earlier. Since Menander was still an *ephebus* at this period it seems impossible to believe that the work was influenced by his comedies. We must rather hold that the young poet was attracted to Theophrastus then in middle life by the reputation of the philosopher in ethics. Moreover, since Philemon, the oldest poet of the New Comedy, first appeared in 329 B.C., it is clear that in general the Characters of Theophrastus antedate the New Comedy. In the case of a type or two there may be evidence for some slight influence from the New Comedy; but on the whole the New Comedy was rather influenced by the characters of Theophrastus than the reverse. Hence we may believe that the mime is largely responsible for

the strongly developed bent towards the objective delineation
of character whether we meet that tendency in the New Comedy
or in Theophrastus.

But such objective and realistic types are precisely those we
find in the pages of Lucilius and Horace. Sometimes these
types are made concrete by the use of proper names, sometimes
they are only designated by the generalized type-names of the
miser, glutton, trader, prostitute, and others. And what is
most important, our range of characters is a wide one as in the
mime, not a limited one as in the more restrained and artistic
comedy of Menander. Similarly, Theophrastus reaches or is at
least conscious of this world in his types of the ἀναίσθητος (14),
δυσχερής (19), ἀηδής (20), and ἀνελεύθερος (25). He further shows
his appreciation for the more racy realism of the mime in con-
trast to the more limited New Comedy of the mime: while he
defines Comedy merely as the imitation of life, he says the μῖμος
ἐστιν μίμησις βίου τά τε συγκεχωρημένα καὶ ἀσυγχώρητα περιέχων.
Theophrastus, also in the free use of slang, proverbs, and popu-
lar idioms is on entire harmony with the diction of the mime.
But this is the characteristic pre-eminently of the diction of
Lucilius—and to a much more limited extent of Horace also, as
this whole study will show. It would be absurd to refer these
characteristic features of satiric diction exclusively to the
mime, but it would be equally dangerous to exclude this influ-
ence in view of the proved connections of Lucilius with Panae-
tius and Clitomachus, and the evidence of his wide acquaintance
with rhetorical theories in relation to the most important genres
of the Hellenistic and Roman literary world. Moreover, the
mime and other popular forms of improvisation were given
literary definition and a somewhat more finished literary form
under Peripatetic influences.[106] How large a part such impro-
visatory theories of satire played in Lucilius' methods of
composition is proved by the criticisms of Horace, and Lucilius'
selection of *schedium* and *ludus* as titles for his work.

Again the Latin writers on rhetoric had a wide interest in the
mime, as we may infer from the full discussion of the mime by
Cicero in the *de oratore* 2, 274–292.[107] In the latter passage,
indeed, and Quintilian 6, 3, 8,[108] *dicacitas scurrilis* and *obscenitas
verborum* are assailed in language which reminds us of Horace's

criticism on Lucilius in *sat.* 1, 10, 1 ff. In the works of Seneca *rhetor* and Seneca the philosopher we have frequent evidence of the influence of the mime. Such rhetorical theories based on the style, content, and tone of the mime belong in all probability to the literary studies of the Peripatetic philosophers.

Finally, the conception of Socratic irony, well-known in the Scipionic circle, not without traces of influence on Lucilius, was even more intensively developed in the rhetorical and critical theories in regard to the mime and even by the mime itself. Thus Timon, the sillographer, declared that the real Socrates was an ἠθολόγος, while Zeno the Epicurean called him an Attic *Scurra*.[109] There is, indeed, some justification for such an attitude in the actual character of Socrates as depicted by Xenophon and by Plato.[110] In the symposium of Xenophon for example (4, 19; 5, 1–9) Socrates ironically praises his own beauty to discomfort Critoboulus who is enamored of his own charms.[111] The language of Socrates also frequently descends to the lower level of the mime. He likes to speak *of* and *to* carpenters, small traders, physicians, bakers, weavers, shoemakers, tanners.[112] In all his life and teaching he illustrates the ideals and methods summed up under τὸ σπουδαιογέλοιον. This ideal was also a fundamental characteristic of the mime for the mimes of Sophron were called in one and the same breath σπουδαῖοι and γελοῖοι. Similarly Hermogenes, the rhetorician,[113] speaks of the Socratic symposium as: πλοκὴ σπουδαῖα καὶ γελοῖα καὶ πρόσωπα καὶ πράγματα. As Reich justly remarks,[114] the great literary accomplishment of Socrates was to secure for humor full civic rights in all the subsequent literary productions of the Greeks. It is due to his life, character, and ironic method of philosophical exposition more than to any other single factor that in the Hellenistic age the temper of the σπουδαιογέλοιος enlivened so many different forms of literary expression. It seems probable therefore that Lucilius, a thorough student of the Academic and Peripatetic learning, in acknowledging his indebtedness as a satirist to the *Socratici carti* (fragment 709) had in mind the relations binding the lighter and more playful side of Socrates to the humor of the mime, as well as the more obvious characteristics of the Socratic irony.[115]

Let us turn next to the influence of the *epistula* or literary epistle in verse upon the satires of Lucilius.[116]

The aphorism quoted by Hirzel:[117] 'Der Brief ist in Prosa was das Lied in der Poesie,' is so far true that the letter is a natural medium for the expression of personal mood. Moreover both the song and the letter were in early Greece addressed to an individual or to a narrow circle rather than designed for the general public. In general conformity with this same tradition the odes of Horace have always an object of address—a person, a god, the Muse, or a personified object. This tradition is as early as Hesiod, Archilochus, and Theognis. In the field of lyric poetry we may regard the lyric in which Alcaeus informs his friend Melanippus of the loss of his shield as a poetic epistle. Its aesthetic form constitutes its main difference from the ordinary epistle.

In the period of the sophistic rhetoric of Gorgias the letter first attained real importance as a dependent literary form. I say dependent because the imaginary or actual letter at the period was still embedded in other narrative forms, such as the histories of Herodotus and Thucydides, and the *Cyropaedia* of Xenophon.

Under the influence of rhetoric, however, the letter shortly appeared as an independent form. It was so employed by Isocrates, Theopompus, and Theocritus of Chios in their advisory (symboleutic) and hortatory (protreptic) writings. In such cases the letter takes the place of oral discourse. In other case professional writing is cloaked under the epistolary form. Thus the engineer Crates wrote to Alexander the Great, and the physician Mnestheus wrote on wine drinking περὶ κωθωνισμοῦ.[118]

In the task of developing the letter as an independent form the influence of Aristotle is of great importance. It was natural that Aristotle, who aimed above all else at the orderly exposition of his theories, should favor the epistle more than Plato. Plato was more enamored of the clash of minds, and enjoyed, therefore, the interruptions and cross questionings, the digressions and the rebuttals in the throes of which the truth is born.

Now the letter differs from the dialogue principally in its compression. It too is a sort of conversation, but it is more easily amenable to rhetorical schematization than the ordinary dialogue. The dialogues of Aristotle, however, had already sloughed off the apparent distinction between the letter and dialogue. Hence it was much easier for Aristotle to pass over into the epistolary form than Plato. So we find him writing a *protrepticus* to King Themison of Cyprus in epistolary form, and probably a περὶ βασιλείας, and a περὶ ἀποικιῶν to Alexander. In Aristotle also both the letter and the dialogue are far on the road leading to the genesis of the technical treatise.

In the Hellenistic period as the result of the decentralization of culture concomitant with the rise of the kingdoms of the Diadochoi the letter as a literary form naturally grew at the expense of the dialogue, whose very existence was so closely bound up with the free life and the free speech of Athens. *Epistolographi* became necessary officials at the courts of the Hellenistic kingdoms. According to Plutarch[119] King Seleucus declared that if people only knew how wearisome the reading and writing of so many letters was, they would not take the crown even if it lay at their feet. The Peripatetics and the immediate students of Aristotle now advanced the form. Thus we hear of a discussion of the text of the physics of Aristotle carried on in epistolary form between Eudemus and Theophrastus.[120] Also we hear of letters of prominent men of this period such as Parmenio, Ptolemy Largus, or Eumenes; nor need we doubt their genuineness; but forgeries were also current. In fact the letter became for a time the dominating literary form. It was thus used to seal friendship or as the medium for philosophical or scientific polemic.

Perhaps the Epicurean sect did more than any other to develop the letter. This was natural because this sect was not heir to the traditional dialogue of the Academy and the Stoa. The Epicurean schools were bound together for scientific ends by an organization which in closeness of intimacy approached a religion. Epicurus himself took care that the scattered communities should not lose this feeling. His letters to the friends in Egypt, in Asia, in Lampsacus, in Mytilene,[121] breathe a spirit in some respects reminiscent of the epistles of St. Paul. We thus gain a picture of the life and activities of the Epicureans resembling that afforded us by the dialogues of the Socratic school.

Far more important, however, for Roman satire is the fact that the letter was one of the forms employed by the humorous popular Cynic and Stoic writers. It was thus used by Crates the Cynic and also by Menippus.

When we turn to Rome we find that letter writing became a Roman literary art under Greek influence and was speedily nationalized as was the dialogue. We know that the epistolary form was used by Spurius Mummius, who appears in Cicero's *de republica* as an intimate friend of Scipio the younger. He received a Stoic education and accompanied his more famous brother to Corinth as a *legatus*. From Corinth he sent a number of poetic epistles to his friends. These did not receive general publicity, but were preserved in the archives of the family where they were read by Cicero, who praises their wit.[122] Lucilius himself clearly used the epistolary form in a satire of the fifth book. This satire is a letter of the convalescent and somewhat hypochondriacal Lucilius to a friend. The subsequent development of the epistle in Roman soil will be more conveniently considered in connection with Horace's epistles.[123]

Of all the forms of popular philosophic exposition employed by the Cynics and the Stoics of the Hellenistic period the διατριβή was probably the most important in its influence on satire. Since the development of this form was in large measure the work of the satiric philosopher, Bion of Borysthenes, it seems best to consider the διατριβή in connection with his life and works. We may thus study as a whole the intricate problem of Bion's influence upon the satires of Lucilius and Horace.

Bion of Borysthenes,[124] (*floruit circa* 280 B.C.) was according to his own account, the son of a freedman, a *salsamentarius*,[125] or saltfish dealer, and a Laconian *hetaera*, named Olympias. His father was later sold again into slavery with his whole family. Bion was purchased by a rhetorician, who, pleased with his ability, left him his whole fortune. Possessed of this fortune Bion went to Athens to study philosophy in the last decades of the fourth century. Apparently his earliest attachment was to the Academy;[126] later he passed over to the Cynics, perhaps studying under Crates; still later he became the pupil of the Cyreniac Theodorus, and finally of Theophrastus. After the completion of his student years Bion became a travelling philosopher, and visited various towns, among others, Rhodes. He was long established at the court of Antigonus Gonatas, where he vigorously defended himself against the jealous attacks of the Stoic philosophers Persaeus and Philonides.[127] In the period following 250 B.C., he delivered lectures on philosophy at Athens. He died after a severe illness about 240 B.C.

Essentially Bion was a Cynic—at times a Cynic of the utmost frankness and bitterness—yet his Cynicism was modified both as regards his life and his philosophy by the strongly hedonistic influence of Cyrenaism.[128] Such an assimilation of tenets apparently diametrically opposed is not an isolated phenomenon at this period. The Cyreniacs Theodorus and Hegesias had in fact made a partial assimilation of Cyreniac hedonism with Cynicism. As the student of Theodorus Bion was naturally inclined to adopt a similar eclecticism. Indeed he even went so far as to count Aristippus among his masters. Bion evidently imbibed his religious scepticism in the schools of Crates and Theodorus. Thus we know that he severely attacked the soothsayers.[129] Indeed the life of Diogenes Laertius, which is in part distinctly hostile, gives him a bad reputation for impiety, asserting that he derived his religious opinions from Theodorus.[130] The strongly satirical element in Bion is illustrated by his famous remark on marriage, that if you marry an ugly woman you will have a punishment (ποινή), and if a handsome one you will have one who is common (κοινή).[131] In similar tone is couched the remark on the three classes of pupils, gold, silver, and bronze; the gold is the class which pays and learns, the silver the class which pays and does not learn, the bronze the class which learns but does not pay.[132] He was probably attracted to Theophrastus by his interest in the delineation of character, a necessary accomplishment for one who was to be the father of the satirical διατριβή.

Although the διατριβή did not begin with Bion,[133] its development is his most striking title to fame. In origin the word διατριβή does not differ from the terms διάλεξις, διάλογος, ὁμιλία. It designates the activity of the master in his school or even the school itself. Thus a work of the historian Theopompus against the school of Plato is called κατὰ τῆς Πλάτωνος διατριβῆς.[134] In point of fact the διατριβή developed historically from the

dialogue as a sort of school declamation. The expositor opposed
to himself an imaginary opponent or opponents, the *adversarius*,
in the place of the clearly conceived speakers of the dramatic
dialogue. As a dialogue transformed into a declamation or
discourse the διατριβή long retained much of the dramatic vigor
of its parent. This is notably true of the διατριβή of Bion.[125] It
was in fact a short disquisition of informal character upon an
ethical theme. Hence the definition of Hermogenes:[126] διατριβή
ἐστι βραχέος διανοήματος ἠθικὴ ἔκθεσις. Such disquisitions were
current under the names of Aristippus, the elder Bryson and
Antisthenes, long before the period of Bion. Following the
precedent set by Antisthenes they were then adopted by the
Cynics and the Stoics. In the Epicurean school, however, they
never gained a footing. We must not forget, however, that,
as in every other genre, the rules for the διατριβή increased in
rigidity with the lapse of time. Consequently the διατριβαί of
the earlier Cynics and Bion resembled more closely the Platonic
dialogues in verve and flexibility than they did their own
scholastic descendents, the διατριβαί of Musonius, Epictetus and
Philo.

Turning now to the διατριβή as conceived by Bion, I wish to
show that certain of his most marked characteristics reveal
similarities in tone, method of delineation, and style with the
sermones of Lucilius and Horace. Hence the selection of this
title on the part of Lucilius can hardly have been an accident;
and that this title had probably certain definite rhetorical
implications from the point of view of humor and style we have
already seen by our study of Panaetius *de sermone*,[127] and the
Ciceronian theory of the relations of the liberal jest to the
plain style. A detailed analysis and comparison of the critical
satires of Lucilius and Horace will tend still further to corro-
borate this point of view. In fact I am inclined to lay greater
weight on this more general evidence of spiritual kinship
between the Greek satirist and the two great Roman satirists
than upon any evidence laboriously reconstructed to prove
similarity of theme. Here our problem is well-nigh insoluble.
At best we can only point out the general indications of the
direction in which the trail seems to run, for we are comparing
the fragmentary remains of Bion as far as they can be recon-

structed from the life of Diogenes Laertius, certain passages
in Plutarch and other ancient *testimonia*, and the remains of
his successor and *epitomator* Teles, with the fragments of
Lucilius. Yet even here I shall hope to adduce some evidence
both internal and external pointing to the possible influence of
Bionean themes upon Lucilius. I must, however, entirely
disclaim any effort to prove that the διατριβαί of Bion are the
exclusive or even the central source of Lucilian satire. On the
contrary I am in essential accord with the point of view which
regards Lucilius as the *inventor* or εὑρετής of satire. The object
of this chapter therefore is rather to show that Lucilian satire
is the product of a highly sophisticated Hellenistic environment
combined with the Italic *penchant* for frank, vigorous, dramatic
expression. Recognizing, therefore, the inevitable limitations
of our problem, let us first consider the evidence regarding
similarity of tone, method of delineation, and style which seems
to point to some spiritual relationship between the διατριβαί
of Bion and the satires of Lucilius and Horace.

The tone of the διατριβαί of Bion affords admirable examples
of the tone of the τὸ σπουδαιογέλοιον. Thus in the letter to
Antigonus Gnatas, in which Bion derides the claims of good
birth by acknowledging and even exaggerating all the charges of
his opponents in regard to his humble origin, we have a striking
example of the favorite Cynic mixture of seriousness and humor.
Such ironical self-depreciation is a mask for the assertion that a
man must be valued for his own inherent worth. So Sto-
baeus:[138] οὕτως οὖν καὶ ἐπὶ τῶν φίλων ἐξέταξε οὐ πόθεν εἰσὶν ἀλλὰ
τίνες. We have here in fact the fundamental elements of the
Cynic commonplace of εὐγένεια or noble birth, a commonplace
which recurs in the satires of Lucilius, Horace, and Juvenal.[139]

The same ironical tone marks Bion's attitude even towards
death itself, as we may infer from the jest:[140] εὔκολον ἔφασκε τὴν
εἰς ᾅδου ὁδόν· καταμύοντες γ'οὖν ἀπιέναι; the way to death is easy
and smooth, one can travel it with closed eyes. In another
passage, apparently known to Accius,[141] Agamemnon, tearing
his hair in his grief is held up to ridicule, for baldness is no cure
for grief. Or again,[142] we have the saying that the inhabitants
of the lower world would be more punished if they carried water
in buckets that were whole than in such as were bored, a

mockery perhaps at the proverbially fruitless task of the Danaides. Such passages anticipate the tone of the dialogues of the dead in Lucian, of certain satires (reconstructed) from Menippus, and of such satires of Horace as 2, 5, a satirical colloquy of the legacy-hunting Odysseus with Tiresias, and its Lucilian analogue.

Evidently then, the διατριβαί of Bion were broadly satirical in tone and atmosphere in distinction from the moral discourses of Plato, Seneca, and Philo.

Teles, too,[142] shares the satiric tone of his master. Thus the grim jest about death: "If no one closes your eyelids, and you die open-eyed and open-mouthed what evil is that?"—is essentially in the spirit of Bion. Again in at least one of the διατριβαί we have a genuinely satirical and highly unexpected conclusion (ἔσχατον εἰς Ἄδου) which reminds us of the abrupt and humorous termination of certain satires of Lucilius and Horace.[144] In short, as Hense well says of Bion: utebatur sermone modo tristi saepe iocoso.

In the second place we have in Bion the same autobiographical interest which we find in the satires of Lucilius and Horace. The healthy egoism of the letter of Bion to Antigonus with its assertion of human worth and artistic independence reminds one of the interview in which that typical egoist and great artist of the renaissance, Benvenuto Cellini refused to give up to Pope Clement VII the uncompleted chalice.[145] The use of the conversational genre as a medium of personal confession is thus seen to have a long descent. While the satires of Lucilius and of Horace are animated by the living spirit of two vigorous personalities, keenly alive to every aspect of contemporary life, and welcoming every chance for self-revelation, the intense personal quality of the two men attracted them to a genre which from the Hellenistic age on was redolent of the assaults of the Cynic and Stoic philosophical humorists upon their times and of their revelations of themselves. Among such Greek satirists Bion occupies a most important position. Apparently his life also like that of Lucilius was open to view in his writings as though traced on a votive tablet. In this sense he is certainly one of the spiritual progenitors of the two Roman satirists.

The life of Diogenes Laertius has two statements which are significant in this connection. In 47 it describes Bion as: καὶ ἀπολαῦσαι τύφου δυνάμενος, having a capacity for the enjoyment of personal vanity or absurdity, and as having left many ὑπομνήματα or memorials of himself.

Again Bion seems to have been the first to intersperse his discourses with χρεῖαι to give humorous illustration to his teachings. Thus the life of Diogenes Laertius, 47, speaks of his ἀποφθέγματα χρειώδη πραγματείαν ἔχοντα. We know that he told anecdotes of Socrates and Xanthippe, of the poets and philosophers.[146] It is difficult to exaggerate the importance of this precedent thus set by Bion for the future development of Roman satire in Lucilius and Horace.[147]

In keeping with the pedantry of the Hellenistic period we find in Bion citations from the epic, from tragedy, and from comedy. These citations were employed, sometimes directly to re-enforce a point, sometimes for purposes of parody. It is naturally a task of much difficulty to determine whether the citations in the remains of Teles are made by Teles himself, or whether he only records those made by Bion.[148] Among the authors quoted, probably by Bion himself are Socrates, Aristippus, Xenophon, Plato, Metrocles, Diogenes the Cynic, Crates. Among the poets we have evidence for the use of Homer, Theognis, Euripides, Antiphanes, Menander.[149]

Here also the similarity between Bion's attitude and that of Lucilius is striking. In Lucilius the same Hellenistic rage for citation has by no means abated, as we may see from the *Index Auctorum* of Marx, where among the authors cited are Homer, Aristophanes, an unknown Greek comic poet, Euripides, Menander, Plato. We also have allusions to Socrates and Aristippus. The large part that Homeric parody played in Lucilian satire has already been discussed.[150] Lucilius also drew freely for imitation or parody upon his Roman predecessors and contemporaries, notably upon Ennius, Caecilius, Pacuvius, while he uses comic scenes from Plautus and Terence, to illustrate his satires. Such a procedure relates Lucilius' method of delineation not merely to that of Bion, but to the habit of the whole tribe of Greek philosophical preachers.

Similes and allegorical personifications play a very important part in the works of Bion. This fact is clear in the life of Diogenes Laertius, notably from chapter 3. In fact the fertility of Bion in this respect reminds us of comedy and of the mime. We know that like Aristhenes, Bion introduced a dialogue between πράγματα and πενία, who play the rôle of slaves against their master. The scene in Horace's satire, 1, 1, 15 in which a god suggests an exchange of rôles on the part of various discontented beings has been proved to be derived from Bion. With the personification of πενία and πράγματα we are reminded of the personification of Death and Life employed by Ennius in his satires,[151] and of the title of *Mortis et Vitae Iudicium*, an Atellana by Pomponius. Similarly Tantalus served in Bion as a stock type of unsatisfied greed. In his use of such comparisons and allegories Bion shows himself a thorough-going Cynic.

We find Bion comparing insatiable avarice with the thirst of a dropsical patient,[152] a simile borrowed from Diogenes. His dictum that avarice was the mother city of all evil also is attributed to Diogenes,[153] while his comparison of *amphorae* containing vinegar seems related to the simile in which Diogenes substitutes alabaster vessels.[154] Animal similes, which are frequent in the works of the Cynics, because the animals as living in accordance with nature are proper guides for man, occur in the works of Bion and are comparatively frequent in the satires of Lucilius and Horace.[155] We find also similes derived from material objects. Thus the avaricious rich, because of their moral poverty are like silversmiths, who have riches in their hands which they cannot use.[156] Just as a purse is estimated at the value of the money it holds, though itself worthless, so rich men are honored on the basis of their possessions. In fact it seems probable that many of the similes of Teles, not expressly assigned to Bion, are derived from him.[157]

Now such a method of delineation or exposition is essentially that of Lucilius and of Horace. Indeed certain of the similes of Bion are actually used by them. The method is, to be sure, common to all the Cynics and the use of these identical similes is not in itself decisive as a proof of direct dependence upon Bion. Taken in connection with other evidence, however, it creates a strong presumption that the actual formulation given to this common Cynic material by Bion was known to both Lucilius and Horace and influenced them in the composition of their own popular philosophic satires.

Bion was an eclectic popular preacher rather than a formal philosopher. His versatile eclecticism reveals an attitude towards literature and life which corresponds strikingly to the ebb and flow of philosophic impulse manifest in the satires and lives of Lucilius and Horace. His successive relations to the Academician Xenocrates, the Cynic Crates, the Cyreniac Theodorus, and finally to the Peripatetic Theophrastus show that like Lucilius and Horace he was rather a witty man of letters than a formal philosopher. The Roman Lucilius apparently starting out with strong Academician predilections was gradually transformed into a liberal Stoic, probably as the result of the influence of the Scipionic circle. So Horace was gradually swept away from the fashionable Epicureanism of the late republic and early empire to the liberal Stoicism of his later years. This advance has often been traced by critics from the restrained and humane Epicureanism of the earlier satires, epodes, and odes to the sincere, but undogmatic Stoicism, still tempered by occasional lapses to the hedonism of Aristippus to which Horace gives urbane expression in the second book of satires, the third and fourth book of odes, and above all in the epistles. None of these three men could ever accept without reservations the more rigid tenets of Stoicism. The very fact that they were satirists made this impossible. As a result we find the pedantry and pretension of the learned world ridiculed with equal freedom by Bion, Lucilius, and Horace.

Thus Bion ridicules the grammarians, mathematicians, musicians, and all serious philosophers. Diogenes Laertius in the life of Bion, 47, declares: ἦν . . . τὰ μὲν ἄλλα πολύτροπος καὶ σοφιστής, ποικίλος καὶ πλείστας ἀφορμὰς δεδωκὼς τοῖς βουλομένοις καθιππάζεσθαι φιλοσοφίας, while in §53 we read: καὶ ὅλως καὶ μουσικὴν καὶ γεωμετρίαν διέπαιζεν.[168] In essential harmony with such an attitude are Horace's assaults on the excesses in matter and manner of Fabius, Crispinus, Damasippus, and the Stoic preachers, which apparently were not without parallels in the satires of Lucilius.

In what is somewhat pedantically, but conveniently called
χαρακτηρισμός, that is in the minute delineation of satiric types
of character, Bion is an adept. This tendency, which started
with the New Comedy, the Ethics of Aristotle, and the Charac-
ters of Theophrastus, came to pervade nearly all the forms of
literature conceived in the half-humorous, half-serious spirit of
the τὸ σπουδαιογέλοιον. Bion is, then, an earlier traveller on this
road which is later so clearly marked for us by the satires of
Lucilius and Horace. As the scholar of Theophrastus he
appraises human types with penetrating accuracy. Examples
of this method may be found in the Diogenes Laertius
4, 7, 50 where we have epigrammatic characterizations addressed
to the chatterer (πρὸς τὸν ἀδολέσχην) and the rich niggard
(πρὸς τὸν πλούσιον μικρολόγον). These same types, it will be
noticed, are found in Lucilius and in Horace. The chatterer or
loquacious bore is the subject of a satire in Lucilius book 6 and
of Horace's *satire* 1, 9. In fact as Hirzel has acutely observed,[159]
descriptions of types by Theophrastus, Lycon, and the Greek
rhetoricians read like sketches from Horatian (and Lucilian)
satire. Such typical characterizations were naturally increased
by the free invention of the Romans. Thus in Horace *sat.*
1, 1, 95 we may regard Ummidius and in *sat.* 1, 2, 55 Marsaeus
as examples of such invented types.

But although all three satirists are profoundly impressed
with the ideal and external aspects of human character, they
never forget that no man precisely fits the mould into which his
temperament and social environment constantly seek to con-
fine him: naturam expellas furca, tamen usque recurret.
Bion quite as much as Lucilius or Horace gets at grips with
contemporary life. He is a supremely realistic satiric philo-
sopher. This is proved by his use of contemporary proper
names in which respect he equals the freedom of Lucilius and
surpasses that of Horace. We see in his satires the figures of
the period of the Diadochoi: Lycinus, Hippomedon, Chremon-
ides, Glaucon, Ptolemaeus, Persaeus, and Philonides, and
Antigonus Gonatas. So the satires of Lucilius give us the most
vivid picture of the contemporaries of the Gracchi and the
Scipionic circle, just as the satires of Horace mirror the life of
the circle of Maecenas and the Augustan age.[160]

Finally we have to compare the style of the Bionean διατρίβαι with that of Lucilius and Horace. In so far as humor is an element in style we have already seen that the works of Bion are closer to the satires of Lucilius and Horace than they are to such later offspring of the διατρίβαι as the works of Seneca the philosopher, Musonius, and Epictetus. In so far as style involves the choice and arrangement of words according to the sometimes conflicting claims of personal genius and rhetorical tradition the style of Bion shows affinities rather with that of the more spirited and more informal Lucilius than with that of the more polished and restrained Horace. In particular we find in Bion as in Lucilius the same surprising contrast between informality of tone, carelessness of finish, and a racy catholicity of diction on the one hand, and a wide and technical command of the instruments of rhetoric, and broad and unpretentious familiarity with the most varied fields of Greek literature on the other. In this unusual combination of personal aggressiveness with a vigorous and catholic sympathy for all the movements of contemporary life the genius of Bion is strikingly similar to that of Lucilius.

With the Gorgianic rhetoric, which exercised[161] such an important influence upon early Roman literature Bion is especially familiar. How profound the rhetorical interests of Lucilius were, as the result of his acquaintance with the Stoic rhetoric of Diogenes of Babylon and Panaetius I have already considered in detail.

Often the rhetorical development of Bion's themes is studied and intricate. Geffcken[162] has shown how the διατριβή on αὐτάρκεια or contentment begins with a consideration of μεμψι-μοιρία or discontent with one's lot, touching first the unjust accusation made by human beings against their poverty, then surveying certain stereotyped professions, which are the target for further discontent, also phases of life like γῆρας, πενία etc., for which individual remedies are proposed. This theme is enlarged to make a transition to physical weakness, and with a return to the simile of the actor found at the beginning of the διατριβή, the circle of the argument is completed, two anecdotes of Socrates forming the close.

Here we have an almost labyrinthine development of the argument, which is not without analogies to that followed by Horace in the first satire of his first book. Possibly a similar intricate sequence may have been followed by Lucilius in one or both of the satires in books 18 and 19, though the meagreness of the fragments makes positive assertion impossible. A detailed examination of the evidence which makes it a plausible hypothesis that Lucilius and Horace followed some Greek original closely related to Bion, and were influenced by his somewhat ambling method of developing his theme must be deferred until we consider Horace's first satire.[168]

In the διατριβαί of Bion, dialogue, even dramatic dialogue is still present, though not so distinctly as in Latin satire. Nevertheless we are not yet reduced to the colorless φησίν' of the later διατριβαί, which recall the *quisquis es* of Persius *sat.* 1, 44:

quisquis es, o modo quem ex adverso dicere feci.

We still have a quasi-discourse, for we find objections interjected to be answered, as well as expressions of approval. Although Bion does not employ dramatic spokesmen for the expression of his ideas as do Lucilius, Horace, and at a later period Lucian, the large number of citations from the poets and philosophers, always in the direct discourse, create a distinctly dramatic atmosphere. For these reasons the style of Bion, like that of Latin satire, is extraordinarily lively. We find those little mime-like scenes by virtue of which he received the title of θεατρικός, copious use of comparisons, metaphors, personifications, citations and parodies. We thus make a measurable approach to ordinary conversation.

Accordingly any summary of the style of Bion demands the analysis of the meaning of the passage of Diogenes Laertius, 7, 5, 52: ἦν δὲ καὶ θεατρικὸς καὶ πολὺς ἐν τῷ γελοίῳ διαφορῆσαι, φορτικοῖς ὀνόμασι κατὰ τῶν πραγμάτων χρώμενος. διὰ δὴ οὖν τὸ παντὶ εἴδει λόγου κεκρᾶσθαι, φασὶ λέγειν ἐπ' αὐτοῦ τὸν Ἐρατοσθένην, ὡς πρῶτος Βίων τὴν φιλοσοφίαν ἀνθινὰ ἐνέδυσεν.

First of all, just what is the meaning of θεατρικός in this passage? Wachsmuth[164] interprets the expression rather narrowly as referring to the fondness of Bion for personification as for instance in the dialogue between Poverty and Property: egre-

griam προσωποποιίαν adhibet ille, igitur θεατρικός audit; varias
quibus homines philosophique decipi colent opiniones evertit
non severe excogitando, sed facete deridendo; igitur est . . .
πολὺς διαφορῆσαι . . . non sublimi dictione utitur, sed ipso
sermone familiari loquiturque ad sensum popularem vulgarem-
que accomodate, igitur notatur φορτικοῖς κ.τ.λ.

The judgment of Hense[165] is more sound and less narrow.
He refers the term θεατρικός with good reason to the whole
stylistic method of Bion, who as a representative writer in the
vein of the τὸ σπουδαιογέλοιον and as a popular philosopher and
pupil of Theophrastus writes in a spirit redolent of contemporary
life as mirrored on the stage, in the mime, and New Comedy.
The term therefore covers both the quasi-dramatic structure
of the Bionean διατριβή and its diction:[166] ad universam igitur
disserendi rationem id refero vocabulum nimium intellegens
orationis ornatum propter crebras similitudines non minus
quam propter alia lenocinia scaenae aptiorem quam philosophiae
sacrario. Theatricus enim mihi audit philosophus qui philo-
sophatur πρὸς ὄχλον καὶ θέατρον (ps. Plat. Axioch p. 370D) qui
in speciem laborat risum captans vel plausum et acclamationem
magnoque intervallo separatur ab illo cui alter philosophus[167]
satis magnum theatrum est (epicur. fr. 208 Usener). So Lucilius
in a satire which forms the analogue to Horace's sat. 1, 4 discussed
the relation between satire and comedy.[168] This is clearly the
correct interpretation of fragment 1029:

sicuti te, qui ea quae speciem vitae esse putamus.

A comparison between the context in which this passage
probably stood in Lucilius and Horace, sat. 1, 4, 45 ff., makes it
certain that Horace and probable that Lucilius asserted that
their satirical style was dramatic (θεατρικός) in the same sense
as was that of Bion. Both are certainly following Hellenistic
rhetorical and critical theories as to the nature of comedy,
when they relate satire to comedy in diction and tone, just as
we see diction and tone coupled with the dramatic manner in
the passage of Diogenes Laertius quoted above. The constant
appeal to comedy as a norm, which pervades the critical theory
of Horace and possibly pervaded that of Lucilius can only be
seen in its proper perspective after a study of Hellenistic satiri-
cal literature.

Moreover, the methods of Bion have something of the sensationalism which so easily comes to be associated with the stage: witness the story of his persuading the sailors of Rhodes to put on the dress of students of philosophy and follow him about. By entering the gymnasium with such a company he made himself the cynosure of all eyes, περίβλεπτος.[169]

The words καὶ πολὺς . . . χρώμενος in the passage cited above seem to refer to the diction of Bion, which is absolutely realistic. As Hense says, Bion's words are: ad nudam vitae veritatem expressa eademque spurciora haud raro vel immundiora. It is not necessary to quote here illustrations of this racy coarseness.[170] Such a theory of diction is clearly in close harmony with that employed by Lucilius' less refined interpretation of the plain style, which permitted the free use of plebeianisms, the interweaving of Latin with Greek words and with words from the Italic dialects, and even the occasional descent to the obscenities and to the vulgarisms of the sermo castrensis, the argot of the Roman armies.

Finally, the passage of Diogenes Laertius informs us that Bion was charged not merely with "bringing philosophy to the people" but with vulgarizing it. This seems to be the natural interpretation of the charge that he was the first who clothed philosophy in a flowery robe, the costume of the prostitute. That is he debased the more austere standard animating the dialogues of Plato and Aristotle by means of broad jests and a loose diction derived from the stage.[171]

Bion adds nothing to the world's store of thought.[172] He simply gives a glittering illumination to the old doctrine. He is master of that negative poetic faculty which lies close to the heart of every true satirist. He accepts life as he finds it; his essential doctrine is a cheerful accommodation to what is, ἀρκεῖσθαι τοῖς παροῦσιν, the same note which so constantly recurs in all the writings of Horace. He has small regard for the world's standard of values, but can offer us no better one. Hence the need of "accommodation." The world hopes or rejoices, the satirist is cynically amused; while mankind frets by the side of the grave, the satirist smiles. In Bion we have at times an attitude reminiscent of that of Aristippus with whose tenets we know he was in sympathy. Thus according to Diogenes Laertius 2, 4, 77 it was

Bion who narrated the anecdote of the servant laboring under a weight of money who was ordered by Aristippus to drop what was beyond his strength and only carry what he could. How far Horace's predilections for Aristippus were imbibed from Bion and how far they were due to independent study of the Cyreniac philosopher it is no longer possible to say.

So far, then, we have examined certain general affinities which related the διατριβή of Bion to the later works of Lucilius and Horace. We have seen a similar interest in self-portraiture, a similar use of popular moralistic anecdotes, a similar fondness for citations or parodies from epic, philosophy, and comedy, a similar distrust of formal learning and pedantry, a similar tendency to a comfortable eclecticism in the appropriation of a loose-fitting philosophical creed, a similar gift for the acute delineation of character by types, a similar power to come to close grips with contemporary life, a similar stylistic tone, half-serious, half-humorous, coupled with a democratic diction and vividly dramatic power of scene-painting. Are not these some of the essential characteristics of the satires of Lucilius and Horace—of Lucilius perhaps even more than Horace—for as a stylist Horace transcends and ennobles the common material that he has received from both his Greek and his Roman predecessors? Even without the evidence afforded by a comparison of the fragments of the Greek satirist with the works of Lucilius and Horace the considerations I have enumerated point in the direction of the probable spiritual kinship—whether conscious, or unconscious—of the Bionean διατριβή with certain widely prevalent moods and methods of Lucilian and Horatian satire.

In view of the fragmentary condition of Bion and Lucilius the analysis of the internal evidence which points in the direction of direct or indirect relationship between certain themes and passages of the διατριβαί of the Greek popular philosopher and the satires of Lucilius and Horace in almost no case warrants us in a positive statement of direct genetic descent leading from the earlier Greek to the later Roman writers. We are dealing rather with probabilities and possibilities in the appropriation by Lucilius and Horace of certain popular philosophic material than with the proved certainties of direct or indirect imitation.

With this *caveat* constantly in mind let us now examine the passages in Lucilius and Horace which betray traces of the influence of Bion.

In the first place, as I shall show in detail below,[173] the first satire of Horace's first book betrays many traces of the influence either of some διατριβή of Bion or of a complex of closely related sophistic sources. This satire is a contamination of two commonplaces of the Cynic popular philosophy, that on μεμψιμοιρία (or discontent with one's lot), and that on φιλοπλουτία (or αἰσχροκέρδεια), or love of riches. The imperfect fusion of these two themes resulting in the peculiar "shuffling" sequence of the argument existed in the Bionean διατριβή. Now Lucilius treated the same theme in two satires in books 18 and 19, which I shall later show influenced Horace's satire. If then we could discover traces of a similar contamination of themes in these Lucilian satires it would be a plausible hypothesis to hold that the parallel contaminations in the two Latin satirists were due to their common acquaintance with Bion.

The διατριβή of Bion, which Horace's satire on the whole most nearly parallels, is that on a αὐτάρκεια or the self-sufficiency of the sage, especially in relation to material advantages. This διατριβή is best preserved to us in the epitome of Teles. Now such a Lucilian line as 557 is clearly animated by the same Cynic-Stoic doctrine, assailing the vice of discontent with one's lot, μεμψιμοιρία, a state of mind which finds one of its most striking illustrations in the insatiable love of wealth, φιλοπλουτία:

> denique uti stulto nil sit satis omnia cum sint

With such a commonplace, which has many parallels in the Cynic-Stoic literature we may compare Bion-Teles 7, 7, 7, H.[174]

ἀλλ' ἡμεῖς οὐ δυνάμεθα ἀρκεῖσθαι τοῖς παροῦσιν, ὅταν καὶ τρυφῇ πολὺ διδῶμεν, καὶ τὸ ἐργάζεσθαι.

The discontent with one's lot, μεμψιμοιρία discussed in Horace's *sat.* 1, 1, 1–7 seems to have a parallel in the Lucilian line 563, which I should therefore place somewhere at the beginning of the satire.[175]

> sic singillatim nostrum unus quisque movetur.

With these two positive statements on *invidia* (μεμψιμοιρία) in Lucilius and Horace I should be inclined to compare the introduction to the same διατριβή in Bion-Teles where the necessity of acquiescence in the dispensation of fate is asserted: The good man, we are told, will play the part assigned to him by chance, as the good actor will act that assigned to him by the poet:

Δεῖ ὥσπερ τὸν ἀγαθὸν ὑποκριτὴν ὅ τι ἂν ὁ ποιητὴς περιθῇ πρόσωπον τοῦτο ἀγωνίζεσθαι καλῶς, οὕτω καὶ τὸν ἀγαθὸν ἄνδρα ὅτι ἂν περιθῇ ἡ τύχη.[175]

It seems fairly evident, therefore, that αὐτάρκεια[176] was first defined in all three writers in relation to its opposite μεμψιμοιρία or discontent. But in all three writers also the transition to φιλοπλουτία (avaritia), the most widely spread manifestation of discontent is almost instantaneous, and furthermore is made in Bion and Horace by one of those dramatic personifications which helped to win for the Greek satirist the epithet of θεατρικός. Bion personifies τὰ πράγματα (Possessions), and makes her speak, and probably also πενία (Poverty). So in Horace a god (15), presently more clearly defined as Jupiter (20), speaks. In Lucilius, while we cannot assert any personification, the imperatives sume in 564, and noli reprehendere in 565 suggest an injunction put into the mouth of someone who speaks with higher authority (than the poet himself?).

Also it seems clear that the commonplace:[177]

tanti quantum habeas sis,

which is of pre-Cynic origin, was formulated in one of its most widely known aspects in Bion. It seems probable that Lucilius was familiar with the particular Bionean aspect of this commonplace. Thus Bion said according to Stobaeus 91.32 (cf. Hense op. cit., p. lxix):

Βίων ἔλεγεν ὥσπερ τὰ φαῦλα τῶν βαλαντίων κἂν μηδενὸς ᾖ ἄξια τοσούτου ἐστὶν ἄξια ὅσον ἐν ἑαυτοῖς τὸ νόμισμα ἔχουσιν, οὕτω καὶ τῶν πλουσίων τοὺς οὐδενὸς ἀξίους καρποῦσθαι τὰς ἀξίας ὧν κέκτηνται.

With this we may compare Lucilius 559:

aurum vis hominem (ne?) habeas. "hominem quid ad aurum?"

Another fragment from Lucilius book 18 which, as we shall see, was known to Horace when he wrote the first satire of his first book seems to show indirect traces of Bionean influence in its resemblance to the general thesis of Bion-Teles on αὐτάρκεια.

The man who is αὐταρκής carries his own power of enjoyment within him, as Lucilius says, fragment 554:

aeque fruniscor ego ac tu.[178]

There seems to be good reason for believing that the second satire of Horace's second book on the *tenuis victus* or plain living recommended by the Cynics was also a theme of Bion's. But here also we have certain fragments of Lucilius which appear to show relationship with Bion as well as with Horace.[179] It is probable, therefore, that Lucilius was familiar with the same detailed treatment or occasional allusions to this theme in Bion. These passages of Lucilius 550, 701, 699 are discussed below in full.

I shall also strive to show below[180] that the sixth satire of Horace's first book treats a theme similar to that contained in the famous letter of Bion to King Antigonus Gonatas. In this letter Bion (Diog. Laert. 4, 46) overwhelmed the malicious slanders of the rival philosophers Persaeus and Philonides by frankly telling the story of his humble birth.[181] Similar in nature is the remark addressed by Antigonus Gonatas to an effeminate youth:[182] παρ' ἐμοί, φησίν, ὦ μειράκιον, ἀνδραγαθίας εἰσὶν οὐ πατραγαθίας τιμαί.

It has been shown by Cichorius that a satire of Lucilius in book 30 treats a theme similar to that of Horace 1, 6, *viz.*, the introduction of Lucilius to a new patron. The question of a possible relation of this Lucilian satire to that of Bion therefore arises. Such a relationship seems probable in the sense that Bion was one of the first to formulate the common theme defining the principles governing the relations of a literary protégé of ignoble birth to his patron.

We find in Bion certain fragments containing assertions of independence in relation to riches and fame parallel to that in Lucilius 669 and to Horace *sat.* 1, 6, 18–22 which I have treated below.[183] Thus in Stobaeus *florilegium* 46, 23 we read: Βίων ἔφη δεῖν τὸν ἀγαθὸν ἄρχοντα παυόμενον τῆς ἀρχῆς μὴ πλουσιώτερον ἀλλ' ἐνδοξότερον γεγονέναι. In Teles 29H. 6, the wise man is to be unmoved by renown or its lack: πρὸς δόξαν καὶ ἀδοξίαν ἴσως ἔχοντα. And in fact the Cynics lead a life indifferent to all such objects of desire as wealth, fame, or good birth (Diog. Laert. 6, 9,

105): ἀρέσκει δ' αὐτοῖς καὶ λιτῶς βιοῦν . . . πλούτου καὶ δόξης καὶ εὐγενείας καταφρονοῦσιν.

Another passage of Bion quoted in Diogenes Laertius 4, 7, 51 of this same general tenor is discussed in connection with Horace's sixth satire.[184] It is clear, then, that both Lucilius and Horace could have found in Bion a commonplace on the appropriate attitude to be assumed by the popular philosopher towards δόξα (ambitio) as well as a defense of the position of the satirist of humble birth in the circle of an aristocratic patron. It therefore seems to me likely that they considered the well-known Bionean treatment of these two related themes in writing their satires on the introduction to a new patron.

The half-popular, half-philosophic analysis of friendship occupies an important place in the διατριβαί of Bion and the satires of Lucilius and Horace. According to Bion the basis of true friendship is similarity in character: τοὺς φίλους[185] ὁμοίοι ἂν ὦσι συντηρεῖν, ἵνα μὴ δοκοίημεν πονηροῖς κεχρῆσθαι ἢ χρηστοὺς παρῃτῆσθαι. It is evident, therefore that Bion accepts the doctrine, which in the writings of Plato, Aristotle, the Cynics, Peripatetics, and Stoics,[186] relates friendship to character. Only the good are capable of true friendship.

Now in book 29 of Lucilius we have a series of senarii, already discussed in another context,[187] which treat of the Socratic theory of love and friendship. We are at least justified in saying that like Bion Lucilius accepted the Platonic doctrine that friendship depends on nobility of soul, for Socrates in fragment 833 ff. disregards the appeal of physical beauty, and imparts his teaching to the boni, a term which seems to refer both to the καλοὶ κἀγαθοί or the gentlemen of Athens in the conventional sense and to the philosophical conception of the virtuous:

> quid? quas partiret ipse doctrinas bonis.

If Bion believed that true friendship, based on similarity of character, must be preserved and bad friendship rejected it is a fair inference[188] that he accepted the corollary of this doctrine, that friendship between the good implies equal partnership or community not only in regard to all that is involved in the ordinary relations of human life, but still more in all life's difficulties and dangers. Thus Diogenes Laertius 7, 1, 124 gives the Stoic doctrine of friendship to which we must infer that Bion subscribed:

λέγουσι δὲ καὶ τὴν φιλίαν ἐν μόνοις τοῖς σπουδαίοις εἶναι διὰ τὴν ὁμοιότητα· φασὶ δ' αὐτὴν κοινωνίαν τινὰ εἶναι τῶν κατὰ τὸν βίον, χρωμένων ἡμῶν τοῖς φίλοις ὡς ἑαυτοῖς. δι' αὐτὸν θ' αἱρετὸν τὸν φίλον ἀποφαίνονται καὶ τὴν πολυφιλίαν ἀγαθόν· ἐν τε τοῖς φαύλοις μὴ εἶναι φιλίαν. μηδενί τε τῶν φαύλων εἶναι φιλονεικεῖν πάντας τε τοὺς ἄφρονας μαίνεσθαι.

Now Lucilius in fragment 909 asserts that community in the ordinary duties of human life binds friends together. Indeed the Latin phrase, *quantum est inter humanum genus*, is virtually a free paraphrase of the Greek τῶν κατὰ τὸν βίον:

cum amicis quantum est inter humanum genus
rerum quae inter se coniungant, communicat.

Above all, friendship is tested in time of stress, fragment 905, and only the most weighty moral cause ought to lead one to disregard the advantage of a friend, 903, 904. The continual maintenance of friendship, τὸ συντηρεῖν τοὺς φίλους (and the antithetical rejection of bad friends), is probably emphasized in fragments 906 and 907.

Further, if we are to use friends as ourselves it follows that we must know ourselves for two reasons: first, that we may give our friends their due; second, lest betrayed by self-deception and excessive self-love we may not be able to distinguish the flatterer from the friend. Hence in connection with friendship, as so often elsewhere, Socrates rightly emphasized the applicability of the Delphic motto γνῶθι σεαυτόν. This application of the motto is apparently alluded to in Lucilius fragment 908.

The distinction between the professional parasite of the Greeks or the *scurra*, his Roman analogue and the friend is easy. It is made by Lucilius in fragment 717 from another satire:

sic amici quaerunt animum, rem parasiti ac ditias.

So in Horace's *Ars Poetica* 422–425 the literary parasites flock about the tables of the wealthy patron. In a Lucilian satire of book 26 a series of fragments suggests a banquet by a wealthy patron by which the applause of the crowd is won.[189]

A more difficult task is to distinguish the true friend from the false, the frank and honest criticism of friendship from the bland and deceitful praise of flattery. Here the doctrine of friendship bounds and defines, at any rate in Roman satire,[190] the doctrine of the satirist's right and duty to employ frankness of utterance, in short the whole theory of the satirist's function and the nature of his humor. Both Lucilius and Horace, and probably Bion before them were fully conscious of this. But before turning to literary theory let us consider the more obvious human aspects of the case.

We know that Plutarch wrote a discourse on the subject *de amici et adulatoris discrimine*. Furthermore in this discourse he quotes Bion and assails his laxity in assigning a high function in friendship to praise (p. 59a):

εὔηθες τοίνυν καὶ ἀβέλτερον τὸ τοῦ Βίωνος· 'εἰ τὸν ἀγρὸν ἔμελλες ἐγκωμιάζων εὔφορον ποιεῖν καὶ εὔκαρπον, οὐκ ἂν ἁμαρτάνειν ἐδόκεις τοῦτο ποιῶν μᾶλλον ἢ σκάπτων καὶ πράγματα ἔχων. οὐ τοίνυν οὐδ' ἀνθρώπους ἄτοπος ἂν εἴης ἐπαινῶν, εἰ τοῖς ἐπαινουμένοις ὠφέλιμος ἔσῃ καὶ πρόσφορος'.

This censure of Plutarch's is, however, unfair for we know that Bion carefully differentiated the insincere praise of the flatterer from the proper and helpful recognition of excellence accorded by friend to friend. Thus he compared those who lend too ready an ear to flatterers to pitchers which are moved around by the ears, Plutarch *de vitioso pudore* 536a: διὸ καὶ Βίων ἀπείκαζε τοὺς τοιούτους (i.e. τοὺς τὰ ὦτα τοῖς κολακεύουσι παραδιδόντας) ἀμφορεῦσιν ὑπὸ τῶν ὤτων ῥᾳδίως μεταφερομένοις. It is evident, therefore, that he sharply distinguished between the true friend and the flatterer. But we find clear evidence of this distinction also in Lucilius and Horace.

Since the distinction is immediately bound up with the Cynic commonplace on freedom of speech, παρρησία, without which neither Greek nor Latin satiric forms could exist, we are not justified in referring its use in Lucilius and Horace exclusively to Bion. The application of this commonplace to literary criticism so far as I have been able to discover is first found in the Latin satirists. I shall show below,[191] that it plays an important part in the critical theory of Horace's *satires* 1, 4; 1, 10 and 2, 1 and the *Ars Poetica* as well as in certain Lucilian satires of books 26 and 30 which traverse similar themes. I must, therefore, content myself with a summary statement here.

In brief the concluding portion of the *Ars Poetica* 425 ff., upon the distinction between sincere and self-interested literary criticism goes back to the distinction between the *verus* and the *mendax amicus* in an eisagogic satire in Lucilius book 26 addressed to Iunius Congus. Here belongs[192] fragment 611 on the duty of the true friend to advise and speak the truth, which corresponds to Horace's *Ars Poetica* 421–424; the simile of the *praeficae* or hired mourners, Lucilius 954–955, which corresponds to *Ars Poetica* 431–433. The true friend or critic, whether Quintilius Varus, *Ars Poetica* 438 ff. or Aristarchus 450, or the *verus amicus* of Lucilius 953, 957, 958, will never lie to his friend.

But besides the *Ars Poetica* Horace's *satires* 1, 3; 1,4 and 2,1 discuss the relation between satire and friendship, and differentiate the frank jest of the true satirist with its friendly tone from the biting invective, which in its desire to impale a victim, rejoices at a laugh raised at a neighbor's expense. It is impossible here[193] to give a detailed analysis of these satires from this point of view; only a few points may be mentioned in anticipation.

In the first place all four of these works of Horace are permeated by the theory of the closed circle of friends, the literary coterie. Hence literary ideals, both in Lucilius and Horace, are in essence based on group ideals. Most assaults, whether in the period of the Scipios or in the Augustan age, whether literary, ethical, personal or political, are directed against those outside of the poet's circle. A study of the use of proper names in these four works and in Horace's *sat.* 1, 10 and in Lucilius will afford complete confirmation of this assertion.

Lucilius[194] perhaps stands somewhat closer to the direct methods of Diogenes the Cynic and the earlier Cynics, while Horace approaches the more human tolerance of Bion and the later Cynics. Hense's[195] summary of the attitude of Bion to freedom of speech admirably characterizes the theoretical attitude of all three satirists: sine veritate amicitia nulla. Libere loquatur amicus et ingenue alterius errorem corrigat corrigique se patiatur libenter. Only as regards the more favorable judgment which Bion accords to praise in the sphere of friendship Horace is somewhat closer to Bion's point of view than is Lucilius. Thus in such passages as *sat.* 1, 3, 69 ff., he desires to play the part of an *amicus dulcis* and asserts that on the principle of give and take he will find *dulces amici* line 140.

Even his satires are only for friends, *sat.* 1, 4, 73, and his criticisms, line 81, never violate the rights of true friendship. Similarly in *sat.* 1, 10 he has the highest praise for the literary productions emanating from the harmonious circle of Maecenas and the related circles of Pollio and Messala while he attacks only the works of the circle of Valerius Cato,[196] the work of the rivals of the circle of Maecenas, and the notoriously vicious.

I shall show below[197] that Lucilius in satires in books 26 and 30 gave theoretical adherence to the same attitude, both as regards the proper spirit of criticism and the claims of friendship. Here he denies with quite as much vigor as Horace himself any charges of social slander, as for instance in fragments 1026. In such a fragment as the *senarius* 821 from book 29, which is probably to be related to the fragments on friendship put into the mouth of Socrates he seems to satirize himself by the term *improbus Lucilius* implying that he is fully conscious that the ingrained frankness of the satirist makes him at times a *persona non grata*:

> amicis hodie cum improbo illo audiuimus
> Lucilio aduocasse.

Nevertheless as I shall show below,[198] we seem to have preserved in two fragments of book 30 a conscious reference to Lucilius' feeling that he continues the tradition established by Diogenes of biting attacks even upon friends. Thus in 1095 he appears to describe the poet's function in terms involving the favorite word play upon κύων Cynic and κύων dog; and in 1097 he touches upon the treacherous mildness and deceitful blandness of the false friend in words which seem to be closely related to line 43 in the Phoenix of Colophon fragment.[199]

In view of these general similarities in the "topic" on the function of friendship in life and in letters it seems certain that both Lucilius and Horace were familiar with the commonplace as formulated by the Cynics, Stoics, and Epicureans. It is probable that they were familiar with the particular formulation of the commonplace developed by Bion in various parts of his work, though this is not susceptible of absolute proof. Their development of the relation between the function of the frank friend and the sincere literary critic seems to be a Roman addition to the commonplace.

Besides these broader resemblances of theme there are certain briefer illustrative examples, similes, and short passages of a miscellaneous nature, in which Lucilius and Horace probably were influenced by Bion. In Lucilius, fragment 764, we apparently have a simile in which some passion of the soul is compared to dropsy:

> ‿—aquam te in animo habere intercutem.

A comparison of Horace *odes* 2, 2, 13 proves that the passion in question is avarice. The longing of the dropsical patient for water is compared with the insatiable thirst of avarice:

> crescit indulgens sibi dirus hydrops
> nec sitim pellit nisi causa morbi
> fugerit venis et aquosus albo
> corpore languor.

The same comparison is found in Bion-Teles περὶ πενίας καὶ πλούτου, p. 28, 13 ff.:

> καὶ εἴ τις βούλεται ἢ αὐτὸς ἐνδείας καὶ στάσεως ἀπολυθῆναι ἢ ἄλλον ἀπολῦσαι μὴ χρήματα αὐτῷ ζητείτω, ὅμοιον γάρ, φησιν ὁ Βίων, ὡς εἴ τις τὸν ὑδρωπικὸν βουλόμενος παῦσαι τοῦ δίψους, τὸν μὲν ὕδρωπα ὑδρωπικὸν μὴ θεραπεύοι, κρήνας δὲ καὶ ποταμοὺς αὐτῷ παρασκευάζοι.[200]

Polybius' use of the same simile in 13, 2 seems to show that he was familiar either with the passage in Bion or with very similar uses of this commonplace in the popular Cynic ethics. Furthermore Polybius was a member of the Scipionic circle.

A favorite simile of the Cynics, which is found in Bion, Lucilius, and Horace is that of Tantalus. Thus in Bion-Teles 25, 5 H., Tantalus is used as a type of the insatiable craving of man, the victim of his passions:

> καὶ ὥσπερ ὁ Τάνταλος ἐν λίμνῃ ἕστηκεν . . . . οὕτως ἐνιών ἡ ἀνελευθερία καὶ δυσελπιστία. κ.τ.λ.

Similarly in Lucilius 140 Tantalus is used apparently of the torment of the sensual passion:

> Tantalus, qui poenas ob facta nefantia, poenas
> pendit.

Whether this passage is to be related to Horace's use of Tantalus as a type of avarice in *sat.* 1, 1, 68 ff.,[201] or to the obscene incident chronicled by Horace in *sat.* 1, 5, 82 ff., is not entirely clear.[202] Since, however, Tantalus was a stock Cynic figure to symbolize the helpless victim of some passion there is no difficulty in referring the allusion to both passages.

With this passage I have completed the analysis of the internal evidence bearing upon the relation of Bion to Lucilius. In view of the fragmentary condition of both authors such an analysis cannot attain certain results. I feel, however, that combining the more cogent evidence deduced from the comparison of Bionean and Lucilian themes with the scattering evidence of somewhat more direct dependence upon Bion in a few individual passages, and with the rather striking similarity between the two authors in methods of delineation, style, and tone, we may venture to say that it is probable that Lucilius was familiar with Bion at first hand. This point of view finds further corroboration in the external evidence afforded by the commentary of Pseudo-Acro on Horace's *epistles* 2, 2, 60, which has already been discussed.

This extended survey of the general relation between satiric forms and Lucilian and Horatian satire was necessary to show that Roman satire is on the whole but another result of the fructifying influence of Greek literature combining with the native Italic gift for half-dramatic, half-satirical improvisation. Lucilian satire, a genre composed in the midst of the most Hellenizing of all the Roman literary coteries, probably owed far more to the influence of the popular Cynic σπουδαιογέλοιον than to the crude beginnings of the Italic drama.[203] It has been my effort to show in these pages that such relationship between the inchoate Greek satiric forms was probably conscious and direct. It is difficult for me to believe that Lucilius could have been unconscious of the streams of influence which relate the spirit, though not the form of his work, to the manifestations of the satiric spirit in Greek literature. Save for his timidity to assert the probability of such conscious influence, Leo has admirably summarized the nature of this relationship.[204] Leo is entirely right in regarding Lucilius as the inventor or εὑρετής of a new genre *satura*. It is in this sense that the famous dictum of Quintilian, *satura tota nostra est* is true. Leo says of the relation of Lucilius to his Greek predecessors:

Von Archilochos und Hipponax mit ihrem Kampflust zu Lucilius geht eine direkte Linie, gleichviel ob er sich dessen bewusst war oder nicht (?). Zu Anfang der hellenistischen Dichtung erneuert und verstärkt sich dieser Strom wie es im Wesen ihrer individualistischen Stimmung lag. . . . Man kann sie auch nicht nach der Form abgrenzen; nicht Verse oder Prosen oder Beides bezeichnet sie, sondern Gegenstand und Ton. Die andern Kyniker und ihre Verwandten, wie der Borysthenite Bion, schreiben wie sie sprächen in einer eigenen Art von Stil und Form, die sich aus dem Dialog zur Predigt entwickelt hatte. . . . Das dritte Jahrhundert, und gewiss auch das zweite, war voll von dieser Literatur der Betrachtung, Lehre, Polemik, mit und ohne eine erzählende Erfindung, die den Stoff lebendig und eindringlich machte. Von einer Gattung, der sich Lucilius angeschlossen hätte, darf man gar nicht reden; er that in seiner Weise und auf lateinisch was unzählige griechen in vielen persönlichen und nachgeahmten Weisen und auch Römer vor und mit ihm taten. Dass etwas daraus wurde was neu und eigen erschien und was in Rom und Italien mehr bedeutete als die Schriften seiner Vorgänger in Griechenland und Rom, das war sein Verdienst.

In these three introductory chapters I have tried to make it clear that among the Romans from the period of the Scipionic circle to the age of Augustus literary criticism and literary creation were two closely allied arts. These arts were often united in the same person. Lucilius, Cicero, and Horace were almost equally eminent as creative artists and as literary critics. As literary artists they consciously based their creative work upon certain well-grounded theories of craftsmanship. The formulation and development of these laws of composition was the task of the Greco-Roman rhetoric, which perfected its discipline by the most scientific and yet appreciative study of the great Greek masterpieces in the various genres. From the period of Plato and Aristotle on, therefore, the literary artist, whatever his field gladly acknowledged his allegiance to a long and glorious tradition, which made it impossible for him to sacrifice the higher symmetry of the whole work to any imaginative power or beauty in the parts. As Aristotle said, the end is the chief thing of all. The rules of which I have said so much find their sole value as guides to the attainment of the perfect work of art, they constitute in fact what Horace calls the *lex operis*. These rules the literary artist regarded as the charter of his ordered literary freedom.[206]

In chapter two on the Relations of Lucilius and the Scipionic Circle to the New Greek Learning and Literature I have sought to trace the direct influence of the Stoic rhetoric and the Stoic theory of the plain style and the restrained humor of the *sermo* or conversation upon the representative writers of the Scipionic circle. In particular I have discussed the influence of the theories of Diogenes of Babylon and Panaetius upon Lucilian satire, and the more exacting definition given to such rhetorical theories by Cicero and the Roman Atticists in the period separating the age of Cicero from that of Augustus. In chapter three we have seen how far the familiarity of Lucilius with the freely-conceived and loosely wrought forms of Hellenistic satire conveniently classified by the common denominator, τὸ σπου-δαιογέλοιον, brought about certain modifications of the laws of the *sermo* and its appropriate type of humor in the satires of Lucilius. On the other hand, I have sought to present Horatian satire as an almost perfect exemplar of the classical theory of literary imitation and literary criticism as realized by one of the most original, and yet one of the most typical works of Augustan literary culture.

I would earnestly beg my readers before criticizing such hypotheses as too rigid or as imposing too narrow limits upon the task of the literary artist of antiquity to divest their minds so far as possible from all the prepossessions of the romantic theory of literary composition, the theory which since the middle of the 18th century has so profoundly influenced literary criticism and composition. Nor is this an easy task today for anyone, even for the professional student of the ancient classics. We are all prone to interpret the literary problems of the past in the light of the prevailing literary mode. In fact so completely have the tenets of the romantic theory of the nature of original composition taken possession of the field that it requires a conscious effort to recall the fact that for centuries the opposing point of view was the prevailing one. And yet the dominance of the romantic theory of composition is a comparatively recent phenomenon.

In contradistinction to the classical theory of composition the romantic theory insists upon the emancipation of the literary artist from models and from rules, and upholds the claims of originality and spontaneity. This theory is incredulous as to the value of imitative discipline, while it is passionately devoted to the sudden flare of sensuous impression, and is relatively indifferent to the glow of the reflective emotions.

The publication in 1759 by Edward Young, better known as the author of *Night Thoughts*, of his *Conjectures on Original Composition* in the form of a letter to Richardson, the novelist, is one of the earliest indications of the reaction from the monotonous perfection of the pseudo-classicism of the 18th century. So far as literature is concerned this work, romantic in spirit, but dressed in the external trappings of the pseudo-classicists, anticipates by a few years the revolutionary outbursts of Rousseau.

Like most later romantic critics Young insists upon the stark contrast between Originals and Imitators, and virtually ignores the alembic qualities of genius in transforming the ore that it gathers from every source. "Originals," he declares,[206] "are and ought to be great favorites, for they are great benefactors, they extend the republic of letters, and add a new province to its dominion: Imitators only give us a sort of duplicates of what we had, possibly much better than before; increasing the mere drug of books, while all that makes them valuable, knowledge and genius are at a stand. . . ." Still further: "An imitator shares his crown if he has one, with the chosen object of his imitation; an original enjoys an undivided applause. An Original may be said to be of a vegetable nature; it rises spontaneously from the vital root of genius; it grows, it is not made: Imitations are often a sort of manufacture wrought up by those mechanics, art, and labor, out of existent materials not their own."

Whereas in the best periods of classical composition the effect of great originals is, as we have seen, to engender in the heirs of the tradition a spirit of generous emulation, according to Young, 'they engross, prejudice, and intimidate:' ". . . they engross our attention, and so prevent a due inspection of ourselves; they prejudice our judgment in favor of their abilities, and so lessen the sense of our own; and they intimidate us with the splendor of their renown, and thus under diffidence bury our strength."[207]

Young shares also that distrust of learning and of the "laws" or "rules," which finds so large a place in the romantic creed of the present day, thus he says:[208]

> Learning, destitute of this superior aid (i.e., the aid of genius)—to which Horace would entirely agree, as I may incidentally remark, see (*A.P.*, 405–411)—is fond and proud, of what has cost it much pains; is a great lover of rules, and boaster of famed examples: as beauties less perfect, who owe half their charms to cautious art, learning inveighs against natural unstudied graces, and small harmless inaccuracies, and sets rigid bounds to that liberty, to which genius often owes its supreme glory, but the no-genius its frequent ruin. . . . For rules, like crutches, are a needful aid to the lame, tho' an impediment to the strong.

Although Young's antitheses are bald and sometimes incorrect, and his contrasts lack shading, his essay is rather a protest against the excesses of a frigid formalism engendered by the eighteenth century cult of rationalism as applied to literature than an iconoclastic attack upon the classics. Indeed the true classicist frequently finds himself in general harmony with Young's point of view, and could quote good classical authority in support of it did time permit.

With Rousseau the movement has entered upon a new phase, much more characteristic of the temperamental quality of the 19th century Romanticism, of which Rousseau and not Young or the 18th century sentimentalists is the real father. The joy of emancipation from any definite sequence of ratiocination, which is so pervasive in modern literature finds consummate expression in a famous passage of Rousseau:

> I love to busy myself with mere nothings; to begin a hundred things and finish no one of them: to go and come as the whim takes me; to change my plans every instant; to follow a fly in all its movements; to turn up a stone to see what is under it, to undertake ardently a task that would require ten years and give it up without regret at the end of ten minutes; in fine, to muse all day long without order and sequence.

The result, however, of such complete surrender of the waking intelligence of the literary artist, especially in the period of literary gestation to the claims of the sensuous imagination is, as Babbitt has shown in the New Laocoon,[209] disastrous to any work of the higher reflective imagination. All literary flights become short and febrile. Art and Literature pass more and more from the domain of directed thought into the region of revery. Art is reduced to suggestion, and suggestion is defended as an attenuated hypnosis. In the words of Bergson: "Art aims to lull to sleep the active powers of our personality and to bring us to a state of perfect docility in which we realize the idea that is suggested to us in which we sympathize with the sentiments expressed. In the methods of Art we find under a refined and in some sense spiritualized form the methods by which hypnosis is ordinarily obtained." Similarly in the field of literary criticism Professor Spingarn, a dithryambic follower of the Italian critic Croce: "has done away with the old rules, has done away with the genres or literary kinds, has done away with the comic, the tragic, the sublime, has done away with the theory of style and all the paraphernalia of Greco-Roman rhetoric, has done away with all moral judgments in literature, has done away with the evolution of literature, and has done away with the rupture between genius and taste. Art is simply organic expression—and to every work is to be addressed the sole question, What has it expressed, and how completely?" To such anarchistic welter of Romanticism I must demur.

I should be the first to recognize the grave danger inherent in the solid virtues of the classical tradition, the danger that the technique will be exaggerated above the art, that the free human spirit, as was the case in the silver age of Latin literature and in the Neo-classical revival of the 18th century will be borne along a captive bound to the wheels of abstract theory. But I must equally protest against the narcotic visions of our latterday romanticists. It would seem as if the noble task of the French Revolution and the Romantic Movement in freeing the human spirit from the formalism of the Neo-classicists had at last been attained, and that we are now facing the opposite danger of drifting into the vortex of a purely sensuous impressionism.

But surely the highest works of art in every age, the *Odyssey* of a Homer, the *Aeneid* of a Virgil, and the *Divina Commedia* of a Dante have blended the many colored rays of the vision into the white radiance of truth and beauty.

And in modern times too we do not lack the testimony of men of genius that the profound truths, on which the classical theory of imitation rests, can never lose their meaning, whether for the literary critic or the creative artist.

Thus Schiller in his recension of Matthison's poems differentiates the material from the function of the poet and artist, following the same distinction made by the Greco-Roman rhetoricians: Es ist niemals der Stoff, sondern die Behandlungsweise, was den Künstler und Dichter macht.

And Heine,[219] speaking of the matter of plagiarism says:

Nichts ist thörichter als der Vorwurf des Plagiats; es giebt in der Kunst kein sechstes Gebot, der Dichter darf überall zugreifen, wo er Material zu seinen Werken findet; und selbst ganze Säulen mit ausgemeisselten Kapitälern darf er sich aneignen, wenn nur der Tempel herrlich ist, den er damit stützt.

In 1830 Alfred de Musset said, with clear understanding of the relation of imitation to inspiration:

Pourquoi désavouer l'imitation, si elle est belle? Bien plus, si elle est originale elle-même? Virgile est fils d'Homère, et le Tasse est fils de Virgile. Il y a une imitation sale, indigne d'un esprit relevé, c'est celle qui se cache et se renie, vrai métier de voleur; mais l'inspiration, quelle que soit la source, est sacrée.

But perhaps the most epigrammatic summary of the relation of invention to imitation is that of André Chénier:

Ainsi donc, dans les arts, l'inventeur est celui
Qui peint ce que chacun peut sentir comme lui.

Book I of John Morley's Recollections is entitled the *Republic of Letters*. It is prefaced by a translation from Doudan, which gives lofty expression to the immortality of the classical tradition of imitation in the imagination of the man of letters:

The Man of Letters properly so called is a peculiar being; he does not look at things exactly with his own eyes; he has not merely his own impressions; you could not recover the imagination which was once his; 'tis a tree on which have been grafted Homer, Virgil, Milton, Dante, Petrarch; hence singular flowers which are not natural any more than they are artificial. With Homer he has looked at the plain of Troy, and there lingers in his brain something of the light of the sky of Greece; he has taken something of the pensive beauty of Virgil as he wandered on the Aventine slopes; he sees the world like Milton through the grey mists of England, like Dante through the limpid burning sky of Italy. Out of all these colors he makes for himself a new color that is unique; from all these

glasses through which his life passes to reach the real world there is formed
a peculiar tint which is the imagination of the man of letters.

We have now completed our extended survey of the rhetor-
ical theory of imitation and of literary composition as pursued
in essential harmony with that theory in the Scipionic and in the
Augustan epoch. We have seen how close—in spite of all the
differences of age, temperament, and training—is the bond
which binds Horace to his great predecessor. Both men unite
the functions of the literary critic and the creative artist.
This is the fundamental fact in the interpretation of the develop-
ment of satire as a genre. In the light of this deeper knowledge
of the constituent elements of the great Satiric tradition we may
now turn to our second task, a close analysis and comparison of
the themes, form, and language of the satires of Lucilius and
the satires and epistles of Horace.

NOTES ON CHAPTER III

[1] A complete and satisfactory history of Greek satiric literature, especially of the τὸ σπουδαιογέλοιον has still to be written. In the meantime the researches of classical philologists have been accumulating a number of valuable studies. I have drawn freely upon the following: J. Geffcken, *Studien zur griechischen Satire* in *N. Jahrb. f.d. Klass Alt.*, 27, pp. 393-411, 469-493; *Kynika*, Heidelberg, 1909; Brandt and C. Wachsmuth, *Corpusculum poesis epicae Graecae ludibundae*, 2 vols., vol. 1 by Brandt, vol. 2 by Wachsmuth, (the preface to volume 2 is especially valuable); Gerhard, *Phoenix von Kolophon*, (important collection of material); Ernst Weber, *De Dione Chrysostomo Cynicorum sectatore* in *Leipziger Studien zur classischen Philologie*, vol. 10, pp. 77-268. The following contain material of value for the study of Cynic popular forms: H. Reich, *Der Mimus*; F. Susemihl, *Geschichte der griechischen Litteratur in der Alexandrinerzeit*, 2 vols. s.v. Bion of Borysthenes especially; R. Helm, *Lucian und Menipp.*, Leipzig, 1906; O. Hense, *Teletis Reliquiae*, 1889; in C. Wessley's *Studien zur Palaeographie und Papyruskunde*, vol. 6, edited by Wilhelm Crönert, *Kolotes und Menedemos* has a series of investigations of value for the history of philosophy and literary history, cf. index.

[2] On this notice see Wachsmuth, *op. cit.*, p. 66, n. 1. For a different rendering see Crönert, *Kolotes und Menedemos*, p. 106, n. 506. This latter reading would evidence the large part played by parody in Greek satiric literature.

[3] Wachsmuth, *loc. cit.* very appropriately quotes the testimony of Didymus, apud Stobaeum *ecl.* 2, 7, 11 g., p. 99, 3 Wachs.

[4] As found in Crönert, *Kolotes und Menedemos*, p. 106, n. 506.

[5] See *infra*, pp. 152-154.

[6] See *infra*, pp. 178-201.

[7] See *supra*, p. 118.

[8] On the παίγνια of Monimus see Diog. Laert. 6, 83. On the παίγνια in the age of the Sophists see Von Arnim, *Leben und Werke des Dio von Prusa*, p. 11.

[9] *De animi tranquillitate* 4.

[10] Diog. Laert. 6, 92.

[11] Weber, *de Dione Chrysostomo Cynicorum sectatore*, pp. 88 ff.; Welcker, *praef. Theog.*, p. xcv, n. 46; Wachsmuth, *op. cit.*, pp. 66-85.

[12] Dio. Chrys., *or.* 8, 281 R.

[13] See *supra*, p. 118. Also Horace, *sat.* 1, 10, 60. On σχέδιον as a rhetorical term, Walz, *Rhett.* 3, 422.

[14] See also *sat.* 1, 4, 120 on the diffuseness of Crispinus; also *sat.* 2, 7, 45.

[15] *Rhet.* 3, 7, 1.

[16] See *infra*, pp. 178-201.

[17] See *supra*, pp. 78-126 *passim*.

[18] See also *infra*, pp. 288-291 on Horace, *sat.* 1, 4, 45.

[19] On Lucilius and Accius see Cichorius, *op. cit.*, pp. 59, 131 f., 153 f., 203 f., 205 f., 261.

[20] See Leo, *op. cit.*, p. 386 ff.

[21] He apparently discussed epic, tragedy, and other genres, as Leo proves.

[22] We cannot prove that the title *satura* was actually employed by Lucilius, but the evidence seems to me to point in that direction. I find myself in general accord with the point of view taken by Ullman in his article *Satura and Satire* in C. P. 8, pp. 187 ff. The MS. evidence that *libri satyrarum* was applied to the corpus 1-25 of Lucilius seems to me weighty, while the evidence for the use of the term by Varro is convincing. For Hendrickson's point of view see his article *Satura, the Genesis of a Literary Form*, in C. P. 6, pp. 129-143.

[23] See *Kolotes und Menedemos, op. cit.*, p. 105.

[24] See Heinze-Kiessling, *Introduction to Horace Sat.*, p. ix.

[25] Theaetetus, p. 150 E.

[26] On Greek satiric poetry in iambics see Gerhard, *op. cit.*, p. 242, 264, and under index iambus; also Cichorius, *op. cit.*, pp. 42 ff.

[27] See Cichorius, *op. cit.* Also *supra*, p. 66.

[28] See Marx, *comment on Lucilius*.

[29] See *infra*, pp. 195 ff.; Cichorius, *op. cit.*, pp. 177-179.

[30] See *infra*, p. 407.

[31] See Cichorius, *op. cit.*, p. 180.

[32] See Cichorius, *op. cit.*, p. 167, 175.

[33] On this commonplace compare my paper *Lucilius and Persius*, Tr. A. P. A., vol. 40, pp. 137 ff.; also *infra*, pp. 436 ff.

[34] See *infra*, pp. 221-228.

[35] The ἴαμβος Φοῖνιξος which I have used freely in my study of Horace, *sat.* 1, 1 below contains several Stoic commonplaces which show affinities with certain passages in Horatian satire. In line 77 we have a reference to the much debated relation between riches and wisdom. One party to the controversy maintained the thesis conveniently called the ἔπαινος πλούτου, that is, the praise of riches on the ground that *ipso facto* the rich man was wise. Of this Greek commonplace there are many variations. Probably such passages as Horace, *sat.* 2, 3, 96 and *ep.* 2, 2, 151 ff. belong here. On the other hand the antithetic ψόγος πλούτου regards riches and stupidity as synonymous. In particular a dog in the manger policy is assailed. Hence the μικρολόγος is attacked. Such a man is said to be ignorant of the principle of the wise use of possessions (*nescius uti compositis*). See Gerhard, *op. cit.*, p. 113. Here belong Horace, *sat.* 2, 3, 67 and 109. The question of κτήματα-χρήματα is thus a stock subject of debate. Under this category we may place Horace, *ep.* 1, 7, 57 and A. P. 170.

Sometimes the question is not of use or non-use, but rather of good or bad use. On this commonplace see Gerhard, *op. cit.*, p. 114 ff. Evidently Horace's story of Servius Oppidius and his two sons Aulus and Tiberius (*sat.* 2, 3, 168 ff.) is influenced by this Greek commonplace.

The spendthrifts spend money for needless grandeur. Hence the Greek satirists develop an elaborate complex of commonplaces on the houses of the wealthy. See Gerhard, *op. cit.*, pp. 115 ff. Here belong Horace, *ep.* 1, 2, 47 and *sat.* 2, 3, 308. In this last passage Horace mocks at himself for building on the scale affected by the rich. On the restlessness accompanying such building see Horace, *ep.* 1, 1, 97. Similarly in the odes we have the favorite contrast of popular philosophy between the great villa and the humble cottage. See *odes* 2, 10, 7 ff.; 2, 3, 17; also *sat.* 2, 6, 71. The extremity of simplicity was reached by Diogenes, who dwells out of doors or sleeps in the temples, who consequently would be ἄοικος or homeless, but for the fact that the universe (κόσμος) is his home.

The true demands of the soul surpass in real value all material possessions. So Horace duplicates the sentiment of line 88 in *Phoenix of Colophon* by *ep.* 1, 1, 52.

Finally the phrase λόγοις χρηστοῖσι σωφρονισθεῖσα in line 90 of *Phoenix* with its emphasis upon the value of philosophic aphorisms as instruments of moral instruction is perhaps directly related to the procedure of Horace's father at the close of the 4th satire. See *infra*, pp. 298 ff. Compare also the sentiments of *ep.* 1, 1, 133 ff.

[36] *Op. cit.*, pp. 97 ff.

[37] *Cf.* Horace *ep.* 2, 1, 93 as a good illustration of the Roman feeling towards literary pursuits.

[38] *Cf.* Gerhard, *op. cit.* index *s.v.* Elegeion.

[39] Leo, *op. cit.*, p. 425.

[40] In Greek parody plays a very important part in the comedies of Aristophanes.

[41] With this we may compare such a passage as the speech of Zeus in Lucian's *Jupiter trag.* 25.

[42] See *infra*, pp. 400-405.

[43] For details see *infra*, and commentary of Marx.

[44] Thus, 223 = Ψ443; 355 Ἄρες Ἄρες = E31; 468 = λ491 and 1319; 836 = α403; 1244 = ε322. (This fragment may possibly be related to the satire on the return of Odysseus, of which I have detected traces in book 30). 1254 = A. 2; 1291 = δ607.

[45] On the ἀληθής ἱστορία see Reitzenstein, *Hellenistische Wundererzählungen*.

[46] On the ἀπομνημόνευμα see E. Kopke, *Ueber die Gattung der Apomnemoneumata in der griechischen Litteratur*, Brandenburg 1857 (not accessible to me); article by E. Schwartz in the Paully-Wissowa, *Realencycl.* 2, pp. 170 f.; Gerhard, *op. cit.*, pp. 248 ff.

[47] Diog. Laert. 7, 4.

[48] See Hirzel, *Der Dialog*, I, p. 144, note 3.

[49] See *infra*, pp. 306-316.

[50] See *infra*, pp. 316-324.

[51] *Op. cit:*, pp. xviii ff.

[52] Diog. Laert. 5, 18.

[53] See Gerhard, *op. cit.*, p. 149.

[54] See Gerhard, *op. cit.*

[55] *Gnomologium Vaticanum.*

[56] Suetonius *Julius* 56, 7; *Gramm.* 21.

[57] See *infra*, p. 389.

[58] See Cichorius, *op. cit.*, p. 348.

[59] *Op. cit.*, pp. 303-315 discusses book 11.

[60] See *infra*, pp. 324-330.

[61] *Sat.* 1, 8 has perhaps more affinities with the mime. *Cf.* Lejay, *op. cit.*, p. xxxix.

[62] For bibliography see Hirzel, *der Dialog*, vol..1, pp. 151-159, pp. 360-366, 440, 2; 454, 1; vol. 2, pp. 7, 19, 40, 44 ff.; Christ-Schmidt, *op. cit.*, vol. VII, 2, 1, p. 39, note 4; R. Helm, *Lucian und Menipp.*, pp. 3, 256 ff.

[63] Diog. Laert. 4, 41.

[64] Athenaeus 4, 134, 7.

[65] Even earlier was the parodic δεῖπνον of Hegemon. This narrative, marked by a strong ironical tone, was told in the first person. Its use of parody was masterly. It probably satirized the parasite Chaerephon. The vice of the speaker, greediness, is wittily revealed. See *Athenaeus* 5, 3, 15; 28 ff., 89, 116 ff. Also Geffcken, *op. cit.*, p. 395.

[66] See Hirzel, *Der Dialog*, vol. I, p. 361, note 2.

[67] See Christ-Schmidt, *op. cit.*, vol. VII; 2, 1, 447.

[68] See Susemihl, *op. cit.*, vol. 2, p. 422.

[69] Athen. 2, 64A.

[70] Athen. 3, 79E.

[71] Hirzel, *op. cit.*, vol. I, p. 363.

[72] See Cichorius, *op. cit.*, pp. 269-273.

[73] See *infra*, pp. 408-415.

[74] See *infra*, pp. 412 ff.

[75] See *supra*, p. 150.

[76] On the fable see Christ-Schmidt, *op. cit.*, 7, 1, pp. 180 ff.; Hausrath, *Untersuchungen zur Ueberlieferung der aesopischen Fabeln* in *Jahrbb. f. Cl. Philologie Supp.*, 21, 1894, pp. 247 ff.; *Das Problem der Aesop Fabel*, *N. Jahrbb. f. d. Class. Alt.* 1, 1898, p. 305 ff.; Pauly-Wissowa, *op. cit. s.v.* Aesopus *s.v.* Fabel; Gerhard, *op. cit.*, pp. 229 and note 5, 246 ff., 251, 252 and note 3, 267 ff., 272, 279, 282, 284, 290 ff. are especially valuable on the part played by the fable as an instrument of Cynic-Stoic instruction.

[77] See Christ-Schmidt, *op. cit.*, vii, 1, p. 181, 7.

[78] See in general Christ-Schmidt, *op. cit.*, 7, 1, pp. 182 ff.

[79] On Socrates' interest in the fable see Gerhard, *op. cit.*, p. 246, n. 4. Antisthenes used the fable of the lion and the hares; Diogenes (Diog. Laert. 6, 80) that of the panther and the ravens. Kerkidas (fr. 3, II 4, p. 541 Bergk) has a speech of the tortoise.

[80] We frequently find the fable in the form of an epigram, or epigrammatic maxims are inserted in the fable, as in Babrius. Leonidas of Tarentum probably had a good deal of influence in moulding this type of fable. See Gerhard, *op. cit.*, p. 268, n. 1; Geffcken, *op. cit.*, p. 93.

[81] *Saturarum libri inc.*, ed. Vahlen. *Cf.* also *fragments* 65 V and 67 V.

[82] Sometimes the similes or proverbs relating to animals are akin to fables though of different origin. See Horace, *sat.* 2, 1, 20, 52, 55; 2, 2, 64; 2, 7, 70. Such similes and proverbs are favorite devices of the popular Cynic preachers.

[83] As Havet has seen. For further details see Lejay, *op. cit.*, pp. lxxix and lxxx.

[84] On the mime see: J. A. Führ, *De Mimis Graecorum*, Berlin, 1860; E. Hauler, *Der Mimus von Epicharm bis Sophron* in *Xenia Austriaca*, I, Vienna, 1893, pp. 81-135; Hermann Reich, *Der Mimus*, 2 vols., Weidmann, Berlin, 1903, the most important comparative study of the mime. For brief discussions, Christ-Schmidt, *op. cit.*, vol. VII, 1, pp. 380 ff.; 2, 136 and 257; Gerhard, *op. cit.*, pp. 141, 222 f., 225 f., 230, 6, 243, 4, 244 ff., 254, 267, 275, 5, 276; Hirzel, *Der Dialog*, vol. I, pp. 20-26 on Epicharmus and Sophron.

[85] Compare Reich, *der Mimus*, 1, 1 pp. 263 ff. on Theophrastus' definition of the Mime.

[86] See Christ-Schmidt, vol. I, pp. 377-380; Lorenz, *Leben und Schriften des Koers Epicharmus*. As Hirzel well says *op. cit.*, vol. I, p. 23, n. 1, he anticipates the liveliness of the Socratic method.

[87] See Gerhard, *op. cit.*, p. 230, n. 6.

[88] See Karl Watzinger in *Mitth. des deutsch. Atth. Instit.* 26, 1901, pp. 1 ff.

[89] See Christ-Schmidt, *op. cit.*, vol. vii, 2, 1, pp. 153-155.

[90] See *supra*, pp. 93-96 for a criticism on the humor of the mime.

[91] Valerius Maximus 2, 108.

[92] Buecheler, *C. L. E.* 361; Dessau, *Inscr. Lat.* 5221.

[93] *Cf. supra*, pp. 95 ff.

[94] On the early history of the mime at Rome see Leo, *op. cit.*, pp. 372 ff.

[95] See *infra*, pp. 336 ff. on the rhetorical background of this satire.

[96] See *supra*, pp. 93 ff.

[97] *Cf.* Reich, *der Mimus*, vol. I, pp. 411 ff.

[98] *Cf.* Lejay, *op. cit.*, pp. xxxviii-xl.

[99] See *infra*, pp. 393-396.

[100] See *infra*, pp. 308-310.

[101] See *infra*, pp. 330-336.

[102] V 1 *saturarum*, ed. Vahlen.

[103] *Cf.* Reich, *op. cit.*, vol. I, 1, p. 305.

[104] Aristotle, *Eth.* 1127 b, 20.

[105] Athenaeus, *op. cit.*, 621 d, e.

[106] *Cf.* Reich, *op. cit.*, vol. I, pp. 237-263.

[107] See *supra*, pp. 93-96.

[108] *Cf.* Reich, *op. cit.*, vol. I, pp. 64-79.

[109] Cicero, *de natura deorum* 1, 93.

[110] *Cf.* Reich, *op. cit.*, pp. 69-73.

[111] For further examples see Reich, *op. cit.*, vol. I, pp. 358 ff.

[112] Plato, *Symposium*, 221 d; *Gorg.* 491 a, 517 d, e; Xenophon, *Memorabilia* 1, 25.

[113] Spengel, *Rhet. Graec.*, vol. II, p. 455.

[114] *Op. cit.*, 1, 1 pp. 354-376; especially p. 359 f.

[115] See *supra*, p. 113.

[116] On the epistula see Misch, *Geschichte der Autobiographie*, pp. 180, 206 ff., 223, 240 f., 267, 369. (Rather on letters in prose than in verse, but some good remarks on Horace): H. Peter, *Der Brief in der* Röm. *Litt.* in *Abh. der sächs. Gess. der Wissenschaft*, B, 20, N. 3, Leipzig, 1901, p. 179, p. 221; P. H. Edwards, *The Poetic Element in the Satires and Epistles of Horace*, part I, Diss., Baltimore, 1905.

[117] *Op. cit.*, p. 301.

[118] Athenaeus 11, p. 483 F.

[119] *An seni resp. ger.* sit 11, p. 799 A.

[120] *Schol. Aristot.*, p. 404 b, 10 ff.

[121] See Usener, *Epicurea*, p. 135 ff.

[122] Cicero, *ad Att.* 13, 6, 4.

[123] See *infra*, pp. 425-468.

[124] On Bion, see *Diog. Laert.* 4, 7, 46-58; Susemihl, *op. cit.*, pp. 32-41; Christ-Schmidt, *op. cit.*, vol. 7, 2, 1 p. 65; C. Wachsmuth, *op. cit.*, 273 ff.; 201 ff.; O. Hense, *Teletis Reliquiae* xlvi-cix; J. Geffcken, *op. cit.*, pp. 404-408; W. Crönert, *Kolotes und Menedemus*, p. 31 ff.

[125] It is a somewhat suspicious circumstance that the father of Horace, a freedman like Bion's father is also called *Salsamentarius*. See Diog. Laert. 7, 4, 46; Plutarch, *quaest. symp.* 631d; Auct. ad Herennium 4, 54, 67; Suetonius *vita Horat.*, p. 44, 4. Reiff.

[126] It is in dispute whether Bion studied under Crates, the Academician, or Crates, the Cynic. The life of Diogenes Laertius asserts the former view. This is denied by Zeller 2⁴, 1, 342, 2, and A. Hense, *op. cit.*, liv; see also Susemihl, *op. cit.*, vol. I, p. 33, n. 98. Hirzel, *Untersuch. zu Cic. philos. Schr.* 2, 60, n. 2, and *Der Dialog* 1, p. 375 note, and Wachsmuth, *op. cit.*, p. 73, accept the text of Diogenes Laertius. On the whole Hirzel and Wachsmuth appear to me to make out the better case.

[127] On this letter see *infra*, pp. 316-317.

[128] *Cf.* Diog. Laert. 2, 4, 77; Bion quoted in Plutarch, *de lib. educ.* 10, 7d. The passage in Horace's *epistles* 1, 2, 28, in which Horace asserts a similar eclecticism and a fondness for the luxury-loving Aristippus is proof of the temperamental sympathy of the two men, and their common acceptance of eclecticism.

[129] Diog. Laert. 2, 18, 135; Plutarch, *de superstit.* 7, 168 D-E, Hense, *op. cit.*, pp. xlvii, Hense believes that the whole passage of Plutarch on superstition is derived from Bion, while Bion himself drew from some comic source.

[130] Susemihl, *op. cit.*, vol. I, p. 35, n. 104g, believes that this statement while true in part is exaggerated, for Bion showed a good deal of reserve in such remarks. See Diog. Laert. 2, 12, 117. We do not know whether like Plato and Aristotle, Bion merely disbelieved in the popular gods, or whether like Theodorus, he became a thorough-going atheist. See further Hense, *op. cit.*, pp. lxii ff.

[131] Diog. Laert. 4, 7, 48.

[122] Stobaeus, *ecl.* 2, p. 218, 16 ff. W. *cf.* Hense, *op. cit.*, p. lxi.

[123] On the διατριβή in general see Hirzel, *der Dialog*, vol. I, pp. 368 ff.; vol. II, pp. 133, 191, 292; 329.4; Lejay, *op. cit.*, pp. xv and xvi; Gerhard, *op. cit.*, index, *s.v.* Diatribe; Norden, *Antike Kunstprosa*, pp. 129 ff.; Susemihl, *op. cit.*, vol. I, p. 36, n. 105 on the διατριβή before Bion.

[124] Athenaeus 11, p. 508C.

[125] See Norden, *Antike Kunstprosa*, vol. 1, p. 129, note 1 for evidence that the essential features of the διατριβή are really implicit in Plato's dialogues, where we find Socrates disputing with imaginary opponents, the introduction of allegory, and the personification of material objects, so common in the διατριβή. The φησί (*inquit*) of the διατριβή has not yet appeared, although the longer formula ἔροιτο ἂν ἡμᾶς is found.

[126] *Rhet. Gr.* 111p, 406 W.

[127] See *supra*, pp. 84-91.

[128] Stobaeus, *Florileg*, 86, 13 M; *cf.* Teles, p. 6, 1, H. and p. lxxix.

[129] In Horace, *sat.* 1, 6; in Juvenal, *sat.* 8. For the relation of Horace's satire to certain Lucilian fragments in book 30, see *infra*, pp. 316-324.

[130] Diog. Laert. 4, 7, 49. On the apothegms of Bion on death see also Geffcken, *op. cit.*, p. 406.

[131] Cicero, *Tuscl. Disp.* 3, 26, 62.

[132] Diog. Laert. 4, 7, 50.

[133] Diog. Laert. 4, 7, 49.

[134] On the abrupt close of Lucilian satires see *supra*, p. 89.

[135] See Cust's translation of the *Life of Benvenuto Cellini*, vol. I, chapter 12.

[136] On Xanthippe and Socrates see Teles, p. 13, 6 and 13, 11H and Hense, introduction, pp. xlv-xlvi. Also Geffcken, *op. cit.*, p. 406, n. 11.

[137] See *supra*, pp. 158-162.

[138] On this point see Susemihl, *op. cit.*, vol. I, p. 38, notes 108c and 108g; Hense, *op. cit.*, pp. xxvi, xxxv, xxxvi, xxxviii, xl, lii, civ, cviii.

[139] On Homer, see Diog. Laert. 4, 7, 46 with parodies on *Odyss.* 10, 335; 47 on *Il.* 6, 211; 52 on *Il.* 3, 182, and 5, 146; on Euripides, 51, on *Hippol.* 424. On Theognis' relation to the apothegm on old age, see *ibid.* 4, 51; also Hense, *op. cit.*, p. lxxi; on Antiphanes' influence on the apothegm of Diogenes see Diog. Laert. 4, 48, and Hense, *op. cit.*, p. lxxiv.

[140] See *supra*, pp. 152-155.

[141] *Cf.* Ennius, ed. Vahlen, *saturarum Lib. Inc.* 20.

[142] See *infra*, p. 200 for discussion of this passage.

[143] Diog. Laert. 6, 2, 50.

[144] Plutarch *de vit. pud.* C. 18, 536a with Maxim 44, p. 198, 43.

[145] See *infra*, p. 200.

[146] *Apud. Telet.* in Stob., *floril.* 3, p. 213, 5 ff.

[147] See Weber, *op. cit.*, p. 184.

[148] See also Susemihl, *op. cit.*, vol. I, p. 37, n. 108, where we find quoted the assertion of Dicaeocles of Cnidus that Bion and the Theodoreans assailed all the philosophers and spared no abuse.

[159] *Op. cit.*, vol. II, p. 10, n. 2, and compare especially Theophrastus *Χαρακ.* 1, 2, 3, 7, 8, 15, 19, 28. See also *Auctor ad Herennium* 4, 63 ff. For such types in Horace see *sat.* 1, 1, 64; 2, 5, 84; ep. 2, 2, 128.

[160] See *infra*, 370, n. 8 for a discussion of the use of contemporary names in Horace's satires.

[161] Leo, *op. cit.*, pp. 34-40, and Hense, *op. cit.*, lxxxiv-lxxxvii.

[162] *Op. cit.*, p. 407.

[163] See *infra*, pp. 219-247.

[164] *Op. cit.*, p. 76.

[165] *Op. cit.*, pp. lvii-lvix.

[166] Hense compares Plutarch's *Moralia*, p. 1076c.

[167] Epicur., *frag.* 208, Usener.

[168] See *infra*, pp. 287-290.

[169] Such a view is further confirmed by Varro, *fragment* 304B from the Menippean satire called Modius:

> sed ó Petrulle né meum taxis librum
> si te pepigat haec modus scenatilis.

On this fragment see Norden's *In Varronis Saturas Menippeas Observationes Selectae*, p. 272 and p. 341. Schanz, *op. cit.*, 8, 1, 2, 3, p. 426, n. 1 for bibliography on the interpretation of the satire *Modius*.

[170] Hense, *op. cit.*, pp. lviii-lix. Wachsmuth, *op. cit.*, p. 76, note.

[171] For a fuller discussion of this whole question including other passages related to that of Diogenes Laertius, see Wachsmuth, *op. cit.*, pp. 74-75.

[172] Geffcken, *loc. cit.*, p. 408.

[173] See *infra*, pp. 219-247.

[174] For detailed proof see *infra*, p. 235-236.

[175] For Horace see *infra*, p. 230.

[176] See also *infra*, pp. 224-225.

[177] See *infra*, p. 237.

[178] Whether the commonplace upon the uselessness of merely amassing a store (of grain or gold) was in Bion as well as in Lucilius 555 and Horace, *sat.* 1, 1, 41 is not so clear. An imitation of Teles quoted by Hense, *op. cit.*, p. 18, parallels the general order of Horace's argument. His words ὁ πλοῦτος . . . κόρον οὐκ ἔχει τοῖς κτησαμένοις might be taken as summarizing the content of Horace's lines 41-72. The theme of the superfluous store of the granary found in Horace's lines 45-46 is evidently a recollection of Lucilius' fragment 555, but it has not survived in any of the imitators of Bion. The nearest approach is in Teles, p. 28, 4 H: ἐπιθυμοῦντες μὲν πολλῶν χρῆσασθαι δὲ οὐ δυνάμενοι.

[179] *Cf. infra*, pp. 378-387 on Horace, *sat.* 2, 2.

[180] *Cf. infra*, pp. 316-324.

[181] Stobaeus, *florileg* 87.13; Plutarch, *de vitioso pudore*, p. 534C and *Apotheg. reg. et duc.*, p. 183 D. See Hense, *op. cit.*, p. lxxii.

[182] See *infra*, pp. 316 ff.

[183] See *infra*, pp. 317 ff.

[184] See *infra*, p. 317.

[18] Diog. Laert. 4, 7, 51, I accept Hense's emendation of ὅμοιοι for ὁποῖοι; see *op. cit.*, p. lxxvii.

[18] Hense, *op. cit.*, p. lxxvii f. for citation of passages.

[187] See *supra*, p. 151.

[188] As Hense has seen *op. cit.*, p. lxxvii.

[189] *Fragments* 662, 664 and especially 665. See also *infra*, p. 458 on the *Ars Poetica* and these lines.

[190] I suspect a still earlier use of this quasi-corollary of the commonplace in Greek literary theory.

[191] See *infra*, pp. 277-280 in *Sat.* 1, 4; pp. 343-345 in *Sat.* 1, 10 and *Ars Poetica*, pp. 458-460.

[192] See *infra*, pp. 458 ff.

[193] See also Ullman, *Horace on the Nature of Satire*, Tr. A. P. A., vol. 48, pp. 111-132.

[194] See *supra*, pp. 114 ff.

[195] *Op. cit.*, p. lxxviii.

[196] See *infra*, pp. 336 ff. and especially Hendrickson's study, *Horace and Valerius Cato* in C. P. 11, pp. 249-269; 12, pp. 77-92; 328-350 *passim*.

[197] Pp. 279-297.

[198] See *infra*, pp. 279 ff.

[199] *Cf.* Gerhard, *op. cit.*, p. 30 ff.

[200] *Cf.* Stobaeus, *Florilegium* 10, 46; 93, 31; Horace, *epp.* 2, 2, 146 and Plutarch, *de cupiditate divitarum*, p. 524A.

[201] See Hense, *op. cit.*, pp. xcvi-cv.

[202] See *infra*, pp. 310-311.

[203] This is not to deny that the strongly dramatic and improvisatory instincts of the Italian Lucilius found free play in satire. My point is rather that the dramatic characteristics of satire of a more formal and conscious sort are to be traced rather to a free adaptation of the spirit of the Greek satiric forms than to any relationship of the beginnings of Latin satire, with the supposed dramatic *satura*, *Atellana*, and other early Italic dramatic forms.

[204] *Op. cit.*, pp. 410-411.

[205] I short I find myself unable to subscribe to the central doctrine of the article by Hack in the *Harvard Studies in Classical Philology*, vol. 27, pp. 1-66: *The Doctrine of the Literary Forms*. Hack holds in substance: "that the poet and the critic are always at war even when the two activities are combined in the same person; Horace the poet disagrees rather violently with Horace the critic." On the contrary the cumulative evidence of the introductory chapters of this book on the development of the rhetorical theory of imitation in Rome, the chapter on the influence of the plain style and the related theory of ironic humor as developed in the Scipionic circle, and subsequently extended and defined by the movement of the Roman Atticists has proved the existence of a traditional rhetorical theory of the content, tone and diction of the *sermo*. My analysis of the satire of Lucilius and Horace in chapters 4-6 seems to me to prove rather that in practice the poet supports and essentially reenforces the literary

critic wherever the two functions are combined in the same person. At times practice lags behind theory, and it goes without saying that the laws of the genre are expressed by each man of genius in a form in essential harmony with the spirit of the age as well as with the principles of the tradition. But there is to my mind no reason for asserting a divorce between theory and practice. The classical theory of the literary forms is not a strait-jacket or a noose into which the creative artist deliberately thrusts his head. On the contrary the evolution of the literary forms rests on the common emotional and spiritual experience of the race. Consequently it defines broadly the *milieu*, in which the ancient literary artist is glad to work. Wordsworth's sonnet, beginning with the words "Scorn not the sonnet," gives admirable expression to a similar point of view as regards one of the most intricate of our modern literary forms.

[206] I quote from a copy of the second edition, p. 10.

[207] *Op. cit.*, p. 17.

[208] *Op. cit.*, p. 28.

[209] See New Laocoon *passim*: especially pp. 129 ff.

[210] This and the following passages are quoted and discussed by Stemplinger, *op. cit.*, pp. 158-162.

CHAPTER IV

THE SATIRES OF BOOK I

SATIRE I

Horace's first satire represents an attempt, only partially successful, to fuse two favorite themes of the Cynic-Stoic popular philosophy. These themes are discontent with one's lot, μεμψιμοιρία, and the love of riches or avarice, φιλοπλουτία or αἰσχροκέρδεια.[1]

The earlier philosophic variants of the commonplace dealing with discontent with one's lot, probably current in the third century B.C., form the basis of Horace's lines 1-22. Today there are extant no complete examples of this commonplace. Its general outlines, however, may be clearly reconstructed on the basis of later Greek epitomatizations and imitations, and of certain earlier fragments. The most important of these are a passage in a letter attributed to Hippocrates, treating of discontent in general, but with an enumeration of types of the discontented varying from that of Horace,[2] and a passage which looks like a summary of a scene from a mime found in Maximus of Tyre, a sophist of the second century A.D. In this latter passage we have two pairs of discontented beings matched off. The γεωργικός, who corresponds to Horace's *agricola*, and the ἀστικός, represented more concretely in Horace by the *iuris consultus*, form the first antithetical pair. The second pair is the military man, στρατιωτικός, and the civilian, εἰρηνικός. To these correspond in Horace, the *miles* and the *mercator*. In fact, the passage of Maximus shows so strong a resemblance to Horace, lines 1-21, that Lejay[3] does not hesitate to assert that we have a [free?] translation of the beginning of Horace's satire. The passage in question is as follows: (pp. 2-3)

καὶ ἴδοις ἂν τὸν μὲν γεωργικὸν μακαρίζοντα τοὺς ἀστικοὺς ὡς συνόντας βίῳ χαρίεντι καὶ ἀνθηρῷ, τοὺς δ' ἀπὸ τῶν ἐκκλησιῶν καὶ τῶν δικαστηρίων καὶ τοὺς πάνυ ἐν αὐτοῖς εὐδοκίμους ὀδυρομένους τὰ αὑτῶν καὶ εὐχομένους ἐπὶ σκαπάνῃ βιῶναι καὶ γηδίῳ σμικρῷ.· ἀκούσῃ δὲ τοῦ μὲν στρατιωτικοῦ τὸν εἰρηνικὸν εὐδαιμονίζοντος, τοῦ δὲ ἐν εἰρήνῃ στρατιωτικὸν τεθηπότος. καὶ εἴ τις θεῶν ὥσπερ ἐν δράματι ὑποκριτὰς ἀποδύσας ἕκαστον τοῦ παρόντος βίου καὶ σχήματος, μεταμφιέσει τὸ τοῦ πλησίον (mutatis partibus). αὖθις αὖ οἱ αὐτοὶ ἐκεῖνοι ποθήσουσι μὲν τὰ πρότερα ὀδυροῦνται δὲ τὰ παρόντα. οὕτω δυσάρεστόν τι ἐστιν ὁ ἄνθρωπος κομιδῆ καὶ φιλαίτιον καὶ δεινῶς δύσκολον καὶ οὐδὲν τῶν αὑτοῦ ἀσπάζεται. 21, 1.

Is this passage a translation of Horace or are we to explain the resemblances to Horace on the theory that both Horace and Maximus depend on some earlier common source in Greek? If we accept this second alternative can we determine what that common source was? Personally, I am strongly inclined to the second alternative for a number of reasons.

In the first place we do not find the same sharp antithesis of concrete types in Maximus which we find in Horace. I find it difficult to believe that the *iuris consultus* of Horace would be loosely rendered by ἀστικός, his *mercator* by εἰρηνικός. I hold it much more probable that Horace, in accordance with his habit, gave concrete expression and Roman coloring to some Greek original whose more generalized antithetical pairs were followed by Maximus of Tyre.

Much more important is the general consideration, which will become clearer as we continue with the analysis of this satire, that Horace is evidently following the well-worn lines of Greek popular philosophical treatises mainly of Cynic origin. And, thirdly, it seems to me reasonable to refer the dramatic interference of the god in Maximus and in Horace, lines 15–22, to some Greek διατριβή of distinctly dramatic character. Let us consider this last point briefly.

Of all the διατριβαί of the Hellenistic period those of Bion, the true founder of this form, stand out most clearly, as dramatic in character, and profoundly influenced by the mime.[4] Now the hypothetical phrasing of the words εἴ τις θεῶν suggests a form imitative of the mime rather than the mime itself. Further, we know that Teles-Bion used this conditional form to introduce a semi-dramatic coloring in the personification of πράγματα or possessions: διὸ καὶ εἰ λάβοι, φησὶν ὁ Βίων, φωνὴν τὰ πράγματα . . . καὶ δύναιτο δικαιολογεῖσθαι.[5] In this same passage Bion (l. 5) also gives a general caution against discontent: μὴ οὖν βούλου δευτερολόγος ὢν τὸ πρωτολόγου πρόσωπον· εἰ δὲ μὴ ἀνάρμοστόν τι ποιήσεις. With this we may compare Horace's *mutatis partibus* (l. 18) and the ὥσπερ ἐν δράματι ὑποκριτὰς ἀποδύσας κ.τ.λ. of

Maximus.[6] In these facts, then, we have somewhat meagre, but distinct indications associating the form of the passage of Maximus rather with Bion than with Horace's satire. If now I can show that the popular philosophers of the Hellenistic period especially affected the themes of μεμψιμοιρία and φιλο-πλουτία it will be a much more natural assumption that the Greek sophistic writings subsequent to Horace drew upon these national Greek sources rather than upon the Roman poets. Furthermore, if I can show resemblances between Horace's method of exposition and that of such earlier Greek writers, I shall measurably increase the probability that the resemblances between Horace and these later Greek writers go back to common, or at least related Cynic sources current in the Hellenistic period. Without pretending to exhaust the widely scattered and fragmentary material upon this subject, I would first invite my reader's attention to certain striking parallelisms in methods of popular expositions between these Cynic writings and Horace's first satire.

The anonymous treatise on αἰσχροκέρδεια or the sordid pursuit of wealth, found in the Heidelberg Papyrus 310, the ἴαμβος Φοίνικος of the same papyrus, the Papyrus Lond. 155 verso, and the Papyrus Bodl. mss. gr. class 1, f.1, (p) which have been edited with a wealth of similar illustrative common-places from the whole range of Greek literature by Gerhard in his *Phoenix von Kolophon*,[7] afford us a remarkable opportunity of examining Horace's relation to such common themes and stock illustrations so widely represented in Greek popular philosophy. Important also is Plutarch's treatise on φιλοπλουτία or the love of riches, which apparently represents a later form of the same tradition. Let us now examine in some detail these tools of popular Cynic exposition.

(1) In line 72 of the Anonymous on αἰσχροκέρδεια we find the bustling activity, which the Greeks called τὸ πολυπράττειν or πολυπραγμοσύνη, associated with the mad pursuit of riches.[8] Especially interesting in this connection is the assertion of Teles-Bion (?) in the διατριβή on poverty and wealth, p. 35,2 f.H., denying that wealth is conducive to the study of philosophy. The reason given is that the pursuit of wealth prevents all leisure: ἢ πάλιν οὐχ ὁρᾷς διότι οἱ μὲν πλούσιοι πλείω πράττοντες κωλύονται τοῦ

σχολάζειν. Similarly Horace holds up to ridicule the excuse that boundless activity in pursuit of wealth is to attain leisure. Such leisure never comes. See 28 ff.

> ille gravem duro terram qui vertit aratro,
> perfidus hic caupo, miles nautaeque per omne
> audaces mare qui currunt, hac mente laborem
> sese ferre, senes ut in otia tuta recedant,
> aiunt, cum sibi sint congesta cibaria.

Here the *laborem ferre*, taken in connection with the varied activities just enumerated, looks like a rendering of πολυπραγμοσύνη, while the *"in otia tuta recedant"* recall the σχολάζειν of Teles, the epitomator of Bion. Plutarch also in the περὶ φιλοπλουτίας, 6, 525 F couples restless activity in the pursuit of wealth with complete incapacity to enjoy it after it is acquired, the same context which we have in Horace, 27 ff.: ἐτέρα δὲ ἐστιν ἡ θηριώδης συκοφαντοῦσα, καὶ κληρονομοῦσα, καὶ φροντίζουσα, καὶ ἀριθμοῦσα τῶν φίλων ἔτι πόσοι ζῶσιν, εἶτα πρὸς μηδὲν ἀπολαύουσα τῶν πανταχόθεν προσποριζομένων.

(2) The *mercator* is one of the commonest types of αἰσχροκέρδεια even before the period of the New Comedy.[9] This type frequently appears in the New Comedy, in Greek popular philosophical works, and in the anthologies of Greek proverbial wisdom. The boldness and adaptability of the sailor-trader in encountering the winds and waves is praised by Teles περὶ αὐταρκείας which Horace's lines 29 ff. reecho:

> miles nautaeque per omne
> audaces mare qui currunt.

and Teles p. 6, l, 7. H.: διὸ δεῖ μὴ τὰ πράγματα πειρᾶσθαι μετατιθέναι ἀλλ' αὐτὸν παρασκευάσαι πρὸς ταῦτα πῶς ἔχοντα, ὅπερ ποιοῦσιν οἱ ναυτικοί· οὐ γὰρ τοὺς ἀνέμους καὶ τὴν θάλατταν πειρῶνται μετατιθέναι, ἀλλὰ παρασκευάζουσιν αὐτοὺς δυναμένους πρὸς ἐκεῖνα στρέφεσθαι.

(3) Many of the later Cynics, following the example of Crates of Thebes, mitigated the earlier Cynic severity of Diogenes by a more genial manner of teaching. Like the physician, they sweeten the bitter dose of philosophy with honey, a method of procedure which is followed by Horace, who cites the precedent of coaxing teachers who help children to study their A B C's by the gift of sweet cakes, (l. 23).[10] With this we may compare Themistius (περὶ ἀρετῆς) (in *Rh.*

Mus. 27 p. 440), who says: "That you may easily follow me, I will weave a pleasing exposition into the beginning of my discourse, as the physicians do if they give a severe remedy; they smear the edge of the cup with honey and wine." This idea, contrary to his true method of teaching, was even attributed to Diogenes himself: οἱ μὲν ἰατροὶ τὰς τῶν ἐκλεικτῶν φαρμάκων πικρίας μέλιτι, οἱ δὲ σοφοὶ τὰς τῶν δυσκολωτέρων ἀνθρώπων ὁμιλίας ἱλαρότητι γλυκαίνουσιν.[11]

(4) The wide use of animal similes and fables by the Cynics has already been noticed.[12] As animals by definition "live in accordance with nature" man can learn much from them. In this satire we find Horace in 33 ff. using the ant as the type of industry, and differentiating her logical economy from unreasonable miserliness, which does not use its store.[13]

This ancient simile is found also in Plutarch περὶ φιλοπλουτίας 6, 525 F, who compares the unaggressive type of avarice with a snail, and with the bath keeper's ass that, carrying wood and fuel for the fires, is filled with smoke and ashes, but is itself neither bathed nor warmed. This type of covetousness, Plutarch continues, "makes a man live the life of an ass or ant": καὶ ταῦτα πρὸς τὴν ὀνώδη καὶ μυρμηκώδη λέγω ταύτην φιλοπλουτίαν.

Similarly in the Anonymous or αἰσχροκέρδεια l. 40 we have the word ἐν θηρίοισι, evidently used in a context similar to that of Horace and Plutarch, as Gerhard[14] has proved by many other illustrative examples of this commonplace.

Again in line 46, Horace appears to have substituted the slave who bears food and yet receives no more than his fellow-slave who carries nothing for the mules who carry gold and silver, but eat only hay. This latter simile was used by Aristo in *Gnomolog. Vatic.* ed. Sternbach N., 120 to portray the wealthy misers by: τοὺς πλουσίους καὶ φειδωλοὺς ὁμοίους εἶναι τοῖς ἡμιονοῖς οἵτινες χρυσὸν καὶ ἀργύριον φέροντες χόρτον ἐσθίουσιν.

(5) The animals, moreover, do not accumulate their stores simply for the sake of accumulation, but against an evil day. When the evil day arrives they employ their stores to meet their physical needs. Therefore, they have not the vice of πλεονεξία, or acquisitiveness. This is the fundamental distinction between the ant and the miser, as Horace points out in lines 36–40.

(6) While the animals recognize the limitations imposed upon the manner of their life by the forces of nature, sea, wind, the mountains, the seasons, etc., the avaricious man is completely indifferent to all physical hardships, even to shipwreck, for example, when engaged in the pursuit of gain. This commonplace is developed by the Anonymous περὶ αἰσχροκερδείας in line 73.[15] Again in the London Papyrus, lines 14 and 15, the words πεςῇ and πλωτήρ seem to suggest that the ἔμπορος, the Greek pattern for Horace's *mercator*, is the incarnation of avarice. In this connection fragment 2 of Aischion,[16] in which the traders are called the ants of the sea, is particularly in point, since in Horace the description of the trader in line 30 is immediately followed by the simile of the ant in line 33. The Greek line was

Στεῶν καθ' Ἑλλήσποντον, ἐμπόρων χώρην,
ταῦται θαλάσσης ἐστρέφοντο μυρμήκες.

(7) And yet all the activities of man are proved to be useless by the simple fact of the limited capacity of the human stomach, often a coarse cynic analogue for the human spirit, for the enjoyment of what has been amassed. So Horace in lines 45 and 46:

milia frumenti tua triverit area centum,
non tuus hoc capiet venter plus ac meus.

In a similar commonplace in the Anonymous περὶ αἰσχροκερδείας the word γαστρός occurs in line 45, evidently in a context implying that one must not be the slave to food or drink, while in line 56 the human passions are compared to horses which need the bit. Among these passions, control of the appetite γαστρὸς κρατεῖν is singled out in the proverbial wisdom of the Greek philosophers. Before Horace Varro[17] had set forth the need for such control in his *Virgula divina* fragment 572 B: praesertim cum ventrem meum coerceam nec murmurari patiar.

(8) In the Anonymous on αἰσχροκέρδεια occur two rallying cries of the Cynic sect; in line 46 we have the personal expression of contentment with one's lot, ἀπαρκεῦμαι by which the writer asserts his allegiance to the principle of the self-sufficiency αὐτάρκεια of the sage. Hence the doctrine of ἀρκεῖσθαι τοῖς παροῦσιν, of satisfaction with what is at our disposal, became a

Cynic proverb. Bion-Teles p. 28, l. 12 H, asserts that Crates promised this reward for his teaching: βιώσῃ ἀρκούμενος τοῖς παροῦσι. Horace, as every reader knows, was temperamentally sympathetic to the spiritual and social implications of this well-worn commonplace.[18] The objective correlative, so to speak, of this subjective attitude of contentment, is called in Greek τὰ ἀρκοῦντα, in Latin *quod satis est*, the modicum required to meet the need of food, clothing, and shelter; an idea which is naturally associated with honest and respected poverty, and in consequence contrasted with envied and hated wealth. This collocation occurs in line 70 ff. of the Anonymous:

ἐγὼ μὲν οὖν, ὦ Πέρσα, βουλοίμην εἶναι
·τἀρκοῦντ᾽ ἐμαυτῷ καὶ νομίζεσθαι χρηστὸς
ἢ πολλὰ πράσσων καὶ ποτ᾽ εἰπεῖν τοὺς ἐχθρούς.

It is the objective aspect of the commonplace, the *quod satis est*, to which Horace gives most frequent expression. The relation between the objective modicum of τὰ ἀρκοῦντα and the subjective sense of independence and self-sufficiency αὐτάρκεια, the product of deliberate acquiescence "with things as they are," perhaps finds definitive expression in Horace's *epistles* 1, 2, 46:

quod satis est cui contingit nihil amplius optet.

Naturally, he desires nothing more for he is by definition αὐτάρκης or self-sufficient. In our own satire these same correlatives, subjective and objective, stand in clear antithesis in line 59:

at qui tantuli eget (=ἀπαρκεῦμαι).
quanto est opus (=τὰ ἀπαρκεῦντα).

(9) But contrasted with this philosophical moderation and content, we have the insatiable monetary philistinism of the crowd, which, ignorant of philosophy, denies the doctrine of sufficiency with its corollary of the limitations set by our spiritual ideals on our physical nature. Thus in the iambic poem of *Phoenix of Colophon* in line 95 of the Heidelberg Papyrus, we have in the words ἀξίους τ[ρι]ῶν χ[αλκῶ]ν, "worth three coppers," an allusion to the low value set on the character of the penurious philosopher by the crowd. Over against this doctrine the crowd sets up the thesis of insatiable greed and measures every man by the size of the money he has amassed.

The *Nil satis est* of the streets is substituted for the *quod satis est* of the schools.

Similarly Plutarch περὶ φιλοπλουτίας 7, p. 526 C, asserts that fathers advise their sons: κέρδαινε καὶ φειδοῦ, καὶ τοσούτου νόμιζε σεαυτὸν ἄξιον εἶναι ὅσον ἂν ἔχῃς. Similarly Horace in line 62 says:

'nil satis est' inquit, 'quia tanti quantum habeas sis.'

The relation of this line to Bionean and Lucilian formulations of the same commonplace I shall discuss presently.[19]

(10) Tantalus[20] is employed as a stock example of insatiate greed in line 68. This is an allegorical interpretation of his punishment in the lower world, found as early as Timon of Phlius, and occurring also in Bion. In Timon 18 we read: διδόασι (sc. οἱ πλούσιοι καὶ φειδωλοί) τὴν δίκην ὥσπερ ὁ Τάνταλος ἄποτοι καὶ ἄγευστοι καὶ ξηροὶ τὸ στόμα ἐπικεχηνότες (*inhians*) μόνον τῷ χρυσίῳ.

(11) In line 34 of the Anonymous περὶ αἰσχροκερδείας,[21] the αἰσχροκερδής is declared to attract wealth to himself from every source: ἔοικεν εἶναι π[άντο]θεν γὰρ ἕλκουσιν. Similarly in Plutarch's περὶ φιλοπλουτίας p. 525 F, we read of φιλοπλουτία . . . : πρὸς μηδὲν ἀπολαύουσα τῶν πανταχόθεν προσποριζομένων. With these last words we may compare Horace's line 70:[22]

congestis undique saccis
indormis inhians, et tamquam parcere sacris
cogeris.

(12) Animals are content to satisfy their needs which are classified by Epicurus as φυσικαί or ἀναγκαῖαι or both;[23] that is the minimum requirements of food and shelter. This commonplace, found also in slightly varying form in the teachings of the Cynics, occurs in Horace's lines 74 ff.:

nescis quo valeat nummus, quem praebeat usum?
panis ematur, olus, vini sextarius, adde
quis humana sibi doleat natura negatis.

These lines Porphyrio rightly interprets of the minimum requirements of food and shelter: quae frigori aut fami repellendae et commodiori mansioni sunt necessaria aliaque similia.

(13) The avaricious, however, instead of leading lives rendered simple and contented by the satisfaction of these needs, thus limited by nature and necessity, are not only tor-

mented by the insatiable craving for greater wealth, but by the
anxiety as to the continual possession of the wealth they have:
the miser has positive "phobias" of robbers, fires, and thievish
slaves. So Horace in lines 76 ff.:

> an vigilare metu exanimem, noctesque diesque
> formidare malos fures, incendia, servos
> ne te compilent fugientes, hoc iuvat?

So in the very fragmentary London Papyrus, 155 verso, line
10,[24] we find the robber as a sort of counter-type to the rich
miser: [... ... ... ἕ]καστος ἔνθεν ἀρπάζη. The suggested restor-
ation for the lacuna of περισκοπεῖ δ' seems plausible. So theft is
condemned in Greek proverbial literature, as the greatest evil
that flesh is heir to:

> ἡ δ' ἁρπαγὴ μέγιστον ἀνθρώποις κακόν.

But it is to this very evil, at least in anticipation, that the
avaricious man deliberately subjects himself. To this self-
inflicted torture of anticipated loss by theft, line 13 of the same
fragment seems to refer.[25]

> ἁρπαγὴν τρισσ(εύων)ἡν ψυχήν.

It will be noticed that the Horatian *compilent* reproduces the
Greek ἁρπάζειν.

(14) From such evils, the inevitable concomitants of the
race for wealth, the true Cynic utters a heartfelt prayer for
deliverance.[26] So Horace continues in line 79:

> horum
> semper ego optarim pauperrimus esse honorum.

With this we may compare the wish of the Anonymous on
αἰσχροκέρδεια in the Heidelberg Papyrus line 70:

> [ἐγ]ὼ μὲν οὖν, ὦ Πάρρε. βουλοίμην εἶναι,
> ἀρκεῖντ' ἐμαυτῷ καὶ νομίζεσθαι χρηστὸς
> ἢ πολλὰ πρήσσειν καὶ ποτ' εἰπεῖν τοὺς ἐχθρούς.

(15) Moreover, the avaricious man is something more than
the mere passive victim of his fears of losing his hoard; he is the
object of the active enmity, not merely of his acquaintances,
neighbors, and friends, but even of those of his own household;
his children, wife, and above all, from motives of self-interest,
his heir, hate him. This envy toward the rich, the φθόνος τῶν

πλουσίων, is a widely-spread commonplace in the Cynic-Stoic popular philosophy of the Hellenistic period and in its later derivatives. This is, in fact, one of the stock arguments in the polemic against wealth, the ψόγος τοῦ πλούτου.[27] It occurs in line 72 of the Anonymous fragment just quoted and is illustrated with a wealth of detail by Gerhard, who shows that almost uniformly the rich are the victims of φθόνος, ἐπιβουλή, and μῖσος. Thus we have a saying, attributed to Democritus: οἱ πένητες ἐκπεφεύγασιν ἐπιβουλὴν φθόνον καὶ μῖσος οἷς οἱ πλούσιοι καθ' ἡμέραν συνοικοῦσιν. Similarly according to Plutarch περὶ φιλοπλουτίας 7 p. 526.D, the avaricious do not succeed even in winning the love of their own children: οὐ φιλοῦντες ὅτι πολλὰ λήψονται, ἀλλὰ μισοῦντες ὅτι μήπω λαμβάνουσι.

This aspect of the general theme of avarice is developed in pretty close harmony with Greek models by Horace in lines 80–91,[28] lines 84 ff., being especially in point:

> non uxor salvum te volt, non filius; omnes,
> vicini oderunt, noti, pueri atque puellae.

(16) Finally in line 106, of Horace,[29] we clearly have an allusion to a proverbial saying of one of the seven wise men of Greece, Cleobulus, μέτρον ἄριστον:

> est modus in rebus, sunt certi denique fines.

I have thus shown by an analysis of no fewer than 16 commonplaces, represented in this satire alone, Horace's complete familiarity with the well-worn tools of Cynic exposition. That he has succeeded in putting the stamp of his own genius upon this mass of traditional material is high proof of his creative power. Moreover, if Horace is so familiar with the expository methods and themes of the great company of popular philosophers which encompass Bion, the great representative of the τὸ σπουδαιογέλοιον, it is unlikely that he escaped the influence of Bion himself. In no sense, however, are we to regard the διατριβαί of Bion as the exclusive sources of this satire, though we have already seen[30] that Horace was evidently familiar with the particular formulation given to these commonplaces by Bion. In regard to this matter of his familiarity with Greek popular philosophy, it is probable that Horace is following though with circumspection, good taste, and full regard for his literary independence, in the steps of his great masters, Bion and Lucilius.

Horace's own words in lines 23–27 are of fundamental importance for an understanding of the whole temper and spiritual heritage of his satires in relation to the various popular Greek philosophical forms conveniently summarized under the designation τὸ σπουδαιογέλοιον, the appropriate designation of the κυνικὸς τρόπος or Cynic manner in popular philosophical exposition. To this Cynic method Horace gives his express allegiance when he says, paraphrasing the Greek technical term:

> quamquam ridentem dicere verum
> quid vetat?

And again, when having given a short and restrained flight to the laughable τὸ γέλοιον (ludus) lines 23–26, he turns to the serious exposition of his doctrine τὸ σπουδαῖον (seria) in line 27:

> sed tamen amoto quaeramus seria ludo.

In such a clear avowal of discipleship to Greek popular philosophy, an avowal supported by the detailed analysis of the Greek popular philosophical elements suffusing the tone and content of this satire, we find further proof of the abiding influence of the whole critical theory of the τὸ σπουδαιογέλοιον, expounded in the Scipionic circle by Panaetius, and first given adequate expression in Latin literature by the satire of Lucilius.[31]

Furthermore, we must remember that the Cynic or Stoic popular preacher was a familiar contemporary figure on the streets of Augustan Rome.[32] Crispinus, Fabius, and Stertinius bear witness to the truth of this assertion. Horace was thus sure to gain first hand acquaintance as well as literary intimacy with all the methods of the Cynic preacher. Bearing in mind, therefore, the intricate mesh of Greek influences which surround this satire, we are now at length in a position to proceed with the analysis of the Lucilian satires on the same theme found in books 18 and 19, and to determine, so far as is any longer possible, the nature of their relation, on the one hand, to these same Greek popular philosophical forms; on the other, to this introductory satire of Horace's first book.

From book 18 of Lucilius, we have only three lines extant, all of which, however, can be definitely related to passages in Horace's satire. From book 19, we have eleven lines, of which nine lines may, on the whole, though with varying degrees of probability, be related to Horace's satire. In the case of two lines, 565 and 566, by a plausible but rather less certain reconstruction, I have attempted to show the possibility of a similar relationship. Moreover, an analysis of these nine lines of Lucilius in book 19 seems to show that he also before Horace contaminated the two related themes of μεμψιμοιρία and φιλοπλουτία, doubtless as the result of his familiarity with these two related commonplaces in the pages of Bion and other popular Greek preachers of philosophy.[33] It need cause us no surprise that Lucilius twice treats this theme, in satires found in books 18 and 19, for Horace himself in *satire* 2, 3, 82–160, retraverses in summary the ground of this first satire.

I should, therefore, be inclined to refer fragment 563 to the theme of μεμψιμοιρία, and hold that it stood near the beginning of Lucilius' satire in book 19. Lucilius, however, announces his theme positively; Horace negatively.

> sic singillation nostrum unus quisque movetur.

Movetur in this line is correctly interpreted by Max as referring to perturbation or *motus animi*, but the cause[34] of this restlessness is discontent, not fear.

Horace begins his first satire with a similar generalization, put negatively:

> Qui fit, Maecenas, ut nemo, quam sibi sortem
> seu ratio dederit seu fors obiecerit, illa
> contentus vivat, laudet diversa sequentis?

Lucilius may even in connection with 564 have introduced the god, who granted each discontented soul the right to select in exchange for his present lot the most beautiful day he could possibly conceive, a stronger touch than Horace's permission, granted by some god (later transformed into Jupiter) to exchange his own lot for that of his envied neighbor, line 55 ff. Lucilius' line reads:

> sume diem, qui est visus tibi pulcherrimus unus.

Horace's lines (15 ff.) are:

> si quis deus 'en ego' dicat
> 'iam faciam quod voltis: eris tu, qui modo miles,
> mercator; tu, consultus modo, rusticus: hinc vos,
> vos hinc mutatis discedite partibus. eia,
> quid statis?' nolint, atqui licet esse beatis.

Here the *sume diem* of Lucilius, suggesting a categorical imperative possibly put into the mouth of a god, corresponds in thought, though not verbally to Horace's *iam faciam quod voltis*. In particular, the *sume* suggests an authoritative command similar to Horace's *eris tu*, while the *pulcherrimus* may perhaps find a faint echo in Horace's *atqui licet esse beatis*.[25]

Long before Lucilius and Horace, the Greek satirists who treated the theme of φιλοπλουτία[26] were familiar with the false excuse of the avaricious that they were laying up their store for old age when they could live upon it in comfortable retirement. This argument is uniformly refuted in the Greek satirists by the observation that the avaricious habits of youth and middle age are continued in old age; the argument that *otium* is the goal of avarice is thus shown to be an absurdity. So Lucilius in fragment 557 asserts that the shrivelled old men pursue all the same gainful occupations:

> rugosi passique senes eadem omnia quaerunt.

Horace's version of this commonplace is found in lines 29–31:

> hac mente laborem
> sese ferre, *senes* ut in otia tuta recedant,
> aiunt, cum sibi sint congesta cibaria.

Horace then proceeds, in lines 32–40, to contrast the impelling force of avarice, which will brave all obstacles, whether imposed by man or nature, in the pursuit of gain, with the natural industry of the ant,[27] which after the period of acquisition in the summer time wisely remains at home to enjoy her store in the winter:

> sicut
> parvola, nam exemplo est, magni formica laboris
> ore trahit quodcumque potest atque addit acervo
> quem struit, haud ignara ac non incauta futuri.
> quae, simul inversum contristat Aquarius annum,
> non usquam prorepit et illis utitur ante

> quaesitis sapiens, cum te neque fervidus aestus
> demoveat lucro neque hiems, ignis, mare, ferrum,
> nil obstet tibi, dum ne sit te ditior alter.

In the surviving fragments of Lucilius, the ant is not mentioned, but the *sic* with which fragment 561 begins, in view of the similarity of the lines of Lucilius immediately following with those of Horace, would seem to make it extremely probable that in Lucilius also the simile of the ant immediately preceded these lines. Thus, in the Lucilian passage, the avaricious man is positively advised to amass his gains that he may be able to use them for his delight at home, when the unfriendly winter [of old age?] arrives:

> sic tu illos fructus quaeras, adversa hieme olim
> quis uti possis *ac* delectare domi te.

In other words, Horace expands negatively the difference between the procedure of the avaricious man, and the true wisdom of the cautious and economical ant, while Lucilius directly exhorts the avaricious man to follow the methods of the ant, which though economical is not miserly.

In view of this difference of procedure between the two poets, it is hard to say whether we should compare the *adversa hieme olim* of Lucilius with Horace's more concrete *universum contristat Aquarius annum*, a vivid description of January, or should refer the line merely to the *hiems* of Horace's line 39. The *quis uti possis* is in any case parallel to Horace's *illis utitur ante quaesitis sapiens*. With *quaesiti* we may also compare Lucilius' *illos fructus quaeras*. The avaricious man, if he were truly a sage, would delight himself at home *delectare domi te*, while that wise sage, the Horatian ant '*non usquam prorepit,*' i.e., remains in her anthill.

We thus see that both in Lucilius and Horace the animal, not man, lives in accordance with nature; in short, we here have a perfect instance of the adaptation of one of those Cynic similes of animal life to philosophic teaching, a procedure already discussed above.[38] In fact, Horace in using the metaphor *sapiens* instead of the simile wishes to emphasize that the ant is an *abnormis sapiens*, while man is a *stultus*; or to state the facts in accordance with a well-known Epicurean dictum,[39] the ant obeys those impulses which are both necessary and natural (αἱ ἐπιθυμίαι αἱ φυσικαὶ καὶ ἀναγκαῖαι).

In the lines of Horace immediately following, the poet seems to traverse ground found in a Lucilian satire in book 18, from which we have today only two fragments, 554 and 555. We may explain this similarity either by saying that Horace deliberately contaminated material found in two Lucilian satires, or by saying that Lucilius twice treated the well-known Cynic commonplace on avarice. As we have already seen that the latter fact is certainly true, it is difficult to decide between these two alternatives. However, the somewhat detailed resemblance between the Horatian passages, which I shall proceed now to discuss, and these two Lucilian fragments from book 18, make the hypothesis of contamination by Horace the more probable one.[40] Corroborative evidence may be found in the fact that the whole course of this investigation will show that Horace was fond of contaminating his Lucilian material. Let us now turn to the two Lucilian passages in question.

In fragment 554 Lucilius makes use of a commonplace upon the capacity of the human stomach for enjoyment. This commonplace, as we are now aware, from the evidence of the Heidelberg Papyrus, supplemented by the illuminating studies of Gerhard, was widely used in the Hellenistic period. Thus the Anonymous, author of the iambic fragment on αἰσχροκέρδεια apparently said, lines 45 and 46:

> ʾ ϳτωφ σ[. . .] . . . [ἐ]στιν, οὐ νενίκημα[ι]
> τ . ʾ. . ϳ. [. . . .] καὶ γαστρ[ὸ]ς ἀλλ' ἀπαρ[κ]οῦμαι.

In these lines the thought seems to be[41] that the speaker has not been conquered by food or drink, but in accordance with the ascetic practice of the Cynics, he has limited his appetite to the rational *modicum* needed to satisfy the demands of life, that is to the τὸ ἀρκεῖσθαι τοῖς παροῦσι already discussed.[42] The ἀπαρκεῦμαι of this unknown iambographer thus expresses the same creed as Horace's *quod satis est* in this satire, and his *quod adest* (cf. τὰ παρόντα) in satire 2, 6, 13.

Again in lines 55 and 56 of our unknown iambographer we have a somewhat similar context:

> ἐγὼ μὲν οὖν, ὦ Π[άρνε], ταῦτ' οὐχὶ[ζηλῶ]
> ἀλλ' ἐν χαλ[ινοῖς]. [.] . . . λωστον . . . [. . .]·
> γαστρὸς κατισχ [. . .]. [. . .] βιά[ζ]ομαι τ[οῦτο].

The meaning of these lines[43] seems to be that: I, Parnes, do not enviously desire this, but rein in close the cravings of the belly and force myself to this doctrine, viz., that the regulating principle of my life be simplicity and lack of expense.

Subjectively, therefore, one who has accepted this ascetic principle of the limitation of the objective desires, or appetites, to the ἐπιθυμίαι φυσικαί and ἀναγκαῖοι is quite as happy as the miser, for the amassing of goods does not bring happiness, which is a subjective state of the soul. This state of happiness or contentment, the result of philosophy, finds expression in the iambographer's word ἀπαρκεῦμαι, in line 46, and οὐχὶ ζηλῶ, line 55. The latter phrase somewhat suggests the nil admirari of Horace's epistles 1, 6, 1. A precisely similar attitude is found in the Lucilian fragment 554:

$$-\smile\ \smile-\smile\ \smile-\text{aeque fruniscor ego ac tu.}$$

That is, I, the philosophic assailant of avarice, (notice that the Greek also uses an emphatic ἐγώ in line 55), am quite as happy as you, the wealthy miser with stores of wine and grain, fragment 555.[44]

Similarly Horace, in line 44 ff.:

> quid habet pulchi constructus acervus?
> milia frumenti tua triverit area centum,
> non tuus hoc capiet venter plus ac meus.

A still later formulation of this same commonplace is found in Plutarch περὶ φιλοπλουτίας 8 527B: τίνων τίς ἡ χρῆσις αὔτη, δι' ἣν θαυμάζεται ὁ πλοῦτος; πότερον τῶν ἀρκούντων ἢ τῶν περιττῶν; εἰ γὰρ τῶν ἀρκούντων, οὐδὲν πλέον ἔχουσιν οἱ πλούσιοι τῶν μέτρια κεκτημένων. It will be noticed that Lucilius' line is the reverse expression of this idea. Plutarch says that the rich have no more than those who have moderate possessions; Lucilius says I, a man of moderate possessions, have just as much pleasure as you, the rich man, with your superfluous possessions.

The belly, the organ measuring the capacity of enjoyment, but itself having a limited capacity of measurement and, therefore, of enjoyment, appears in the anonymous iambographer in lines 46 and 57 (γαστρός) and in Horace's venter of line 46, but is absent from the extant fragments of Lucilius.

It is worthy of record, however, that among the fragments of Lucilius, cited without reference to any particular book, the line 1167 reads *et ventrem et gutturem eundem.* Of course, these words are conceivable in various contexts. Marx, for example, refers them to the description of a fish. It is a tempting conjecture, however, in view of the resemblance we have just been establishing to assign this line to book 18 of Lucilius, and place it in pretty close connection with fragment 554. Thus the philosophic speaker might have gone on and said: I can enjoy as much as you for I have the same kind of stomach and throat as you. The addition of *guttur* would then be a typical Lucilian pleonasm. *Guttur,* moreover, is associated with *uenter* in Plautus' *Captivi* 3, 1, 8, and is a natural word to use in such a context because of the association of the throat with gluttony.

The concept of superfluous, and from the Cynic's point of view, meaningless external possessions is represented in Lucilius fragment 555 by the 1200 *medimni* of wheat taken from the threshing flour or the 1000 casks of wine stored in the cellar:

> milia ducentum frumenti tollis medimnum,
> uini mille cadum.

Precisely the same example recurs in Horace's line 45, quoted above.[46]

These two fragments from book 18 of Lucilius, therefore, deal rather with the subjective feeling of contentment, the ἀπαρκεῦμαι of the iambographer, which is emphasized as the result of philosophic study in all the Hellenistic popular schools, though preeminently so by the Cynics and Stoics. But correlative with this is the impersonal τὰ ἀρκοῦντα, the *quod satis est* of worldly possessions, the modicum required to minister to our physical needs. These two correlative terms, the "slogans" of the Cynics, constantly recur in ancient philosophical literature, and indeed in the satires of Horace himself. Their appearance in the present satire is almost inevitable.

But if the sage can be happy without the superfluities of wealth we have been describing in Lucilius and Horace, the miser, on the other hand, innocent of the first principles of philosophy and the freedom such knowledge brings, does not possess the secret of contentment even when he has everything in the way of external possessions; he is a *stultus,* because he tries to measure spiritual satisfaction, ἀπαρκεῦμαι by the material standard of τὰ ἀρκοῦντα, i.e., (the extent of external possessions), whereas the true philosopher will adopt precisely the reverse standard; he will measure the value of his material possessions by the amount of spiritual satisfaction they bring him, and thus measuring will find that nature itself sets appropriate limits to mere accumulation.   These limits are those of our physical necessities and a modicum of social comfort and repute.   The mistake of the *stultus*, as announced in another well-worn Cynic commonplace, which, however, dates back to a pre-Cynic origin, is due to the fact that he measures the value of men in terms of money.

To an analysis of this complex of ideas present in Lucilius' book 19, in the lines of Horace beginning with 61 ff., and widely spread in the literature of the Cynics and the Stoics we now turn.

In fragment 558 of the 19th book of Lucilius, we read:

> denique uti stulto nil sit satis omnia cum sint.

That is the man without knowledge of philosophy, *stultus*, is marked by insatiable greed for material possessions.   Therefore he never attains contentment or satisfaction, though he has the world at his disposal.

Similarly Horace in line 61 ff.:

> at bona pars hominum decepta cupidine falso
> 'nil satis est' inquit, 'quia tanti quantum habeas sis.'

The *stultus* of Lucilius thus clearly corresponds to the generality of mankind, deceived by the false passion of avarice, for the passions blind men to true reason.   The iuxta-position of *cupidine falso* possibly recalls the Epicurean concept of meaningless desire, κενὴ ἐπιθυμία.[46]

This Horatian commonplace *tanti quantum habeas sis* is of pre-Cynic origin, though its widest currency is in the popular Cynic literature.   It appears at least as early as Pindar's Isthmian ode 2, 11, χρήματ' ἀνήρ.   The formulation of this commonplace in the Anonymous περὶ αἰσχροκερδείας and in Plutarch I have already discussed.[47]

Both Lucilius and Horace appear to be influenced more nearly by the formulation given to this commonplace in Bion,

p. LXIX H.: Βίων ἔλεγεν, ὥσπερ τὰ φαῦλα τῶν βαλαντίων, κἂν μηδενὸς ᾖ ἄξια τοσούτου ἐστὶν ἄξια ὅσον ἐν ἑαυτοῖς τὸ νόμισμα ἔχουσιν. οὕτω καὶ τῶν πλουσίων τοὺς οὐδενὸς ἀξίους καρποῦσθαι τὰς ἀξίας ὧν κέκτηνται.

Horace was certainly familiar with two formulations of this commonplace found in Lucilius 1119 and 559. In 1119 we read:[48]

> aurum atque ambitio specimen uirtutis virique est:
> tantum habeas, tantum ipse sies tantique habearis.

Essentially the same "topic" is found in Lucilius 559:

> 'aurum uis hominem <ne?> habeas.' "hominem? quid ad aurum?"
> quare, ut dicimus, non uideo hic quid magno opere optem.

Somewhat further elucidation of this passage is perhaps required.

When confronted with the choice between a man, *hominem*, "or a human value," as we should say, and gold, Lucilius' *adversarius* scornfully rejects the man as unworthy of comparison with gold. The last line, 560, however, seems to be spoken by Lucilius himself, who voices the conclusion of the typical Cynic preacher, saying: "Wherefore, as we say, I do not see in this situation what I should earnestly pray for"; that is, why should I, a philosopher who has a better understanding of the true objects of prayer, of what really brings happiness, desire the sort of thing which in the case of the avaricious man brings only unhappiness. A typical Cynic prayer, therefore, would ask freedom from such material desires and material possessions. Such prayers are clearly represented in the Anonymous iambographer,[49] line 70. The same well-marked tradition is continued in Horace line 79 ff.:

> horum
> semper ego optarim pauperrimus esse honorum.

That is, the spiritual values, such as honor, affection, a good reputation even when accompanied by poverty, are far preferable to material possessions.

In this connection, Horace, line 68, employs as a type of the insatiable pressure of the passions, Tantalus, an allegorical figure used in the writings of the Hellenistic popular philosophers on the basis of the *Odyssey*, λ 580 ff. Here Horace was probably influenced by the employment of this same allegorical figure by Teles-Bion, as we have already seen.[50]   Even before Horace, Lucilius' line 140 from the third satire had used Tantalus as a type, but rather for the torments of unsatisfied sexual passions.

So far, then, from bringing contentment in their train, material riches produce exactly the reverse effect.   The victim of avarice, just as in the Greek popular philosophical fragments,[51] is assailed by endless anxieties; he mistrusts his slaves, fears robberies and fires, Horace line 76 ff.:

> an vigilare metu exanimem, noctesque diesque
> formidare malos fures, incendia, servos
> ne te compilent fugientes, hoc iuvat?

Fragment 1055 of Lucilius must have stood in a similar context, as Marx has seen, for it clearly refers to the anxiety of the misers lest their servants rob them, *subducere* being used as Nonius explains in the sense of *subripere*:

> neu qui te ignaro famuli subducere.

The context of the passage, as restored by Marx, must be approximately correct in view of the similarity the line discloses with the Greek and Latin commonplaces we have been discussing:

> Vehementer tu curas ne res tibi furto pereat neu qui te ignaro famuli quicquam subducere possint.

So far I have tried to show the relationship of eight of the eleven lines in Lucilius' book 19 with definite passages in the first satire of Horace.   In the case of several of these lines, we have seen clear evidence that Lucilius' familiarity with Greek satiric literature in general, and Bion in particular, is almost as marked as that of Horace.   Lines 565, 566, and 567 still remain to be discussed.   In the case of these lines, our conclusions are much less certain, but I think a plausible, perhaps even a persuasive case can be made out for their relation with a passage found in this same satire of Horace.   Moreover, the fact that eight of the eleven lines now extant in book 19 have already been so clearly connected with Horace's satire, raises a strong presumption that these remaining fragments were found in the satire of Lucilius, for we have no evidence in the content of any of the fragments cited from this book that the book contained more than one satire. Let us first consider lines 565 and 566,[12] which belong closely together.

The relations of these two lines to Horace's satire can only be seen when we compare them on the one hand with what appears to be a fuller paraphrase of the same general context in Juvenal 14, 205 ff., and on the other hand with the passage in the present satire beginning with line 23. Such a comparison will incidentally afford us an interesting concrete illustration of the workings of the rhetorical principle governing the author's right to appropriate the material traditional in his genre and to transform it according to the dictates of his own genius and contemporary taste. It will be noticed that in tone and content Juvenal, who evidently had both Horace and Lucilius in mind, is much closer to Lucilius than Horace is. In fact, without the key afforded to the interpretation of the Lucilius passage by Juvenal I had previously sought in vain to establish any relation between Lucilius and Horace. The passages in question read as follows:

Lucilius:

> peniculamento uero reprehendere noli,
> ut pueri infantes faciunt, mulierculam honestam.

The Juvenal passage reads:

> illa tuo sententia semper in ore
> versetur dis atque ipso Iove digna poeta:
> "unde habeas quaerit nemo, sed oportet habere."
> hoc monstrant vetulae pueris repentibus assae,
> hoc discunt omnes ante alpha et beta puellae.'

The Horace passage reads:

> praeterea ne sic, ut qui iocularia, ridens
> percurram (quamquam ridentem dicere verum
> quid vetat? ut pueris olim dant crustula blandi
> doctores, elementa velint ut discere prima:
> sed tamen amoto quaeramus seria ludo).

Marx has correctly divined the basis for the interpretation of the Lucilian lines. *Peniculamentum* means the trailing skirt of the robe, what the Greeks call *syrma*. The two lines, therefore, mean: Do not pull by the train of the dress, a respectable woman as baby boys do. Marx, however, is mistaken in refer-

ring these words to the habit of pulling a person's garment in
the street to attract his attention. The passage, so far as I can
see, has no reference to the respect accorded to women of good
station, who should not be accosted in this manner on the
street, even when summoned to appear before a court. On the
contrary, the simile, at least, refers exclusively to the habits[65]
of children.

In this connection two questions naturally arise: first, who
is the *muliercula honesta*, and second, under what circumstances
are the children pulling at the train of the *muliercula honesta*.

In regard to the first question, we must remember that
Lucilius is writing in the age of Cornelia, the mother of the
Gracchi. Therefore, it seems likely that the *muliercula honesta*
is either the mother herself, or, what is more probable, some
respectable female relative who assists the mother in the care of
the child. The well-known passage in the *Dialogus* of Tacitus,
chapters 28 and 29, in which the education of the child in the
good old days was contrasted with the careless and indifferent
ideals in vogue in the empire, when the child was left to the
tender mercies of an ignorant *ancilla* of the slave class: iam
pridem suus cuique filius ex casta parente natus, non in cella
emptae nutricis sed gremio ac sinu matris educabatur, cuius
praecipua laus erat tueri domum et inservire liberis, eligebatur
autem maior aliqua natu propinqua, cuius *probatis expectatisque
moribus* (*cf.* Lucilius' *mulierculam honestam*) omnis eiusdem
familiae suboles committeretur; coram qua neque dicere fas
erat quod turpe dictu neque facere inhonestum factu videretur.

Then follows in 29 the contrasted picture of the empire,
which reads like a commentary on Juvenal's 14th satire: At
nunc natus infans delegatur Graeculae alicui ancillae, cui
adiungitur unus aut alter ex omnibus servis, plerumque vilissi-
mus nec cuiquam serio ministerio adcommodatus. Horum
fabulis ac erroribus teneri statim et rudes animi imbuuntur;
nec quisquam in toto domo pensi habet quid coram infante
domino aut dicat aut faciat.

This passage, therefore, essentially corroborates my conjec-
ture that in Lucilius the *muliercula honesta* is some respectable
female relative acting as the child's nurse. Juvenal contem-
porizes this figure by substituting the *assa*, or dry nurse, of

whom the scholiast says: assa nutrix dicitur quae lac non praestat infantibus, sed solum diligentiam et munditiam adhibet. Such a nurse, judging by the teachings imputed to her in line 207, resembles the *Graecula ancilla* of Tacitus in character.[54] For the *muliercula honesta* of Lucilius and the *assa* of Juvenal, Horace apparently substitutes the *blandi doctores*, where functions begin at a somewhat later period in the child's educational career.

In the scholiast on Juvenal, furthermore, we have a line: *hoc nutricula sicca vetusta infantibus monstrat*, which Friedlander believes to be a verbal paraphrase of verse 206, which has by mere chance fallen into the metrical form of the hexameter. To me it seems much more probable that we have here a quotation by the scholiast of a Lucilian line of which Juvenal's line 208 is a paraphrase. If this conjecture seems reasonable, the line might well be assigned to book 19, which we are now analyzing. More than that the preceding line of Juvenal, *unde habeas quaerit nemo sed oportet habere*, may well be a decidedly free variant paraphrase of such a Lucilian line as 559:

'aurum uis hominem<*ne*> habeas?' "hominem? quid ad aurum?"

Certainly the idea at the root of the latter phrase; "A man?" "What is that in comparison with money?" is decidedly suggestive of Juvenal's more epigrammatic line.

The key to the solution of the words of Lucilius, *peniculamento reprendere mulierculam honestam*, is found in Juvenal's *pueris repentibus*. The children of Lucilius are either creeping and clinging to their nurse's dress, or else, which seems to me more probable, learning to walk, while they support their toddling steps in this manner. The scene is, therefore, in the nursery and not on the street. In other respects the attitude of the children is similar to that of the children represented on the *Ara Pacis* of Augustus.[55] The *"repentibus"* of Juvenal is perhaps an exaggeration of the youthfulness of the child in accordance with his satiric manner.

Our next inquiry is as to the occupation of the nurse. On this matter we have no information at all in Lucilius, but a comparison of the passage of Juvenal with Horace may offer us some suggestion of what may conceivably have stood in the now lost context of the two Lucilian lines. In both Horace and Juvenal, we have a simile derived from teaching the letters to children. In Horace, however, we have the *blandi doctores* substituted for the nurses. In the rest of the passage the resemblance between Horace and Juvenal is so close as to leave no doubt that Juvenal had Horace as well as Lucilius in mind. To Horace's *ut pueris* corresponds Juvenal's *pueris repentibus*. Horace's *elementa velint ut discere prima* is reproduced by Juvenal's *hoc discunt omnes ante alpha et beta puellae*. More than that, Juvenal in line 205 explains the *sententia*; *unde habeas quaerit nemo, sed oportet habere*, by the words; *illa sententia semper in ore versetur dis atque ipso Iove digna poeta*. Such a *sententia* is worthy of the poetic composition of the gods and Jove himself.

If now we look at the lines immediately preceding this passage in Horace, we shall see that in line 15 some god, *si quis deus*, who in line 20 is transformed to an angry Jupiter of the comic stage, is represented as proposing to the discontented representatives of the *comédie humaine* a change of rôles. But all, actuated by avarice, refuse this offer. Whereupon the angry god swells out his cheeks and declares that he will never again lend so willing an ear to their prayers. Juvenal rhetorically heightens this idea by saying that the *sententia* of line 207, familiar to him from fragment 559 in Lucilius' satire and from line 62 in Horace is worthy of Jove himself, *i.e.*, of being put into the mouth of the speaker in Horace's dramatic scene. Furthermore, we have already noticed[46] that in the *sume diem* of Lucilius, fragment 564, it is possible in view of the similarity of the line to Horace's lines 15 ff. to regard *sume* as a categorical imperative put in the mouth of the god.

Finally in Lucilius' use of *noli* we seem to have some suggestion that the prohibition is against being "tied to the nurse's apron strings," as children are. On the contrary, the context no longer extant, may have asserted that we must like men seriously learn the lessons of life by personal experience, depending absolutely on ourselves. The simile of Lucilius may, therefore, have been used to contrast a nursery scene with the deep seriousness of later life, the real object of the satirist's discourse.

But this is just the attitude assumed by Horace in his use of the simile beginning with line 23. With his tongue in his cheek, the poet at first affects to reprobate the use of the laughable:

> praetera ne sic, ut qui iocularia, ridens
> percurram.

Here the *ne sic percurram* to my ears has some echoes of the Lucilian prohibition *noli reprendere.* Then with a sudden characteristic shift Horace recalls that he is by spiritual descent a σπουδαιογέλοιος, and may justly employ the wheedling methods of teachers, who give their boys cakes to arouse in them the desire to learn their A B C's.[57] Yet in line 27 we again by a second shift of the point of view[58] return to the hard school of grown men with its more serious tasks:

> sed tamen amoto quaeramus seria ludo.

Even if we decline to let our fancy play about the Lucilian context now lost we are bound to acknowledge that *noli* when taken in connection with *ut pueri infantes* must imply the antithesis of seriousness to childishness.

If, finally, both the *blandi doctores* of Horace and the *assae* of Juvenal teach, it does not require a great stretch of imagination to make the same assumption in the case of the *muliercula honesta* of Lucilius, especially as we have the support of the passage of Tacitus' *dialogus*[59] for such a conjecture.

To many this may seem an over-bold reconstruction, but let us remember:

(1) that in Lucilius, Horace, and Juvenal we have a simile derived from the nursery;

(2) that we have the teaching of the alphabet both in Horace and Juvenal;

(3) that we have the creeping child in Juvenal;

(4) that Juvenal was certainly employing a well-known *sententia* on the philistinism of making money the sole standard of value, and that his readers were also the readers of Lucilius and Horace;

(5) that the satirist's procedure is to be different from that of the teacher (Horace and Juvenal), and the reader's from that of the child (Lucilius and Juvenal).

I have therefore filled in the outlines of the Lucilian passage following the indications afforded in the later passages in

Horace and Juvenal, which clearly deal with the same scene and employ the same simile.

Our only real leap into the unknown is perhaps the conjecture that the *muliercula honesta* of Lucilius was also a teacher. Yet that is supported by Tacitus. Of the kindergarten method of such teaching Horace alone speaks in full, yet we may have a trace of Lucilian coloring in this passage in Porphyrio's quotation of fragment 1183 apropos of this very line.

In line 117 towards the end of the first satire Horace uses the simile of the satisfied banqueter, who retires contented from the banquet of life. This simile is even better known as employed by Lucretius 3, 138. The origin of the simile, however, is perhaps to be traced back to Bion:[60] οὐχ ὑπομένω, ἀλλ' ὥσπερ ἐκ συμποσίου ἀπαλλάττομαι οὐδὲν δυσχεραίνων· οὕτω καὶ ἐκ τοῦ βίου, ὅταν ὥρα ᾖ 'ἔμβα πορθμίδος ἔρμα.'

I close my consideraton of the Lucilian passage in book 19, with fragment 567. Here, although other interpretations are, of course, not excluded, it seems to me likely that with a passing allusion to some contemporary incident from the stage we have the close of the Lucilian satire.[61] Lucilius would then compare himself to some tragic actor, who ranted himself hoarse in the part of Orestes. The implication is that if he continues much longer he too will spoil his verses (*carmina perdit*). He therefore like Horace closes abruptly and humorously. So Horace, contemporizing, this Lucilian allusion closes with a side-attack on the tiresome street preacher Crispinus. He too, like Lucilius will not add a word:

> ne me Crispini scrinia lippi
> conpilasse putes, verbum non amplius addam.

Besides these relations between whole lines, we have also certain briefer indications, more or less definite of Lucilian coloring in Horace's first satire, which must now be summarily indicated.

In line 86 *post* is separated from *ponas* by tmesis:

> miraris, cum tu argento post omnia ponas.

Such a use of tmesis according to Ausonius and Eugenius of Toledo is characteristic of the style of Lucilius.[62]

In line 103, Naevius[63] seems to be a type-name taken from Lucilian satire as Porphyrio's comment on the line shows: Naevius autem fuit in tantum parcus ut sordidus merito haberetur Lucilio auctore. This Naevius may well be identical with the Naevius mentioned in Horace's satires 2, 2, 68, as the *simplex Naevius*, who cares so little for decent household arrangements that he furnishes his guests with greasy water.[64]

Whether Nomentanus is also a Lucilian name is less certain. In any case the allusion is in part to a contemporary of the Ciceronian period. The name, however, was restored by Scaliger's conjecture to Lucilius lines 56 and 69. Personally, I am convinced by Cichorius' argument[65] in support of this emendation, especially as we know that a mint-master, L. Atilius Nomentanus issued a denarius about the year 136 B.C. He would, therefore, be about 50 years old at the time of the case of Scaevola, and is probably mentioned in these passages of Lucilius as a witness for Scaevola whose credibility is attacked. While Horace, of course, does not have this Lucilian character in mind either here or elsewhere, but rather the spendthrift L. Cassius Nomentanus of the Ciceronian period his readers would at once remember that there was a Nomentanus in Lucilius' satires also, especially when the name stands in sharp contrast to the well-known Lucilian name Naevius.

Again in line 104, and apparently with direct reference to the opposed characteristics of Naevius and Nomentanus Horace uses the two Lucilian words *vappa* and *nebulo*. That *nebulo* is taken directly from Lucilius has long been recognized. It seems to have escaped notice that *vappo* is also a Lucilian word. Thus in Lucilius 1358 we read *hos uappones*. Here, as Dousa has seen, we must regard the ascription of the words to Lucretius as an error for Lucilius. Whether the words were found in the 19th book of Lucilius or not it is no longer possible to say. In changing *vappo* to *vappa* Horace gains variety, and avoids the double use of the favorite Lucilian plebeianism ending in -o, often a somewhat contemptuous designation.[66]

If we accept the exposition of Heinze-Kiessling *ad loc.* on the basis of Pliny *N.H.* 14, 25, that *vappa*, which first denoted the lees of wine, then came to mean *probrum etiam hominem, cum degeneravit animus*, we may regard the word as meaning "slack"[87] rather than prodigal, and contrast the word rather sharply with *nebulo*, which clearly refers to Nomentanus. The word *nebulo* Horace evidently took over from Lucilius for in line 468 we have the term *lucifugus nebulo*.

In concluding our survey of this satire of Horace let me briefly reconstruct what seems to me on the basis of the resemblances to Horace's development of this theme, a plausible sequence for the argument of Lucilius' satires in book 19. As we have just seen all the eleven lines actually assigned to this satire, 557–567, may be related to Horace's first satire. To the same satire of book 19 I add line 1119 and 1183 not cited specifically by book.

Towards the beginning of the satire Lucilius raised the question of discontent or μεμψιμοιρία. The effect of this discontent is seen in the mental perturbation or restlessness which assails every one of us (567 *cf*. Horace, 1–4). And yet if some god says: Take the which seemed to you the fairest conceivable day (564) in exchange for your present lot, they would refuse this chance of happiness (*cf*. Horace, 15–16). Put away therefore a childish attitude, do not like children tug at the skirt of the honored nurse (565 and 566), when she would teach you your first lessons in life (*cf*. Juvenal 14, 208 and Horace 23–26). Our inquiry is to be that of serious-minded adults.

We find, then, that wrinkled and dried-up old men follow these same pursuits, *i.e.*, the search for gain (557 *cf*. Horace 30–32). Though you say the ant is your model, your procedure is different. You should seek to amass that store, which you might use like her in unkindly winter and delight yourself in your home, (561 *cf*. Horace 32–40).

But the man without knowledge is marked by the insatiable craving of avarice even when he has everything (558 *cf*. Horace 60–62). The reason for this error is that he judges men by a monetary standard, not money by a human standard; for such wealth, why should a philosopher raise any prayer (559 and 1119 *cf*. Horace 60–61, and for prayer 79).

Such goods only bring the fear of loss by thievish servants (1055 from a different satire *cf*. Horace 76). They are the reverse of satisfactory. But I must not spoil my poetry by ranting, as the tragic actor spoiled his part of Orestes by ranting until he was hoarse, (567 cf. Horace 120 and 121).

Just as Horace twice treated this commonplace of avarice, as a symptom of the emotional discontent of man, first in this satire and then in satire 2, 3, lines 82–160, so Lucilius treated the same theme in satire 18, from which survive fragments 554 and 555, to which I should be inclined to add fragment 1167. In these fragments Lucilius formulated the well-worn Cynic commonplace, that as the acquisitive capacity of the human belly is limited, so is the acquisitive capacity of the human heart limited so far as material satisfactions are concerned. These lines of Lucilius were clearly in the mind of Horace when he wrote lines 44–45. Whether other elements in Horace's satire are derived from this 18th satire, I find it impossible to say.

No satire better illustrates the unbroken line of the classical tradition of free imitation than these two satires of Lucilius and the first satire of Horace where both Roman satirists are the devoted students of the common wisdom of the Greek Hellenistic satirists, οἱ σπουδαιογέλοιοι and especially of the diatribe of Bion. In fact, Horace's first satire serves as an almost perfect example of the thesis of my introductory chapters on the distinction between the rhetorical theory of imitation as employed by a great literary artist, and the romantic theory of originality and isolated self-inspiration.

In fact in this satire Horace shows the same attitude towards tradition that we find Constable expressing in relation to the art of painting.[48] Constable too followed a tradition. "A self-taught artist," he said, "is one taught by a very ignorant person"; and the sentences with which he prefaced a series of four lectures in 1836 on the history of landscape painting are typical:

> I am here on behalf of my own profession, and I trust it is with no intrusive spirit that I now stand before you; but I am anxious that the world should be inclined to look to painters for information on painting. I hope to show that ours is a regularly taught profession; that it is scientific as well as poetic, that imagination alone never did and never can produce works that are to stand by a comparison with realities; and to show, by tracing the connecting links in the history of landscape painting, that no great painter was ever self-taught.

SATIRE 2

The theme of Horace's second satire is the praise of moderation in the satisfaction of the sexual desires. His view of virtue even here is Aristotelian; virtue is a μεσότης.[69] And yet when one considers the contrary excesses into which men run in their folly, the verdict must almost be that in practice there is no mean; *Nil medium est* (28). Yet upon examination we shall find where the mean as set by nature lies; for this mean set by nature must be our test. Horace, therefore, is entirely out of sympathy with any application of the Stoic theory of the equality of offences to the sexual question. Fornication and adultery are not, as formulated in Cicero's *Paradoxa* 3, 20 equal sins, for Horace denies that there is any sin *per se* in the satisfaction of the sexual desires. His view is rather a blend of Epicurean and Cynic theories, grafted upon the crass insensibility of the Roman *mos maiorum*, that unwritten moral code of early Rome, which judged such matters not by the standard of the lapse in morality, but by the test of whether or not there was any consequent loss in property or reputation to the young man.[70]

With the Epicureans Horace holds that pleasure is the *summum bonum*, and that nature is the unerring guide of what constitutes pleasure. Horace first tests the case of the adulterer by this Epicurean standard of pleasure in lines 37 ff. He denies that adultery is a pleasure, because the pleasure involved is uncommon (*rara*), spoiled by pain,[71] and even attended by severe dangers:

> utque illis multo corrupta dolore voluptas
> atque haec rara cadat dura inter saepe pericla.

But these are exactly the "prudential checks" which lead the Epicurean according to Origen *contra Celsum* 8, 63 to avoid adultery:[72]

διὰ τὸ νενομικέναι τέλος τὴν ἡδονήν, πολλὰ δ' ἀπαντᾶν κωλυτικὰ τῆς ἡδονῆς τῷ ἐξάπτι μιᾷ τῇ τοῦ μοιχεύειν ἡδονῇ καὶ ἔσθ' ὅτε φυλακὰς ἢ φυγὰς ἢ θανάτους, πολλάκις δὲ πρὸ τούτων καὶ κινδύνους κατὰ τὸ ἐπιτηρεῖν τὴν τοῦ ἀνδρὸς ἔξοδον ἀπὸ τῆς οἰκίας καὶ τῶν τὰ ἐκείνου φρονούντων.

Again in lines 73 ff., Horace, after having dramatically set forth the folly of Villius, who defended the practice of forming a *liaison* with a *libertina* as against adultery, sets forth the Epicurean principle that the bounty of nature is limited and easy to secure, while vain desires are insatiable. Thus Horace:

> at quanto meliora monet pugnantiaque istis
> dives opis natura suae, tu si modo recte
> dispensare velis ac non fugienda petendis
> inmiscere. tuo vitio rerumne labores
> nil referre putas?

And Epicurus according to Diogenes Laertius 10, 144 said:[73]
ὁ τῆς φύσεως πλοῦτος καὶ ὥρισται καὶ εὐπόριστός ἐστιν.

Moreover, Epicurus also held that one must differentiate the unavoidable from that which is to be sought, both in the case of pleasure and of pain. Thus in Diogenes Laertius 10, 129 ff., he delcares: πᾶσα οὖν ἡδονὴ διὰ τὸ φύσιν ἔχειν οἰκείαν ἀγαθόν, οὐ πᾶσα μέντοι γ᾽ αἱρετή (*petenda*), καθάπερ καὶ ἀλγηδὼν πᾶσα κακόν, οὐ πᾶσα δὲ ἀεὶ φευκτὴ (*fugienda*) πεφυκυῖα, τῇ μέντοι συμμετρήσει καὶ συμφερόντων καὶ ἀσυμφόρων βλέψει ταῦτα πάντα κρίνειν καθήκει.

The commonplace which is expressed in Horace's lines 76 and 77, just quoted, that it makes all the difference, whether our sufferings are due to our own faults or to some external cause, seems to be related rather to a passage in Bion-Teles, p. 92 H: ἀνιάσῃ οὐχ ὑπὸ τῶν πραγμάτων (*rerum vitio*), ἀλλ᾽ ἀπὸ τῶν ἰδίων τρόπων καὶ τῆς ψευδοῦς δόξης (*tuo vitio laborabis*).

Towards the close of the satire in lines 109 ff. Horace allows the Epicurean elements in his argument to appear most clearly of all. The Epicureans distinguish between desires that are natural and necessary (ἐπιθυμίαι φυσικαὶ καὶ ἀναγκαῖαι), desires that are natural, but not necessary (φυσικαὶ καὶ οὐκ ἀναγκαῖαι) and those that are neither natural nor necessary (οὔτε φυσικαὶ οὔτε ἀναγκαῖαι). Horace reproduces this classification, at least in part. Thus in lines 111–113 he paraphrases the concept of the desires which are both natural and necessary, what we should rather call today the indispensable minimum:

> nonne, cupidinibus statuat natura modum quem,
> quid latura sibi, quid sit dolitura, negatum,
> quaerère plus prodest et inane abscindere soldo?

In the last line the two terms *inane* and *soldo* are also to be defined in strict accordance with the Epicurean terminology. By *inane* (κενόν) is really meant the δόξα κενή, that which rests upon empty illusion; by *soldo* we mean in the Epicurean physics, the στερεόν that which is material and has real substance (*i.e.*, the atoms in distinction from the void); in the ethical field, by a natural transfer of meaning, that which has solid objective reality in distinction from mere appearance. Moreover, this latter state, as an objective fact of nature, is readily attainable, the former, as resting upon subjective appreciation, is difficult of attainment, for as Epicurus teaches: τὸ μὲν φυσικὸν πᾶν εὐπόριστον, τὸ δὲ κενὸν δυσπόριστον. (Epic. p. 63, Us.) In line 119 Horace makes a further application of this Epicurean test to sexual passion by translating εὐπόριστος by *parabilis*. The women of the brothel offer a love easy of attainment and ready at hand:

> namque parabilem amo Venerem facilemque.

On the other hand, the pleasures which are neither necessary nor natural are ruled by δόξα κενή, mere imaginative illusion. Examples of pleasures of this type are enumerated in lines 114–118; their stimulus, whether in food, clothing, or in matters of sex, lies in the extraneous attractions of luxury. Horace's examples, the *aurea pocula* (113), the *parvo* and *rhombus* (114), and the picture of the woman of natural beauty in distinction from the woman whose charms are artificially heightened (123 ff.), read like concrete illustrations of the Epicurean definition of ἐπιθυμίαι οὔτε φυσικαὶ οὔτε ἀναγκαῖαι.[74] For Epicurus says (Epic. frag. 456 Us.): ἡ δὲ τοιῶνδε σιτίων ἢ τοιᾶσδε ἐσθῆτος ἢ τοιῶνδε ἀφροδισίων (ἐπιθυμίαι) οὔτε φυσικὴ οὔτε ἀναγκαία.

Horace does not expressly discuss the intermediate class of desires, those which are in accordance with nature, but not necessary.[75] I cannot help feeling, however, that the position assigned to the women of the intermediate class of *libertinae* is in some measure influenced by the Epicurean classification of such intermediate passions.[76] Relations with this class of women are the result of a natural stimulus; one cannot be deceived as to the quality of their wares (lines 101 ff.). The desires they satisfy are evidently, therefore, in accordance with nature, but on the other hand it is not necessary to go to them, because by reason of their cupidity the pleasures they purvey fall rather under the concept of the δυσπόριστον than the εὐπόριστον. Or in other words, they approximate, on the one side, to the women of

the brothel, so far as their physical charms are concerned, but
on the other side to the amorous married women, so far as their
cupidity renders relations with them difficult rather than cheap
and easy. Why then have recourse to them when the brothel
stands open?

Besides these Epicurean theories, stating the functions and
defining the types of sexual desire, Horace, and probably Luci-
lius before him, depended upon the erotic literature of the
Hellenistic period, as expressed in the popular Cynic philosophy,
in the New Comedy, and in the Anthology.[77] Let us briefly
consider these points.

In the first place the whole satire is characterized by a
frankness, not to say a crudeness of speech, which recalls in
every tone the somewhat brutal παρρησία or freedom of speech
affected by the Cynics.[78] But more than that we can show
relationship with at least one Cynic production of a predecessor
of both Lucilius and Horace. It seems probable, indeed, that
both Lucilius and Horace, whether directly or indirectly, were
influenced by this work or by similar Cynic productions of the
same general type.[79] The work in question is a fragment by
Cercidas of Megalopolis, who flourished in the second part of
the third century B.C. Cercidas was a Cynic philosopher, who
apparently played a considerable part as a lawgiver, practical
politician, and general in the life of his native city.[80]

The second of the two poems associated with his name in
one of the Oxyrynchus papyri (vol. 8, No. 1082) is on the
subject of love. "It is addressed to a friend Damonomus, and
opens with a reference to a passage in Euripides, in which
Cupid is represented as having two kinds of breath, one making
the course of love run smooth, the other stormy. The choice
rests with the individual, who is counselled to prefer the gentle
breeze, and, aided by temperance to make a safe and easy
voyage." Here there is a break, and the following column,
(with which we are now especially concerned) is unfortunately
mutilated; but it contains a few significant verses, which advo-
cate the simplest and cheapest satisfaction of animal instincts.
Cercidas adopts the attitude expected in a follower of Diogenes,
who decried marriage (Diog. Laert. 6, 54, 72) and described love

as the occupation of the idle (*id.*, 51) and a painful pursuit of pleasure (*id.*, 67).[81]

The lines in question, 13–15 of Col. 5, read as follows (in Grenfell-Hunt p. 33):

καὶ μ[. . . . . ὀ]δύναν ἀ δ' ἐξ ἀγορᾶς Ἀφροδίτα
καὶ τὸ μη[δε]νὸς μέλειν ὁπ[α]νίκα λῇς ὅκα χρῄσῃς.

And a second fragment line 15, p. 34:

οὐ φόβος, οὐ ταραχά· τα[ύ]την ὀβολῷ καταχλίνας
Τ[υν]δαρίοιο δόκει γαμβρὸ [ς τό]<κ>' ἦμεν.

In precisely the same way Horace in line 119 recommends a cheap and easy love, as we have already seen. And again in line 121 Philodemus, an Epicurean contemporary of Cicero, is quoted as favoring a woman, who was cheap and came at call:

hanc Philodemus ait sibi quae neque magno
stet pretio neque cunctetur cum est iussa venire.

The *parabilis Venus* of the earlier passage corresponds to the ἀ δ' ἐξ ἀγορᾶς Ἀφροδίτα in Cercidas; the *nec magno pretio* to the ὀβολῷ of Cercidas.

To the man who once has such a woman in his embrace she seems a very Helen or to express it by an epic periphrasis he seems to be the son-in-law of Tyndareus (see the last line of Cercidas). To this thought exactly corresponds Horace's line 125 f.:[82]

haec ubi supposuit dextro corpus mihi laevum,
Ilia et Egeria est; do nomen quodlibet illi.

In such cases the element of fear and anxiety is removed. As Cercidas says:

οὐ φόβος οὐ ταραχά.

In Horace's lines 127 ff. we have a detailed picture of some of the anxieties which added the zest of danger to the pursuit of the married woman:

nec vereor ne dum futuo vir rure recurrat,
ianua frangatur, etc.

At this point Cynic and Epicurean doctrines meet, for as Cicero says in the Tusculan Disputations 5, 33, 94: (Epicurei) obscenas voluptates de quibus multa ab illis habetur oratio, . . . si

natura requirat, non genere aut loco aut ordine sed forma,
aetate, figura metiendas putant.[83]

We may even continue our comparison further. Horace's
metaphor of the waves of passion in lines 109–110 may be
compared with the more detailed description of the man on
whom love blows from the left cheek in lines 12–14 of Cercidas:[84]

τοῖς δὲ τὰν ἀριστερὰν λύσας ἐπόρσῃ
λαίλατας ἢ λαμυρὰς πόθων ἄέλλας,
κυματίας διόλου τούτοις ὁ πορθμός.

"But they on whom he looses the left cheek and stirs forth the
storms and wanton blasts of desire have their course ever set
on a surging sea." Horace's lines read:

hiscine versiculis speras tibi posse dolores
atque aestus curasque gravis e pectore tolli

In spite of its lack of euphemistic refinements the atmosphere
of the satire also shows traces of the influence of the New Com-
edy.[85] In line 20 we have a direct allusion to the *Heauton-
timoroumenos* of Terence. The principle of *in medio virtus*,
(line 29) (ἡδὺ τὰν τὸ μέτριον) is a commonplace in the New
Comedy, being found both in Alexis (fr. 216 Kock vol. 2, p.
376 and 259) and Antiphanes (fr. 258 vol. 2, pp. 392 and 120).

The antithesis of Horace's lines 84–85:

nec siquid honestist
iactat habetque palam, quaerit quo turpia celet.

is found in Alexis fr. 98 Kaibel:[86]

καλὸν ἔχει
τοῦ σώματός τι· τοῦτο γυμνὸν δείκνυται.

We have moreover in the *Adelphi* of Philemon and in the
Nannion of Euboulus two long fragments, which may be
brought into comparison with the more general argument and
tone of this satire. These two passages also share certain
common features.

In the passage in the *Adelphi*[87] Philemon approves of the
brothel as an institution established by Solon, which permits
the young men of Athens to satisfy the necessary demands of
passion in a natural way. Solon here plays a rôle analogous
to that of Cato in Horace's lines 31 ff. The married women are
thus spared. Everything in the brothel is frank and without

concealment. The price is cheap; the women are lined up for inspection. We have, in fact, precisely the theme developed in Horace's lines 84–101,[88] a passage too long to quote, but which should be compared in detail with the following fragment from Philemon (quoted by Athenaeus, 13, 569 D).

> Σὺ δ' εἰς ἅπαντας εὗρες ἀνθρώπους, Σόλων.
> σὲ γὰρ λέγουσι τοῦτ' ἰδεῖν πρῶτον <βροτῶν>,
> δημοτικὸν ὦ Ζεῦ πρᾶγμα καὶ σωτήριον,
> (καί μοι λέγειν τοῦτ' ἐστιν ἁρμοστόν, Σόλων)
> μεστὴν ὁρῶντα τὴν πόλιν νεωτέρων,
> τούτους τ' ἔχοντας τὴν ἀναγκαίαν φύσιν,
> ἁμαρτάνοντάς τ' εἰς ὃ μὴ προσῆκον ἦν,
> στῆσαι πριάμενόν τοι γυναῖκας κατὰ τόπους
> κοινὰς ἅπασι καὶ κατεσκευασμένας.
> Ἑστᾶσι γυμναί· μὴ 'ξαπατηθῇς· πάνθ' ὅρα,
> οὐκ εὖ σεαυτοῦ τυγχάνεις ἔχων; ἔχεις
> <ἑστηκότως>πως; ἡ θύρα 'στ ἀνεῳγμένη.
> εἷς ὀβολός· εἰσπήδησον· οὐκ ἔστ' οὐδὲ εἷς
> ἀκκισμὸς οὐδὲ λῆρος, οὐδ' ὑφήρπασεν,
> ἀλλ' εὐθύς, ὡς βούλει σύ, χῶν βούλει τρόπον.
> Ἐξῆλθες; οἰμώζειν λέγ', ἀλλοτρία 'στί σοι.

The fragment of Euboulus resembles that of Philemon so far as the commendation of the public exhibition of the charms of the prostitutes is concerned, but prefaces this commonplace on a cheap and natural love by a definite assault upon adultery.[89]

> ὅστις λέχη γὰρ σκότια νυμφεύει λάθρᾳ,
> πῶς οὐχὶ πάντων ἐστὶν ἀθλιώτατος;
> ἐξὸν θεωρήσαντι πρὸς τὸν ἥλιον
> γυμνὰς ἐφεξῆς ἐπὶ κέρως τεταγμένας,
> ἐν λεπτοπήνοις ὕφεσιν ἑστώσας, οἵας
> Ἠριδανὸς ἁγνοῖς ὕδασι κηπεύει κόρας
> μικροῦ πρίασθαι κέρματος τὴν ἡδονήν,
> καὶ μὴ λαθραίαν κύπριν, αἰσχίστην νόσων
> πασῶν, διώκειν, ὕβρεος. οὐ πόθου χάριν.
> Ἑλλάδος ἔγωγε τῆς ταλαιπώρου στένω,
> ἣ κυδίαν ναύαρχον ἐξεπέμψατο.

In this fragment lines 4 and 5 seem especially close to Horace's line 101 ff.:

> Cois tibi paene viderest
> ut nudam, ne crure malo, ne sit pede turpi;
> metiri possis oculo.

The contrast between natural desire, an ἐπιθυμία which is
εὐπόριστος, is emphasized by Horace in lines 116–119, while the
spice of danger and luxury which adds a factitious attraction to
the relations with married women appears in lines 111–117,
and in 126–132. This whole antithesis is briefly summed up by
Euboulus in lines 9 and 10, especially in the words ὕβρεος οὐ
πόθου χάριν, which in tone though not verbally recall Horace's
distinction between *inane* and *soldum* in line 113. The reproba-
tion of adultery, purely on the ground of expediency, pervades
both writers.

Finally, a word should be said of certain scattering indica-
tions of the influence of the poets represented in the Greek
Anthology. From them Horace borrows descriptions, songs,
and even anecdotes and names. Thus in verse 92, the exclama-
tion of admiration for feminine charms *"o crus, o bracchia!"*
harks back to such cries as that of Philodemus in the Palatine
Anthology 5, 132 (*cf.* ep. 15 Kaibel):

> ὦ ποδός, ὦ κνήμης, ὦ τῶν ἀπόλωλα δικαίως
> μηρῶν κ.τ.λ.

In lines 105–108 Horace partly paraphrases, partly trans-
lates a well-known poem of Callimachus (A. P. 12, 102, 31)
upon the pleasures of the chase in hunting and in love:

> Ὡγρευτής, Ἐπίκυδες, ἐν οὔρεσι πάντα λαγωόν
> διφᾷ καὶ πάσης ἴχνια δορκαλίδος,
> στείβῃ καὶ νιφετῷ κεχαρημένος· ἢν δέ τις εἴπῃ,
> "τῇ τόδε βέβληται θηρίον," οὐκ ἔλαβεν.
> χοὐμὸς ἔρως τοιόσδε, τὰ μὲν φεύγοντα διώκειν
> οἶδε, τὰ δ' ἐν μέσσῳ κείμενα παρπέταται.

And Horace:

> leporem venator ut alta
> in nive sectetur, positum sic tangere nolit,
> cantat, et adponit 'meus est amor huic similis: nam
> transvolat in medio posita et fugientia captat.'

Finally in line 120 we have an allusion to an epigram of
Philodemus in favor of a *"Venus parabilis."*[90] Not one of the
fourteen epigrams, however, attributed to Philodemus in the
Greek Anthology corresponds to this line. On the contrary we
have an extant epigram of precisely the reverse strain:

> οὐ γὰρ ἑτοῖμα βούλομαι, ἀλλὰ
> ποθῶ πᾶν τὸ φυλασσόμενον.

It is essential to bear in mind this highly developed erotic tradition of the Greeks, which influenced the erotic satires of Lucilius as well as those of Horace, if we would appraise correctly the nature of Horace's relations in this satire to certain themes of Lucilius found in three satires, whose subject matter and tone are dexterously interwoven and transformed by Horace.

The most important of these satires, as Cichorius has already discovered,[91] is found in book 29. This satire we may fairly regard as furnishing Horace with the framework for his argument, and a considerable number of illustrative details. But Horace also drew upon material from satires of Lucilius in book 7 and 8, which also dealt with the sexual question. As nearly all of the modern editors have pointed out,[92] this is probably the earliest of Horace's satires as it is the most Lucilian of all in directness and crudity of diction, and in ruthlessness of personal attack.

Now we know from a passage in Arnobius,[93] (2, 6 p. 51, 20, Reiff.), which evidently refers, not to the general characteristics of Lucilian satire as a whole, but to the title of an individual satire, that one of the satires of Lucilius bore the title *Fornix*, just as a satire in book 16 was entitled *Collyra*. Such a title would suit satires in books 7, 8, or 29, 3, all of which were known and studied by Horace. In the passage in question the speaker says: . . . quia Fornicem Lucilianum et Marsyam Pomponi obsignatum memoria continetis. Personally I should be inclined to assign this title to the last of the three satires, because there we have, as Cichorius has conclusively shown,[94] the same threefold contrast between relations with married women, with *libertinae*, and with the inmates of the *fornix* or brothel, which we find in Horace's satire. Lucilius' argument like that of Horace was strongly in favor of this class of women, as we shall see. The title *fornix* therefore seems more appropriate for this satire than for either satires 7 or 8, where it is scarcely possible to prove from the extant fragments such an explicit approval of the brothel as an institution.

The first passage of Horace, which contains a clear Lucilian reminiscence, is found in line 31, where Horace repeats the well-known apothegm of Cato on seeing a man leaving a brothel:

> quidam notus homo cum exiret fornice, 'macte
> virtute esto' inquit sententia dia Catonis.

Here Cato, as we have just seen,[96] plays the same function in the Roman erotic literature that Solon did in the *Adelphi* of Philemon.

Horace's verse-tag *sententia dia Catonis* is a recollection of the Lucilian periphrasis, *Valeri sententia dia*, fragment 1316.[96] Such periphrases, often in part, (as here) for metrical reasons are common in epic poetry. It seems likely that Lucilius used these words to contrast the epic dignity of the original, who is perhaps Ennius, with the frivolity implied in the application of the language to a vulgar incident in the life of a great city. Thus *dia* is an archaism and *macte virtute* a somewhat formalistic expression of praise for military daring. If, moreover, the Valerius mentioned in Lucilius was Valerius Valentinus,[97] a satirist contemporary with Lucilius, who wrote a *lex Tappula*, a sort of parody of a legal instrument to govern the proceedings of an organization of boon companions, the absurdity of the contrast with the epic hero would be still further intensified. Similarly in Horace, the hard-hitting and blunt Cato is the satirical antithesis of an epic figure and his remark is anything but *dia*. More than that we are told that Valerius Valentinus boasted[98] in one of his satirical compositions of having seduced a free-born girl. If that is so Lucilius might have used this incident to point a moral in the very satire in which he praised *per contra* the institution of the brothel. Would it then be possible to regard the periphrasis *Valeri sententia dia* as being the sardonic introduction of Lucilius to this outrageous boast made by Valerius? We no longer have the evidence for a conclusive answer, but the idea seems an attractive one. If we accept it we should interpret Cato's remark in Horace as standing in sharp antithesis, though couched in a similar verbal periphrasis, to the dictum of Valerius.

The extant fragments of the third satire found in Lucilius' 29th book apparently begin with line 851, which is addressed in tones of earnest admonition, even of epic seriousness, to the friend whose close attention Lucilius would invite to the intricate problems presented by the nature of the relations between the sexes:

praeterea ut nostris animos adtendere dictis
atque adhibere uelis.

Now Horace begins his formal discourse in line 37 in similar tones of epic admonition, which, as Porphyrio saw, parody a line from the Annals of Ennius (465 Vahlen). Ennius' line, as quoted by Porphyrio reads:

> audire est operae pretium procedere recte
> qui rem Romanam Latiumque augescere vultis.

Evidently then, the line of Ennius emphasizes the need of right progress or advance on the part of those who wished to increase the Roman state and Latium. This line Horace wittily adapts (the *urbane abutitur* of Porphyrio) to his context by changing *vultis* to *non vultis*: "It is worth while to give ear, you who do not wish to make a successful advance on the road of adultery, to the story of how the adulterers are involved in all kinds of difficulties."[99]

It seems likely, therefore, that the lines of Lucilius with the same tone of epic seriousness stood as an introductory exhortation in the satires of Lucilius. This probability receives additional corroboration from the nature of the succeeding Lucilian fragments, which I shall now analyze.

Fragment 853 of Lucilius is evidently addressed to some young noble, with his public career still before him (*oriundus*), to whom Lucilius dedicates his satire.[100] Since Horace's satire is of general application, we have no parallel to this line:

> consilium patriae legumque oriundus rogator.

Lines 854 and 855 of Lucilius are, I think, rather to be regarded as the words in the first person spoken by some character in a dramatic dialogue than to be assigned to the poet in *propria persona*.[101] If this is so, these lines:

> cum manicis catulo collarique ut fugitiuum
> deportem.

are naturally to be put into the mouth of the angry husband, who expresses the will or wish to lead off or banish somebody (probably the lover of his wife) like a fugitive slave with shackles on his hands and a fetter on his neck. The fragment would then stand in some context similar to Horace 40–44 in which the dangers that beset the adulterer are set forth. Here *fugiens* is actually mentioned in line 42. Obviously the husband, though not actually mentioned, is the prime-mover in all such punishments or perils as Horace enumerates.[102]

> hic se praecipitem tecto dedit; ille flagellis
> ad mortem caesus; fugiens hic decidit acrem
> praedonum in turbam; dedit hic pro corpore nummos;
> hunc perminxerunt calones.

In a passage immediately following, lines 44 and 45, Horace enumerates castration and amputation of the *penis* as one of the penalties sometimes meted out to the detected adulterer:

> quin etiam illud
> accidit, ut cuidam testis caudamque salacem
> demeterent ferro; 'iure' omnes: Galba negabat.

It is probable that here he was influenced by a scene representing castration and amputation of the *penis* found in a different satire of Lucilius dealing with sexual problems. At any rate, in a satire in book 7, lines 279 ff. apparently represent the husband of the guilty woman as castrating himself to take vengeance upon her.[103]

> hanc ubi vult male habere, ulcisci pro scelere eius,
> testam sumit homo Samiam sibi, 'anu noceo' inquit,
> praecidit caulem testique una amputat ambo.

Again in fragment 282, Lucilius speaking in his own person with a more masculine aggressiveness than Horace, says that it would have been better for the hero in such a story to flog his leacherous old wife:

> dixi. ad principium uenio. uetulam atque uirosam
> uxorem caedam potius quam castrem egomet me.

Horace, however, with a clearer dramatic feeling, keeps the incident, but makes castration the penalty forced upon the adulterer by the angry husband. Apparently also Horace avoided the crude Lucilian word play, *testa, testis* by substituting *ferro* as the instrument used in the castration for *testa*.

But when all is said your bargains in lust are better purchased in the second class who furnish satisfaction, that of the *libertinae*. So Lucilius in line 318:

> uerum et mercaturae omnes et quaesticuli isti.

With this use of *mercatura*,[104] we may compare Horace lines 47, 48, 83, and 105. Line 47 reads:

> tutior at quanto merx est in classe secunda,
> libertinarum dico.

In this line of Horace *merx* is used essentially in the sense of a satisfaction bought over the counter like a ware offered for sale.

We may now return to our main-travelled road, the comparison of the satire in Lucilius 29, 3 with Horace's line of argument and illustrative examples. It seems clear from a comparison of Lucilius' lines 857 and 858 with lines 864 and 865, that we have in this satire of Lucilius the same classification of the women who satisfy sexual desire under the three divisions of married women, freedwomen, and prostitutes which we find in Horace.[106] In lines 864 f. I accept the ingenious emendation of Cichorius by which *uoluisse* is substituted for the corrupt *uel sese* and read these lines as follows:

>   nunc tu
> contra uenis, uel qui in nupt*is* uoluisse neges te.
> nec sine permitie.

These lines demand somewhat fuller elucidation before we proceed to compare them with Horace. It is clear that the subject under discussion is the question of *liaisons* with married women. The words *nunc tu contra uenis* are uttered by the poet himself, who anticipated a supposed objection of his *adversarius*:[106] "At this juncture you come forward with the objection . . . " Now the *adversarius'* objection must obviously have to do with the question of *liaisons* with married women and must have clearly been stated in some infinitive concealed under the corruption *uel sese*. If now we read *uoluisse*, the *adversarius* will emphatically deny that he has any relations with women of this class, *uoluisse* being used as often in Plautus in the sense of sexual desire. Consequently, the *adversarius* is unaffected by Lucilius' diatribe against adultery. The words *nec sine permitie* will then again fall to Lucilius, who rejoins for his part, "Good, but the *liaisons* that you carry on are also not without their dangers." To what class of relations do these dangers then attach? Obviously, it seems to me, to the class of freedwomen who play so prominent a part in Horace's satire, though they are not expressly mentioned in Lucilius.

The answer of the Lucilian *adversarius* is thus seen to be in essence that of the Horatian Sallust and Marsaeus in lines 54 and 57. In the former passage Sallust is so eaten up with self-love and self-praise, that he plumes himself on the fact that he refrains absolutely from adultery, although he madly spends his substance on the *demi-monde:*

> verum hoc se amplectitur uno,
> hoc amat et laudat, 'matronam nullam ego tango.'

He is just like Marsaeus, the lover of Origo the *mima* or "chorus girl" who cries out in line 57:

> 'nil fuerit mi' inquit 'cum uxoribus umquam alienis.'

Lucilius' rejoinder *"nec sine permitie"* is clearly reechoed in fuller form in Horace's lines 58 and 59, as well as in the incidental indications of the extravagance towards the freedwomen and *meretrices* found in lines 48–59. As Horace justly says, the *liaisons* with *demi-monde* involve even severer loss of reputation than of property:

> verum est cum mimis, est cum meretricibus, unde
> fama malum gravius quam res trahit.

It will be most convenient to consider in close connection with these lines of Lucilius lines 857 and 858 which belong to the admonitory verses of Lucilius and assert that a certain type of sexual passion must be torn from the heart:

> ubi erat †scopios[107]
> eicere istum abs te quam primum et perdere amorem.

That the passion in question is the love for married women seems clear by a comparison with two passages in Horace's satire as well as with line 864. In lines 77 ff. Horace, in precisely similar tone, although without direct verbal imitation, warns against the pursuit of married women, which "involves only wasted labor and purely illusory results, unfounded on solid natural facts":

> quare, ne paeniteat te,
> desine matronas sectarier, unde laboris
> plus haurire mali est quam ex re decerpere fructus.

Later in lines 110–119 Horace, following Epicurus, introduces his explicit warnings in regard to the distinction to be made between the different types of sexual pleasure. Here *liaisons* with married women are explicitly disapproved, because they belong *par excellence* to the ἐπιθυμίαι οὔτε φυσικαί οὔτε ἀναγκαῖαι inasmuch as their attractiveness rests on their external surroundings.[108]   But these surroundings are luxurious (96 ff., 115 ff. *aurea pocula*, a metaphorical symbol of luxury), and dangerous (103 ff., 126 ff.).   Also the charms of the married women are concealed, and therefore uncertain, that is impossible to observe.   In line 109–110 Horace, following the Greek erotic tradition,[109] which prefers a calm course of love to a tempestuous one, always seeking and never attaining as in the chase, sums up the disadvantages of both married women and *meretrices* in contradistinction to the epigram of Callimachus:

> hiscine versiculis speras tibi posse dolores
> atque aestus curasque gravis e pectore tolli?

The Epicurean analysis of the three types of desire and the decision in favor of a *Venus parabilis*, which follows in lines 111–119 we have already considered.

Fragments 854, 857, and 864 of book 29, 3 of Lucilius evidently belong to that part of the satire in which the young man, addressed by the poet in fragment 853, was warned against excesses with married women.   To this same general argument against recourse to married women I should be inclined to refer, line 856.   Obviously here other interpretations are not excluded, but in view of the general tone of the satire, an allusion to a strategem on the part of a married woman against her overfond lover seems a natural interpretation.   The *nupta* herself may be regarded as the speaker.   She asserts that she laid a plot at the hour of assignation (taking *conventus* as a genitive singular):

> haec tum conventus tela insidiasque locavi.

So Horace in line 103 asks much the same question of the foolish pursuer of the veiled charms of the matron:

> an tibi mavis
> insidias fieri pretiumque avellier ante
> quam mercem ostendi?

The *insidiae* in both Horace and Lucilius are probably laid by the same person, whether that person be the matron, the enraged husband, or possibly, but less probably, the lover himself.[110]

On the other hand, I am inclined to refer the corrupt fragment 861 to the class of freedwomen.   The rapacious *meretrix* of this class is compared to a *polypus*. The poet suggests the unhappy results that will ensue if one surrenders himself even for a brief period to this rapacious class. Such must be the general force of this simile, though the line is too corrupt to admit of an exact restoration of all the details:[111]

>   cui
> paulisper me dem, *iam* ede*t* haec, se ut polypus, ipsa.

Like the *polypus* the voracity of the *meretrix* is so great that it involves its own undoing (*edet se*).

Here we seem to have a context similar in some respects to Horace's lines 47–63 ff., where the *mimae* and *meretrices*, the representatives of the *libertinae*, or *demi-monde* devour both the property and the good name of their lovers. Lines 55–59 seem especially in point, for the fate of Marsaeus at the hands of Origo was a *cause célèbre*:

> ut quondam Marsaeus, amator Originis ille,
> qui patrium mimae donat fundumque laremque,
> 'nil fuerit mi' inquit 'cum uxoribus umquam alienis.'
> verum est cum mimis, est cum meretricibus, unde
> fama malum gravius quam res trahit, an tibi abunde
> personam satis est, non illud quidquid ubique
> officit evitare? bonam deperdere famam,
> rem patris oblimare, malum est ubicumque. quid inter
> est in matrona, ancilla peccesne togata?

Similarly the Lucilian fragment declares: "She to whom I give myself even for a little time, will eat these things, (i.e., property and reputation) at once (*iam*), even as the polypus consumes itself."

In contradistinction, therefore, to the married women or to the rapacious freedwomen, both Lucilius in book 29, 3 and Horace recommend recourse to the women of the *fornix* or brothel. According to both writers this class of women have one preeminent advantage over the matrons in that their good physical points, as they line themselves up for inspection,[112] entirely nude, cannot be concealed.

So Lucilius in 859 declares with reference to these women:

> hic corpus solidum inuenies,[113] hic stare papillas
> pectore marmoreo.

In Horace this advantage is shared by both the freedwomen and prostitutes in distinction from the married women.[114] Thus in line 83 ff. Horace says:

> adde huc quod mercem sine fucis gestat, aperte
> quod venale habet ostendit, nec siquid honestist
> iactat habetque palam, quaerit quo turpia celet.

Later in lines 94 and 101 Horace emphasizes the fact that while the physical defects of the married woman may be concealed, the Coan garments worn by the women of the other two classes by reason of their transparency render any concealment impossible. The strong influence of the Greek erotic literature of the Hellenistic period upon this particular commonplace we have already discussed. Horace's lines follow:

> altera, nil obstat; Cois tibi paene viderest
> ut nudam, ne crure malo, ne sit pede turpi;
> metiri possis oculo latus.

Finally in lines 866 and 867 of book 29, 3 Lucilius speaks of a class to whom his friend may have recourse without fear of reproach (*sine flagitio*), who are less rapacious (*poscent minus*), and with whom a relation is subject to far fewer objections (*multo rectius*). What is this class, whose gender is concealed under the corruption *quiete?* It is, I think, more probably the women of the *fornix*, in view of the title of the Lucilian satire, and of the praise of this class by Horace. Cichorius' emendation of *quae et* is therefore to be preferred to the *qui et* of Mercier and Marx, since the love of boys receives an only passing mention by Horace in line 117, and is not mentioned at all in the other extant fragments of this satire.

> quae *et* poscen*t* minus et praeb<*eb*>unt rectius multo
> et sine flagitio.[115]

The cheapness of these women, as we have seen, was emphasized by Solon, Cercidas, and Euboulus. They constitute in fact the perfect type of an ἐπιθυμία φυσικὴ καὶ ἀναγκαία as defined by Epicurus, and of the *Venus parabilis* as set forth by Horace in lines 119 ff., for they are cheap, and come on call. They absolutely fulfill the requirements laid down by the philosopher Philodemus in his epigram:[116]

namque parabilem amo Venerem facilemque

. . . .

hanc Philodemus ait sibi quae neque magno
stet pretio neque cunctetur cum est iussa venire.

It has seemed best to pursue this comparison between
Lucilius' *sat.* 29, 3 and Horace's *sat.* 1, 2 through to the end, as
this satire is the main thread in the somewhat complicated
mesh of Horace's sources. Certainly the general argumentative
structure of Lucilius in this satire is strikingly similar to that of
Horace. It is now necessary to retrace our steps and examine
the question of the relations between this satire of Horace, and
the erotic satires of Lucilius preserved in books 7 and 8, from
which we shall find Horace interweaves material with great
skill. *Satire* 29, 3 is so to speak, the warp of Horace's satire,
while the threads of the woof are found in these two satires.

From book 7, the following fragments demand consideration,
arranged in the order in which they appear to have influenced
Horace whether directly or indirectly: In book 7: 269, 271,
288, 267, 1222, 266, 293(?), 268, 264; in book 8, the following,
318, 307, 296, 313, 314, 315, 302, 303, 305, 306.[117] It will be
more convenient, as the fragments from these two books are
ingeniously interwoven, to follow the order of Horace's lines
before attempting a separate reconstruction of the themes of
these two books of Lucilius.

The use of *merx* in line 47 in a sense which recalls that of
mercaturae in fragment 318 of book 8, and the use of fragments
279 and 282 from book 7, in a scene representing castration as
one of the dangers attendant upon adultery has been fully
discussed already.

In line 68, according to Porphyrio's annotation we have a
Lucilian imitation: Muttonem pro virili membro dixit Lucilium
imitatus. The imitation, however, probably consists rather in
the personification of the *animus* which speaks in the name of
the *mutto* in a fashion following that of Lucilius just as both
Roman writers follow such satiric personifications as those
popularized by Bion in the case of πενία, Poverty. The *quid
responderet* of Horace's line recalls Bion's τί ἂν ἔχοις ἀντειπεῖν;
Horace's lines are:

huic si muttonis verbis mala tanta videnti
diceret haec animus 'quid vis tibi?

Lucilius' line 307 is:

> at laeua lacrimas muttoni absterget amica.

The resemblance to Lucilius' refers, however, only to the word *mutto*, or possibly to the personification of the *mutto* by Lucilius in this immediate context. The actual words of Lucilius, as the parallels quoted by Marx prove, refer to masturbation, a practice approved by the Cynics.

I turn next to a somewhat extended passage in Horace's satire, lines 86–95. Here Horace first describes the method employed by the shrewd buyer, on his guard against over-valuing a fine head and face alone, in appraising the "points" of a horse. Then in lines 93–95 the application of this illustration is made to the question of the "fine points" of a woman, especially to the danger of disillusion in the case of the matron, whose beauty of face alone is visible. Here Horace seems to have had in mind, and to have paraphrased certain passages from both the 7th and the 8th books of Lucilius. The Horatian passage is as follows:

> regibus hic mos est, ubi equos mercantur: opertos
> inspiciunt, ne si facies, ut saepe, decora
> molli fulta pede est, emptorem inducat hiantem,
> quod pulchrae clunes, breve quod caput, ardua cervix.
> hoc illi recte, ne corporis optima Lyncei
> contemplere oculis, Hypsaea caecior illa
> quae mala sunt spectes. 'o crus, o bracchia!' verum
> depugis, nasuta, brevi latere ac pede longost.
> matronae praeter faciem nil cernere possis,
> cetera, ni Catia est, demissa veste tegentis.

The discussion on beauty of face was clearly found in Lucilius, book 7, as we may see from fragments 269 and 271. In fragment 269, a speaker presumably a lover, expresses his love for a girl addressed in the second person, shows that he is an admirer of her youthful beauty and face, and promises to be a lover:

> qui te diligat, aetatis facieque tuae se
> fautorem ostendat, fore amicum polliceatur.

In line 271 the exact meaning of the simile is uncertain:

> aetatem et faciem, ut saga et bona conciliatrix.

but apparently both the words of 269 and of this line are put into the mouth of a procuress, who recommends her human wares, stressing solely *aetas* and *facies* and possibly slurring over other points. In both poets these lines clearly have reference to the Epicurean standard to be applied to *obscenae voluptates*, as can be seen by a comparison with Cicero's Tusculan Disputations 5, 33, 94: (Epicurei) obscenas voluptates de quibus multa ab illis habetur oratio . . . si natura requirat non genere aut loco aut ordine sed *forma*, aetate, figura metiendas[118] putavit. Now *forma, aetate, figura* are precisely the natural charms, which both Lucilius and Horace emphasize as the only solid bases for sex attraction.

Notice also that in fragment 288, the good points of a high bred horse were apparently described by Lucilius: they toss their head and locks; their forelocks fall loosely far down over their forehead, as was their custom.[119]

> iactari caput atque comas, fluitare capronas,
> altas, frontibus immissas, ut mos fuit illis.

This line, to my mind, though entirely without verbal similarity, describes the points of a good horse, just as Horace does in line 89:

> quod pulchrae clunes, breve quod caput, ardua cervix.

This cautious behavior in the traffic of love is especially necessary, for love is blind. The lover whose sight is as keen as Lynceus to certain physical defects, may be blinder than Hypsaea when it is a question of surveying his lady's blemishes. So Horace, line 90 ff., just quoted.

It is clear that line 267 of Lucilius, whether or not with Marx we put the words into the mouth of a *meretrix*,[120] must refer to a similar commonplace on the blindness of love. The more racy Lucilius, however, deprives the infatuated lover of the sense of smell as well as of sight: "What sort of men are these," says the speaker, "have they neither eyes nor nose?" And what are these things? (*i.e.*, imperfections that the blinded lover will overlook?):

> quos? oculi non sunt neque nasum? et qualia sunt!

The *qualia sunt* seems to introduce an enumeration of such ugly features, now lost, but possibly similar to that in Horace's line 93 quoted above.[121]

In fragment 315 of Lucilius' eighth book we have a simile in which something or somebody is compared to a river, a huge stone from the top of the mountain, and a pinnace in full sail with favoring breeze.[122] The *meliambic* fragment of Cercidas affords material, I think, for the correct interpretation of this simile.[123] In that fragment, as we have seen, Cupid is represented as having two kinds of breath, the one making the course of love run smooth, the other stormy; the individual who chooses the cheap and simple means afforded by the brothel for satisfying his sensual appetites will make a safe and easy voyage. Probably, then, the lines of Lucilius refer to this easy voyage of love by the man who follows the promptings of passions that are natural and necessary:

> verum flumen uti, atque ipso de vortice < *montis* >
> < *saxum* > *ingens*, pedibus *cercurum currere ut* aequis.

This interpretation receives additional support from the emphasis in fragments 303, 305, and 306 of this same book upon the gratification of sensual pleasure, apparently by means of the brothel. In Horace's lines 109 and 110 we have a summarized expression of the reverse side of this common erotic simile, the picture of the waves of passions and the mental anxieties which result from recourse to married women or to the *meretrices*:

> hiscine versiculis speras tibi posse dolores
> atque aestus curasque gravis e pectore tolli?

The similes of Cercidas and Lucilius, and the metaphor of Horace are probably not uninfluenced by the Epicurean antithesis between the tempest of the soul χειμὼν τῆς ψυχῆς (Epic. III, p. 62 Us.), and the calm of the soul γαλήνη.

The relation of the argument of lines 110–119 to certain passages in Lucilius satire 29, 3, and of both Lucilius and Horace to the Epicurean threefold division of the passions and to the Epicurean antithesis between the τὸ κενόν and the τὸ στερεόν, we have already analyzed in full. But the illustrative examples contained in these lines seem to have been developed in relation to certain passages in Lucilius' eighth book. Thus in line 303 ff., a very corrupt passage, the speaker seems to say that when he drinks from the same cup as his love, presses his lips to hers, and embraces her, he is smitten with the unceasing craving for love, he does not care whether his love is of noble or base birth, beautiful or ugly. Such is the plausible interpretation of Marx, (cum tentigine rumpor non curo bonane sit an mala pulchra honesta an turpis), for the context in which these lines stood:

> cun poclo bibo eodem, amplector labra labellis
> fictricis compono, hoc est cum psolo copumai.

Evidently the speaker is inflamed with desire, and therefore under utterly natural compulsion he prefers to satisfy his appetite with a love ready and easily procurable. The context therefore seems to resemble in general that of Horace from lines 111–119, but more particularly that of lines 116–118:[124]

> tument tibi cum inguina num, ni
> ancilla aut verna est praesto puer, impetus in quam
> continuo fiat, malis tentigine rumpi?

After praising the ready complaisance of the inexpensive girls of the *lupanar* in line 121,[125] Horace then proceeds to enumerate the practical excellencies which may be expected from the ordinary prostitute, lines 123–124; such a woman does not seek to heighten her charms artificially or to increase her height. She has the *modicum* of beauty bestowed on her by mother nature, and, another very important advantage, she always comes on call, without any of the tantalizing delays affected by the married women or *meretrices* with their catch phrases, *post paullo, sed pluris, si exierit vir* (lines 120–122.)

This last virtue is emphasized by Lucilius in lines 925–927 which evidently stood in a satire from book 29 written in iambic senarii:

> Lucilius scribit de Cretaea, cum ad se cubitum uenerit,
> [sua uoluntate] sponte ipsam suapte adductam ut tunicam
>   et cetera
> reiceret.

It seems probable that Lucilius in book 7 treated the same erotic commonplace. Thus fragments 268, 266, and 264 seem to contrast, with somewhat coarser details than the refinement of the Augustan age permitted Horace, the obvious physical attractions of one class of women, not to be sure unaccompanied by non-essential physical defects with the artificial perfections of a Phryne.[136]

Thus in line 268, we evidently have the desire of a prostitute (compare Horace's *sit* in line 123 with Lucilius' *siem*) that though she have a neck as long as that of a swan and goose she may be passionate and well-knit:

> calda *siem* ac bene plena, *si* olorum atque anseris collus.

Again as in Horace she is to be *munda hactenus*, passably "smart." So Lucilius expresses a *caveat* against unclean ears and worms in the ear:

> ne auriculam obsidat caries, ne vermiculi qui.

How different is the procedure of the extravagant wantons of whom Phryne is the historical representative, and whose toilet Lucilius enumerates!

> rador, subvellor, desquamor, pumicor, ornor
> expilor, <ex>pingor.

When locked in the embrace of love, the average inmate of the *fornix* will suffice, says Horace in line 125 as quoted above. Porphyrio by quoting line 306 recognizes its close connection with this line; and 305 is clearly from the same Lucilian context which describes the embrace of love:

> tum latu componit lateri, et cum pectore pectus
> . . . et cruribus crura diallaxon ◡ ◡ — ◡.

This completes the enumeration of Lucilian passages which testify to the identity of Horace's theme with that presented by Lucilius in 29, 3, and the use of illustrative material from satires in books 7 and 8 of Lucilius. How profoundly the atmosphere of the Greek erotic literature of the Hellenistic period, and the erotic elements in the philosophy of Epicurus affected both Lucilius and Horace we have examined in full. This common dependence on the Greeks, however, in no way excludes the importance of Lucilius' influence in developing the argument, coloring the language, and suggesting the appropriate atmosphere of this early study of Horace. The general atmosphere of the satire is in fact rather Lucilian than Hellenistic. This appears first of all in the frankness and coarseness of the personal invective. From no other satire, as the commentators point out, do we have such an extensive portrait gallery of contemporaries: Tigellius, Fufidius, Maltinus, Rufillus, Gargonius, Cupiennius, Sallustius, and Marsaeus; Villius and Longarenus; Galba and Fabius; the women, Fausta, Hypsaea, Catia. Here too are names high in society: Tigellius and Cupiennius, close to Augustus, and Maltinus, if we trust Porphyrio and the commentary of the so-called Pseudo-Acro, Maecenas himself.[127]

(2) The vocabulary is distinctly Lucilian.[128] We may especially notice *vappa* (H. 12 = L. 1358), *nebulo* (H. 12 = L. 468, 577), *Maltinus cf. Malta* (H. 25 = L. 732), *permolere* (H. 35 = L. 278, 294), *Mutto* (H. 68 = L. 307, 959), *depugis* (H. 93 cf. L. *noctipuga* 1222), *nasutus* (H. 93 = L. 242). Also *balatro* (2), *ingluvies* (8), *cunnus* (36, 70), *tentigo* (118), by their distinct atmosphere of the *sermo plebeius*, though not found in any extant fragment, suggest to me a Lucilian coloring.

As the tendency of this study of Horace's satire is to show that the Lucilian fragments follow a somewhat different sequence than that adopted by either Marx or Cichorius, it will be worth while to indicate briefly my own idea as to the original order of the fragments in the development of these three related Lucilian themes.

In book 29, 3 the most important of Horace's sources I should arrange the fragments in this order: 851, 853, 854, 864, 861, 859, 856, 857, 866, and 868 (a theme not treated by Horace). The theme of this satire clearly follows the general argument later employed by Horace. It too accepts the Epicurean classification according to which the matrons, *nuptae*, represent the ἡδόναι οὔτε ἀναγκαῖαι οὔτε φυσικαί; the freedwomen, *libertinae* or *meretrices*, the ἡδόναι φυσικαὶ ἀλλ' οὐκ ἀναγκαῖαι, the women of the *fornix*, from whom the satire probably received its name, the ἡδόναι φυσικαὶ καὶ ἀναγκαῖαι. Lucilius also was clearly familiar with formulations of this theme current in the New Comedy, the popular literature of the Cynics, and probably the Greek Anthology, a tradition best represented to us today by the meliambic fragment of Cercidas, and the *Nannion* of Euboulus. The argument of Lucilius' satire perhaps ran somewhat as follows:

The poet (851) makes a general appeal for attention to his warnings against the dangers in sexual relations. Especially is he concerned for his young friend, an *adulescens optimae spei*, who may some day deserve well of the state (853). [Let him remember] the occasion when the angry husband dragged off the fleeing adulterer, like a fugitive slave (854). But, says the poet, you assert that you have no relations with married woman; so far, so good, but let me tell you that the freedwomen class has its dangers also (864). Even a peccadillo with the harpy-like *libertina* will eat into your good name and property even as a polypus consumes itself (861). Only in the *fornix* or brothel will you find a love that has objective reality, that is (*solidum*), and therefore free from the illusory stimulus, the κενὴ δόξα, which surrounds the *liaisons* with matrons (859). The dangers that dog the path of the adulterer are illustrated by the plots that the wife [or possibly the angry husband] has planned against the paramour at the hour of assignation (856). Therefore tear from your heart, such a love which can only bring you pain (857). Better far, as I told you above, is the love of the girls in the brothel, who cost little, and will involve you in no disgrace (866).

This completes all the fragments which stand in any relation to the satire of Horace. Apparently, however, Lucilius treated in this satire the question of seduction also, perhaps at the close of the satire. Since Valerius Valentinus had boasted of having seduced a girl of good character, the Lucilian allusion to *Valeri sententia dia* may have referred sardonically to this (fragment 1316). If we venture to assign this fragment to book 29, 3 we may then perhaps associate it with fragment 868, which has been correctly interpreted by Cichorius:

> at non sunt similes neque dant.   quid, si dare vellent?
> acciperesne?   doce.

Above all, says the poet to his young friend, do not follow the outrageous standard represented today by my fellow satirist Valerius Valentinus with his "inspired" dictum on seduction. You hesitate. But let me remind you that freeborn maidens are utterly different from these three classes; they do not bestow their favors. But even assuming that they did; would you be willing to accept them? Inform me as to that.

From book 7 of Lucilius we have the following fragments, which I should be inclined to arrange, though with much greater hesitation, as follows: 278, 279, 282, 269, 271, 288, 267, 266, 293(?), 268, 264. Here I can only venture to say that Lucilius treated of the following scenes. Whether his argument varied from that in 29, 3, and wherein the difference lay, I am unable to determine. (1) We have a discussion of adultery and a scene representing the castration of a man (but whether the husband or the adulterer is uncertain) (278, 279, 282). (2) We have a scene in which "the points" of a woman were compared with the points of a horse, and judgment upon the basis of beauty of face alone was disapproved as misleading (269, 271, 288, 267). This scene apparently stood in a context, which like Horace (86–102), favored the women of the *fornix*, as against married women. (3) Possibly we have an aphorism, similar in its application to the epigram of Callimachus on the joys of the chase, Horace (105–109), with a reproval of our tendency to reject the goods that are freely offered 293(?). (4) A scene in which the everyday physical attractions, with a modicum of compensating defects thrown in, of the women of the *fornix* were contrasted with the artificially heightened beauty of the *meretrices* 268, 266, 264(?).

From the satire in book 8 I have discussed the following fragments:[139] 318, 307, 300, 315, 303, 302(?), 296, 305, 306. Here too I find it impossible to determine the exact sequence of the Lucilian theme. I may content myself with pointing the disconnected commonplaces treated in this satire, which it seems to me were as follows. (1) A discussion of the wares of love offered by the *libertinae* occurred (318). (2) A scene differing somewhat from anything in Horace, in which the Cynic practice of masturbation was discussed (307). (3) Following the tradition of the Greek erotic literature, the easy life of those who had recourse to the women of the brothel was compared to that of a ship sailing before a fair breeze (315). (4) The satisfaction to the cravings of our natural appetites easily gained by recourse to these women of the brothel was set forth (302(?), 303), and perhaps contrasted with the factitious stimulus aroused by luxurious married women. (5) The sexual act was depicted as the sole natural attainment of desires, for which a woman of good physical parts, but no exceptional claims to beauty will suffice (305, 306).

In spite of the repulsive brutality of the subject, this satire like the first repays the most careful study and affords concrete illustration of the ever shifting relation between the rhetorical tradition of imitation and the author's desire to give independent expression to his personal message to the men of his own times. Above all we see how the base metal of the Greek erotic literature and philosophy was twice reminted to circulate anew among the men of the Scipionic period and the Augustan age. Horace's second satire is inconceivable without the previous works of Cercidas and Euboulus, the erotic poems of the Greek Anthology, the Epicurean and Cynic philosophy of the passions, and the satiric moulding of this material by his great master Lucilius.

Satire 3

Unlike the first and second satires, the third satire seems to be written without the direct consciousness of a Lucilian model. It is the poet's ethical defence for satire as distinct from censoriousness. It is therefore placed between the second satire, whose Cynic frankness of utterance might by the uncritical be confounded with censoriousness, and the fourth satire, the poet's aesthetic defence of satire.

The thesis of the satire appears to be a free adaptation of the Epicurean attitude towards friendship. A poet, whose standard of ethics is so completely socialized as Horace, naturally gave his adherence to this Epicurean teaching, which as Lejay says,[130] made of friendship "un institution et un rite." On the other hand, he attacks the Stoic doctrine of the self-sufficiency and the autocratic isolation of the individual. Among the Roman poets this satire, as is well known, stands in the closest relation to Lucretius, especially to book 4, 1136 ff., where occurs the passage on the illusions of lovers, and to Lucretius, 5, 783 ff., which sets forth the Epicurean theory that the development of morality, justice and civilization was the result of enlightened expediency. The former commonplace, as Lejay has shown,[131] goes back at least as far as Plato and the Greek moralists, but is known to Horace rather from Lucretius, and also as I shall presently show from Lucilius. Except for this commonplace, on the illusions of the lover we seem to have

only a few stray traces of Lucilian influence. To the analysis of
this influence we may now turn.

Porphyrio was aware of the Lucilian tone of line 38 ff., for his
annotation is: *Luciliana urbanitate usus in transitu amaritu-
dinem aspersit.* Marx compares with this passage of Horace,
Lucilius 1068:

> contra haec inuitasse aut instigasse uidentur.

The *haec,* evidently body defects, *uitia,* were perhaps described
in one of the fragments now lost. The verbs *inuitasse* and
instigasse seem to imply that these very physical defects of his
mistress act as a stimulus to the imagination of the fond lover.
So Horace delcares:

> illuc praevertamur, amatorem quod amicae
> turpia decipiunt caecum, vitia aut etiam ipsa haec
> delectant, veluti Balbinum polypus Hagnae.[133]

Besides this "topic" we have a few other stray Lucilian
reminiscences. In line 21 the Maenius mentioned by Horace
is apparently a personage of Lucilian satire:

> Maenius absentem Novium cum carperet, 'heus tu'
> quidam ait, 'ignoras te an ut ignotum dare nobis
> verba putas?' 'egomet mi ignosco?' Maenius inquit.

He is mentioned by the Pseudo-Asconius on Cicero's *divinatio
in Caecilium* 50, as reserving for himself a column from which
he might see the gladiatorial games, when he sold his lot for the
basilica Porcia. He had a reputation as a wit and a spendthrift.
Porphyrio's note on this Horatian passage seems to refer to this
column.[133] Thus in Lucilius line 1203:

> [Maenius] columnam
> cum peteret.

In line 56 the phrase *vas incrustare* is evidently a recollection of a
Lucilian collocation for the Pseudo-Acro on this passage quotes
a line from Lucilius' book 3, line 134: Incrustari vas dicitur cum
aliquo vitioso suco inbuitur atque inquinatur, secundum quod
et Lucilius in III:

> nam mel regionibus illis
> incrustatus calix rutai caulis habetur.

In Lucilius fragment 537 we seem to have a characterization of the man lacking in social tact or *communis sensus*, which runs parallel to Horace's line 63. This type of the *comédie humaine* was probably developed in the Hellenistic[124] writers long before it was used by either Lucilius or Horace. Although there is no direct verbal imitation, the general parallelism in thought is clear. Moreover, the passage of Lucilius seems to be in keeping with doctrine as to appropriateness of time and place enunciated by Panaetius, a member of the Scipionic circle in Cicero's *de officiis* 1, 144. Lucilius' line asks, Why do you ask so tardily especially at this time?

> cur tam ignaviter hoc praesertim tempore quaeris?

So Horace:

> simplicior quis et est qualem me saepe libenter
> obtulerim tibi, Maecenas, ut forte legentem
> aut tacitum impellat quovis sermone: 'molestus
> communi sensu plane caret' inquimus.

Finally in book 28[125] we have in the first trochaic satire belonging to the book a humorous parody on the Stoic paradox on the self-sufficiency and universal potential capacity of the Stoic *sapiens*. He is the best tailor says Lucilius and the best shoddy-maker. (747)

> sarcinatorem esse summum, suere centonem optume.

This line probably refers to the real words of a tailor and is not a proverb. We may then compare the line with Horace's 1, 3, 124 where the Stoic wise man in precisely the same humorous manner is declared to be the best shoemaker:

> si dives, qui sapiens est,
> et sutor bonus et solus formosus et est rex,
> cur optas quod habes?

This interpretation of Lucilius receives corroboration from the fact that Lucilius is fond of poking fun at the Stoics in his early works. Moreover, we know that in 1225 he treated this same Stoic paradox; a passage, which is, so far as the limitation of desires (expressed by *habebit*) is concerned, even closer to Horace's satire:

> ⌣⌣⌣⌣⌣ nondum etiam[hic] haec omnia habebit
> formonsus diues liber rex solus ut extet.

According to Marx this second fragment is to be associated with a satire dealing with philosophy in book 15 and placed directly after 515.

It seems possible to refer line 747 to the same context as 746. The man who is there described as boasting of his capacity for accomplishment, even if the activity be a ridiculous one, may well be the Stoic sage who by virtue of his wisdom asserts that he can do everything:

> in re agenda, ipsa ridicula iactat se de re t . . .

This completes the short list of Lucilian recollections in this satire.

Satire 4

The fourth satire is Horace's aesthetic defence of the satiric form.[126] Since, however, satire as a literary form had been profoundly influenced by the ethics of the Cynic-Stoic σπου-δαιογέλοιοι ever since the days of Lucilius, it was equally necessary to establish its moral validity: to show on the one hand that its method of direct attack differed from mere censoriousness, satire 3, and on the other hand that this method of attack had honorable literary antecedents, both in Greek rhetorical theory and in Greek satiric literature. Hence satire is shown to derive much of its spirit of outspoken frankness, (παρρησία libertas), from the Old Comedy, much of its fondness for the delineation of character (χαρακτηρισμός) from the New Comedy. The satirist's tendency to induce the general principles of human conduct from the observation of one's neighbor's faults and self-examination into one's own is the normal procedure of the popular Cynic ethics. Moreover, it was necessary for Horace to define the position of satire with relation to other literary genres, especially its relation to Epic, to which it was most nearly allied in metre, and to Comedy to which the inchoate Greek satire owed so much. Horace, then, is writing upon the proper limits of the laughable τὸ γέλοιον, both aesthetically and ethically. But he is doing much more than this. The two Stoic philosophers Diogenes of Babylon and Panaetius had, as we have already seen evolved a body of principles governing the grammatical foundations of the plain style, and finding appropriate expression in the subject matter, tone, diction, and humor of the *sermo* or conversation, whether oral or written. To these stylistic theories, which gained general adherence in the Scipionic circle Lucilius had given a somewhat loose adherence. Thus in one or more satires in book 30 and elsewhere, he appears to have defined his position in relation to such questions, in so far as they related to the genre which he himself called a *sermo*. These satires thus became Horace's models in so far as he followed the spirit of Lucilian satire, his point of departure in so far as he felt that a restatement and modification of the Lucilian theory of satire was required by the more urbane spirit of Augustan ethics and aesthetics.

But this Augustan urbanity, of which Horace is perhaps the most famous exemplar rests in large measure upon later and more refined definitions of the diction and humor appropriate to the *sermo* or discourse in the plain style. These later definitions we may reconstruct by the study of the rhetorical theories of the Roman Atticists, and preeminently from the rhetorical works of Cicero. The critical satires of Horace cannot be seen in their proper perspective until we realize that they restate and recast in conformity with the tenets of Augustan literary criticism the essentials of a continuous tradition of the subject matter, diction, and humor, appropriate to the *sermo*, or discourse in the plain style. The writers giving the most explicit definition to this rhetorical tradition are Diogenes of Babylon, Panaetius, Lucilius, and Cicero.

The influence of Panaetius in giving a broader and more stylistic development to the grammatical rhetoric of Diogenes of Babylon, and in establishing certain of the fundamentals of Ciceronian and Horatian literary criticism deserves especial emphasis. The fourth and tenth satires of the first book, the first satire of the second book, the literary epistles and above all the *Ars Poetica* of Horace must be examined in the light of these facts. Only thus is it possible to determine the relation of Horace's literary and aesthetic theories to the aesthetic and rhetorical tradition, which, as we have seen, exercised such an important influence in the development of the *sermo*, or informal discourse, half-serious, half-humorous, written in the plain style.

In fact, Horace's fourth satire may be regarded as an aesthetic and ethical analysis of the Lucilian theory of satire;

a criticism, however, presented under the guise of an attack upon those contemporaries who believed in a direct revival of Lucilian invective presented in the traditional Lucilian form of improvisation.

Now ethically Lucilius stands closer to the direct methods, the obscenity, and the brutal frankness of Diogenes and the earlier Cynics, while Horace represents a reversion to the more humane tolerance and greater restraint of the later Cynics of the Bionean type. Indeed, we seem to have in Lucilius a conscious allusion to this feeling that he continues—or at least was regarded by contemporary criticism as continuing—the tradition established by Diogenes of biting attacks even upon his friends. Both the Greek and the Roman believed that such frank criticism was the true province of friendship,[137] while the more kindly and laudatory attitude was often but a mask for hypocrisy. Thus in book 30, line 1095, the poet, with an allusion to the favorite word play of the Cynics on κύων, says of his function:[138]

> inde canino ritu oculisque involem.

In 1097 he speaks of the reverse character, the pleasant-spoken, but treacherous flatterer and hypocrite:

> est illud quoque mite malum blandum atque dolosum.

With the first we may compare the well-known apothegm of Diogenes:[139] The other dogs bite their enemies, but I my friends in order to save them. Hence the Cynic often adopted the manner of the enemy, whom he was fond of contrasting with the false friend, and whom he found much less dangerous. Indeed, the second passage of Lucilius is so close to line 43 in the fragment of *Phoenix of Colophon*,

> τὸ μαλιχῶδες καὶ προσηνὲς δὴ τοῦτο

as to indicate the Cynic provenance of the line.[140] Horace, on the other hand, is at pains to assert that his own theory of criticism is not at variance with the *urbanitas* which should characterize true friendship.[141] Thus in line 90 ff., he recognizes the presence in society of the back-biter, from whom in lines 34 ff. and lines 66 ff., he has already differentiated the true satirist, and in line 100 ff., he promises to keep his works free from that

fault. He would be *dulcis amicis* (135). The whole third satire
in fact, is a plea for human tolerance, with few Lucilian recollec-
tions and in a spirit alien to the prevailing tone of Lucilian
satire.

Now the criticisms cited by Horace in this satire, charging
the poet with the unsparing use of personal abuse and invective,
are in no real sense applicable to Horatian satire. On the
contrary, they are only a concrete picture of the general concep-
tion of satire as formulated in the poet's time under the influ-
ence of the Greco-Roman rhetorical tradition applicable to the
diction and humor of the *sermo*, which we have already sought
to analyze. In this connection, however, it is worthy of remark
that Horace, unlike the loose-constructionist Lucilius, but in
harmony with the theories of Panaetius (and Cicero) as to the
province of the laughable, rejects entirely the slashing and
biting type of humor favored by the earlier Cynics.

Panaetius, it will be remembered, assailed the aesthetic and
moral coarseness of Cynic speech, as a sin against social pro-
priety, the test for which he called *approbatio aurium*, an expres-
sion having certain analogies with Horace's ideal of *urbanitas*.
Also Panaetius[142] asserted that such coarseness of speech was
inimical both to moral and stylistic sensibility and was therefore
altogether to be rejected. Accordingly, he eliminated coarse-
ness and abuse and favored the definition of the liberal jest,
as enunciated by Aristotle, in preference to the coarser and
franker humor affected by the Cynics.[143] Horace's definition
of the type of humor appropriate to the *sermo*[144] goes back in
ultimate analysis to Aristotle. Since, however, the stylistic
theories of Panaetius evidently played a vital part in popular-
izing such Aristotelian theories of the province of the laughable
in the Scipionic circle and exercised an important influence
upon the Lucilian theory of satire, it seems reasonable to regard
Panaetius—as well as Cicero—as one of the principal mediating
influences in transmitting this Aristotelian tradition to Horace.

Aesthetically Lucilius, like Persius and Juvenal, is less con-
cerned with form than with content and spirit. He seeks above
all to reproduce the rapid informality and inconsequence of the
Cynics with their constant recollection of the swashbuckling
spirit of the Old Comedy. Nevertheless, Lucilius, like Horace,

seems to have made the attempt to give his theories literary justification by asserting that his form was not poetry at all.

Lucilius appears also to have formulated a definite theory of the province of the laughable in relation to satire. In this formulation, as we have seen,[145] he was influenced by the teaching of Panaetius as well as by those of the Cynics. Thus Panaetius cites[146] the Old Comedy among the appropriate examples of the liberal jest. It seems probable that Lucilius was familiar with this doctrine of Panaetius. In support of this view I am inclined to cite line 1111 from the fragments of Lucilius grouped by Marx under the caption *incertae sedis reliquiae* and to assign this fragment to the critical satire of Lucilius now under discussion. This line is as follows:

> archaeotera . . . unde haec sunt omnia nata.

Here Marx refers the *archaeotera* to Homer, and explains the passage as an expression of the preeminence assigned to Homer in the critical and rhetorical theories of the ancients. This interpretation is, of course, possible, though the use of the comparative as referring to Homer seems strange to me. Hence I am inclined to explain the line as referring to the Old Comedy upon whose theory of the laughable, as Lucilius here expressly asserts, his own writings (*haec*) depend. This interpretation of the Lucilian line finds further support in the marked similarity of this Lucilian line with the initial lines of Horace's fourth satire:

> Eupolis atque Cratinus Aristophanesque poetae
> atque alii quorum comoedia prisca virorumst
> . . . .
> hinc omnis pendet Lucilius, hosce secutus.

My readers will notice that Horace's enumeration of the leading writers of the Old Comedy corresponds to Lucilius *archaeotera*, and that the *hinc omnis pendet Lucilius* looks like a paraphrase of *unde haec sunt omnia*. In short I am inclined to believe that these lines of Horace in thought and form contain a direct and significant allusion to the critical theories of Lucilius. Such an interpretation sheds much light upon the relation between this fourth satire of Horace and the literary theories of Lucilius set forth in his satire or satires in book 30.

This assertion of the dependence of Lucilius upon the great writers of the Old Comedy is probably primarily in reference to Lucilius' employment of the aggressive censorious wit of the Old Comedy and relative indifference to other and more estimable stylistic qualities of that form. Horace himself is in closer harmony than Lucilius with post-Aristotelian literary theory,[147] which while assigning certain virtue to the *vis comica* of the Old Comedy adopts a theory of the laughable in accord rather with the more subtle and restrained humor of the New Comedy.[148] But the literary theories of the two satirists will emerge most clearly by a detailed analysis and comparison of both the Lucilian and the Horatian satires to which I now turn.

I arrange the fragments of Lucilius in the following order: 1021, 1019, 1020, 1022, 971, 1014, 1015, 1016, 970, 1027, 1028, 1029, 1279, 1010, 1294, 1033, 1289, 1030, 1079, 1031, 588, 596, 1290, 1038, 1017, 1025, 1096, 1268(?), 1026, 1018(?), 1060, 1063, 1064, 1070, 1067, 1054, 1038, 1032.

Horace begins with a protest against certain aesthetic imperfections in Lucilian satire: (1) its harshness in composition (8); (2) its improvisatory character (9–10); (3) its redundancy (11–12); and the tendency to favor garrulity and redundancy by street-preachers like Crispinus, who like Lucilius favor improvisatory composition (13–16). He differs from Lucilius and his modern analogue Fannius[149] in not writing "best sellers" for the man in the street (20–24). And why? Because "the man in the street" is suspicious of satire as a literary genre, feeling rightly that he is the subject of attack.

Up to this point we have, naturally, Horace's own words. In lines 20–24 there follows the skilful transition by which Horace insinuates himself into his real theme. This theme is more clearly stated in verse 64:

> nunc illud tantum quaeram, meritone tibi sit
> suspectum genus hoc scribendi.   ·

In the development of this theme Horace traverses essentially the same ground as Lucilius in book 30, and the resemblances, sometimes in theme, sometimes in illustrations, sometimes in language as well, are frequent.

In lines 21–34 Horace illustrates the reason for the general popular disfavor of the satiric form by attacking the different

weaknesses of typical men of the day.   Naturally those who are
hit, fear satire and dislike the satirist:

> Beatus Fannius ultro
> delatis capsis et imagine, cum mea nemo
> scripta legat volgo recitare timentis ob hanc rem
> quod sunt quos genus hoc minime iuvat, utpote pluris
> culpari dignos.   quemvis media elige turba:
> aut ob avaritiam aut misera ambitione laborat;
> hic nuptarum insanit amoribus, hic puerorum;
> hunc capit argenti splendor; stupet Albius aere;
> hic mutat mercis surgente a sole ad eum quo
> vespertina tepet regio, quin per mala praeceps
> fertur uti pulvis collectus turbine, nequid
> summa deperdat metuens aut ampliet ut rem:
> omnes hi metuunt versus, odere poetas.

This same sequence is set forth in Lucilius 1021, 1019, 1020,
as Marx has seen.   In 1021, the *adversarius* appears to accuse
Lucilius as the author of a *suspectum genus*, who though he
assails, and blames, accomplishes nothing:

> quod tu *nunc* laedes culpes, non proficis hilum.[160]

So Horace fears (lines 23–24) to recite his writings for he knows
that his audience is sensitive to blame.   Both poets as we have
seen above[161] are writing with due regard to such rhetorical
formulations of the tone of the *sermo*, as are found in Cicero
(Panaetius) where the question of faultfinding was discussed,
and censure of the absent forbidden.

   In the mouth of the *adversarius* also are to be put 1019 and
1020.   The *adversarius* of Lucilius, apparently a spokesman for
his sinful fellows, (compare Horace's *quemvis media elige turba*)
asks why the poet should be concerned with the enumeration of
the various forms of vice.   The speaker of the line is probably
the same victim of sexual passion, who clearly appears in 1020
where Nonius p. 387, 26 glosses *servare* by *sollicite et suspiciose
observare*, and where, as Marx shows, we are to think of the man
who frequents the brothel as the speaker.   Both lines thus
appear to be used in a context similar to Horace *sat.* 1, 4, 24 ff.
This seems likely from the common use of *voluter* in the sense of
"wallowing" in sin.[162]   The two lines are as follows:

> quid tu istuc curas, ubi ego oblinar atque voluter?
> quid servas quo eam, quid agam? quid id attenet ad te?[163]

The thought of the last Lucilian line is reproduced by Horace's line 27:

> hic nuptarum insanit amoribus, hic puerorum.

Horace then proceeds (34–38) to reproduce the current criticism of the satirist, as a dangerous bull, who in the fury of his charge, spares neither friends nor self, a man who likewise would have the whole city familiar with his casual lampoons. We have here, as so often in satire, an adaptation of one of the typical animal similes of the Cynics.[154]   The "satirist armed and an object of terror," does not stop at the illiberal form of jest attributed by Aristotle to the βωμολόχος,[155] and held to be characteristic of the Old Comedy. Thus Horace in line 34:

> faenum habet in cornu, longe fuge: dummodo risum
> excutiat sibi, non hic cuiquam parcet amico;
> et quodcumque semel chartis inleverit, omnis
> gestiet a furno redeuntis scire lacuque,
> et pueros et anus.

Now we have preserved in Lucilius's book 30, lines 1022, 971, 1014, 970, 1015, 1016, several of the essential illustrations used in this exposition. In fact there seems reason to believe that Lucilius, influenced probably by the Panaetian interpretation of the Aristotelian theory of the laughable made in this satire a differentiation between the type of humor he employed as a satirist, and the more coarse, unrestrained, and vulgar type of jest. Theoretically, therefore, he and Horace may have occupied a common ground, but the two satirists differed widely in their application of their common rhetorical formula to actual composition. Both agreed, as Cicero says *de officiis* 1, 104, that in jesting *modus retinendus est*, but differed as to the nature of the limit to be applied to the liberal jest, and its point of application.

Moreover, if we assign to a Lucilian *adversarius* certain of these lines Lucilius, like Horace, may have rebutted a charge of βωμολοχία, or scurrility directed against his satires. On this matter in the case of fragments we can of course only speak of probabilities. Let us now turn to the fragments in question.

In place of Horace's comparison of unrestrained satirist with the enraged bull (l. 34) Lucilius uses the equally apt comparison of the dreaded satirist with a set mouse trap or a scorpion with tail raised ready to sting.[156]

A person impelled by such a conception of the comic spirit, the typical βωμολόχος of Aristotle's *Eth. Nicom.* 4, 14, 1128 a, 36 spares neither himself nor others, if he can raise a laugh. This is, of course, the ultimate source or rather the rhetorical formula justifying Horace's lines 34 and 35 quoted above. It seems likely that line 971 of Lucilius stood in a similar context, though it is difficult to decide whether we should put the line in the mouth of the poet himself or of an *adversarius*. If we accept the former alternative the line will express the satirist's determination to arouse the laughter of the crowd by unrestrained jest. Or if—and this second alternative seems to me the more probable in view of the influence of Panaetius upon Lucilius—we assign the line to an *adversarius*, the poet is charged with employing in his satires the very type of unrefined humor, which he like Horace reprobates:[157]

> Quae quondam populi *risu* res pectora rumpet.

Line 1014 is referred by Marx either to Horace's line 34 or line 83. The reference seems to be to the abusive character of Lucilian satire of which someone, perhaps the *adversarius*, complains. Lucilius employs savage invective, perhaps as Marx suggests in the words with which he attempts to weave a context around this line, in order to raise a laugh at all costs:[158]

> idque tuis factis saeuis et tristibus dictis.[159]

That is, as Marx continues, *te consequi cupis, ut risum excutias.* In other words, as Aristotle would say, Lucilius is in the opinion of the *adversarius* a typical βωμολόχος.

Moreover, the satirist wishes to record his caustic personal observations in his *sermones*, and to have these widely circulated, 1015 and 1016. Thus in 1015:

> gaudes, cum de me ista foris sermonibus differs.

and 1016:

> et male dicendo in multis sermonibus differs.

Taken together, these two Lucilian lines seem to suggest a context parallel to that of Horace in lines 36 ff.:

> et quodcumque semel chartis inleverit, omnis
> gestiet a furno redeuntis scire lacuque,
> et pueros et anus.
> •

In view of Lucilius' fondness for word plays it seems reasonable
to assume that 1015 and 1016 stood pretty closely together.   In
the first passage, as *foris* shows, *differs* was used in the sense of
disseminating malicious reports about a person, or as Nonius
says p. 284, 14, in the sense *diffamare, divulgare*. In the second
passage *differs* seems to be used in the sense of libeling a person
in the works of a writer rather than in the broader sense of
circulating subsequently such a written libel.   Somewhat
similar is Horace's use of *chartis inleverit*.   Marx refers
1015 to Horace 1, 4, 78 a similar context, but *laedo*
there does not so clearly imply the spreading abroad of
evil report which plays such an important part in the
earlier Horatian passage and is emphasized in the Lucilian
passage by *foris*.   Both Lucilius and Horace seem to emphasize
the fact that according to their respective *adversarii* the satirist
succeeds in making his abuse the talk of the town.   Here also
we have traces of the rhetorical theories of Aristotle and Panae-
tius.   The type of satire represented by the βωμολόχος appeals
to the groundlings, for as Aristotle says, he does not jest like the
εἴρων for his own amusement, but for the defamation of his
neighbor, Aristotle *Rhetoric* 3, 18 *ad fin*: ἔστι δὲ εἰρωνεία τῆς
βωμολοχίας ἐλευθεριώτερον· ὁ μὲν γὰρ αὑτοῦ ἕνεκα ποιεῖ τὸ γελοῖον,
ὁ δὲ βωμολόχος ἑτέρου.[160]

This penchant of the βωμολόχος for the defamation of his
neighbor carries with it as a necessary corollary a considerable
audience.   Both Lucilius and Horace emphasize the spreading
of the satirist's ill-natured jest, when once uttered, among the
crowd.   Thus Lucilius in line 970:[161]

> multis indu locis sermonibus concelebrarunt.

This looks like a generalization.   Horace in accordance with his
custom substitutes a more concrete picture of the slaves and
old wives returning from the bakery and the fountain, line 37:[162]

> omnis
> gestiet a furno redeuntis scire lacuque,
> et pueros et anus.

Probably, therefore, Lucilius in these lines reprobated, like Horace, the illiberal jest, which Cicero, following Panaetius, describes in the *de officiis* 1, 134 as proceeding *severe, maledice, contumeliose.* One is even tempted to compare the use of *maledice* in this passage with Lucilius' *maledicendo* in line 1016 as pointing towards the probable familiarity of Lucilius with Panaetius' formulation of the Aristotelian differentiation between the liberal and the illiberal jest.

In lines 39–62 Horace turns to the discussion of the relation of satire to the New Comedy and to Epic. He expressly denies to himself (and to Lucilius, line 57) the title of poet, asserting that it is not enough to write mere prose in metrical feet to receive the designation of poet. In truth the position of satire is analogous to that of the New Comedy, both the dialogue of the New Comedy and satire are *sermones* or everyday conversations in the plain style. Both lack, therefore, as Horace rightly argues, the essential poetic qualities best realized in the Epic. These are inspiration (*mens divinior*) and the grand style (*os magna sonaturum*). Satire is rather, like the New Comedy, an attempt to versify the language of everyday life. All this is asserted in language which derives its technical stylistic definitions of the characteristics of the Old and the New Comedy from Aristotle and shows conspicuous points of analogy with the traditional criticism set forth in the Coislinian treatise περὶ κωμῳδίας.[163] That Lucilius was interested in such rhetorical discussions of what constituted true poetry is conclusively proved by the differentiation between *poema* and *poesis* in lines 338–347 in book 9.

In fragments 1027, 1028, 1029, 1279, 1010, 1294, I believe we can find traces, much less detailed to be sure, of the existence in this Lucilian satire of a similar effort to establish the laws of satiric technique, and to define the relation of satire to Comedy and to epic poetry.

Horace, it will be remembered, begins his aesthetic discussion with a professional baldness of diction in line 38:

> agedum, pauca accipe contra.

With this we may compare Lucilius line 1027:[164]

> summatim tamen experiar rescribere paucis.

Both passages certainly look like transitions prefacing brief rejoinders by way of digressions. In view of the relation previously set forth between the Lucilian satire and Horace's fourth satire, it is a plausible conjecture to associate the Lucilian transition with Horace's transition to the discussion of the stylistic qualities of satire. The drift of the following fragments adds further confirmation to such a conjecture.

Horace begins at once (line 39) by denying to his genre the name of poetry, and to himself the name of poet:

> primum ego me illorum, dederim quibus esse poetis,
> excerpam numero.

With this general context I shall venture to compare Lucilius 1028 written in the more elevated epic strain of one to whom the muses entrust their keys. That is, Lucilius too declines the title of poet. The diction and careful finish of this excursion of Lucilius into the epic style may be compared with Horace's adaptation of the lines from the *Annales* of Ennius (266 V) in lines 60 and 61.

Cichorius[165] has seen in these lines an allusion to the temple of the *Camenae* at Rome in which Accius,[166] a leading spirit in the *collegium poetarum*, had his statue set up. I am inclined to agree to the possibility of this interpretation, especially as we know that Horace too had his quarrels with the guild of poets.[167] In this very satire, in fact, the Fannius in line 21, who has voluntarily offered his MS. and his portrait bust to some public library at Rome occupies a position similar to that assigned to the epic poet of the Lucilian line, probably Accius with his exaggerated statue in the temple of the *Camenae*. In fact, in the Heinze-Kiessling edition of Horace we find the plausible conjecture that the new work of Fannius was received in the library of the *collegium poetarum*. According to this interpretation, we may guess that Lucilius differentiated his verses from those of Accius, just as Horace differentiated his from those of Fannius. Neither does Lucilius any more than Horace accept the name of poet, though he once called his work a *poema*, and often favors the terms *sermo*, *schedium*, *ludus*, as we have seen.[168] It seems likely, therefore, that Lucilius like Horace refused to take any part in the organization known as the *collegium poetarum.* Hence his "gibe at the poet" Accius, whose statue acts as janitor to the muses.

Again Lucilius in 1029 seems to have contrasted himself with a comic poet:

> sicuti te, qui ea quae speciem uitae esse putamus.

Marx has clearly suggested the right context to be supplied for this line:[169] versibus exsequeris, dicam vix esse poetam. Upon comparing the many parallel passages there quoted we see that it was a commonplace of Greek rhetorical criticism that the function of comedy was to hold the mirror up to daily life. Hence Horace denied that it any more than satire was true poetry; both were *sermoni propriora* (42). Comedy (48) is *sermo merus*. Even its more spirited passages (48–52) are like the spirited passages in our everyday life (52):[170]

> numquid Pomponius istis
> audiret leviora, pater si viveret?

In this passage Horace and possibly Lucilius before him—though on this point the direct testimony of our surviving fragments fails us—evidently restated the main points made by certain Hellenistic rhetoricians and critics, the *quidam* of Horace's line 45, who denied to the New Comedy the right to pass as poetry. Cicero in the *orator* 20, 67, re-echoes the essentials of this Hellenistic theory. Moreover,[171] the affinities between this Ciceronian passage and Horace's lines are most striking. To my mind they go far to establish the complete familiarity of Horace[172] with the *orator* of Cicero, as one of the most important mediating agencies between the literary criticism of the Hellenistic period, and that of the Augustan age, especially that of the Augustan Atticists. In the passage in question Cicero says: video visum esse nonnullis Platonis et Democriti locutionem, etsi absit a versu, tamen quod incitatius feratur et clarissimis verborum luminibus utatur, potius poema putandum quam comicornun poetarum, apud quos nisi quod versicula sunt, nihil est aliud cottidiani dissimile sermonis. Here the *incitatius ferri* of Cicero corresponds to the *acer spiritus et vis* of Horace. Again Horace's statement in lines 47 and 48:

> nisi quod pede certo
> differt sermoni, sermo merus.

seems in close harmony with Cicero's statement in the *orator* 180 as to the nature of prose rythms:

quibusdam non videtur numerosa oratio, quia nihil inest in ea certi ut in versibus.

In this connection Lucilius' lines 1294 f. deserve passing notice:

— — seruandi numeri et uersus faciendi,
nos Caeli Numeri numerum ut seruemus modumque.

There is, to be sure, no direct parallel to these lines in Horace's fourth satire. Marx, however, in his commentary on this passage has shown that *numerus* was first introduced into Latin literature by Lucilius as a translation of the Greek μέτρον and *modus* as a translation of the Greek ῥυθμός. Horace and Horace's readers would, therefore, probably think of Lucilius' technical use of these terms when they read such lines as this line 47 with its allusion to *pede certo* or lines 6 and 7 at the beginning of the satire in which it is asserted that Lucilius followed the writers of the Old Comedy except that by substituting the dactyl for the iambus he gave to his verse a new rhythm. One wonders whether the passage in question may have stood in a context in this satire in book 30, and have set forth Lucilius' justification for this metrical innovation. Moreover, to substitute the dactyl for the iambus is to substitute for a prosaic foot an heroic foot according to Roman rhetorical theory. Hence Lucilius might on this basis have felt justified in applying the term *poema* to his writings, a term which he actually uses in 1013.

With this same general context in the satire of Lucilius in book 30, one is inclined to associate 1279, in which Lucilius gives us the informal title of his verse,[173] *schedium*, and may also like Horace—though this is a purely conjectural context— have denied to his satires the title of poetry.

In fact, Marx's restoration of the mutilated verse, *qui schedium fa*—as ego non poeta sum, qui schedium faciam, tantum non carmina vera—seems ingenious and plausible. The line which may have stood in this same Lucilian satire from book 30 is perhaps best referred to some context similar to Horace's satire 1, 4, 39 ff., in which Horace denied that mere metrical correctness is the touchstone of true poetry, and asserts, line 42, that his writings are *sermoni propriora*, a correct definition because as the *auctor ad Herennium* 3, 13, 23 explains, sermo est oratio remissa et finitima cottidianae locutioni. The term *schedium*, which from originally meaning a raft, had come to mean anything hastily knocked together is in point of fact, as we have seen,[174] an appropriate designation for the improvisatory character of Lucilian satire, just as the master employed *ludus*, a term referring to the informal play of humor so characteristic of the plain style, to distinguish his writings from such productions in the grand style as epic or tragedy.

More than that, Lucilius may himself have applied the term *poema* to his works as fragment 1013 also in book 30, seems to imply:

> et sola ex multis nunc nostra poemata ferri.

If these words are to be put into the poet's own mouth, it may be that Horace approving of such designations of his master's poetry as *schedium, ludus, sermo* voices an objection to the use of the more pretentious term *poema* in line 63, where he says:

> alias iustum sit necne poema.
> nunc illud tantum quaeram, meritone tibi sit
> suspectum genus hoc scribendi.

In lines 64–70 Horace returns to his main theme. He claims that the comparison of the satirist with a public prosecutor is unfair. At any rate, only thieves like Caelius and Birrus need fear the prosecutor. Unlike my predecessor, who traces his spiritual descent from the writers of the Old Comedy, he would seem to say, I shall not assume the rôle of *censor morum*, even though you assume the rôle of bandit. Why then should you fear me?

Horace here directly disavows the rôle, which Lucilius perhaps under the influence of a rhetorical theory of humor associating the liberal jest with the reforming spirit of the Old Comedy deliberately assumes in book 30[175] in such lines as 1033, 1289, 1030, 1031.

In line 1033 Lucilius seems to assume directly the rôle of a *censor morum*, perhaps deliberately selecting the word *nota* in view of its inevitable associations with the *nota censoria*.

Here *nota* is glossed by Nonius by the word *turpitudo*. This suggests, as we have already noticed, some connection of the passage with the theory of the illiberal jest which employs obscene words in the assault upon an indecent subject.[178] Possibly a similar charge of censoriousness was brought against Lucilius by the *adversarius*, and naturally enough the poet rejoins, "in the case of one whom you know knows all your blemishes and faults," *i.e.*, (brands). Compare Horace lines 64–70:

> nunc illud tantum quaeram, meritone tibi sit
> suspectum genus hoc scribendi. Sulcius acer
> ambulat et Caprius, rauci male cumque libellis,
> magnus uterque timor latronibus: at bene si quis
> et vivat puris manibus, contemnat utrumque.
> ut sis tu similis Caeli Birrique latronum,
> non ego sim Capri neque Sulci: cur metuas me?

In line 66 of this Horatian passage the professional prosecutors or *delators*, Sulcius and Caprius, are represented as walking around with their long indictments, hoarse from their long prosecutions. Lucilius' line 1289 may possibly be referred to a somewhat similar context, though of course in the case of so mutilated a line we are on highly conjectural ground. Such an interpretation seems favored by the interpretations of this fragment both by Cichorius and Marx[177] on the basis of the definition of Paulus ex Fest, p. 282, who after defining rava vox as rauca et parum liquida . . . adds unde etiam causidicus pugnaciter loquens ravilla. Festus, p. 282.14 quotes the fragment of the hexameter:

$$— — — — — — — — \text{ t ravi}$$

Marx restores the missing word as *clamarent*, but Cichorius, more aptly in my opinion in view of the etymology of *ravilla*, suggests *latrat*. Doubtless, as he points out, the allusion is to L. Cassius Longinus, a contemporary of Lucilius called *Ravilla*, not from his eloquence, but from his much speaking for Cicero, *Brutus* 97 declares: L. Cassius multum potuit non eloquentia, sed dicendo tamen.

Is it not possible, therefore, to refer this mutilated line in which the aggressive and long-winded *causidicus* Cassius is satirized by Lucilius to a context in this apologetic satire of

book 30? In that case the *acer Sulcius et Caprius* of Horace
who are *rauci male* and have bundles of indictments may be
regarded as a transformed contemporary allusion, bringing up
in the minds of Horace's readers the picture of the pugnacious
and long-winded Cassius Longinus, who barks until he is hoarse.

The Lucilian line 1030[178] belongs in the same context. The
words are possibly those of the poet to the *adversarius* in which
like Horace, Lucilius disclaims any intention to use unrestrained
invective for the purposes of indiscriminate attack. No upright
citizen need fear the shafts of this earlier satirist:

> nolito tibi me male dicere posse putare.

Doubtless also Lucilius wrote this line in more or less complete
recognition of the theory of the liberal type of jest appropriate
to the *sermo*. In this respect the line reiterates the rhetorical
doctrine of line 1016 in which Lucilius resents the charge of
βωμολοχία, or scurrility brought against his satire by the undis-
criminating.[179] It will be noticed that the term *male dicere*
occurs in both passages, a term applied to the definitions of the
illiberal jest given by Panaetius in the *de officiis* 1, 134.

In spite of this recognition of the limits and nature of the
liberal jest, Lucilius, unlike Horace, was ready in the reforming
spirit of the Old Comedy to play the part of the public prosecu-
tor. Thus in 1031 we read:[180]

> et Mutonis manum perscribere posse tagacem

Here *tagax* means *furunculus a tangendo*. This verse is perhaps
with Marx to be put into the mouth of an *adversarius* who
assails the aggressive invective of Lucilius: quid magnum,
inquit furunculi manum sinistram perscribere posse versibus.
Apparently the allusion in the name Muto is to a Quintus Muto,
the principal perhaps in some *cause célèbre* of the Gracchan age.
If so, we may have in the Lucilian prototype of Horace's sub-
stituted paraphrase an allusion parallel to the case of theft
charged against Petillius Capitolinus in lines 93 ff.[181]

In lines 71–78, Horace defines his attitude toward his readers.
His tone is aristocratic. He will read only for the innermost
circle of his friends, and that only on compulsion. He will have
nothing to do with the public *recitatio*. On the contrary he
affects to hope that his book will not reach the common herd

through sales in the book stores. There are more than enough to recite publicly, and to enjoy the sound of their own voices:

> nulla taberna meos habeat neque pila libellos,
> quis manus insudet volgi Hermongenisque Tigelli,
> nec recito cuiquam nisi amicis, idque coactus,
> non ubivis coramve quibuslibet, in medio qui
> scripta foro recitent sunt multi quique lavantes:
> suave locus voci resonat conclusus, inanis
> hoc iuvat, haud illud quaerentis, num sine sensu,
> tempore num faciant alieno.

This passage illustrates Horace's highly artistic method of "contemporizing" Lucilian satire.[182] It is written with direct reference to and reaction from Lucilius' preference for an audience recruited from men of general culture rather than from men of professional learning, as set forth in book 26, lines 582–596. The bookseller's shop with its pillar and the *public recitatio*, introduced by Pollio, are of course allusions to contemporary Augustan life, but the private reading in the home of a wealthy patron could not have been unknown in the age of Lucilius.[183]

Thus Lucilius in 588 from book 26, another apologetic satire, contrasts the audience *he* seeks with that sought by a certain class of *scriptores*. He seeks the *illi*, or men of well-known culture, not the *populus*. This passage, as Marx rightly saw,[184] is parallel to Horace 1, 4, 72:

> nunc itidem populo <*placere nolo*> his cum scriptoribus:
> voluimus capere animum illorum.

Horace then returns to his main theme, the definition and defence of satirical humor in line 78:

> 'laedere gaudes'
> inquis, 'et hoc studio pravus facis.'

These words, as Hendrickson has shown,[185] are a further application to the definition of the liberal type of humor appropriate to the *sermo*, couched in the plain style of the Aristotelian assault on the βωμολοχία or scurrility of the Old Comedy. Thus of the βωμολόχοι Aristotle says:[186] μᾶλλον στοχαζόμενοι τὸν γέλωτα ποιεῖν ἢ τοῦ λέγειν εὐσχήμονα καὶ μὴ λυπεῖν (*laedere nocere*) τὸν σκωπτόμενον. Similar is the *Ars Poetica* 283 ff., where we find that criticism and tradition assigning to the Old Comedy a function

of hurting analogous to that assigned by rhetorical criticism to
satire. With the loss of this privilege of aggression the Greek
prototype of satire declined:

>   turpiter obticuit
>   sublato iure nocendi.

In Cicero's *de oratore* 2, 236 we have traces of a similar rhetorical
theory of coarse and aggressive humor, which suggests Aris-
totle's characterization of the spirit of the Old Comedy by the
words αἰσχρολογίᾳ λυπεῖν:

> haec enim ridentur vel sola vel maxime, quae *notant* et designant turpitudi-
> nem aliquam non turpiter.

This last formulation suggests the formulation of the nature of
the true type of jest made by Cicero in the *de officiis* 1, 104,
which defines the illiberal type of humor as unworthy of any
freeborn man since the subject is indecent and the words
obscene. If then Lucilius in line 899 expresses the desire that
verba obscena may be removed from his page, he even before
Horace may well have been familiar with this same Aristotelian
theory, through its formulations by Panaetius.

Later Greek aesthetic criticism, retrograding from the high
standard of Aristotle, recognized βωμολοχία, as for instance in
iambic poetry and the Old Comedy, as an actual merit. So in
the Coislinian treatise περὶ κωμῳδίας we read: ὁ σκώπτων ἐλέγχειν
θέλει ἁμαρτήματα τῆς ψυχῆς καὶ τοῦ σώματος. These words illus-
trate the set purpose attributed to Horace's satire by the *adver-
sarius* who declares *hoc studio facis*.

Yet before Horace, a similar charge appears to have been
levelled against Lucilius, who in 1035 is reproved by name
for his deliberate attacks, the reproof being apparently assigned
to his *adversarius* by the earlier poet.

>   nunc, Gai, quoniam incilans nos *laedis*, vicissim

With the last word we may compare the Horatian *laedere
gaudes*. The *incilans* of Lucilius glossed by Nonius by *increpare
vel improbare* seems quite as close to such Aristotelian expres-
sions as αἰσχρολογίᾳ λυπεῖν (compare also the use of *male dicere*
in lines 1016 and 1033) as anything in Horace's satire. Here
then we have a further bit of evidence for Lucilius' familiarity
with the rhetorical definitions of the *genus iocandi* and for

Horace's familiarity, and thorough-going analysis of the Lucilian theory of satiric humor as presented in this satire of book 30.

To such attacks of their respective *adversarii*, both authors reply in *propria persona*. So Horace line 79 ff.:

> unde petitum
> hoc in me iacis? est auctor quis denique eorum
> vixi cum quibus?

And Lucilius 1017:

> haec tu me insimulas? nonne ante in corde uolutas.

The first part of this Lucilian line is parallel to the stone-throwing in Horace; the last sounds like a *tu quoque* addressed to the *adversarius;* he should think twice before he accuses Lucilius of deliberate malice. This charge reminds us of Horace's remark also attributed to an *adversarius, et hoc studio pravus facis* (line 79).

In verses 81–85 Horace then proceeds to amplify the description of the satirist summarized under *laedere gaudes*. This further description of the βωμολόχος corresponds to that in lines 34–38. The βωμολόχος is the slave of laughter:[187] ὁ βωμολόχος ἥττων ἐστὶ τοῦ γελοίου. So completely is he enslaved that he disregards the two fundamental virtues of truthfulness and loyalty to friends. Even assuming, then, for the sake of argument, that the writer of satire has the quality of βωμολοχία, is his freedom on the written page worse than the freedom of speech allowed to the slanderer in society at large, who has a reputation for refined wit gained by assaults on friends and hosts? May not the satirist, then, make fun of the physical peculiarities of a Rufillus or a Gargonius? Thus Horace in lines 86 ff.:

> saepe tribus lectis videas cenare quaternos,
> e quibus unus amet quavis adspergere cunctos
> praeter eum qui praebet aquam; post hunc quoque potus,
> condita cum verax aperit praecordia Liber.

Lucilius, however, in line 1025 seems to allude to the same contrasted types of the true satirist previously mentioned, apparently in a line now lost, and another more virulent type, the social slanderer or oral βωμολόχος, who joins a reputation for urbanity (cf. line 1096) with real social treachery. Which he virtually asks is the worse, the frankness of the satiric jest or malignant scurrility, βωμολοχία?

Thus in 1025,[188] referring to the social slanderer of this type in contrast with someone discussed above, presumably the satirist, Lucilius says:

> improbior multo quam de quo diximus ante:
> quanto blandior haec, tanto uehementius mordet.

And in 1096:

> est illud quoque mite malum blandum atque dolosum.

The *blandior* in 1025, the *mite* and *blandum* in 1096 correspond to the Horatian *comis et urbanus liberque* of line 91. The greater treachery of such speech as contrasted with the frank spirit of the true satirist, whose very frankness in ancient aesthetic theory was closely related to the παρρησία of the Old Comedy and the Cynics, is suggested in the Horatian *infesto nigris* of line 91, the *lividus et mordax* of line 93. In this connection compare especially the Lucilian phrases *dolosum malum* in the former fragment and the *mordet* in the latter fragment.[189]

In the same Lucilian context and perhaps immediately following 1096 belongs 1026:

> omnes formonsi, fortes tibi, ego improbus. esto.

These lines are rightly to be compared with Horace's lines 90 ff.:[190]

> hic tibi comis et urbanus liberque videtur,
> infesto nigris: ego, si risi quod ineptus
> pastillos Rufillus olet, Gargonius hircum,
> lividus et mordax videor tibi?

That is both Lucilius and Horace rightly ask, in defence of their theory of the truly liberal humor appropriate to satire, whether the purveyor of social slander is to be regarded as a refined wit, while the satirist is considered a malignant enemy to society.[191]

With line 100, *hic nigrae sucus loliginis, haec est aerugo mera*, Horace completes his definition of τό γέλοιον or the true nature of the laughable in social life and in satire. This negative exposition is an attempt to differentiate the true comic spirit from that of βωμολοχία or scurrility, with which it was at times confounded by writers of the Old Comedy, by certain schools of rhetorical criticism, and even by Lucilius himself, the heir to conflicting traditions. The true satirist, Horace holds, will hark back, not to the spirit of the Old Comedy, but to that of the New, to that of Theophrastus,[192] and that of the more mellow later Cynics like Menippus and Bion who are rightly grouped together under the common designation of σπουδαιογέλοιοι or serious humorists. Accordingly, in lines 102–142 Horace lets us see τὸ σπουδαῖον, the earnest features of the satirist beneath the comic mask.

Now Horace's father in this satire is not merely the sturdy representative of the Roman *mos maiorum* in education,[193] but even more a mouthpiece for the empirical morality of the Cynics,[194] expounded with all the artistic reserve of the Greek εἴρων.[195] Such a conception does not reduce the older man to a myth or seek to deny the real part he played in forming the Horatian attitude towards life. It merely advances the postulate that to the cosmopolitan Horace, imbued with the teachings of Greek philosophy, his old father, seen through the mist of the years seemed like what we should call a "natural" Cynic, just as Ofellus is pictured as an *abnomis sapiens*. Nor is it impossible that Horace rendered forgetful by the passage of the years and led on by his own philosophic studies may at times attribute expressions and ideals to the older man which would have surprised the simple *praeco*. The self-made father in many an age has undergone a similar fate at the hands of an affectionate and highly sophisticated son. Let us dissect the pedagogy of the old man in the light of this theory.

He teaches morality (a) by precept (*cf.*) *hortaretur*, 107; *deterreret* 112; (*sapiens uitatu quidque petitu sit melius causas reddet tibi*; *formabat puerum dictis* 121); similar is Horace's own emphasis on *aetas, amici,* and *consilium proprium* in training. But in the second place (b) the older man teaches morality by example (*exemplis vitiorum quoque notando*; examples of prodigality (109–111), lapses in sexual morality (111–115), a type from the jury panel for every act).

Now this method is essentially Cynic, as can be seen by anyone who will study the Cynic commonplaces collected by Gerhard in his edition of Phoenix of Colophon. (1) Thus the

Cynics laid great stress upon the part of λόγοι χρηστοί in educa-
tion.[196] This is especially illustrated by their use of the
poetical χρεῖαι assigned to the seven wise men.[197] (2) The
Cynic examples are drawn mostly from contemporary
life.[198] (3) Literary examples, when used, are mainly from the
New Comedy with its careful delineation of types.[199] So also
the examples cited by Horace's father, the *filius Albi, Scetanus,
Trebatius*, are all New Comedy types, and his method of using
these examples of warning and encouragement (*cf.* 115) is
identical with that of those educational realists, the *patres
severi* of the New Comedy. Compare Demea in the *Adelphi*,
line 414, with Horace's line 104. (4) Horace's father and
Horace himself adopt the Cynic method of character drawing
χαρακτηρισμός, and in particular both seek to contrast their own
ideals with those of the world.[200] But (5) the Cynic ideal, as
Gerhard has shown, is νομίζεσθαι χρηστός; the good opinion of
the world is the main argument for morality.[201] This is also
the ideal of Horace's father, who finds in *fama* his principal
argument. So in line 113 ff.: *deprensi non bella est fama Tre-
boni*, and in 124 ff., on the evil of *flagrare rumore malo*.   (6)
Horace's own ethical therapeutics are allied to those of the
later Cynics and to the philosophical theories of the laughable.
Thus in developing the portrait of himself he adopts the tone of
the εἴρων, who uses self-mockery, τὸ γέλοιον αὐτοῦ ἕνεκα, as
Aristotle puts it.[202] With such self-mockery we may compare
the close of the satire lines 140 ff.:[203]

> cui si concedere nolis,
> multa poetarum veniet manus, auxilio quae
> sit mihi (nam multo plures sumus) ac veluti te
> Iudaei cogemus in hanc concedere turbam.

(7) The satirist-sage of the Cynics will therefore employ the
method of self-examination and self-blame.[204] He will thus in
part avert a reputation for censoriousness when analyzing
before the public the character of his friends, in part like the
εἴρων he will thus cloak his self-praise.[205]

Horace's method of procedure is similar. In fact, the self-
examination in lines 133–140 is conducted absolutely in the
spirit of the Cynic εἴρων. Especially to avoid self-praise for his

literary virtues and in accordance with the doctrine that humor
is a quasi-vice do we have the words of 139–140:

> hoc est mediocribus illis
> ex vitiis unum.

(8) The fruit of this self-examination, a sort of autodialectic,
is sincerity. Therefore, the Cynic sage and the Roman satirist
alike insist on the right of free speech, free thought, and free
composition.[206] With this assertion, humorously put, Horace
closes the satire. That is, seriously put, we will make a convert
of you to the method and ideals of the σπουδαιογέλοιοι.

The ironical humor which pervades this whole passage is
worthy of the Platonic Socrates. Under the impulse of this
mood of Socratic self-depreciation, in which both father and son
share, the father (lines 114 ff.), like Socrates refuses to accept
the title of *sapiens* or professional philosopher, while Horace,
the son, even affects to designate his habit of making humorous
jottings for his satires as a *mediocre uitium* or petty fault. In
using this appellation Horace is doubtless influenced by the
tendency of Aristotelian and Hellenistic rhetorical criticism to
assign only a limited function to humor. We have already seen
traces of this point of view in the analysis of the laughable
reproduced by Cicero from the teachings of Panaetius in the
first book of the *de officiis*. In 108, for example, Panaetius has
without the slightest suggestion of reprobation characterized
Socrates as the typical εἴρων. In 109 also he classes irony with
those dissimulations of nature and character which are least
blameworthy. In Aristotle, however, irony belongs to the
extreme marked by deficiency, and is almost as far removed
from truthfulness as is the opposed extreme of boastfulness or
ἀλαζονεία—almost as far from truthfulness yet not quite as far—
for boastfulness is the more blameworthy extreme. Hence as
a corollary irony becomes comparatively speaking a peccadillo,
or petty fault (compare the *mediocre uitium* of Horace) or even
a relative virtue.[207]

Now in the first satire of book 29 of Lucilius we have a
similar exposition of the educational theories of the Greek
philosophers adapted to Roman needs. It is not clear from the
extant fragments, whether Lucilius speaks in his own person

or through a dramatic spokesman. Fragments 808, 806, 810, 811, 812, clearly bear evidence to the similarity of theme, and merit detailed comparison with Horace's lines 101–120.

In 808 Lucilius emphasizes the Socratic and Cynic commonplace that the source of sin is the heart of man; hence, the sinful desire changed, the sinful act will not be committed. In the case of lust, however, this is almost hopeless. Thus in line 808:

> .   non tollas prius
> quam sustuleris animum ex homine atque hominem ipsum interfeceris.

Horace in line 103 holds to the same psychology, when he promises to keep the vice (vitium) of censoriousness out of his writings, and before that out of his heart (animo):

> quod vitium procul afore chartis.
> atque animo prius, ut siquid promittere de me
> possum aliud vere, promitto.

In Lucilius 806 we read:

> cupiditas ex homine — ◡ — ◡ — ◡ — ◡ — ◡ — ◡ —³⁰⁸
> — ◡ — ◡ — cupido ex stulto numquam tollitur.

If Marx's plausible restoration of the context of these lines is accepted we seem to have a parallel to the Cynic method of Horace's father of teaching by precept. Thus Marx: cupiditas ex homine <tolli poteris bonis praeceptis, at quae innata est mala> cupido ex stulto nunquam tollitur. So Horace in line 105:

> insuevit pater optimus hoc me,
> ut fugerem exemplis vitiorum quaeque notando.

This conjecture to my mind finds further confirmation in the relation of the Horatian praecepta to the χρηστοί λόγοι of the Cynics.

The acceptance of this Cynic method of preaching by the disciple will bring relative contentment. This is the idea contained in the Anonymous against αἰσχροκέρδεια lines 90–91 of the Heidelberg Papyrus.²⁰⁹

> [ὅπως λ]όγοις χρηστοῖσι σωφρονισθεῖσα
> [καλῶς] τὰ χρηστὰ καὶ τὰ συμφέροντα εἴδη <ι>.

It is found in Lucilius 811:

> . . . cum cognoris, uitam sine cura exigas.

and is repeated by Horace 107–108:

> cum me hortaretur, parce frugaliter atque
> viverem uti contentus eo quod mi ipse parasset.

Lucilius 812 could, of course, be thought of in various other contexts, but in the sequence now partly established, this line seems to summarize a thought similar to that of Horace's father in lines 115–119. How close the two passages are, may be seen by the fact that Marx's commentary might without violence stand as a note on the Horatian passage: praeter virtutem et sapientiam omnia quae iactamus, ne multa dicam, inepta sunt flexa, fragilia. The Lucilian line is:

> omnia alia, in quibus ecferimur rebus, ne ego multis loquar.

Horace 115–119:

> 'sapiens, vitatu quidque petitu
> sit melius, causas reddet tibi. mi satis est si
> traditum ab antiquis morem servare tuamque,
> dum custodis eges vitam famamque tueri
> incolumem possum.'

Horace then proceeds to set forth (lines 129-end) the results of his father's teachings as seen in his own habits of life. First he asserts that he is free from the deadly sins, and that he can free himself from the *mediocria vitia* of Cynic theory by the advice of a frank (*i.e.*, a Cynic) friend or by the Cynic practice of self-examination.

> fortassis et istinc
> largitur abstulerit longa aetas, liber amicus,
> consilium proprium.

In two passages, 805 from this same satire in book 29, 1 and 1054 from book 30, Lucilius expounds a similar theory of life:

> aetatem istuc tibi laturam et bellum, si hoc bellum putas.

Horace in lines 136 ff., apparently uses the word *belle* in recollection of this Lucilian passage:

> Hoc quidam non belle: numquid ego illi
> imprudens olim faciam simile?

The second passage also emphasizes the disciplinary value of experience:

> non nunquam dabit ipse aetas quod possit habendo.

We may conjecture that the importance of the frank Cynic friend and of self-examination may have been found in other Lucilian passages no longer extant, but in the same context. Indeed, in line 1036, which must be assigned to Lucilius himself, the poet in addressing his *adversarius* says: If I may be permitted to adopt this procedure and cast into metrical form this which I now speak; (*do = dic* according to Nonius on this passage). That is, the poet Lucilius like Horace asks indulgence for his methods of composition. That these were even more improvisatory than those of Horace is not expressly stated, but requires no demonstration to any student of the two writers. So Horace in 137 ff.:

> haec ego mecum
> conpressis agito labris; ubi quid datur oti,
> inludo chartis. hoc est mediocribus illis
> ex vitiis unum: cui si concedere nolis.

And Lucilius 1036:

> si liceat facere et iam hoc versibus reddere quod do.

Compare the use of *liceat* in Lucilius with the *cui concedere nollis* of Horace.

Finally Marx is right in placing 1038 at the close of the Lucilian satire in book 30. Lucilius too with a sudden shift of mood ended his satire with a humorous allusion. The *adversarius* says:

> quin totum purges, devellas me atque deuras,
> exultes <et> sollicites.

That is: I can't say a word in criticism of you as a satirist without your striking me, plucking me like a fowl, singeing me like a pig, assaulting, and picking upon me. Horace, however, renders the central idea of this line, the satirist's assertion of his right to free criticism and to make his assaults in virtue's cause, by making a band of partisan poets, like a company of proselytizing Jews, force their common views upon the reluctant *adversarius*:

> multa poetarum veniet manus, auxilio quae
> sit mihi (nam multo plures sumus), ac veluti te
> Iudaei cogemus in hanc concedere turbam.

Both satirists, therefore, in closing their remarkable defences of the satiric art and the satiric humor, resume the tone of the γέλοιος or humorist.[210]

It is perhaps impossible to determine whether the material contained in Lucilius' aesthetic and ethical defence of satire was divided between two satires in book 30 or concentrated in a single satire. Nevertheless, I shall venture in the light of my detailed analysis to reconstruct briefly certain argumentative sequences, which Horace probably found in one or more Lucilian satires of book 30 and which in my opinion profoundly influenced the tone and content of his fourth satire.

The following lines of Lucilius apparently develop the same general theme contained in Horace's lines 21–38, an indirect defence of the humor of satire against the charge of indiscriminate, bitter, and malicious assaults on human weakness, such assaults as in traditional rhetorical theories, covering a long development from Plato and Aristotle to Panaetius, are associated with the illiberal jest. Most of these lines are apparently put into the mouth of an *adversarius*—possibly a comic poet, in the case of certain lines—who advances boldly to the attack. Lucilius, he says, is the author of a *"suspectum genus"* who, though he injures and blames, accomplishes nothing (1021). Why, says another victim of the satirist's lash, are you concerned as to whether I besmirch myself (with vice) and wallow in iniquity? (1019). Why do you narrowly observe whither I am going, what I am doing? What is that to you (1020)?

Such a man as the satirist is, as Aristotle would say, a βωμολόχος or scurrilous jester who sets no reasonable bounds to his bitter humor: he is like the mouse trap stretched to catch its victim or the scorpion with tail raised ready to sting (1022). This type of humor seeks to raise a laugh from the *populus* at all costs. Compare line 971, which may be attributed either to the poet himself or his *adversarius*. Lucilius, then, is charged by the *adversarius* with being a typical βωμολόχος whose aim is to raise a laugh at the expense of his victim by his cruel acts and bitter words (1014). You rejoice, says the *adversarius*, to record your caustic personal observations and me in your *sermones* and to circulate these lampoons widely (1015, 1016).

The true satirist, like the βωμολόχος, the *adversarius* continues, demands a popular audience (970).

In lines 1027, 1028, 1029, 1294, 1279, 1013, Lucilius in a series of lines, which seem to set forth a theme similar to that of Horace's lines 39–62, tries to establish the laws of the satiric genre and to define its relation to Comedy and Epic. In line 1027 the poet announces his intention to make a brief rejoinder to the assaults of the *adversarius*. He is not the mortal to whom the *Camenae* entrust their keys (1028), for he does not write true poetry (*i.e.*, epic). The function of satire is like that of the New Comedy, to hold the mirror up to life. Like you who give metrical form to what we regard as a cross section of life I should scarcely assume the title of *poeta*, (1029). Lucilius even translates into Latin the technical terms μέτρον and ῥυθμός (1294). Yet he prefers to give an improvisatory title to his poetry, a creation hastily knocked together by one who does not claim true poetic inspiration. Hence he speaks of his work properly as a *schedium* (1279). Yet for all that his poems alone—and he calls them *poemata*—of all that is produced by his contemporaries are widely current (1013).

Then turning to the function of his *sermones*, Lucilius in lines 1033, 1289, 1030, 1031, 1035, 1017, 1025, 1096, 1026, defends the ethos of his humor which he relates to the high purposes of moral reform in a sequence that shows certain affinities to Horace's exposition of the satiric vs. the scurrilous type of humor in lines 64–70, 78–100. Lucilius speaking of himself assumes the rôle of a *censor morum*, and replies to his *adversarius*. He is one whom you know, knows all your stains and blemishes (1033). Although he is an assailant of vice the poet will not emulate the methods of the long-winded L. Cassius Longinus surnamed Ravilla, hoarse from his much speaking (1289). Do not think he declares, that I employ my "*carmen maledicum*," merely to assail you (1030). I am not a βωμολόχος without any restraint. And yet the poet Lucilius, unlike Horace, is ready to assail the thieving hand of a Mutto, (1031), so declares the *adversarius*.

The *adversarius*, proceeding and now accusing Lucilius by name says (1035): "Now, Gaius since advancing to the attack, you assail us in your turn." To this the poet replies: "Do you bring this accusation against me, and have you not first revolved these things in your heart" (1017)? The back-biter of society is much more to be reprehended than the satirist, previously described, whose frankness is redeemed by the purpose of moral reform (1025), for the milder such a social back-biter is the more violent his invective (behind your back). Such a character is a mixture of gentleness, malignity, flattery, deceit (1096). Shall all men of this type be acquitted in your eyes, as fine and gallant fellows, while I the satirist am to pass as an impudent nuisance (*improbus*) (1026)?

The lines of Lucilius from book 29, 1 which correspond in a general way to Horace's lines 100–138 need no further treatment. In lines 1036 and 1038, however, which are both from book 30, Lucilius returns to his humorous defence of the satiric jest, just as Horace does in the concluding lines of the satire. In 1036, he says: "If I were permitted to adopt this procedure and put into metrical form my jottings." And finally the hard-pressed *adversarius* cries out (1038): "I can't say a word without your striking me, plucking me like a fowl, singeing me like a pig, assaulting and picking upon me."

SATIRE 5

The fifth satire of Horace is a ὁδοιπορικόν a direct contemporary paraphrase of Lucilius' book 3, which recounts a journey to the Sicilian straits.[211] We have the explicit testimony of Porphyrio to this effect in his commentary on line 1: Lucilio hac satyra aemulatur Horatius iter suum a Roma Brundisium usque describens, quod et ille in tertio libro fecit, primo a Roma Capuam usque, et inde fretum Siciliense. In this passage the word *aemulatur* gives explicit external evidence that Horace followed the principle of generous rivalry in his imitative relations to the great founder of the satiric genre. Evidently, then, Porphyrio is familiar with this aspect of the problem of rhetorical imitation, which I have analysed in my introduction. The nature of Horace's relation to Lucilius in this satire may, therefore, in a sense be regarded as a norm for the measurement of his attitude to Lucilius as revealed by the same methods of critical analysis of Horace's satires, and their comparison with their Lucilian prototypes. For, in view of the small part that verbal imitation plays in the "rivalry" of Horatian with Lucilian themes, one hesitates to use the word "model."

Other examples of this anecdotic genre are the *Propempticon* of Cinna for Pollio,[212] the *Iter* of Julius Caesar, and the ὁδοιπορ-ικόν, no longer extant of Persius. Let us now proceed to the examination of Horace's satire.

The first stage of Horace's journey was from Rome to Aricia, the second from Aricia to Forum Appi. In line 5, he then continues:

> hoc iter ignavi divisimus, altius ac nos
> praecinctis unum; minus est gravis Appia tardis.

In the *altius ac nos praecinctis unum* Horace's readers would see an allusion to the greater strenuousness of the earlier satirist on his first day's journey, for, as Marx has seen, it is a fair inference from Lucilius' lines 110 ff., that he made the whole journey not to *Forum Appi* alone, but to *Setia* on the hills above in a single day, and found all except the last steep stretch mere play:

> verum haec ludus ibi, susque omnia deque fuerunt,
> susque et deque fuere, inquam, omnia ludus iocusque:
> illud opus durum, ut Setinum accessimus finem,
> aigilipes montes, Aetnae omnes, asperi Athones.

Lucilius, however, did not stop at *Forum Appi*, but pushed up the mountain road three miles further to Setia. The reason is that given by Horace in line 7 and by Porphyrio's commentary on this passage, bad water:

> hic ego propter aquam, quod erat deterrima, ventri
> indico bellum,

On this Porphyrio, perhaps in allusion to Lucilius, says: hodieque Foro Appi viatores propter aquam, quae ibi deterrima est, manere vitant.

From Lucilius' book 15, line 514, Horace evidently got the word *cerebrosus* and possibly the hint for the incident of lines 20 and 21, in which a hot-headed passenger belabors with a willow cudgel the sleeping boatman and his mule. Perhaps in Lucilius[213] a horse was treated in the same fashion by one of the slaves, whom Lucilius then belabored and along with him the *bubulcus* and *mediastinus* in line 512 for his cruelty: 514 is as follows:

> te primum cum istis insanum hominem et cerebrosum.

Householders abutting on the great Roman roads were bound by law to furnish shelter, wood, and salt to those travelling on public missions. Lucilius refers to this in line 131:

> . . . . *si* dent hi ligna videte.

So Horace and his fellow-travellers put up for the night at a tiny farm house near the *pons Campanus* over the Savo: where the requirements of the law are complied with, lines 45–46:

> proxima Campano ponti quae villula, tectum
> praebuit parochi quae debent ligna salemque.

In both the Journies of Lucilius and of Horace there occurred a stop of some length. In that of Lucilius it was either at Capua or at the inn at the promontory of Palinurus.[214] During this pause both companies were entertained by a performance of *scurrae*. In Lucilius this determination to rest is announced in line 115:

> — ◡ ◡ et spatium curando corpori honestum
> sumemus.

We may notice that Horace's company rests at Capua. The mules drop their saddle bags there in good season: (47 *hinc muli Capuae clitellas tempore ponunt*). Maecenas recuperates by playing ball (48 *lusum it Maecenas*). Horace and Virgil enjoy a nap (*dormitum ego Vergiliusque*).[215]

Then follows in Horace, 51–70, the contest between the *scurra*, Sarmentus and the Oscan, Messius Cicirrus. To this passage we may relate the Lucilian lines 117–122. These lines may be interpreted either as referring to a gladiatorial conflict or to a contest between two clowns or *scurrae*, described in language parodying a gladiatorial conflict just as Horace parodies an epic combat.[216] In view of the apparent aversion of Lucilius to gladiatorial combats, this second interpretation seems preferable.[217] Indeed in Lucilius' line 117 we have a description of one of the combatants, who is evidently the Lucilian analogue to Messius:

> broccus Bovillanust:[218] 'dente adverso eminulo hic est
> rinoceros.'

This line of Lucilius is the prototype of Horace's line 56:

'equi te
esse feri similem dico.'

The allusion to the horn of the unicorn in Horace is parallel to the horn of the rhinoceros in Lucilius. The point in the use of *brocchus*, *i.e.*, with swollen upper lip, and prominent tooth (*dente adverso eminulo*) seems to be the aim to designate those physiognomies which resemble the donkey and the ape and are therefore regarded as idiotic.[219] Again in line 58 we read:

'O tua cornu
ni foret exsecto frons'

To the same context, although we may not assert that Horace used the lines in any direct imitation, belong lines 120, 119, 121. Line 120 was evidently a boast on the part of one of the Lucilian champions that he could "hit in the wind" *conturbare animam* whoever attacked him:

conturbare animam potis est quicumque adoritur.

In a similar vein the Horatian Messius asserts his prowess in lines 57 ff.:

ridemus et ipse
Messius 'accipio,' et caput et movet.

In line 119 of Lucilius I am inclined to believe that we have an extremely coarse allusion, a parody on the heroic pedigrees of epic poetry, to the birth of one of the champions. His mother did not give birth to him, but thrust him forth from the rear, a remark employed as a gibe against his opponent by one of the Lucilian *scurrae:*

non peperit, verum postica parte profudit.

It is possible to see in Horace's sardonic account of the pedigree of his two champions, Messius, of the former race of the Osci, perhaps with a side allusion to the scornful popular etymology of *obscaenus* from Obscus,[220] and Sarmentus, who as a *libertus* had no family at all, an Augustan mitigation of a similar, but much more Lucilian mock heroic pedigree.

The position of Lucilius' line 121 must have been somewhere at the close of the contest. It must refer to that combatant who corresponds to the victorius Messius, and whom Lucilius compares to the well known type of gladiator called the *pinnirapus* because he tried to tear the feathers from the helmet of his opponent:

> ille alter abundans
> cum septem incolumis pinnis redit ac recipit se.

The simile in line 1342 might of course be referred to various contexts. It is probable, however, that it refers to a one-eyed man who looks like a split pig with only one eye visible. Such a comparison might be carried further by asking the one-eyed man to impersonate the Cyclops, whose personal appearance he certainly resembled. If we assign these words to one of the rival *scurrae* in Lucilius, we would then have a bit of personal abuse parallel to Horace's lines 60–64. To me such a reference seems more plausible than to assign the fragment to the discussion on the Cyclops in book 15, lines 480 ff.[21] Messius, with a scar in the centre of his forehead is Horace's analogue for the one-eyed *scurra* of Lucilius. Lucilius' line reads:

> uno oculo, pedibusque duobus, dimidiatus
> ut porcus.

And the Horatian passage:

> Campanum in morbum, in faciem permulta iocatus.

We have no precise parallel to the bustling Syrian *caupona* of Lucilius' lines 128, 129, 130. We may compare, however, the bustling character of the *sedulus hospes* of Beneventum, who burns the skinny thrushes in lines 71 ff.:

> Tendemus hinc recta Beneventum, ubi sedulus hospes
> paene macros arsit dum turdos versat in igni.

These thrushes, however, may be a recollection of the *macrosque palumbes* in Lucilius 14, 453.

Whether the Syrian hostess played a part recalling that of the *sedulus hospes*—she at once puts on her shoes, line 129, and frisks around like a young colt 130, perhaps dances for her guests like the *copa* of Virgil—or whether she figures in an incident like that assigned by Horace to the *mendax puella* of Trivicum, lines 82–85, it seems evident that the latter incident occurred in Lucilius.[22] Thus in line 140:

> Tantalus, qui poenas ob facta nefantia, poenas
> pendit.

may be a comparison in the mock-heroic tone of the tortures
suffered by Lucilius while waiting in vain for the appearance of
the girl.[223]   With this line, we may closely connect line 1248,
in which *permixi* is not used of urination, but probably of the
result of a sexually exciting dream:[224]

> permixi lectum, inposui pede pellibus labes.

The Horatian scene in which *pellibus labes imponere* is freely
rendered by line 85 (*maculant etc.*) is as follows:

> hic ego mendacem stultissimus usque puellam
> ad mediam noctem exspecto: somnus tamen aufert
> intentum Veneri: tum immundo somnia visu
> nocturnam vestem maculant ventremque supinum.

In another satire Lucilius alludes to a word which is metri-
cally impossible in the hexameter.   Although this passage,
fragment 228 from book 6[225], finds its immediate context in
that book, Horace may well have been partly influenced to
adopt this typical bit of Hellenistic pedantry in line 87 from
consciousness of such a Lucilian precedent.   The Lucilian line
follows:

> servorum est festus dies hic,
> quem plane hexametro versu non dicere possis.

In Horace, according to Porphyrio in allusion to a town called
Equus Tuticus, we have a similar statement in line 87:

> mansuri oppidulo.   quod versu dicere non est.

On the whole, it was the effort of Horace by dexterity of
phrase to avoid the prosaic turns given to the Lucilian narrative
by the repetition of the figures of the miles covered.[226]   Such
indications are found in Lucilius in lines 107, 114, 124, 126.
In only two passages in Horace do we have such definite allu-
sions, in lines 25 and 86.   In each case there is an explicit
reason for giving the exact number of miles; in the former lines
because Horace's company only made three miles in a whole
day; in the latter lines because of the speed of the day's journey,
24 miles, and to indicate the name of the town at which a stop
was made.   It is not clear whether Lucilius gave a more detailed
enumeration of the number of miles covered.   The three cita-
tions mentioned above offered no sufficient basis for a conclusion

on this point. Consequently, Horace's practice may represent a deviation from Lucilius' method, or may be in essential harmony with it. In one place, however, Horace paraphrases a Lucilian allusion to the wretched condition of a certain stretch of road. The Lucilian line is 109, the Horatian paraphrase is 94 ff. Lucilius says:

> praeterea omne iter est hoc labosum atque lutosum.

Horace 94 f.:

> Inde fessi pervenimus, utpote longum
> carpentes iter et factum corruptius imbri.

Here the last part of the second line is clearly a more concrete paraphrase of *labosum et lutosum.*

Although I am unable to accept Cichorius' view that the fragments of Lucilius in which the future tense occurs, 102–104, 107–108, belong rather to a *propempticon* than to the description of a journey, the generic outlines of the *propempticon*, the farewell to the departing traveller, are so close to those of the ὁδοιπορικόν, that we may assume that they have certain common rhetorical features. Such a common feature is the inevitable enumeration of the different stations on the journey. Thus the Greek rhetorician Menander (Spengel, *Rhet. Gr.* 3, p. 398, 29) in his directions for the composition of λόγοι προπεμπτικοί says: κἂν μὲν πεζεύειν μέλλῃ, διάγραφε τὴν ὁδὸν καὶ τὴν γῆν δι' ἧς πορεύται.

Now this is precisely what Lucilius does in lines 99 and 100, which Cichorius restores to read as follows:

> locosque uiamque
> degrumabis, uti castris mensor facit olim.

The words of the rhetorician, ὁδός and γῆ offer at least a starting point for the emendation *locosque.* The line would then refer to laying out the itinerary on the map with careful indications of the main stations, just as the surveyor lays out the camp and indicates by flags the position of the main streets, corners, tents, etc. (see Polybius 6, 41, a contemporary of Lucilius). Perhaps the actual stations for the proposed journey were even marked on the map by little flags, just as we did with our maps of the war. The meaning of the lines will then be: if you, exactly as the surveyor for the camp, have determined the points at which you plan to rest—then it will be possible to decide on the details of the journey *e.g.*, whether you will accomplish any given stage by sea or by land. Everything from the dash on is, of course, a purely conjectural context now lost. It is quite true that in these two lines, as in 102–104 and 107–108, the future tenses refer to a journey in prospect, but this does not force us to imagine a separate poem, a *propempticon*, included in this same book on account of similarity to the description of an accomplished journey. On the contrary it is quite possible to assume that Lucilius in retrospect first gives his *proemium* a dedication to a friend, who for some reason has not been able to make the journey with him as he intended. The point of view in this fragment 99–100 is naturally that of the time when the completed satire was sent as a compliment and a sort of consolation to the friend who was unable to take the journey which he and Lucilius had planned together. Lucilius then naturally goes on to tell how they mapped out the proposed trip together (100–101), and how he told his friend what he would see on the trip to the Sicilian straits (102–104), (107–108), a trip which of course Lucilius must have made many times. Naturally, the future tense would be dramatically used in this part of the narrative even though the journey is seen and told in retrospect. Horace does not follow this part of the Lucilian narrative, first because it perhaps involved a certain amount of repetition to give the proposed itinerary, and then recount the actual incidents of the real journey; and second, because he actually made his journey in the company of Maecenas to whom the satire is implicitly dedicated. Nevertheless, he is careful to give most of the stations on the road, as anyone may see who examines the itinerary which is prefixed to this satire in Heinze-Kiessling's fourth edition.

Certain other incidents occur in both the satire of Lucilius and that of Horace. In lines 6 and 7 Horace complains of the poor quality of the water at Forum Appi, which brought on an attack of indigestion:

> hic ego propter aquam, quod erat deterrima, ventri
> indico bellum, cenantis haud animo aequo
> exspectans comites.

A similar incident occurs in the third book of Lucilius, but apparently at the inn on the promontory of Palinurus, where a dirty dish of rue is considered as great a delicacy as honey, and the simplest ingredients of a meal are lacking (132, 133).

> nam mel regionibus illis
> incrustatus calix rutai caulis habetur.

The result is an acute attack of indigestion on the part of some member of the company, described by Lucilius with coarse frankness:

> ——⌣⌣—— exhalas tum acidos ex pectore ructus.

Both poets take a line or two to describe the circumstances of their getting up in the morning. Thus Lucilius in line 143 speaks of waking up and calling his slaves:

> ergo
> e somno pueros cum mane expergitus clamo.

Horace describes how after the night on the canal boat the company suddenly became aware that they have not stirred all night long, line 19:

> iamque dies aderat, nil cum procedere lintrem
> sentimus.

Doubtless to Horace's readers the journey on the canal boat, lines 9–23, would seem like a contemporary paraphrase of the trip made by Lucilius along the coast from Puteoli to some point which afforded a view of the Liparai Islands (fragment 124–147). Similarly English readers of Dr. Johnson's *London* are reminded, by the voyage on the Thames, as the author intended, of the trip of Umbricius, who leaves Rome by the *Porta Capena* in Juvenal's third satire.

It will perhaps be appropriate to reconstruct the journey of Lucilius as well as we can on the basis of the surviving fragments, that these details of my analysis may fall into their proper perspective.

The satire begins with a proem, which is not imitated by Horace, possibly because it involved needless repetition of the details of the journey. To this belong lines 97 and 98, 99, 102, 105, and 107. The satirist begins by telling his friend, who for some reason was prevented from making the journey with him as they originally planned, that if he had taken part in the journey he would have his share in the fame and pleasure attendant upon it (97). He then narrates one of the immediate causes for the journey (*praeterea*), the illness of his cowherd Symmachus on his Sicilian estate (105). He then proceeds to recall to the mind of his friend, how they mapped out the itinerary together, exactly as a surveyor lays out his camp (99), and how he told his friend of the sights he would enjoy as he approached the Sicilian Straits (102). He figures up some of the stages of the journey as they planned it (107).

We now pass to the account of the actual journey. The first day's journey is a long one, but an easy one save for the last stiff stretch of three miles from *Forum Appi* to *Setia* (110–114). At some town or inn on the road perhaps, either at Capua or at the inn kept by the Syrian woman, at the promontory of Palinurus, the company stopped for a considerable rest (115). Here took place a conflict between two *scurrae* of which we have a free paraphrase in the episode of Messius and Sarmentus in Horace's satire (46–70). The occasion was probably a banquet. One of the contestants was a man from Bovillae with a protruding tooth like the horn of a rhinoceros (117). One of the two *scurrae* reproaches his rival with an obscene account of the manner of his birth (119). One of them asserts that he can "knock out" anyone who attacks him (120). The other imitates the gladiatorial *pinnirapus* by tearing seven feathers from the crest of his adversary.

The stages of the journey are then narrated; first to Puteoli where they take ship (123), pass the bay of Naples and the promontory of Minerva (125), and so on to Salerno (124), and then to the Portus Alburnus (126), and to the promontory of Palinurus, which they reach at night (128).

Here a Syrian woman who keeps the inn is waked up, puts on her shoes (129), bustles about (130), and furnishes the company a meal which is not above criticism, though the wine is good enough to lead them to change their plans and stay over night (131–139).

This water trip of Lucilius suggests the briefer trip of Horace on the canal through the Pomptine marshes (9–23).

Perhaps Lucilius, like Horace, was disappointed in an amorous adventure involving the hostess or one of the maids.

In spite of his torment (140), the result is the same as in the case
of Horace (1248). Finally the travellers see the Lipari Islands
with sparks flying from Stromboli as from a glowing forge (144).

It is needless to repeat in this summary those scattering
passages in which Lucilian words or methods of exposition were
followed or readapted by Horace. As thus outlined the satire, I
venture to say, affords strong corroboration for the thesis that
Horace drew his theme in large measure from Lucilius. This
satire also affords us the opportunity to study the free and
thoroughly artistic nature of Horace's imitations of his great
predecessor.[27]

SATIRE 6

While the fourth satire was an aesthetic defence of the form,
tone, and style of satire as conceived by Horace, the sixth is a
defence of the poet's position within the aristocratic circle of
Maecenas, for which he writes. The poet's position in that
circle is justified because membership in the circle is based not
upon birth, but upon character, and because the circle is united
by its community of literary and philosophical convictions.
In the circle of Maecenas, therefore, the vice of *ambitio* or social
self-assertion, which was so widely spread in the great capital,
was unknown. As proof of this the poet is naturally led to set
forth the origin of his friendship with Maecenas. The con-
tinuance of this relation is assured because Horace, Maecenas,
and all the members of the circle have the same unostentatious
social philosophy, which like that of Epicurus finds happiness in
the midst of a congenial company of friends, rather than in
the vulgar rivalry for social or political advancement (*ambitio*).

In short, the relation of Horace to Maecenas has certain
analogies to that of Bion of Borysthenes to Antigonus Gonatas,
as we have already seen. Bion too sought to disarm attacks
upon his humble origin by proudly and frankly acknowledging
it and laying stress upon his worth as a man. Hence the text
of this satire is essentially that of Bion's famous letter to
Antigonus Gonatas: οὕτως οὖν καὶ ἐπὶ τῶν φίλων ἐξέταζε οὐ πόθεν
εἰσὶν ἀλλὰ τίνες.

Bion's attitude towards δόξα or reputation, the Greek pro-
totype of Horace's *ambitio*, is essentially similar to that of

Horace. In the first place we have a series of passages in the praise of fame which are apparently put into the mouth of an interlocutor in order that they may be refuted. Such a passage is that in Diogenes Laertius 4, 51, in which ignoble birth is said to be a poor companion for freedom of speech: τὴν δυσγένειαν πονηρὸν ἔλεγεν εἶναι σύνοικον τῇ παρρησίᾳ. δολοῖ γὰρ ἄνδρα, κἂν θρασύσπλαγχνος τις ᾖ. Bion's own feelings, however, are those of the typical Cynic. He is equally indifferent to fame or its absence: πρὸς δόξαν καὶ ἀδοξίαν ἴσως ἔχοντα. (Tel. p. 8, 1; cf. Diog. Laert. 7, 117). We may further-more infer that Bionean material is latent in a passage of Plutarch's de aud. poet. p. 28 d, where the same passage of Euripides is refuted. A man's reputation depends on his own wisdom and not on the ignorance or ignobility of his father: διὰ τί δέ, ἂν ἐκ πατρὸς φαύλου καὶ ἀνοήτου γεγονώς, αὐτὸς ὦ χρηστὸς καὶ φρόνιμος, οὐ προσήκει μοι διὰ τὴν ἐμὴν ἀρετὴν μέγα φρονεῖν, ἀλλὰ καταπεπλῆχθαι καὶ ταπεινὸν εἶναι διὰ τὴν τοῦ πατρὸς ἀμαθίαν; So also Plutarch in the same dialogue, p. 22A, opposes Bion to the aristocratic counsels of Theognis, who had declared that poverty inhibits action and speech: χαρίεν δὲ καὶ το τοῦ βίωνος πρὸς τὸν Θέογνιν λέγοντα

'πᾶς γὰρ ἀνὴρ πενίῃ δεδμημένος οὔτε τι εἰπεῖν
οὔθ' ἔρξαι δύναται, γλῶσσα δὲ οἱ δέδεται.

πῶς οὖν σὺ πένης ὢν φλυαρεῖς τοσαῦτα καὶ καταδολεσχεῖς ἡμῶν'; In a sense, therefore, the present satire of Horace may be said to combine two traditions widely represented in Hellenistic philosophy. The first is the assault on fame or social striving (ambitio, δόξα). The second is the assertion of human worth on the part of the man, who has risen to eminence from humble position by virtue of his genius. Juvenal's eighth satire has certain affinities to these two themes.

The form of this discourse of Horace, the justification of the poet, just as 1, 4 was the justification of the genre, is at once an apology for his relations with Maecenas, and a eulogy of his patron and his own sincerity. This theme is developed in accordance with the strict rhetorical sequence of the schools under the headings of γένος, τροφή, ἀγωγή, φύσις ψυχῆς καὶ σώματος, ἐπιτηδεύματα, πράξεις.[228] Under nearly every one of these headings the material is presented in the form of a σύγκρισις or comparison, in which the negatived or deprecated practice is put first, followed by a statement of the positive and commendable practice. This is the figure of ἀναίρεσις. This sixth satire standing midway in the first book is like a second dedication to Maecenas at the beginning of the second quintad of satires.

Now in the dedicatory verses of a satire in book 30, as Cichorius[229] has shown, we have several fragments which set forth in similar tone the relations of Lucilius to some patron. These are the three fragments 1009, 1010, 1011. First, however, I must discuss fragments 669, from book 26; and 1227, probably from book 30, which seem to have influenced earlier lines in the sixth satire.

In lines 18–22 Horace asserts proudly his purpose to preserve his own identity as a poet, and to avoid any criticism which would be sure to fall upon the freedman's son who ventured into public life:

> namque, esto, populus Laevino mallet honorem
> quam Decio mandare novo, censorque moveret
> Appius ingenuo si non essem patre natus:
> vel merito, quoniam in propria non pelle quiessem.

So Lucilius will preserve his poetic independence. He will not enter into the commercial operations, nor change his skin. These commercial operations are perhaps those of the usurer whose reputation was a bad one. Hence Lucilius says: But a freedman, a fellow with triple hide, a Syrian himself, a whipping post, with whom I am to change my skin and with whom I change all things:

> at libertinus, tricorius, Syrus ipse, at mastigias
> quicum versipellis fio et quicum commuto omnia.

In this passage in particular *versipellis* apparently is the original of Horace's paraphrase *in propria non pelle quiessem*. The Lucilian passage places the integrity of the poet's calling above the lure of wealth, the Horatian above political ambition.[229a]

In the same satire of book 30 probably belongs line 1227 for Horace imitates its verse movement and transitional formula in line 45:

> nunc ad te redeo, ut quae res me impendet, agatur.

Possibly the danger threatening Lucilius was an assault upon the nature of his relations with his patron. Lucilius was of good birth and it would seem of assured social position, but perhaps after the death of his patron Scipio he was assailed, as Horace was, for this friendship granted to a provincial, and was thought to be socially ambitious. Hence he sets forth his need for a new patron and proceeds to describe how the new relationship grew up. If we refer *te* to the new patron, this fragment may have preceded the account of his introduction to this new patron contained in lines 1009, 1010, 1011 from book 30:

> producunt me ad te, tibi me haec ostendere cogunt.
> neminis ingenio tantum confidere oportet
> gratia habetur utrisque illisque fibique simitu.

That is, the poet, constrained by his friends, draws near his patron and presents him with these verses (1009); for no one has so fine an understanding [of poetry] *ingenium* as the patron (1010). Finally (1011), the poet expresses his gratitude for the closeness of the relationship thus established to his new patron and to the friends who introduced him. These lines are carefully wrought and marked by a tone of respectful courtesy, uncommon in Lucilius. The whole situation is essentially identical with that in Horace's satire 1, 6. Thus with the first half of 1009 we may compare Horace 54 and 55:

> nulla etenim mihi te fors obtulit; optimus olim
> Vergilius post hunc Varius dixere, quid essem.

With Lucilius' disinclination to recite his poems, set forth in the last half of line 1009, we may compare Horace's stammering embarrassment on the occasion of his introduction to Maecenas, 56–60:

> ut veni coram, singultim pauca locutus
> (infans namque pudor prohibebat plura profari)
> non ego me claro natum patre, non ego circum
> me Satureiano vectari rura caballo,
> sed quod eram narro.

With the praise of the good taste of the patron of Lucilius, we may compare Horace 62-64, a sort of amplification of Lucilius' tribute to the natural qualities of his new patron:

> magnum hoc ego duco
> quod placui tibi, qui turpi secernis honestum,
> non patre praeclaro, sed vita et pectore puro.

These lines also express Horace's gratitude to Maecenas, corresponding to the *gratia tibi habetur* of Lucilius line 1011. The *gratia illis habetur*, on the other hand, is implied in the affectionate allusion to Virgil and Varius in lines 52–55.

If this whole Horatian passage is painted in Lucilian colors, the note of Heinze-Kiessling on line 59 immediately preceding gains added effect. In brief the adjective *Satureianus* is a bold and incorrect transliteration for the more correct *Saturinus*. Of himself Horace, unless influenced by the appearance of this form of the adjectives in the pages of his predecessor, would hardly have employed this archaic transliteration of the Greek Σατύριον, a name applied to the district watered by the river Taras in which Tarentum was founded. Lucilius, it would seem, therefore, must have said something about riding round his country estates on a Tarentine nag. Horace, whose descent resembled that of the ignoble Bion rather than that of the well-to-do Lucilius, must here take on a tone quite different from that of his predecessor, because he was, as he tells us in satires 2, 1, 75, *infra Lucili censum*. He therefore makes a virtue of complete frankness, and tells the exact facts:

> non ego me claro natum patre non ego circum
> me Satureiano vectari rura caballo
> sed quod eram narro.

This interpretation, although the exact Lucilian parallel has been lost, seems to have some support in Lucilius line 1109:

> Apulidae pe<dibus stlembi>.

Here the adjective *stlembus* seems to mean an *equus piger et tardus*. Lucilius avoids by the use of this patronymic in the genitive case the use of the unmetrical cretic *Apuli* — ◡ —. Horace avoided the adjective by substituting *Satureianus*, which he may have found in Lucilius, perhaps in this very same satire. Horace's *caballus*, a plebeianism used by Lucilius in line 163, would reproduce the idea of *Stlembus = gravis, tardus*. In this latter passage from book 4 we read:

> succusatoris taetri tardique caballi.

Moreover, if the *Satureianus caballus* relates to Lucilius, the words *claro natum patre* must also refer to him. Horace, then, says in effect that he is neither so rich as his great predecessor, nor of such distinguished ancestry. This interpretation possibly finds further support in the scholion on Horace's satire 2, 1, 29; *fuit enim valde nobilis* Lucilius. Moreover, it seems a fair inference to hold with Cichorius that Lucilius had estates near Tarentum,[221] a view which is supported by some internal evidence.

Horace owes to his father, not a lofty social position, but a pure life and a pure heart (64). Accordingly in lines 65 ff., he describes the education ἀγωγή and the training, τροφή, which he owed to his father. Have we any similar biographical material in Lucilius? So far as I can discover, we have nothing in this satire of book 30, but in the 12th book of Lucilius we have at least eight lines which may be compared with the biographical element in the present satire so far as general tone and content are concerned, though there is no exact verbal imitation. These lines are 427, 428 and 429, 430, 431, 432, 433. At least three of these lines look as if they were uttered by the father of Lucilius 427, 428, and 429; while 431 is susceptible of that interpretation, though it might also be conceived in the mouth of any counsellor to the young. In 427, Lucilius' father seems to recommend a man who would be faithful whatever might happen to Lucilius or his brother:

> hunc, siquid pueris nobis, me et fratre fuisset.

The passage is rightly referred to a guardian of some sort to be placed over the young men. Marx thinks of a tutor. Evidently, then, the father of Lucilius did, unlike the father of Horace, furnish him with a *paedagogus*, whereas Horace's father undertook that duty himself, as we see in line 81 ff.:

> ipse mihi custos incorruptissimus omnis
> cirum doctores aderat.

Moreover, Horace's father thought no expense too great to give his son, thus dispatched to the great city, the assured social essentials required of those who possessed an ancestral estate; clothing and slaves were not stinted, lines 78–80.

> vestem servosque sequentis,
> in magno ut populo, siqui vidisset, avita
> ex re praeberi sumptus mihi crederet illos.

He had in fact to the full all the traditional indifference to expense which the self-made man always shows in the case of his children. On the other hand, the father of Lucilius was much more canny about money matters and reproved the prodigality of his son by saying that he would need a "state treasurer," (*quaestor*) and a *choragus*, the ancient equivalent for a millionaire friend, to keep him in funds from the public chest:

> huic homini quaestore aliquo esse opus atque corago
> publicitus qui mi atque e fisco praebeat aurum.

Apparently Horace contrasts the liberality of his father with the greater shrewdness of the father of Lucilius. Undoubtedly the contrast was in keeping with the facts of the case, yet we must remember that the rhetorical principle of ζῆλος or generous rivalry with the master is also at work in such passages.[22]

Fragment 430 may be taken as the description of the teacher, who belonged to what we might call the emaciated professorial type. The description well suits the ascetic appearance of the philosopher, whose plain diet is described in lines 501 and 502:

> rugosum atque fami plenum ‿‿ — ‿‿ — ‿

This figure, therefore, may be taken as corresponding to the *doctores* of Horace's line 82.

Line 431 is distinctly didactic in tone. It might be put into the mouth either of Lucilius' father or one of his teachers. It fits exactly the tone of a commonplace on ἀγωγή or τροφή:

> firmiter hoc pariterque tuo sit pectore fixum.

Line 432 represents the pupil's assent to the teaching of his father or master. It has no exact parallel in Horace except the glad acknowledgment that Horace gives in this satire and in lines 105–139 of the 4th satire of the merits of his father's pedagogy and the lasting effects wrought on his own character.

If we take the verb *decolavi* in a transitive sense in the difficult and perhaps mutilated fragment 434 we might regard these lines as a tribute to the influence of popular philosophical teaching, whether imparted by his father or his teacher, upon the life of Lucilius who says "upon which fruits of life I have fertilized myself":

> quibus fructibus me de
> colavi victus.

So Horace in lines 82–84 tells how he owed his inner purity of character and unstained reputation to his father's loving care and expresses his deep gratitude in line 88:

> quid multa: pudicum,
> qui primus virtutis honos, servarit ab omni
> non solum facto, verum opprobrio quoque turpi:
> . . . . at hoc nunc.
> laus illi debetur et a me gratia maior.[228]

Porphyrio on line 106 rightly noticed the direct imitation of a Lucilian line 1207. This line from the time of Dousa has been assigned to book 3, and is so assigned by Marx. I am inclined to relate it rather to this particular satire in book 30, in which Lucilius may have set forth to his new patron the simplicity of his life on one of his country estates,[224] possibly that at Tarentum. Horace's passage substitutes *lumbos* for *costas, ulceret* for *premeret, onere* for *gravitate*. Lucilius 1207:

> mantica cantheri costas gravitate premebat.

Horace 106:

> mantica cui lumbos onere ulceret atque eques armos.

In line 1034 Lucilius, as Cichorius has shown,[225] assailed the comic poet Afranius (?) for his immoral life. The line contains a word play on *lustra* in the sense of "dives," and the verb *lustro* to survey, a punning antithesis which Horace avoids in his adaptation of the fragment in line 111. The Lucilian line, as Marx has seen, contained a reference to the archways of the circus, the lurking places of the prostitutes of the city.[226] *Oppida* in this Lucilian line is used of the *carceres*, a meaning which is supported by a Varronian definition.[227] We may then refer *lustrans* to the poet Lucilius himself, who strolling about, as Horace does, detects the extravagant expenditure of his rival upon the women of the *lupanar*.[228] The Lucilian line:

> quem sumptum facis in lustris, circum oppida
> lustrans.

So Horace, paraphrasing *lustrans* by *pererro* says:

> quacumque libidost
> incedo solus, percontor quanti olus ac far
> fallacem circum vespertinumque pererro
> saepe forum, adsisto divinis.

In one earlier passage in Horace's satire also we have traces of
the influence of this passage of Lucilius at least in the use of the
word *lustra*, and possibly in the denial on the part of the satirist
that he pursued immoral courses in their lowest forms, line 68 f.:

> si neque avaritiam neque sordis nec mala lustra
> obiciet vere quisquam mihi.

Finally the sixth satire of Horace shows traces of Lucilian
coloring in the use of certain Lucilian words. The *oenophorus*,
or wine basket, found in Lucilius line 139 is used in line 109, in
both cases as a part of the necessary equipment of a journey.

In line 117 ff. Horace describes the common furnishings of
his table which was marked by Epicurean simplicity:

> cena ministratur pueris tribus et lapis albus
> pocula cum cyatho duo sustinet, adstat echinus
> vilis, cum patera guttus, Campana supellex.

In commenting on this line Porphyrio quotes the Lucilian
line 1158:

> echinus
> †chinnabam infectas.

The line is hopelessly corrupt, but it proves that Horace found
the word *echinus*, which is extremely rare, in the sense of a vessel
for the table of uncertain material and purpose in the pages of
Lucilius.

Finally in lines 125 f. Horace tells us that when the hotter
rays of the sun have warmed him to go to the bath he avoids the
Campus Martius and the three-cornered game of ball. Lucilius
in fragment 1134 likewise alluded to this same game, though in
a satire which apparently had relation to the second satire of
Horace's second book rather than to the present satire:

> Coelius, conlusor Galloni, scurra, trigonum
> cum ludet, solus•••
> ludet et eludet.

SATIRE 7

The seventh satire of Horace's first book is a χρεία, for, as
Lejay has seen,[239] this *memoratio dicti vel praecipui* is in substan-
tial harmony with the outlines and tone of this favorite Hellen-
istic form.[240]   As Horace recounts an anecdote of his campaign

under Brutus, our satire belongs to that particular genus of
χρεία which is technically known as an ἀπομνημόνευμα,[241] a type
of composition which has exercised an even more considerable
influence upon the second book of Horace's satires.

But this χρεία or reminiscent anecdote might also from the
point of view of subject matter be called an ἀγών. Here we have
a trial scene, in which Horace introduces to us in mock heroic
lines the two litigious heroes, Publius Rupilius Rex of Praeneste
and the Greek Persius. In bitterness and directness of invec-
tive the tone of their argument before the court of Brutus is
reminiscent of the confrontations or ἀγῶνες of the Old Comedy,[242]
though its direct antecedents belong rather to the Hellenistic
period.

But the closest structural parallel to the Horatian χρεία is a
satire of Lucilius in book 2. In that book also we have a trial
scene, that of Quintus Mucius Scaevola, who is charged with
peculation in the province of Asia by Titus Albucius.[243]

In this charge,[244] certain of the members of the suite of
Scaevola were also involved. In considering the relations
between the Lucilian and the Horatian satire, we are to expect
rather that similarity of language and thought, which springs
from the observance of the simple expository forms conven-
tional in the χρεία of the law suit. No explicit verbal imitation
is to be anticipated. Horace's satire, moreover, is a mere
incident, a *dictum* towards which the whole exposition moves.
On the other hand, Lucilius' satire, which also contained a
similar *dictum*, or humorously turned retort, evidently depicted
with much greater detail the trial of Q. Mucius Scaevola. It is
then only in the most general way that the second satire of
Lucilius is to be regarded even as a structural model for this
seventh satire of Lucilius.[245] To me it seems probable in view
of the general principles of rhetorical imitation, which so
profoundly influenced the continuation of any literary tradition,
that the existence of the Lucilian satire acted as a direct chal-
lenge to the inventive powers of Horace. Structurally also
both satires have the following points in common:

(1) Both satires are introduced as anecdotes and told by
the poets;

(2) Both satires deal with court scenes;

(3) And with incidents of provincial administration.

(4) The combatants in both seek to outdo each other in invective.

(5) Both satires seem to be built up with direct reference to the rhetorical climax, which consists in the *dictum*, by which the opponent is given his *coup de grâce*.

(1) The setting of the Horatian trial is given in lines 1–2:

> proscripti Regis Rupili pus atque venenum
> ibrida quo facto sit Persius ultus, opinor
> omnibus et lippis notum et tonsoribus esse.

More matter of fact is Lucilius' introduction to the court scene in line 55:[346]

> ———————— fandam atque auditam iterabimus <*famam.*>

Horace seems to have adopted a tone much closer to that of Lucilian invective than is usual with him. The description of the venomous character of Rupilius Rex, while not directly reminiscent of such Lucilian passages as line 44 from book 1, or 493 f. from book 15, retain the general flavor of Lucilian vituperations. The earlier fragment describes the loathsomeness of the appearance of Lupus, a new arrival at the council of the gods:

> vultus item ut facies mors cetera,[347] morbus, venenum.

In 493, a very corrupt fragment, perhaps referring to Trebellius, Lucilius overwhelms the man with abuse (*obruit hominem conviciis*), as Marx who cites the first line of Horace's satire remarks:

> in numero quorum nunc primus Trebellius multost
> Lucius, narce, saeva i febris, senium, vomitum, pus.

The *vomitum* and *pus* of Lucilius are surely not far removed from the *pus atque venenum* of Horace.

(2) Both satires deal with court scenes, as is at once apparent. In this connection certain details deserve fuller treatment. On line 23 of Horace's satire Porphyrio cites line 348:

> ut praetoris cohors et Nostius dixit aruspex.

This line is by Baehrens assigned to book 11 and placed immediately after line 308, as line 309(8). Marx, on the other hand, prefers to refer the line to book 14 where it may stand in close connection with line 473. The argument in favor of either of these assignments rests on the fact that both in book 11, line 398 (M) and in book 14, line 469, the *cohors* of the *praetor* is mentioned. In both of these passages the commander (*praetor*), Scipio himself, seems to be engaged in purifying his camp of loose characters, and therefore is represented in opposition to the lax organization and immorality of the *cohors*. On the other hand, line 1348 shows no traces of such opposition.

As, then, the line is quoted by Porphyrio in connection with the 7th satire of Horace's first book, it seems more reasonable to assign this line to book 2 of Lucilius, which on general grounds stands in somewhat definite relations to this satire of Horace. The words of the fragment might be interpreted as implying that some act or saying of the *cohors* and *haruspex* of Scaevola was introduced as evidence by Albucius. Thus further support would be afforded for the conjectural exposition of Cichorius (*op. cit.*, p. 237 ff.) that a lawsuit brought against Scaevola in Asia and involving members of his *cohors* was rehearsed in the indictment brought by Albucius. In fact, it seems probable that more than one member of the *cohors* of Scaevola was involved in this famous trial. In line 56, the argument of Cichorius (p. 244 ff.) in favor of Scaliger's reading *Nomentane* in place of *Montane* seems to me convincing. Again in lines 69–70, if we read *Nomentane*, in place of the conjecture of Marx, *nunc <in> nomen iam*, we have a relatively simple context. The plaintiff who utters the lines says that by examination of the witnesses he will bring out (*exculpo*) the guilt of Nomentanus, possibly to break down his credibility as a witness in behalf of Scaevola, and involve him in the same guilt as the principal defendant.

If now, we associate line 1348 with these two lines, Nostius the *haruspex* may be a witness cited by Albucius from the *cohors* of Scaevola against Scaevola and Nomentanus.

In Horace's satire on the other hand, the *cohors* of Brutus is not directly involved in the trial, but is present as a *consilium* to the provincial governor, who holds court. So in line 23:

> laudat Brutum laudatque cohortem,
> solem Asiae Brutum adpellat stellasque salubris
> adpellat comites, excepto Rege.

(3) As has already been made abundantly clear, both satires deal with incidents of provincial administration. Cichorius[344] analyses the charge of *iniuria* made against Scaevola in lines 57 to 59, and of *repetundae* in lines 64, 68, and 71.

(4) Each contestant seeks to outdo the other in invective.[349] Yet we notice a difference; Lucilius seems to prefer the direct Latin style of Scaevola rather than the highly elaborated style of Albucius. This contrast between the two styles of invective is one of the outstanding methods of characterizing the combatants both in Lucilius and in Horace.

Thus the highly elaborated style of Albucius, of which the oriental gorgeousness of Persius is in a sense an analogue, is compared in lines 84–85 to a mosaic pavement of tortuous pattern. This comparison is probably put in the mouth of Lucilius himself, though it is not entirely impossible to assign it to Scaevola:[350]

> [*]'quam lepide lexis *composlae* ut tesserulae omnes
> arte pavimento atque emblemate vermiculato'.

In this passage evidently the nicely adjusted and balanced clauses of Albucius are the subject of the satirical comparison.

Horace, on the other hand, describes the swollen style of Persius by comparing it to the rush of a torrent swollen by the winter's rains, lines 26 f.

> ruebat
> flumen ut hibernum, fertur quo rara securis.

In contrast to this copiousness we have the concentrated style of Italian abuse employed by Rupilius. Thus Horace in line 27 ff.:

> tum Praenestinus salso multoque fluenti
> expressa arbusto regerit convicia, durus
> vindemiator et invictus, cui saepe viator
> cessisset magna conpellans voce cuculum.

The only clear example of Scaevola's invective is equally direct and personal in line 86:

> 'Crassum habeo generum, ne rhetoricoterus tu seis.'

The use of the Greek comparative here is in part a parody of the fondness of Albucius for Greek terms, but it also suggests, as uttered by the blunt and precise lawyer the indifference to

rhetorical embellishments natural to a convinced adherent of
the unadorned grammatical rhetoric of the Stoics.

(5) The vituperative battle in both satires must have been
fought out to a decision. It is clear that this is the case in
Horace where the pun on Rupilius Rex with which the satire
closes forms the humorous incident toward which the whole
narrative moves. The issue is thus the complete discomfiture
of Rupilius Rex. It is not possible to assert this absolutely of
the satire in Lucilius, which seems to have been much longer,
and may have had a much more serious purpose. Nevertheless,
it seems probable that this satire, too, whether at the end of the
whole satire or somewhere in its course, contained a similar
χρεία towards which, like a humorous climax, the narrative of
the immediate context moved. In this sense, then, we may
speak of the joke played on the Hellenomaniac Albucius by the
cohors of Scaevola at Athens, a parallel humorous climax.
Evidently this story told at the trial, probably by Scaevola,
resulted in quite similar fashion in the discomfiture of Albu-
cius. Thus in lines 88–94 we read:

> 'Gracum te, Albuci, quam Romanum atque Sabinum,
> municipem Ponti, Tritani, centurionum,
> praeclarorum hominum ac primorum signiferumque,
> maluisti dici. Graece ergo praetor Athenis[361]
> id quod maluisti, te, cum ad me accedis, saluto:
> chaere, inquam, Tite, lictores, turma omnis chorusque:
> "chaere Tite." Hinc hostis mi Albucius, hinc inimicus.

And Horace lines 33 ff.:

> Persius exclamat, 'per magnos, Brute deos, te
>   oro, qui reges consueris tollere cur non
> hunc regem iugulas? operum hoc, mihi crede, tuorumst.

The satire of Lucilius, therefore, evidently contained a χρεία
or humorous anecdote, which structurally exercised consider-
able influence on Horace, who like Lucilius had had provincial
experience. Horace was thus led with no thought of direct
verbal imitation to accept the challenge held out to him as a
later satirist by the existence of the amusing and popular narra-
tion of the trial of Scaevola, and the complete discomfiture of
Albucius in the second book of Lucilius, to write a similar but
lighter incident from his own provincial career. In this limited

sense we are justified in regarding the Lucilian satire as the
model for Horace.

SATIRE 8

Satire 8 is a *Priapeum*, a genre which seems to have devel-
oped at Rome at a period subsequent to the time of Lucilius.
So far as I can see there are no traces of Lucilian influence.[252]

SATIRE 9

The ninth satire is a character study of the bore.[253] The bore
seems to combine features from the two related χαρακτῆρες of
Theophrastus, that on ἀδολεσχία or garrulity, 3, and on λαλία or
loquacity, 7. These closely allied types are well differentiated
by Jebb.[254] The main difference between the two seems to be
brought out in the fact that the garrulous man is incapable of
pursuing a subject, while the loquacious man pursues his subject
with relentless fury to the bitter end. Horace has fused these
characteristics in his delineation of the bore. Thus in line 33:

> garrulus hunc quando consumet cumque; loquacis,
> si sapiat, vitet simul atque adoleverit aetas.

and in line 12:

> cum quidlibet ille
> garriret, vicos urbem laudaret.

He emphasizes rather the discursiveness of the bore. On the
other hand, Horace's bore has the pertinacity and aggressive-
ness of the λάλος. In fact, his bore exactly follows the charac-
terization of Theophrastus: τοὺς ἀπιέναι φάσκοντας δεινὸς προ-
πέμψαι καὶ ἀποκαταστῆσαι εἰς τὴν οἰκίαν.[255] With this we may
compare the procedure of Horace's bore as announced by him-
self in lines 15, 19, and 42. I may add that the tone of the
bore's remarks with their rapidity and insistent interruptions
exactly corresponds to the description of Theophrastus:[256]
καὶ ἑτέρας ἀρχὰς τοιαύτας πορίσασθαι ὥστε μηδὲ ἀναπνεῦσαι τὸν
ἐντυγχάνοντα. It seems probable, therefore, that Horace was
familiar with these two types of Theophrastus either directly
or through some satirical treatment in a Cynic διατριβή. But
Horace's more immediate model for his study of the bore was a
satire in the sixth book of Lucilius. Iltgen[257] deserves the credit
for having been the first to point out the close relationship of
this Lucilian satire to Horace's ninth satire.

Satire 9 begins with a verse movement, which harks back metrically to two Lucilian passages, book 16, 534; and *dubia* 1138. The resemblance to the former passage is confined to the introductory verse movement. Horace's line is:

Ibam forte via sacra.

and Lucilius:

"ibat forte aries, inquit, iam quod genus! quantis
testibus! uix uno filo hosce haerere putares,
pellicula extrema exaptum pendere onus ingens.

In 1158 of the *dubia*, however, we have a passage in which Lucilius narrates an incident, which he has put into metrical form (*dicto*). This incident clearly was concerned with the abuse that Scipio heaped, (*intorquet*)[258] upon a *sectator*, as Lucilius calls him. In view of the setting of the scene as given in line 1142, it seems reasonable to assume that the fellow sought to enroll himself among the followers of Scipio at a time when Lucilius and the other members of his suite were escorting him home.

The terms *deliciae, lux effictus*, and *cinaedus* are, I think, to be set in quotation marks and interpreted as typical specimens of the abuse poured upon the would-be *sectator* by Scipio. Lucilius, partly in view of the implications these words contain, partly to explain the situation, adds that the person in question was only the *sectator* of Scipio. He then in 1142 begins his narrative. The meaning of the passage will then be somewhat as follows: If you ask me what I am doing, I will say that I am writing a poem on the story of the abuse that our Publius Cornelius Scipio at the hour when it was time for recreation hurled against his dear favorite, his fair-formed light, his *cinaedus*—that is his follower that you may apply the more correct term to him. (Then follows the introduction to the story). It chanced one day that he was on his way home. We follow many in number and thronging round him. The passage in question follows:

Cornelius Publius noster
Scipiadas dicto tempus quae intorquet in ipsum
oti 'et deliciis, luci effictae atque cinaedo' et
sectatori adeo ipse suo quo rectius dicas.
ibat forte domum. sequimur multi atque frequentes.

Now if my interpretation of this incident is correct, we have a situation similar to that in Horace's ninth satire. In heaping insults upon the bore who seeks to attach himself to his suite Scipio adopts the treatment prescribed by Theophrastus for the garrulous man.[259] ταρασείσαντα δὴ δεῖ τοιούτους τῶν ἀνθρώπων καὶ διαράμενον ἀπαλλάττεσθαι, ὅστις ἄπυρετος βούλεται εἶναι· ἔργον γὰρ συναρκεῖσθαι τοῖς μήτε σπουδὴν μήτε σχολὴν διαγιγνώσκουσιν. Horace with a more subtle irony under similar circumstances, represents himself after a useless struggle as yielding himself to the victorious bore.

I am inclined, therefore, to place this fragment at the beginning of book 6, which, as we shall see, contained a satire characterizing the bore.[261]

Horace, lines 16 and 17, like Scipio tried to shake off the bore by saying that he was going to an acquaintance's, whom the bore did not know:

> nil opus est te
> circumagi: quendam volo visere, non tibi notum.

We find a close resemblance to this broad hint in the first part of Lucilius' line 234 where the speaker, probably Scipio, tells the bore that they (perhaps the members of Scipio's suite) do not prevent you from moving on, a hint even broader than that in Horace:

> — ◡ ◡ — non te porro procedere porcent.

With the last part of Horace's statement we may possibly compare Lucilius' line 230, which I should assign to Scipio rather than refer to greetings to be extended to Lucilius at a time of sickness.[262] Scipio says he is to extend wishes for good health to a friend:

> salvere iubere salutem est mittere amico.

Iltgen[263] recognized the epic tone of Lucilius 247:

> quem neque Lucanis oriundi montibus tauri
> ducere protelo ualidis ceruicibus possent.

and compared it with the mock-heroic prophecy of the *Sabella anus* in Horace's lines 31–34. Thus Lucilius might have said in a preceding line now lost, speaking of the bore: <loquacem si sapiat vitet> quem neque etc. That is, no force can pull the bore from his intended victim. For this description of the victim's fate, Horace substitutes his mock-heroic oracle:

> hunc neque dira venena, nec hosticus auferet ensis,
> nec laterum dolor aut tussis, nec tarda podagra:
> garrulus hunc quando consumet cumque; loquacis,
> si sapiat, vitet simulatque adoleverit aetas.

In Horace lines 40 ff., also the situation is developed in a way that reminds us of Lucilius lines 235–237. In Horace's lines the bore remembers that he is to appear in a law suit, and is doubtful whether to let his suit go by default or follow Horace. He finally decides to continue with his victim, who follows him like a captive:

> 'dubius sum quid faciam' inquit,
> 'tene relinquam an rem.' 'me, sodes.' 'non faciam' ille,
> et praecedere coepit. ego, ut contendere durum
> cum victore, sequor.

With line 40 we may especially compare the Lucilian line 235, put into the mouth of the Lucilian bore and addressed to Scipio.[264]

> —◡◡—◡◡—◡ quid <hic> ipsum facere optes.

After the Lucilian bore announced his decision Scipio, his victim, likewise felt that the failure of the anticipated escape capped the climax of his misfortunes, line 236:

> id solum aduersae fortunae reque resistit.

It is not possible to make out the exact meaning of the corrupt line 233.[265] An examination of the whole Horatian context, lines 45–60, however, makes it probable that the Lucilian line expressed the renewed determination of the bore to gain the favor of the Scipionic circle. Let us first examine the lines of Horace.

In line 43 the bore abruptly turns the conversation to Horace's relations with Maecenas, and in lines 45–48 frankly says that he can further the social ambitions of Horace if he is introduced to the circle of Maecenas. Horace, then, lines 48–52, in words that surely apply with equal truth to the Scipionic circle, sets forth the wide diversity of taste and social standing which, once frankly recognized, only serve to unite this simple circle. Then in line 52, the bore breaks in:

> 'magnum narras, vix credibile.' 'atqui
> sic habet.'

rejoins Horace.   Then the bore utters the words which may be
brought into more direct relation with the Lucilian line:

> accendis quare cupiam magis illi
> proximus esse.[266]

And Lucilius 233:

> hortare, illorum si possim <*pacis*> potiri.

That is: You encourage me to see if I may win the favor of those
famous men.   Horace then replies in line 54:

> 'velis tantummodo: quae tua virtus,
> expugnabis: et est qui vinci possit, eoque
> difficilis aditus primos habet.'

Here we have signs of a situation similar to that suggested in
the Lucilian line just quoted. *Accendis* corresponds to *hortare*;
quae cupiam si possim potiri state the social determination of the
bore; *potiri* answers to Horace's despairing *expugnabis* and to the
evidence of vulnerability expressed by Horace's phrase in line
55 *et est qui vinci possit*. With the *illorum* of Lucilius' line we
may compare the *magis illi proximus esse* of Horace.

Finally we have certain Lucilian lines which have to do
with an allusion parallel to the close of Horace's satire.   These
are 228, 231, and perhaps 1339.   Line 228 is as follows:

> seruorum est festus dies hic,
> quem plane hexametro uersu non dicere possis.

The reference in this line has usually been regarded as to the
Sigillaria, but Marx (following Van Heusde) makes the line
refer to the birthday of Servius Tullius, the Ides of August.
We are not here concerned with the reference, but rather, I
wish to point out that Horace deliberately substitutes for the
servorum festus dies, the *tricesima sabbata* of the Jews.   The
object, of course, is to give his paraphrase contemporary color,[267]
but the motivation of both festivals in their similar contexts
is identical.   Horace's line is:

> 'memini bene, sed meliore
> tempore dicam: hodie tricesima sabbata: vin tu
> curtis Iudaeis oppedere?'

The Lucilian line must then have stood towards the close rather than towards the beginning of the satire in book 6. But we can perhaps go further if we accept the attempt of Cichorius to associate fragment 1339 with line 228 in this sixth book and to hold that he gave in this passage alluded to by Arnobius an obscene account of the origin of the festival of Servius Tullius, in which his claims to divine birth advanced by his mother Ocrisia were perhaps assailed. The passage of Arnobius is as follows: Ocrisiam, prudentissimam feminam divos inseruisse genitali, explicuisse motus certos: tum sancta efferventia numina vim vomuisse Lucilii ac regem Servium natum esse Romanum. Such a passage might well be regarded by the slaves as an insult extended to their patron. In fact, such an insult would be quite similar to Horace's phrase *Iudaeis oppedere*.

Finally the closing line of the Horatian satire was directly modelled on that of Lucilius, as is proved by Porphyrio's quotation of line 231:

> <*nil*>ut discrepet ac 'τὸν δὲ ἐξήρπαξεν 'Απόλλων'
> fiat.

The immediate context of this line is well stated by Marx, except that for his *male mulcatus pugnis et fustibus*, we must substitute the unfortunate victim of the Lucilian bore, perhaps Scipio himself. Thus Marx: "iam miser optat homo celebri haec illi Hectoris pugnae nil ut discrepat ac," τὸν δὲ ἐξήρπαξεν 'Απόλλων fiat. Horace, in keeping with his aversions to the mixture of Greek and Latin, translates this into Latin, lines 77 and 78:

> rapit in ius: clamor utrimque,
> undique concursus. sic me servavit Apollo.[248]

We may conclude, therefore, that the sixth book of Lucilius contained a satire upon the bore, which was the direct model for Horace's ninth satire of the first book. We may even with some degree of plausibility reconstruct the general outlines of this satire upon the basis of the surviving fragments; 1138–1142, 234, 230, 247, 235, 236, 233, 228, 231, 1339. Lucilius announces his intention to narrate the story of the abuse heaped upon the bore, who attempted to attach himself to the suite of

Scipio as the great man's period of recreation was approaching (1138–1142). When direct abuse proved ineffective, Scipio apparently attempted to shake off the bore by saying that they (*i.e.*, the members of my suite) do not prevent you from moving on (234). He further announces that he is on an errand to extend greetings to a friend (230). [If Scipio were wise, he would avoid the bore] whom the bulls of the Lucanian (247) mountains with their sturdy necks could not drag forward. Some incident arises which causes the bore to hesitate as to what "you desire me to do" (235). When he announced his decision to stick to Scipio, this capped the climax of misfortune (236). To some objection of Scipio the bore rejoins: You encourage me to see if I may win the favor of these famous men (238).

At the close of the satire Lucilius may have used the festival of Servius Tullius as an excuse for the escape of Scipio, who may have described in an obscene manner the origin of the festival and the circumstances attending the birth of Servius Tullius, 228 and 1339. Finally, some incident arose by which Scipio the victim was borne off just as Apollo rescued Hector in the famous Homeric combat of Iliad *Y* 443 (231).

SATIRE 10

The conditions which called forth the tenth satire of the first book are well known.[269] In one sense this satire is a reiteration with additions of the criticisms on the form and spirit of Lucilian satire made in Horace's fourth satire. Since, however, that somewhat subtle attack on the tone of Lucilian satire had been received with violent protests by the contemporary champions of the poet, the present satire inevitably assumed a more polemical tone. In fact the attack of Horace is directed even more against the good taste of these contemporary adherents of Lucilian satire, Pompeians, *novi poetae*,[270] and others, than against the weaknesses of Lucilius' own aesthetic theories. Yet even in the midst of this very real and contemporary literary quarrel we may surmise that Horace was not uninfluenced by the polemical tone of one or more critical satires in book 30 with their attack upon literary contemporaries, possibly upon Afranius and Accius.[271] I shall endeavor to show that it is probable that Lucilius differentiated sharply the position and

ideals of the closely knit Scipionic circle from those of Accius
and the guild of poets, just as Horace sets forth the aims and
ideals of the circle of Maecenas as against the *profani*, who
frequent the now unfashionable temple of the Muses.[272]

As was inevitable in the heat of a contemporary controversy,
the line of cleavage between Horatian and Lucilian satiric
theory is much more sharply drawn than in the fourth satire.
Now as the portions of the fourth satire which deal with Lucilius
and are repeated here are mainly criticisms of his stylistic
defects, and as the body of the satire deals with a contemporary
literary quarrel as to the proper canon for satire, it follows that
the direct influence of Lucilius on the form of this satire is less
significant than is the case with the earlier satire. On the other
hand, we have a considerable body of evidence attesting the
complete familiarity of Horace with the long established theory
of the style and humor appropriate for the *sermo* as set forth in
the rhetorical doctrines of Panaetius and Cicero and as further
developed by the meticulous studies of the Roman Atticists.

In line 8 ff. Horace recognizes that Lucilius has the virtue of
vis comica, but asserts that he misses in his predecessor certain
literary qualities. These were always indispensably bound up
with the theory of the plain style from the days of Diogenes of
Babylon and Panaetius and the writers of the Scipionic circle to
the later and nicer definitions of that style developed by Cicero,
Brutus, the Roman Atticists, Messala Corvinus, Pollio,
and the purists of the Augustan age.

Let us examine Horace's relation to these more general rhe-
torical principles before considering the scattering evidences of
his dependence upon Lucilius. Horace sets the following stylistic
requirements for the satirist in lines 8 ff.:

> est brevitate opus, ut currat sententia neu se
> inpediat verbis lassas onerantibus auris,
> et sermone opus est modo tristi, saepe iocoso,
> defendente vicem modo rhetoris atque poetae,
> interdum urbani, parcentis viribus atque
> extenuantis eas consulto.

The first of these qualities brevity, συντομία, a prerequisite of
good style, is indirectly reasserted in line 59 by the side thrust at
the rapid and diffuse Etruscan Cassius and in line 67 where

Horace asserts that Lucilius would employ the file vigorously were he alive today.

The second quality of the plain style is σαφήνεια, clearness, but Lucilius partly because of his prolixity is muddy (line 50, *at dixi fluere hunc lutulentum, saepe ferentem plura quidem tollenda relinquendis*). But perhaps the most important quality of the plain style, that indeed on which the rhetorical theory of the *sermo* is based, is that of *Latinitas* or purity of diction, a direct translation of the technical Greek rhetorical term of Ἑλληνισμός. A closely related designation to this more generic term is the Greek ὀρθογραφία. Both of these virtues of the Stoic rhetoric and of contemporary Atticism are inculcated at some length in the critical satires of Horace. Thus in 1, 4, 12 we are expressly told that Lucilius chafes under the labor by which correctness is attained (*atque piger scribendi ferre laborem, scribendi recte*), where the phrase *labor scribendi recte* is clearly a Latin paraphrase for the Greek technical term ὀρθογραφία. The procedure necessary to attain this ideal, to which alone the true critic of literature will extend his need of praise is set forth in much detail in lines 67–73 of this satire.

An even more significant aspect of this problem of good Latinity was the question of the use of foreign words, especially of Greek words. In view of the Greek origin of Latin grammatical, rhetorical, and aesthetic theories, and of the literary relations between Latin and Greek, we need not be surprised that the right to intersperse Latin with Greek, especially with Greek technical terms was the subject of lively debate from the time of Lucilius and Scipio to that of Horace and Maecenas. In the Augustan age we apparentlyfi nd the Grecizing poets of the school of Calvus, Catullus, Helvius Cinna, Valerius Cato, Propertius, and the other νεώτεροι, asserting a large freedom in this matter, while the poets of the interrelated circles of Messala Corvinus, Pollio, and Maecenas are animated by a more nationalistic spirit, and a nicer sense for the development of the Latin vernacular. The tenth satire, thus seen, affords detailed evidence as to Horace's position in this contemporary debate.[273] We must not forget, however, that long before Horace this question had been the subject of debate in the Scipionic circle.[274] This we may see from the evidence afforded by the dictum of

Panaetius on the use of Greek contained in Cicero's *de officiis* 1, 111 and from the attitude of Lucilius himself.

Lucilius, indeed,[175] while no purist, recognized limits to the employment of Greek and even ridiculed the affectations of the Hellenomaniacs of the period. His style was probably the informal mixture of Greek and Latin current in the Scipionic circle, and may be fairly compared, therefore, with that of Cicero's letters. When his treatment is serious or earnest, his speech, as Hendrickson points out, is pure Latin. It is evident, therefore, that such passages as lines 27 ff., are to be interpreted in the light of this long-standing controversy. The controversy as conceived in the Augustan age, breathes the nationalistic spirit of the circle of Maecenas, "which sought not to follow in the traces of the popular neo-Hellenism, but to produce a literature in language and spirit thoroughly Latin, though drawing its inspiration, and where necessary, its material from Greek models." There is in these lines, of course, a contemporary patriotic appeal, but the appeal is one which re-echoes the larger nationalism both political and literary, in which the writers of the Scipionic circle moved and lived. We may perhaps even find traces of Lucilian coloring in the very wording of the Horatian passage.

Horace, speaking of Greek versifying, says:

> scilicet oblitus patriaeque patrisque Latini,
> cum Pedius causas exsudet Poplicola atque
> Corvinus, patriis intermiscere petita
> verba foris malis Canusini more bilinguis;
> atque ego cum Graecos facerem, natus mare citra,
> versiculos, vetuit me tali voce Quirinus,
> post mediam noctem visus, cum somnia vera:
> 'in silvam non ligna feras insanius ac si
> magnas Graecorum malis inplere catervas.'

Now Porphyrio in his commentary on the phrase *Canusini more bilinguis* quotes the Lucilian phrase *Bruttace bilingui* (lines 1124 Marx) as used by both Lucilius and Ennius. It seems possible, therefore, that Horace's phrase is a deliberate variation on that of Lucilius. A patois of mingled Greek, Oscan, and Latin, must have been spread through Magna Graecia by the time of Lucilius, as Porphyrio assumes. These words may then have been used in a satire on literary criticism, in which Lucilius perhaps defended his habit of mixing the two languages by the analogy of the patois of southern Italy to which he had been accustomed from his youth, and in which he perhaps owned estates.[276] To this well-known defence the more puristic Horace rejoins that he too was *"mare citra natus,"* in fact a south Italian from Venusia, but father Latinus forbade him to write Greek verses when he made the attempt. In these verses then, Horace not only condemns the self-conscious and deliberate Grecising tendencies of such writers as Catulus, Porcius Licinus, Laevius, Catullus, Calvus, Hortensius, Cinna, and Memmius, but also the more unconscious and easy-going practice of the cosmopolitan Lucilius.

And in this condemnation of Lucilius, as Hendrickson has seen, Horace is doubtless assailing Valerius Cato and his followers, who, confounding the colloquial jargon of Lucilius and the exotic productions of the *novi poetae*, favored such a blending of Greek and Latin. So in line 23 we read:

> 'at sermo lingua concinnus utraque
> suavior, ut Chio nota si commixta Falernist,'

This argument rests upon the theory, more fully developed in Quintilian 12, 10, 27–34, that the sound of Greek was far more pleasing and musical than that of Latin. Indeed Quintilian concludes his argument with a remark which is reminiscent of the attitude of the defenders of Lucilius in the present passage: itaque tanto est sermo Graecus Latino iucundior, ut nostri poetae, quotiens dulce carmen esse voluerunt illorum id nominibus exornent. Whether Lucilius himself, who recognized limits to the employment of Greek, would have accepted this defence advanced by his posthumous Hellenizing champions may be doubted.

We may assume, then, with Hendrickson "that Horace was the recipient of doctrines of Latin purity which had come to him through the medium of Pollio and Messala from the purists of the Ciceronian time, Caesar, Calvus, Brutus and others." But we are justified in the further assuming that the basis for the teaching of the Atticists of the Ciceronian period was laid by the rhetorical and grammatical studies of Diogenes of Babylon and Panaetius and the literary theories and practice of the

great writers of the Scipionic circle. We may further assume, I
think, in view of the analysis of the critical satires of Lucilius
in his 30th book, that Lucilius made a deliberate effort to apply
these stylistic theories, which were originally applicable to
oratory and prose to the more informal and conversational
poetic genre, which he called *sermo*.[277]

Of the fourth virtue of the plain style, appropriateness,
τὸ πρέπον, which is raised in the stylistic system of Panaetius
to a position coordinate with the all-embracing concept of
Latinitas we have no direct discussion in this satire beyond the
implication that it is inappropriate for one who is by virtue of
birth a Latin to write Greek.[278] Such a procedure is contrary
to nature, a Stoic dictum. Perhaps also the criticism on the
harshness of the poetry of Lucilius might be referable to this
theory for the question is raised whether the nature of the man
himself or the intractability of his material was responsible for
the harshness of his verse (56–63).

The fifth virtue of the plain style, κατασκευή or ornamenta-
tion, is as we have seen, secured in the main by a nice sense for
rhythmical and phonetic combinations, εὐσυνθεσία. In this
respect, however, the harsh measures of Lucilius merit severe
criticism, for he is *durus*, an antonym of the quality of *mollitudo*.

Now this ideal of *Latinitas*, the central stylistic virtue of the
sermo, as expounded by Horace, demands the constant labor
of revision, by which alone brevity, purity of diction, appro-
priateness, and euphonious composition may be secured. In
this respect Lucilius is relatively deficient as judged by the
exacting standards of the Augustan age. If he were alive today
he would set a far stricter standard in these respects. Hence
the declaration of Horace in the well-known lines 67–73:

> sed ille,
> si foret hoc nostrum fato dilatus in aevum,
> detereret sibi multa, recideret omne quod ultra
> perfectum traheretur, et in versu faciendo
> saepe caput scaberet, vivos et roderet unguis.
> saepe stilum vertas, iterum quae digna legi sint
> scripturus, neque te ut miretur turba labores,
> contentus paucis lectoribus.

The true models for style are those forged by the laborious
methods of the Atticists of the Ciceronian period and their

Augustan successors, Pollio, Pedius Publicola, and Messala. In fact, as I have already pointed out, the ideal of what we may call the *tenuis poeta* as sketched in lines 8–15 of this satire and lines 240 ff. of the *Ars Poetica* stands in striking relationship to that of the *orator tenuis* as set forth by Cicero. In particular both lay stress on the virtues of restraint and good taste. Thus Horace, lines 13 and 14, speaks of the *tenuis poeta*, as *interdum urbani parcentis viribus atque extenuantis eas consulto* with which we may compare Cicero's description of the *tenuis orator* as *summissus et humilis consuetudinem imitans.*[270]

These principles of refinement and restraint are in large measure the result of a careful attention to the proper choice of words and their joining, as Horace declares in the *Ars Poetica*, lines 45 and 46. In these respects also, Messala, Horace's model, displays a minute care. In comparison with Cicero, Tacitus, *Dial.* 18 describes him as *in verbis magis elaboratus;* he is also elegant (*nitidus*), clear and pure (*candidus*)—all virtues of the plain style—and in his translations from the Greek he vies with Hyperides *in illa difficillima Romanis subtilitate* (Quintilian 10, 1, 113 and 5, 2). In this latter quality of *subtilitas*, akin to our modern term suggestiveness or connotation, Messala realizes the stylistic ideal of the *tenuis orator* emphasized by Cicero's description: nam orationis subtilitas imitabilis illa quidem videtur sed nihil est experienti minus. So in our passage Horace applies the verb *exsudet* to the method of Pedius Publicola and Corvinus, and in the *Ars Poetica*, speaking of the attempt to attain the same result by less exacting methods, he declares in line 240:

sudet multum frustraque laboret.

In short Messala exhibited an unremitting zeal in the effort to attain and to inculcate a pure Latinity. Thus he is aptly characterized by Seneca *rhetor.* (*Cont.* 2, 4, 8): fuit Messala exactissimi ingenii in omni studiorum parte, Latini utique sermonis observator diligentissimus. This feeling for Latin reveals a tendency which may have descended to a "pedantic preciosity." Quintilian tells us of whole books devoted to single letters (1, 7, 35). If this is so Messala evidently followed the tradition of the grammatical and lexicographical studies of the Scipionic circle, for Lucilius himself in book 9, lines 350 f., discusses the letter *a*, in 377 the letter *r*, in 379 the letter *s*. To this last letter Messala devoted a whole book according to Quintilian 1, 7, 23.

Asinius Pollio is a much more pedantic adherent of the same school. He composed a special monograph against Catullus whom he criticises for using *pugillaria* (42, 5) instead of *pugillares*. He seems also to have upheld the claims of Rome to the dictatorship of Latin speech. This seems the natural interpretation of his criticism upon the *Patavinitas* of Livy. In fact, as Hendrickson well says: "It was difficult and probably impossible for the non-Roman to meet all the refinements of usage and tradition which to city-born purists like Asinius and Messala constituted the essence of good Latin. There must, in fact, have been much in the language of the brilliant group of poets from Northern Italy and Gaul, which to ears so fastidious was open to the charge of provincialism and defective Latinity."

The beginnings of such efforts to assert this Roman primacy may be traced to the stylistic controversies of the Scipionic circle. Of this Quintilian was well aware. In 1, 5, 56 he relates Lucilius' assault on the provincialisms of Vettius, probably a member of the *gens Vettia* of the Sabine district[280] to Pollio's assaults on the *Patavinitas* of Livy: Taceo de Tuscis et Sabinis et Praenestinis quoque: nam ut eorum sermone utentem Vettium Lucilius insectatur, quemadmodum Pollio reprehendit in Livio Patavinitatem. One wonders whether this criticism of Vettius may have stood in one of the critical satires of Lucilius in book 30.

The theory of the liberal jest, which finds its complete realization in the ideal of εἰρωνεία, is intimately related, as I have shown, to the rhetorical theory of the plain style. In lines 11 to 14 we have a brief summary of the irony of the *urbanus* who is, as Horace declares (*epp.*, 1, 9, 9) *dissimulator opis propriae*, marked by reserve in the use of his powers and by studied under-statement. A style which is enlivened by this refined humor is, as Cicero declares, *de oratore* 2, 67, 269, a *genus perelegans et cum gravitate salsum*. Horace declares, therefore, in favor of the playful humor of the εἴρων, as against the fierce invective, so frequently employed by Lucilius:

ridiculum acri
fortius et melius magnas plerumque secat res.

This is in essence, a precept of Gorgias which had become the common property of rhetorical theory: δεῖν ἔφη, Γοργίας τὴν μὲν σπουδὴν διαφθείρειν τῶν ἐναντίων γέλωτι (Arist. *Rhet.* 3, 18). Aristotle then continues: ἔστι δ' ἡ εἰρωνεία (corresponding to *ridiculum* as defined by the preceding *urbani parcentis*, etc.) τῆς βωμολοχίας (corresponding to *acri* as defined by the preceding description *risu diducere rictum* and *sermone tristi*), ἐλευθεριώτερον, This Aristotelian doctrine had become a commonplace of Roman literary criticism as the result of the teachings of Panaetius in the Scipionic circle, and the popularization of the formal definitions of the types of the laughable in the rhetorical works of Cicero and his contemporaries. Even Lucilius was influenced by the earlier formulations of such theories and denied that his wit was to be regarded as scurrilous.[20] Thus, line 1014, which seems to contain such a charge put into the mouth of an *adversarius*, evidently stood in an argumentative context not unlike that of our Horatian passage:

idque tuis factis saevis et tristibus dictis.

Moreover, in regard to the nature of the humor of the Old Comedy, Horace is in sympathy rather with the post-Aristotelian formulations. These formulations found in the humor of the Old Comedy a liberal spirit of jest in addition to the scurrilous wit condemned by Aristotle, and justified the presence of both (et est quaedam hic quoque virtus). From such criticism developed the general formulation of comic theory (Hermogenes, π. μεθόδου δεινότητος ch. 36, Sp. 11p. 455, 18): κωμῳδίας δὲ πλοκὴ πικρά (acri) καὶ γελοία (*ridiculum*). Panaetius was, as we have shown, one of the most important influences in domiciling this later tradition of the wit of the Old Comedy at Rome. He cites the wit of the Old Comedy as an illustration of the liberal jest (*Atticorum antiqua comoedia*) *de officiis* 1, 104.

It seems probable, moreover, that as the result of its loftier flights and more unrestrained use of all the instruments of poetry and rhetoric, the Old Comedy was classed by rhetorical theorists rather with the grand style than with the plain style, for which the style of the New Comedy was a more appropriate analogue. Thus we read in Tzetzes περὶ κωμῳδίας p. 18 K: ἡ δὲ παλαιὰ κωμῳδία ἔχει τὸ δεινὸν καὶ ὑψηλόν. With this we may compare Horace's line 12 in which Horace's *vicem rhetoris* suggests a free paraphrase of the ideal of τὸ δεινὸν and *vicem poetae* of the ideal of τὸ ὑψηλόν.

It seems evident, therefore, that literary criticism, stimulated perhaps by certain passages in the pages of Lucilius himself, had attributed to Lucilius poetical qualities which Horace felt were alien to the true spirit and purpose of satire. Furthermore, there was a well established literary tradition which related the rhetorical theory underlying the humor of Lucilian satire with the humor of the Old Comedy. In view of the studies of Panaetius we may perhaps assume that the fundamentals of the humor of the Old Comedy were well known in the Scipionic circle, and that it is likely that Lucilius, a thorough-going student of the Old Comedy and of Greek rhetorical theories had sought to relate the theory of the jest appropriate for satire with the traditional definitions of the jest of the Old Comedy.

This mass of rhetorical criticism may have been summarized, reshaped, and given new currency by a prolegomena to Valerius Cato's edition of Lucilius, entitled *de Lucilio*, whose general outlines Hendrickson endeavors to reconstruct.[182] Yet without falling back upon any such supposition, the analysis I have made of the relations between Horace's 4th satire and Lucilius' critical satires in book 30 has brought out so clearly the nature of Lucilius' theory of humor as to make Lucilius' adherence to such Hellenistic theories of the laughable extremely probable.

Horace then goes on, lines 16 ff., to praise the writers of the Old Comedy because in their blend of the qualities of the *ridiculum* and the *acre* they lay stress rather on the former:

> illi scripta quibus comoedia prisca viris est
> hoc stabant, hoc sunt imitandi.

Lucilius is, therefore, not even a true or rather a discriminating imitator of the spirit of the Old Comedy, for as we have already seen at the beginning of satire 1, 4 he reproduces only the license of speech and the harsh wit of these writers.

Through the writings of Panaetius and through his acquaintance with the τὸ σπουδαιογέλοιον of the Hellenistic period, Lucilius must have been familiar with the Greek theories limiting the free play of humor and associated it preeminently with the informal conversation or *sermo*. Influenced in some degree by these theories he designates his satire by such names as *sermo*, related to the Greek διατριβή, *ludus* perhaps related to the Greek παίγνιον, and *schedium*, a Greek term. Thus in line 1039 f. from book 30, he uses the two terms *ludus* and *sermo*:

> cuius vultu ac facie, ludo ac sermonibus nostris
> virginis hoc pretium atque hunc reddebamus honorem.

Similarly Horace in line 37 uses the verb *ludo* to designate his satiric composition, with no purpose of closely reproducing this particular passage but in the full consciousness that he had Lucilian precedent for the use of the verb as a literary definition of the informality of the satiric genre. Thus:

> haec ego ludo
> quae neque in aede sonent certantia iudice Tarpa
> nec redeant iterum atque iterum spectanda theatris.

Indeed, in this passage (lines 36–48) Horace proceeds to define the relation of satire, his genre to other genres in the development of which his friends in the circle of Maecenas had won fame. With ironical humility he disclaims the purpose of writing a composition dignified enough to be recited before the guild of poets in their official gathering place, the temple of the Muses, where Tarpa is judge. His own field is that of Lucilian satire left vacant after the unsuccessful attempt of Varro Atacinus, and the *quidam alii* (*i.e.*, the contemporaries perhaps, as Heinze-Kiessling suggests, more numerous than we can today realize) who followed the looser theories of improvisation after the model of Lucilius. In this field Horace demands of his critics the same right of free criticism which their master Lucilius exercised towards Homer, towards Accius, and towards Ennius,[283] lines 51–56:

> age, quaeso
> tu nihil in magno doctus reprendis Homero?[284]
> nil comis tragici mutat Lucilius Acci
> non ridet versus Enni gravitate minores
> cum de se loquitur non ut maiore reprensis?

Now with the allusion to the *collegium poetarum* in line 37, we may fairly compare Cichorius' exposition[285] upon fragments 1028 and 794. It seems clear from a consideration of these two passages and from a perusal of the interesting article by E. G. Sihler:[286] (1) that this *collegium*, in which the functions of the *poetae* were but imperfectly differentiated from those of the *scribae* or *librarii*, played originally an important part in the practical civic beginnings of Roman literary history; (2) that as a result of the growth under Greek influence of the more enlightened system of literary patronage Lucilius in the Scipionic circle, like Horace in the circle of Maecenas, held himself apart from the professionally organized *poetae*. Hence the criticism of Tarpa and the *recitatio* at the *collegium* by Horace is the counterpart of Lucilius' criticism of Accius. Thus in 794, Lucilius satirizes the heroic statue of himself, which the pompous little poet had erected in the temple of the Muses, the gathering place of the guild:

> quare pro facie, pro statura Accius.

On the other hand, 1028 seems to show that Accius was like Tarpa the *magister collegii*, taking in their literal sense the words of the fragment:

> cui sua committunt mortali claustra Camenae.

Again the members of the *collegium* would receive most of their compensation for compositions in heroic hexameters and elegiac pentameters to serve as the *praeconium virorum illustrium*. Hence both Lucilius and Horace, who pride themselves upon the traditional satiric *libertas*, deny that they write poetry or call themselves *poetae*.[287]

It is worth noticing in this connection that the *beatus Fannius* of satire 1, 4, 22, who is also characterized in this satire, line 79 as *ineptus Fannius*, occupies a position in Horace's satires somewhat similar to that of Accius in the satire of Lucilius. Accius had presented a huge statue of himself to the temple of the Muses, Fannius without being asked offered copies of his books and a bust to be set up, perhaps in the library of the *collegium poetarum*.[288]

On line 53 Porphyrio says: Facit autem haec Lucilus cum alias tum vel maxime in tertio libro: meminit 8 et 10. Here as

Marx rightly notes the criticism in book 9[289] was on Accius' theory of orthography.

Finally, in lines 72 ff., Horace returns to the topic of the audience for which he would write, a theme already developed with reference to Lucilius' lines 589, 592, 593, 594, 595, in the fourth satires lines 71–76.[290] The passage in question is as follows:

> saepe stilum vertas iterum quae digna legi sint
> scripturus, neque te ut miretur turba labores,
> contentus paucis lectoribus an tua demens
> vilibus in ludis dictari carmina malis?
> non ego: nam satis est equitem mihi plaudere ut audax
> contemptis aliis explosa Arbuscula dixit.

The present development of the Lucilian commonplace upon the character of the poet's readers is at once similar to and different from the treatment in the fourth satire. It is similar in its tone of aristocratic aloofness and indifference to popular judgment. Thus in the fourth satire Horace will have nothing to do with the public *recitatio* or the public book stores. He writes for the intimate circle of his friends (70–74). So here again he is content with a few readers (74) and does not care for the crowd, while he dreads becoming a "school classic," as he does the recitation in the fourth satire. On the other hand, the present passage is nearer Lucilius in two respects. First, it definitely enumerates the members of the aristocratic circle of Maecenas for whom Horace writes just as Lucilius enumerated certain members of the Scipionic circle. Second, like Lucilius, Horace in the phrase *nam satis est equitem mihi plaudere*, clearly implies that he too writes neither for the crowd nor for the men of technical scholarship, but for the men of general or rather of average culture. Thus Lucilius in 588 which is a generalized statement closest to Horace, lines 73 and 74:

> nunc itidem populo < *placere nolo* > his cum scriptoribus:
> voluimus capere animum illorum.

Closer to line 76 are Lucilius 592 first part and 595. Thus in 592: *Nam ut Lucilius—dicere solebat neque se ab indoctissimis neque a doctissimis legi velle, quod alteri nihil intellegerent, alteri plus fortasse quam ipse* etc. So in 595:

> nec doctissimis nec scribo indoctis nimis.

On the use of the proper names of the circle of Maecenas we may compare the Lucilian enumeration of readers by name in 592, 593, 595. Thus 592:[291]

de quo etiam scripsit 'Persium non curo legere' *hic fuit enim, ut noramus, omnium fere nostrorum hominum doctissumus,* 'Laelium Decumum uolo,' *quam cognouimus uirum bonum et non inlitteratum, sed nihil ad Persium, sic ego.* . . .

And 593:

> Persium non curo legere, Laelium Decumum uolo.

And 594:

Nec uero ut noster, Lucilius, recusabo, quominus omnes mea legant! Vtinam esset ille Persius! Scipio uero et Rutilius multo etiam magis: quorum ille iudicium reformidans Tarentinis ait se et Consentinis et Siculis scribere.

And the last line of fragment 595:

> Man<il>ium
> Persium <ue>haec legere nolo, Iunium Congum uolo.

In this satire, then, far more than in the fourth, Horace under the smart of hostile criticism, perhaps from Valerius Cato and others of the Neoteric school, allows himself to be swept off his feet, and gives utterance to a sweeping and uncompromising *critique* upon the stylistic deficiencies of Lucilius and the critical standards of his contemporary admirers. By way of compensation he defines for us with much nicer precision than in the fourth satire his own stylistic ideals and theory of humor, and thus definitely takes his stand on the side of the purists and the Atticists in the long literary controversy, which from the time of Cicero had continued to agitate the literary circles of Rome. For any unfairness in his strictures upon Lucilius he ·makes full and generous amends in the first satire of the second book.

NOTES ON CHAPTER IV

SATIRE I

[1] The theme of φιλοπλουτία is best represented for us by such extant Greek treatises as Plutarch's φιλοπλουτία, the anonymous treatise on a αἰσχροκέρδεια found in the Heidelberg Papyrus 310, edited by Gerhard, *Phoenix von Kolophon*, pp. 1-103; the ἴαμβος Φοίνικος of the same papyrus (*idem*, pp. 103-140), the Papyrus Lond. 155 Verso, and the Papyrus Bodl. ms. gr. class f. 1 (p) (*idem*, pp. 156-176). The third century B.C. original of the commonplace on μεμψιμοιρία, Horace lines 1-22, has been successfully reconstructed by R. Heinze, *De Horatio Bionis Imitatore*, on the basis of Hippocratis, *epist.* 17, vol. 9, p. 368, Littré; Maximus of Tyre, *diss.* 21, 1, ed. Reiske and others, *cf.* pp. 15-17. Compare Gercke, *Rh. Mus.* 48, 1893, pp. 41-52, *Die Komposition der ersten Satire des Horaz*, for some limitations on the use of Bion in this satire.

[2] *Cf.* Lejay, *op. cit.*, p. 7.

[3] *Op. cit.*, p. 7.

[4] *Cf. supra*, pp. 180-201 on the relation of Bion to Lucilius.

[5] *Cf.* p. 3, L 15 f. H.   *h. b.*

[6] *Discour.* 21, 1. Also *cf. infra*, p. 230. The resemblance between the beginning of Horace's satire and this passage is striking.

[7] In my discussion of the sixteen different commonplaces represented in this satire of Horace, I constantly draw upon Gerhard's carefully arranged material.

[8] Gerhard, *op. cit.*, p. 92, *s.v.* πολλὰ πρήσσειν.

[9] *Idem*, p. 97 ff.

[10] *Idem*, p. 41 foot.

[11] *Anton. Mel.* 2, 32, Sp. 1084 D.

[12] Gerhard, *op. cit.*, pp. 23 ff., *s.v.* θηρία.

[13] *Idem*, p. 53.

[14] *Idem*, pp. 48 ff.; on the absence of πλεονεξία from animals *idem*, p. 53.

[15] *Idem*, pp. 95 ff.; also pp. 160 ff.

[16] *Idem.*, p. 160.

[17] *Idem*, p. 55 f., 71 f., 285 ff.

[18] *Idem*, pp. 56-62, *s.v.* ἀπαρκεῦμαι.

[19] *Idem*, pp. 136 ff. *s.v.* ἀξίους τριῶν χαλκῶν.

[20] For Bion see p. 25, 5 H.

[21] Gerhard, *op. cit.*, p. 13 *s.v.* ἕλκειν.

[22] *Cf.* also Horace, *sat.* 2, 3, 127 ff.

[23] *Idem*, pp. 48-49.

[24] *Idem*, p. 159 *s.v.* ἅρπα. τὴν κ.τ.λ.

[25] *Idem*, p. 159.

[26] *Idem*, p. 91 *s.v.* βουλοίμην.

[27] *Idem*, p. 92 ff. *s.v.* καὶ ποτ' εἰπεῖν

[28] *Cf.* also *sat.* 2, 2, 96 f. adde | iratum patruum vicinos, te tibi iniquum, etc.

[29] *Cf.* Gerhard, *op. cit.*, p. 269, n. 6.

[30] *Cf. supra*, pp. 192-194. On the relations between Bion and Horace *cf.* R. Heinze, *De Horatio Bionis Imitatore*, Bonn, 1889. Lejay, *op. cit.* in the introduction to this satire, pp. 7 and 8, regards Heinze's conclusions with scepticism, and holds that the Greek philosophical writings subsequent to Horace are more likely to have drawn upon Horace than upon Bion. In view, however, of the pervasiveness of the theme of φιλοπλουτία in Greek literature from the third century on, as established by Gerhard's *Phoenix von Kolophon*, and the comparative unfamiliarity of the Greek writers later than Horace with the Latin classics, it is much more probable that these writers were familiar with some formulation of the commonplace of ultimate Bionean origin than that their familiarity with Horace's formulation of the theme in this satire rests on first-hand knowledge. This argument holds true especially of Plutarch's treatise.

[31] For Lucilius' relation to the διατριβαί of Bion *cf. supra*, pp. 180-201; also the Pseudo-Acro on Horace, *epist.* 2, 2, 60.

[32] *Cf.* Heinze, *op. cit.*, p. 9.

[33] That is long before Horace we may trace the same partially successful efforts to fuse the two themes of μεμψιμοιρία and φιλοπλουτία in the fragments of Bion and the same "tacking" development of the argument. See *supra*, pp. 192-194. This is a more satisfactory explanation of the apparent lack of unity in the satire than Lejay's theory, set forth in his introduction to this satire, p. 1, of the use of *avarus* in this satire in the double sense *homme cupide* and *homme avare*. This does not help us, as *invidia* rather than *avaritia* is still involved in lines 1-22, and line 108. Teichmuller, *Grundgedanke und Disposition von Hor. Sat. 1, 1, Rh. Mus.* 53, pp. 436-452, seems to me forced especially in the treatment of lines 1-22.

[34] *Movetur* is, of course, used metaphorically of the emotional influence of the passion of discontent *invidia* or some other passion. Compare for its use Cicero, *pro Font.* 12, 27: Movetur eo timore quo nostrum unusquisque, quoted by Marx, *ad loc. Invidia* is, so to speak, a universal *motus animi*.

[35] Both Lucilius and Horace appear to have in mind the Greek commonplace of the αἵρεσις or choice granted by the god. Compare for example the formulation of Menippean or Bionean origin by the sophist Maximus quoted by Heinze-Kiessling[4], *ad loc.* or Heinze, *op. cit.*, p. 16, note 1. Similarly Dio Chrysos. *or.* 38, p. 151 R: εἰ τις ὑμῖν ἄνδρες Νικομηδεῖς αἵρεσιν ἔδωκεν e.q.s. In Horace, *sat.* 2, 7, 24, we have a similar choice of lots granted by the divinity. *Cf.* also Plato Axiochus, p. 368, quoted by Heinze, *loc. cit.*

[36] Marx's *comment.* on Lucilius 557 cites *Ars Poet.* 169, the same commonplace. *Cf.* Aristotle, *rhet.* 2, cap. 13, p. 1389 b, 28 ff. and Simonides apud Plutarch, *an seni g.s. resp.* 5 p. 786 B. *Quaero* in Lucilius suggests the search for gain, *cf. quaestus*.

[37] Gerhard, *op. cit.*, pp. 48 ff.   Especially close to our passage is the Greek formulation of the commonplace, *cf.* p. 161 *idem*, in the *Papyrus Lond.* 155 verso:

ἀεὶ δὲ περιφέρουσι τοῦτο τὸ ῥῆμα
κέρδαιν', ἑταῖρε, κἢν θέρους κἢν χειμῶνος.

[38] Pp. 13 f.

[39] *Cf.* Usener, *Epicurea*, p. 77.18.

[40] Compare Horace's treatment of avarice as a form of madness in *satire* 2, 3, 82-160.

[41] Gerhard, *op. cit.*, pp. 55 ff.; 71 ff.; 285 ff.

[42] *Cf.* Gerhard, *op. cit.*, pp. 56 ff.; 86 ff., especially *s.v.* ἀρκοῦμαι, p. 46: Denn das persönliche ἀρκοῦμαι Ich lasse mir genügen einerseits und als Korrelat dazu das unpersönliche τὰ ἀρκοῦντα *quod satis est*, anderseits sind Schlagwörter der Sekte.   *Cf.* Horace c. 3, 1, 25; 16, 44; *ep.* 1, 2, 46; *sat.* 2, 3, 127; 2, 6, 13.   With the personal ἀταρκοῦμαι *cf.* line 59 of this satire: at qui tantuli eget quanto est opus.   *Cf.* Lejay, *Introduction to Satire*, vol. I, p. 8.

[43] *Cf.* for details Gerhard, *op. cit.*, p. 69.

[44] Horace does not imitate the topic of the well-stocked wine cellar in his first satire, but compare *sat.* 2, 3, 110 ff. where both grain and wine are mentioned.

[45] *Cf.* p. 301.

[46] For a contrary opinion *cf.* Lejay, *op. cit.* Introduction to *Satire* 1, p. 5.

[47] This commonplace appears constantly in the popular literature of the Cynics and others.   *Cf.* Gerhard, *op. cit.*, pp. 136 ff.; *supra*, p. 225. Gercke, *op. cit.*, pp. 50 ff. shows conclusively that Horace had the Lucilian treatment of this commonplace in mind.   The same "topic" is found in Petronius 77; Seneca, *de benef.* 115, 4; Juvenal, 3, 143; Apuleius, *Apol.* 23; Cicero, *Paradox* 44.   *Cf.* Otto, *Sprichwörter der Römer*, p. 157.

[48] I read *virique* with Bergk, but even if we accept *utrique* with Marx and Cichorius, and regard the allusions (*cf.* Cichorius *Untersuch*, pp. 333 ff.) as referring to a contemporary political event, I should still on account of the similarity with 559, be inclined to place the fragment in book 19 rather than in book 11.

[49] *Cf.* Gerhard, *op. cit.*, p. 70 and *supra*, p. 227.

[50] *Cf. supra*, p. 200.

[51] *Cf. supra*, pp. 226 f. on the topic of anxiety for loss of wealth.   Also Gerhard, *op. cit.*, p. 16, n. 4.

[52] These lines are explained by Marx as referring to the courtesy which must be shown to women of good standing on the public streets.

[53] So Marx, comment. *ad loc.* is correct in the Homeric citations for this habit of children, but incorrect so far as I can see in inferring that the scene is the street.

[54] This *Graecula ancilla* apparently plays a part similar to the *assa* of Juvenal.

[55] *Tab.* 6, 22, 23 edit. Peterson.

[56] *Cf. supra* pp. 230 ff.

[57] The *elementa* of Horace and the *alpha* and *beta* of Juvenal.

[58] Compare the excellent note in Morris' edition of Horace's satire.

[59] *Cf. supra*, pp. 240 ff.

[60] Stobaeus, 5, 67 = Teles, p. 11, 2 H.

[61] Notice that in Horace, *sat.* 2, 3, 132-141, the avaricious man on the comic stage is compared with Orestes who is declared to be even less mad than the man impelled by the insatiate love of gold.

[62] *Cf.* Lejay, *op. cit.*, note on line 86.

[63] *Cf.* Lucilius line 1212.

[64] *Cf.* cit. Marx, comment. *ad loc.*

[65] *Op. cit.*, p. 245.

[66] *Cf.* Heinze-Kiessling's *Horace* on line 104, and Cooper's *Word Formation in the Sermo Plebeius*, pp. 53 ff.

[67] *Cf.* Cichorius, *op. cit.*, 317 f.

[68] Julius Meier-Graefe, *The Development of Modern Art*, Constable and Claude, p. 102.

SATIRE 2

[69] *Cf. sat.* 1, 1, 105 ff.; 2, 2, 54 ff.; 2, 3, 48 ff.; *epp.* 1, 18, 9; 2, 2, 190-204, quoted by Heinze, *op. cit.*, p. 22.

[70] Lejay, *op. cit.*, Introduction to *Satire*, 1, 2, p. 31.

[71] For this antithesis of *voluptas* and *dolor* compare the Epicurean antithesis of ἡδονή and ἀλγηδών. Epicurus himself taught differently. *Cf.* Heinze-Kiessling[4] on this satire of Horace, line 37.

[72] Compare also the instances of punishment meted out well-known adulterers in Roman history, chronicled by Valerius Maximus 6, 1, 13.

[73] *Cf.* Cicero, *de finibus* 1, 13, 45; cupiditatum ea ratio est, ut necessariae nec opera multa nec impensa expleantur: ne naturales quidem multa desiderant, propterea quod ipsa natura divitias quibus contenta sit, *et parabiles et terminatas* habet.

[74] Epicurus, *fragment* 456. Compare also Lucretius 4, 1063-1072, and Heinze-Kiessling, *op. cit.*, note on Horace line 109.

[75] *Cf.* Lejay, *op. cit.*, p. 31.

[76] There may be an element of sardonic malice, as Lejay has suggested, in the application of the niceties of the philosophical nomenclature of the Epicureans to these three classes of women, especially in the forcible relation of the ἐπιθυμίαι φυσικαί ἀλλ' οὐκ ἀναγκαῖαι to the freedwomen.

[77] *Cf.* Lejay, *op. cit.*, pp. 33 ff.

[78] *Cf. supra*, pp. 84 f.

[79] *Cf.* Leo, *Geschichte der Römischen Literatur*, vol. I, p. 410.

[80] On Cercidas see *Oxyrynchus Papyri*, vol. 8, pp. 20-59, no. 1082, Cercidas, Meliambi.

[81] *Idem*, p. 22.

[82] Compare *infra*, p. 270 and Lucilius lines 305 and 306.

[83] *Cf.* Horace line 123 ff. and *infra*, pp. 268-270.

[84] Oxyrynchus Papyri *loc. cit.*, p. 54 for notes; p. 33 for text.

[85] See Lejay, *op. cit.*, p. 33.

[86] *Idem*, p. 34.

[87] Quoted by Lejay, *op. cit.*, p. 34.

[88] *Cf. infra*, pp. 263-265.

[89] Kock, *Comicorum Atticorum Fragmenta*, vol. 2, *Nannion*, p. 187, no. 67.

[90] On Philodemus of Gadara, who lived in the family of Piso, consul in 58 B.C., see the note in Heinze-Kiessling[4] on Horace, line 120. Also Cicero, *in Pisonem* 28, 29. He probably maintained relations with Horace's friends Varius and Quintilius, and possibly with Siron the teacher of Virgil.

[91] *Op. cit.*, pp. 159-163.

[92] *E.g.*, Lejay, Heinze-Kiessling[4], Morris.

[93] See commentary of Marx on 1177. Probably Arnobius did not have the text of Lucilius, but bases his statement on an excerpt.

[94] *Op. cit.*, pp. 159-163.

[95] *Supra*, p. 253. See also *infra*, p. 271.

[96] *Cf.* Cichorius, *op. cit.*, p. 348; also Cichorius on line 1307, p. 341 ff.; and *infra*, p. 272.

[97] *Cf.* Cichorius, *op. cit.*, p. 163, and Lucilius line 1316.

[98] Lucilius, *fragment* 1307, with commentary of Cichorius, *op. cit.*, pp. 341-345. Valerius Maximus 8, 1, 8.

[99] 465 Vahlen. The parallel of Horace's parody with Lucilius was noted by Skutsch. See Cichorius, *op. cit.*, p. 162, n. 1.

[100] Cichorius, *op. cit.*, p. 158. Perhaps *consilium* is used as an abstract noun applied concretely to the young man because of his future functions in the state.

[101] The first person can hardly be the poet himself as Cichorius assumes, *op. cit.*, p. 159. The first person is used again in 856 and 861. In 856 since *locavi* means *paravi* the reference must be either to the matron or the enraged husband, hardly to the poet. So in line 861 the reference in the phrase *cui paulisper me dem* must rather be to the young man who has formed a loose and temporary *liaison* with a woman belonging to one of the three classes discussed. Lines 854 and 855 fit in much better with the same assumption of a dramatic dialogue with a speaker in the first person.

[102] It is possible also to think of these lines in some such context as 131 ff.:

cruribus haec metuat, doti deprensa, egomet mi;
discincta tunica fugiendum est ac pede nudo.

but this is far less probable for the main emphasis of the passage is upon the guilty man, not on the vengeance of the wronged husband.

[103] Or perhaps like the mediaeval cuckold he feels that his own impotency is to blame. In view of line 282 I think we should read *sibi* with Lachmann rather than *tibi*. It is true that *tibi* would give a context closer to Horace 45, and that in both passages we should then have castration as the legal penalty for detected adultery, probably inflicted by the wronged husband upon the adulterer.

[104] For this use of *mercatura* see Plautus, *Trinummus* 2, 2, 51.

[105] So Cichorius, *loc. cit.*, pp. 157 ff.

[106] *Idem*, pp. 160 ff.

[107] No satisfactory emendation for *scopios* has yet been discovered.

[108] Compare following pages.

[109] See *supra*, pp. 251-256.

[110] See also Cichorius, *op. cit.*, p. 163, note 1.

[111] Cichorius, *op. cit.*, p. 161. I accept Cichorius' tentative interpretation of the corrupt fragment. I punctuate with a comma before, not after *se*, unlike Marx.

[112] Compare the fragment of Euboulos, lines 3 and 5, quoted above on p. 334.

[113] The use of *solida* in this passage may suggest also that Lucilius was conscious of the Epicurean contrast between the τὸ κενόν and τὸ στερεόν.

[114] The class of freeborn virgins stands at the other end of the scale from the women of the *fornix*. See Lucilius, *fragment* 868 and *infra*, p. 272 f.

[115] I accept the emendation of Cichorius, *op. cit.*, p. 162 of *quae* for *quiete*. Marx reads *qui et*.

[116] We have another epigram of his to the contrary effect:

οὐ γὰρ ἕτοιμα βούλομαι, ἀλλὰ ποθῶ
πᾶν τὸ φυλασσόμενον· 2κ

[117] These fragments are not discussed by Cichorius in his treatment of book 7. *Cf.* pp. 287 ff.

[118] So in Horace 103 we are told, see *supra*, p. 263, that both the excellencies and defects of the women of the *fornix* are at once visible without chance of concealment.

[119] Cichorius, *op. cit.*, p. 32 regards this as a description of the long-haired Lusitanian warriors and refers this to one of the Spanish campaigns of Lucilius. Against this is the fact that the words seem to be used of horses in a semi-technical manner. With the *ut mos fuit illis* of Lucilius we may compare Horace's *regibus hic mos est*, line 86.

[120] Compare also *fragment* 798; Martial 3, 8; Lucretius 4, 120.

[121] While such a Lucilian line as 293 is conceivable in various contexts it might possibly be compared in tone with such a passage as Horace 105–108. We reject scornfully the goods at our disposal and capriciously seek the love which always eludes us, just as the huntsman pursues the boar:

tristis, difficiles sumus, fastidimus bonorum.

[122] This line is compared by Marx to a running horse.

[123] See *supra*, p. 251-256.

[124] One is tempted to wonder whether the word *vinibuas* in line 302 might not have been used in a context similar to that of *aurea pocula* in Horace, line 113:

Num tibi cum faucis urit sitis, aurea quaeris
pocula?

[125] It is possible that in book 8, 296 may have stood in a similar context, which treated the merits of the youthful girl in the *fornix*:

— ᴗ ᴗ quod gracila est, pernix, quod pectore
puro quod puero similis.

[126] *Fragment* 264 clearly contained an incident illustrating the capricious treatment meted out by Phryne to a lover. It is possible that Lucilius may have used this incident to show that a girl from the *fornix* less capricious, luxurious, and expensive will be a Phryne in his eyes. Phryne would then be parallel to Helen in Cercidas (see p. 88 above) and to the use of Ilia and Egeria in Horace, line 125.

[127] Compare the commentaries on line 24. Horace may have had in mind the use of *malta* in Lucilius 732. See Porphyrio on 24 and Nonius, p. 27.8 on the Lucilian line.

[128] Some of these words have been discussed above.

[129] Here any exact sequence is difficult to establish. It is to be noticed, however, that 1306, 306, 307 are expressly quoted by Porphyrio as parallels to this satire.

SATIRE 3

[130] *Op. cit.*, pp. 61 ff.

[131] *Op. cit.*, pp. 64 ff. See *Republic* 5, p. 474 d.

[132] *Cf.* Lucretius 4, 1160 *immunda et fetida acosmos.*

[133] Lucilius seems to be referring to the *columna Maeniana.* Porphyrio on the passage of Horace quotes the Lucilian fragment in the text. Maenius also had a reputation as a wit according to the commentary of the pseudo-Asconius on Cicero's *divinatio in Caecilium* 50: qui de personis Horatianis scripserunt aiunt Maenium et scurrilitate et nepotatu notissimum Romae fuisse. See also Horace, *epp.* 1, 15, 26-41, especially line 30:
quaelibet in quemvis opprobria fingere saevus.
In Horace's passage from this third satire the word play on *ignosco* and *ignoro* may be reminiscent of Lucilius.

[134] *Cf.* Gerhard, *op. cit.*, pp. 245, 266, 290 ff. on the fondness of this literature for characterization.

[135] *Cf.* Cichorius, *op. cit.*, pp. 150 ff. The use of this common paradox by both writers need not imply more than that both were familiar with this well-known theme in Cynic-Stoic sources. However, it is significant that Lucilius was the first to establish the use of such popular philosophical material for satire, thus setting the tradition which was developed and modified by Horace.

SATIRE 4

[136] *Cf.* Hendrickson, *Horace Serm. 1, 4: A Protest and A Programme* in *A. J. P.*, vol. 21, pp. 121-142. Especially apposite is page 124. "I do not believe that Horace is here justifying himself before the harsh criticism of a public which felt aggrieved and injured by his attacks, nor do I believe that the contents of the satire and the criticism of himself which it presents are drawn from life. It is, *on the contrary a criticism of literary theory put concretely.*" I believe that this is the correct point of approach to the interpretation of the satire, and that the necessity impelling Horace to define his own position depended in no small measure upon the current acceptance by Augustan Rome of the famous formulation of the satirist's

art made by Lucilius in book 30 (not considered by Hendrickson). For three reasons, however, Horace was induced to present his critique in the guise of a contemporary literary polemic. (1) That was the form adopted by Lucilius in book 30 in which he may have attacked his contemporaries, (possibly Afranius and Accius, if Cichorius, *op. cit.*, pp. 193-208 is correct). Horace, therefore, felt a strong impulse to follow the literary convention of the genre set by his great predecessor. (2) Satire 2, probably the earliest experiment in the Lucilian manner must have aroused some real resentment among Horace's contemporaries, if we can lay any stress at all upon the repetition of 2, 27 in line 92 of this satire. (3) The satire is a protest against the actual attempts to revive Lucilian satire in a form rooted in the rude, direct, and interminable street preaching of a Diogenes, rather than in the more finished literary conversations on ethical topics of the Bionean διατριβαί. The improvisatory methods of such Stoic preachers as Crispinus, Fannius, and Fabius in the decade between 40-30 B.C. show decided analogies to the ideals and methods of Lucilius. *Cf.* Hendrickson, *Satura, the Genesis of a Literary Form*, in C. P., vol. 6, No. 2, pp. 129-143, especially p. 142. Moreover, the appearance of Valerius Cato's edition of Lucilius tended, as Hendrickson has shown, to bring the controversy between Horace and these neo-Lucilians to a focus. See Hendrickson's three articles on *Horace and Valerius Cato*, in C. P., vol. 11, pp. 249-269; vol. 12, pp. 77-92; and pp. 329-350. Compare on lines 45 ff. the article on *Horace's View of the Relations between Satire and Comedy*, in A. J. P., vol. 34, pp. 183-193 by H. B. Fairclough. I find myself in accord with Fairclough's criticism on Knapp's interpretation of the passage in the article, *The Sceptical Assault on the Roman Tradition concerning the Dramatic Satura*, in A. J. P., vol. 33, pp. 143 ff. The article by B. L. Ullman, *Horace on the Nature of Satire*, Trans. A. P. A., pp. 111-132, is a valuable contribution to the interpretation of this satire, but interprets Horace in the light of contemporary conditions rather than from the point of view of his sources.

[137] Interwoven with the ethical and literary theory of Horace's satire also, as Lejay has recognized, *op. cit.*, p. 99, is the theory of the closed circle of friends, the literary coterie. This point of view is even more prominent in *satire* 1, 10. Hence literary ideals both in Lucilius and in Horace tend to be based on group ideals, and ethical and literary polemics are directed against those outside the group. The strong part that philosophy played in cementing the earliest literary circle at Rome, the Scipionic circle, is perhaps in part a reflection of the influence on Roman soil of the philosophical έταιρία of the Greeks. *Cf.* Lejay, *op. cit.*, pp. 61 ff. and Cicero's *Laelius, passim*.

[138] *Cf.* my paper on Lucilius and Persius, vol. cit., pp. 125 ff.

[139] Stobaeus 13, 44: 111, p. 462 H. *Cf.* Joel, *op. cit.*, 2, p. 933; Gerhard, *op. cit.*, pp. 37 ff. In this Horatian satire the use of *rodere*, line 81, and of *mordax*, line 92, seems to be referable in ultimate analysis to the same technical terminology of the Cynics.

[140] See Gerhard, *op. cit.*, p. 30 ff.

[141] In this he is in agreement with the later and more lax Cynics. *Cf.* Zeller 2, 1⁴, 1889, p. 334, and Gerhard, *op. cit.*, p. 41 ff. on Crates of Thebes. Thus in *sat.* 1, 1, 25 the simile of the *blandi doctores* with the *crustula* is perhaps adapted from some such later Cynic similes of the "sugar-coated pill," as we find fathered even on Diogenes himself. *Cf.* Gerhard, *op. cit.*, p. 41, also *cf.* Horace's *satire* 1, 3, *passim.*

[142] See *supra*, pp. 84-85. Also Cicero, *de officiis* 1, 128 and 148.

[143] See *supra*, pp. 91-93. Also Cicero, *de officiis* 1, 101-104.

[144] *Cf.* Hendrickson, *loc. cit.*, p. 128 ff.

[145] See *supra*, pp. 90-93.

[146] See Cicero, *de officiis* 1, 104. Also *supra*, p. 91.

[147] On this see the article by Hendrickson on *Horace and Lucilius* in the *Studies in Honor of Gildersleeve*, especially pp. 154 ff., and also the article on this satire, vol. cit., pp. 140 ff.

[148] In proof of this see *infra*, pp. 287-290.

[149] I accept Hendrickson's argument as proof that both Crispinus and Fannius must be understood as imitators of the Lucilian style. See *C. P.* 6, p. 131. *Satura—The Genesis of a Literary Form*, in *C. P.*, vol. VI, no. 2, pp. 122-143.

[150] I accept the reading of Cichorius, *op. cit.*, p. 194 note for the MS. *tua lades*. *Laudis* read by most of the editors seems out of point in the context. Moreover, *laedere* is virtually a technical term descriptive of the satiric method. With *culpes* compare Horace's *utpote pluris culpari dignos*.

[151] See *supra* pp. 277 ff., especially p. 279.

[152] With *voluter* in this sense see Cicero, *ad fam.* 9, 3, 1; *cum omnes in omni genere et scelerum et flagitiorum volutentur*. So Horace uses the more restrained *laborat*.

[153] While it is possible with Cichorius to refer these lines to a particular rival of Lucilius, it seems better in view of the general similarity with the Horatian lines to put them in the mouth of the ordinary anonymous *adversarius.*

[154] For other examples see *sat.* 2, 1, 52; *epodes* 6, 15; Persius 1, 115 by implication. Also see Hendrickson, *op. cit.*, pp. 127 ff. on these lines. On such animal similes in general see Gerhard, *op. cit.* index *s.v.* θηρία.

[155] Similar is Horace's picture of the armed satirist in *sat.* 2, 1, 39-46, and the simile of the cuttlefish as an example of *nigror* in line 100. *Cf. infra*, p. 297.

[156] Cichorius, *op. cit.*, p. 205, regards these lines as referring to Accius, famed for the severity of his criticism, but as the "topic" of the biting character of the satiric poet is so widely spread it seems better to put them in the mouth of the Lucilian *adversarius* with reference to the abusive tone of Lucilian satire.

[157] I accept Madvig's emendation of *risu res* for *oris aures* of the MS. Compare also Horace, *sat.* 1, 10, 6 a rather similar line.

[158] Cichorius, *op. cit.*, pp. 193 ff. refers this to the complaint of the comic poet that Lucilius had insulted him.

¹⁵⁹ See also *sat*. 1, 10, 11 and 2, 1, 21, where *tristis versus* is also applied to satire. It is difficult to say whether the line is best referred to line 34 or 83, where we have a further delineation of the character of the βωμολόχος. *Cf.* Hendrickson, *op. cit.*, p. 133.

¹⁶⁰ Hendrickson, *op. cit.*, p. 128.

¹⁶¹ Lines 970 and 971 are assigned by Marx to the first satire in book 30. 970 is referred to the gossip of the town, and 971 is compared with Horace, *epp*. 2, 2, 184. These are both possible interpretations, but it seems better to associate the lines with lines 1015 and 1016 in view of the evident similarity in tone and theme.

¹⁶² Among our surviving fragments there is no passage that exactly corresponds to line 35. The use of *differre* in the sense of *diffamare* in 1015, and of *male dicendo* in 1016 makes it well nigh certain that the satirist's failure to spare his friends was a topic discussed also by Lucilius.

¹⁶³ *Cf.* Hendrickson, *op. cit.*, p. 130, note 2.

¹⁶⁴ Here *contra* reproduces the force of *-re* in *rescribere*. This line is referred by Cichorius, *op. cit.* 195, to an answer to be indited by Lucilius to an attack made upon him by the comic poet, his rival Afranius. I am doubtful of the probability of the reference to Afranius. If Cichorius is correct, however, it might be said that it would be especially appropriate for Lucilius to discuss with some warmth in his reply the relation between satire and comedy.

¹⁶⁵ *Op. cit.*, pp. 205 ff.

¹⁶⁶ Pliny, *N. H.* 34, 19.

¹⁶⁷ *Cf. sat.* 1, 10, 38 for a more detailed imitation, treated *infra*, pp. 347 ff.

¹⁶⁸ Lucilius speaks of his works as *poemata* in 1013. On the use of these terms see *supra*, pp. 117 ff.

¹⁶⁹ See comment. *ad loc.*

¹⁷⁰ *Cf.* also Fairclough, *op. cit.*, p. 131.

¹⁷¹ As Heinze has seen.

¹⁷² Of this we shall find further corroborative evidence in the *Ars Poetica.* See *infra*, pp. 449-468 *passim*.

¹⁷³ *Cf.* Ingersoll, *Roman Satire: Its Early Name?* in *C. P.* 7, 1, pp. 59-65. My paper on *Lucilius and Persius*, *Trans. Am. Ph. Assn.*, vol. 40, pp. 250-251.

¹⁷⁴ *Cf. supra*, pp. 118.

¹⁷⁵ Hendrickson, *op. cit.*, p. 131 says: "It is possible that from some such source (the treatise περὶ κωμῳδίας), the same claim of the performance of a public service had been transferred to Lucilius by Roman critics and so had entered the theory of satire." In view of Lucilius' own words in this satire of book 30 is it too bold to conjecture that he himself claimed in his poetry to combine the functions of the Roman censor with a function of free criticism analogous to the παρρησία assumed by the writers of the Old Comedy? To such a παρρησία Horace apparently refers by the use of the term *libertas* in the opening lines of the present satire (1-5), in which he derives this characteristic of Lucilian satire from the writers of the Old

Comedy. Such Lucilian lines as 671 and 675 seem to attest the insistence placed upon such *libertas* by Lucilius himself. Compare also Cicero, *pro Murena* 11, for an implied comparison of the task of the prosecutor with that of the *censor morum*. Again Cicero, *Brutus* 130, characterizes M. Junius Brutus as *magnum dedecus generi vestro . . . is magistratus petivi sed fuit accusator vehemens et molestus*, a passage which is quoted by Heinze Kiessling[4] on lines 63 ff. of this satire.

[176] See *supra*, pp. 93-96.

[177] See Marx, comment. *ad loc.*; Cichorius, *op. cit.*, pp. 340 f.

[178] Or if we accept the interpretation of Cichorius, *op. cit.* 194: "lebe so dass du zu einem Tadel keinen Anlass bietest und also eine Schmähung von mir nicht zu fürchten brauchst," we may compare more specifically the Horatian line 68 above; nor does Cichorius' conjecture that we have a more explicit reference to Afranius militate against this general similarity.

[179] See *supra*, pp. 284 ff.

[180] I accept *Muto*, the reading of, Cichorius, *op. cit.*, pp. 206-208, and the allusion to a Quintus Muto of the Graechan age.

[181] This parallel seems closer than Marx' comparison of the line with Horace, *sat.* 2, 1, 21.

[182] In the last two lines we may have a trace of the influence of the rhetorical doctrine of propriety as applied to the *sermo*. Compare especially p. 85 *supra*. With the *alieno tempore* of Horace we may compare the statement of Cicero (Panaetius), *de officiis* 1, 135: *neque enim isdem de rebus nec omni tempore nec similiter delectamur.*

[183] See the story of the first meeting of Terence and Caecilius recorded by Suetonius, ed. Roth., p. 292, in the Suetonius-Donatus life of Terence.

[184] Compare also Persius 1, 14 ff. in my paper on Lucilius and Persius, vol. cit., p. 126. I am now inclined to compare this Lucilian passage with Horace, *sat.* 1, 4, 72, as well as with *sat.* 2, 2, 60. As so often in Persius we have two Horatian passages contaminated in the imitation. Notice that *populo* occurs in line 16. It seems needless to quote lines 592-596 of Lucilius, for the definite individuals serving as types of the three classes of readers enumerated by Lucilius are not the object of specific imitation in this satire. Rather do we have such a detailed differentiation by *name* of desirable and undesirable readers in Horace, *sat.* 1, 10, 75 ff., where the *eques* may well be compared with the Lucilian *nec doctissimis < nec scribo indoctis nimis >* of Lucilius 595. *Cf. infra*, pp. 348-349. Compare Cichorius, *op. cit.*, pp. 104-109, for an attempt to remove the difficulties in these passages and to assign to their proper classification the *docti* and *indocti*. 587 assigned by Lejay, *op. cit.*, p. 103, to the same context belongs rather to the *Ars Poetica* 11-13. *Cf.* my paper, *Lucilius, the Ars Poetica of Horace, and Persius*, in *Harvard Studies in Classical Philology*, XXIV, p. 5.

[185] *Op. cit.*, p. 132 ff.

[186] *Nichomachean Ethics* 14, 1128 a6. *Cf.* also Cicero, *de oratore* 2, 239.

[187] Aristotle, *Eth. Nic.* 14, 1128 a, 35.

[188] Referred by Cichorius, *op. cit.*, p. 202 to an attack upon a second opponent of Lucilius; placed by Marx in a second satire of book 30. The

resemblance to the Horatian lines noted in the text makes it more probable that the fragment finds its proper place in a general debate on satire and the satirist's art. Whether this debate was carried on by Lucilius with two actual opponents Afranius and Accius, as Cichorius conjectures, I do not venture to say.

[189] On the relation of these lines to Cynic satiric theories cf. supra, pp. 279 ff. Also Gerhard, op. cit., pp. 30 ff. In view of the similarity of theme between Horace's lines 34-38 and 83-85 it is difficult to assign the Lucilian fragments with any degree of dogmatism to the corresponding Horatian lines. For example, 971 might refer to 83 as well as to 35; 1014 to 34 or 83. On the whole, however, the relation of these two Lucilian fragments seems closer to 1022, 1015 and 1016 than to the fragments discussed above as parallel to verses 83 ff. One is inclined to assign to this satire of book 30 and place in this same context line 1268: *prodes amicis.* With *mordax* and *mordet* we may compare the dog-like viciousness of the attack in Lucilius 1095.

[190] Cf. Cichorius, op. cit., p. 195. Also Persius 1, 111, noted by Skutsch, and my paper *Lucilius and Persius,* vol. cit., p. 134. The ultimate source of such lines is a Greek rhetorical and ethical commonplace akin to Aristotle's *Ethics* 1128 a, 14: οἱ βωμολόχοι εὐτράπελοι προσαγορεύονται ὡς χαρίεντες.

[191] While 1018 of Lucilius is conceivable as standing in various contexts, it seems possible to compare it with Horace 92, where Horace speaks of the ill-smelling Gargonius. Thus Marx has shown by comparing Cato, de agri cultura 70, 1 that *fabuli* means *stercus caprarum;* compare the Greek σφυράδες. Horace has perhaps ameliorated to a small degree the coarseness of the Lucilian line in 1, 2, 27, but apparently not enough to satisfy Augustan taste. Lucilius 1018 reads:

hic in stercore humi fabulisque, fimo atque sucerdis.

[192] I do not mean to imply direct verbal imitation, but only that the stock satiric types are drawn in a manner not unlike that of Theophrastus in his χαρακτῆρες. Compare *infra,* pp. 330-336 on satire 1, 9.

[193] So Lejay in his introduction to this satire, pp. 96-98.

[194] He is the empirical Cynic, not the theoretic *sapiens* of the Stoics, cf. lines 115-116.

[195] Still more true of the tone of Horace himself 129-143 in defending satire as a *mediocre vitium.*

[196] Gerhard, op. cit. s.v. λόγοις χρηστοῖσι σωφρονισθεῖσα, pp. 125-126. Cf. also Horace, epp. 1, 1, 33:

fervet avaritia miseroque cupidine pectus:
sunt verba et voces, quibus hunc lenire dolorem
possis, etc.

Compare the *formabat puerum dictis* of Horace's father.

[197] Cf. op. cit., pp. 269 and 277.

[198] Op. cit., pp. 32-45, 65 ff., and 229 ff.

[199] Cf. Horace 48-52; Lucilius *fragment* 1029. Also Gerhard, op. cit., pp. 142, note 3, bibliography and index s.v. Komödie.

[200] Cf. Gerhard, op. cit., pp. 245 ff., and note 4. Geffcken, *Studien*

sur griechischen Satire, N. *Jahrb. f. d. Kl. Alt.*, vol. 27, p. 408.

[201] *Op. cit.*, pp. 87 ff. Also Horace, *sat.* 2, 2, 94 ff.: *das aliquid famae*, etc.

[202] It is worth while quoting the whole passage (*Rhet.* 3, 18 *ad. fin.*): ἔστι δὲ εἰρωνεία τῆς βωμολοχίας ἐλευθερώτερον. ὁ μὲν γὰρ αὑτοῦ ἕνεκα ποιεῖ τὸ γέλοιον ὁ βωμολόχος ἑτέρου.

[203] *I.e.*, deny the right to compose urbane satire.

[204] See Gerhard, *op. cit.*, p. 40.

[205] See Gerhard, *op. cit.*, pp. 40 ff. Compare also 17-18: *pusilli animi raro et perpauca loquentis;* l. 20 *fortasse et minora* (*i.e.*, vitia); and 136 the *mediocria vitia* of Horace. But this attitude pervades the whole satire.

[206] It is hardly necessary to quote illustrations of the *libertas Cynicorum*, but *cf.* Gerhard, *op. cit.*, index *s.v.* παρρησία. The Cynic prides himself on being ἀληθής rather than a κόλαξ. *Cf.* pp. 34 ff. For the assertion of the satirist's ethical and aesthetic sincerity see Lucilius, *frags.* 590, 632; Horace, *sat.* 2, 1, 30-34; *A. P.* 102, 103; Persius 1, 45; Juvenal 1, 1, 79. Also my article *Lucilius and Persius*, in *Trans. A. P. A.*, vol. 40, pp. 129 ff.

[207] Compare for fuller discussion of this point Hirzel, *Untersuchungen zu Cicero's philosophischen Schriften*, vol. 2, pp. 365 ff.

[208] Closer to Lucilius is Persius 5, 120. See my paper *Lucilius and Persius*, vol. cit., p. 144, n. 3.

[209] Gerhard, *op. cit.*, pp. 36 ff.

[210] Both Marx, comment. *ad loc.* and Cichorius refer these words to the poet himself. But the language seems better suited to an attack on the satirist's traditional reputation for bitter language made by an *adversarius* who has suffered. Finally, I have no doubt that 1032:

> *hoc etiam accipe quod dicam: nam pertinet ad rem.*

belongs in the Lucilian defence of satire. It is suited to the more direct method of Lucilius, and may have stood in some context in which the poet makes the transition to his own defence. A context similar to Horace 140 is conceivable, though Horace there speaks with ironical understatement. The lines are, I think, too general to admit of a more exact assignment to a context.

SATIRE 5

[211] I am unconvinced by the argument of Cichorius, *op. cit.*, pp. 251-261 that book 3 contained also a *propempticon* for a future journey as well as an account of the journey already accomplished. For a discussion of the point see *infra*, pp. 312-313.

[212] For the *propempticon* of Cinna, *cf.* Schanz, *Litteraturgesch.* 8, 1, 11, p. 85 and 86; for Caesar's *iter*, *ibid.*, p. 126; for Persius', see Schanz 8, 2, 2 p. 8. Cinna and Persius may have been influenced by the Lucilian model. Thus Cichorius, *op. cit.*, p. 259 compares Lucilius 1309: *mali superat carchesia* with Cinna fragment 4 *summi* carchesia mali. For later ὁδοιπορικά see Marx' commentary on *fragment* 96, and Lejay, Introduction to *Satire*, pp. 140-142.

[213] Marx' conjectural development of the scene may seem overbold, but in any case the word *cerebrosus* is Lucilian.

[214] Marx argues that this rest took place at Capua; see his commentary on 117; Cichorius, *op. cit.*, p. 254 at the inn on the promontory of Palinurus.

[215] We might associate line 115 with line 117 of Lucilius and compare both with Horace 70:

> prorsus iucunde cenam producimus illam.

Consequently it might be a natural conjecture to believe that in Lucilius also the contest was in connection with a dinner.

[216] Cf. Cichorius, op. cit. 253.

[217] If the studies of Dieterich are correct, Pulcinella, pp. 94, 194, 237, Cicirrus is the name of the rôle of Messius in a fabula Atellana. This is made probable by the gloss of Aeschius: κικιρρός, ἀλεκτρυών. This character which wore a mask with extended beak was perhaps the progenitor of Pulcinella. In the libri physiognomi we find notice of this typical character, the man-cock. I am inclined to believe that Messius wore some sort of rude mask and high shoes, a costume which Sarmentus parodies in line 64 by comparing it with the conventional tragic costume. Accordingly he challenges Messius to dance the latest character dance of the metropolis, the Cyclops, and declares he will not need his tragic mask and cothurni for that rôle. Above in line 56 we may assume that Sarmentus is thinking of the long beak of the cock, which to spite Messius he says looks like the horn of a unicorn. In line 58 when Messius moves his head up and down, he is carrying out the convention of the cock's character. See Lejay, op. cit., p. 159, for the cock according to the Anonymous de physiog. 13, is: capite parvo mobili. The reference of Sarmentus is, however, not merely to the cock's beak, but also to the actual physical deformity of the Oscan scurra, the great scar left on his forehead from the removal of a wen. This morbus Campanus made Messius look like an animal which had been dehorned or like the Cyclops with shaggy brow and single eye. Samentus virtually says then: Drop your mask and your foolish rôle of cock. In your own person you are more like the wild horse, dehorned and harmless, or you can without any mask appear as the Cyclops with your shaggy scar, which looks like a single eye in your forehead. Similarly in line 65, Cicirrus's retort is an allusion to the servile origin of Sarmentus, who is really a libertus, but is called a fugitivus.

[218] I accept the conjecture of Turnebus as the most probable restoration for the corrupt Novitlanus. Marx's commentary ad loc. suggests Novi<Ae>clanus.

[219] See the scriptor Physiognomicus quoted by Marx, ad loc.

[220] See Heinze-Kiessling[4] on line 54.

[221] In view of the comparison, ut dimidiatus porcus Iltgen, op. cit., p. 11, is more likely to be right in assigning the fragment to book 3 than Marx in assigning it to book 5. It is difficult to connect this fragment with 15, 480 ff. since in line 482 Lucilius appears to have completed the enumeration of the physical appearance of the Cyclops and then passes on to his staff, bacillus.

[222] Lejay, op. cit., p. 137 suggests, though doubtfully, that the Syra of Lucilius: ait eu plus de complaisance que la mendax puella de Trivicum.

[223] So Marx, ad loc. and Cichorius, op. cit., p. 255. Tantalus was a favorite Cynic-Stoic type of punishment. See also Horace, sat. 1, 1, 68 and pp. 200 and 226 supra.

[204] Dousa compared this line with Horace's lines 84, 85, and L. Mueller assigned it to book 3. So also Cichorius, *op. cit.*, p. 255, n. 3. This seems more probable to me than Marx' reference to the line to Horace, *sat.* 1, 3, 90.

[205] Perhaps Archestratus was the first to employ this pedantry. *Cf.* Heinze-Kiessling, *ad loc.* See also *infra*, p. 334 on Horace's ninth satire, line 69.

[206] *Cf.* Cichorius, *op. cit.*, p. 260 on these fragments, 107, 114, 123, 124, 126.

[207] Iltgen, *op. cit.*, pp. 9-13, discusses the relations of Lucilius to Horace's fifth satire. Some of his parallels have been accepted by others. I have indicated above those that seem to me sound. I must reject, however, either as "forced" or as resting on insufficient evidence the following: $127 - 12$; $1255 - 18$. The study of E. Desjardins, *Voyage D'Horace à Brindes*, in *Revue de Philologie*, vol. II, 1878, pp. 144-175; of H. Duntzer, *Eine Reisesatire und eine Reise-epistel des Horaz*, in *Philologus*, vol. 55, 1896, pp. 256 ff.; of A. Bischoff, *De Itinere Horati Brundisino*, Progr. Landau, 1880, do not treat of Lucilius book 3.

SATIRE 6

[208] As Hendrickson has seen. *Cf.* Hendrickson, *A. J. P.*, vol. 23, pp. 388-399.

[209] *Op. cit.*, pp. 181-192. In pp. 183-192 Cichorius endeavors to show with considerable plausibility that the new patron addressed is C. Sempronius Tuditanus, the victor of the Istrian war. The other lines, however, which refer to our poet's relation with this patron and to this war seem not to have influenced Horace in this satire. See *infra*, pp. 375 ff.

[210] Here I strongly suspect the paraphrase of a Greek satiric commonplace in these lines of Lucilius and of Horace. In the Horatian passage the *vel merito* looks like a translation of a Greek commonplace akin to that found in *Phoenix of Colophon* line 96, καὶ μάλα δικαίως. I have not, however, discovered in Greek, the Horatian antithesis between satiric independence and *ambitio*. On the other hand, the Lucilian fragment with its antithesis of personal independence and wealth, seems to stand in a more or less close relation to the complex of commonplaces on this theme discussed by Gerhard, *op. cit.*, pp. 126 ff., lines 92-96, of the Phoenix fragment. Of course this does not exclude a personal allusion in the case of both Roman writers, for the Romans, as is well known, were wont to compare even their personal conditions with those of Greek writers in similar literary forms, wherever there was a convenient handle for such comparisons.

[211] On the estates of Lucilius see Marx, *Prolegomena* XX, and also Cichorius, *op. cit.*, pp. 22-29.

[212] Compare Chapter 1, *supra*, pp. 43 ff. *Fragment* 428 is referred by Marx to Horace, *sat.* 1, 4, 105 ff.

[213] Line 76 of this satire shows at least an external resemblance to Lucilius 425, as Iltgen noticed. In view of the isolation of this fragment in a satire in book 11, I am inclined to regard this resemblance as merely a

coincidence. The use of the third person *venit* is an insuperable objection to referring this line to Lucilius and the age is an unsuitable one for his arrival at Rome:

> inde venit Romam, tener ipse atque puellus.

[294] This description to book 30 perhaps finds support in the Lucilian echo in line 59, which also referred to riding in the country; *cf. supra,* p. 320 ff.

[295] *Op. cit.,* p. 194.

[296] *Cf. Juvenal* 3, 65.

[297] *De L. L.* 5, 153.

[298] In the following line Lucilius continued with some verb in the first person.

SATIRE 7

[299] *Op. cit.,* Introduction pp. xvii-xxii; also comment on 1, 7, p. 202.

[300] On the χρεία see Gerhard, *op. cit.,* pp. 248 ff., 269 ff.; *supra,* pp. 158-162.

[301] *Supra,* pp. 156-158.

[302] *E.g.,* Euripides and Aeschylus in the *Frogs,* 1378-1499; the Good and the Bad Argument in the Clouds 889-1104. On the ἀγών in the Old Comedy *cf.* Zielinski: *Gliederung der Altattischen Komödie,* pp. 79-119.

[303] The date is probably not earlier than the first half of 119 or later than the first half of 118 B.C.

[304] *Cf.* Cichorius, *op. cit.,* pp. 237-251 for a detailed discussion of the Lucilian lines.

[305] See Kiessling-Heinze⁴, *op. cit.,* Introduction to *Satire.*

[306] Notice that the *fandam atque auditam* are in harmony with the technical definition of the χρεία given *supra,* p. 158.

[307] *Cetera* seems out of place in this inventory of abstract terms of abuse. Cichorius, *op. cit.,* p. 230, n. 1 prefers to read *icterus* with *Scaliger.*

[308] Cichorius, *op. cit.,* pp. 239-240.

[309] Cichorius assigns to the invective of Albucius, *fragments* 62, 63, 57-59, 66, 67, 71, 72, 73, 78-80, 81, 82, 83. See pp. 238-241; against Montanus 61, 70, 56; to the invective of Scaevola, 88, 84, 86, 87, 94. To the narrative speech of Scaevola in his own defence, 64, 65, 60, 61, 51, 58.

[310] So Iltgen.

[311] With *ergo praetor Athenis* compare Horace's *mise-en-scène,* (18), *Bruto praetore tenente ditem Asiam.*

SATIRE 8

[312] Iltgen, *op. cit.,* pp. 16-17, tries, unsuccessfully in my opinion, to prove the Lucilian provenance of this satire. He cites the following fragments which I give in the order of their supposed Horatian correspondence: 1031 and 1066=77 ff.; 1218=25; 1110=27; 999, 949=32 ff.; 1095=33; 1058=37 ff.; 1170=contents of magic brew; 1075=40. These parallels are, however, strained. Some of these fragments are better referred to other Horatian contexts; others have since found more apt explanations in the commentaries of Marx and Cichorius. Buecheler in

his *Vindiciae Priapeorum, Rh. Mus.*, vol. XVIII, 1863, p. 381, shows that Afranius is the first Roman even to mention Priapus. Hence the development of the genre was probably post-Lucilian.

SATIRE 9

[283] For similar character studies in Greek satire *cf.* the φιλοψευδής and ἀπιστῶν of Lucian. *Cf.* also Geffcken, *op. cit.*, p. 491.

[284] Translation of the *Character of Theophrastus*, p. 101.

[285] See Lejay's comment on satire, p. 230.

[286] See Charak. λαλίας VII, 3, ed. Diels.

[287] *Op. cit.*, pp. 18 and 19.

[288] See Marx, comment. *ad loc.* for this sense of *intorquet*; also Cicero, *Tuscl. Disp.* IV, 36, 77.

[289] *Cf.* Jebb's edition, p. 102.

[290] With σχολή *cf.* the *otium* of Lucilius' line 1140.

[291] Both Cichorius, *op. cit.*, p. 101 and Marx argue that the use of present *intorquet* means that the line must have been written in the lifetime of Scipio, but I believe we should rather regard the present tense here as the universal literary present, related with *dicto*, what Lane, Latin grammar 1591, calls the annalistic present used to note brief historical or personal memoranda. The present tense therefore does not militate against an assignment to book 6, written after Scipio's death. A further argument for placing the fragment in book 6 is to be found in the resemblance between the initial movement of the Horatian line and the Lucilian *ibam forte domum*.

[292] So Iltgen, p. 19.

[293] Iltgen. p. 19.

[294] One is inclined to read *me* in this line with Lucian Mueller.

[295] I take *re* as genitive parallel to *fortunae*. Nonius saw that it must be so construed, but did not understand the form. See p. 50a, 21: *Ablativus pro genetivo.*

[296] I believe that *potiri* is correctly restored, but instead of *pacis* I should prefer some word which would imply membership in a close circle of friends. Perhaps by a natural extension of meaning *pax* might be applied to the harmonious relations uniting the members of the Scipionic circle.

[297] So for example in Samuel Johnson's *London*, the Frenchman is substituted for the Greek of Juvenal's third satire.

[298] Iltgen, p. 19 refers to this context the scene in book 18, 552, where also we have the *iniectio manus*, but the reference there is clearly to a master and a slave.

SATIRE 10

[299] On this satire see the important article by Hendrickson, *Horace and Lucilius; A Study of Horace Serm.* 1, 10, in *Studies in Honor of Gildersleeve*, pp. 151-168; and *Horace and Valerius Cato*, in *C. P.* XI, pp. 249-269, XII, pp. 77-92, 329-330. In these three articles Hendrickson successfully establishes the genuineness of the initial verses 1-8, and shows the conflict

between the stylistic ideals of Horace and those of the *Novi poetae* and Valerius Cato. Ullman in *C. P.*, X, pp. 270-296, considers the identity of .Tigellius, and the relationship between the stylistic ideals of Catullus and Horace. While he overstates the case for the identity of ideals between Horace and the *Novi poetae*, his article is of great value for the demonstration of the Atticizing tendencies of both writers.

[270] As Hendrickson has demonstrated, *loc. cit. passim*. See also Marx, *Prolegomena*, p. li. Here Marx rightly emphasizes the fact that Lucilius, who was the uncle of Pompey's mother, had come to be regarded as the special favorite of the grammarians of the house of Pompey and of the Pompeian adherents.

[271] Cichorius, *op. cit.*, pp. 193-215.

[272] See 35-39 of this satire. This passage involves a restatement of certain passages showing Lucilian coloring already treated in the fourth satire. See *supra*, pp. 288 f.

[272] As Hendrickson has seen in the third of his articles on Horace and Valerius Cato, which discusses *The Neoteric Poets and the Latin Purists*, in *C. P.*, XII, pp. 329-350.

[274] See *supra*, pp. 109 ff.

[275] See *supra*, pp. 111 ff.

[276] See Cichorius, *op. cit.*, pp. 22-29 on the estates of Lucilius.

[277] See *supra*, pp. 117 ff. on the titles given to his works by Lucilius.

[278] On the other hand the *Ars Poetica* of Horace is permeated with this doctrine of appropriateness as Hack has shown. See his article, *The Doctrine of the Literary Forms*, in *Harvard Studies in Classical Philology*, XXVII, pp. 21 ff. On the Lucilian influence on the form and content of the *Ars Poetica* and the possible Panaetian influence upon this doctrine of propriety see *infra*, pp. 446 ff. *passim*.

[279] See the article by Jackson on *Molle atque Facetum*, vol. cit., pp. 132-137 for an interesting analysis of the passages in which Horace asserts his general sympathy with the theory of the plain style.

[280] Marx 1322. Cichorius, *op. cit.*, pp. 16 and 348 f.

[281] *Supra*, pp. 90 ff.

[282] *Op. cit.*, pp. 77 ff.

[283] On Homer see 480; on Ennius 1190 and *cf.* Marx, *Index Auctorum s.v.* Ennius; on Accius, 148, 348, 384, 794, and in book 30, 1028. Also Cichorius, *op. cit.* index *s.v.* Accius.

[284] Line 52 is addressed to the champion of Lucilius. It seems probable that Horace wishes to remind him that his master Lucilius had not believed that Homer was impeccable. Thus we read in line 345 from book 9 of Lucilius on the distinction between *poema* and *poesis*:

> nemo qui culpat Homerum
> perpetuo culpa, nequequod dixi ante poesin:
> versum unum culpat, verbum, entymema
> *locum* <unum.>

[285] On 1028 *op. cit.*, p. 205; on 794 *op. cit.*, pp. 153 ff.

[286] *A. J. P.*, vol. 26, pp. 1-21; on the recitations at the *collegium* see pp. 18 ff.   Sihler does not cite these two fragments of Lucilius.

[287] *Cf.* Horace, *sat.* 1, 4, 39 and *supra*, pp. 288 ff. for Horace's use of the more literary implications in Lucilius' line 1028.

[288] See Heinze-Kiessling, comment. *ad loc.*

[289] Comment on Lucilius 348 ff.

[290] See *supra*, pp. 293 ff.

[291] It is worth noticing, however, that while Lucilius in this, his first satire, speaks hesitatingly about his ability to win the approval of the Scipionic circle, Horace speaks with confidence in this, his concluding satire of the first book of the approval already given his form by the men of letters in the circle of Maecenas.   Here, then, we seem to have a deliberate contrast with Lucilius to the advantage of Horace.   On these Lucilian fragments see Fairclough, *Horace's View on the Relations between Satire and Comedy*, in *A. J. P.*, vol. 34, p. 191.

CHAPTER V

THE SATIRES OF BOOK II

Horace published the second book of satires in the year 30 B.C. During the interval of five years since the publication of the first book the passions aroused by the controversy as to the merits of Lucilian satire had cooled. The publication of the first book of the satires had at least settled the question that a revival of the Lucilian genre in the sense apparently advocated by Valerius Cato and his followers among the *novi poetae* and professional Grecizing critics[1] was no longer possible. Satire must be modified in diction, style, and tone to make it acceptable to the more urbane Augustan age. In these essential points Horace, not his opponents, had carried the day. And yet Horace himself had probably come to feel that the strictures of these opponents that his work was *nimis acer*[2] were in some measure justified. No longer could he regard as truly Augustan such direct Lucilian studies as the second satire or such bitterly waged literary controversies as that contained in the tenth satire. His position in the circle of Maecenas was now assured. The time was now ripe, therefore, for a more dispassionate statement of Horace's views upon Lucilius and his work, for a judgment matured by a larger experience with life, and moulded by contemporary criticism. It was especially necessary in publishing a second collection of satires in the Lucilian form to emphasize again the fact that his previous criticism had in the main been based on aesthetic rather than on ethical grounds.[3] Again, the consciousness that the public had recognized Horace's mastery of the satiric form made it unnecessary to repeat for a third time his unchanging belief that brevity and discrimination of phrase, carefulness of finish, variety of movement, and urbane restraint were aesthetic elements essential to satire.

On the other hand, Horace now found himself in complete sympathy with two essential characteristics of Lucilian satire. In the first place, Lucilius had learned from his studies in the Old Comedy and in the loose satiric forms of the popular Cynic and Stoic philosophers to imitate the παρρησία of his older masters and the didactic frankness of these later masters. This appears in his outspoken attack upon Accius, Afranius, and other literary opponents,[4] in the virulence of such political satires as those against Lupus and Metellus, and in his strictures upon the political incapacity of the nobility and the populace.[5] On the other hand, like the literary and moral censors of every age, he tolerated no attack upon himself. This we may see from the libel suit brought before the court of Caelius against a comic poet who had assailed him by name.[6]

In the first satire of the second book, then, Horace asserts the satirist's right to freedom of speech. He makes this right essential to the very existence of satire. Stylistically, however, he finds it necessary to reemphasize the fundamental difference between the grand style of epic and the studied informality of the conversational satire or *sermo* written in the plain style. In line 12 he too makes the acknowledgment which had become a literary convention in the Augustan age that his powers are inadequate for epic:

> cupidum, pater optime, vires
> deficiunt.

In frank assertion and in disclaimer Horace can be shown to be following a traditional treatment of this scheme found in a satire in Lucilius, book 26.[7]

But the legal conditions under which satire could be produced in the Augustan age formed a very real restriction upon the freedom of speech traditional in satire. We are upon the eve of the stricter interpretation and application of the laws for libel and *maiestas*. There is a touch of serious anxiety beneath the jest upon the *mala* and *bona carmina* with which the satire closes.[8]

In the second place Lucilius made his satire a medium of personal confession. He frankly reveals his personal habits and life, his views upon contemporary men and manners. This characteristic sprang from the utter sincerity of the man. It is, however, probably not fanciful to regard it as influenced by Lucilius' acquaintance with the Greek ὑπομνήματα,[9] as developed in the popular philosophic literature of Cynics and Stoics. Horace also found himself in perfect accord with this more amiable characteristic of Lucilian satire. He thus established the note of personal confession as a part of the tradition of the satiric genre. His dependence upon Lucilius in this respect is frankly recognized in this satire in lines 28–34.

In frankness of speech and fullness of self-revelation, therefore, Horace asserts that he is the spiritual heir of Lucilius. In coupling these two points together Horace seems to be following no direct Lucilian model, though he draws freely from material found in Lucilius, books 26 and 30.[10] Thus Lucilius also seems to have defended his right to the fullest and freest criticism of contemporary life, advancing the plea that everything that he wrote was an inevitable expression of his nature. In this general sense we may consider that certain portions of these satires have influenced this satire of Horace,[11] to which I now turn.

I begin with a consideration of two points related rather to the general atmosphere and setting of the satire than to any question of direct verbal imitation. These are (1) the origin of the legal setting of the Horatian satire, and (2) the origin of the passages in which Horace expresses his creed that satiric freedom of utterance must be maintained because it is an assertion of the right of freedom of thought and of sincerity.

In the fifth satire, book 30, lines 1078–1098, we have a number of fragments dealing with political and legal questions, which may have suggested the legal setting of Horace's satire. These fragments 1089, 1088, 1093, 1098, 1078, have been brilliantly and convincingly interpreted by Cichorius,[12] as referring to the political events between the years 129 and 123 B.C. Thus 1089 refers to the undue severity meted out to the revolting allies by the destruction of Fregellae. 1088 refers to the passage of the *Lex Iunia Penni* in 126 B.C., by which the Italian allies resident at Rome lost legal status, and were ordered to be deported. 1093 and 1098 refer to the death of Scipio, and to the unfair charges of tyranny made against him in his lifetime. 1078 refers to his services in the cavalry, *equo publico*.

Now it is obvious that the prevalence at Rome of such an embittered public opinion against Italians would be most unfavorable to Lucilius, and especially would tend to restrict his freedom as a satirist. Marx,[13] indeed, believes that Lucilius was

an Italian, not a Roman citizen, in which case his position since
the death of Scipio would be especially precarious. Cichorius,[14]
however, asserts that Lucilius was a Roman citizen. Whichever
may be the correct view, it is certain that Lucilius was silent
from 123 B.C., the period just after the passage of the *Lex Iunia
Penni* until 119 B.C., when the second book of the satires
appeared. It therefore seems probable to me that this fifth
satire of book 30, written between 129 and 123, connected
these references to political conditions at Rome, so inimical to
bold political criticism, with the idea that in this period of
enforced silence, so clearly approaching, Lucilius should write a
personal epic to celebrate the exploits of Sempronius Tuditanus
in the Istrian war.[15] Lucilius, while courteously rejecting such
an idea (1086), apparently reasserted passionately his intention
to continue as the guardian of political and social morality. We
should then have a legal and literary situation of some general
similarity to that which Horace in conscious recollection of his
great predecessor seeks to paraphrase at the beginning of the
second book.

From this point of view Lejay's summary of the libel laws of
Rome gains new point. Later in the reign of Augustus, Cassius
Severus[16] was actually banished for defamatory writings and the
lex maiestatis revived. Even before that period there must have
been an influential body of public opinion inimical to freedom
of speech. As Lejay says:[17] Le satire des moeurs privées
exposait à des risques definis. Si l'on nommait des personnes
vivantes, comme faisait Horace, on pouvait toujours être
conduit devant le préteur. C'est sur ce point que le poete veut
consulter Trebatius. That Horace felt this danger is shown by
the limited extent to which he indulged in the *satire des moeurs
privées* in the second book, as tested by the investigation of
Filbey.[18] Again Seneca *de beneficiis* 3, 27, 1 tells us that: sub
divo Augusto nondum hominibus verba sua periculosa erant,
iam molesta. The immediate cause of Horace's first satire,
then, was perhaps a desire to make the traditional satiric plea
for freedom of speech in the form of a humorous sally against
undue sensitiveness to the application of the laws on *mala
carmina*. Trebatius Testa, equally famous as a learned
iuris consultus and as a humorist, was a happy foil for the figure

of the anxious satirist. No one could better suggest to Roman
readers the attitude which Horace believed the law should take.
Perhaps it was still early enough to laugh away repressive
tendencies which might later become dangerous to the state
and the individual.[19] At any rate, in dedicating the second
book of his satires, Horace could define his own position on the
great question of satiric freedom of speech in a satire which
would recall to all the attitude taken by Lucilius in one of his
boldest satires, written at a critical period for himself and the
state.

But free speech is endurable only upon the assumption of ·
complete sincerity of motive, and upon complete revelation of
the speaker's most intimate ideals in regard to the social and
ethical problems of his day. This is the atmosphere which
pervades both the satires in book 26 and in book 30 of Lucilius
and this satire of Horace.

In two passages in the first satire of book 26, Lucilius
asserted that his message was sincere for it came from the
heart and must therefore be delivered and heard, whatever its
literary form might be. These fragments are 590 and 631.
590 is as follows:[20]

> ego ubi quem ex praecordiis
> ecfero versum.

In 631 we find expressed the same moral compulsion to satiric
composition coupled with the conventional satiric indifference
to artistic expression:

> — ◡ evadet saltem aliquid aliqua, quod conatus sum.

Similarly, Horace, though with ironic reserve, asserts in
three passages that he will follow Lucilius in the faithful trans-
cription of life as he sees it. Thus in line 6 when Trebatius
Testa categorically advises him not to write satire he answers:

> peream male, si non
> optimum erat: verum nequeo dormire.

In lines 24 to 34 he shows that all men are allowed to follow
their bent. Why then should he who has a knack for simple
metrical composition after the style of Lucilius be checked?

With this Horatian context we may compare[21] Lucilius 628
and 629 where Lucilius similarly invokes the argument of

diversity of tastes and implies his own insufficiency [for the task of epic composition?]. These Lucilian lines read:

> ut ego effugiam quod te in primis cupere apisci intellego,
> et quod tibi magno opere cordiest, mihi vementer displicet.

The Horatian lines are:

> Quid faciam? saltat Milonius ut semel icto
> accessit fervor capiti numerusque lucernis:
> Castor gaudet equis ovo prognatus eodem
> pugnis: quot capitum vivunt, totidem studiorum
> milia: me pedibus delectat claudere verba
> Lucili ritu.

Horace then continues in line 34 with the famous eulogy of Lucilian satire as "a human document":[22]

> ille velut fidis arcana sodalibus olim
> credebat libris, neque si male cesserat usquam
> decurrens alio neque si bene; quo fit ut omnis
> votiva pateat veluti descripta tabella
> vita senis. sequor hunc Lucanus an Appulus anceps.

That is Horace follows Lucilius in the faithful transcription of the life of his times. So also in lines 57–60 Horace asserts that he will write, whatever the circumstances of his life, whatever the color of his fate may be:

> seu me tranquilla senectus
> exspectat seu Mors atris circumvolat alis,
> dives, inops, Romae seu fors ita iusserit exsul,
> quisquis erit vitae scribam color.

I turn next to certain passages where we evidently have a more direct use of Lucilian material. In view of the meagreness of our testimony, it is impossible to decide with certainty whether Horace "contaminated" material from two Lucilian passages in book 26, satire 1, and book 30, satire 5, or whether he imitated the latter book alone. In this case we should have to regard the resemblance to 26, 620, 621, 622, as due to the fact that Lucilius twice treated the same theme of the incapacity of the satirist to compose epic poetry. To me it seems probable that Horace had both passages in mind though it is of course now no longer possible to say which his paraphrase resembled the more.

The three fragments of book 26 occur, as Cichorius first showed,[23] in an εἰσαγωγή addressed to a young historian, Iunius Congus, in which the poet urges his young friend to abandon ancient history for the more profitable epic treatment of some contemporary event, the battle of Popilius Laenas and the deeds of Cornelius Scipio. Lucilius asserts that such a composition is contrary to his nature.[24]

The situation in lines 1079–1087 is, as we have just seen, not dissimilar, except that there Lucilius himself considers the problem of his capacity for epic composition. The poet evinces a clear feeling that an attempt to celebrate the warlike exploits of his new patron (C. Sempronius Tuditanus) in the Istrian wars (?) in an encomiastic epic would benefit his literary and social position, the same attitude taken by Trebatius Testa in the interview with Horace. Now that Scipio was dead Lucilius was left unprotected and was exposed to some danger as the result of the irritated state of public feeling against the Latins and the *socii*. We even have a tentative effort in the epic, an untried form for Lucilius, which he will not venture upon seriously.

Now both groups of fragments stand in especially close relation to the treatment of the same theme in Horace's satire lines 11–17. There Horace is advised to sing the exploits of Caesar, a more profitable form of composition than satire. Horace too, like Lucilius gives an example of what he might do in epic in the way of eulogy of a patron, were not his whole heart in satire. All the fragments in question show close correspondence. Thus in 621 an encomiastic epic is suggested upon the fight of Popilius and the deeds of Scipio:

> percrepa pugnam Popili, facta Corneli cane.

Similarly in 1079 from book 30, the bold exploits of Sempronius Tuditanus seem to the poet like the forlorn hope led by the tribune Caelius, a proper epic theme, treated by Ennius in the sixteenth book of his annals:

> ut semel in pugnas, Caeli, te invadere vidi.

So Trebatius Testa proposing to Horace the composition of an epic upon the exploits of Augustus says, lines 10–11:

> aut si tantus amor scribendi te capit aude
> Caesaris invicti res dicere.

In the second place epic themes are profitable and bring renown besides. So Lucilius 620:

> hunc laborem sumas laudem qui tibi ac fructum ferat.

In 1085 and 1084, Lucilius, as Cichorius shows, first emphasizes his conviction that such a theme is beyond his powers; let one suited to such a famous composition soon appear. He then asserts that such memorials of the valor of the general are being established on the firm foundation of literature 1084. Thus 1085:[25]

> et virtute tua et claris conducere cartis.

and 1084:

> haec virtutis tuae <c>artis monumenta locantur.

So Horace in line 11:

> Caesaris invicti res dicere, multa laborum
> praemia laturus.' cupidum, pater optime, vires.
> deficiunt.

So in 622 Lucilius expresses his incapacity for epic composition:

> ego si, qui sum et quo folliculo nunc sum indutus, non queo.

This is in thought identical with Horace's lines just quoted.

Nevertheless, both Lucilius in 1085, 1089, 1080, 1081, 1095, and Horace in lines 13–15 make informal attempts in the epic manner. Lucilius prefaces his attempt in 1086 with the frank statement that this is all that is to be expected of him for the present.[26]

> his te versibus interea contentus teneto.

He then begins with an expression of his desire to write in the epic strain 1008:

> quantum haurire animus Musarum e fontibus gestit.

In 1080 he shows how this desire was brought to decision by the fame of the glorious battle:

> sicubi ad auris
> fama tuam pugnam <prae> claram adlata dicasset.

and the prodigies of endurance undergone by the commander, 1082:

> quantas quoque modo aerumnas quantosque labores,
> exanclaris.

1094[27] perhaps contained a picture of the dazzling effect of the battle line upon the eyes of the beholders:

> praestringat oculorum aciem splendore micanti.

So Horace in 13–15 essays the epic manner with a description of battle:

> neque enim quivis horrentia pilis
> agmina nec fracta pereuntia cuspide Gallos
> aut labentis equo describit volnera Parthi.

Trebatius Testa then urges Horace, lines 16 ff., at least to celebrate the justice and bravery of Caesar as Lucilius celebrated Scipio in his satires:[28]

> attamen et iustum poteras et scribere fortem
> Scipiadam ut sapiens Lucilius.

In lines 40–56 in a series of similes Horace then retraverses the traditional theme that satire is the natural weapon of the satirist, and that therefore he cannot be blamed for using it. He asserts, however, that his own satire will be used only for defensive purposes, but that as he will not hold back when attacked his enemies will rue the day when they arouse him. Here then we have a restatement in somewhat altered form of the doctrine already familiar to us from the fourth and tenth satires of the first book and from the satires in Lucilius book 30. The present satire of Horace contains rather a freely wrought summary of this satiric commonplace already familiar to us than any deliberate imitation of Lucilius.[29]

In line 60–79 Horace ironically denies that his freedom of speech can injure him in the eyes of this patron by referring to the perfect harmony that existed between Lucilius and the members of the Scipionic circle notwithstanding—but in reality, of course, on account of—Lucilius' attacks on the enemies of that circle, Metellus,[30] Lupus,[31] the corrupt nobles,[32] and the people tribe by tribe.[33] However, he adds in line 70:

> scilicet uni aequus virtuti atque eius amicis.

This is, of course, a direct allusion to the famous fragment of
Lucilius on virtue, 1326 ff., which may have stood in one of the
satires of book 30. Horace seems to have lines 1334 ff. especi-
ally in mind:

> hostem esse atque inimicum hominum morumque malorum.
> contra defensorem hominum morumque bonorum
> hos magni facere, his bene velle, his vivere amicum.

We may notice also incidentally that in this fragment Lucilius,
like Horace, affects to act on the defensive, and like him asserts
the closeness of his relationship with the *boni viri* who comprise
the most aristocratic circle of the day.

Thus the whole passage from 62–74 presents those aspects of
Lucilius' character which won him the liking of all Romans, as a
hard-hitting and cultivated gentleman of the old school. We
have, however, no direct imitation until we come to line 85.
There I believe that Horace fully conscious of Lucilius' employ-
ment of the stock Cynic metaphor of the κύων who bites and
barks for the good of his friends and disciples, but only against
the wicked gives his own free paraphrase of the commonplace.
Thus Lucilius in line 1095:[34]

> inde canino ritu oculisuqe
> involem.

And Horace 84-85:

> si quis
> opprobriis dignum latraverit integer ipse?

With this fragment my analysis of this satire closes. To me
it seems evident that the fifth satire of book 30 was its principal
model as seen by the use direct or indirect of lines 1078, 1088,
1089 for legal setting; 1079, 1080, 1082, 1084, 1085, 1086, 1094,
1095 for imitation of the first formulation of the stock theme of
the contrast of epic with satiric composition. Certain other lines
from book 26 were also used viz.: 590, 633, 669(?), 675(?), 621,
620, 622 mainly to contrast the tone of satiric and of epic compo-
sition and their rewards.

SATIRE 2

Just as in satire 1, 2 Horace applied in a form suited to Roman
tradition the Aristotelian theory of "the mean" to the sexual
passion, so in the second satire of this book he applies the same

theory to the pleasures of the table. Just as there his doctrine, though ultimately derived from Aristotle, may be more immediately traced to the Epicurean classification of pleasures,[35] so here he endeavors to establish the true norm of diet, midway between sordidness on the one hand (53–69, 82, 88) and meaningless show, κενοδοξία, on the other (25–26). Especially does excess on the side of κενοδοξία bring the traditional penalties of Cynics and Stoics, infamy and loss, (dedecus damnum). The observance of the right mean in diet brings the same result as the like procedure in the matter of sex as indicated in 1, 2;[36] in fama (94), res (98) and in addition in good health, (70–81) especially menaced by gluttony. The practical conclusions on this subject of diet are the same as those of satire 1, 2; we must grant nature satisfactions that are εὐπόριστα, easy to secure (15–20). The very human Horace even permits occasional indulgences (83, 116–122).

In this satire Ofellus is a Romanized counterpart of the popular Cynic preacher, who is used as the mouthpiece for Horace's own philosophical ideas, just as Horace's father was in satire, 1, 4.[37] He is represented as a rude, but sturdy Italian peasant, now a tenant farmer, but in his more prosperous days, a peasant proprietor. Hense has shown that it is a favorite device in the Cynic διατριβαί to oppose the plain, rude peasant, the type of the natural man of the Cynics to the "high liver."[38] Moreover the later Stoics, and indeed the Epicureans themselves, as is well known, sought to inculcate an irrational asceticism,[39] which could be more easily criticized by Horace under the disguise of Ofellus.

Under his Roman exterior, however, Ofellus unmasks[40] a moral discourse which perfectly accords with the manner of the popular Cynic preacher. He is even called, as was the boast of the Cynics, an abnormis sapiens.[41] His discourse like the διατριβαί of the Cynics is a violent harangue (8–69; 94–111). The speech bristles with rhetorical questions (27–28, 31–33, 48, 76–77, 86–88, 127–128). Some of these, as is the habit with preachers, are uttered only to be immediately answered by the speaker (7–8, 18–20, 35–37, 63–64).[42]

I have endeavored to set forth briefly the subject of the satire, and to describe the personality of the preacher. I will next speak of the Greek sources of the satire.

In general it may be said that the satire skilfully interweaves
into a harmonious whole a number of commonplaces of the
popular philosophic teachings of Epicureans, Cynics, and
Stoics. This makes anything like dogmatism in the attribution
of Greek sources dangerous. Nor is it within my scope to ana-
lyze such sources of Lucilius and Horace in detail. It will be
necessary, however, to summarize briefly the most marked lines
of relationship.

In the first place the satire seems to follow, in some measure,
though with artistic informality, the epistolary scheme of the
letter of Epicurus to Menoecus.[43] Thus: καὶ μᾶζα καὶ
ὕδωρ τὴν ἀκροτάτην ἀποδίδωσιν ἡδονήν, ἐπειδὰν ἐνδέων τις αὐτὰ προ-
σενέγκηται (9-21), τὸ συνεθίζειν οὖν ἐν ταῖς ἁπλαῖς καὶ οὐ πολυτελέσι
διαίταις καὶ ὑγιείας ἐστὶ συμπληρωτικὸν (71-77), καὶ πρὸς τὰς ἀναγ-
καίας τοῦ βίου χρήσεις ἄοκνον ποιεῖ τὸν ἄνθρωπον (80-81), καὶ τοῖς
πολυτελέσιν ἐκ διαλειμμάτων προσερχομένους κρεῖττον ἡμᾶς, διατίθησι
(82-88), καὶ πρὸς τὴν τύχην ἀφόβους παρασκευάζει. The Hora-
tian satire is, of course, not a bald reiteration of such
dogmatic ethics, but an application of them to life, and a
justification of them on the basis of common human experience.
Hence we have[44] several illustrations, features not found in
Epicurus.

It is, however, a nice question to determine how much
Horace owes to the direct use of Epicurean material, how much
to the popularization of such teachings in the philosophical
works of Cicero, who certainly played a large part as a mediat-
ing agent between the Epicureans and Horace. Thus the
commonplace that hunger is the best sauce is found in Cicero *de
finibus* 2, 90, Cicero *Tuscl. disp.* 5, 90, and in Horace lines 10,
14, 9-21, 21-32, 77-79. The praise of poverty, a widely spread
commonplace in the schools of Greek philosophy, is found in
Cicero *Tusculan Disputations* 5, 89, and in Horace lines 97-100.
From Cicero also came the use of *tenuis victus*,[45] plain living with
the connotation of high thinking. In fact, Lejay believes that:
Ciceron est peut-être encore plus complètement l'inspiration des
grandes lignes de la satire.

In the third place there seems to be some evidence that
there existed a διατριβή of Bion[46] represented also in the work
of Teles upon this very theme. Thus we find in Bion certain

commonplaces used in this satire. These are: (1) hunger is the best sauce (Horace 9–21); (2) our goods are a loan not a gift of fortune; τὰ χρήματα τοῖς πλουσίοις ἡ τύχη οὐ δεδώρηκεν ἀλλὰ δεδάνεικεν (Horace 129–130); (3) life is a war (Horace 111).

But when all is said this satire is rather encompassed by a great cloud of witnesses of the Cynic and Stoic persuasion than related to any one source or complex of related sources. An examination of the Cynic commonplaces collected and discussed by Gerhard in his *Phoenix von Kolophon* shows that the following Cynic Stoic commonplaces occur in this satire. (1) Pleasure after toil: ἡδοναὶ μετὰ τοὺς πόνους (*cf.* lines 9 and 30). The reason is that labor transforms itself into joy.[47] (2) The principle of εὐτέλεια thrift (*cf.* lines 70 ff.); this is rendered by *victus tenuis* in Horace, a regimen which escapes the penalties of gluttony.[48] (3) The Cynic "topic" that praise ἔπαινος,[49] is the sweetest feast for the human ear (*cf.* line 94). (4) The Cynic "topic"[50] that an evil reputation is an important punishment for sin (lines 94–99). (5) The ψόγος πλούτου or invective against wealth.[51]

The large mass of popular Greek philosophy implicit and explicit in this satire has unfortunately tended to obscure the fact that the mind of Lucilius was also steeped in these same Cynic teachings. Our satire, therefore, like the first satire of the first book, contains much Greek popular philosophy, but the application of these commonplaces of Cynic asceticism to satire was attempted long before Horace by Lucilius. Horace, therefore, in this satire as in the first satire of the first book, was quite familiar with these experiments in the form of Cynic *sermones* when he made his own study in the same form. Let us now examine in detail the passage found in Lucilius bearing upon this problem in the present satire.

In line 17 Horace refers to the proverb which declares that bread and salt were the simplest means of satisfying the gnawing stomach. Thus:

> cum sale panis
> latrantem stomachum bene leniet.

But this proverb was also well known to Lucilius, as we may see from line 813,[52] which occurs in the first satire of book 29,

where the rough but satisfying fare of the slave is jocosely
alluded to:

> ⏑ — ventrem alienum, maestum fovere ex molito hordeo
> uti cataplasma.

In lines 19–22 Horace expounds the theme that hunger is
the best appetizer. The pleasure of the culinary Epicurean in
detecting flavors in expensive foods is an over-refinement;
when he is fat and pale from over-indulgence he can no longer
enjoy the nicety of flavors:

> non in caro nidore voluptas
> summa sed in te ipso est. tu pulmentaria quaere
> sudando: pinguem vitiis albumque neque ostrea
> nec scarus aut poterit peregrina iuvare lagois.

We seem to have traces of a similar development in Lucilius'
book 9, the first satire. Probably[53] certain fragments of this
satire contained an attack on Lutatius Cerco, the younger, an
older contemporary of Lucilius, and a famous gourmet. Thus
Horace's generalization of a flavor that is expensive *caro nidore*
may be a generalization from a more concrete Lucilian illustra-
tion. So in 327, as Marx has shown, the reference is to buying
one hundred oysters at a high price, 1000 sesterces:

> tu milli nummum potes uno quaerere centum.

The following fragment 328 refers to the loss of pleasure because
the oysters to the over-nice palate of the gourmet have the
savor of the slime and mud of the river. In both Lucilius and
Horace, then, the context emphasizes the fact that the pleasures
of the table lose their edge. Hence Horace argues that a
simple diet should be preferred. This conclusion is not found
in our surviving Lucilian lines. Lucilius makes the feeling of
disgust arise from over-refinement of taste; Horace, as the
result of disease caused by high living. It may be that the
diseased old man in Lucilius' lines 331 and 332 was a former
glutton. Both use the oyster as an article of luxury. So
Lucilius:

> Quid *ergo*? si ostrea Cerco[54] . . . . .
> cognorit fluvium limam ac cenum sapere ipsum.

With this line should perhaps be joined 1106:

> anseris herbilis virus.

Here the point lies in the complaint that the goose has been fattened on herbs instead of carefully fattened in an enclosure on a special diet. Doubtless Cerco is still the subject with some such phrase as *aut si senserit* to be supplied. So Horace alludes to the flavor of the moorhen.

Five fragments from Lucilius book 27 seem to show that Lucilius wrote on a similar theme. This, indeed, was recognized by Marx, who in commenting on the book says: Agitur libro 27 (688–715) de fortuna humana et de vitae humanae vicissitudinibus quas aequo animo ferendas indicat secundum Archilochi praeceptum. . . . The general applicability of this summary to the *sermo* of Ofellus seems, however, to have escaped the notice of both Marx and Cichorius. Thus fragment 716 attacks κενοδοξία in the menu; 699 and 700 assert the necessity of courage and resignation; 701 reiterates the popular philosophic commonplace that fortune bestows her favors as a loan subject to call, not as a permanent possession. 704 denies, so far as the speaker is concerened, envy for the luxury of neighbors. As Horace has scattered his allusion to these points over the various parts of this satire and made occasional use of passages from other books of Lucilius as well, it will be most convenient to follow the order of his lines.

In line 716 Lucilius apparently asserted that the brilliant tail feathers of the cock were a matter of indifference to the cook provided the bird was fat. This Lucilian example of κενοδοξία is contemporized by Horace by the substitution of the peacock with his glittering tail, first introduced by Hortensius as an accessory of Roman table luxury. Otherwise we have close verbal imitation:[55]

cocus non curat caudam insignem esse illam, dum pinguis siet.
sic amici quaerunt animum, rem parasiti ac ditias.

And Horace lines 24–27:

vix tamen eripiam, posito pavone, velis quin
hoc potius quam gallina tergere palatum,
corruptus vanis[56] rerum; quia veneat auro
rara avis et picta pandat spectacula cauda:
tamquam ad rem attineat quicquam num vesceris ista
quam laudas pluma?

In Horace 31–32 we have another allusion to the over-refinement of the sense of taste which characterizes the Roman gourmet. This time he is able to detect by the flavor whether the *lupus* of the Tiber was caught up stream or between the two bridges near the *insula*—whence came the fattest fish—or at the mouth of the river. This is a direct imitation and expansion of a Lucilian passage, 1174–1176:[57]

> fingere praeterea, adferri quod quisque volebat.
> illum sumina ducebant atque altilium lanx,
> hunc pontes Tiberinus duo inter captus catillo.

Horace 31–32:

> unde datum sentis lapus hic Tiberinus an alto.
> captus hiet, pontisne inter iactatus an ammis
> ostia sub Tusci?

In line 46[58] Horace alludes to the huge sturgeon served by the parvenu Gallonius, a *praeco*, famous in the days of Lucilius. This scene, which is taken from one of the *cenae* or banquet satires of Lucilius, is found in Marx fragment 1238:

> 'O Publi, o gurges Galloni, es homo miser' inquit
> 'cenasti in vita numquam bene, cum omnia in ista
> consumis squilla atque acupensere cum decimano.

It seems possible that in this satire of Lucilius the praise of plain living was advocated by Laelius for it looks as if lines 1235–1237 were uttered in the same context with their praise of the humble sorrel. Gallonius may well have been one of the *gumiae* addressed in due order by Laelius.[59]

So Horace in line 45 gives us a direct allusion to the famous Lucilian scene:

> haud ita pridem
> Galloni praeconis erat acipensere mensa infamis.

In line 69 Horace borrows Naevius from Lucilius as a type of the *sordidus victus*. Thus Porphyrio on Horace *serm.* 1, 1, 101–102 where Naevius was also used as a type says: Naevius autem fuit in tantum parcus ut sordidus merito haberetur, Lucilio auctore. Hence Horace describes him as a *sordidus*, a type representing the excess of economy:

> nec sic ut simplex Naevius unctam
> convivis praebebit aquam: vitium hoc quoque magnum.[60]

In line 111 ff., Horace describes the simple unostentatious feast of Ofellus. The feasts are kept with a stranger or a neighbor when the rain prevents work in the fields. On these occasions raisins, nuts, and split figs constitute the *secunda mensa* or dessert. Thus in 121 ff.:

> tum pensilis uva secundis
> et nux ornabat mensas cum duplice ficu

So also shown in Lucilius 1101 we read of the *asiduas ficos*, the inevitable figs of the *cena rustica*. And in 1173 we read:

> fici comeduntur et uvae.

These two are the ingredients of the rustic banquet mentioned here.

The conclusion of Horace's satire lines 122–136 is certainly modelled on a corresponding passage in Lucilius book 27, although it is difficult in view of the general nature of the brief Lucilian fragments to make a line for line comparison. Ofellus here inculcates the doctrine of equanimity in the face of "the slings and arrows of outrageous fortune," and points out that human folly, and the fickleness of fortune make it impossible to believe that our property, so-called, is more than a loan.

The duty of courage tempered with resignation to the vicissitudes of fortune is enunciated by Horace in lines 126, 135, 136:

> saeviat atque novos moveat Fortuna tumultus.

and in 135–136:

> quocirca vivite fortes
> fortiaque adversis opponite pectora rebus.

So Lucilius in 699:

> re in secunda tollere animos, in mala demittere.

and in 700:

> ceterum quid sit quid non sit ferre aequo animo ac fortiter.

Probably also in 703 the vicissitudes of fortune were compared to the top of a shoe, narrower at the neck, so to speak, which is pulled up when you put the shoe on, that is assume fortune dropped down, that is the mind is resigned, when you take the shoe off.:[41]

> modo sursum modo deorsum tamquam collus cernui.

In view of the instability of fortune and the inconsistency of mankind, it is foolish to envy anyone in the temporary possession of wealth. This is the attitude of Ofellus to the soldier proprietor Umbrenus, who has displaced him in the ownership of his old farm (129–135):

> nam propriae telluris erum natura neque illum
> nec me nec quemquam statuit: nos expulit ille;
> illum aut nequities aut vafri inscitia iuris
> postremum expellat certe vivacior heres.

So the speaker in Lucilius can also say,[42] lines 704–705:

> nulli me invidere, non strabonem fieri saepius
> deliciis me istorum.

The reason for such an attitude is summed up in the popular Cynic proverb already quoted and found first in Bion, that the riches of the wealthy are a loan of fortune not a gift. This "topic" is found twice in Lucilius, once in this satire of book 27, line 701:

> cum sciam nihil esse in vita proprium mortali datum.

This fragment should clearly, I think, precede 704 and we should read the three lines continuously. The immediate relation of 701 is especially to Horace's line 129 as the use of *proprium* shows, but also to 133 and 134:

> num ager Umbreni sub nomine, nuper Ofelli
> dictus, erit nulli proprius, sed cedet in usum
> nunc mihi nunc alii.

The other passage is fragment 550 from book 16:[43]

> cetera contemnit et in usura omnia ponit
> non magna: proprium vero nil neminem habere.

To sum up the evidence of Horace's relationship to Lucilius in this second satire: in the first place we must observe that, like the first and second satires of the first book this satire represents a congeries of philosophical commonplaces.[44] In this satire the commonplaces are from the Cynic, Stoic, and Epicurean *armory* upon the *tenuis victus* as a necessary concomitant to the attainment of *virtus;* the whole fused into unity by the art of Horace. In these three satires, therefore, as well as in the third satire of his book which follows, the raw material is essentially

Greek, but the setting as always in Roman satire has been most skilfully nationalized, that is popularized to meet the taste of cultivated Augustan readers.

Horace, however, was not the first to draw upon this Greek store of proverbial ethics for we have abundant evidence that Lucilius in several satires went to the same sources for examples and precepts. Accordingly, Horace is influenced both by the original Greek form of these commonplaces, and also by their earlier employment in transmuted form in Lucilian satire.

We have ten fragments 813, 327, 328, 1106, 1174, 1238, 1181, 1101, 1173, 550 containing traditional commonplaces scattered through the satires of Lucilius. Of these fragments 1174 and 1181 are perhaps taken from a second banquet of Granius, parallel to that in book 20. Finally, the close of the Horatian satire, in which is emphasized the doctrine that the *tenuis victus* is a direct preparation to the attainment of ἀταραξία by building up an habitual indifference to the vicissitudes of capricious fortune is clearly modelled on portions of a Lucilian satire in book 27. In this satire Horace shows traces of the influence of fragments 716, 699, 700, 703, 704, 701 in the Lucilian exposition.

SATIRE 3

The third satire is a διατριβή or rather a satiric parody upon a Stoic διατριβή on the paradox πᾶς ἄφρων μαίνεται. The satire is designed, on the one hand, to give a picture of the various types of human folly engendered by the passions, on the other, to ridicule the exaggerated manner of the Stoic street preachers in attacking these passions. This secondary purpose becomes clear if we compare the treatment of avarice by Stertinius (82-162) with Horace's earlier treatment in the first satire of book one.[65]

The διατριβή, however, is not put directly into the mouth of Stertinius. Instead Damasippus, the converted spendthrift, whom he has saved from suicide, repeats the discourse which Stertinius delivered to him. By this device the διατριβή is made to fall under the category of ἀπομνημονεύματα, in which the disciple recounts the sayings of his master.[66] This form of setting makes it possible to satirize contemporary social phenomena without direct attack. Consequently, as we have seen,[67] it is employed by Horace several times in the second book.

Horace is at pains to combine the serious elements in the technique of such Stoic popular discourses with occasional persiflage at the pedantry or extravagance, well-nigh inevitable in their method. It will be worth our while to illustrate this feature of the satire by summarizing the essential points in Horace's method.[68]

In the first place the Stoic preachers begin their formal discourses with exact definition of their terms. So Stertinius defines madness in (41), and with reference to the traditional definition of the sect in (43-45).[69] In the second place, the Stoic method of proof is empiric. It is a $\phi\iota\lambda o\sigma o\phi\iota a$ $\epsilon\kappa$ $\tau a\rho a\delta\epsilon\iota\gamma\mu\acute{a}\tau\omega\nu$. Hence the larger the number of examples of madness cited and appraised the more cogent the nature of this inductive method.[70] Third, the tribunal to which the Stoic preacher appeals is the law of human nature, built up by the accumulated experience of the individual members of the human race, and expressed in public opinion. Compare the use of *dicatur* (108), *videatur* (120), *habebitur* (209).[71] Fourth, the Stoics have a fondness for the conditional rather than for the normal categorical syllogism (104-130; 208-218), and for argumentation on the basis of hypothetical examples (*e.g.*, 131-132, 159-160, 212-213, 219-220, 253, 272-275).[72] The technique of the Stoic dialectic is therefore observed by Horace.

In addition, Horace makes Stertinius observe the strongly marked stylistic mannerisms of the Stoic preachers. Such are (1) the use of sharp rhetorical questions often answered by the preacher himself (*e.g.*, 65, 89, 97, 157-160, 162, 200, 295);[73] (2) the use of a pseudo-dialogue, a sort of atrophied survival of the genuine Socratic dialectic, represented by the use of *inquam* (276), and interrupting interjections (117 and 160);[74] (3) the use of a shadowy *adversarius*, a shifting personality, but usually regarded as a man of straw to be refuted, rather than as a fellow seeker for the truth.[75]

Finally, we have the regular linguistic marks of the $\delta\iota a\tau\rho\iota\beta\acute{\eta}$, such as asyndeton, the use of miniature illustrative scenes, frequent metaphors, brutal directness of language, and above

all the effort to relieve the seriousness of the central argument
by conscious lapses into the *sermo plebeius*.[76] Stertinius also
employs the technical philosophical terminology of the Stoics.
Thus sin is a disease *morbus* (27, 80, 122, 161, and 254).[77] In lines
208-209 we have the Stoic theory of καταληπτικὴ φαντασία,[78]
the notion that the image seized by the conscience is derived
from reality. The characters of Homer and of the Greek trage-
dians and comedians are quoted as types of the cardinal passions
of the Stoics.[79] Anecdotes of philosophers or χρεῖαι, to use the
technical term, are found.[80] For the reasons enumerated,
therefore, we may regard this satire as one of the most carefully
wrought, and certainly the most consciously didactic of all the
satires of Horace.

The complex question of the Greek sources of the satire is
beyond the scope of this work. I wish merely to call attention
to the fact that the doctrines of Stertinius are eclectic, as is,
of course, to be expected from the fact that he represents
Horace. Therefore, we find many general affinities with the
related doctrines of the Cynics, as the following inventory of
passages from our satire cited by Gerhard in his *Phoenix von
Kolophon* will show. Thus (1) in line 94 we have a "topic"
on the influence of wealth;[81] (2) in line 96 the relation between
wisdom and riches;[82] (3) in line 100 the χρεία of Aristippus in the
Libyan desert;[83] (4) in lines 111 and 142 the stock picture of
the miser watching his hoard;[84] (5) in 115, 142 the commonplace
on the use of sour wine;[85] (6) in line 127 on the faithlessness,
ἀπιστία, of the rich;[86] (7) in line 145 we may compare the use of
εὐάζω by the Anonymous on αἰσχροκέρδεια;[87] (8) in line 146 the
commonplace of the laughing heir;[88] (9) in line 164 the sacrifice
of the avaricious man;[89] (10) in line 296 the Cynic warrior
against sin;[90] (11) in line 308 the use of wealth.[91]

The influence of Bion was probably felt in formulating the
traditional anecdote of Aristippus in the desert.[92]

Horace's relations with his Latin predecessors are clearer.
Thus Varro's *Eumenides*, which was upon the same theme,
was written under the direct influence of such popular philo-
sophic theories current in Rome. The treatment of Varro
shows both similarities and differences when compared with
the present satire.[93] Iltgen, so far as I have discovered was

the first commentator to point out that Lucilius wrote on the same paradox in book 30.[94] I shall endeavor to show that book 17 of Lucilius probably contained a second and similar discourse on this favorite Stoic theme.

In book 30, we can trace the development of a parallel Lucilian theme in lines 1005, 1006, 1007, 1178 (?), 995, 1092.

We have some indications, quite vague to be sure, which seem to show a Lucilian coloring for the lines which stand at the beginning of Horace's satire. It is just possible that the motive for the opening lines may have been similar in Lucilius. Thus Horace in line 13 ff. following the allegorical method of interpreting mythology favored by the Stoics, represents Damasippus as urging that the Siren sloth be avoided:

> Vitanda est improba Siren
> desidia, aut quicquid vita meliore parasti
> ponendum aequo animo.

Now in Lucilius 1005 we have a clear allusion to the effect of the song of the Sirens upon Ulysses. In addition the note of Nonius seems to imply that Lucilius also used the scene allegorically to imply that some influence lures the hero away from the search for true philosophy (*quaerimus*).[95] Thus: induci est aliquibus fallaciis decipi. The Lucilian line in question reads:

> — ◡◡ — ◡◡ — ◡◡ — quid quaerimus? acri
> inductum cantu, custoditum.

Horace, line 16 ff. immediately continues the conversation by jeering at the long hair and flowing beard of Damasippus. These are the stock characteristics of the street philosopher:

> Di, te, Damasippe, deaeque
> verum ob consilium donent tonsore.

The essential correctness of my interpretation of Lucilius 1055 as given above finds further confirmation in the fact that we probably have the same stock allusion in Lucilius 1007, which Marx rightly places immediately after fragment 1005.[96]

> — ◡◡ — ◡◡ — neque barbam inmiseris istam.

In line 41 Stertinius begins his discourse by a definition, after the formal scheme of Stoic discourses, of what madness is.

Lucilius in fragment 1178 which may be plausibly referred to this satire does the same. Thus Horace 41:

> primum nam inquiram quid sit furere.

Horace then proceeds to answer his own rhetorical question by giving the correct definition of madness:

> hoc si erit in te
> solo, nil verbi, pereas quin fortiter addam
> quem mala stultitia et quemcumque inscitia veri
> caecum agit, insanum Chrysippi porticus et grex
> autumat.

So Lucilius also,[97] if we may trust Porphyrio on this very passage, has a similar rhetorical question preparatory to the definition of madness:

> ostendit quid sit furor, ut Lucilius.

In the course of the development of the picture of the miser, Stertinius (117-119) pictures the old man of seventy-nine who sleeps on a wretched bed of straw, while he allows the decent coverings in his strong box to become the prey of moths and worms. Thus:

> age, si et stramentis incubet unde
> octoginta annos natus, cui stragula vestis,
> blattarum ac tinearum epulae putrescat in arco.

The last line appears to have much in common with the Lucilian line 995:[98]

> lana, opus omne perit: pallor tiniae omnia caedunt.

In lines 142-156 we have a scene in which the physician cures the sick miser, Opimius, by having his sacks of money brought in and counted, while he utters the warning that the greedy heir is even now ready to sweep them off. Then in line 152 the dialogue proceeds as follows:

> 'men vivo? ut vivas igitur vigila. hoc age.

Now in Lucilius 1092 we have the following line:

> [quod] nos esse arquatos: surgamus, eamus, agamus.

Here the reference is to jaundice, the cure for which lies in activity. We have no direct mention of avarice in the line, but in view of the other resemblances to Horace in the satire and especially in view of the similarity in the energetic tone of the last part of the line, one is inclined to conjecture that the line may have stood in a context which described the sick miser.[99]

This completes the analysis of the fragments from the satire in book 30. Before turning to Horace's use, mainly in lines 259-271, of material from a satire of similar theme in book 27, I wish to consider certain sporadic traces of Lucilian influence which appear mainly in the central portions of Horace's satire.

In Horace 123-126 we have described as an external mark of the avaricious man, an uncombed and unoiled head, full of dandruff. Such a man also uses wretched oil for his salad:

> ne tibi desit
> quantulum enim summae curtabit quisque dierum,
> unguere si caules oleo meliore caputque
> coeperis inpexa foedum porrigine?

This description seems to be an imitation of Lucilius 523 ff. in book 16, where the νεόπλουτοι are said to oil their frowzy hair:[100]

> et
> hi quos divitiae producunt et caput ungunt
> horridulum.

In line 175 Horace uses Nometanus, a name probably of Lucilian origin, as a type of the spendthrift. It may well be that in Cicuta, the avaricious man, his foil, we have another Lucilian name. Doubtless the use of the name here is determined by the same considerations which led to its introduction by Horace in satires 1, 1, 102.[101]

In Horace 250-256 the famous χρεία narrating the conversion of the drunken young debauchee, Polemon, to philosophic truth as the result of the preaching of Xenocrates is set forth. Now for the idea of interweaving such χρεῖαι in the texture of satire Horace had ample precedents in Lucilius.[102] Moreover, in book 27 of Lucilius we find a discussion of the succession of the masters of the Academy. Polemon, we are told, handed on his school to his favorite pupil [Crates]. Thus lines 755:

> Polemon et amavit, morte huic tranmisit suam
> scolen quam dicunt.

I believe that it is natural to refer 757 also to the same context.[108] The speaker accosts a neophyte and says: But what of your attitude? Address me that I may know:

> verum tu quid agis? interpella me, ut sciam

This direct appeal appears to me quite in the tone of Horace 253:

> quaero faciasne quod olim
> mutatus Polemon.

If so, the incident of Polemon's conversion may have been told in the same Lucilian context in a verse now lost.[104]

This completes my list of sporadic Lucilian reminiscences. I turn next to a consideration of certain lines from a Lucilian satire in book 27 in which the madness of love was discussed. In this satire we may trace Horatian resemblances to the following fragments: 732, 729, 730, 737, 734, 731, 732, 735.

Horace in 76-81 enumerates the headings under which he will treat madness.[105] These are the Stoic passions of ambition, avarice, luxury, superstition, sexual love:

> audire atque togam iubeo componere quisquis
> ambitione mala aut argenti pallet amore,
> quisquis luxuria tristive superstitione
> aut alio mentis morbo calet: huc propius me,
> dum doceo insanire omnis vos ordine adite.

Fragment 732 would seem to show that Lucilius in this satire made a similar enumeration of the types of madness:

> Insanum vocat quem maltam ac feminam dici videt.

This example would, of course, fall under *luxuria*.

The other fragments in the sequence just enumerated all refer to the madness of love. In fact they throw an interesting light on the sympathetic attitude of Lucilius toward the work of Terence, an older member of the Sciponic circle.

We know that it was a convention in the διατριβή to draw examples from the stage of the New Comedy. Thus the unlucky lover Thrasonides from the μισούμενος of Menander often served as a warning example. So in Horace lines 259-271 of this satire we have a paraphrase of certain lines from the *Eunuchus* of Terence, Act 1, scene 1. The excluded, abused, but completely enslaved lover, Phaedria, debates with himself and with his slave Parmeno whether to return to Thais if she will receive him. The slave Parmeno seeks to dissuade him and asserts that love is a madness. The editors of Lucilius and Horace seem not to have observed that the fragments just enumerated contain a much freer working over of the same scene. Lucilius, therefore, was the first satirist, following the precedent of the διατριβή to paraphrase a scene from the New Comedy as vivid means of moral teaching. In this precedent he was followed by Horace and by Persius in their satires upon the same Stoic paradox.[106]

In considering the two paraphrases of the scene, it is interesting to observe that both Lucilius and Horace are closer to Terence than they are to each other. That is, Horace was influenced rather by the Lucilian convention of using a scene from the *palliata* than by a desire to reproduce closely the Lucilian adaptation of such a scene.

The Horatian passage 259-271 runs as follows:

> amator
> exclusus qui distat, agit ubi secum, eat an non,
> quo rediturus erat non arcessitus, et haeret
> invisis foribus: 'nec nunc cum me vocet ultro,
> accedem? an potius mediter finire dolores?
> exclusit, revocat redeam? non, si obsecret,' ecce
> servus non paullo sapientior: 'o ere, quae res
> nec modum habet neque consilium, ratione modoque
> tractari non volt. In amore haec sunt mala bellum
> pax rursum; haec siquis tempestatibus prope ritu
> mobilia et caeca fluitantia sorte laboret
> reddere certa sibi; nihilo plus explicet ac si
> insanire paret certa ratione modoque.

The first Lucilian line, 729, reads:

> cum pacem peto, cum placo, cum adeo et cum appello, 'meam'

The situation, therefore, is clearly that of the lover excluded from the house of his mistress, who seeks to "make up" and to regain peace. We may compare *Eunuchus* 53-54 rather as standing at the same point in the sequence of the scene than for direct verbal imitation. Lucilius 730 must have stood in the same context, I think. It has, however, no precise parallel in the *Eunuchus*. I should prefer to make it a question raised by the excluded lover, who in soliloquy says, "When my humblest slaves accost m(, am I not to address my lady-love." The lines are taken by Marx, mistakenly I think, as referring to the unwillingness of the lover to use the phrase *domina mea* of his *amica* in the presence of slaves. The whole tone of the line makes it well-nigh certain that it must have had a place in this same scene.

> Infécta pace ultro íd eam venies índicans.

In lines 60 and 61 of Terence also we have the contrasts of love compared to those of war and peace. The parallel Horatian lines are 259-263.

The greed of the *meretrix* was expounded by the slave much more fully apparently in Lucilius than in Terence. Horace with finer artistic perception emphasized rather her capriciousness of temper. Thus Lucilius 737:

> quam non solum deuorare se omnia ac deuerrere.

These words recall the more generalized remark of Parmeno lines 54 and 55:

> actumst, ilicet
> perísti: eludet, úbi te victum sénserit.

Horace did not reproduce this touch in his paraphrase.

In 734 the lover Phaedria queries whether he can ever succeed in making the course of love run smooth. Thus:

> ego enim an perficiam ut me amare expediaí
> —‿‿—?

The corresponding lines of Terence are 56-58, put into the mouth of Parmeno, who emphasizes the irrationality of love:

> Proin túí dum est tempus, étiam atque etiam cógitas,
> ere: quaé res in se néque consilium néque modum
> habet íllum, cum consílio regere nón potes.

The corresponding Horatian lines are 264-267 above. We may compare also 270-271 for the slave's conclusion. Lucilius 731 belongs to a context, in which the lover asserted his right to work out the problem, and his determination to adopt a firm course:

> iam qua tempestate uiuo, certe sine: ad me recipio.

The corresponding lines of Terence, 64–66, are spoken by Parmeno, but are referred by him to an imaginary monologue, which he imputes to his master:

> et quód nunc tute técum iratus cógitas
> Egon íllam quae illum, quaé me quae non . . .! síne modo,
> morí me malim: séntiet qui vír siem.

We have no precise parallels to these lines in Horace. 263, however, is parallel perhaps to a Lucilian line now lost, which closely followed 731, and expressed the lover's determination to die.

In 735 Lucilius expresses the fear attributed to Phaedria by Thais, that the reason that he was excluded was her love for another. The line is, therefore, to be assigned to Thais, I think, and *aspectu* and *capiare* are to be referred to masculine not feminine beauty; or with Dziatzko we may read *capiar alterae* and put the remark in the mouth of Phaedria:

> at metuis porro ne aspectu et forma capiare altera.

The parallel would in the first case not be line 83 cited by Marx but the speech of Thais in line 95:

> ne crúcia te obsecro, ánime mi, mi Phaédria.
> non pól quo quemquam plús amem aut plus díligam
> eo féci; sed ita erát res, faciundúm fuit.

Thais does not appear in the Horatian adaptation of the scene from the *Eunuchus*.

At the conclusion of the τόπος on the madness of love, Horace makes fun of "the baby talk" of the full grown lover in lines 273 and 274:[107]

> cum balba feris annoso verba palato
> aedifacante casas qui sanior.

This seems to be a recollection of 915 in book 29:

> subplantare aiunt Graeci — ‿ — ‿ —

The Lucilian passage probably also contained the Greek verb ὑποσκελίζω as Marx suggests, but the reference was, I think, to affected utterance like that of the lover rather than to translation from the Greek.[108]

Finally Horace ends the formal argument of the satire in 305 with a quizzical acceptance of the preacher's dogma, and confesses his own madness:

> stultum me fateor (liceat concedere veris)
> atque etiam insanum.

Now 724 might, to be sure, be interpreted of yielding to superior force in any form, but in view of the Horatian parallels already established it seems not too bold to believe that it stood somewhere near the close of the Lucilian satire, and referred to yielding to superior argument.

> id concedere unum atque in eo dare, quo superatur, manus.

To sum up then the results of my study of this satire. Its theme is a διατριβή upon the widely spread Stoic paradox ὅτι πᾶς ἄφρων μαίνεται. The ultimate origins of the satire are, therefore, to be sought in the various formulations of this commonplace by the hands of Cynic and Stoic popular philosophers. But long before Horace this theme had been formulated in Latin satire by Lucilius in two satires in books 27 and 30. The form of Horace's satire is accordingly influenced to a very considerable extent by Lucilius' treatment of the theme. In the satire in book 30, Lucilius set forth the importance of the uninterrupted search for philosophy (fragments 1005), ridiculed the professional beard of the philosopher (1007), defined what he meant by madness (1178), proved the folly of avarice by one or more examples (995, 1092). In the satire in book 27, Lucilius evidently had a discussion on luxury (732) and a scene from the *Eunuchus* of Terence as an illustration from the New Comedy of the folly of love (729, 730, 737, 734, 731, 735). At the close of the satire, the speaker (whether he was Lucilius himself we do not know), acknowledged that he must yield to the truth of the indictment (that all men are mad save the sage—fragment 724).

Finally we have evidence from other Lucilian satires that he was as well acquainted as Horace with the ordinary commonplaces and examples of Cynic-Stoic argumentation. It, therefore, seems not unreasonable to hold that Horace in developing his own parallel study of this well worn Cynic-Stoic paradox probably regarded the working over of these *loci* in Lucilius. Thus we find in other books of Lucilius five fragments, 523, 755, 757, 742, 915, which attest his complete familiarity with such well worn examples of Stoic preaching. This satire, therefore, the most academic of all the Horatian satires, deserves most careful study, as an example of the double indebtedness of Horace to the Greek popular philosophic literature, and to the earlier satiric adaptations of the teachings of that literature by Lucilius.

SATIRE 4

Satire four is the second of the three culinary satires of the second book. As the introduction to the satire in the fourth Heinze-Kiessling edition rightly emphasizes, this satire is at once a companion piece and a foil to the second satire. That is, while the second satire lays stress on the *praecepta tenuis victus*, this satire emphasizes the proper place of a cultivated and restrained enjoyment of the pleasures of the table,[109] as an aid to the *beate vivere* of the Epicureans.

The development of such culinary themes in Greek literature is wide-spread.[110] Thus in Greek comedy the cooks vaunt their arts and formulate their precepts. Here we may compare the extracts from Poseidippus, Euphron, Sosipater preserved in book 9, 376 ff. of Athenaeus. For example in the σύντροφοι of Damoxenus,[111] a cook gives a theory of the rôle of chyme, and the need of a philosophic system, not only for the actual practice of cooking, but as a directive principle of the culinary art.

Archestratus of Gela wrote the 'Ηδυπάθεια a manual of gluttony. This was in the form of a parody in hexameters on Homer and Hesiod. Its framework was a gastronomic voyage of discovery. At each step the specialties of the district were celebrated and the best recipes for their preparation were given. This poem was only one representative of the genre. At Rome, however, it was the best known, owing to the translation of Ennius, entitled the *Heduphagetica*. Another work in the same form was apparently Varro's περὶ ἐδεσμάτων.

While Horace's satire has many affinities the theme is more definitely subordinated to Epicurean philosophy. This was natural for the Stoic Chrysippus regarded Archestratus as the ἀρχηγός of the Epicureans.[112]   Now the Epicureans emphasized the fact that the necessary condition precedent to a happy life was the knowledge of nature (*rerum natura*).   In accordance with this principle Horace in enunciating the culinary precepts of this satire lays stress on the *natura* of the ingredients (21, 45), and repeats the word in giving the recipes.   He follows the tradition, then, of such culinary discourses by presenting his theme under two *quasi*-philosophical aspects: (1) the culinary inventions (*inventa* εὑρήματα) are related to the general theory of *inventio;* (2) we have a list of viands with their provenance, really a sub-division of the products of a general geographical district;   (3) we have a third method of exposition in the use of precepts dealing with the period most favorable for eating the dish discussed (*e.g.*, line 30).

The theme of this satire is further related to popular philosophic literature in the fact that this material is presented to the reader as an ἀπομνημόνευμα[113] or report of the words of the master by a disciple.   This device of Greek popular philosophy is employed three times by Horace in this second book.   In the third satire Damasippus rehearses the teachings of Stertinius; in this satire Catius rehearses the gastronomic philosophy of an unknown master, and in the seventh satire the slave Davus rehearses the teachings imparted to him by the janitor of Crispinus.   The philosophical setting of the satire is therefore in every way so carefully drawn by Horace as to be easily detected and defined even today.   On the other hand, it is perhaps impossible to discover the precise mood in which Horace writes the satire, nor is such a discovery essential to my present purpose.[114]

Although we cannot today prove that any of the culinary satires of Lucilius[115] presented their teachings in precisely the form adopted by Catius, there is evidence that Lucilius was equally familiar with the Greek literature on this subject, and that his incidental treatment of culinary lore in certain of the satires has influenced the fourth satire of Horace.

Horace in line 30 in describing the *gustatio* says that the waxing of the moon swells oysters!

lubrica nascentes implent conchylia lunae.

This piece of gastronomic lore is directly imitated from Lucilius 1201:

> luna alit ostrea et implet echinos.

In accordance with Greek gastronomic lore, as set forth in the introduction to this satire,[116] both Lucilius and Horace laid stress on the provenance of shell-fish. Thus Horace lines 31 ff.:

> sed non omne mare est generosae fertile testae:
> murice Baiano melior Lucrina peloris,
> ostrea Circeiis, Miseno oriuntur echini,
> pectinibus patulis iactat se molle Tarentum.

So Lucilius in 1210 speaks of the *murex marinus*, which is quoted by the *pseudo-Acro* on this line. That we have a reference to Lucilius in the Horatian passage becomes probable, in addition to the fact of the citation of Lucilius by the *pseudo-Acro*, when we observe that Horace in terms of contemporary luxury asserts that the giant mussel from the Lucrine lake is better than the *murex* of Baiae, *i.e.*, the *murex marinus* of Lucilius, localized at Baiae by Horace for direct contemporary satiric effect.[117] Then follows the discussion on the boar, the *pièce de résistance* of the *cena* proper. Horace in lines 40 ff. especially recommends the Umbrian boar which has fattened on wild acorns:

> Umber et iligna nutritus glande rotundas
> curvat aper lancis carnem vitantis inertem:

Lucilius also discussed the boar in a surviving line 1341:

> uiscus aprinum.

It is impossible to say whether this discussion was introduced in connection with a banquet which *uiscus* would suggest.

SATIRE 5

The framework of the fifth satire is a Νέκυια in which Odysseus descends to the lower world to consult Tiresias on the best lot in life. Following the Homeric Νέκυια, *Odyssey*, book 11, Menippus of Gadara had written similar parodies whose main features may in part be reconstructed from Horace's free imitation, and from the closer reconstruction of Menippean themes by Lucian.[118] Lucian's Νεκυομαντεία in particular[119] seems to contain a theme derived from Menippus, which shows certain external analogies to this more freely wrought Horatian satire. Thus (1) the motive for the visit to the lower world on the part of Menippus in Lucian, and of Ulysses in Horace is to question the seer Tiresias as to the best means of improving their fortunes. (2) Hence both themes appear to be sarcastic attacks on the teaching of Chrysippus and the earlier Stoa that the sage is a χρηματιστικός. Originally, of course, this doctrine, which is implicit in the conception of the omniscience of the Stoic sage, referred only to his capacity in assessing wealth and property at their correct moral and material values. Since, however, the doctrine easily lent itself to perversion by recreant Stoics it was frequently made the subject of attack by Epicureans and other opponents of the Stoics. In fact Caesar's attack on Cato Uticensis, the ideal Stoic sage of the Ciceronian and Augustan period may have made considerable use of this commonplace, and may in some respects be related to Horace's attitude towards Cato.[120] (3) Menippus is directed in Lucian to call himself either Heracles, Odysseus, or Orpheus. (4) In line 3, Horace speaks of Tiresias as laughing at the crafty-minded Odysseus, who after having been told he will return to Ithaca in safety immediately asks how he may recoup his fortunes. Similarly in Lucian's *Menippus* 21 the sarcastic Tiresias smiles as he recommends to Odysseus the life of a private citizen as the best: ὁ δὲ γελάσας (quid rides?) . . . καὶ πολὺ τῶν ἄλλων ἀποστάσας ἠρέμα προσκύψας πρὸς τὸ οὖς φησιν ὁ τῶν ἰδιωτῶν ἄριστος βίος καὶ σωφρονέστερος. (5) As corroborative proof of the probable use of Menippean material by Horace and Lucian we may cite Varro's Menippean satire περὶ ἐξαγωγῆς, a sort of Νεκυία.

The cumulative weight of these five considerations makes it probable that at least the framework of Horace's satire goes back to Menippus. How far the development of the theme follows a Menippean sequence it is impossible to say.[121]

The character of Ulysses, a stock Stoic hero, the exemplar of all the virtues, in these three works is transformed under a Cynic assault. The ground for the assault rests upon indications of the more crafty and unscrupulous sides of the hero's character, which implicit in Homer, were intensified by tragedy[122] and further developed by comedy.[123] The Cynic attitude towards the Homeric hero is well illustrated by the *Sesculixes* of Varro, a Menippean satire, in which these characteristics were apparently multiplied by 1½. The Cynic attack upon Ulysses as a Stoic χρηματιστικός was especially bitter. In a sense also both his character and the ideal recommended for him by Tiresias seem to suggest the κόλαξ as distinct from the true friend, though there are no direct rhetorical similarities in the detailed methods of delineating the two types of flatterer and hunter of inheritances.[124]

This brief summary will be sufficient to show that this satire is related with special definiteness to certain tendencies, and stock types of popular Cynic-Stoic exposition, while the parallels between Lucian and Horace make it probable that Menippus at least suggested the framework of the Horatian satire.

Now we have indications that Lucilius was familiar with the use of Odysseus and Tiresias as exemplars of traditional Cynic-Stoic characteristics, which, while falling short of proof on account of the brevity and paucity of the fragments, point to the possibility that Lucilius in book 17 wrote a satire which, like that of Horace, assailed the shiftiness of the Homeric hero. I will first consider the more general class of indications, and then turn to book 17 of Lucilius.

Tiresias is mentioned twice in Lucilius' lines 226-227, and lines 1107-1108. In the first fragment it is clear that he serves only as the type of extreme age, for the subject of the fragment is evidently the death of an aged slave, as old as the venerable prophet:

> uerum unum cecidisse tamen senis Tiresiai
> aequalem constat.

In the second fragment Marx, reading *quidam*, refers the passage to an aged slave excluded from the *triclinium*, but if we fill out the last two syllables of the line by *em* (*i.e.*, read *quidem* with the earlier editors) there is no reason why we should not see in the two lines an allusion to Tiresias himself. In any case weakness of voice and great age are ascribed to Tiresias in Lucian, while Lucilius with concrete exaggeration speaks of a hacking cough:

> ante fores autem et triclini limina quidem
> perditus Tiresia tussi grandaeuus gemebat.

Lucian *Nekuia* 11, 21: ὁ δὲ γελάσας . . . ἐστι δὲ τυφλόν τι γερόντιον καὶ ὠχρὸν καὶ λεπτόφωνον.[125]

We may now turn to the lines in book 17. The content of this book is not easily determined, but it apparently contained a satire in the parodic Cynic vein upon the return of Ulysses, a theme which was apparently treated also by Lucilius in a satire in book 30.[126] Clearly as in Horace 2, 5, 75-83, an attempt was made by Cynic innuendo to assail the fidelity of Penelope to her absent husband. Lucilius, however, apparently assigned this assault either to her maid Eurychia or to her father Icarius,[127] while Horace represents Tiresias as implying that Penelope's chastity will readily yield to gold, if Ulysses gives her the opportunity to advance their joint fortunes. That is, she like her lord is χρηματιστική. So in 538 Lucilius has a dialogue carried on either by father or maid upon Penelope's disinclination to remarry:

> nupturum te nupta negas, quod uiuere Vlixen
> speras.

And Horace 75 ff:

> scortator erit: cave te roget; ultro
> Penelopam facilis potiori trade.' putasne,
> perduci poterit tam frugi tamque pudica,
> quam nequiere proci recto depellere cursu?
> 'venit enim magnum donandi parca iuventus
> nec tantum Veneris quantum studiosa culinae.
> sic tibi Penelope frugi est: quae si semel uno
> de sene gustarit tecum partita lucellum,
> ut canis a corio numquam absterrebitur uncto.

Here, then, Tiresias is represented as urging that Ulysses voluntarily turn over Penelope to the aged *scortator*, and Ulysses is represented as asking whether the frugal and chaste Penelope could be seduced; for ten years she has withstood the suitors.

Probably lines 1296 and 540 ff. are also to be put into the mouth of the same personage who addresses Penelope, reminding her of other matrons who fell from the path of virtue, Alcmene and Helen, and suggesting that their dazzling beauty was not without its blemishes. Thus 1296:

> si <*facie*>facies praestat, si corpore corpus.

and 540 ff.:

> num censes calliplocamon callisphyron ullam
> non licitum esse uterum atque etiam inguina tangere mammis,
> conpernem aut uaram fuisse Amphitryonis acoetin
> Alcmenam, atque alias, <Ηε>lenam ipsam denique—nolo
> dicere: tute uide atque disyllabon elige quoduis—
> <κου>ρην eupatereiam aliquam rem insignem habuisse,
> uerrucam, naeuum, punctum, dentem eminulum unum?

We have no precise parallel to these lines in the Horatian satire, but the sardonic tone in which the same epic heroine is treated in both satirists is similar and suggests Cynic influence (in this case perhaps Menippean).

It is difficult to reconstruct the exact context in which line 552 was used, but certainly, on the one hand, the quotation from a law of the twelve tables referring to deceit is apropos in a satire on the wily Ulysses. It is worth while citing Horace 27 ff. in which Ulysses is urged to defend the rich rascal in a law suit for certainly we have the process of serving a warrant and a case involving fraud in Lucilius. In Lucilius, then, it is possible that Ulysses was advised to appear in behalf of a rascal involved in a fraudulent law suit. Thus Horace says:

> magna minorve foro si res certabitur olim,
> vivet uter locuples sine gnatis, inprobus, ultro
> qui meliorem audax vocet in ius, illius esto
> defensor.

So also in Lucilius 552 we seem to have the description of the process of serving the warrant as in the last line of Horace:

> 'si non it, capito' inquit 'eum, et si caluitur.' "ergo
> fur dominum?"

Finally line 550 seems to re-echo the idea present in the *Nekuomanteia* of Lucian that Fortune's favors are a gift not a loan. It therefore serves in some degree to strengthen the suspicion, although as we have seen,[128] we are here dealing with a philosophical commonplace, that Lucilius like Horace may be using Menippean material, for the commonplace is found in both writers. Lucilius' lines 550-51:

> cetera contemnit et in usura omnia ponit
> non magna: proprium uero nil neminem habere.

With this we may compare Lucian *Nek.* 16, of those who are compelled to give up the costumes lent them by fortune: Ἔνιοι δὲ ὑπ᾽ ἀγνωμοσύνης ἐπειδὰν ἀπαιτῇ τὸν κόσμον ἐπιστᾶσα ἡ τύχη, ἄχθονται τε καὶ ἀγανακτοῦσιν ὥσπερ οἰκείων τινῶν στερισκόμενοι καὶ οὐχ ἃ πρὸς ὀλίγον ἐχρήσαντο ἀποδιδόντες.

This completes the enumeration of the fragments in book 17, which stand in any relation to the satire of Horace. It is perhaps worth adding, however, that lines 547-48, which appear to refer to the boxing match between Ulysses and Irus, afford further proof of the Homeric material employed in this satire. The allusion is to the discovery of the massive bones and biceps of Ulysses as he strips for the battle:

> magna ossa lacertique
> adparent homini.

One other fragment of Lucilius, 882-83 from book 29, may be brought into relation with this Horatian satire.[129] In these lines we have a conventionalized description of the attitude of the comic slave when embarrassed from the consciousness of guilt or fraud. This parallelism should not pass unnoticed, though by itself it affords insufficient proof of direct dependence upon Lucilius, since such descriptions are commonplaces of the New Comedy. The Lucilian line:

> — ∪ — ∪ — ∪ — ∪ — ∪ — hic me ubi uidet,
> subblanditur *fur*, palpatur, caput scabit, pedes legit.

And Horace 2, 5, 91:

> Davus sis comicus atque
> stes capite obstipo, multum similis metuenti.

Satire 7

The subject of the seventh satire,[130] like that of the third of this book is a Stoic paradox: μόνος ὁ σοφὸς ἐλεύθερος καὶ πᾶς ἄφρων δοῦλος. The method of presenting the paradox is also similar to that employed in the third satire. We have another example of an ἀπομνημόνευμα for Davus, Horace's slave, is represented as preaching to his master a Stoic sermon, the doctrines of which he has imbibed from the *ianitor* at the house of Crispinus (45). In this confrontation of the slave philosophically free with the master, philosophically the slave of his passions, Horace is following a Cynic method of developing the theme, which may be traced back ultimately as far as a passage in the *Protrepticus* of Aristotle. For Aristotle there says:[131] If a master were worse than his own slaves, he would be ridiculous: εἰ τις τῶν οἰκειῶν αὐτοῦ χείρων εἴη, καταγέλαστος ἂν γένοιτο.

A further Cynic development of the theme is found in the Διογένους πρᾶσις of Menippus, which seems to have influenced fragment 404 B of Varro's περὶ ἐδεσμάτων.[132] The conception of the sale is that the unphilosophic master is worthless. Thus Varro declares: Si quantum operae sumpsisti ut tuus pistor bonum faceret panem, eius duodecimam philosophiae dedisses, ipse bonus iam pridem esses factus. Nunc illum qui norunt, uolunt emere milibus centum; te qui novit, nemo centussis. With this we may compare Horace (42-43).

> quid, si me stultior ipso
> quingentis empto drachmis deprenderis?

The same paradox is expounded by Cicero *paradoxa* 5, with which—or with allied popular philosophical treaties—Horace's satire is closely related.[133]

Not only is the theme a well-worn Stoic commonplace, but Horace's method of presentation is essentially that of the Stoics, as Lejay has shown in his introduction to the satire. This is seen most clearly in Davus' method of developing his thesis by the use of stereotyped Stoic examples. Thus (1) Davus engages *more Stoicorum* in a running fire of rhetorical questions.[134] (2) He uses technical philosophical terms such as *peccare*.[135] (3) He employs the blunt coarse vocabulary of the Cynics, and describes the most brutalized aspects of sexual love.[136] (4) We find such stereotyped Stoic illustrations as: (a) the god who gives men a change of lot (24);[137] (b) the simile of the beast who has broken its chain (70-71);[138] (c) the simile of the marionettes (82);[139] (d) the simile of the struggle to escape the mire of sin (27);[140] (e) *cheragra* (and *podagra*) as the earthly punishment for sin.[141] (5) We find examples of the slavery to the passions, viz.: (a) to love (46-71); (b) to aesthetic dilettanteism (90-101); (c) to gluttony (102-111); (d) to inconsistency of temper (111-115). All these are Stoic commonplaces.

In the treatment of slavery to sexual passion (46-94), Horace retraces in summary the ground of the second satire of book 1.[142] The only new point of view presented here is that the lover as the corruptor of the faithless wife deserves the greatest condemnation. In this development of the theme of the slavery to love Horace as in the second satire[143] seems to depend on the Lucilian treatment of this same theme. We have also other stray Lucilian reminiscences in the satire.

In line 50, Davus sets forth his simple method of gratifying desire by means of the ordinary prostitute. Thus we read in lines 46-52:

> te coniunx aliena capit, meretricula Davum.
> peccat uter nostrum cruce dignius? acris ubi me
> natura intendit, sub clara nuda lucerna
> quaecumque excepit turgentis verbera caudae,
> clunibus aut agitavit equum lasciva supinum,
> dimittit neque famosum neque sollicitum ne
> ditior aut formae melioris meiat eodem.

Here lines 48-50, as Marx has pointed out, seem to resemble the general tone of Lucilius 1267, evidently spoken to Hortensius in a similar context:

> podicis, Hortensi, est ad eam rem nata palaestra.

Here palaestra[144] is used in the sense of exercitatio, somewhat similar to the agitavit of Horace.

In line 90 of Horace we have the particular phase in the commonplace of the slavery to love, which represents the excluded lover.[145] He is drawn to the threshold of his mistress by his passion only to be thrust out, and drenched with hot or cold water.[146] This "topic" of the excluded and insulted lover is found also in Lucilius book 29. Here fragments 837, 839, 840, 843, 844, 845, elaborate upon the attempts of the excluded lover to break into the house with his slave, and the counter-defence of the occupants of the besieged house. In 841 and 845 we have the particular turn which gives the key to the interpretation of Persius' phrase udas ante foras (5, 165-166), and which is the starting point for the tradition. Thus in 841:

> ‿ — ‿ — has e fenestris in caput
> deiciunt, qui prope ad ostium aspirauerint.

That the allusion is to a deluge of water[147] poured upon the
lover from the windows becomes clear from a comparison with
845 and the Horatian passage.   845 reads:

> Gnato, quid actum est? 'depilati omnes sumus.'

Here the commentary of Marx rightly explains the *depilati*
as referring to the use of hot water in the process of plucking
fowls.[148]   The master and slave drenched with hot water are
like plucked fowls.   This completes the scanty evidence of
Lucilian influence upon the composition of this satire.[149]

SATIRE 8

The eighth satire, in which Fundanius gives the poet Horace
an account of the dinner of the rich *parvenu* Nasidienus, belongs
to the literary form known to the Greeks as the δεῖπνον.[150]
The characteristics of this genre which flourished in close
relation to the New Comedy have already been analyzed.[151]
Before the period of Horace the genre had early passed over
to Latin literature.   The *Heduphagetica* of Ennius is a theme
closely related to that of the banquet.   In Lucilius we have a
number of satires on banquets; in books 4, 5, 13, 20, and 21.
In view of the spread of table luxury in the period following
the Macedonian Wars this theme was naturally attractive to
so vigorous a satirist of contemporary manners as Lucilius.
In a later period we have the field represented by the *Nescis
quid serus Vesper vehat* and the περὶ ἐδεσμάτων of Varro, and
under the empire by the famous episode of the *Cena Trimal-
chionis* in Petronius.

The relation of the Lucilian banquets to the eighth satire
of Horace is not entirely clear.   Of book 21 we have no extant
fragments.   Lejay regards book 5 as the model of Horace, but
this is true only in the most general sense for book 5 is rather
a *cena rustica*, marked by parsimony on the part of the host
than a banquet satire of the ordinary type.   The principal
model of Horace's satire was perhaps Lucilius' book 20, al-
though he did not hesitate to employ other *motifs* characteristic
of the genre drawn from other Lucilian satires.

It is evident also that such δεῖπνα gained part of their effect
by the characterization of the host, who is usually a wealthy
parvenu, but sometimes as in the case of Lucilius' Granius, a

man of clever and overpowering wit, one who indeed owes his success partly to that quality. On the other hand, Nasidienus in Horace and Trimalchio in Petronius are both types of the *parvenu* host.[152] It follows that although traces of close verbal imitation of Lucilius are scanty, we do have substantial evidence that the free studies of Lucilius and Horace in the genre of the δεῖπνον show parallel methods of delineation. We may consequently infer with some degree of certainty that Horace was influenced both by Greek originals and by the previous Lucilian studies in this genre. In fact, the nature of Horace's relations to Lucilius revealed in this satire may be compared with his method in satire seven of the first book.[153] Let us now examine the satire in detail following the order of the Horatian lines.

Fragment 1180, for Marx, is apparently correct in assigning it to book 20, makes it probable that the host was the *praeco Granius*. In social position, therefore, we have in Lucilius an appropriate companion to Nasidienus, and the *sevir* Trimalchio. Thus Cicero: Multae deinde causae (L. Licinii Crassi oratoris): sed ita tacitus tribunatus ut nisi in eo magistratu (anno 647 107 B.C.) cenavisset apud praeconem Granium idque nobis naravisset Lucilius, tribunum plebem nesciremus fuisse.

This fragment makes it possible that the Lucilian satire like that of Horace was an ὑπόμνημα, in which L. Licinius Crassus told the story of the banquet to the earlier poet, as Fundanius did to Horace.

The banquet began with a description of the *gustatio*, whose general nature we may assume was similar to that described by Horace in lines 6-9. The purpose of this course is, as with us, to open the banquet with such appetizers as will at once satisfy the fasting stomach and whet the appetite for the more elaborate and substantial courses that are to follow. The nature of these appetizers is asked by Horace in lines 4 and 5:

> dic, si grave non est,
> quae prima iratum ventrem placaverit esca.

This inquiry may perhaps be regarded as a commonplace for in another satire of Lucilius' book 29, lines 813-814 we read:[154]

> — ᵕ ventrem alienum, maestum fovere ex molito
> hordeo uti cataplasma.

At the close of this first course in both banquets the viands
were removed by a slave, and the tables were wiped with a pur-
ple frieze cloth.   Thus in Lucilius 568:

> purpureo tersit tunc latas gausape mensas.

and Horace 10 ff.:

> his ubi sublatis puer alte cinctus acernam
> gausape purpureo mensam pertersit et alter
> sublegit quodcumque iaceret inutile.[155]

Naturally the quality of the wines was a stock theme in
such banquet satires.   Among Greek wines the Chian was held
in especially high esteem.   It is alluded to in Lucilius, line 1131,
which Marx suggests may be a quotation from some Greek
poet like Archestratus.   If so it is tempting to assign the brief
fragment to satire 20 and regard it as a remark of the *parvenu*
Granius.   Such an assignment will gain some measure of sup-
port from Trimalchio's praise of Opimian wine and his fondness
for quoting Greek.   The Lucilian line is:

> Χῖος τε δυνάστης

which evidently refers to the lordship of "Chian."   Also in
the dinner of Nasidienus we find the same traditional praise of
wine by the host for there the Caecuban and Chian are brought
on with almost religious veneration.   Thus 13-15:

>   ut Attica virgo
> cum sacris Cereris procedit fuscus Hydaspes
> Caecuba vina ferens, Alcon Chium maris expers.

Marx closely connects Lucilius 569 with 1174.   569 reads:

> illi praecisco atque epulis capiuntur opimis.

Line 1174 reads:[156]

> fingere praeterea, adferri quod quisque uolebat
> illum sumina ducebant atque altilium lanx,
> hunc pontes Tiberinus duo inter captus catillo.

Marx believes that the allusion is to the *caput cenae*, and cer-
tainly in Petronius 36 the *altilia* and the *sumina* do appear at
the very beginning of the *cena* proper.   He therefore compares
these lines to Horace's line 26 ff.:

> nam cetera turba,
> nos, inquam, cenamus avis, conchylia, piscis.

It can of course be argued that we have here the equivalent of Lucilius' fish and fattened fowl,[187] but a closer connection can, I think, be made out for lines 85 ff. of Horace:

> deinde secuti
> mazonomo pueri magno discerpta ferentes
> membra gruis, sparsi sale multo non sine farre,
> pinguibus et ficis pastum iecur anseris albae.

Here the *discerpta membra* are certainly similar to *praeciso*, and the *pinguibus* recalls the Lucilian *opimis*.

That the *raconteur* in such banquet satires should attack the wretched mixture of extravagance, bad taste, and sordidness of the host was an almost inevitable commonplace. The tone of Lucilius' criticism upon the banquet of Gallonius with its huge sturgeon has a parallel in the Horatian satire. Possibly Horace drew from this second satire because Gallonius as an inept and stupid host was in some respects closer to Nasidienus than the witty Granius. In spite of his absurd extravagance, Lucilius says to Gallonius, *es homo miser*. This phrase is closely reproduced by Horace's exclamation "divitias miseras!" in line 18. Thus Lucilius 1238-1240:

> 'O Publi, O gurges Galloni, es homo miser' inquit
> cenasti in uita numquam bene, cum omnia in ista
> consumis squilla atque acupensere cum decimano.

And Horace 16-18:

> hic erus "Albanum, Maecenas, sive Falernum
> te magis adpositis delectat, habemus utrumque."
> divitias miseras!

An amusing incident of the Horatian banquet, lines 24-25 was the way in which Porcius, true to his name, ate up all the cakes:

> Nomentanus erat super ipsum, Porcius infra,
> ridiculus totas simul absorbere placentas.

Now apparently fragment 1183 stood in the dinner of Granius in book 20. In this line the speaker, probably some parasite of Granius, narrated a similar incident of himself. Thus Lucilius:

> gustaui crustula[188] solus.

Naturally the host would use the best olive oil and boast of the brand. So Lucilius in 961, a fragment cited without book from a satire in trochaic septenarii (*i.e.*, somewhere in books 26-29), speaks of the oil of Casina, which is pressed from green olives. Thus:

> ὠμοτριβὲς oleum Casinas.

And Horace 44 ff. makes Nasidienus offer and praise the oil of Venafrum of the first of the three pressings:[159]

> oleo quod prima Venafri
> pressit cella.

After the accidental falling of the awning in line 54 ff., which threw the company into temporary confusion, Nomentanus tries to rally his friend by an exhortation in the grand style on the uncertainty of fortune and the tricks she plays upon mortals 58-60. With this Balatro sarcastically pretends to agree and ends his discourse in lines 73-74 by comparing the genius of the host, revealed by the conquest over the domestic difficulties attendant upon the banquet with that of the general, whose genius is revealed by his resourcefulness under disaster. Now in book 13 of Lucilius, a banquet satire, we have a series of fragments, 447, 448, 449, 450, 452, which clearly refer to a conversation on fortune and the battlefield. Although it is, of course, possible to take these quite literally of military events, as Marx does, it is certainly tempting to regard them as in some way involving a simile in connection with the banquet. This interpretation finds some support in the use of it in a comparison in line 452:

> ut perhibetur iners, ars in quo non erit ulla.

Moreover, the caprice of Fortune is the topic of a conversation in the banquet of Trimalchio, (55) after a parallel catastrophe (in 53) in which an acrobatic performer falls on the neck of Trimalchio. It is clear, therefore, that we are dealing with a traditional incident of the δεῖπνον, perhaps of Greek origin. I shall first quote the two Horatian passages 59-62 and 73-74. The words of Nomentanus are as follows:

> quis esset
> finis, ni sapiens sic Nomentanus amicum
> tolleret, "heu, Fortuna, quis est crudelior in nos

> te deus: ut semper gaudes inludere rebus
> humanis."

And at the close of Balatro's speech, 73-74:

> sed convivatoris ut ducis ingenium res
> adversae nudare solent, celare secundae.'

With the first we may compare 447, which shows the high position assigned someone (the host?) by fortune:

> cui parilem fortuna locum fatumque tulit fors.

whose talent rises above that of the ordinary man who in 448 is contrasted with him:

> — ᴗ ᴗ unus modo de multis qui ingenio sit.

With lines 73 and 74 of Horace we may compare 449-451 of Lucilius in which at greater length than in Horace Lucilius apparently argues that even in war fortune cannot triumph over *ingenium*, and 451 in which the comparison (*ut*) between the art of the noble *convivator* and the noble general was perhaps made. These two personages Lucilius implies in his comparison are not considered *inertes* because both have *ars* (*ingenium* in Horace). Thus in 449-451 we read:

> acribus inter se cum armis confligere cernit,
> aut forte omnino ac fortuna uincere bello,
> si forte ac temere omnino quid, *quor*sum? ad honorem?

And 452:

> ut perhibetur iners, ars in quo non erit ulla.

In connection with the last line one might add that we have a similar conflict between art and fortune in Horace line 84, where Nasidienus returns with a changed brow to improve bad fortune by art:

> Nasidiene, redis mutatae frontis, ut arte
> emendaturus fortunam.

In the Horatian banquet we find that Varius, unable to restrain his laughter in the face of this absurd bombast, tries to conceal his amusement behind his napkin. Thus in line 62:

> Varius mappa conpescere risum
> vix poterat.

With this, I am inclined to compare Lucilius line 1164 which might, to be sure, be thought of in other contexts, but which suits well the Horatian incident. Napkins are caught up (*velli*)—I believe by more than one guest and perhaps for a similar reason:

> et velli mappas.

This completes the scene from book 13.

Returning, therefore, to the principal satire of Lucilius on the *cena* of Granius in book 20, we find that both the satirists refer to the nose as the seat of anger or scorn, a well-known commonplace of Greek origin.[160] No other resemblance, however, seems to exist between the Lucilian and Horatian lines. The Lucilian line refers to a law of Calpurnius Piso, the Horatian line is a remark of the scornful Balatro. Lucilius says perhaps using the orator Crassus as his spokesman, 573-74:

> Calpurni saeua lege in Pisonis reprendi,
> eduxique animam in primori <s fauc> ibus naris.

And Horace quotes Balatro 64-65:

> Balatro, suspendens omnia naso,
> "haec est condicio vivendi" aiebat.

In view of the number of fragments from book 20 of Lucilius already related more or less closely to Horace, satire 2, 8, one is inclined to imagine some nearer relation between the close of Horace's satire and Lucilius 575. In Horace the guests are disgusted with the descriptions of the *natura* and the *causae* of all the viands which Nasidienus insists on inflicting upon them. They take vengeance by suddenly leaving the banquet refusing to taste anything, just as if Canidia had breathed upon it with her breath more deadly than African serpents. Now 575 has a comparison with a. Marsian snake charmer who makes serpents swell by his song until they burst. Perhaps the point of the comparison in Lucilius was in relation to Granius, the host who forced food upon one of his guests, who feeling himself about to burst, fled. This is, of course, pure conjecture, but so is the interpretation of Marx, and certainly *disrumpto* might well be taken literally in a banquet satire instead of being referred with Marx to *ira* or *invidia*. The Lucilian lines are:

> iam disrumpetur, medius iam, ut Marsus colubras
> disrumpit cantu, uenas cum extenderit omnis.

The Horatian lines:

> quem nos sic fugimus ulti
> ut nihil omnino gustaremus, velut illis
> Canidia adflasset, peior serpentibus Afris.

In the examination of this Horatian satire I have sought to show that book 20 of Lucilius contained a satire on a banquet of Granius, which was in general theme and methods of delineation the principal model of Horace's free contemporary study in the same genre. This I have endeavored to illustrate by the use of fragments, 1180, 568, 1131(?), 1174, 569, 1183, 543, 575. Thus 1180 shows similarities between Nasidienus and Granius, in the method of narration; for perhaps Crassus told the story of the Lucilian banquet as Fundanius told the story of Horace's banquet. 568 shows direct verbal imitation; 1131 shows the common praise of Chian wine; 1174 shows that while Lucilius' Granius gave choice of viands, Horace's Nasidienus gave choice of wines; 569 rehearses a list of viands similar to that in Horace. 1183 satirizes the greed of a banqueter, perhaps a *scurra*. 573 speaks of the curling nostrils as the seat of sarcastic scorn. 575 uses, as does the Horatian satire, a simile in which the common element of the poisonous serpent occurs. The cumulative evidence, therefore, for the structural relationship of Horace's satire to that of Lucilius in book 20 is strong. Moreover, this hypothesis is further strengthened by parallel incidents and methods of delineation found in the *Cena Trimalchionis* of Petronius. We thus see that Lucilius, probably strongly influenced by Greek models as well as by the spread of lavish banqueting in the Scipionic epoch, was the first to establish the traditions of the δεῖπνον in Latin satire.

But Horace also made use of commonplaces which he probably found in other banquet satires of Lucilius, as may be seen by the use of the fragments, 813, 1238, 961, 447, 448, 449, 450, 452, 1164. Among these the commonplace upon the caprice of fortune and the development of the *ingenium convivatoris* in the face of adversity probably played an important part in the banquet satire of book 13. All in all, then, the eighth satire is an excellent example of the high literary art of Horace, who succeeds at once in giving a vivid picture of contemporary life, and in reproducing certain of the traditional features of the Greek δεῖπνον and its successor, the Latin *cena*.

NOTES ON CHAPTER V

SATIRE I

[1] See the three articles by Hendrickson on *Horace and Valerius Cato*, in C.P., vol. 11, pp. 248–269; vol. 12, pp. 77–92, 329–350.

[2] *Sat.* 2, 1, 1.

[3] Ethical criticism is, of course, involved in the differentiation between the liberal and the illiberal jest. See the discussion on Horace's satires 1,3 and 1,4 above, pp. 274–277, 277–294.

[4] *Cf. supra*, pp. 283 ff.; Cichorius, pp. 59, 131 f., 153 f., 203 f., 205 f., 261 on Accius; pp. 133, 197 f., on Afranius.

[5] On the nobility see lines 259 and 260; compare Cichorius, *op. cit.*, pp. 284–286; on the people 1229, 1259–1263; Cichorius, *op. cit.*, pp. 335–338.

[6] *Auctor ad Herennium* 2, 13, 19; Marx, *proleg.* XXVII; *testimonia* 17, line 1345.

[7] For Horace's use of material from book 26 in satires 1,4 and 1,10 see *supra*, pp. 294 ff., 348 ff.

[8] Lejay, *op. cit.*, pp. 289–292, gives an admirable analysis of the legal background of this satire as well as a summary of the course of Roman legislation on freedom of speech from the time of the XII tables to the Augustan age. He shows that it was necessary for Horace to proceed with caution if he would directly attack contemporaries. These conclusions are confirmed by a study by E. J. Filbey, University of Wisconsin thesis, 1903, *Satire by Direct Criticism of Contemporaries and Satire by Types in Lucilius, Horace, and Persius*. In this study Filbey brings out the striking difference of procedure between Horace's first and second book. "In book 1 out of 72 persons criticized, 24 or 33 per cent are contemporaries; if the number of probable contemporaries, 19, be added we have 43 persons or 60 per cent. The number of instances of satire by types of various kinds is 17 persons indicated by typical names or 24 per cent." See p. 31. On the other hand in book 2 we have a total of only 33 persons criticised. Of this number only 4 are contemporaries; if the probable contemporaries are added the number is 11 or 33 per cent. The number of instances of satire by the use of typical names of various kinds is 9 or 27 per cent. See p. 52. The shrinkage of the number of persons satirized by more than half in the second book, together with the slight increase in the number of types criticized under proper names is therefore clearly significant of a deliberate change in Horace's theory of satire in book 2. On the other hand Lucilius (*cf.* p. 77) was free in political satire. Of 27 persons criticized 7 were politicians and of these 6 were contemporaries. There is no evidence that Lucilius ever felt it necessary to satirize a contemporary under cover of a typical pseudonym. In Horace no severe direct criticism of political contemporaries occurs. Of 105 persons criticized in

the two books of Horace's satires only 14 are politicians (*cf*. p. 77). Filbey also shows that the increasing severity of legal restrictions is directly reflected in these later satires of Horace and of Persius. (*Cf*. pp. 85 ff.)

On the other hand in the present satire Horace, as Cartault and Lejay have seen (*op. cit*., p. 293) allows himself one final fling in the bold use of proper names, though these names are in the main those of victims of little social prominence.

[9] *Cf*. Gerhard, *op. cit*., pp. 248, n. 3.

[10] As in 1,4 and 1,10. See *supra*, pp. 277–306 for 1,4; pp. 336–349 for 1,10.

[11] Most of the material in these satires bore in greater detail upon Horace's more detailed treatment of the aesthetic and ethical principles of the satirist's art presented in 1,4 and 1,10. In view of the fragmentary condition of Lucilius and the fact that he too like Horace treated the same topic more than once it is difficult to relate passages of Horace in 1,4; 1,10 and 2,1 to corresponding passages of Lucilius with complete certainty.

[12] *Op. cit*., pp. 208–215.

[13] *Prolegomena*, p. xix.

[14] *Op. cit*., pp. 14–22.

[15] *Op. cit*., pp. 183 ff.

[16] Tacitus, *Ann*. 1, 72.

[17] *Op. cit*., p. 287.

[18] *Supra*, p. 370, note 8.

[19] In line 59 Horace uses the word *exsul*, perhaps a passing reflection upon the possibility of *relegatio*, which later became the actual penalty for offences under the laws of *maiestas* as administered by Augustus.

[20] See also my paper on *Lucilius and Persius*, in *Tr. A. P. A*., vol. 40, pp. 127 and 129 where I discuss another Horatian use of this commonplace in the *Ars Poetica* and in the first satire of Persius. Also my paper, *Lucilius, the Ars Poetica of Horace, and Persius*, in *Harvard Studies in Classical Philology*, vol. xxiv, p. 8. Juvenal I, 79 f., is the same commonplace.

> si natura negat, facit indignatio versum
> qualecumque potest, quales ego vel Cluvienus.

[21] So Lejay, *op. cit*., p. 294. It is conceivable that these lines might have stood in various contexts, but their presence in a satire in book 26 on a theme similar to Horace's satire 2,1, lends weight to this attribution of Lejay. Moreover, the attitude of all the Latin satirists is essentially identical with the Cynic commonplace undoubtedly known to them: οὐκ ἔστιν οὐδὲν σεμνὸν ὡς παρρησία. See Gerhard, *op. cit*., p. 280 or Diogenes cf. text 6, 69: ἐρωτηθεὶς τί κάλλιστον ἐν ἀνθρώποις, ἔφη παρρησία. *Cf*. also Gerhard, *op. cit*., index *s.v.* παρρησία.

[22] The lines 669, 671, 675 from the second satire of book 26 contain similar expression of independence, but since these lines express rather the economic independence of the landed proprietor who scorns commercial gains, than the spirit of free speech, they can hardly have influenced the general form of this satire, unless we should see a vague recollection of them

in lines 34 and 35 where Horace asserts his descent from the sturdy race of Lucanian or Apulian *coloni*. This, however, seems rather strained.

²³ *Op. cit.*, pp. 109–127.

²⁴ Although this **ἀσαγωγή** exercised great influence on the *Ars Poetica* of Horace, see Chapter VI *passim*, I am unable to find that these three fragments were imitated there.

²⁵ See Cichorius, *op. cit.*, p. 185 for the interpretation of these fragments. In *epistles* 2, 1, 250–263, Horace reiterates his predilection for satire as against the demand that he should write an encomiastic epic on the exploits of Augustus.

²⁶ This point is not found in the surviving fragments of the **ἀσαγωγή** to Iunius Congus.

²⁷ See Marx, comment. *ad loc.* for the textual difficulty. It seems to me possible that this arose from a word play upon the two meanings of *acies* (1) battle line, (2) eyesight, which not understood by copyists was the source of corruption.

²⁸ See *fragments* 394, 688, 1139 as examples of the praise of Scipio.

²⁹ Thus we have Cynic animal similes in 50–52 and 55 applied to the satirist's weapons in a way that recalls the treatment in 1, 4, 34; see *supra*, pp. 284 ff.; the half-ironical pretense that satire is used only in self-defense *cf.* 1, 4, 65–70 and *supra*, pp. 291 ff.; the stock suggestion of the *adversarius* that as satire is inseparable from *malice* it is justly suspected, see 1, 4, 20–23; it is a *triste carmen* see 1, 4, 33 ff., 65, 78–80. In general compare my treatment of satire, 1, 4, *passim*. On *triste* compare 1, 10, 15 and p. 343 *supra*.

³⁰ *E.g.*, book 26, 676, 678.

³¹ Lupus book 1, and 27, 784 ff.

³² *E.g.*, 258, 260.

³³ On the tribes see Marx' comment on 1259, 1260; Cichorius, *op. cit.*, pp. 335–338; the scholiast on Persius I; 114 who says: *quia tribus omnes xxxv laceravit.*

³⁴ See also *supra*, pp. 279 ff.

SATIRE 2

³⁵ See *supra*, pp. 248–251.

³⁶ For the more detailed comparison of the two satires see Lejay, *op. cit.*, pp. 324–325.

³⁷ See *supra*, pp. 298 ff.

³⁸ *Rh. Mus.* xlvii, p. 238.

³⁹ Lejay, *op. cit.*, pp. 322–323.

⁴⁰ See Cartault, *op. cit.*, p. 151.

⁴¹ Like Horace's father, another *abnormis sapiens*, masked as a sturdy old Roman from the country.

⁴² I follow here Lejay's admirable summary of the stylistic peculiarities of the satire, *op. cit.*, p. 325.

⁴³ Diog. Laert. x, 131. Usener, *op. cit.*, p. 641.

⁴⁴ As Lejay as pointed out, *op. cit.*, pp. 315 ff.

⁴⁵ *Tusc. Disp.*, 3, 49; 5, 26, 89; *De finibus* 2, 90; *Lael.* 86; *Parad.* 12.

⁴⁶ Lejay, *op. cit.*, p. 317 denies the direct influence of Bion upon this satire, but in my opinion without sufficient reason.

⁴⁷ *Op. cit.*, pp. 73-75.

⁴⁸ *Op. cit.*, pp. 72-73.

⁴⁹ *Op. cit.*, pp. 40-42.

⁵⁰ *Op. cit.*, pp. 89 ff.

⁵¹ *Op. cit.*, pp. 92-94. On this last see Hermes, xlii, 645, where we have a defence of poverty by Metrodorus.

⁵² See Marx, comment. *ad. loc.*; also *infra*, p. 410.

⁵³ As Cichorius has shown, *op. cit.*, pp. 296-298.

⁵⁴ I accept Cichorius' plausible reconstruction of this corrupt line.

⁵⁵ Lucilius, however, uses the simile to differentiate the true friend from the parasite.

⁵⁶ *vanis rerum* is Latin paraphrase for κενοδοξία.

⁵⁷ Assigned by Marx to book 20, Juvenal 5, 104 ff., is also an imitation of this commonplace.

⁵⁸ Zawdaski, *op. cit.*, p. 19 compares Lucilius 946: (◡ — ◡ — ◡ atque omnes mandonum gulae with Horace 39 ff.:) porrectum magno magnum spectare catino vellem ait Hapyiis gula digna rapacibus. Both passages have in common an abusive attack on gluttony and the use of the plebeianism *gula*. It is quite possible therefore that the Lucilian passage came from a context similar to the Horatian, but unfortunately we have no Lucilian context for the fragment so as to justify a more definite statement.

⁵⁹ Marx treats all these passages together in his commentary.

⁶⁰ One is tempted to compare Horace 99 ff., with Lucilius 1181, especially as we have lines 31-33 an imitation of Lucilius 1174, which as Marx has shown probably belong to a satire on the dinner of Granius, who speaks in the former fragment. At least it seems probable that Horace and Lucilius, perhaps following Greek sources characterized the conceit of the wealthy *parvenu*. Thus Lucilius:

> Granius autem
> non contemnere se et reges odisse superbos.

And Horace line 99 ff.:

> 'iure' inquit 'Trausius istis
> iurgatur verbis: ego vectigalia magna
> divitiasque habeo tribus amplas regibus.'

⁶¹ I accept Marx's explanation, comment. *ad. loc.*

⁶² Compare also Horace's *epistles* 1, 14, 37.

⁶³ See also Horace's *epistles*, 2, 2, 170.

⁶⁴ In *satire*, 1, 2, however, the commonplaces are mainly Epicurean.

SATIRE 3

⁶⁵ See Lejay, *op. cit.*, commentary on this satire, p. 385.

⁶⁶ *Cf.*, the *Memorabilia* of Xenophon; Lucian's *Memorabilia* of Sostratus, the Cynic, and of Demonax.

⁶⁷ See *supra*, pp. 156-158.

⁶⁸ I follow in general the admirable introduction of Lejay on this satire, *op. cit.*, pp. 356–390.

⁶⁹ See Lejay, *op. cit.*, p. 356, who cites Cicero, *de. off.*, I, 7; *de finibus* IV, 4, 8; *Tuscl. Disp.*, 3, 56, on the importance of *definitio* in the Stoic dialectic.

⁷⁰ Lejay, *op. cit.*, p. 357.

⁷¹ Lejay, *op. cit.*, p. 358.

⁷² On line 253 see Lejay's note; in general see Lejay, pp. 358–359.

⁷³ Lejay, *op. cit.*, pp. 359–360.

⁷⁴ Lejay, *op. cit.*, p. 362.

⁷⁵ Lejay, *op. cit.*, p. 362.

⁷⁶ For detailed enumeration of examples see Lejay, *op. cit.*, pp. 363–364.

⁷⁷ Lejay, *op. cit.*, pp. 364–365.

⁷⁸ Lejay, *op. cit.*, p. 365.

⁷⁹ Lejay, *op. cit.*, pp. 367–368 for tragedy; p. 370 for comedy.

⁸⁰ *E.g.*, that of Aristippus, 100 ff.; the conversion of Polemon, 254 ff.

⁸¹ Gerhard, *op. cit.*, p. 164.

⁸² Gerhard, *op. cit.*, p. 105.

⁸³ Gerhard, *op. cit.*, p. 100.

⁸⁴ Geffcken, *loc. cit.*, p. 484.

⁸⁵ Lejay, comment. *ad loc.*

⁸⁶ Gerhard, *op. cit.*, p. 45.

⁸⁷ Gerhard, *op. cit.*, p. 20.

⁸⁸ Gerhard, *op. cit.*, p. 94,2 and 189,2.

⁸⁹ Gerhard, *op. cit.*, p. 164.

⁹⁰ Gerhard, *op. cit.*, p. 191.

⁹¹ Gerhard, *op. cit.*, pp. 109 and 167.

⁹² See Lejay, *op. cit.*, p. 374. M. Heinze, *op. cit.*, p. 25. Lejay is inclined to doubt the influence of Bion in this place. On Aristo of Ceos, Bion and Horace *cf.* pp. 370 ff.

⁹³ Discussed by Lejay, *op. cit.*, pp. 381–382.

⁹⁴ *Op. cit.*, p. 15.

⁹⁵ I interpret *quaero* rather of the search for the *summum bonum* than with Marx as used in the sense of an important inquiry. The fact that Ulysses in the *Sesculixes* of Varro was a philosophical figure adds some incidental support to this view. For this meaning see Cicero, *Acad.* I, 5, 19: *negabant ulla alia in re nisi in natura quaerendum esse illud summum bonum. Quaero* would thus be in meaning not unlike Horace's *aut quicquid in vita meliore parasti.*

⁹⁶ The Lucilian passage might also be compared with Horace, line 34:

tempore quo me

solatus iussit sapientem pascere barbam

This line shows closer verbal resemblances to Lucilius, but the close parallel between the Horatian and the Lucilian sequence with the occurrence of the allusion to the Siren in both authors makes it more natural to refer Lucilius

1007 to the earlier Horatian passage. Of course Lucilius as well as Horace may have alluded more than once to the *barba sapeiens*.

[97] Marx line 1178, which is referred to book 27, 732, a similar theme, *cf. infra*, p. 393.

[98] Referred by Marx to a woman who neglects her household duties of spinning and weaving, but the similarity with the Horatian line and the other fragments in book 30 parallel to this satire make the reference suggested above more probable.

[99] Varro, *Eumenides* 148 B, while used in a different context may be quoted as confirming the probability that in this Lucilian fragment jaundice was used as a Stoic symbol for the effects of madness: nam ut arquatis lutea quae non sunt et quae sunt lutea videntur, sic insanis sani et furiosi videntur esse insani.

[100] See also Horace, *sat.* 2, 2, 25.

[101] See fragments 57 and 69. Also see *supra*, p. 245. Marx doubts whether the name is Lucilian, but with insufficient reason I think.

[102] *Cf. supra*, pp. 158–162 on the use of χρεῖαι in satire.

[103] Marx refers it to a philosophical dispute between the champions of two different schools.

[104] Lucilius also used in book 28, line 742, a χρεῖα upon the volumes sent to the tyrant Dionysius by the philosopher Aristippus. Horace in lines 99–102 quotes another χρεῖα told by Aristippus; the story of how he ordered his slaves to leave the gold in the Libyan desert that they might travel more rapidly.

[105] For such Stoic definitions see *supra*, p. 388. Marx assigns line 1178 to this satire where apart from its relation to other fragments of book 30 it might well stand.

[106] For Persius *cf.* 5, 161–174.

[107] I accept the interpretation of Heinze-Kiessling[4] on *annoso*.

[108] For Lucilius' attitude towards Greek words see *supra*, pp. 111 ff. and 338 ff.

SATIRE 4

[109] For Lejay's entirely different interpretation of the aim of Horace in this satire see *infra*, p. 399, n. 114.

[110] Here I follow the introduction of Lejay to this satire, *op. cit.*, pp. 441–455.

[111] *Cf.* Athenaeus, III, 102a, ed. Kaibel.

[112] *Cf.* Athenaeus, VII, 310a, ed. Kaibel.

[113] On this genre see *supra*, pp. 156–158.

[114] Lejay's theory, precisely the reverse of the traditional one, represented by Heinze-Kiessling is certainly in keeping with the refined irony of Horatian satire. According to him Catius is a simple Roman, who confines his gastronomic wanderings to Italy, who presents culinary *inventa*, traditional as early as Cato, and who differentiates true taste, expressed in nicety of service and moderation of expense from the lavish display of imported and costly viands. Thus under the mask of the

earnest, pompous, provincial gourmet, Horace could on the one hand satirize the pretentiousness of the professional culinary discourses of the schools, on the other hand such a satire may reflect the tone of conversations on the refinements of the table carried on within the Epicurean circle of Maecenas.

[115] We have a very large number of brief fragments from such culinary satires of Lucilius as those in books, 4, 5, 8, and scattering lines in books 13, 14, 30. Mention of viands that appear also in this satire of Horace is naturally common. Since most of these viands would recur in most Roman banquets, it is impossible to assert Lucilian influence exercised on Horace in this respect, in the absence of description of the provenance, preparation, or effects of such viands in Lucilius. See also my discussion of 2,8 passim, infra, pp. 408 ff.

[116] See supra, pp. 399 ff.

[117] Lucilius like Horace regarded sorrel as a dish of value. So in lines 1235 ff., we have Laelius addressing the gluttons in praise of sorrel. This passage as we have seen is more probably to be related to a theme similar to that of Horace, 2,2. See supra, pp. 378–387. It will be noticed, however, that the first Lucilian line implies an exposition in the manner of the Epicureans on the nature of sorrel.

> o lapathi, ut iactare, nec es satis cognitu qui sis!

Therefore it is at least possible in the immediate context now lost that Lucilius set forth the fact that the true nature of sorrel was a laxative. At any rate it is for this purpose that sorrel is praised by Horace, line 27 ff.:

> si dura morabitur alvus
> mitulus et viles pellent obstantia conchae
> et lapathi brevis herba, sed albo non sine Coo.

SATIRE 5

[118] Lejay, op. cit., holds that the similarities between Lucian and Horace are due rather to Lucian's familiarity with Horace than to the use by both authors of Menippus as a common source.

[119] See R. Helm, Lucian and Menipp., pp. 17–62.

[120] See Dryoff, Caesar's Anticato und Cicero's Cato, Rh. Mus., 63, 1908, pp. 587 ff.; A. Bonhöffer, Die Ethik des Stoikers Epiktet, p. 324 ff., 240. Apparently in his Anticato, Caesar, an Epicurean, attacked Cato of Utica, a Stoic as χρηματιστικός.

[121] Since Menippus lived in Thebes, cf. Helm, op. cit., p. 21, n. 3, it is tempting to conjecture that the incident of the anus improba Thebis, which look like a Greek χρεία, lines 84–88, is taken by Horace from him. For other parallels between Lucian and Horace, see Helm, op. cit., p. 205 ff. Helm believes these are due to Lucian's knowledge of Horace.

[122] E.g., in the Philoctetes of Sophocles.

[123] See Mahaffy, The Degradation of Odysseus in Greek Literature, Hermathena, Dublin, 1875, I, pp. 265 ff.

[124] Lejay, op. cit., pp. 484 ff.

[125] In the absence of any indications that Tiresias appeared in book 17 we are not justified in assigning the fragment to book 17.

[126] *Cf. supra*, pp. 154 ff., for a discussion of the Homeric material in book 30.

[127] So in Ovid, Heroides I, 81.

[128] See *supra*, pp. 386 ff., for a discussion of this commonplace in connection with Horace's *satire*, 2, 2.

[129] See Cichorius, *op. cit.*, p. 172.

SATIRE 6

[130] The sixth satire, an expression of gratitude to Maecenas for the gift of the Sabine farm, and an encomium, perhaps not uninfluenced by Epicurean coloring, upon the life of the country in contrast to that of the town, appears to be free from Lucilian influence.

SATIRE 7

[131] Stobaeus III, 3, 35; *fr.* 57, Rose *cf. Ox. Pap.* IV, p. 82.

[132] Lejay, *op. cit.*, p. 540.

[133] Lejay, *op. cit.*, pp. 539–541.

[134] Lejay, *op. cit.*, p. 545.

[135] Cicero, *paradoxa* III, 20, 22.

[136] Lejay, *op. cit.*, pp. 548–550.

[137] See Teles quoted by Max. of Tyre, *Disc.* 21, 1, and *satire* 1, 1, 15, *supra*, pp. 230 ff.

[138] Lejay, *op. cit.*, p. 546.

[139] Lejay, *op. cit.*, p. 546.

[140] Lejay, *op. cit.*, p. 547.

[141] Lejay, *op. cit.*, p. 547.

[142] Lejay, *op. cit.*, pp. 556–558.

[143] See pp. 248–274.

[144] See also Terence, *Phormio* 484: Plaut. *Bacch.* 66; Martial 10, 55, 4.

[145] We find the same scene satirically pictured in Persius 5, 156–66. Compare my note on *Udas ante fores* in *Classical Philology* 11, pp. 336, 338, for a brief discussion of the traditional satiric in distinction from the *erotic* manner of depicting exclusion scenes.

[146] See Cicero, *Paradoxa* 5, 36 for the rhetorical outline of this commonplace.

[147] *Has* perhaps refers to some such word as *ollas; cf.* Marx, *ad loc.;* also Juvenal 3, 276 ff.

[148] See Apicius 6, 221.

[149] Unless perhaps we see a vague Lucilian recollection in line 15 ff., where the gouty condition of the *scurra, Volanerius* is regarded as the result of a life of excess:

> Scurra Volanerius, postquam illi iusta cheragra
> contudit articulos, etc.

The physical defects of sin are a favorite topic for the Latin satirists. So Lucilius 331:

quod deformis, senex arthriticus ac podagrosus
est, quod mancus miserque, exilis, ramice magno.

With these passages from Horace and Lucilius we may compare also Persius 5, 57–59.

Again in line 97 the allusion to an Augustan gladiator Pacideianus would suggest the Lucilian gladiator of the same name in the fourth book line 151:

Pacideiano . . . optimus multo
post homines natos gladiator qui fuit unus.

SATIRE 8

[150] Cf. Christ, Griechisch. Literaturgesch., 4th ed., p. 766.

[151] On possible relations between Horace and Lucian, especially in regard to the συμπόσιον ἢ Λαπίθαι, see Helm, op. cit., p. 265, n. 5, and Lejay op. cit., p. 582. We have banquet scenes also in the ἀλεκτρυών 9–11, and the Ἑρμότιμος 11–12.

[152] Graius can hardly have been the laughing stock of his guests, but like Trimalchio and Nasidienus he may have had a weakness for foolish ostentation.

[153] Cf. supra, pp. 324–330.

[154] Horace imitates this commonplace more closely in sat. 2, 2, 18. See supra, p. 382.

[155] On this last line of Horace cf. Petronius 34 where the lecticarius sweeps away a silver dish which had fallen from the table.

[156] Lejay, op. cit., p. 581 points out that just as Nasidienus (16–17) gives his guests the choice between the better wines, Granius gives his guests the choice between the more delicate viands in line 1174. Cf. Petronius 36 for the altilia and sumina, also served at the beginning of the cena proper. On the Lucilian line 1176 cf. Horace sat. 2, 2, 31–32, supra, p. 384 ff.

[157] We may notice that in book 4, line 168 we have an allusion to the grus. This book contained an assault on table luxury, but the context appears quite different.

[158] Cf. the scholiast on Juvenal 9, 5 Crustula species operis pistorii.

[159] Cf. Columella 12, 52, 11.

[160] Cf. Petronius 62, mihi animam in naso esse.

CHAPTER VI

THE EPISTLES AND ARS POETICA

The three books of the odes were published in 23 B.C. After their publication Maecenas had apparently pressed Horace[1] to return to poetical composition, perhaps with the hope that he would continue his experiments in the Archilochian iambics by publishing a second book of epodes. But ten years had elapsed since the publication of the epodes, and in the meantime Horace's interests had changed! *non eademst aetas, non mens.*[2] Lyrical poetry also with its dalliance with the mood of the passing hour no longer attracted him. The flight of time, as he later declared,[3] had robbed him of his taste for such themes:

> singula de nobis anni praedantur euntes,
> eripuere iocos, Venerem, convivia, ludum;
> tendunt extorquere poemata; quid faciam vis?

Such pursuits he is now ready to put aside. So in the first epistle of the first book, an introduction to the earlier collection of twenty letters, he declares:[4]

> nunc itaque et versus et cetera ludicra pono.

His whole aesthetic and moral nature was now addressing itself to the most serious of all human problems, the art of life.[5] Again in the first epistle line 11: .

> quid verum atque decens curo et rogo, et omnis
> in hoc sum.

Hence we find in the first book of the epistles, or rather in the more formal letters of that collection, a renewed effort to adopt and restate the theories of the popular Epicurean, Cynic, and Stoic philosophy in a form suited to Roman society and morals. This is the same source of inspiration which first appeared in such satires as 1, 2, 3 in the first book, but which is given adequate and almost professional expression in several satires of the second book. In fact, these satires of the second book with their more systematic presentation of the questions

of social ethics are in content the direct precursors of the first
book of the epistles. Thus the second satire on the relation
between plain living and high thinking, the *tenuis victus*, the
third, on the Stoic paradox ὅτι πᾶς ἄφρων μαίνεται, the seventh
on the parallel paradox, ὅτι μόνος ὁ σοφὸς ἐλεύθερος, differ only
superficially from the treatment of similar themes in the
epistles.

The epistles, indeed, are simply a subdivision of the satiric
form. Like the satires they are not poetry in the strict sense
of the term. They are rather *sermones*[6] in the sense that they
are discourses, but while the satires are *sermones* addressed
directly to the reader, the epistles are either real letters ad-
dressed to some member of the poet's circle of friends, or else
they are discourses to the general public presented under cover
of an introduction to a friend in the epistolary form. Such a
convention is not so far removed from the device of employing
such dramatic spokesmen as Ofellus, Damasippus, Davus, and
others in the second book of satires.

In antiquity the *Epistulae* were reckoned with the *sermones*
as representations of the poetical form *satira*.[7] This is proved
by the testimony of Quintilian, Suetonius, Statius, Sidonius
Apollinaris, Porphyrio. Horace himself in *epp.* 2, 2, 58 is rightly
adduced in support of the same contention:

> denique non omnes eadem mirantur amantque:
> carmine tu gaudes, hic delectatur iambis,
> ille Bioneis sermonibus et sale nigro.

Here the satires (*sermones* and *epistulae*) are called *sermones*
in contrast with lyric poetry *carmen*, and the epodes *iambi*.
The epithet *Bioneis* also suggests an equivalent for διατριβαί
or λόγοι.

The use of the epistolary form represents, as we have
already seen, a long historical development.[8] In the period
separating Lucilius from Horace Catullus had written his
elegy to M. Allius in this form.[9] But the most important
influence in determining Horace's use of the form was its
employment by Lucilius in his fifth book. This book clearly
contained an epistle in which the poet laments to a friend
the wretched state of his health and blames the friend for his

failure to visit him, a *motif* which is not without direct influence upon the epistles of Horace.

Since the epistles are even more personal than the satires themselves, as they deal, now with contemporary life, now with the application of the laws of conduct to that life, it follows that the mould of satiric tradition is partly broken. Such imitations as we have from Lucilius are usually stray allusions to individual passages or illustrations with whose expression or teaching Horace for the moment finds himself in sympathy. The situation thus differs radically—if we except the *Ars Poetica*—from that revealed by my analysis of the satires of Horace's first and second books. Moreover, after the long years of study and experiment, of imitation of, and modification of the great Lucilian tradition of satire, Horace, never a slavish imitator, and now in the maturity of his powers, had come to feel that by the recomposition of all these elements of contemporary life and past tradition he had fused the new mould of Horatian satire. He had, in fact, attained the complete mastery of the form best suited to express his critical judgment upon the aesthetic and moral ideals of the Augustan age. As a result of such consciousness—and we may trace a similar intellectual development in the three books of fables by Phaedrus—we find a diminution of Lucilian influence in the epistles. Horace has now attained complete literary maturity. I now turn to the scattered evidence of Lucilian imitations or influence disclosed by a study of the epistles.

If my assumption, discussed in detail in connection with the first satire of the first book of Horace is correct, that Juvenal 14, 207 is to be regarded as a verse of Lucilian origin,[10] we probably have in line 53 of Horace's first epistle yet another passage which betrays the influence of the Lucilian formulation of the commonplace that money is power, as all the world knows. In both Horace and Juvenal we are told that all classes of Romans had learned this lesson by rote and hold that money must be gained by any and every means, just as the school boys have learned their lessons from dictation and then rehearse them. The Horatian passage which may be compared for details with the passage of Juvenal already quoted is as follows:

> vilius argentumst auro, virtutibus aurum:
> 'o cives, cives, quaerenda pecunia primumst;
> virtus post nummos; haec, Ianus summus ab imo.
> prodocet, haec recinunt iuvenes dictata senesque
> laevo suspensi loculos tabulamque lacerto.

It will be observed that in the Horatian passage, Ianus, who repeats the assignment for dictation, acts as the schoolmaster. The general resemblance of this aphorism with such Lucilian fragments as 559 adds to the probability that Buecheler's conjecture that the line is Lucilian is correct. It will be noticed that Horace's phrase *virtus post nummum* recalls the comparison between *aurum* and *homo* in the Lucilian fragment. I am, therefore, inclined to connect this recovered Lucilian line with fragment 559 and assign it to book 19 of Lucilius. That line reads:

> 'aurum vis hominem <ne> habeas' hominem?' quid ad aurum?'

In lines 70 ff. Horace uses the fable of the sick lion and the fox to illustrate the fact that he is terrified by the fashion in which all individual judgments are consumed in the capacious maw of the many-headed beast, *Demos*. Many tracks lead into the cave, but none are turned in the reverse direction to mark the return to personal independence of judgment on the part of those who have yielded to the unthinking judgment of the crowd. This same fable, doubtless a favorite apothegm in the Cynic-Stoic armory, was used in fuller form by Lucilius in fragments 980, 981, 983, 985, 988, while Horace in lines 73-76 briefly summarized its climax. Thus Horace:

> olim quod volpes aegroto cauta leoni
> respondit, referam: 'quia me vestigia terrent,
> omnia te adversum spectantia, nulla retrorsum.'
> belua multorum es capitum. nam quid sequar aut quem?

And Lucilius:

> leonem
> aegrotum ac lassum
> tristem, et corruptum scabie, et porriginis plenum
> inluuies scabies oculos huic deque petigo
> conscendere.
> deducta tunc uoce leo: 'cur tu ipsa uenire
> non uis huc?
> sed tamen hoc dicas quid *sit*, si noenu molestum est.

'quid sibi uult, quare fit ut intro uorsus *et* ad te
spectent atque ferant uestigia se omnia prorsus?

The second epistle in accordance with the allegorical method
of interpretation favored by the Cynics and Stoics interprets
Homer as a treasure house of ethical theory and precept.[11]
It contains only one stray allusion to Lucilius.

In line 26 Horace uses the name of an animal, the *sus*, as a
monosyllabic verse tag. Lucilius, however, approved only of
the use of the smaller animals in such cases.[12] Thus Servius
on the *Aeneid* 8, 83 says under the *lemma, conspicitur sus*:
Horatius 'et amica luto sus:' sciendum tamen hoc esse vitiosum:
nisi forte ipso monosyllabo minora explicentur animalia, ut
'parturient montes nascetur ridiculus mus!' gratiores enim
versus isti sunt secundum Lucilium.

The third epistle is a letter addressed to Julius Florus, a
friend of Horace, who is a member of the suite of Tiberius
serving at the time in the east. To him was also addressed
ep. 2, 2. Porphyrio on line 1 informs us that Florus made an
anthology of the older Latin satirists: Hic Florus scriba fuit,
saturarum scriptor cuius sunt electae ex Ennio, Lucilio, Var-
rone saturae. In view of this familiarity of Florus with Latin
satire and with Lucilius the relationship between lines 15 ff.
and Lucilius fragment 549 is of some significance. Doubtless,
such a student of Lucilius would, in accordance with the inten-
tion of Horace, be reminded by the warning against literary
plagiarism given Celsus Albinovanus, that Lucilius had also
protested against this practice in 549:

si messis facis <*et*> Musas si vendis Lavernae.

In Horace Celsus is warned against the habit of pillaging the
library of Apollo. Now since we know that the temple of the
Muses was the *rendezvous* of the poets and *scribae* of the age of
Lucilius we are justified, I believe, in regarding Horace's allusion
to the new library and temple of Apollo on the Palatine as in
part a recollection of a parallel institution of the age of Lucilius.[13]
Marx's suggested context for the Lucilian line seems to me
essentially correct: Itaque 'si messis facis' antecedenti versu
habebat quo explicaretur veluti 'agris alienis si messis.' In this
connection we may further note that such an allusion would be

especially appropriate in a letter to Florus, a member of the
guild of *scribae*. Also the sarcastic allusion in *ep*. 2, 2, 93
seems to me to show that in connection with the new library
there was an adjacent room (*procul*) in which poets might
recite their works:[14]

> adspice primum
> quanto cum fastu, quanto molimine circum—
> spectemus vacuam Romanis vatibus aedem.
> mox etiam, si forte vacas, sequere et procul audi,
> quid ferat et quare sibi nectat uterque coronam.

To the same general effect may be cited *ep*. 2, 1, 214:

> verum age, et his, qui se lectori credere malunt
> quam spectatoris fastidia ferre superbi,
> curam redde brevem, si munus Apolline dignum
> vis complere libris et vatibus addere calcar,
> ut studio maiore petant Helicona virentem.

The Horatian passage in this third epistle, lines 15-20, evidently
is related to the same general context:

> quid mihi Celsus agit? monitus multumque monendus,
> privatas ut quaerat opes et tangere vitet
> scripta Palatinus quaecumque recepit Apollo,
> ne, si forte suas repetitum venerit olim
> grex avium plumas, moveat cornicula risum
> furtivis nudata coloribus.

It will be noticed that the idea of literary theft which in the
Lucilian passage is somewhat baldly stated as selling the
Muses to Laverna, the patron divinity of thieves, is more
gracefully presented in Horace's epistle under cover of the
fable of the crow in stolen plumage.

The next three epistles, 4, 5, 6; two short letters to Albius
Tibullus and to Torquatus, and the third a longer philosophical
exposition of the doctrine of *nil admirari*, addressed to Numicus
are apparently without Lucilian influence.

In the seventh epistle, however, we have two possible
Lucilian echoes. Thus in line 29, Horace uses the fable of the
dormouse and the weasel. Horace, now middle-aged, can no
longer meet the demands of Maecenas in the same manner as
in his youth. He is like the dormouse of the fable. The dor-
mouse after having crawled through the narrow hole and then

stuffed himself with the contents of the bin was then unable to return by the same passage. At this juncture the weasel, observing his plight, remarked that to get out the dormouse must keep as thin as when he went in. As applied to Maecenas the point of the fable is that he must restore to Horace his youth if he would keep him constantly at his side; as applied to Horace, that since he has grown fat on the bounty of his patron he must now resign everything if he would free himself from the corresponding obligation to meet the restrictions imposed by the patron's wishes. And, in fact, in lines 35-40 Horace does answer that he is willing to pay this price to secure his leisure and independence.

This fable was perhaps used in Lucilius' fragment 208 which may well refer to a thieving animal:[16]

> dic quam cogat uis ire minutim
> per commissuras rimarum noctis nigrore.

This interpretation is the more probable because fragment 203 seems to show that, like Horace, (lines 34-35) Lucilius in this epistle recognized that wealth was not synonymous with contentment of spirit. Thus Lucilius:

> nam si, quod satis est homini, id satis esse potisset,
> hoc sat erat: nunc cum hoc non est, qui credimus porro
> diuitias ullas animum mi explere potisse?

So Horace in lines 34-36:

> hac ego si conpellor imagine, cuncta resigno;
> nec somnum plebis laudo satur altilium nec
> otia divitiis Arabum liberrima muto.

In view of the indications of a context thus partially indicated it seems reasonable to compare with Lucilius 208, the Horatian lines 29-33:

> forte per angustam tenuis nitedula rimam
> repserat in cumeram frumenti, pastaque rursus
> ire foras pleno tendebat corpore frustra.
> cui mustela procul 'si vis' ait 'effugere istinc,
> macra cavum repetes artum, quem macra subisti.'

In line 65 of this epistle occurs the rare Lucilian word *scruta*, a further slight indication of Lucilian coloring in this epistle.

Without asserting any direct imitation it is surely worth
noticing that the hypochondriacal tone of complaint which per-
vades the eighth epistle to Celsus Albinovanus is similar to that
so marked in the Lucilian epistle found in book 5, and repre-
sented by fragments 181, 184, 189, 1292, 1277. These frag-
ments, in fact, show distinct general resemblances to the tone
of the first twelve lines of the Horatian epistle, although in
Lucilius the poet complains that he is not visited while ill by
his friend, whereas Horace complains rather of his own ill-
health, peevishness, and discontent.

Fragment 181 gives the general setting for the letter of
Lucilius:

ὁμοιοτέλευτα—ceteraque huius modi scitamenta—quam sint insubida et inertia
et puerilia, facillissime hercle significat in quinto saturarum Lucilius. Nam
ubi est cum amico conquestus, quod ad se aegrotum non uiseret, haec ibidem
addit festiuiter:

    quo me habeam pacto, tam etsi non quaeris, docebo,
    quando is eo numero mansi quo in maxima non est
    pars hominum . . .

And 184

    ut per<i>sse uelis, quem uisere nolueris, cum
    debueris. Hoc 'nolueris' et 'debueris' te
    si minus (quod atechnon) et Eissocratium hoc
    lerodesque simul totum ac si miraciodes,
    non operam perdo, si tu hic.

With the general tone of these Lucilian lines we may especially
compare lines 3 and 4 of the complaint of Horace which is found
in lines 3-14:

    si quaeret quid agam, dic multa et pulchra minantem
    vivere nec recte nec suaviter:

In the same neurasthenic tone Lucilius continues in fragment
189:

    si tam corpus loco ualidum ac regione maneret
    scriptoris, quam uera manet sententia cordi.

This is somewhat like Horace lines 7 ff.:

    sed quia mente minus validus quam corpore toto
    nil audire velim, nil discere, quod levet aegrum;
    fidis offendar medicis, irascar amicis,
    cur me funesto properent arcere veterno.

Similarly in 1292, which is assigned by Marx to the same epistle, Lucilius says that his physical health was as great a danger to him as two pirates, Rhondes and Icadion, whose names he gives, were a source of danger to sailors:

Rhondes Icadionque

cum dixit Lucilius duo nomina piratarum posuit, tam infestum sibi corpus et ualitudinem referens quam i li essent saluti nauigantium.

Perhaps also Lucilius complained (1277) of chills and headaches:

querquera consequitur * capitisque dolores

The next five epistles 9, 10, 11, 12, 13, are intimate personal letters, which naturally contain no Lucilian recollections. Thus 9 is a letter introducing Septimius to Tiberius. 10, written to his friend Aristius Fuscus, praises the life of the country above that of the town as freer from anxieties and more likely to secure contentment and true freedom. 11, which is written to Bullatius, who is travelling in Asia Minor in search of mental distraction, urges him to remove his disquietude by the discipline of contentment, not by long journeys. 12 is a purely personal epistle written in a tone of gentle irony to Iccius, who is torn between the conflicting claims of business and philosophy. 13 is really a note designed to be presented to Augustus to accompany a copy of the three books of the odes, but written as a set of fussy directions to Vinnius Asina, the mutual friend of Horace and Augustus, who is the bearer.

On the other hand, the fourteenth epistle shows traces of Lucilian influence, though I hesitate to go as far as Tyrrel in affirming that the whole epistle follows a Lucilian model.[16] The epistle is ostensibly addressed to the bailiff of Horace's estate. Horace, after remarking that his servant scorns the farm which he himself loves, humorously suggests that they engage in a contest to see whether the bailiff is more of an adept in plucking the thorns out of the ground than Horace is in plucking the faults out of his heart, and in consequence whether Horace or his estate is in the better condition. Thus:

Vilice silvarum et mihi me reddentis agelli,
quem tu fastidis habitatum quinque focis et
quinque bonos solitum Variam dimittere patres,

> certemus, spinas animone ego fortius an tu
> evellas agro et melior sit Horatius an res.

Now in Lucilius it seems natural to regard fragment 213, which might, to be sure, be taken literally of a man wandering through a thicket of thorns,[17] as referring to the sins, which like the biblical tares encumber the human heart. *Plenum*, the gloss of Nonius on *stat* accords well with such an interpretation. Thus:

> — ◡ ◡ — ◡ ◡ interea stat sentibus pectus.

The passage would, therefore, mean that in the meanwhile (*interea*), that is while you neglect the duty of reformation, your breast is full of brambles.

Again in line 19 Tyrrel is perhaps right in believing that the rare word *tesqua* is an archaism borrowed from Lucilius, for Lucilius is familiar with such technical terms though this word does not occur in our surviving fragments.

It is also worth noticing that Lucilius in two places refers to the *uilicus*. The reference in fragment 512 is purely general and shows no relation to this epistle. On the other hand, fragment 532 certainly suggests the theme of a *uilicus*, who like his Horatian counterpart is indifferent and slack with his work on some country estate (presumably one belonging to Lucilius). Thus:[18]

> 'fundi delectat uirtus te, uilicus paulo
> strenuior si euaserit.'

Probably also Dousa, the first great Lucilian scholar was right in seeing in fragment 704 in book 27 a parallel to lines 36 and 37 for both passages refer to the sidelong glances of envy. Thus Horace:

> non istic obliquo oculo mea commoda quisquam
> limat, non odio obscuro morsuque venenat.

And Lucilius 704:

> nulli me inuidere, non strabonem fieri saepius
> deliciis me istorum![19]

The fifteenth epistle is addressed to a certain Numonius Vala, who apparently belonged to a family of some importance on the peninsula of Sorrento. Horace, who has been advised to take the cold water cure by his physician Antonius Musa, therefore asks Vala various questions about bread, water, game, and sea food in a district, which, in contrast to the more fashionable peninsula of Baiae, might seem very "primitive." He then pokes fun at his own inconsistency, in that he, the constant preacher of the simple life, should make such inquiries. He is like the Lucilian spendthrift Maenius, "who was a preacher against prodigals, but who always returned with delight to his old life." Or he is like Bestius after his reformation, perhaps a Lucilian character. With the exception of these two Lucilian allusions, the epistle appears to refer entirely to contemporary events.

The Maenius referred to is probably the one mentioned in fragment 1203:[30]

> [Maenius] columnam
> cum peteret.

The incident referred to in this fragment is explained by Porphyrio's commentary on Horace *sat.* 1, 3, 21, which contains an allusion to the same Lucilian character:[31]

> Hic post patrimonium adrosum Kalendis Ianuariis in Capitolio clara voce optaret ut quadringinta milia nummorum aeris alieni haberet <et> quaerente quodam, quid sibi vellet, quod tam sollemni die aes alienum habere optaret, 'Noli mirari' inquit octingenta debeo. Hic fertur domo sua quam ad forum spectantem habuerat divendita in unam columnam inde sibi excepisse, unde gladiatores spectaret, quae ex eo Maeni columna nominabatur. Cuius et Lucilius sic meminit.[32]

Doubtless, also some passages from Lucilian satire are the basis for the delineation of his character in lines 26-46. Line 31 looks especially like a repetition in substance of a Lucilian characterization of Maenius, for it is quite in the Lucilian manner:

> pernicies et tempestas barathrumque macelli
> quidquid quaesierat ventri donaret avaro.

In Horace's lines this Lucilian worthy is described, doubtless, in Lucilian colors, as a reckless and witty spendthrift, who, after he had run through two fortunes became a *scurra*, who had no regular crib to eat from. He was, however, so savage in the jests with which he repaid chance hospitality that at last he could find no patrons. Then as hungry as three bears, he would eat whole platters of cheap lamb and tripe, all the while maintaining that the bellies of gluttons should be seared with hot plates of metal. He spoke, in fact, like a reformed Bestius. Yet this very man if he had captured a greater prize would praise as the best thing in the world a fat thrush or a large sow's matrix.

The *correctus Bestius*[32] here mentioned is doubtless another Lucilian type. If we may judge from Persius *sat.* 6, 37, he assailed like Cato the censor the fashionable immigrant philosophers, whose teaching corrupted the city. Even the haymakers, the type of rustic simplicity, spoil their porridge with thick oil. Thus:

> et Bestius urget
> doctores Graios: "ita fit; postquam sapere urbi
> cum pipere et palmis venit, nostrum hoc maris expers
> faenisecae crasso vitiarunt unguine pultes."

The sixteenth epistle while nominally addressed to Quinctius is in reality a discourse on the Stoic text, ὅτι αὐτάρκης ἡ ἀρετὴ πρὸς εὐδαιμονίαν,[33] designed actually for the general reading public. The epistle begins (1-16) with the well-known description of the Sabine farm which assures the poet bodily health and peace of spirit. The poet then turning to his friend Quinctius expresses his fears (18) lest, led astray by popular estimates, Quinctius shall forget the true ideal of the virtuous Stoic *sapiens.* He then, (lines 21 ff.) proceeds with his admonition by employing the well-known and well-worn Stoic commonplace which compares the πάθη σώματος with the πάθη ψυχῆς, while he incidentally insists upon the Cynic-Stoic theory of simplicity of diet.

Now this commonplace was also employed but apparently in much greater detail by Lucilius in book 26 fragments 635, 639, 638, 640, 643, 641, 645, 647, 648, 642. The topic was later reproduced by Persius 3, 88-109. Lucilius announces his general thesis in 635 and again in 639. His text is the interdependence of soul and body:

> principio physici omnes constare hominem ex anima et corpore
> dicunt.

The rich glutton appears in all three satirists. In Lucilius and in Persius he consults a doctor and is ordered to rest. The Horatian passage, which is in effect a summary allusion rather than a developed exposition of the commonplace, does not contain this preliminary exposition, but begins when under the influence of gluttony the patient ignores the signs of fever at meal time. The result is a chill. Horace also omits the conclusion of the commonplace, the sudden attack of nausea, brought on by gluttony, and consequent death.[28] Horace's lines 21-24 follow:

> neu, si te populus sanum recteque valentem
> dictitet, occultam febrem sub tempus edendi
> dissimules, donec manibus tremor incidat unctis.
> stultorum incurata pudor malus ulcera celat.

In the Lucilian formulation 638 asserts that an overmastering passion reacts on the body:

> animo qui aegrotat, uidemus corpore hunc signum dare.

640 describes the false hope engendered by a temporary improvement:

> idcirco omnes euasuros censent aegritudinem.

And 641 the consequent visit to stadium and gymnasium:

> cum <in> stadio, in gymnasio, in duplici corpus siccassem pila.

In 643 the doctor tries to drive out the chill by warm clothes:

> uestimentis frigus atque horrorem exacturum putet.

Here we may notice that the *tremor* of Horace reproduces the *frigor ac horror* of Lucilius. 645 suggests that an *eluuies uentris* may relieve the over-burdened stomach:

> — ◡ — ◡ ut, si eluuiem facere per uentrem uelis,
> cura, ne omnibus distento corpore expiret uiis.

647 describes the disgusting details of the illness:

> si hic uestimenta * * eluit luto,
> ab eo risum magnum imprudens ac cachinnum subicit.

In 642 the doctor feels the patient's pulse:

> neque prius quam uenas hominis tetigit ac praecordia.

In fragment 659 from the same book 26 Lucilius asserts the dangers of avarice and the advantage of a simple diet:

> mordicus petere aurum e flamma expediat, e caeno cibum.

The last clause refers to the ideal simplicity of diet advocated by the Cynics. Persius expands this idea in his satire 3, 111-114 into a picture of the disinclination of the wealthy man for the simple fare of the people—and we may add of the Cynic,— their philosopher. The Horatian line 24 is in fact directly imitated, expanded, and heightened by Persius 113-114:

> tenero latet ulcus in ore
> putre, quod haud deceat plebeia radere beta.

But the germ of the thought in both writers is the line of Lucilius. On the other hand, the spirit at least of the first part of the Lucilian line is reproduced later in this same epistle in lines 63 ff.:

> qui melior servo, qui liberior sit avarus,
> in triviis fixum cum se demittit ob assem,
> non video.

This is in turn given by Persius 5, 111 ff.:

> inque luto fixum possis transcendere nummum
> ne gluttu sorbere salivam Mercurialem?

The seventeenth epistle, which Kiessling holds was written to justify Horace's relation to Maecenas, is nominally addressed to a young acquaintance Scaeva. This defence is made in the terms of the philosophy of Aristippus, whose creed and personality were especially attractive to Horace. Although Lucilius, as we may see from fragment 742 in book 27 was familiar with the teachings of Aristippus, I have been unable to discover any traces of Lucilian influence in this epistle. The eighteenth epistle, a companion piece to the seventeenth, upon the relation between protégé and patron is addressed, as is epistle 1, 2, to Lollius Maximus. After discussing the tact with which the defendant must adapt himself to the mood of his patron Horace concludes by a brief summary of directions for the attainment of peace of mind. There is no evidence of the influence of Lucilius in this epistle.

The nineteenth epistle, while addressed to Maecenas, is in substance an attack on Horace's critics, doubtless in many cases the same critics already assailed in satires 1, 4 and 1, 10, and who now ignore the three books of the odes. Horace attacks these critics for plagiarism and clannishness. He asserts his originality, although like Sappho and Alcaeus he has dealt freely with his models. He will remain independent of the organization of these professional critics nor will he take part in their recitations. However, he will not after their example indulge in personal abuse. Especially in lines 33-40, Horace reasserts his desire that his work should gain the approval of that reading public which is marked by general culture and appreciation; that is, he aims at an audience which embodies the virtues of the golden mean. On the one hand, he does not seek the applause of the inconstant crowd, whose votes are purchasable and therefore worth less. On the other hand, he will not court as hearer (*auditor*) nor as avenging rival (*ultor*) the notice of the professional guild of poets:[26]

> iuvat inmemorata ferentem
> ingenuis oculisque legi manibusque teneri.
> scire velis, mea cur ingratus opuscula lector
> laudet ametque domi, premat extra limen iniquus:
> non ego ventosae plebis suffragia venor
> inpensis cenarum et tritae munere vestis,
> non ego nobilium scriptorum auditor et ultor
> grammaticas ambire et pulpita dignor.

It is abundantly clear from this outline and from the passage quoted that Horace here asserts, probably with relation to his odes and epistles, the essential points of the satiric commonplace upon the choice of an audience, which he had already announced in relation to his satires in 1, 4, 71-76, and 1, 10, 72-90.[27]

As I have already shown that those passages stand in direct and close relation to Lucilius book 26, fragments 588, 589, 592, 593, 594, 595, it follows that the present passage, in which Horace has in mind rather his own earlier proclamation of his aesthetic creed in relation to the choice of his readers is a sort of indirect reflection of the Lucilian theory.

The twentieth epistle is an epilogue to the book, written in the year 20 B.C. at the time when the first collection of epistles was arranged for publication. It is at once an expression of the mingled hopes and fears with which the writer gives his work to the world, and a brief life of the author,[28] (21-28, following in miniature the topical arrangement of the standard literary biographies, such as are preserved in Suetonius). Here naturally we have no trace of Lucilian influence; indeed the content of the epistle suggests rather the genius of the elegiac epigram than the epistolary satire.

THE SECOND BOOK OF THE EPISTLES

The second book of epistles was written during the concluding years of Horace's life. These epistles seem to have been published at about the same time as the fourth book of the odes, that is about 14 or 13 B.C. The mood in which Horace composed these three delightful literary essays is well expressed in the second epistle, line 141 ff.:

> nimirum sapere est abiectis utile nugis,
> et tempestivum pueris concedere ludum,
> ac non verba sequi fidibus modulanda Latinis,
> sed verae numerosque modosque ediscere vitae.

Horace accordingly abandoned all thought of independent composition, and decided to write for the benefit of the younger generation his theories of the literary art. With this purpose were written the second epistle to Iulius Florus, composed at a time when Horace was still firm in his devotion to philosophy, but incidentally giving a vivid picture of literary conditions in Rome, and the *Ars Poetica*, a more formal εἰσαγωγή or introduction to poetic composition addressed to the Pisos, Cn. Piso the consul of 23 B.C. and his two sons. To these two epistolary treatises Horace prefixed the first epistle dedicated to Augustus. This epistle was written according to the *vita* of Suetonius at the direct request of Augustus. The emperor who had read some of the *sermones* of Horace complained that the poet had made no mention of him adding: an vereris apud posteros infame tibi sit, quod uidearis familiaris nobis esse. Apparently the *sermones* referred to were the second epistle and the *Ars Poetica*, which most closely resemble the first epistle in tone. This is probably one of Horace's last published works. "Its contents are general. It discusses the attitude of the literary critics of that day towards contemporary writers, it contains an eloquent plea for the worth of the poet, a partial sketch of the growth of Roman literature, a severe condemnation of the degeneracy of dramatic taste, an appeal to Augustus on behalf of less pretentious poets and a warning to the poets themselves to avoid some decided blunders in approaching their patrons."[29] The epistle was perhaps dedicated to Augustus in 13 B.C. on his return from a three years' absence in Gaul.

The epistle contains a few traces of Lucilian influence. In line 50 ff. the characterization of Ennius repeats the tradition first proclaimed by Ennius himself,[30] but repeated by Lucilius that the father of Roman poetry was the reincarnation of Homer:

> Ennius et sapiens et fortis et alter Homerus.
> ut critici dicunt, leuiter curare uidetur
> quo promissa cadant et somnia Pythagorea.

Lucilius, fragment 1189, spoke of Ennius as *alter* Homerus, according to Saint Jerome:[31]

> Homerus alter ut Lucilius de Ennio suspicatur.

Here Marx plausibly infers from *suspicatur* that Lucilius may have ridiculed the dream by which at the beginning of the *Annales* Ennius described the transmigration of the soul of Homer to his body after it had passed through an intermediate incarnation as a peacock.[32]

Although it is impossible to speak with certainty in view of the vagueness of the fragments, it is tempting to conjecture that in a Lucilian satire in book 9, which dealt with literary criticism, there was a comparison between Ennius and the crude beginnings of Italian poetry as typified by the hymns of the *Salii*. Thus fragments 319 and 320 clearly refer to the Salii and their dance:

> hinc ancilia, ab hoc apices capidasque repertas,
> praesul ut amptruet inde, ut vulgus redamptruet inde.

I shall venture to bring these lines into relation with Horace's allusion in line 86 to the *saliare Numae carmen*:

> iam Saliare Numae carmen qui laudat, et illud
> quod mecum ignorat solus volt scire videri
> ingeniis non ille favet plauditque sepultis
> nostra sed impugnat, nos nostraque lividus odit.

Now the possibility of this comparison once granted it is worth noticing that in Lucilius 338 and 341 we have a definition of the nature of *poesis* and *poema*, and an insistence on the importance of structural unity as revealed in the *Annales* of

Ennius and the Iliad of Homer.   Hence I am inclined to think
that such finished works of art were contrasted by Lucilius
with the rude, brief and inchoate remains of early Latin, such
as the hymns of the *Salii*.   So in 338 Lucilius says that the
distinction between poetic forms is not understood.

> non haec quid ualeat, quidue hoc intersiet illud,
> cognoscis primum hoc, quod dicimus esse poema.
> pars est parua poema.

In the same spirit Horace (72-75) protests like Lucilius
against a theory of literary criticism which is based merely on
the beauties or defects of individual passages without regard
to the structural perfection of the whole work.   Hence we may
compare with these lines of Horace Lucilius 345 ff.; and we
may further notice that Horace uses *poema* as does Lucilius.
The Lucilian fragment reads:

> — ⌣ espistula item quaeuis non magna poema est.
> illa poesis opus totum, (tota [que] Ilias *una*
> est, una ut *θέσις* annales Enni) atque *opus* unum
> est, maius multo est quam quod dixi ante poema.
> qua propter dico: nemo qui culpat Homerum,
> perpetuo culpat, neque quod dixi ante poesin:
> uersum unum culpat, uerbum, entymema, *locum* < *unum* >.

So Horace also directs his criticism in lines 69-75 to details
substituting the Odyssey of Livius Andronicus as an example
of archaic poetry:

> non equidem insector delendave carmina Livi
> esse reor, memini quae plagosum mihi parvo
> Orbilium dictare: sed emendata videri
> pulchraque et exactis minimum distantia miror.
> inter quae verbum emicuit si forte decorum et
> si versus paullo concinnior unus et alter
> iniuste totum ducit venditque poema.

Furthermore, if we recall Porphyrio's note on Horace *sat.* 1,
10, 53, it seems clear that this same satire contained dramatic
criticism at any rate on Accius, and perhaps on other poets:

> "Nil comis tragici mutat Lucilius Acci?"   Facit autem haec Lucilius
> cum alias tum vel maxime in tertio libro: memenit[23] VIIII et X

Later in this epistle (line 123) the simple fare of the poet is
described.   The line is imitated from Lucilius fragment 501,

which described the *tenuis victus* or "simple life" prescribed by
the Stoic philosophy. The Lucilian passage is:

> quae gallam bibere ac rugas conducere uentris
> farre aceroso, oleis, decumano pane coegit.

And Horace's words:

> vivit siliquis et pane secundo.

Here the Lucilian *panis acerosus* is exactly the equivalent of the
panis secundus of Horace: the allusion, however, is transferred
from the philosopher to the poet.[34]

In lines 245 to 263 Horace recurs for the third time to the
expression of the favorite commonplace,[35] that the gifts of the
satirist are lower than those of the epic poet, and hence that he
can never hope to essay with success the grand style of epic
composition. The satirist must rather recognize the deficiency
of his powers, however willing his spirit may be, or at most be
satisfied with a short flight on epic wings, such as the description
of Augustus' battles in *sat.* 2, 1, 10-15 already fully discussed,
but which may be repeated here for comparison with the present
formulation of the commonplace:

> aut, si tantus amor scribendi te rapit, aude
> Caesaris invicti res dicere, multa laborum
> praemia laturus. Cupidum, pater optime, vires
> deficiunt; neque enim quivis horrentia pilis
> agmina nec fracta pereuntias cuspide Gallos
> aut labentis equo describat volnera Parthi.

Compare lines 250-255 in the present epistle:

>   nec sermones ego mallem
> repentis per humum quam res conponere gestas,
> terrarumque situs et flumina dicere et arcis
> montibus inpositas et barbara regna tuisque
> auspiciis totum confecta duella per orbem
> claustraque custodem pacis cohibentia Ianum
> et formidatam Parthis te principe Romam,
> si quantum cuperem possem quoque; sed neque parvum
> carmen maiestas recipit tua nec meus audet
> rem temptare pudor quam vires ferre recusent.

On the other hand, the satirist Horace suggests slyly that a
caricature fastens itself more firmly in the minds of men than a
noble picture, and therefore that he will continue to pursue his
half-serious, half-mocking art.

It is at once clear that these lines show a refracted influence, so to speak, from such Lucilian passages as fragments 620, 621, 622, in book 26, and more particularly from fragments 1079, 1085, 1086, 1088, 1080, 1081, 1095 in book 30. In this book Lucilius declines to celebrate the exploits of a patron, perhaps Sempronius Tuditanus on precisely similar grounds, but like Horace attempts a short epic flight, which he then immediately abandons with a frank confession of incapacity for such composition. I must refer my readers to the discussion of these lines in connection with Horace's *sat.* 2, 1.

Here also in lines 260-270 Horace asserts the decisive power of ridicule represented by satire, which is also the natural expression of the satirist's inner nature. These lines may be compared with the similar argument in *sat.* 2, 1, 40-56. Just so Lucilius in fragment 1095, as we have seen, compared his frank attacks to the rush of the mad dog, the analogue of the cynic philosopher:

> inde canino ritu oculisque
> inuolem.

The second epistle is addressed to Julius Florus, who is still, as in *epistle* 1, 3 absent from Rome in the suite of Tiberius. After excusing himself humorously for his deficiencies as a correspondent, Horace declines to write verses for several reasons. He has feathered his nest, like the soldier of Lucullus; hence the financial motive is gone. The years also have robbed him of the inclination to poetry; but above all the social and literary atmosphere of Rome is inimical to true poetry. The poets of the day are enrolled in a mutual admiration society. The dilettante may be happy, but the true poet now dreads the labor necessary to perfect his work. It is better to avoid the harmonies of poetry and seek to attain the harmonies of life. Most of all the folly of avarice should be shunned. Horace so far has been able to avoid hurtful extremes and to practice the doctrine of the Golden Mean, and thus grow in happiness with the declining years.

An epistle, which reflects so faithfully the personal experience of Horace, his attitude towards the external life of the capital, towards the aesthetic and philosophical ideals of the

Augustan age, is naturally little influenced by Lucilius. I have noticed only three traces of Lucilian influence.

In line 75 Horace used the monosyllabic name of an animal *sus* as a verse tag:

> hac rabiosa fugit canis, hac lutulenta ruit sus:

This is an expansion of the rule by which Lucilius theoretically limited such monosyllabic closes to the names of *minora animalia*, a principle which I have discussed above.[36]

In line 95 we may notice that according to Porphyrio *ad loc.* Horace in dividing *circum spectemus* between two lines follows a precedent set by Lucilius. No examples of this practice are preserved in our extant fragments. Horace's lines are:

> adspice primum
> quanto cum fastu, quanto molimine circum
> spectemus vacuam Romanis vatibus aedem.

Porphyrio here comments: Una pars orationis est divisa in duos versus Luci(l)i more et antiquorum.

The relation of the allusion in the last line to the *aedes Musarum* to the other passages in Lucilius and Horace referring to the meeting place of the guild of poets has already been fully discussed. In the present passage there appears to be no consciousness of the Lucilian treatment of that theme.

Finally in lines 158-163 and 171-177 Horace in accordance with common philosophic theory denies the philosophic validity of the legal principle of perpetual possession. Thus in the first passage:

> si proprium est quod quis libra mercatus et aerest,
> quaedam, si credis consultis, mancipat usus;
> qui te pascit ager tuus est, et vilicus Orbi;
> cum segetes occat tibi mox frumenta daturas,
> te dominum sentit.

And 171-176:

> tamquam
> sit proprium quicquam, puncto quod mobilis horae
> nunc prece, nunc pretio, nunc vi, nunc morte suprema
> permutet dominos et cedat in altera iura.
> sic, quia perpetuus nulli datur usus et heres
> heredem alterius velut unda supervenit undam,
> quid vici prosunt, etc.

Here in line 172 the phrase *puncto horae* duplicates the same Lucilian phrase in fragment 472, where, however, the allusion is to the sudden attack of the enemy:

— puncto uno horae qui quoque inuasit $\smile — \smile$.

The present commonplace recalls rather the use of the same popular Cynic aphorism by Horace in *sat.* 2, 2, 129-130. The most widely popular formulation of the aphorism was that by Bion who looked upon possessions as a loan made by fortune, not an outright gift. This commonplace as we have already seen[37] was twice used by Lucilius in fragments 550 and 701.

I turn now to the *Ars Poetica*, which to an extent hitherto scarcely realized reflects the influence of those theories of literary criticism first formulated by Lucilius on the basis of his studies in Greek rhetorical theory.

THE *Ars Poetica*

So far as the influence of Lucilius upon the *Ars Poetica* is concerned,[38] I accept the result of Norden's investigation, *Die Composition und die Litteraturgattung der Horazischen Epistula ad Pisones*,[39] and Cichorius' reconstruction of a satire in Lucilius in the eisagogic form, addressed to a young historian Iunius Congus.[40] I shall endeavor to show, however, that the traces of Lucilian influence are not confined to the closing lines of the *Ars Poetica*, 422 ff. Here Cichorius has ingeniously demonstrated the parallel development of the τόπος of the *verus* and the *mendax amicus* in Lucilius and in Horace. But traces of Horace's Lucilian studies are also to be found elsewhere in the poem. First, however, it is necessary to recapitulate briefly certain characteristics of the eisagogic form established by Norden's study, for only thus shall we be able to appreciate the nature of the relationship of Lucilius to Horace intelligently.

By the term εἰσαγωγή Norden understands a manual of the laws governing an art or science, arranged in accordance with a carefully formulated rhetorical scheme under the two topics— not of course mutually exclusive—of *ars* and *artifex*. Thus in the *Ars Poetica* verses 1–294 are *de arte poetica* and verses 295–476 are *de poeta*. This scheme as Norden shows[41] is the one followed in the *de architectura* of Vitruvius in the *institutiones oratoriae* of Quintilian, in the Pseudo-Galen and the Pseudo-

Soranus *ad filium* on Medicine, and in many other introductions to the Arts and Sciences. Such εἰσαγωγαί might be composed in the form of a catechism (σχῆμα κατὰ πεῦσιν καὶ ἀπόκρισιν) or in the form of an exhortation to scientific study delivered by an expert to a tyro.[42] In the *Ars Poetica* of Horace this parainetic or advisory element is very strong. All such εἰσαγωγαί are examples of the transfer from philosophic rhetoric to the respective arts or sciences in question of definitely formulated theories of argumentative and expository sequences. The influence of the Stoic rhetoric is particularly strong in the development of such schemes. For example the *Ars Poetica* in lines 347–452 outlines the characteristics of the perfect poet (*de perfecto poeta*); lines 453–476 give the companion picture of the mad poet (*de insano poeta*). Now the perfect poet is really the counterpart of the ideal Stoic sage trained in Stoic philosophy and working in the field of poetry. On the other hand, the mad poet who depends on the *afflatus* of inspiration is really the antithetical figure of the Stoic *stultus* transferred to the field of poetry.[43]

In the case of Horace's *Ars Poetica* the influence of Cicero's *orator* and *de oratore*, the argumentative development of which follows the same rhetorical and philosophical themes, is profound, as Norden has shown and Hack has illustrated even more fully.[44] The whole subject, however, calls for extended investigation, and will afford one of the most convincing demonstrations, if I am not mistaken, of Horace's intimate acquaintance with the fundamental principles of Ciceronian rhetoric.[45] In all εἰσαγωγαί then, whether their field be rhetoric, poetry, or the sciences, we usually find the discussion of certain "topics" naturally with considerable freedom as to the admission or exclusion of any particular topic, and with such variations in the detailed formulation of the "topic" as arise from the application of the general principles to the art or science in question. In the case of oratory and poetry, as I have shown the parallelism is remarkably close. Among the topics discussed under the *Ars* were the age, invention and perfection of the art, as well as its aims, advantages, and pleasures, and the formulation of its laws; under the *artifex*, the training relation between training and talent, character of the *perfectus artifex* as contrasted with the μαινόμενος or inspired enthusiast.[46]

We find certain formal characteristics of the εἰσαγωγή reproduced in Lucilius, book 26, as well as in the *Ars Poetica*. Thus (1) the categorical address in or to the second person is essential to the εἰσαγωγή. This is found frequently both in Horace's *Ars Poetica* and in Lucilius, book 26. In Horace, for example: 6, *credite Pisones;* 38, *sumite materiem vestris—versate diu;* 153, *tu, quid ego—audi;* 269, *versate manu, versate diurna;* 292, *vos, o Pompilius sanguis, reprehendite;* 366, *O maior iuvenum tolle memor.*[47] In Lucilius, book 26, cf. frag. 603, *vide ne—;* 609 *quid cavendum* etc.; 610 *haec tu si voles;* v. 620 *hunc laborem sumas;* v. 621, *percrepa—cave.* (2) Teaching by personal example is a further common practice of this form. Thus Horace tells of his own literary practice and ideals and with some pedagogic insistence, as we can see from the frequent use of *ego* in verses 35, 55, 87, 234, 301, 304, 306, (*ipse*); 409–410 and Lucilius in frags. 590, 609, 628, 630, 650. (3) By definition the εἰσαγωγή necessarily insists on training by study rather than an over-confident dependence on natural gifts.[48] Thus Lucilius 612, and especially 627:

> quare hoc colere est satius quam illa, studium omne hic
> consumere.

This insistence on *studium*, which recurs several times in the *Ars Poetica* (e.g., 240–243, 268, 269, 291–295, 385–390, and the satirical description of the *demens poeta* 453 ff.), finds its clearest expression in 409–415, especially in the words:

> ego nec studium sine divite vena
> nec rude quid prosit video ingenium.

And again in 412:

> qui studet optatam cursu contingere metam
> multa tulit fecitque puer, sudavit et alsit,
> abstinuit Venere et vino; qui Pythia cantat
> tibicen, didicit prius extimuitque magistrum.

(4) Study implies the critical teacher. Thus Lucilius in 944 probably promised his help to some aspirant for literary honors:

> a me auxiliatus sies.

Horace 304–308[49] describes his critical function more fully:

> ergo fungar vice cotis, acutum
> reddere quae ferrum valet, exsors ipsa secandi:

> munus et officium, nil scribens ipse, docebo,
> unde parentur opes, quid alat formetque poetam,
> quid deceat, quid non, quo virtus, quo ferat error.

Similarity of form finds expression in similarity of language. Without asserting, therefore, any direct borrowing from Lucilius, I wish to compare two Lucilian passages with Horace's *Ars Poetica* to show that the satire to Iunius Congus from book 26 was evidently written in the same general eisogogic form as the *Ars Poetica*. In both writers we find the same mixture of friendly interest with critical advice. Similar in tone are Horace's strictures when discussing the order of the argument, (*ordo*), which involves acceptance of only that which is instantly appropriate to be uttered and the rejection or postponement of all other argumentative material. A similar process of restrained, cautious, and appropriate selection is advocated in the matter of diction, to which the poet passes in line 46:[50]

> hoc amet, hoc spernat promissi carminis auctor.
> in verbis etiam tenuis cautusque serendis
> dixeris egregie, notum si callida verbum
> reddiderit iunctura novum.

Horace here has in mind that parsimony in the use of argument and diction which plays so strong a part in the conception of the *tenuis poeta* as a counterpart of the *tenuis orator*, as sketched in the *orator* of Cicero, an ideal which he had already defended before the critical world of Rome in his *sat.* 1, 10, 8 ff.[51]

Indeed the experienced teacher who tempers severity with friendly sympathy for youthful aspiration seems typical of the εἰσαγωγή. In this temper Lucilius says to Congus, 617:

> tuam probatam mi et spectatam maxume adulescentiam.

Horace similarly recognizes the earnestness and good sense of the Pisos, already developed under wise paternal training and precept, in 366:

> o maior iuvenum, quamvis et voce paterna
> fingeris ad rectum et per te sapis.[52]

We may now turn to a detailed examination of the passages in Horace's *Ars Poetica* which show either direct imitation or traces of Horace's general familiarity with the theme of this satire of Lucilius, in book 26. The most important difference in Lucilius' treatment of the material of the εἰσαγωγή is that he perhaps in writing to Congus, then engaged in writing history of the great past of Rome, sought to dissuade him from that task, and assuming a rôle analogous to that of Trebatius Testa in Horace *sat.* 2, 1, tries to persuade his young friend to enter upon the task of writing an epic drawing its subject from contemporary history.[13] Of this commonplace, which compares epic composition with that in another genre we of course find no traces in the *Ars Poetica*. In this comparison it will be convenient to follow the order of Horace.

Lucilius 587:

> nisi portenta anguisque uolucris ac pinnatos scribitis.

began his literary polemic against the tragedians with a discussion on the grand style of tragedy which he distinguishes from the simple language and direct purpose of his satire, 590. He evidently criticized the use of stock tragic monsters. Horace transfers this commonplace of Greek origin[14] to a different context by using these traditional tragic monsters as a text to inculcate the necessity of unity and congruence in a true work of art. Thus in verses 11–13:

> scimus, et hanc veniam petimusque damusque vicissim
> sed non ut placidis coeant inmitia,[15] non ut
> serpentes avibus geminentur, tigribus agni.

In verses 45–72 in the *Ars Poetica* we have a discussion on the choice of words ἐκλογὴ ὀνομάτων. Horace insists on the importance of deftly fashioned verbal complexes (the famous *curiosa felicitas*) as a means of giving well worn words an aspect of newness, but also defends the right of the poet to coin new words in moderation and on the analogy of Greek formations. Thus in 48 ff.:

> si forte necessest
> indiciis monstrare recentibus abdita rerum, et
> fingere cinctutis non exaudita Cethegis[16]
> continget, dabiturque licentia sumpta pudenter,
> et nova fictaque nuper habebunt verba fidem, si
> Graeco fonte cadent parce detorta.

Later, he by implication asserts the right to revive old words
and restore them to their former position of honor. Good usage
is the only test of such matters, lines 70–72.

> multa renascentur quae iam cecidere cadentque
> quae nunc sunt in honore vocabula, si volet usus,
> quem penes arbitrium est et ius et norma loquendi.

Of metaphorical language he says nothing, either for the
simple reason that it was not his purpose to write an exhaustive
treatise, or else, as I think more probable, because the *tenuis
poeta*, like the *tenuis orator* is chary in the use of metaphor.
Without pushing this argument *ex silentio* too far, it is at least
worth notice that with this exception we have a classification of
verba singula or single words strikingly similar to that of Cicero
in the *de oratore* and the *orator*. Thus in the *de oratore* 3, 149 ff.
Cicero begins his detailed discussion of the theory of *ornate
dicere*, which depends (1) upon the individual words selected,
(2) upon their combination, (a) as regards arrangement, (b) as
regards rhythm. Then follows a discussion upon metaphorical
language subdivided into figures of speech and figures of
thought. Now in 152 Cicero tells us that there are three classes
of words which one may use to polish his discourse and render
it luminous; these are *verba inusitata, verba novata, verba trans-
lata*. Of the *inusitata*, he declares, 153: inusitata sunt prisca,
fere ac vetustata ab usu cotidiani sermonis iam diu intermissa,
quae sunt poetarum licentiae liberiora quam nostrae; sed tamen
raro habet etiam in oratione poeticum aliquod verbum dignita-
tem. After giving a number of examples of such archaisms he
concludes: aut alia multa, quibus loco positis grandior atque
antiquior oratio saepe videri solet.

Section 80 of the *orator* repeats substantially the same doc-
trine with variations in phraseology and some slight amplifica-
tion. Moreover, it is important to notice that this discussion
on the choice of words falls under the treatment of the *genus
tenue* or plain style, (75–90) where it is clearly regarded as one
of the most important instruments of the *orator tenuis*. Simi-
larly in accordance with the arguments presented in this book
in connection with my analysis of the plain style in the Scipionic
circle, in the theory of the Roman Atticists, and in Horace's
critical satires, 1, 4; 1, 10; and 2, 1, one may regard Horace as

showing such general sympathy with the tenets of this style as
to deserve the title of *tenuis poeta*. And in fact he too under
his treatment of the choice of words does use the adjective
tenuis with reference to one of the most important subdivisions
of the τόπος of the ἐκλογή ὀνομάτων or choice of words, that of
iunctura. Horace's ideal poet will be *in verbis etiam tenuis
cautusque serendis* (line 46). It now seems appropriate to
quote 80 and the first part of 81 of the *orator* that my readers
may have the material on which my comparison of Cicero's
and Horace's theories of diction, as involved in the choice of
words and the combination of artistic verbal complexes, before
them. It is worth noticing that these sections are marked by
the same persistence on artistic restraint and discrimination
which figures so prominently in Horace's discussion in the
Ars Poetica. Compare Cicero's adjectives *verecundus, tenuis,
elegans, nec—audax, parcus, demissior*, with Horace's epithets
tenuis, cautus, callidus, sumpta pudenter, parce detorta in lines
45 ff. of the *Ars Poetica*, where the same theme as that of
Cicero is discussed. Somewhat similar is the use of *sanus
cultus* in the parallel discussion on diction in *epp*. 2, 2, line
122. The passage of Cicero is as follows:

verecundus erit usus oratoriae quasi supellectilis. supplex est enim quo-
dom modo nostra, quae est in ornamentis, aliis rerum alia verborum;
ornatus autem <verborum> duplex, unus simplicium, alter collocatorum:
simplex probatur in propriis usitatisque verbis x x quod aut optime sonat
aut rem maxime explanat: in alienis aut translatum et sumptum aliunde
ut mutuo, aut factum ab ipso et novum, aut priscum et inusitatum; sed
etiam inusitata ac prisca sunt in propriis, nisi quod raro utimur; collocata
autem verba habent ornatum si aliquid concinnitatis efficiunt, quod verbis
mutatis non maneat, manente sententia; nam sententiarum ornamenta
quae permanent, etiam si verba mutaveris, sunt illa quidem permulta, sed
quae emineant pauciora—Ergo ille tenuis orator modo sit elegans, nec in
faciendis verbis erit audax et in transferendis verecundus et parcus [et]
in priscis, reliquisque ornamentis et verborum et sententiarum demissior.

So far as the use of archaisms is concerned, little more need be
said. A comparison of the two passages of Cicero with the
passage in the *Ars Poetica* and with Horace, *epp*. 2, 2, 115 ff.
shows almost complete accord between the views of the two
writers.

Horace and Cicero also agree that the test in all such matters
is that of good usage, the consensus of what Diogenes of Babylon

long before either had called οἱ εὐδοκιμοῦντες Ἕλληνες.[57] So
Cicero in the 3, 150 of the *de oratore* speaks of the importance
of an established reputation for sound Latinity, *consuetudo
bene loquendi* (cf. the Greek Ἑλληνισμός and ὀρθογραφία) in the
problem of the choice of words: sed in hoc verborum genere
[propriorum] delectus est habendus quidam atque is aurium
quodam iudicio ponderandus est; in quo consuetudo etiam
bene loquendi valet plurimum. Again in 170 Cicero limits the
usage of archaisms by the test of what usage, *consuetudo*, will
bear: ita fit, ut omnis singulorum verborum virtus atque laus
tribus exsistat ex rebus; si aut vetustum verbum sit quod
tamen consuetudo ferre possit; aut factam vel coniunctione vel
novitate, in quo item est auribus consuetudinique parcendum.
So Horace makes usage the test in the matter of the employ-
ment of new words by the poet. In *epp.* 2, 2, 119:

> adsciscet nova, quae genitor produxerit usus.

And again in lines 70-72 of the *Ars Poetica* of the rise and fall
and rebirth of words, he makes good usage the sole standard
of speech:

> multa renascentur quae iam cecidere cadentque
> quae nunc in honore vocabula, si volet usus
> quem penes arbitrium est et ius et norma loquendi.

In such passages by usage is meant precisely what Diogenes
of Babylon called the standard of οἱ εὐδοκιμοῦντες Ἕλληνες, and
what Quintilian aptly described 1, 6, 45 as the *consensus
eruditorum*. Such a standard of good usage is as Gellius
declares 12, 13, 15, *cum domina omnium rerum tum maxine
verborum*.

On the topic of the coinage of new words, again, Cicero, *de
oratore* III, 154, gives the same categories of actual invention,
the building up of new compounds — where we must notice
that, owing to his greater sympathy with earlier Latin poetry
and its freer use of such compounds we have no limitation
based on the analogy to the Greek—and in the third place
striking collocations (like '*di genitales*'). So again in the
orator 68 Cicero contrasts the freedom of the orator and the
poet in the matter of coining new words and of making striking
collocations:[58] ego autem, etiam si quorundam grandis et ornata

vox est poetarum, tamen in ea cum licentiam statuo maiorem esse
quam in nobis faciendorum iugendorumque verborum. And
Horace in theory, as we may see from such passages as 48 and
240-242 lays great stress on this larger freedom of the poet in
the matter of striking verbal collocations. His masterly
employment of this most delicate tool of style is perhaps the
most peculiarly individual of all the characteristics of his literary
art. In the *orator* 81, indeed, we have a discussion on *collocatio*
which deserves more detailed analysis and comparison with
Horace's theory of *iunctura* or *collocatio* as phrased in lines 47
and 48. Of the collocation of words Cicero says: collocata
autem verba habent ornatum si aliquid concinnitatis efficiunt,
quod verbis mutatis non maneat manente sententia; nam
sententiarum ornamenta, quae permanent, etiam si verba
mutaveris, sunt illa quidem permulta, sed quae emineant
pauciora.

This *dictum* seems to mean that verbal collocations have the
quality of stylistic adornment only in case that something in
the nature of a nice blending of phrase (*concinnitas*) results
which would not remain if the words were changed, even though
the thought still remained the same. For such adornments of
the thought (σχήματα διανοίας) as remain if you change the
words are to be sure numerous enough, but those which are
striking are relatively few. Cicero clearly, then, classes a
deftly arranged *iunctura* or *collocatio* resulting in a perfectly
blended phrasing, *concinnitas*, as an instrument of speech, not
an instrument of thought. Horace seems to be of the same
opinion for he classes *iunctura* among the devices of diction, not
of thought. Indeed his phrase *callida iunctura* is used in a
sense quite analogous to Cicero's *si aliquid concinnitas efficiunt*,
for by it a well-known word is made to perform the function of
a new word—as for instance in such a collocation as the famous
splendide mendax, applied to the loyalty of Hypemnaestra to
her husband. Since clearly questions of thought are not pri-
marily involved Horace does not even take the trouble to
mention them.

Of the category of metaphorical language, however, of
which Cicero speaks in detail in the *de oratore* 3, 155, 170 and
in the *orator* 81-86 Horace says nothing. While this omission

may be due solely to the fact that Horace is not writing a complete eisagogic treatise but only conveying a limited body of instruction carefully thrown into the mould of an εἰσαγωγή under cover of a letter to the youthful Pisos, I am inclined to see somewhat greater significance in this omission. This significance emerges when we compare Horace's theoretical adherence to the tenets of the plain style, the 'genus tenue'[59] with Cicero's explicit injunctions of the very narrow limitations within which the tenuis orator may avail himself of those beauties of style which are derived from metaphorical language. In short the tenuis orator may only use those metaphors which are usual in everyday life. It is impossible for me to go into this point in detail, but Cicero's remarks in 81 must suffice to summarize his conception of the limits within which metaphorical language is admissible in the plain style: Ergo ille tenuis orator .modo sit elegans, nec in faciendis verbis erit audax et in transferendis verecundus.

What latitude is permissible by this verecundia transferendorum verborum, so to speak, is set forth in the succeeding sections of the orator. I am inclined therefore to associate this passage in the orator with the significant passages collected by Jackson at the close of his article on Molle atque Facetum[60] in support of the thesis that the bucolics of Virgil and the odes of Horace were written in essential harmony with the tenets of the rhetorical theory of the plain style. That the satires of Horace were so written I have constantly emphasized in this study. But it is not possible for me to pursue this digression into the interesting field of Ciceronian and Horatian relationships further. It was necessary, however, to say this much in order to see in their correct perspective the evidence that Lucilius was probably an adherent at least of some of the same rhetorical theories as to the choice of words.

In fragment 650 Lucilius evidently discussed the question of the use of unusual words and grammatical problems:[61]

siquod verbum inusitatum aut zetematium offenderam

Offendo here used in the sense of invenio is parallel to the use of fingere in Horace in the passage quoted above[62] from his Ars Poetica lines 48–53, while the Greek loan word zetematium recalls

Horace's criticism (*sat.* 1, 10, 20) on Lucilius' freedom in the use
of Greek expressions. The *parce detorta* further reenforces the
same point especially as Horace's own coinage *cinctutis* is a
natural Latin formation. That Lucilius had the conventional
rhetorical treatment on the ἐκλογή ὀνομάτων under which the
use of loan words and the poets' right to coin new words were
defended becomes even clearer upon comparison with the
preceding line 649, which I believe taken with this line refers to
a grammatical, not to a philosophical controversy.[63]

> quid ni et tu idem inlitteratum me atque idiotam diceres.

So Horace in verse 55 ff.:

> ego cur adquirere pauca
> si possum, invideer, cum lingua Catonis et Enni
> sermonem patrium ditaverit et nova rerum nomina protulerit?

In lines 86-130 Horace sets forth the theory of the *verborum
colores* from the proper variation of which we attain *decus*, or as
we should say, an appropriate and congruous style. The style,
he says, must harmonize (86-98) with the literary form or
εἶδος. The tragic and the comic style are contrasted, yet even
within the limits of either of these genres, Horace recognizes
that we may suddenly shift to the other to express fittingly a
change of mood. This forms the transition to the discussion
of πάθος, the appropriate language for the expression of the
moods of grief, joy, anger, sobriety. Then follows (114-130)
the discussion of the style appropriate to the traditional charac-
ter types of comedy, tragedy, epic poetry. Their language
(*cf.* 112) must accord with their station and fortune.

Apparently the satire in book 26 of Lucilius, devoted to a
literary controversy, contained a somewhat similar argument, at
least in part. Lucilius first differentiated the style suitable for
the εἶδος of satire from that of tragedy. Here he incidentally
satirized the swollen diction of the tragic poet Pacuvius.[65] He
asserted that simplicity and sincerity were the true emotional
tests of style, πάθος.[66] Such a style, the plain style of the *sermo*
as affected by Lucilius, is in no sense to be considered an
ignobilitas—much less should such a style descend to that level.
So in 608:

> — ⏑ nunc ignobilitas his mirum ac monstrificabile.[67]

What seems to the tragic poet an *ignobilitas* is in reality the simple expression of real feeling. It is not a strange, but a natural style, and will be used by you too, my tragic friend, when you would stir the hearts of your auditors with true pathos, 610:[68]

> haec tu si uoles per auris pectus inrigarier.

Turning back now to Horace we find a similar argument. Horace too satirizes the tragic bombast, 95 ff., and insists that true pathos finds expression in the simple language of the plain style:[69]

> et tragicus plerumque dolet sermone pedestri,
> Telephus et Peleus cum pauper et exul uterque
> proicit ampullas et sesquipedalia verba,
> si curat cor spectantis tetigisse querella.

The necessity of sincerity was emphasized by Lucilius in 590:

> ego ubi quem ex praecordiis ecfero uersum.

This is re-echoed in spirit by Horace, 102:

> si vis me flere, dolendumst
> primum ipsi tibi.

Horace, however, returned later to the defence of the plain style and those aspects of the middle style which are derived from the plain style when he outlined the style appropriate to the satyr drama, and by implication for satire, in words which support my hypothesis, that the *ignobilitas* of Lucilius is to be interpreted as a stylistic term, for in verses 246–247 the *ignominosa dicta* is certainly to be regarded as a technical rhetorical term, and probably one suggested by the *ignobilitas* of Lucilius:

> aut nimium teneris iuuenentur versibus umquam
> aut inmunda crepent ignominiosaque dicta.

In contrast with the use of *ignobilitas* by Lucilius and *ignominiosa verba* by Horace the description of the tragic trimeters of Accius in line 259 as *nobiles trimetri* is significant of the contrast between the diction of the grand and the plain style, especially in view of the literary polemics waged between Lucilius and Accius.[70] Horace, on the contrary, in accordance with a well-established rhetorical tradition,[71] speaks of his own *sermones* as *repentis per humum* (*epp.* 2, 1, 251) a virtual paraphrase of the stylistic epithet *humilis*, and of his *musa pedestris* (*sat.* 2, 6, 17) a collocation parallel to the *sermo pedestris* just quoted from line 95 of the *Ars Poetica*.

The Lucilian influence, however, is most apparent in the concluding lines of the *Ars Poetica*.[72] Here in lines 419–420, as the auctioneer attracts the crowd to buy his wares, so the wealthy poet readily gathers to his poems those who bid highest with flattering criticism:

> ut praeco, ad mercis turbam qui cogit emendas,
> adsentatores iubet ad lucrum ire poeta
> dives agris, dives positis in fenore nummis.

This simile is clearly borrowed from Lucilius,[73] 1282:

> quidni et scruta quidem ut uendat scrutarius laudat,
> praefractam strigilim, soleam inprobus dimidiatam.

The *scrutarius* is Horace's *praeco*, the *scruta* are the *merces*, the *laudat* is the *adsentatores iubet* of the later poet. The simile is introduced by *quidni*, which corresponds to the *ut* of Horace.[74]

Horace then proceeds with the contrast between the *verus* and the *mendax amicus* closely imitated from the εἰσαγωγή of Lucilius, and relates this distinction to that between sincere and self-interested literary criticism. Thus Lucilius asserts the duty of frank criticism which the true friend will not hesitate to assume in 611:[75]

> porro amici est bene praecipere, veri bene praedicere.

In Horace this function of friendly critic is assumed by Quintilius (438), who is soon generalized (445) into the *vir bonus et prudens*, or the ideal Stoic sage, projected into the field of literary criticism, and seeking to form the *sanus poeta*, by virtue of his literary teachings. These lines read like an expansion of the thought of Lucilius:

> vir bonus et prudens versus reprendet inertis,
> culpabit duros, incomptis adlinet atrum
> transverso calamo signum, ambitiosa recidet[76]
> ornamenta. parum claris lucem dare coget
> arguet ambigue dictum, mutanda notabit,
> fiet Aristarchus nec dicet: cur ego amicum
> offendam in nugis?"[77]

The concluding verses of the passage, as Cichorius rightly emphasizes, form a striking parallel to Lucilius 953:[77]

> Homini amico et familiari non est mentiri meum.

Perhaps in the same context Lucilius with his usual emphasis and redundancy added 957 and 958:[78]

> mihi necesse est eloqui
> nam scio Amyclas tacendo periisse.

This proverb would then characterize the dangers of relying upon the hypocritical silence of the *mendax amicus*, for as Horace says, 451:

> hae nugae seria ducent
> in mala derisum semel exceptumque sinistre.

With the same context I am inclined to associate fragment 624, in view of the fact noted above that the *vir bonus et prudens* is really the Stoic *sapiens* carrying on his activities in the field of literature. The line in question is referred by Marx to the Epicurean sage. Since, however, Cichorius has brought forth convincing evidence that 626, which Marx takes in close connection with 625, refers rather to the calm gained by the writing of history, as a refuge from the contemplation of contemporary political dissensions,[79] I am inclined to interpret 624 rather of the Stoic than the Epicurean sage, and associate the line with this same context of the true and the false friend. For instance if put into the mouth of Lucilius, the analogue in the dialogue with Iunius Congus of the kindly and truthful but severe Stoic critic in Horace, the lines might be spoken in rejoinder to an objection of undue severity on the part of Congus or youthful writers in general: "If they see this, that the wise man always seeks what is good and thinks:"

> sin autem hoc vident, bona semper petere sapientem, et putant.

Possibly the lost context might go on, "They do not then chafe under the frank criticism designed to secure excellence in the field of literature" or some similar thought. On this interpretation the *sapiens* would be a more philosophically defined countertype to the *vir bonus et prudens* of Horace.

After the simile of the auctioneer Horace sketches the bribe which the wealthy dilettante offers: about his luxurious table flocks the brood of literary parasites. How shall he distinguish between true friends and false? (verses 422-425):

> si vero est, unctum qui recte ponere possit
> et spondere levi pro paupere et eripere artis
> litibus inplicitum, mirabor si sciet inter
> noscere mendacem verumque beatus amicum.[80]

This bribe of the luxurious dinner is present also in Lucilius, fragments 662, 664, 665, where we have a banquet. 664 in particular seems to breathe the condescension of the wealthy patron, *unctum qui recte ponere posset*:

> munifici comesque amicis nostris videamur viri.

The praise of such *adsentatores* is like the lamentations of the professional mourners, hired and therefore excessive. So Horace, line 432:

> ut qui conducti plorant in funere dicunt
> et faciunt prope plura dolentibus ex animo, sic
> derisor vero plus laudatore movetur.

This simile is distinctly borrowed from Lucilius, 954, which clearly belongs to book 26:

> — mercede quae conductae fient alieno in funere
> praeficae, multo et capillos scindunt et clamant magis.[81]

This passage completes my survey of the fragments of book 26.

But the indebtedness of Horace to Lucilius is not confined to the two satires of book 26, for we have evidence of the use of considerable Lucilian material from other satires. Especially does there seem to be evidence that Horace was influenced by a satire in book 27, although the baffling nature of the surviving fragments makes it difficult to establish so clearly the sequence of the argument for this satire. I shall therefore endeavor to state my inferences with caution. Still the dedication, fragment 688, the allusion to Archilochus, 698, and the references to the *Socratici carti* in 709, seem to show that literary discussion was found in this book also.

Line 693 was, perhaps, used by Horace:

> rem cognoscas simul, et dictis animum adtendas postulo.

While the ordinary contrast between word and deed (so Marx) is, of course, not excluded as the interpretation of the fragment, the direct address *animum adtendas*, and especially the presence of *simul* seems to imply the insistence on two harmonious qualities such as subject matter and language rather than an antithesis. Moreover, as all students of ancient rhetoric know, such terms as *res, materia, dicta, verba* are constantly used in rhetorical discussions on the functions of the orator (or poet). *Inventio* is a prerequisite of composition, but it must be supplemented by the complete mastery of the other functions of the orator (or poet). I mean particularly such functions as *ordo*, and *facundia* or *elocutio*. Now this same insistence on the importance of combining knowledge of the subject, the source of good writing (*Ars Poetica*, 309), with style, the fruit of such intellectual mastery of the material, recurs in the *Ars Poetica*, 310-312:[82]

> rem tibi Socraticae poterunt ostendere chartae,
> verbaque provisam rem non invita sequentur.

This is, of course, Cato's famous definition: *rem tene verba sequentur*, and therefore goes back to the rhetorical discussions contemporaneous with the older Scipionic circle and only slightly antedating the appearance of the satires of Lucilius. Related to this idea is the Stoic definition of the orator as a *vir bonus dicendi peritus*.[83] Evidently then Cato's definition was the product of contemporary Stoic rhetoric, with its insistence on the truth, the plain style, and on moral values in the art of speech. So here Horace immediately adds a definition of *virtus* 311 ff. based on Stoic sources, and perhaps largely influenced by the theories of Panaetius, but previously passed through the medium of the well-known definition of Lucilius.

But the source of moral knowledge is Greek philosophy, especially the philosophy of Socrates and the Academy which is so closely allied to life. It was the Greek poets, however, who combined inspiration with style; therefore, the Roman poet must draw his *dicta* (diction) from them as he draws his *res* (subject matter) from the study of philosophy. Thus Horace of the Greek in 324 f.:

> Grais ingenium, Grais dedit ore rotundo
> Musa loqui, praeter laudem nullius avaris.

In Lucilius philosophy and the artistic gift (?) of the Greeks
are related in precisely the same way in 709:

> †nec sic ubi Graeci? ubi nunc Socratici carti?   # quidquid
> quaeritis.

I have already given the evidence that Lucilius in laying
stress on the study of the Socratic dialogues, as a source for his
sermones, apparently assumes precisely the attitude of his
fellow member of the Scipionic circle, Panaetius in the *de
officiis* 1, 134, that the *Socratici* (*cf.* Lucilius *charti Socratici*)
furnish the model for the *sermo*. Further we have seen the
importance of the studies of Lucilius and Panaetius in the
field of Academic philosophy, and have learned that Plato,
Xenophon, Antisthenes, and Aeschines were the writers figur-
ing most prominently in this canon. And finally we have seen
the high value that Horace set on the philosophy of Panaetius.[34]
Evidently then we are dealing in this doctrine of the value of
the dialogues of the Socratic school for literary composition
with a well-established literary and rhetorical tradition extend-
ing from Panaetius himself and Lucilius through the rhetorical
works of Cicero to the Augustan age and the critical theories
of Horace himself.

Lucilius evidently rejected the defence of the youthful poet
that his mediocre work was "not so bad," 702:

> paulo hoc melius quam mediocre, hoc minus malum quam
> ut *pessumum.*

So Horace in 372[85] with some emphasis denies the right of
mediocrity to live in poetry:

> mediocribus esse poetis
> non homines, non di, non concessere columnae.

Lucilius, fragment 698:

> metuo ut fieri possit: ergo <*anti*>quo ab Arciloco excido.

denies the possibility of the animals of the field, by a reversal
of Nature's order, changing place with the dolphin; this par-
ticular ἀδύνατον—and Lucilius' words *metuo ut fieri possit* seem
to be a paraphrase of the technical rhetorical term—first
appears in Archilochus (fragment 71, H-B).

μηδεὶς ἰθ ὑμῶν εἰσορῶν θαυμαζέτω.
μηδ' ὅταν δελφῖσι θῆρες ἀνταμείψωνται νομὸν
ἐνάλιον καὶ σφιν θαλάσσης ἠχέωντα κύματα
φίλτερ' ἠπείρου γένηται, τοῖσι δ'[ἡδὺ ἦν ὄρος].

This was possibly used by Lucilius also as a simile to assail literary incongruity, at least we have this turn given in Horace, lines 29 f.:

> qui variare cupit rem prodigialiter unam,
> delphinum silvis adpingit, fluctibus aprum.

From the tenth satire of Lucilius,[36] declared by the scholiast to have inspired the first satire of Persius, we have two passages to consider, the first on the question of that subjective aspect of *ordo*, which involves the use of discrimination in arguments or material by the poet or the orator. The selection of those arguments which need to be uttered at just that point in the discourse or poem and the rejection of all others is closely related to Horace's discussion of *ordo* in lines 40–45 of the *Ars Poetica*. Lucilius 386 says:

> horum est iudicium, crisis ut discribimus ante,
> hoc est, quid sumam, quid non, in quoque locemus.

And Horace declares:

> cui lecta potenter erit res,
> nec facundia deseret hunc nec lucidus ordo,
> ordinis haec virtus erit et venus aut ego fallor,
> ut iam nunc dicat iam nunc debentia dici,
> pleraque differat et praesens in tempus omittat,
> *hoc amet, hoc spernat* promissi carminis acutor
> in verbis etiam tenuis cautusque serendis.

The rhetorical coloring of both passages may be illustrated by a selection of a few passages from the wealth of material bearing on this subject in the rhetorical works of Cicero. But first of all we may notice that Demetrius π. ἑρμ. rightly asserts the importance of introducing movement into the argumentative sequence, even at the expense of completeness: ὅτι οὐ πάντα ἐπ' ἀκριβείας δεῖ μακρηγορεῖν (cf. Horace's *differat* and *omittat* and Lucilius' *quid non sumam*), ἀλλ' ἔνια καταλιπεῖν καὶ τῷ ἀκροατῇ συνιέναι καὶ λογίζεσθαι ἐξ ἑαυτοῦ.

On the important part played by movement and judgment in all that is involved in the subjective problems affecting the effort of the literary artist to secure a *lucidus ordo* Cicero says, *de oratore* 1, 142, speaking of the orator: ut deberet reperire primum quid diceret. deinde inventa non solum ordine sed etiam momento quodam. (*Cf.* Horace *iam nunc*) atque iudicio dispensare atque componere.

Again in the *de oratore* 2, 307–332, where *ordo* is discussed, Cicero declares that *ordo* must be considered under two heads, (1) that type of order which is inherent in the nature of the case (*altera, quam adfert natura causarum*), and (2) that which is the result of what we may describe as the wise treatment of the problem of selection and arrangement (*tractatio*) of the material at the disposal of the orator (*altera quae oratoris iudicio et prudentia comparatur*). He then goes on in sections 308 to show that it is the function of the second or subjective subdivision of *ordo* to make proper selection out of all the arguments and argumentative sequences at the orator's disposal of that particular set of arguments best suited to the case in hand. Selection is one of the most fundamental tasks of the orator therefore: ut vero statuamus ea quae probandi et docendi causa dicenda sunt, quam ad modum componamus id est vel maxine proprium oratoris prudentiae.

Clearly the same principle of artistic selection lies at the very heart of the lines of Lucilius and Horace. Lucilius actually uses the quasi-technical rhetorical terms *crisis* and *iudicium*, while Horace paraphrases the idea correctly with the words *hoc amet, hoc spernat*. Moreover, in line 31 above, in speaking of the delicate question of the discrimination between the conflicting claims of unity in the whole composition and congruous variety in its individual parts, Horace uses the term *Ars* of the poet's function in a sense virtually synonymous to that of *iudicium*: *in vitium ducit culpae fuga, si caret arte.*

It may be—but this is not quite so certain—that the great Homer nodded in Lucilius (taking *quietis*, as genitive of *quies*) as in Horace, and long works were then also soporific, even to their authors. Thus Lucilius 391:

> languor, obrepsitque pigror torporque quietis.

and Horace 358 ff.:

> indignor quandoque bonus dormitat Homerus:
> verum operi longo fas est obrepere somnum.

I turn next to scattered similarities from other books of Lucilius. Horace in the *Ars Poetica*, 139, in *Epp.* 1, 2, 26 and 2, 2, 75 used the monosyllabic name of an animal to close a verse. Only in the passage in the *Ars Poetica*:

> parturient montes, nascetur ridiculus mus.

does he strictly follow the Lucilian injunction, fragment 1209 Marx, which limited the employment of this verse tag to *minora animalia*.

Lucilius 881 is taken from a comic scene directly rather than one satirically used by Lucilius. This line according to Cichorius[87] is uttered by the *senex* and refers to the tricks against him played by the *adulescens* his son, and a crafty slave. It is possibly a scene derived from the Hymnis of Caecilius:

> in me illis spem esse omnem, quouis posse me emungi bolo.

Horace clearly has this same scene in mind when in 236 he differentiates the style of the satyr drama from tragedy on the one hand and the *palliata* on the other.

> nec sic enitar tragico differre colori,
> ut nihil intersit Davusne loquatur et audax
> Pythias emuncto lucrata Simone talentum,
> an custos famulusque dei Silenus alumni.

Horace also clearly accepted, as did Lucilius 437, the derivation of tragedy from τρύξ.[88] Thus Diomedes G.L. 1 p. 487, 23:

> Alii autem putant a faece, quam Graecorum quidem appellant, tragoediam nominatam—est Horatius testis (*Ars Poetica*, 275)—Alii <a> vino arbitrantur propterea <quod> olim τρύξ vinum dictitabatur a quo τρύγητος hodieque vindemia est, quia Liberalibus apud Atticos die festo Liberi patris vinum cantoribus pro corollario dabatur cui rei testis est Lucilius in duodecimo.

Horace 275 reads:

> ignotum tragicae genus invenisse camenae
> dicitur et plaustris vexisse poemata Thespis
> quae canerent agerentque peruncti faecibus ora.

A comparison of line 312 ff. with Lucilius' 1326 ff., at once shows that Horace was familiar with the passage in which Lucilius assimilated to Roman needs the Stoic doctrine of the *vir bonus* and of *virtus*, conceived in terms of "service" as the *summum bonum.*[89] Notice especially the concluding lines of the fragment:

> virtus id dare re ipsa debetur honori
> hostem esse atque inimicum hominum morumque malorum,
> contra defensorem hominum morumque bonorum,
> hos magni facere, his bene uelle, his uiuere amicum,
> commoda praeterea patriaí prima putare,
> deinde parentum, tertia iam postremaque nostra.

Horace 312:

> qui didicit patriae quid debeat et quid amicis
> quo sit amore parens, quo frater amandus et hospes,
> quod sit conscripti, quod iudicis officium, quae
> partes in bellum missi ducis, ille profecto
> reddere personae scit convenientia cuique.

Lucilius as well as Horace was familiar as we have already seen in *sat.* 1, 4, 42,[90] with the theory of the Greek rhetoricians derived ultimately from Aristotle, that comedy (*i.e.*, the New Comedy) held the mirror up to nature. In view, therefore, of the strong Lucilian coloring of the context it seems that Horace here also in lines 317–318, which immediately follow, reproduced the Lucilius formulation of the same commonplace in book 30, 1029.

> sicuti te, qui ea quae speciem uitae esse putamus.

Nonius, who glosses *speciem* by *specimen vel exemplar*, indirectly emphasizes the closeness of the passage to Horace:

> respicere exemplar vitae morumque iubebo
> doctum imitatorem et vivas hinc ducere voces.

My endeavor, then, has been to show:

(1) that the εἰσαγωγή to Iunius Congus in book 26 of Lucilius was necessarily like Horace's *Ars Poetica* addressed in terms of kindly criticism and warning to a tyro, and insisted on the importance of training and study as against mere talent.

(2) I have tried to show that both in this satire and in the literary polemic in book 26 Lucilius formulated at least some of the laws of poetic composition which Horace follows in the *Ars Poetica*, and discusses some of the same conventional topics. I have further brought forth some evidence from the rhetorical works of Cicero, in order to set the relation of the

εἰσαγωγαί of Horace and Lucilius in the correct perspective as regards rhetorical theory. A brief summary may be helpful: Thus:

    I. Lucilius 587 and Horace 1-13. Unity and appropriateness are essential.

    II. Lucilius, 649 and 650, and Horace 48 ff. ἐκλογή ὀνομάτων with special reference to new formations.

    III. Lucilius, 597, 599, 601, 602, 605 and Horace 85 to 98. The differentiation of style by εἶδος literary genre, with special discussion of tragedy.

    IV. Lucilius, 590, 603, 608, 610, and Horace, 99-113, the differentiation of style in harmony with the principle of πάθος with special reference to the simplicity of the plain style (that of the *sermo* or satire).

(3) In the concluding portion of the *Ars Poetica*, verses 419 ff. the "topic" of the sincere friend and critic is developed so closely in harmony with Lucilius 611, 953, 957, 958, 624, 664, that we must assume that Horace was using Lucilius as a direct model.

(4) Within the framework of the common rhetorical scheme, transferred by both Lucilius and Horace from rhetoric to poetry, the following passages may be especially noted as showing evidence of direct verbal imitation or of the influence of the thought of Lucilius upon Horace:

Lucilius 587 = *Ars Poetica* 1-13
Lucilius 608 = *Ars Poetica* 246-247
Lucilius 953 = *Ars Poetica* 450.
Lucilius 954 = *Ars Poetica* 431
Lucilius 611, 953, 954, 957, 958, 624, the distinction between the true and false friend = model for *Ars Poetica* 425-450.

(5) A comparison of passages which I have discussed shows that Horace drew also from other satires of Lucilius besides book 26:

    (1) Three passages 693, 698, 709 come from book 28, evidently another important source for the *Ars Poetica*.

    (2) Two passages from book 10, 386, 391.

    (3) From book 29 we have one passage 881 in which an illustration is drawn from comedy. And from book 30

Horace for a second time quotes Lucilius' definition of *virtus*.

It is somewhat difficult to give a compact classification of these scattering evidences of Lucilian coloring in the *Ars Poetica*, but we seem to have eight instances in which the thought of Lucilius is adopted with more or less close imitation in the verbal form, viz: 386, 391, 693, 698, 709, 702, 1029, 1326; one case of a similar metrical clausula 1209, and of a similar etymology used as the basis for a literary argument, 437; in 881 the employment of an allusion or perhaps even a scene from the New Comedy, and the quotation of a long fragment of philosophical import, with apparent approval.

In conclusion, then, it seems fair to assert that the evidence afforded by a comparison of the fragments of Lucilius with Horace's *Ars Poetica* tends to support the belief that Lucilius' theory of literary criticism was formulated according to the same rhetorical σχήματα, and under substantially the same rhetorical influences—mainly emanating from the Stoic rhetoric of Diogenes and Panaetius, but reinterpreted before the Augustan period by Cicero and the Roman Atticists—as Horace's *Ars Poetica*. Furthermore such a detailed comparison, involving the use of words, scenes, argument, and illustration, shows that Lucilius was the first Latin exponent of several of the theories of literary criticism, hitherto regarded as peculiarly Horatian as well as the direct model of no inconsiderable portions of the *Ars Poetica*.[91]

NOTES ON CHAPTER VI

[1] *Epp.* 1, 1, 2.

[2] *Ibid.* 4.

[3] *Epp.* 2, 2, 55 ff.

[4] *Epp.* 1, 1, 10.

[5] *Epp.* 2, 2, 144.

[6] *Cf.* R. Hirzel, *Der Dialog*, vol. 2, p. 10.

[7] See Hendrickson, *Are the Letters of Horace Satires?* in *A. J. P.*, vol. 18, pp. 313-324.

[8] See *supra*, pp. 176-178.

[9] 68 a. *Cf.* also Schanz, *op. cit.*, 8³, 2, 1, p. 163.

[10] See *supra*, pp. 205 ff.

[11] See *supra*, pp. 153-155 on Lucilius and Homer.

[12] See *infra*, p. 445; p. 465 ff.

[13] See *supra*, pp. 288 ff. and 346 ff. on this institution and Lucilius, *fragments* 794 and 1028.

[14] See *infra*, p. 445.

[15] This interpretation is quite as plausible as that of Marx, who sees in these lines an allusion to a thieving slave.

[16] *Cf.* his *Latin Poetry*, p. 182.

[17] So Marx, comment. *ad loc.*

[18] This Lucilian fragment comes from a satire in book 16 called the Collyra, because it is dedicated to the mistress of Lucilius. One wonders whether this fact has any influence on Horace's allusion to his mistress Cinara in line 33.

[19] Here also *fragments* 707, 708, 711, and 712 evidently refer to country life; but I am unable to detect any traces of relationship with this epistle.

[20] See Marx, *ad loc.*

[21] See also Horace, *sat.* 1, 3, 21, *supra*, pp. 275 ff.

[22] *Cf.* also Asconius, *ad Ciceronis divinationem* in *Caecil.* 16, 50, p. 1200, and Livy, 39, 44, 7.

[23] As Kiessling says: Bestius wird wohl wie Maenius ein Gestalt der Lucilischen Satire sein, die in derselben die Rolle des allvaterischen Eiferers gegen die eingerissene Sittenverderbniss spielte; auch Persius scheint auf Lucilius zurückzugehen. Bestius, if we may judge from Persius 6, 37 (Bestius urget doctores Graios), like Cato the censor, assailed the fashionable immigrant philosophers, whose teaching corrupted the city. Even the haymakers, he says, spoil their porridge with thick oil:

> et Bestius urguet
> doctores Graios: ita fit: postquam sapere urbi
> faenisecae crasso vitiarunt unguine pultes.

[24] *Cf.* Cicero, *Paradoxa 2.*

²⁵ *Cf.* my paper *Lucilius and Persius*, vol. cit., pp. 137-139. For a fuller discussion of this commonplace of the sick glutton see K. Joel, *Der echte und der Xenophontische Sokrates*, 2, p. 454.

²⁶ The parallel in Juvenal, *sat.* 1, 1, 1:

> semper ego auditor tantum, nunquamne reponam?

shows, I think, that Horace's *auditor et ultor* are to be taken sarcastically. Furthermore, the *nobilium scriptorum* are probably to be referred to writers of epic and tragic compositions in the grand style. I base this inference on the allusions to epic, elegy, and tragedy in Juvenal's first satire and Lucilius' contrast in book 26, *fragments* 588, 592, 594, 595 between the tone of his satire and that of tragedy, and the reference to different classes of readers, parallel to Horace's classification in a general way.

²⁷ See *supra*, pp. 293 ff. and pp. 348 ff.

²⁸ We may compare Propertius 1, 22 and Ovid, *Amores* 3, 15.

²⁹ Kirtland-Kiessling introduction to epistle.

³⁰ *Annales*, frag. 5 and 11, ed. Vahlen.

³¹ Hieronymus, *comment. in Michaeam* book 2, cap. 7, vol. 6, pl. 578, 519 Vallars.

³² *Cf.* also scholiast on Persius 6, 10.

³³ One may speculate whether the more modern and elegant Terence, as representative of the cultivated literary interests of the Scipionic circle was not held up as a model in contrast with the more popular and less finished dramatists. We have seen that Lucilius betrays traces of the influence of Terence. See Marx *index auctorum* and *supra*, pp. 393 ff. It thus becomes conceivable that the Horatian passage, lines 55-59 which, in terms of Alexandrian scholarship establishes the canon of comic poetry, and assigns to their respective ranks the Roman comic poets may have had some counterpart in this Lucilian satire.

³⁴ For a discussion of the elaborate imitation of these two passages in *Persius* 3, 54-56 see my paper *Lucilius and Persius*, vol. cit., pp. 136 and 137.

³⁵ Already expressed in part in *Sat.* 1, 4, 60 and more fully in *Sat.* 2, 1, 10-16. See *supra*, pp. 287 ff. and pp. 370 ff. Similar is the refusal to write a contemporary epic on Agrippa, *Carm.* 1, 6.

³⁶ See *supra*, pp. 429.

³⁷ See *supra*, pp. 385 ff.

³⁸ Hack's article on the *Doctrine of the Literary Forms*, vol. cit., is of the utmost importance for the study of the *Ars Poetica*. Especially valuable is Hack's evidence for the influence of Plato and Cicero upon Horace. Also he rightly emphasizes the fundamental importance for the interpretation of this epistle of the doctrine of propriety. On the other hand, I cannot accept his fundamental conception as to the cramping influence of the doctrine of the literary genres or the disregard of the laws of the genre in practice by Greek and Roman writers. The whole tendency of this book is to show Horace's free and independent acceptance of the laws of the genre of satire. This is not the place to discuss the matter in detail,

but in general I feel that Hack's article represents a misconception as to the origin, development, and value of the Doctrine of the Literary Forms.

In my opinion it is an overstatement to say that the content of a given poem is in the most cases predetermined by the genre selected by the poet. On the contrary the genres are a *reflection* in literature of the *common* emotional and aesthetic experiences of man. Hence certain subjects in course of time, and as the result of the workings of the human spirit come to express themselves in certain given forms, because aesthetic experience convinced the literary artist that these particular forms were the most appropriate modes for the expression of that body of human emotion. We, therefore, have here no biological analogies, and the ancients even the much abused Alexandrian critics, were not concerned with biological analogies.

The evolution which I have thus broadly outlined has a profound influence on the successors of the great tradition in each genre. Such a successor is by no means precluded from adding new material if in his judgment—and here *each individual* poet is the final arbiter—the new material is adapted to the genre in which the successor chooses to work. It is a profound error therefore to regard the theory of the *Literary Forms* as something mechanical, external, or constraining. On the contrary the doctrine of the genres is an expression of *common* human experience, alike emotional and aesthetic.

I believe that it can be demonstrated that Horace in practice as well as theory followed in his epodes, odes, and satires the essential principles of which these genres were the expression, and also that the εἰσαγωγή is a logical instrument used by Horace in the present epistle. We are dealing, however, with an εἰσαγωγή expressed in the epistolary form. Nor are these two concepts mutually exclusive or destructive.

³⁹ Hermes 40, pp. 481-528.

⁴⁰ *Op. cit.*, pp. 109-127.

⁴¹ *Op. cit.*, pp. 508-514.

⁴² Cicero's *de partitione oratoria* is such a catechism. The arithmetic lesson, *Ars Poetica* 326 ff. is a humorous extract from such an εἰσαγωγή εἰς ἀριθμητικήν. See Norden, p. 519. As further examples of such exhortations see Cato, *ad Marcum Filium*, which shows that the form probably antedates *Lucilius* at Rome, Livy to his son on the excellencies and defects of the orator (*Quintil.* 10, 1, 39). Other examples are quoted by Norden on pp. 520, 521.

⁴³ For proof see Norden, p. 498 ff.

⁴⁴ Yet Hack seems not to be aware of the implications of his belief that Cicero, in his rhetorical works, is profoundly influenced by Plato, and that Horace in turn was influenced by Cicero's *orator* and *de oratore*, to which I entirely agree. These implications are that Cicero studies his Plato, both directly when writing his philosophical works, but that in his rhetorical works he was influenced rather by previous adaptations of Plato's theories made by the Greek rhetoricians and rhetorical philosophers.

Among such mediating agencies it is difficult to exaggerate the influence of Panaetius, a profound student of Plato, a member of the Scipionic circle, and one who made τὸ πρέπον, τὸ καθῆκον decorum and propriety the very centre of his ethical and aesthetic system. One may well query therefore whether Horace, who as Hack has admirably shown, places propriety in the very centre of complex of literary theories presented in the *Ars Poetica*, was not influenced by Panaetius as well as by Cicero's popularization of the doctrines of this important philosopher. I reserve a fuller answer to this question to some future occasion.

⁴⁵ This subject is treated in part by Miss Grant, in a Wisconsin doctoral thesis soon to be published, on *The Rhetorical Theory of the Laughable in Cicero and in Horace*.

⁴⁶ We find the following points in Horace's *Ars Poetica*: age, inventor, perfector, 391 ff. (275 ff. on drama, 220 on satyr play) aim 333 ff. parts 488 ff.; training of *artifex* 309 ff.; talent versus study 408 ff.; perfect artist 502 ff. See Norden, p. 517 note 1.

⁴⁷ *Cf.* Wickham's introduction to *Ars Poetica*, p. 383. Wickham rightly emphasizes the fact that, "The places where a name or other personal appeal occurs are . . . where the chief points of the epistle are to be enforced."

⁴⁸ Here we are dealing, as Professor Shorey has shown, *Transactions of the American Philological Association*, vol. 40. pp. 185-201, with the Greek rhetorical commonplace on φύσις, μελέτη, ἐπιστήμη. *Cf.* especially pp. 185-188.

⁴⁹ On the image of the whetstone *cf.* Shorey, *op. cit.*, p. 188, note 4.

⁵⁰ I believe the order of the lines as found in the MS. is correct. Line 45 refers to the subjective function of *ordo*, which leads a writer to select at any given place in his argument the point most apposite for proof or illustration, and to reject for the time being all the other arguments in his armory. Line 46 will then mark the transition to the choice of words, ἐκλογὴ ὀνομάτων. Here Horace places first his favorite device of *iunctura*. This is a reversal of opinion from my position in the article on *Lucilius, the Ars Poetica of Horace, and Persius*, where I transposed these lines with Bentley, Kiessling and Norden.

⁵¹ This application of rhetorical theories of prose composition to poetry had perhaps been made as early as the period of the Scipionic circle. For instance in fragment 603 the discussion on the artifical use of *commiseratio* in oratory may have been associated with a consideration of the proper diction and tone of the pathetic in poetry. On the *tenuis orator* see Cicero's *orator* 81-85. In 84 Cicero emphasizes the *parsimonia* or restraint of this type of oratory. Jackson in his article *Molle atque Facetum, op. cit.*, pp. 132 ff. gives an interesting collection of passages in proof of the contention that Horace accepted in essence the stylistic implications defining the functions of the *tenuis poeta*.

⁵² *Cf.* also 291, *vos, o Pompilius sanguis*, etc.

⁵³ See *Cichorius, op. cit.*, pp. 109-127. On Horace's *satire* 2, 1 see *supra*, pp. 369-378.

⁵⁴ This criticism is at least as old as the Frogs of Aristophanes; cf. 930 ff. the strictures on the ἰσπαλακτρωῶν of Aeschylus.

⁵⁵ Cf. serpentes avibus geminentur with anguis volucris et pinnatos.

⁵⁶ Epp. 2, 2, 109-125, should be regarded as an earlier exposition of Horace's theories as to choice of words and be carefully compared with our present passage in the Ars Poetica. It contains essentially the same doctrines and shows several coincidences in language.

⁵⁷ See supra, pp. 86 ff.

⁵⁸ So Kroll, but compare Sandys' orator, who has a different interpretation of this passage.

⁵⁹ As discussed supra, pp. 78 ff. and pp. 337 ff.

⁶⁰ Op. cit., pp. 132 ff.

⁶¹ Cf. Cichorius, op. cit., p. 128.

⁶² Nonius, p. 359, 12.

⁶³ Cf. Marx, comment. ad loc., but wrongly.

⁶⁴ A study of the Lucilian ἰδιώτης (a term used in Plato's Phaedrus, 258 of the prose writer as opposed to the poet, and frequently of a layman in distinction from the expert), suggests that Lucilius may have defended his right to coin new words in a context similar to that of Horace, and that he may have compared himself as the abused craftsman of satire, a form analogous to prose, with the more honored creators of other literary forms. So Persius in the prologue 6 calls himself semipaganus. Cf. also Horace's abused tone in invideor and the reference to other Roman men of letters. The nova rerum nomina is not unlike inusitatum, and setematium interpreted linguistically is not so far from Horace's line 49, especially the monstrare abdita rerum. To me the Horatian passage looks like a free adaptation of the formulation of a rhetorical doctrine found in Lucilius. If ἰδιώτης should be regarded as standing in possible contrast with artifex we should have here another bit of evidence for an εἰσαγωγή in book 26.

⁶⁵ Cf. fragments 597, 599, 601, 602, 605.

⁶⁶ But no surviving fragments of Lucilius discuss the ἦθος of style.

⁶⁷ Here the monstrificabilis satirizes the heavy compound words of tragedy. Cf. Cichorius, op. cit., p. 130.

⁶⁸ Notice the emphatic position of the haec tu which I have therefore interpreted in connection with the other evidences of a controversy as an assertion by Lucilius of the part which simple sincerity of diction plays even in tragedy.

⁶⁹ The sesquipedalia verba, like the monstrificabile of Lucilius, satirizes bombastic compounds.

⁷⁰ See Cichorius, op. cit. index s.v., Accius.

⁷¹ Cf. Cicero, orator 76 of the ideals of the orator Atticus or tenuis: summissus est et humilis.

⁷² As Cichorius has seen, op. cit., pp. 115-120.

⁷³ Not from book 26. Marx places it under the unassigned fragments from 1-25, 28-30.

⁷⁴ The simile is used by Horace in Epp. 1, 7, 65 and Epp. 2, 2, 10. Marx tentatively suggests that the Lucilian fragments may belong under

book 10, a satire on literary criticism, which was also imitated by Horace in the *Ars Poetica*. See *infra*, p. 463.

[73] On the origin of this distinction in the commonplaces of the Stoics and Cynics, *cf.* my paper on *Lucilius and Persius*, vol. cit., p. 125, n. 4. In fragment 611 I accept Cichorius' emendations of *veri* and *praedicere* which are paleographically easy and give a reading well suited to the tone of these eisagogic fragments.

[74] With this phrase compare in *Epp.* 2, 2, 122, where the same topic is discussed, *luxuriantia compescet*. So Cicero, *de oratore* 2, 33, 96: *interdum* in *summa ubertate inest luxuries quaedam quae stilo depascenda est*. *Cf.* also *orator* 81.

[75] *Op. cit.*, pp. 119 ff.

[76] *Op. cit.*, p. 119, n. 1.

[77] *Op. cit.*, p. 111 ff.   Compare Livy's *praefatio* 5.

[78] The last line of the passage closely resembles in tone *frags.* 611 and 953.

[79] Notice with Cichorius the close imitation: *quae conductae*, Lucilius; *qui conducti*, Horace; *flent in funere*, Lucilius; *Plorant in funere*, Horace; *multo magis*, Lucilius; *prope plura*, Horace; *capillos scindunt et clamant*, Lucilius; *dicunt et faciunt*, Horace.

[80] See Norden, *op. cit.*, p. 500, note 1.

[81] See Radermacher, *Rh. Mus.* 54, pp. 284 ff. and 57, p. 314, who proves its Stoic origin. So Strabo 1, 17 according to Stoic sources: οὐχ οἷον τε ἀγαθὸν γενέσθαι ποιητὴν μὴ πρότερον γενηθέντα ἄνδρα ἀγαθόν.

[82] See *supra*, p. 113.

[83] Or should we rather regard the line as a humorous recognition by *Lucilius* of the informal character of his own *sermones* and so parallel to Horace's humorous turn on himself in 303.

> Non alius faceret meliora poemata; verum
>   nil tanti est.

[84] In my original treatment of these passages, *cf.* my article, *Lucilius and Persius*, vol. cit., pp. 121 and 124, I considered the reference was to *iunctura*. I now prefer to interpret them as referring to the subjective aspects of *ordo*.

[85] *Op. cit.*, p. 171. *Cf.* Pseudo-Acro on line 238, who seems to be conscious of such a scene in Lucilius, if we accept the MS. reading.

[86] Perhaps both were influenced by the διδασκαλικά of Accius, book 2.

[87] Probably derived from the teachings of *Panaetius*. In *sat.* 2, 1, 75, Horace also alludes to this famous commonplace. *Cf. supra*, p. 73, and pp. 377-378.

[88] *Cf.* Marx, comment, *ad loc.*, for the rhetorical testimonia on this commonplace. *Cf. supra*, pp. 289 ff. for a fuller discussion.

[89] After careful examination I find myself unable to agree with Tyrrel's view, *op. cit. passim*, that there are considerable traces of the influence of Lucilius in the odes and epodes. We have no right to attribute to *Lucilius* on the general ground of coarseness of expression such a phrase as *olentis uxores mariti* in *odes* 1, 17, 7. On the other hand the comparison of the

thirst attendant upon dropsy with avarice is clearly a recollection of Lucilius *fragment* 764. See *supra*, pp. 200 ff. We have allusion to Lucilius in the following passages in Porphyrio's commentary on the *odes* 1, 7, 1 = 1291; 1, 22 in which *canto Lalagen* is explained by Collyra the title to the sixteenth book of Lucilius; 1, 27, 1-2 in which Lucilius' lines 1267:

Podicis Hortensi est ad eam rem nata palaestra

is quoted in support of the perfectly natural turn of *nata* in the sense of *facta*; and 2, 21, 7-8, where on *descende promere* Porphyrio cites for the infinitive of purpose Lucilius 222, *da bibere*. It is obvious that these are parallels cited only for exegetical purposes.

Nor can I feel that we have any clearer evidence for Lucilian influence on the epodes, and this in spite of Lucilius' familiarity with Archilochus, *frag.* 698. The tenth epode which Tyrrel regards as Lucilian and compares explicitly with the Lucilian line 870 ff.:

⏑ — ⏑ — ⏑ — ⏑ nec ventorum flamina flando suda iter secundent.

is to be regarded rather as influenced by an Ennean tragedy, perhaps the Thyestes, than as a *propempticon*, such as we have in this epode and in Horace's *odes* 1, 3, the ode to Virgil's ship.

CHAPTER VII

CONCLUSION

The central thesis of this book has been so fully set forth in the preface, the three introductory chapters, and the analysis of Horace's aesthetic creed in the *Ars Poetica*, that little further need be said by way of summary upon these points. Just as this study was going to press, however, Babbitt's *Rousseau and Romanticism* appeared. In this work Babbitt subjects to a searching analysis the whole modern philosophical and literary movement which is best typified by the name of Rousseau. The work thus lays down the fundamental principles, ethical, psychological, and aesthetic upon which the classical, the neo-classical, and the romantic interpretation of life and literature rest. Every student of the Greek and Roman classics owes Professor Babbitt a profound debt of gratitude for his penetrating interpretation of the real meaning and value of the classical spirit for our modern world.

The conclusions of my own study in the Classical Theory of Imitation, as illustrated by the literary and aesthetic theories of Lucilius and Horace, and the nature of the imitative discipleship which binds Horace to his great predecessor confirm and supplement Babbitt's conclusions in all essential points. It will be profitable therefore to outline the salient theses of Babbitt's book and to point out certain anticipations of these theories in ancient literary criticism. I shall then proceed with a concrete demonstration of the essential harmony of the Classical Theory of Imitation as realized in the aesthetic theory and creative practice of the satirists, Lucilius and Horace, with Babbitt's analysis of classicism. Next I shall consider in some detail the part played by decorum, the feeling for restraint, proportionateness, and centrality in the evolution and perfection of what at first sight seems so free and spontaneous a genre as Latin satire. Finally, I shall endeavor to show that willing submission to these fundamental tenets of classicism in no manner hampers the true genius, but rather that from his adherence to these humanising principles there evolves the literary masterpiece.

In his preface Babbitt quotes as the key to his argument the lines of Emerson:

> There are two laws discrete
> Not reconciled,—
> Law for man, and law for thing;
> The last builds town and fleet
> But it runs wild
> And doth the man unking.

In essence Babbitt's book on the negative side is, as he says, in his preface, a protest against the undue emphasis on the "law for thing," which finds its expression in literature in the emotional naturalism of Rousseau and the romanticists. On its positive side his argument aims to reassert the "law for man" and the supreme value for modern democratic society of the special discipline on which that law rests against the prevalent forms of naturalistic excess in life and letters. In short, Babbitt seeks to reconcile literature and the man of letters with life once more by reasserting that the task of literature is to interpret the experience of the individual in terms of the common experience of the race, not as something unique and eccentric. Or to quote his own words: Life does not give here an element of oneness and there an element of change. It gives a *oneness that is always changing*.

Now Roman satire is just such an interpretation of life as Juvenal realized, when he said (*Sat.* 1, 85 f.):

> Quidquid agunt homines votum timor ira voluptas
> Gaudia discursus, nostri farrago libelli est.

In these lines the oneness is the struggle of man, the outward expression of his seething emotions, against the ever-changing stream of life down which he is swept. In fact, to an unusual degree Latin satire from Lucilius to Juvenal displays in its ethical and aesthetic aspects this quality of a oneness which is ever-changing, a fact which has not escaped my thoughtful readers.

In this life is a oneness that is always changing, that is an element that is permanent and real, inextricably blended with something ever vanishing or transforming itself. Hence the interpretation of life requires the inextricable union within man of the discriminating faculty which we usually call reason or judgment with that of the imagination which gives intuitive penetration into the veil of illusion. The dream of life may, therefore, best be managed—and the classicist emphatically holds that it requires management—through the right use of illusion by the imagination. We thus gain access to a higher reality, to an interpretation of man and life resting on the observed facts of human experience as tested by the laws of reason and probability, but employing intuitive insight, if I may be permitted the pleonasm, to picture man and his works *sub specie aeternitatis.*

Such a oneness within the soul of man may alone lay hold of the oneness in the universe. Such a working partnership between the reason and the imagination is alone capable of erecting a sound model for imitation in the sphere of human conduct and in the sphere of literature which mirrors human life.

The romantic creed is, of course, a reaction from the reason, logic, and good sense of the eighteenth century just as this neo-classical reason was itself a recoil from the intellectual romanticism with its elaborate system of conceits and preciosities of the seventeenth century, and the cult of the romantic deed that had flourished in the mediaeval romances. For the transforming, contemporizing, and progressive imitation of the true classicist, the type of imitation I have illustrated in Chapters IV, V, and VI of this book, the neo-classicist substituted a tame, servile, and external type of imitation such as Horace himself has protested against in the nineteenth epistle of the first book, and has carefully differentiated from his own standard of free imitation in the well-known lines:

> O imitatores servum pecus ut mihi saepe
> bilem saepe meum vestri movere tumultus.

For a true standard of appropriateness or decorum, shifting with the nature of the genre, such as that set forth by Horace in the *Ars Poetica,* the neo-classicist substituted the oppressive external standards of an artificial etiquette. Romanticism, therefore, is a revolt from the domination of the feelings by the reason, from a false theory of imitation, and a perverted sense of decorum. The romanticist is first and foremost an impassioned rebel, but a rebel whose creed needs to be carefully analyzed.

In the first place the romanticist insists on spontaneity or originality, and denies the value of imitation and decorum. Thus Rousseau declares that the prime work of the genius is to refuse to imitate. We have already seen how Young in his *Conjectures on Original Composition* glorifies the spontaneous growth of genius, misinterprets, as is only natural after the frigidity of the neo-classicists, the nature of true imitation and even insinuates that "one is aided in becoming a genius by being brainless and ignorant." He holds in essence "that genius flourishes most in the primitive ages of society before originality has been crushed beneath the superincumbent weight of culture." (See Babbitt, p. 38). In fact, this insistence on an untutored Arcadian primitivism is one of the most widely spread manifestations of the romantic spirit. Romantic poetry constantly glorifies the savage, the simple peasant, the unconscious child. Rousseau has been called the first of the great anti-intellectualists.

This "return to nature" of the romanticist is admirably described by Babbitt: "To follow nature in the classical sense is to imitate what is normal and representative in man and so to become decorous. To be natural in the new sense one must begin by getting rid of imitation and decorum. Moreover, for the classicist, nature and reason are synonymous. The primitivist, on the other hand, means by nature the spontaneous play of impulse and temperament, and inasmuch as this liberty is hindered rather than helped by reason, he inclines to look on reason, not as the equivalent, but as the opposite to nature." (Babbitt, pp. 38-39).

It follows, therefore, that the romanticist, who has thrown over imitation and decorum is resentful of all discipline whether ethical or aesthetic. Since his nature is the spontaneous expression of his expansive emotions he is unwilling to impose any inner checks upon those emotions.

Not only is the conscience in the ordinary sense transformed into an expansive principle of affirmation, sympathy, and overflowing feeling for humanity, but the artistic conscience also regards itself as emancipated from all aesthetic restrictions, from nearly all of those traditions of sound craftsmanship which the experience of the great masters of literature has slowly built up, and among which imitation and decorum or appropriateness occupy a central position, both ethically and aesthetically. In short, from the days of Shaftsbury and Rousseau the romanticist throws off the yoke of both the Christian and the classical discipline in the name of temperament, perhaps the essential aspect of the movement in favor of original genius. (Babbitt, pp. 45 ff.)

How exacting is the yoke which the sincere Christian takes upon himself in imitation of Christ, his master, needs no demonstration. The severity of the imitative discipline voluntarily assumed by the aspirant for literary fame under the classical dispensation is too little known, and yet some of the main articles in that creed have been sketched by Horace in the *Ars Poetica* with a sure hand. Thus Horace takes sound ground on the question of spontaneous genius versus traditional culture by asserting that the poet must first be born and then be made. He holds to the formula *poeta nascitur tum fit*, not to the romantic doctrine *poeta nascitur non fit*. Thus in lines 408-411 he declares:

> Natura fieret laudabile carmen, an arte,
> quaesitum est: ego nec studium sine divite vena,
> nec rude quid prosit video ingenium; alterius sic
> altera poscit opem res et coniurat amice.

That is, natural genius and patient art should not be opposed as if they were enemies: they are really friends.

Horace then continues, strongly emphasizing the severe discipline by which alone true literary success can be attained (lines 412-414):

> Qui studet optatam cursu contingere metam,
> multa tulit fecitque puer, sudavit et alsit,
> abstinuit venere et vino.

In a sense the spontaneous romantic genius is right in taking a stand for self-expression, for assuredly none of the conventions whether national or literary are a final expression of truth. The neo-classicists erred in expressing in terms of finality certain rules and conventions which are in part sound, if used with discretion, in part mechanical and external. As against this false doctrine of external convention the romanticist was justified in revolting in favor of the change and novelty in things. But the romanticist erred in not extricating from the shifting law or convention of a particular time or place the higher law of the ethical imagination of which the latest convention is but an imperfect image. If he had acted thus he would have laid hold of the "unwritten law of heaven," the law of oneness which binds together human experience in all ages and lands.

In discarding this law, and proceeding upon the hypothesis that everything that limits temperament is artificial or mechanical the romanticist is turning his attention to multiplicity, infinite change, and the exaltation of wonder. On the contrary the classicist, who strives to develop his reflective and ethical self and thus to lay hold of that unity which transcends his personal experience, is unwilling to lay final emphasis on wonder. His motto is like that of Horace (*Nil admirari*). With an attitude approximating to the humility of the Christian he experiences awe rather than wonder. He respects himself and is awed by the common humanity within him, but resolutely refuses to be stupified by the uniqueness of his own genius, the supposed abyss which separates him from the common herd.

Moreover, the romantic attitude towards life and letters tends to assert the desirability of giving free rein to the dominant faculty, bent, or ruling passion to what we commonly call today the "artistic temperament" at the expense of a rounded development of all the powers. As Babbitt well says (p. 63): "The partisans of expression as opposed to form in the eighteenth century led to the fanatics of expression in the nineteenth, and these have led to the maniacs of expression in the twentieth. . . . But the more the element of proportion in beauty is sacrificed to strangeness the more the result will seem to the normal man to be not beauty at all, but rather an esoteric cult of ugliness. The romantic genius, therefore, denounces the normal man as a philistine and at the same time, since he cannot please him, seeks at least to shock him and so capture his attention by the very violence of his eccentricity."

The final result of this anarchical freedom which the romantic genius grants to his temperament is an eccentricity hardly distinguishable from madness.   The works of the post-impressionists, cubists, futurists, vorticists in modern French art, the esoteric cult of the monstrous and the ugly which plays such a part in modern German art, the absurdities of many of our new poets in "free verse," afford unhappy evidence of the truth of this contention.

In short, the romanticist is in certain respects the modern analogue to the picture of the *demens poeta* or mad poet sketched by Horace in the concluding lines of the *Ars Poetica*, as the foil to the picture of the slowly maturing perfect poet.   This mad poet under the influence of his inspiration is so oblivious of reality that while he mouths his verse he falls into a well, and in addition "so temperamental" that after having called for assistance, he is unwilling to accept it when it comes.   And worst of all, as Horace wittily suggests:

Nec semel hoc fecit, nec, si retractus erit, iam
fiet homo et ponet famosae mortis amorem.

As Babbitt suggests, the romanticist is often poetical without being wise.   The neo-classicist, like Dr. Johnson, for example, is wise without being poetical, while the classicist from the inner fusion of the critical reason and the creative imagination aims to produce a work of art which shall be both wise and poetical.

This abbreviated and, therefore, over-dogmatic presentation of the creed of the romanticist will not, I trust, satisfy my readers.   I must content myself with referring all who are interested in the subject to Babbitt's discriminating analyses of these romantic theories.

At the very heart of the classical creed lie the two doctrines of imitation and decorum.   Since these two doctrines are constantly illustrated from the point of view of psychology, ethics, and aesthetics in Babbitt's book, and from the point of view of rhetorical theory and literary composition in the present study, I shall confine my attention to them.   It will be found, I believe, that in actual practice Horace does follow the essential features of Babbitt's analysis of classicism.   Hence the nature of his free imitative discipleship to Lucilius in the composition of his satires harmonizes to a remarkable degree with Babbitt's view of the fundamental aspects of the classical theory of imitation. I am inclined to think, however, that as a literary problem the relation of the perpetuator of a great tradition to its inventor leads, at any rate in the earlier stages of discipleship to a somewhat closer and more direct type of imitation, especially to a franker appropriation of traditional themes, than Babbitt has apparently recognized. We have something much more direct, concrete, and self-conscious than the imitation of soul by soul. Yet even in this doctrine of imitation the insistence on restraint and proportion may be discovered, for such restraint and proportion are of the very essence of the classical spirit. The classicist having decided what is normal either for man or some particular class of men takes this normal "nature" for his model and proceeds to imitate it. Whatever accords with the model he has thus set up he pronounces natural or probable. The classicist, therefore, affirms a general nature, a core of normal experience. From this central affirmation derives the doctrine of imitation and from imitation in turn the doctrine of probability and decorum. (Babbitt, pp. 16-17)

The romanticist believes that it is impossible to conform and imitate and at the same time to be free and original and spontaneous. Above all it is impossible to submit to the yoke of either reason or imitation and at the same time be imaginative. He holds that the creative imagination can be restored to its rights only by repudiating imitation. The imagination is supreme the classicist grants, but adds that to imitate rightly is to make the highest use of the imagination. This is perhaps the central point in the debate between classicist and romanticist. (Babbitt, p. 69 in substance)

Now the romanticist's rejection of all imitation is due to his confounding what we may call the plagiaristic imitation of the neo-classicist with the free and transforming imitation of the true classicist. And yet it must be acknowledged, I think, that the classicist like the romanticist has the defect of his virtue. Consequently the peculiar danger of classicism is that an original apprenticeship of free and transforming imitation of the model will degenerate into that stupid and uninspired plagiaristic imitation which exalts artistic technique above creative imagination. And this is the actual fate that overtook Latin literature in so many genres during the so-called silver

age. The barren epics of Lucan, Statius and Silius Italicus
stand in essentially this relation to Virgil's Aeneid.   The
antithetical dangers to which the romanticist is exposed I
have just discussed.   The imitative relationship of Virgil's
Aeneid to Homer, the Alexandrian epyllia, and Euripidean
drama, or the relation of Horace's satires to those of
Lucilius as set forth in this book are examples of classical imita-
tion at its best.   Moreover, the classicist, as I have tried to
show in my first chapter, does not confound plagiarism with
free imitation, but clearly discriminates between them, as Horace
has again and again emphasized in his critical writings.

I am chary of applying biological analogies to the field of
human action and expression.   Nevertheless when one con-
siders the part that imitative instinct plays in the actions of
the young of animals, in the development of children, and in the
initial stages of instruction in the fine arts one wonders whether
we in America are justified in making so little use of that
principle in the literary training of boys and girls in their teens
and in our American colleges.   With the Greeks and Romans
at any rate reading and literary paraphrase went hand in hand
and little attention was paid to the process of recording the
spontaneous observations of still untutored minds upon the
world around them.

Certainly spontaneity as a working creed for the tyro in
the literary art stands at the farthest remove from the exacting
discipline sketched for the young Pisos by Horace in the *Ars
Poetica*.   In this exposition Horace insists on exact knowledge,
on discrimination in the choice of words and their collocation,
on a strictly limited use of loan words, on good metrical tech-
nique, on complete submission to the admonitions of one's own
aesthetic conscience, on repeated revision, on the value of a
stern and dogmatic criticism—and I have by no means ex-
hausted the list of prescriptions. (See *Ars Poetica* 86 ff.,
119 ff., 130 ff., 240 ff., 260 ff., 290 ff., 370 ff., 410 ff.)   That is,
to become a literary artist it is necessary for the spontaneous
genius (*rude ingenium*) to submit himself to a prescribed cur-
riculum of the most thorough-going character.   For genius
without such schooling accomplishes nothing.

Such a school for the poet is doubtless utterly antipathetic to the sensibilities of many of my readers, and in truth some aspects of Horace's programme seem to anticipate the formalism of the neo-classicist's programme. Nevertheless, we must remember that in this school were formed not only an extraordinary number of polished and technically proficient versifiers, but poets of such varied gifts, broad humanity, and high inspiration as Tibullus, Propertius, Ovid, Horace, and Virgil. The mere citation of these names is a sufficient refutation of the theory that a patient art founded upon an exacting imitative discipline necessarily stifles genius.

The part that Greco-Roman rhetoric played in evolving this well-articulated theory of imitation I have described in detail in my first chapter. I need not retraverse that ground here, but I would beg my readers to remember that at their best the ancient rhetoricians evolved an objective and discriminating literary criticism based on wide reading, sound linguistic and phonetic training, and real sensitiveness and appreciation which has scarcely been equalled since. The analysis of the relation between Horace's satires and those of Lucilius in chapters IV, V, and VI, I believe affords concrete proof that Horace in practice accepted this rhetorical theory of imitation.

Also, I would once more emphasize the fact that the classical tradition did not stifle or constrain originality according to the ancient point of view, because the type of imitation it evolved was in no sense plagiaristic and only sporadically was close verbal imitation employed. The themes which a Terence or a Horace employed as the raw material (*publica materies*) for his invention were not so narrowly limited as to involve a task in any sense reminiscent of the reweaving and unweaving of Penelope at the loom. New themes might be developed, if consonant with the laws of the genre. Even in the first book of satires Horace's third satire seems to be such a theme, while the principle of *contaminatio* gave wide scope for new combinations of the traditional material, as in the second satire of the first book for example. The principles of contemporization and of generous rivalry with the inventor of the genre acted as a real stimulus to the genius of the continuator of the great tradition, and at the same time were a real source of pleasure to the relatively small body of highly cultivated readers, in whose minds such literary echoes produced an effect analogous to that of the refrain.   In short, each writer endeavored to transmit the tradition of his genre by transmuting it. And finally, and perhaps most important of all, the ancient reader and ancient critic were far more sensitive to architectonic symmetry and harmony of form and phrase than are even the most cultivated of our modern readers.   In fact, originality in the modern sense of the insatiate hunger for the novel, or the strange in plot or theme entered but a small degree into their aesthetic consciousness.

From the patient art and the austere imitative discipline to which the true classicist gladly sends his genius to school, because to him, as Aristotle says the end is the chief thing of all, is born a feeling of proportionateness or appropriateness, the τὸ πρέπον of the Greek rhetoricians.   This feeling for what is proportionate, appropriate, decorous, manifests itself in almost every aspect of literary composition, in the choice of words appropriate to the genre, in the ordering of the words according to the principles of prose rhythm or metre, and rhetorical effect, in the symmetrical relations of the parts of a work of art to the whole, and in that delicate discrimination by which the lex operis or law of the genre was built up, and from whose nice application the various genres evolved.   This tradition for appropriateness or decorum has maintained itself more fully in such modern Latin literatures as French and Italian than in the more spontaneous creations of German, English and American literature.   The words of Daunou (translated by Babbitt, p. 100) in his La Harpe show how firmly established the tradition for decorum was in the age of Madame de Staël. "One of the services that he (La Harpe) should render nowadays is to fortify young people against vain and gothic doctrines which would reduce the fine arts to childhood if they could ever gain credit in the land of Racine and Voltaire.   La Harpe uttered a warning against these doctrines when he discovered the first germs of them in the books of Diderot, Mercier, and some other innovators. . . .   He did not distinguish two literatures.   The literature that nature and society have created for us and which for three thousand years past has been established and preserved and reproduced by masterpieces appeared to him alone worthy of a Frenchman of the eighteenth century. He did not foresee that it would be reduced some day to being only a particular kind of literature, tolerated or reproved under the name of classic, and that its noblest productions would be put on the same level as the formless sketches of uncultivated genius and untried talents. Yet, more than once decadence has thus been taken for advance, and a retrograde movement for progress. Art is so difficult. It is quicker to abandon it and to owe everything to your genius. . . . Because perfection calls for austere toil you maintain that it is contrary to nature. This is a system that suits at once indolence and vanity."

Whatever may be thought of this pronouncement today, it is beyond cavil that it is in complete harmony with the literary theories of the Augustan age and shows many striking similarities with the doctrine of Horace in the *Ars Poetica*. On the other hand Rousseau and all the great romanticists are hostile to decorum. Yet as Babbitt well says (p. 201): "True decorum is only the pulling back and disciplining of impulse to the proportionateness that has been perceived with the aid of what one may term the ethical or generalizing imagination. To dismiss like the romantic expansionist everything that limits or restricts the lust of knowledge or of power, or of sensation as arbitrary or artificial is to miss true decorum and at the same time to sink as a Greek would say from ethos to pathos."

There must then be a warfare in the aesthetic cave within the soul of man corresponding to the war within the ethical cave in his soul between expansive impulse and the limiting principle of conscientious control. True decorum which emerges from such a warfare is not antipathetic to the creative imagination because through such a struggle the creative imagination learns to generalize its impulses into forms of pure humanity and therefore truly interpretative of life. Through decorum rightly conceived one attains a higher unity inextricably blended with reality, not a unity that is, as Babbitt aptly phrases it, a dream unity.

We have already seen that in obedience to the principle of imitation Horace takes up, so to say, the literary cross, and with a simplicity which reminds us of the Christian grace of humility gladly submits to the critical homily of Quintilius. (See *Ars Poetica*, 437) Indeed the law of decorum has certain correspondences with the law of the Christian life. Like that law it is not only evolved by the practice of imitation, but is deliberately imposed on the human heart from within.

The principles of decorum or appropriateness were worked out by ancient rhetoric and philosophy with the utmost nicety of detail; in fact, to a point which to us moderns seems almost to savor of preciosity. Nevertheless, the result of adherence to this body of principles was a perfection of finish, a symmetrical beauty which is much less common today. Thus Panaetius, as we have seen, in his treatise περὶ τοῦ καθήκοντος made appropriateness the foundation not only for aesthetics but for ethics. Since we have constantly found these principles of decorum operative in the critical and satirical writings of Lucilius and Horace it will be profitable to study them in somewhat greater detail.

In the first place it is interesting to notice that the ancients recognized the expansive element in the heart of man, the free play of the emotions, but dealt with this problem not along Rousseauistic lines, but in pretty close accord with the principles of decorum. Thus in the *de officiis*, 101-104, Cicero freely translating Panaetius recognizes the conflict between reason and appetite or expansive emotion, ὁρμή. His solution of the conflict is that reason must command, appetite obey. Hence every action should be based on reason. The wise control of the passions is the first law of duty. Consequently even jesting, an emotional outburst which has a recreative value,—a term frequently used by Babbitt—may be used as a means of relaxation, but is subject to the restraints of reason; that is to the law of decorum. Cicero then proceeds to enumerate those laws. This method is in direct contrast to the dalliant mood— one may hardly speak of method—of Rousseau and his followers in dealing with the outpourings of human emotion.

Did time permit it could probably be shown in a most interesting way how these principles of decorum permeated the whole theory and practice of composition in the Augustan age, and notably the compositions of Horace. Even the more temperamental Lucilius I have shown to be influenced by them far more than has hitherto been realized.

The doctrine of decorum absolutely interpenetrates Horace's theory of the poetic art at almost every phase, as Hack has convincingly shown in his article on the doctrine of the literary forms. It is significant that in passing from the discussion of the *ars* to the task of the *artifex* or literary artist, Horace asserts the fundamental importance of this guiding principle, *Ars Poetica*, 306 ff.:

> Munus et officium nil scribens ipse docebo,
> unde parentur opes, quid alat formetque poetam,
> quid deceat, quid non, quo virtus, quo ferat error.

So also at the very beginning of the treatise the winged serpents of tragedy are used as a symbol of the importance of unity and congruity in a true work of art.

Later when discussing the choice of words in lines 45-72 Horace permits the coinage of new words only if the privilege is used with discretion (*dabitur licentia sumpta pudenter*), and compounds formed on the analogy of the Greek laws of composition must be sparingly employed (*parce detorta*). Even in the matter of nicely articulated verbal complexes, the very core of Horace's claim to a *curiosa felicitas* he advocates the same principle of restraint. His ideal poet will be *in verbis etiam tenuis cautusque serendis*, like the *tenuis orator* of Cicero. Again in the question of the order of words (*ordo*) the poet will accept only that which is instantly appropriate to be uttered, and will reject or postpone all other argumentative material. (See *Ars Poetica*, 40-45) Finally in the range of his vocabulary also Horace shows how the doctrine of decorum had been perfected in the period separating the age of Lucilius and the Scipios from his own as the result of the puristic studies of the Atticists of the Ciceronian and Augustan period. This point has been fully considered in connection with my analysis of satires 1, 4; 1, 10, and the *Ars Poetica*. On the other hand we have found that the more expansive Lucilius, while recognizing many of the limitations to a "wide open vocabulary" prescribed by the less developed doctrines of decorum prevalent in the

Scipionic circle, nevertheless travelled a considerable distance
on the road of the great romanticist Victor Hugo, who boasted
that he had put the liberty cap on the dictionary.

A decorous and restrained art is a reticent art. I do not
need to labor the point of Horatian reticence, which is one of
the commonplaces of literature. And indeed in the *Ars Poetica*,
(line 145) he expressly couples *pudor* with the *lex operis* in dis-
cussing the difficult problem of imitation. Reticence, indeed,
lies at the very root of the quality of *curiosa felicitas*. In all
his critical writings Horace has repeatedly expressed his feeling
for the desirability of brevity, and emphasized the lack of that
quality in the improvising Lucilius. Perhaps this humorous
reticence is best illustrated in satire 1, 4, 17 where in declining
the contest in improvisation proposed by Crispinus he raises
a prayer of thanksgiving that his temperament is that of one,
raro et perpauca loquentis.

In the field of language and style, the evolution of the three
styles, plain, middle and grand is perhaps the most notable
product of the orderly and logical development of the principles
of restraint, propriety, and good taste which we have been
describing. While from one point of view propriety, τὸ πρέπον,
is only one of the five stylistic virtues in the system of Diogenes
of Babylon, it is difficult to exaggerate its power of interpene-
trating all the aspects of the Stoic rhetoric. Under the influence
of the more humane Panaetius and the Roman Atticists, and
aided by the generally eclectic tendencies of philosophical and
literary studies in the Ciceronian and Augustan period, and, I
may add by the strong mediating tendency of the Greco-Roman
civilization, this quality at last disputed the supremacy with
the doctrine of good Latinity itself.

In the correlation of invective with the grand style, of irony
with the plain style, and in the elaborate formulation of the
distinction between the liberal and the illiberal jest in Greco-
Roman rhetoric, in Cicero and in Horace, which I have dis-
cussed in my second and third chapters, and in connection with
Horace's fourth satire of the first book we have another striking
example of the working of the same principle of decorum.

It is perhaps worth emphasizing the fundamental distinction
between romantic and Socratic irony. The former, as Babbitt

has shown, is an expression of bitter personal disillusion on the part of the romanticist at the gap between the Arcadian dreamland into which he would project himself and the real world of struggling humanity, from which he would fain escape but to which sooner or later he is irrevocably recalled. The Socratic and the Horatian irony, on the other hand, and I have tried to show the close relation existing between them, are completely socialized. They represent a restrained and humorous recognition of the gap which separates the half-educated mass of men from what is truly central in existence, a larger and deeper knowledge of life and its hidden meaning, a goal which ever eludes even the wisest of us but in the pursuit of which with the united force of our reason and imagination, the only true happiness is to be found. There is no note of acrid disdain or disillusion in the irony of a Socrates or a Horace, which only seeks to tell the truth under cover of a jest:

> ridentem dicere verum
> quid vetat? ut pueris olim dant crustula blandi doctores
> elementa velint ut discere prima.

From such *blandi doctores* the children of men will ever take the sweetened cakes, and cling to their robes as they learn from them the *prima elementa vitae*.

But the literary genres are perhaps the noblest expression of the classical tradition clearly discriminated by the reason, wrought by an arduous imitative discipline, fused into harmony by the brooding imagination of the noblest minds of the Greeks and Romans, they enshrine in firm and radiant forms the visions of the human spirit. And so while we may well give all praise to Lucilius, the inventor of Roman satire, our deepest affection and devotion go out to Horace, to Horace the conscientious artist, to Horace our kindly and quizzical guide on a long but friendly journey, to Horace the humane discoverer of our daily life.

> "Ainsi donc, dans les arts, l'inventeur est celui
> Qui peint ce que chacun peut sentir comme lui."

FINIS

BIBLIOGRAPHY

Arnim, H. von. *Leben und Schriften des Dio von Prusa. Berlin. 1898.*

Babbitt, Irving. *Rousseau and Romanticism. Boston. 1919.*

Billeter, G. *Der Wettkamp als Mittelpunkt des griechischen Lebens.*

Bischoff, A. *De Itinere Horati Brundisino. Progr. Landau. 1880.*

Bonhoffer, A. *Die Ethik des Stoikers Epiktet. Stuttgart. 1890.*

Brandt, P. and C. Wachsmuth. *Corpusculum poesis epicae Graecae ludibundae. 2 vols., vol. 1 by Brandt, vol. 2 by Wachsmuth.*

Brinkmann. *Rh. Mus. Vol. 63, pp. 618 ff.*

Buecheler, F. *Vindiciae Priapeorum. Rh. Mus. Vol. XVIII, 1863.*

Buttner, R. *Porcius Licinus. Leipzig. 1893.*

Cartault, A. *Etude sur Les Satires D'Horace. Paris. 1899.*

Christ, W. *Griechische Literaturgeschichte. 4th ed.*

Cichorius, C. *Untersuchungen zu Lucilius. Berlin. 1908.*

Cooper, F. T. *Word formation in the Sermo Plebeius. New York. 1895.*

Cronert, Wilhelm. *Kolotes und Mendemus in C. Wessley's Studien zur Paleographie und Papyruskunde. Vol. 6. Leipzig. 1906.*

Cust, R. H. H. *Translation of Life of Benvenuto Cellini. 2 vols. London. 1910.*

Deajardins, R. *Voyage D'Horace à Brindes. Revue de Philologie. Vol. II. 1878. Pp. 144-175.*

Dieterich, A. *Pulcinella. Leipzig. 1897.*

Dryoff, M. *Caesar's Anticato and Cicero's Cato. Rh. Mus. 63, 1908. Pp. 587 ff.*

Duff, J. W. *Literary History of Rome. London. 1909.*

Duntzer, H. *Eine Reisesatire und eine Reise Epistel des Horaz. Philologus, vol. 55, 1896. Pp. 256 ff.*

Edwards, P. H. *The Poetic Element in the Satires and Epistles of Horace, part I. Diss. Baltimore. 1905.*

Fairclough, H. B. *Horace's View of the Relations between Satire and Comedy. A. J. P. Vol. 34, pp. 183-193.*

Filbey, Edward J. *Satire by Direct Criticism of Contemporaries and Satire by Types in Lucilius, Horace, and Persius. University of Wisconsin Thesis. 1903.*

Fiske, G. C. *Lucilius, the Ars Poetica of Horace and Persius. Harvard Studies in Cl. Phil. Vol. 24, pp. 1-36.*

Fiske, G. C. *Lucilius and Persius. Tr. A. P. A. Vol. 40, pp. 121-151.*

Fiske, G. C. *Udas ante foras. C. P. pp. 336-338.*

Fuhr, J. A. *De Mimis Graecorum. Berlin. 1860.*

Geffcken, J. *Studien zur griechischen Satire. N. Jahrb. fur das Klass. Alt. vol. 27, pp. 394-403.*

Geffcken, J. *Kynika. Heidelberg. 1909.*

Gercke, A. *Rh. Mus. 48. 1893, pp. 41-52. Die Komposition der ersten Satire des Horaz.*

Gerhard, G. A. *Phoenix von Kolophon. Leipzig. 1909.*

Grant, Mary. *The Rhetorical Theory of the Laughable in Cicero and Horace. University of Wisconsin Thesis. 1919.*

Greenidge, A. H. J. *Roman history. New York. 1905.*

Hack, R. K. *The Doctrine of Literary Forms. Harvard Studies in Classical Philology. Vol. 27, pp. 1-66.*

Hartman, J. J. *de Phaedri fabulis commentatio. Leyden. 1889.*

Hauler, C. *Der Mimus von Epicharm bis Sophron in Zenia Austriaca I. Vienna. 1893, pp. 81-135.*

Hausrath, A. *Untersuchungen zur Ueberlieferungog der aesopischen Fabeln in Jahrb. f. d. Klass. Alt. Suppl. 21, 1894. Pp. 274 ff.*

Hausrath, A. *Das Problem der aesopischen Fabel. N. Jahrb. f. d. Klass. Alt. 1. (1898) p. 305 ff.*

Heinze, R. *De Horatio Bionis Imitore. Bonn. 1888.*

Heitland, W. E. *The Roman Republic. Cambridge (England) 1909.*

Helm, R. *Lucian und Menipp. Leipzig. 1906.*

Hendrickson, G. L. *Horace and Lucilius. A Study of Horace Serm. 1. 10. Studies in Honor of Gildersleeve. Pp. 151-168.*

Hendrickson, G. L. *Are the Letters of Horace Satires? A. J. P. 18, pp. 312-324.*

Hendrickson, G. L. *Horace, Sermo. 1, 4. A Protest and a Programme.* A. J. P. 21. Pp. 121-142. *Quoted on Horace's theory of humor.*

Hendrickson, G. L. *Horace and Valerius Cato.* C. P. Vol. 11, pp. 249-269; Vol. 12, pp. 77-92, 328-350 passim.

Hendrickson, G. L. *The Origin and Meaning of the Ancient Characters of Style.* A. J. P. 26. pp. 249 ff.

Hendrickson, G. L. *Satura, the Genesis of a Literary Form.* C. P. pp. 129-143.

Hense, O. *Teletis Reliquiae.* Freiburg. 1889.

Herwig, M. A. *Horatius quatenus recte de Lucilio iudicaverit.* Halle. 1873.

Hirzel, R. *Der Dialog.* 2 vols. Leipzig. 1895.

Hirzel, R. *Untersuchungen zu Cicero's philosophischen Schriften.* 3 vols. Leipzig. 1877-1883.

Iltgen, J. J. *de Horatio, Lucilii aemulo.* Montabauer. 1872.

Ingersoll, J. W. D. *Roman Satire. Its Early Name?* C. P. VII, pp. 59-65.

Jackson, C. F. *Molle atque Facetum.* Harvard Studies in Classical Philology. ᵈ 24, pp. 117-137.

Jebb, R. C. *The Characters of Theophrastus.* London. 1909.

Joel, K. *Der echte und der Xenophontische Sokrates.* 2 vols. Berlin. 1893-1901.

Kiessling, H. and Heinze, R. *Q. Horatius Flaccus. Satiren.* 4th edition. Berlin. 1910.

Knapp, C. *The Sceptical Assault on the Roman Tradition concerning the Dramatic Satura.* A. J. P. Vol. 33, pp. 131 ff.

Kock, T. *Comicorum Atticorum Fragmenta.* 3 vols. Leipzig. 1880-1888.

Kroll, W. *M. Tulli Ciceronis Orator.* Berlin. 1913.

Lejay, P. *Satires.* Paris. 1911.

Leo, F. *Geschichte der römischen Literatur.* Berlin. 1913.

Lindsay, W. W. *Nonius Marcellus' Dictionary of Republican Latin.* Oxford. 1901.

Lorenz. *Leben und Schriften des Koers Epicharmus.*

Mahaffy, J. P. *The Degradation of Odysseus in Greek Literature.* Hermathena. Dublin. 1875.

Marx, F. *C. Lucili carmina reliquiae.* 2 vols.

Meier Graefe, Julius. *Modern Art.* New York. 1908.

Misch, G. *Geschichte der Autobiographie. Leipzig and Berlin.*
1907.

Mommsen, T. *Roman History.* (*Eng. Trans.*)

Morley, John. *Recollections. New York. 1917.*

Mullach, F. W. *Fragmenta Philosophorum Graecorum. 3 vols.*
Paris. 1860.

Norden, E. *Die Composition und die Literaturgattung der*
Horazischen Epistula ad Pisones. Hermes. 40 pp. 481-528.

Norden, E. *Virgil's Aeneis im Lichte ihrer Zeit. Neujahr-*
bücher für das Klass. Alt. Vol. 7, pp. 251-265.

Norden, E. *In Varronis Saturas Menippeas Observationes*
Selectae. Leipzig. 1891.

Norden, E. *Antike Kunstprosa. 2 vols. Leipzig. 1898.*

Ogle, M. B. *Horace an Atticist. C. P. 11, pp. 156-168.*

Otto, A. *Sprichwörter der Romer. Leipzig. 1890.*

Peter, H. *Wahrheit und Kunst. Geschichtsschreibung und*
Plagiat im Klassischen Altertum. Berlin. 1911.

Peter, H. *Der Brief in der rom. Litt. Abh. der sachs. Gess. der*
Wissenschaft. Vol. B. 20, N. 3. Leipzig. 1901. p. 179.
p. 221.

Rademacher, L. *Studien zur Geschichte der antiken Rhetorik.*
Rh. Mus. 54. p. 284 ff., p. 314.

Reich, H. *Der Mimus. 2 vols. Berlin. 1903.*

Reitzenstein, R. *Scipio Aemilianus und die Stoische Rhetorik.*
Strassburger Festschrift zu 46 vers. der deutschen Philologer
und Schulmanner. Strassburg. 1901.

Reitzenstein, R. *Hellenistische Wundererzählungen. Leipzig.*
1906.

Reitzenstein, R. *Werden und Wesen der Humanitat in Alter-*
thum. Strassburg. 1907.

Ribbeck, Otto. *Rh. Mus. 31, 381 ff. Ueber den Begriff des*
εἴρων.

Rohricht, Aug. *Quaestiones scaenicae. Dissert. Argent. 1885.*

Sandys, J. E. *M. Tulli Ciceronis ad M. Brutum Orator. Cam-*
bridge. 1885.

Schanz, *Romische Literaturgeschichte.*

Schmekel, A. *Die Philosophie der mittleren Stoa. Berlin.*
1892.

Shorey, P. φύσις, μελέτη, ἐπιστημή, *Transc. Am. Phil. Assn.* Vol. 40, pp. 185-201.

Sihler, E. G. *The Collegium Poetarum at Rome.* A. J. P. Vol. 26, pp. 1-21.

Smiley, Charles Newton. *Latinitas and* Ἑλληνισμός. *University of Wisconsin Thesis.* 1906.

Spengel, L. *Rhetores Graeci. 3 vols. Leipzig.* 1854-56.

Stemplinger, E. *Das Fortleben des Horazischen Lyrik seit der Renaissance. Leipzig.* 1906.

Stemplinger, E. *Das Plagiat in der griechischen Literatur. Berlin.* 1912.

Striller. *De Stoicorum Studiis rhetoricis. Breslauer Phil. Abhandlungen.* Vol. I, pp. 1-112.

Susemihl, F. *Geschichte der griechischen Litteratur in der Alexandrinerzeit. 2 vols. Leipzig.* 1891.

Suss, W. *Ethos. Leipzig.* 1910.

Teichmüller, *Grundgedanke und disposition von Hor. Sat. 1, 1. Rh. Mus.* pp. 436-452.

Topffer, J. A. *Attische Genealogie. Berlin.* 1889.

Triemel, L. *Ueber Lucilius und seine Verhaltniss zu Horatius. Kreusn.* 1877.

Tyrell, R. Y. *Horace and Lucilius. Hermathena.* 4, 355.

Tyrell, R. Y. *Latin Poetry. Johns Hopkins Lectures.* 1893. pp. 162-215.

Ullmann, B. L. *Horace, Catullus, Tigellinus.* C. P. 10, pp. 270-296.

Ullman, B. L. *Horace on the Nature of Satire.* Tr. A. P. A. Vol. 48, pp. 111-132.

Ullman, B. L. *Satura and Satire.* C. P. Vol. 8, pp. 187 ff.

Usener, H. *Epicurea. Leipzig.* 1887.

Wachsmuth, G. *Corspusculum Poesis Epicae Graecae Ludibundae.* 1888.

Wartensleben, G. von. *Begriff der gr. Chreia und Beitrage zur Geschichte ihrer Form. Heidelberg.* 1901.

Weber, Ernst. *De Dione Chrysostomo Cynicorum sectatore in Leipziger studiene zur classischen Philologie,* Vol. 10, pp. 77-268.

Wendland, J. T. P. *Die Hellenistiche-Romische Kultur. Tubingen.* 1907.

Wessley, C. *Studien zur Palaeographie und Papyruskunde. Vol. 6. ed. by Wilhelm Cronert. Kolotes und Menedemes.*

Wilkins, A. S. *M. Tulli Ciceronis de Oratore. 3 vols. Oxford. 1888.*

Witzinger, *Mitth. der Atth. Instit. 26, p. 1 ff.* (*1901*).

Young, Edward. *Conjectures on Original Composition. 1759.*

Zawadski, V. *Quatenus in satiris Horatius videtur imitatus esse Lucilium. Erlangen. 1881.*

INDEX

Porphyrio, on *epistula* a form of satire, 426; on Horace, 26, 32, 76, 110, 243, 244, 257, 266, 271, 275, 276, 306, 307, 311, 323, 327, 335, 340, 385, 390, 429, 435, 443, 445.
Propriety, appropriateness, decorum, τὸ πρέπον, 79, 85 f., 340; virtue of plain style, 129; in Diogenes, 129; Panaetius περὶ τοῦ καθήκοντος, 72, 84 ff., 124, 276; in Panaetius' system co-ordinate with *Latinitas*, 129, 341; principles of applied to the laughable, 91 f.; incidental discussion of in Horace's Odes, 129; main theme of *Ars Poetica*, 85, 129;. rejected by Romanticists, 478 ff.; lies at heart of classical creed, 482 ff.; discussion of true decorum, 487; foundation for aesthetics and ethics, 488; principles of decorum operative in Lucilius and Horace, 488.

Quintianus, 27.
Quintilian, formulated and developed rhetoric, 16, 80; assails coarseness, 174; describes the perfect orator, 44; discusses relation of *epistula* to satire, 426; compares Horatian and Lucilian satire, 129; quotes Lucilius on pure Latinity, 111; discusses Messala's zeal for pure Latinity, 342; use of the χρεία in education, 160; *consensus eruditorum*, 453; *iunctura*, 124; the laughable, 7, 6; value of *loci communes*, 54; modernization, 51; reading, 36; rivalry in imitation, 43; *urbanitas*, 164; use of Greek, 240; *Inst. Or.* cited as example of εἰσαγωγή, 446. 1, 5, 56: 343; 1, 6, 45: 453; 1, 7, 23: 343; 1, 7, 35: 342; 1, 9, 3: 160; 6, 3: 76; 6, 3, 8: 174; 6, 3, 20: 124; 6, 3, 104: 117; 6, 3, 107: 117; 8, 3, 49: 117; 9, 4, 32: 124; 10, 1, 66: 51; 10, 1, 94: 106, 117, 129; 10, 1, 113: 342; 10, 2, 1: 38; 10, 2, 2: 36; 10, 2, 28: 43; 10, 5, 2: 342; 10, 5, 4: 36; 10, 5, 12: 54; 12, 10, 27 ff.: 340.

Reading, see ἀνάγνωσις.
Recitatio, 390; introduced by Pollio, 294; Horace on, 293 f.
Rhetoric, a study of masterpieces, 33; lay at foundation of Classical Theory of Imitation, 485; pre-requisite for literary composition, 32; placed on scientific basis in Hellenistic period, 16; aim defined by Aristotle, 78; tenets codified by Isocrates, 40; formulation and development of laws of composition, 32 ff.; ancient manuals of, 35; fostered reading, interpretation, paraphrase, and translation, 36 ff.; Stoic rhetoric, 38, 76, 116, 123, 461, natural expression in plain style, 70; indifferent to excessive elaboration, 109; fondness for etymology, 108; regard for phonetic values, 131; principles of expounded for Romans by Diogenes and Panaetius, 17, 76, 107, 112, 202; laid foundation for Roman rhetoric and critical theory, 80; nationalized and developed in circles of Scipio and Maecenas, 16, 76 f.; influence on Lucilius and Horace, 107 ff. 466; Stoic theory of plain style, see under Plain Style. See also Aristotle, Cicero, Horace, Imitation, Lucilius, Paraphrase, Reading.
Rivalry, in imitation, 43 f.
Romanticism, 205 ff.; anarchistic attitude of, 206, 478 ff.; confounds plagiarism with free and transforming imitation, 483. See Imitation.
Rousseau, father of Romanticism, quoted, 205; emotional naturalism of, 477; Rousseauism, conflict of humanism and humanitarianism, 73.
Rufillus, 271.
Rupilius Rex, Publius, 53, 103, 162, 325 ff.
Rutilius Rufus, Publius, exponent of plain style, 81; interest in biography, 81; *de vita sua, responsa*, 51; judgment of feared by Lucilius, 112, 123.

Sal, pungent wit, marks transition from plain style in narrower sense to invective (grand), 106; Cicero on two types of, 119.
σαφήνεια, clearness, 79, 129, 338.
Sappho, 42, 439.
Scaliger, on Lucilius, 245, 327.
Sarmentus, 308, 309, 315.
Scaevola, Publius Mucius, Quintus Mucius, models of plain style, 81 ff., 162, 245, 325 ff.

ζῆλος, aemulatio, rivalry, in imitation, 43, 322.
Zeno the Epicurean, on Socrates, 175.

Zeno the Stoic, 53, 86, 100, 159; divided men into two classes, 144; ἀπομνημονεύματα of, 156.
Zeus, 153.

Table of Parallel Passages and Citations from Lucilius and Horace.

The following is a list of Lucilian fragments discussed in the text in connection with Horatian passages either by way of comparison or contrast in theme, treatment, form, or diction:
Lucilius, line 44 f., cf. Horace Sat. 1, 7, 1 ff., 326; l. 84 f., cf. Sat. 1, 7, 26 ff., 109, 328; ll. 88 ff., cf. Sat. 1, 7, 33 ff., 53, 111, 329; l. 107, cf. Sat. 1, 5, 25 and 86, 311; l. 109, cf. Sat. 1, 5, 94 ff., 312; l. 114, cf. Sat. 1, 5, 25 and 86, 311; l. 115, cf. Sat. 1, 5, 46 ff., 308, 315; ll. 117 ff., cf. Sat. 1, 5, 51 ff., 172, 308 ff.; ll. 124 ff., cf. Sat. 1, 5, 9 ff., 25 and 86, 311, 314; l. 126, cf. Sat. 1, 5, 25 and 86, 311; ll. 128 ff., cf. Sat. 1, 5, 71 ff., 310; l. 131 ff., cf. Sat. 1, 5, 9 ff. and 45 f., 308, 315; ll. 132 f., cf. Sat. 1, 5, 6 f., 313 f.; l. 134, cf. Sat. 1, 3, 56, 275; l. 139, cf. Sat. 1, 6, 109, 324; l. 140, cf. Sat. 1, 1, 68 ff., 200 ff., 238, also Sat. 1, 5, 82 ff., 310; l. 143, cf. Sat. 1, 5, 19, 314; l. 163, cf. Sat. 1, 6, 59, 320; l. 181, cf. Epp. 1, 8, 110, 432; l. 184, cf. Epp. 1, 8, 3 ff., 432; l. 189, cf. Epp. 1, 8, 7 ff., 432; l. 203, cf. Epp. 1, 7, 34 f., 431; l. 208, cf. Epp. 1, 7, 29 ff., 431; l. 213, cf. Epp. 1, 7, 29 ff. and 14, 1 ff., 168, 434; ll. 228 ff., cf. Sat. 1, 5, 87 and 9, 68 ff., 89, 334; l. 231, cf. Sat. 1, 9, 77 ff., 90, 335; l. 233, cf. Sat. 1, 9, 53 ff., 334; l. 234, cf. Sat. 1, 9, 16 f., 332; ll. 235 ff., cf. Sat. 1, 9, 40 ff., 333; l. 242, cf. Sat. 1, 2, 93, 271; l. 247, cf. Sat. 1, 9, 31 ff., 352; ll. 264 ff., cf. Sat. 1, 2, 120 ff., 269; l. 267, cf. Sat. 1, 2, 93, 267; ll. 269 ff., cf. Sat. 1, 2, 93 ff., 266; l. 278, cf. Sat. 1, 2, 35, 271, 273; l. 279 ff., cf. Sat. 1, 2, 44 f., 259; l. 282, cf. Sat. 1, 2, 44 f., 259, 265, 273; l. 288, cf. Sat. 1, 2, 89, 267; l. 293(?), cf. Sat. 1, 2, 105 ff., 273; l. 294, cf. Sat. 1, 2, 35, 171; ll. 303 ff., cf. Sat. 1, 2, 111 ff., 268 f.; ll. 305 f., cf. Sat. 1, 2, 125, 270; l. 307, cf. Sat. 1, 2, 68, 265 f., 271; l. 315, cf. Sat. 1, 2, 110,

268; l. 318, cf. Sat. 1, 2, 47, 48, 83, 105: 259 f., 265; ll. 319 f., cf. Epp. 2, 1, 86 ff., 441; ll. 327 f., cf. Sat. 2, 2, 19 ff., 382; ll. 331 f., cf. Sat. 2, 2, 19 ff., 382; ll. 338 ff., cf. Sat. 1, 4, 39 ff. and Epp. 2, 1, 72 ff., 287, 442; ll. 345 ff., cf. Epp. 2, 1, 69 ff., 442; l. 348, cf. Sat. 1, 7, 23, 326; ll. 346 f., cf. A. P. 40 ff., 110, 132, 387, 463; l. 391, cf. A. P. 358 ff., 464; l. 425, cf. Sat. 1, 6, 76, 233; l. 427, cf. Sat. 1, 6, 81 ff., 321; ll. 428 f., cf. Sat. 1, 6, 78 ff., 321; l. 430, cf. Sat. 1, 6, 82 ff., 322; l. 434, cf. Sat. 1, 6, 82 ff. and 88, 323; l. 437, cf. A. P. 275, 465; ll. 447 f., cf. Sat. 2, 8, 59 ff., 412; ll. 449 ff., cf. Sat. 2, 8, 73 f., 413; l. 452, cf. Sat. 2, 8, 54, 413; l. 453, cf. Sat. 1, 5, 72, 310; ll. 464 ff., cf. Sat. 2, 6, 88; l. 468, cf. Sat. 1, 2, 12, 271; l. 472, cf. Epp. 2, 2, 172, 446; ll. 493 f., cf. Sat. 1, 7, 1 f., 326; l. 501, cf. Epp. 2, 1, 123, 442; l. 514, cf. Sat. 1, 5, 20 f., 307; ll. 523 ff., cf. Sat. 2, 3, 123 ff., 392; l. 532, cf. Epp. 1, 14, 1 ff., 434; l. 534, cf. Sat. 1, 9, 1, 331; l. 537, cf. Sat. 1, 3, 63, 276; l. 538, cf. Sat. 2, 5, 75 ff., 403; l. 549, cf. Sat. 1, 3, 15 ff., 2, 1, 214 and 2, 93: 429 f.; ll. 550 f., cf. Sat. 2, 2, 129 and 133 f., Epp. 2, 2, 171 ff.: 194, 386, 405, 445 f.; l. 552, cf. Sat. 2, 5, 27 ff., 404; ll. 554 f., cf. Sat. 1, 1, 44 ff., 234, 247; l. 557, cf. Sat. 1, 1, 29 ff., 231, 246; ll. 558 ff., cf. Sat. 1, 1, 60 ff. and 79, Epp. 1, 1, 52 ff., 237, 246, 427 f.; l. 561, cf. Sat. 1, 1, 32 ff., 56, 231, 246; l. 563, cf. Sat. 1, 1, 1 ff., 192, 230; l. 564, cf. Sat. 1, 1, 15 ff., 193, 231, 242, 246; ll. 565 f., cf. Sat. 1, 1, 23 ff., 193, 241 f., 246; l. 567, cf. Sat. 1, 1, 1 ff. and 120 f., 89 f., 244, 246; l. 568, cf. Sat. 2, 8, 10 ff., 410; l. 569, cf. Sat. 2, 8, 26 ff., 85 f., 410 f.; ll. 573 f., cf. Sat. 2, 8, 64 f., 414; l. 575, cf. Sat. 2, 8, 93 ff., 414 f.; l. 577, cf. Sat. 1, 2, 12, 271; ll. 582 ff., cf. Sat. 1, 4, 71 ff., 10, 72 ff., Epp. 1, 19, 33 ff., 294, 348, 439; l. 587, cf. A. P. 11 ff., 109, 450; l. 588, cf. Sat.

1, 4, 72 and 10, 73 f., 294, 348;
l. 590, *cf. Sat.* 2, 1, 6 f. and 24 ff.,
A. P. 11 ff. and 99 ff., 109, 133, 373,
450, 457; ll. 592 ff., *cf. Sat.* 1, 10, 76,
348 f.; l. 595, *cf. Sat.* 1, 10, 76,
348 f.; ll. 608 ff., *cf. A. P.* 29 f.,
95 ff., 246 f., 419 ff., 438 ff., 109,
198, 457 f., 463, 467; l. 612, *cf. A. P.*
240 ff., 268 f., 291 ff., 385 ff., 409 ff.,
453 ff., 448; l. 617, *cf. A. P.* 366,
449; ll. 620 ff., *cf. Sat.* 2, 1, 11 ff.,
Epp. 2, 1, 250 ff., 374 ff., 443; l. 624,
cf. A. P. 451 f., 459; l. 627, *cf.*
A. P. 240 ff., 268 f., 291 ff., 385 ff.,
409 ff., 453 ff., 448; ll. 628 ff., *cf.*
Sat. 2, 1, 24 ff. and 50, 133, 374;
l. 633, *cf. Sat.* 2, 1, 6 f. and 24 ff.,
373; ll. 635 ff., *cf. Epp.* 1, 16, 436 f.;
ll. 649 f., *cf. A. P.* 48 ff., *Sat.* 1, 10,
20, 109, 455 f., 467; l. 659, *cf. Epp.*
1, 16, 24 and 63 ff., 437 f.; ll. 662 ff.,
cf. A. P. 422 ff., 196, 460; l. 669,
cf. Sat. 1, 6, 18 ff. and 2, 1, 64,
168, 194, 318; ll. 671 and 675, *cf.*
Sat. 2, 1, 50, 133; l. 693, *cf. A. P.*
309 ff., 109, 461; ll. 699 f., *cf. Sat.*
2, 2, 122 ff., 194, 385; l. 701, *cf.*
Sat. 2, 2, 129 and 133 ff., *Epp.* 2, 2,
171 ff., 194, 386, 445 f.; l. 702, *cf.*
A. P. 372, 462; l. 703, *cf. Sat.* 2, 2,
122 ff., 385; ll. 704 ff., *cf. Sat.* 2, 2,
129 ff., *Epp.* 1, 14, 36 f., 386, 434;
l. 709, *cf. A. P.* 324 f., 461 f.; l. 710,
cf. A. P. 310 ff., 113; l. 716, *cf. Sat.*
2, 2, 24 ff., 172, 383; l. 724, *cf. Sat.*
2, 3, 305, 397; ll. 729 f., *cf. Sat.* 2, 3,
259 ff., 394; l. 731, *cf. Sat.* 2, 3, 263,
396; l. 732, *cf. Sat.* 1, 2, 25 and 2, 3,
76 ff., 271, 393; l. 734, *cf. Sat.* 2, 3,
264 ff. and 270 f., 395; l. 735, *cf.*
Sat. 2, 3, 95, 396; l. 747, cf. *Sat.*
1, 3, 124, 276; l. 755, *cf. Sat.* 2, 3,
250 ff., 25 ff., 53, 392; l. 757, *cf.*
Sat. 2, 3, 253, 393; l. 764, *cf. Odes*
2, 2, 13, 200; l. 794, *cf. Sat.* 1, 10,
37, 347; l. 805, *cf. Sat.* 1, 4, 129 ff.,
302; ll. 806 ff., *cf. Sat.* 1, 4, 101 ff.,
301 f.; ll. 813 f., *cf. Sat.* 2, 2, 17
and 2, 8, 4 f., 381, 409; ll. 837 ff.,
cf. Sat. 2, 7, 90, 407 f.; ll. 851 ff., *cf.*
Sat. 1, 2, 37 ff., 257 ff.; l. 881, *cf.*
A. P. 236, 465; ll. 882 f., *cf. Sat.* 2,
5, 91, 405; l. 899, *cf. Sat.* 1, 4, 78 and
A. P. 283 ff., 294 f.; l. 915, *cf. Sat.*
2, 3, 273 f., 396; l. 944, *cf. A. P.*
304 ff., 448; l. 953, *cf. A. P.* 438 ff.
and 450 f., 198, 459, 467; ll. 954 f.,
cf. A. P. 431 ff., 168, 198, 460, 467;

ll. 957 f., *cf. A. P.* 438 ff. and 451 f.,
198, 457; l. 959, *cf. Sat.* 1, 2, 68, 271;
l. 961, *cf. Sat.* 2, 8, 44 ff., 412; ll.
970 f., *cf. Sat.* 1, 4, 34 ff., 285 f., 304;
ll. 980 ff., *cf. Epp.* 1, 1, 73 ff., 428;
l. 995, *cf. Sat.* 2, 3, 117 ff., 391;
ll. 1005 ff., *cf. Sat.* 2, 3, 13 ff., 390;
l. 1008, *cf. Sat.* 2, 1, 13 ff., 376;
ll. 1009 ff., *cf. Sat.* 1, 6, 52 ff., 88,
319 f.; l. 1013, *cf. Sat.* 1, 2, 63, 290 f.,
305; ll. 1014 ff., *cf. Sat.* 1, 3, 19, 4,
33 ff. and 81 ff., 10, 79: 87, 92, 285,
287, 293, 304, 344; l. 1017, *cf. Sat.*
1, 4, 79 ff., 296, 306; ll. 1019 ff., *cf.*
Sat. 1, 4, 21 ff., 282 f., 304; l. 1022,
cf. Sat. 1, 4, 34 and 10, 50: 133,
284 f., 304; l. 1025 f., *cf. Sat.* 1, 4,
90 ff., 297, 306; ll. 1027 ff., *cf. Sat.*
1, 4, 38 ff. and 60 f., 1, 10, 37, *A. P.*
317 f.: 189, 287 ff., 305, 347, 466;
ll. 1030 ff., cf. *Sat.* 1, 4, 64 ff., 78 ff.,
93 ff., 291 ff., 305; l. 1034, *cf. Sat.*
1, 6, 68 f. and 111 f., 323 f.; l. 1035,
cf. Sat. 1, 4, 78, 305; l. 1036, *cf. Sat.*
1, 4, 137 ff., 303, 306; l. 1038, *cf.*
Sat. 1, 4, 141 ff., 90, 303, 306; ll.
1039 f., *cf. Sat.* 1, 10, 37, 346; l.
1054, *cf. Sat.* 1, 4, 129 ff., 302; l.
1055, *cf. Sat.* 1, 1, 76 ff., 238, 246;
l. 1068, *cf. Sat.* 1, 3, 38 ff., 275;
ll. 1078 ff., *cf. Sat.* 2, 1, 11 ff., 40 ff.,
84 f., 2, 3, 152, *Epp.* 2, 1, 260 ff.,
372, 375 ff., 381, 444; l. 1096, *cf.*
Sat. 1, 4, 91, 297, 306; l. 1101, *cf.*
Sat. 2, 2, 111 ff. and 121 ff., 385;
l. 1106, *cf. Sat.* 2, 2, 19 ff., 382;
l. 1109, *cf. Sat.* 1, 6, 58 ff., 320;
l. 1111, cf. *Sat.* 1, 4, 1 ff., 109; l.
1131, *cf. Sat.* 2, 8, 13 ff., 410;
l. 1134, *cf. Sat.* 1, 6, 125 f., 324;
ll. 1138 ff., *cf. Sat.* 1, 9, 89, 172, 331;
l. 1158, *cf. Sat.* 1, 6, 117 ff., 324,
331; l. 1164, *cf. Sat.* 2, 8, 62, 414;
l. 1167(?), *cf. Sat.* 1, 1, 44 ff., 234,
247; l. 1173, *cf. Sat.* 2, 2, 111 ff. and
121 ff., 385; ll. 1174 ff., *cf. Sat.* 2, 2,
31 f., 8, 26 ff. and 85 ff., 384, 410,
411; l. 1178, *cf. Sat.* 2, 3, 41, 391;
ll. 1180 ff., *cf. Sat.* 1, 8, 6 ff., 409;
l. 1183, *cf. Sat.* 1, 1, 27 and 2, 8,
24 f., 244, 411; l. 1189, *cf. Epp.* 2, 1, 50
ff., 441; l. 1201, *cf. Sat.* 2, 4, 30, 399 f.;
l. 1203, *cf. Sat.* 1, 3, 21, *Epp.*, 1, 15,
26 ff., 275, 435; l. 1207, *cf. Sat.* 1, 6,
106, 323; l. 1210, *cf. Sat.* 2, 4, 31 ff.,
400; l. 1222, *cf. Sat.* 1, 2, 93, 271;
l. 1225, *cf. Sat.* 1, 3, 124 ff., 276;
l. 1227, *cf. Sat.* 1, 6, 45, 88, 318;

ll. 1235 ff., *cf. Sat.* 2, 2, 45, 384; ll. 1238 ff., *cf. Sat.* 2, 2, 46 and 8, 16 ff., 384, 411; l. 1248, *cf. Sat.* 1, 5, 85, 311; l. 1267, *cf. Sat.* 2, 7, 48 ff., 407; l. 1277, *cf. Epp.* 1, 8, 432 f.; l. 1279, *cf. Sat.* 1, 4, 39 ff., 305; l. 1282, *cf. A. P.* 419 f., 458; l. 1289, *cf. Sat.* 1, 4, 64 ff., 292, 305; l. 1292, *cf. Epp.* 1, 8, 432 f.; ll. 1294 f., *cf. Sat.* 1, 4, 6 f. and 47, *Epp.* 1, 18, 59, 110 f., 305; l. 1316, *cf. Sat.* 1, 2, 31 f., 256 f.; ll. 1326 ff., *cf. Sat.* 2, 1, 70, *A. P.* 312 ff., 66, 377 f., 465; l. 1339, *cf. Sat.* 1, 9, 70, 335; l. 1341, *cf. Sat.* 2, 4, 40 ff., 400; l. 1342, *cf. Sat.*, 1, 5, 60 ff., 310; l. 1358, *cf. Sat.* 1, 1, 104 and 2, 12, 245, 271.

The following Lucilian fragments are cited without special reference to Horace:

Line 1, 48; 15, 111; 19, 48(n); 24 and 26, 153; 33, 108; 37, 153; 44, 326; 54, 153; 56, 245; 57 ff., 328; 63, 108; 64, 328; 68, 328; 69, 245; 71, 328; 97 ff., 314 f.; 99 ff., 312 f.; 107 f., 312 f.; 137, 165; 148, 48; 165 ff., 165; 171, 108; 189, 165; 191, 48; 192 ff., 165; 308, 326; 350 f., 343; 351, 356, 357, 358, 362, 364, 367, 369, 371, 373 ff., 377, 379, 381, 382: 108; 377 f., 110, 131, 343; 388 f., 66, 110, 148; 397 ff., 67; 398, 327; 411, 162; 421, 103; 437, 108; 438 ff., 165; 452, 114; 454 ff., 165; 462, 48; 467, 67; 469, 327; 480 ff., 154; 490, 67; 492 ff., 154; 501 f., 322; 506 ff., 154; 519, 108; 534, 167; 554, 194; 557, 192; 558, 89; 559, 193; 564, 111; 585, 152; 587, 48; 592, 123 f.; 594, 112; 596, 82; 597 and 599, 48; 604, 110; 605 f., 48; 612, 98; 665, 165; 669, 98; 688 and 698, 460; 700, 98; 707, 99; 709, 175, 460; 717, 196; 718, 173; 736, 98; 737, 395; 738, 112; 742, 112, 161; 751, 66, 150, 165; 752, 150, 165; 753, 66, 150, 164 f.; 754, 66, 112, 161, 165; 755, 66, 150, 161, 165; 756, 150, 165; 757 ff., 165; 762, 66, 150, 165; 764 ff., 150; 771, 98; 773 ff., 150; 794, 75; 821, 199; 830 ff., 114, 151; 833 ff., 151, 195; 834, 114, 151; 839 ff., 151; 868, 272; 895, 96; 899, 95, 171; 900, 96, 151; 902 ff., 114, 151, 196; 923 ff., 151; 957, 98; 964, 83, 112; 980 ff., 167; 996 ff., 1000 ff., 154; 1007, 157;

1009 ff., 158; 1012 f., 147 f.; 1014, 117; 1016, 118; 1026, 199; 1027, 89; 1028, 75; 1032, 89; 1039, 118; 1076, 164; 1094, 98; 1095 and 1097, 199; 1100, 107; 1104, 66; 1111, 109, 113; 1117, 110; 1119, 237, 246; 1121, 172; 1128 and 1130, 108; 1132 f., 110; 1134, 108; 1137, 110; 1138, 157; 1142, 331; 1150 and 1156, 165; 1167, 131; 1168, 110; 1172, 164; 1190, 108; 1201 and 1205, 165; 1209, 110, 465; 1212, 165; 1215, 108; 1227, 79; 1228, 67; 1235, 161, 165; 1238, 161; 1241, 108 f.; 1250, 165; 1251, 66; 1279, 89; 1280, 102; 1284, 108; 1315, 165; 1316, 161, 272; 1322, 106, 111; 1326 ff., 67, 73; 1334, 108; 1342 f., 155; 1344, 95, 108, 171; 1348, 327; 1368, 165; 1370, 165; 1915, 111.

The satires and epistles of Horace are discussed with reference to Lucilian fragments as follows:

Sat. 1, 1 and Lucilius ll. 565, 566, 563, 564, 557, 561, 554, 555, 558, 1119, 559, 560, 1055, 1183, 567, 1358, 468, pp. 219-247.

Sat. 1, 2 and Lucilius ll. 1316, 851, 853, 854, 855, 279 ff., 282, 318, 857, 858, 864, 965, 961, 859, 866, 867, 269, 271, 288, 267, 1222, 266, 293(?), 268, 266, 264(?), 318, 307, 296, 313, 314, 315, 302, 303, 305, 306, pp. 248-274.

Sat. 1, 3 and Lucilius ll. 1068, 1203, 134, 537, 747, 1225, pp. 274-277.

Sat. 1, 4 and Lucilius ll. 1095, 1097, 1021, 1019, 1020, 1022, 971, 1014, 1015, 1016, 970, 1027, 1028, 1029, 1279, 1010, 1294, 1033, 1289, 1030, 1079, 1031, 588, 596, 1290, 1038, 1017, 1025, 1096, 1268(?), 1026, 1018(?), 1060, 1063, 1064, 1070, 1067, 1054, 1038, 1032, pp. 277-306.

Sat. 1, 5 and Lucilius ll. 110 ff., 115, 117 ff., 128, 129, 130, 140, 107, 114, 124, 126, 109, 102 ff., 107 ff., 132, 133, 124 ff., 97, 98, 99, 102, 105, 107, 453, 514, 512, 480 ff., 228, 1342, 1248, pp. 306-316.

Sat. 1, 6 and Lucilius ll. 1009, 1010, 1011, 669, 1227, 427, 428, 429, 430, 431, 432, 433, 501, 502, 1207, 1034, 139, 1158, 1134, pp. 316-324.

Sat. 1, 7 and Lucilius ll. 55, 44, 493 f., 348, 473, 398, 469, 56, 69 f., 1348, 57 ff., 64, 68, 71, 84 f., 86, 88 ff., pp. 324-330.

Sat. 1, 8 no traces of Lucilian influence.

Sat. 1, 9 and Lucilius ll. 534, 1138, 1158, 1142, 234, 230, 235 ff., 236, 233, 228, 231, 1339, pp. 330-336.

Sat. 1, 10 and Lucilius ll. 1124, 350 f., 377, 379, 1039 f., 1028, 794, 589, 592, 593, 594, 595, 588, pp. 336-349.

Sat. 2, 1 and Lucilius ll. 1078-1098, 590, 633, 628, 629, 620, 621, 622, 1008, 1326 ff., pp. 369-378.

Sat. 2, 2 and Lucilius ll. 813, 327, 328, 331, 332, 1106, 688-715, 716, 1174-1176, 1238, 1235-1237, 1101, 1173, 704-705, 701, 550, pp. 378-387.

Sat. 2, 3 and Lucilius ll. 1005, 1006, 1007, 1178(?), 995, 1092, 523 ff., 755, 757, 732, 729, 730, 737, 734, 731, 732, 735, 915, pp. 387-398.

Sat. 2, 4 and Lucilius ll. 1201, 1210, 1341, pp. 398-400.

Sat. 2, 5 and Lucilius ll. 226-227, 1107-1108, 538, 1296, 540 f., 552, 550-551, 547-548, 882-883, pp. 400-405.

Sat. 2, 6 no Lucilian influence.

Sat. 2, 7 and Lucilius ll. 1267, 837, 839, 840, 843, 844, 845, 841, pp. 405-408.

Sat. 2, 8 and Lucilius ll. 1180, 813-814, 568, 1131, 569, 1174, 1238-1240, 1183, 447, 448, 449, 450, 452, 573-574, 575, pp. 408-415.

Epp. 1, 1 and Lucilius ll. 559, 980, 981, 983, 985, 988, pp. 427-428.

Epp. 1, 3 and Lucilius l. 549, pp. 429 f.

Epp. 1, 7 and Lucilius ll. 208 and 203, pp. 430-431.

Epp. 1, 8 and Lucilius ll. 181, 184, 189, 1292, 1277, p. 432.

Epp. 1, 14 and Lucilius ll. 213, 532, 704, pp. 433-434.

Epp. 1, 15 and Lucilius l. 1203, pp. 434-436.

Epp. 1, 16 and Lucilius ll.635, 639, 638, 640, 643, 641, 645, 647, 648, 642, 659, pp. 436-438.

Epp. 1, 19 and Lucilius ll.588, 589, 592, 593, 594, 595, pp. 438-440.

Epistle 1, 2 shows only one stray Lucilian allusion in the use of a monosyllabic verse tag, p. 429, and epistles 4, 5, 6, 9, 10, 11, 12, 13, 17, 18 and 20 show no Lucilian influence, pp. 430, 433, 438, 439.

Epp. 2, 1 and Lucilius ll. 1189, 319, 320, 338, 341, 345 ff., 501, 620, 621, 622, 1079, 1085, 1086, 1088, 1081, 1095, pp. 440-444.

Epp. 2, 2 and Lucilius ll. 472, 550, 701, pp. 444-446.

Ars Poetica and Lucilius διαγωγή to Iunius Congus, ll. 603, 609, 620, 590, 628, 630, 650, 612, 627, 944, 617, 587, 649, 608, 1282, 611, 953, 958, 624, 662, 664, 665, 954, 688, 698, 709, 693, 702, 386, 391, 1209, 881, 437, 1326 ff., 1029, 597, 599, 601, 602, 605, 610, 957, pp. 446-468, with summary of parallels, pp. 467 f.

The following Horatian passages are cited without special reference to Lucilian influence:

Sat. 1, 1, 15, 184; 17, 57; 68, 56; 75, 57; 85 f., 28; 95, 186; 1, 2, 31, 99; 55, 186; 1, 3, 44 ff., 121; 69, 198; 136 ff., 89; 140, 198; 1, 4, 1 ff., 93, 115; 3, 115; 8, 132; 9 ff., 128; 11, 129; 13, 127 f.; 18, 121; 34, 120; 35, 122; 36, 157; 49, 126; 53, 130; 60, 126; 73, 199; 76 f., 120; 80, 122; 81 ff., 120, 199; 86 ff., 120; 93 ff., 121; 137, 157; 139, 53; 1, 6, 48, 67; 1, 10, 1 ff., 132, 175; 3, 106, 171; 5, 94; 8, 128; 9 ff., 125; 10 ff., 97; 12, 126; 13, 117, 122; 14 ff., 119; 19 ff., 127; 27 ff., 125, 127; 30 ff., 106; 31 ff., 126; 36, 130; 37, 75, 118; 40 ff., 41; 43 ff., 117, 122; 46 ff., 28, 117; 50 ff., 129; 56 ff., 132; 60 ff., 128; 65, 93, 107; 66 ff., 126; 81 ff., 122; 82, 77; 2, 1, 2, 130; 6, 157; 13 ff., 126; 28 ff., 29; 30 ff., 53, 157; 34 ff., 64; 39 ff., 66; 40 ff., 121; 62 ff., 29, 89, 115; 68, 115; 71 ff., 88; 74, 29; 77, 65, 168; 2, 3, 99 ff., 161; 111 and 142, 56; 186, 168; 250 ff., 161; 314 ff., 168; 2, 6, 41 ff., 88; 64 ff., 172; 65 ff., 126; 79 ff., 126, 168; 83, 172; 2, 7, 70 f., 56; *Epp.* 1, 1, 14, 67; 3, 15 ff., 27; 17 ff., 45; 6, 1, 234; 18, 59, 111; 2, 1, 170 ff., 98; *A. P.* 47, 124, 133; 56, 128; 119, 34; 128 ff., 40; 130 ff., 49; 131 ff., 45; 134 ff., 44; 135, 130; 234, 130; 240 ff., 126, 129; 242, 133;

268 ff., 30, 36; 270, 98; 310, 99;   2, 19, 31; 3, 2 and 3, 67; 3, 1, 31;
405 ff., 205; 408 ff., 30; 453 ff., 31;   30, 12 ff., 29; 4, 2, 27 ff., 45; 4,
Odes 1, 29, 13, 113; 2, 7, 9 ff., 67;   18 ff., 77.

CPSIA information can be obtained at www.ICGtesting.com
Printed in the USA
BVOW03s0414030214

343790BV00017B/688/P